Geophysical Monograph Series

Geophysical Monograph Series

Geophysical Monograph 214

Extreme Events

Observations, Modeling, and Economics

Mario Chavez
Michael Ghil
Jaime Urrutia-Fucugauchi
Editors

This Work is a co-publication between the American Geophysical Union and John Wiley and Sons, Inc.

WILEY

This Work is a co-publication between the American Geophysical Union and John Wiley & Sons, Inc.

Published under the aegis of the AGU Publications Committee

Brooks Hanson, Director of Publications
Robert van der Hilst, Chair, Publications Committee

Published by John Wiley & Sons, Inc., Hoboken, New Jersey
Published simultaneously in Canada

Library of Congress Cataloging-in-Publication data is available.

ISBN: 978-1-119-15701-4

Cover images: **Left top panel:** A space weather event registered in October 2003. A large active region (upper left panel) on the Sun erupted with a bright area (upper right panel), followed within minutes by a coronal mass ejection (lower left panel), see http://sohowww:nascom:nasa:gov/hotshots/. In the lower right pannel the aurora borealis due to the event (photograph by *Andy Keen*, http://www.aurorahunters.com). *Rusmaikin et al.* [2016], Drivers of Extreme Space Weather Events: Fast Coronal Mass Ejections, Chapter 7 in this Monograph. **Right top panel:** The 26th of December 2004 a Mw 9.1 to 9.3 magnitude subduction earthquake with epicenter in the Sumatra-Andaman, Indonesia, region, generated a Mega-Tsunami that caused ~ 300,000 casualties. The map shows the maximum Tsunami amplitudes derived from a numerical simulation of this event. *A. Piatanessi*, www.ingv.it/%7eroma/reti/rms/terremoti/estero/indonesia/indonesia.htm. **Left bottom panel:** Global-scale comparison of changes in historical (1901–2010) annual maximum daily precipitation between station observations (compiled in HadEX2) and the suite of global climate models contributing to the fifth phase of the Coupled Model Intercomparison Project (CMIP5). *Asadieh B. and Krakauer N. Y.* [2015], Global trends in extreme precipitation: climate models versus observations, Hydrol. Earth Syst. Sci., 19, 877–891, 2015; www.hydrol-earth-syst-sci.net/19/877/2015/ doi:10.5194/hess-19-877-2015. **Right bottom panel:** Modeling of damage cost of one- to three- floor dwelling built stock in Guadalajara, México, for a Mw 8.5 magnitude subduction earthquake scenario. *Chavez et al.* [2016], Extreme Magnitude Earthquakes and their Direct Economic Impacts: A Hybrid Approach, Chapter 17 in this Monograph.

Printed in the United States of America

10 9 8 7 6 5 4 3 2 1

CONTENTS

CONTRIBUTORS

Lubna A. Amir
Department of Geophysics
Faculty of Earth Sciences
University of Earth Sciences and Technology
Bab Ezzouar, Algiers, Algeria

Mike Ashworth
Scientific Computing Department
STFC Daresbury Laboratory
Sci-Tech Daresbury
Warrington, UK

Cinzia Bianchi
Istituto di Ricerca per la Protezione Idrogeologica
Consiglio Nazionale delle Ricerche
Perugia, Italy

Jochen Bröcker
Max Planck Institute for the Physics of Complex Systems
Dresden, Germany
Department of Mathematics and Statistics
University of Reading
Reading, UK

Eduardo Cabrera
Institute of Advanced Research Computing
School of Engineering and Computing Sciences
Durham University
Durham, UK

Suzana J. Camargo
Lamont-Doherty Earth Observatory
Columbia University
Palisades, NY, USA

Heriberta Castaños
Instituto de Investigaciones Económicas
Universidad Nacional Autónoma de México
México, DF, México

Erik Chavez
Centre for Environmental Policy
Imperial College London
London, UK

Mario Chavez
Instituto de Ingeniería
Universidad Nacional Autónoma de México (UNAM)
México, DF, México

Néstor Corona
Centro de Estudios en Geografía Humana
El Colegio de Michoacán
Michoacán, México

Servando De la Cruz-Reyna
Instituto de Geofísica
Universidad Nacional Autónoma de México
México, DF, México

Walter Dudley
Marine Science Department
University of Hawaii at Hilo
Hilo, HI, USA

Patrice Dumas
Environmental Research & Teaching Institute
Ecole Normale Supérieure
Paris, France
Centre de coopération Internationale en Recherche
Agronomique pour le Développement
Nogent-sur-Marne, France
Centre International de Recherche sur
l'Environnement et le Développement
Nogent-sur-Marne, France

Cecilia Enriquez-Ortiz
Instituto de Ingeniería
Universidad Nacional Autónoma de México
México, DF, México

Angélica Felix
Instituto de Ingeniería
Universidad Nacional Autónoma de México
México, DF, México

Joan Feynman
Jet Propulsion Laboratory
California Institute of Technology
Pasadena, CA, USA

Andrei Gabrielov
Departments of Mathematics & Earth
and Atmospheric Sciences
Purdue University
West Lafayette, IN, USA

Silvia Garcia
Instituto de Ingeniería
Universidad Nacional Autónoma de México (UNAM)
México, DF, México

Michael Ghil
Geosciences Department, Environmental Research &
Teaching Institute (CERES-ERTI), and Laboratoire
de Meteorologie Dynamique (CNRS and IPSL)
Ecole Normale Supérieure
Paris, France
Department of Atmospheric & Oceanic Sciences
and Institute of Geophysics & Planetary Physics
University of California
Los Angeles, CA, USA

Kazuhisa Goto
Disaster Control Research Center
Graduate School of Engineering
Tohoku University
Sendai, Japan
Present address: International Research Institute
of Disaster Science
Tohoku University
Sendai, Japan

Andreas Groth
Department of Atmospheric & Oceanic Sciences
University of California
Los Angeles, CA, USA
Environmental Research & Teaching Institute
Ecole Normale Supérieure
Paris, France

Fausto Guzzetti
Istituto di Ricerca per la Protezione Idrogeologica
Consiglio Nazionale delle Ricerche
Perugia, Italy

Stéphane Hallegatte
Centre International de Recherche sur
l'Environnement et le Développement
Nogent-sur-Marne, France
The World Bank
Climate Change Group
Washington, DC, USA

Solomon M. Hsiang
Goldman School of Public Policy
University of California Berkeley
Berkeley, CA, USA

Fumihiko Imamura
Disaster Control Research Center
Graduate School of Engineering
Tohoku University
Sendai, Japan
Present address: International Research Institute
of Disaster Science
Tohoku University
Sendai, Japan

Holger Kantz
Max Planck Institute for the Physics of Complex
Systems
Dresden, Germany

Richard W. Katz
National Center for Atmospheric Research
Boulder, CO, USA

Vladimir Keilis-Borok[†]
Institute of Geophysics & Planetary Physics
and Department of Earth & Space Sciences
University of California
Los Angeles, CA, USA
Institute of Earthquake Prediction Theory &
Mathematical Geophysics
Russian Academy of Sciences
Moscow, Russia
[†]Deceased (2013).

Shunichi Koshimura
Disaster Control Research Center
Graduate School of Engineering
Tohoku University
Sendai, Japan
Present address: International Research Institute
of Disaster Science
Tohoku University
Sendai, Japan

Yochanan Kushnir
Lamont-Doherty Earth Observatory
Columbia University
New York, USA

Upmanu Lall
Department of Earth and Environmental Engineering
Columbia University
New York, USA

Timothy M. Lenton
Earth System Science
College of Life and Environmental Sciences
University of Exeter
Exeter, UK

Valerie N. Livina
National Physical Laboratory
Teddington,
Middlesex, UK

Cinna Lomnitz
Instituto de Geofísica
Universidad Nacional Autónoma de México
México, DF, México

Ismael Mariño-Tapia
Departamento de Recursos del Mar
CINVESTAV-Mérida
Yucatán, México

Brian G. McAdoo
Department of Geography
Vassar College
Poughkeepsie, NY, USA

Edgar Mendoza
Instituto de Ingeniería
Universidad Nacional Autónoma de México
México, DF, México

Ana Teresa Mendoza-Rosas
Instituto de Geofísica
Universidad Nacional Autónoma de México
México, DF, México

Jennifer Nakamura
Lamont-Doherty Earth Observatory
Columbia University
New York, USA

Philippe Naveau
Laboratoire des Sciences du Climat et de
l'Environnement LSCE-IPSL-CNRS
Gif-sur-Yvette, France

Catherine Nicolis
Institut Royal Météorologique de Belgique
Brussels, Belgium

Gregoire Nicolis
Interdisciplinary Center for Nonlinear Phenomena
and Complex Systems
Université Libre de Bruxelles
Brussels, Belgium

Narciso Perea
Instituto de Ingeniería
Universidad Nacional Autónoma de México (UNAM)
México, DF, México

Ligia Pérez-Cruz
Programa Universitario de Perforaciones en
Océanos y Continentes
Departamento de Geomagnetismo y Exploración
Geofísica
Instituto de Geofísica
Universidad Nacional Autónoma de México
México, DF, México

Horst Punzmann
Research School of Physics and Engineering
The Australian National University
Canberra, Australian Capital Territory, Australia

María-Teresa Ramírez-Herrera
Laboratorio Universitario de Geofísica Ambiental
(LUGA) and Instituto de Geografía
Universidad Nacional Autónoma de México
México, DF, México

Pierre Ribereau
Institut de Mathématiques et de Modélisation de
Montpellier – UMR 5149
Montpellier, France

Andrew W. Robertson
International Research Institute for Climate
and Society (IRI)
Columbia University
New York, USA

Mauro Rossi
Istituto di Ricerca per la Protezione Idrogeologica
Consiglio Nazionale delle Ricerche
Perugia, Italy
Dipartimento di Scienze della Terra
Università degli Studi di Perugia
Perugia, Italy

Alexander Ruzmaikin
Jet Propulsion Laboratory
California Institute of Technology
Pasadena, CA, USA

Alejandro Salazar
Instituto de Geofísica
Universidad Nacional Autónoma de México (UNAM)
México, DF, México

Paola Salvati
Istituto di Ricerca per la Protezione Idrogeologica
Consiglio Nazionale delle Ricerche
Perugia, Italy

Michael G. Shats
Research School of Physics and Engineering
The Australian National University
Canberra, Australian Capital Territory, Australia

Stefan Siegert
Max Planck Institute for the Physics of Complex Systems
Dresden, Germany
College of Engineering
Mathematics and Physical Sciences
University of Exeter
Exeter, UK

Rodolfo Silva
Instituto de Ingeniería
Universidad Nacional Autónoma de México
México, DF, México

Alexandre Soloviev
Institute of Earthquake Prediction Theory &
Mathematical Geophysics
Russian Academy of Sciences
Moscow, Russia

Stilian Stoev
Department of Statistics
University of Michigan
Ann Arbor, MI, USA

Gerardo Suárez
Instituto de Geofísica
Universidad Nacional Autónoma de México
México, DF, México

Gwladys Toulemonde
Institut de Mathématiques et de Modélisation de
Montpellier – UMR 5149
Montpellier, France

Jaime Urrutia-Fucugauchi
Instituto de Geofísica
Universidad Nacional Autónoma de México (UNAM)
México, DF, México

Hua Xia
Research School of Physics and Engineering
The Australian National University
Canberra, Australian Capital Territory, Australia

Hideaki Yanagisawa
Disaster Control Research Center
Graduate School of Engineering
Tohoku University
Sendai, Japan
Present address: Faculty of Liberal Arts
Tohoku Gakuin University
Sendai, Japan

Ilya Zaliapin
Department of Mathematics and Statistics
University of Nevada
Reno, NV, USA

PREFACE

In statistical terms, extreme events can be defined as events that largely deviate from the statistical mean. From the physical point of view, it is widely accepted that such events are generated by systems that are both nonlinear and complex. Due to their infrequent occurrence, on the one hand, and to the complexity of the processes involved, on the other, extreme events have been difficult to study and, even more so, to predict. For these reasons, their analysis has mainly focused on studying their frequency-size distribution, while their prediction has been limited, by-and-large, to applying extreme value theory (EVT) to estimate the expected time intervals for the occurrence of an event that exceeds a certain threshold. It has become clearer and clearer, though, that the applicability of classical EVT theory to complex and nonlinear phenomena may be limited, while novel methods for their study are becoming available.

This monograph aims to present an overview of methods recently developed for the description, understanding and prediction of extreme events across a range of phenomena in the geosciences, with an emphasis on the study of their socio-economic impacts. It is the outcome of four American Geophysical Union sessions on *Extreme Events: Observations, Modeling and Economics*, held in 2007, 2008, 2011 and 2013. The editors of this volume organized these four sessions in order to examine the broad topic of extreme events in the geosciences from an interdisciplinary perspective. The primary objectives of these sessions were to provide an open forum for the theoretical and empirical developments that could improve: (i) the understanding, modeling and prediction of extreme events in the geosciences, as well as (ii) the quantitative evaluation of their economic consequences. Most of the articles in this monograph emerged from these four AGU sessions.

The monograph covers the causes and consequences of extreme geophysical phenomena like space weather, asteroid impacts, climatic change, earthquakes, tsunamis, hurricanes, landslides, volcanoes, and flooding; it also addresses their associated socio-economic impacts, locally, regionally and globally. The understanding and modeling of these phenomena is critical to the development of timely strategies worldwide for the prediction of natural and anthropogenic extreme events, in order to mitigate their adverse consequences.

We would like to dedicate this Monograph to the memory of V. Keilis-Borok (1921–2013) and of Emilio Rosenblueth Deutsch (1926–1994) for their visionary contributions in the geosciences and in seismic risk engineering.

Vladimir I. Keilis-Borok

Keilis-Borok was a Russian mathematical geophysicist and seismologist. He was the founding Director of the International Institute of Earthquake Prediction Theory and Mathematical Geophysics of the Soviet, and then Russian, Academy of Sciences in Moscow. His major contributions to the geosciences included, at first, important studies of seismic-signal propagation and of Earth structure. The second part of his research life was dedicated to applying concepts and methods from the theory of nonlinear and complex systems to the prediction of both natural and socio-economic crises. Starting with the study of premonitory seismic patterns, he and his numerous and diverse collaborators applied related methodologies to make socio-economic predictions with notable success. The mathematics of pattern recognition was thus brought to bear to correctly predict the popular vote winner of presidential elections in the United States, as well as to predicting rises in murder rates in Los Angeles, recessions, spikes in unemployment and terrorist attacks.

Keilis-Borok served as the President of the International Union of Geodesy and Geophysics (1987–1991), Chair of the Mathematics and Natural Sciences Section, International Council of Scientific Unions (1988–1991), Founding Chairman, International Committee for Geophysical Theory and Computers (1964–1979), and an Expert for the Soviet side in the technical meetings on the Nuclear Test Ban Treaty (1960–1990). He was elected to the American Academy of Arts and Sciences (1969), Austrian Academy of Sciences (1992), U.S. National Academy Sciences (1971), Pontifical Academy of Sciences (1994), Soviet Academy of Sciences (1988), and the Academia Europaea (1999). He received the first L.F. Richardson Medal of the European Geosciences Union, a Doctorate Honoris Causa from the Institut de Physique du Globe, Paris, and the 21st Century Collaborative Activity Award for Studying Complex Systems from the McDonnell Foundation. He was also an exceptionally warm and supportive colleague and human being.

Emilio Rosenblueth Deutsch

Rosenblueth Deutsch was a Mexican civil engineer and professor of the Universidad Nacional Autonoma de Mexico (UNAM, Institute of Engineering). His published work, characterised by conceptual formulation of rational frameworks and probabilistic theories, the use of innovative mathematical models and of their application, mainly in seismic engineering, had a major influence on developments in seismic risk and design worldwide. His and coauthored books and over 300 publications, reveal his original thoughts on risk analysis, concepts of reliability, optimisation in seismic design, education, and ethics in technology.

His contributions were recognized worldwide, among others by the National Academy of Sciences of the United States, the American Academy of Arts and Sciences, the American Society of Civil Engineers (ASCE), the American Concrete Institute, and the International Association for Earthquake Engineering. He was a member of the Colegio Nacional of Mexico, and President of the current Mexican Academy of Sciences. Academic honors conferred on Rosenblueth Deutsch, to name only a few, include the Freudenthal Medal and the Newmark medal of the ASCE, the Prince of Asturias Prize from Spain, the Bernardo Hussay Interamerican Science Prize, the Huber Research Prize, the Moiseff Award, the National Science and Arts Prize of Mexico, and honorary doctorates from the University of Waterloo, the Carnegie Mellon University and the UNAM.

Incidentally, Emilio Rosenblueth Deutsch, was the co-editor (with Cinna Lomnitz) of the book *Seismic Risk and Engineering Decisions*, Elsevier (1976), for which Jim Brune wrote a chapter on *The Physics of Earthquake Ground Motions* in which he followed fundamental results on the seismic source suggested by Keilis-Borok in 1959 (Ann. Geofis. 12, 205-214), and therefore the latter indirectly also contributed to the book. Thus, the present monograph's being dedicated to their memory brings them together again ...

M. Chavez, M. Ghil, J. Urrutia-Fucugauchi

ACKNOWLEDGMENTS

It is a pleasure to thank the organizers of the AGU meetings held in 2007, 2008, 2011, and 2013; the first two and the last one were held during the Joint Assemblies in Acapulco, Fort Lauderdale, and Cancún (in 2007, 2008, and 2013, respectively), while the third one was held during the San Francisco Fall meeting of 2011, for having approved and encouraged the holding of four sessions on *Extreme Events: Observations, Modeling, and Economics*, and especially the authors and participants in the sessions. We are also grateful to the American Geophysical Union and to Wiley for their editorial and management support. Victoria Forlini (AGU), Telicia Collick (AGU), Mary Warner (AGU), Colleen Matan (formerly AGU), Brooks Hanson (AGU), Rituparna Bose (Wiley), Mary Grace Hammond (Wiley), Danielle LaCourciere (Wiley) and F. Pascal Raj (SPi Global) helped make the publication of the monograph a reality. Most of all, we thank our thoughtful and talented authors and reviewers, without whom this book would not have been possible.

1

Introduction

Mario Chavez,[1] Michael Ghil,[2,3] and Jaime Urrutia-Fucugauchi[4]

The recent occurrence of events like the European 2003 heat wave, the Sumatra 2004 earthquake, the 2005 Hurricane Katrina, the Tohoku 2011 earthquake, the 2012 Hurricane Sandy, and the Nepal 2015 earthquake represented not only climatic or geophysical extremes, but they have had or will have large and long-lasting consequences in large segments of the world population. In each case, these events impacted systemic, structural, and socioeconomic weaknesses in the societies found in their path. The common characteristic of these events is that they reached larger intensities, durations or both, when compared with previous observations of the same phenomena; they also had or still have an impact on health, infrastructures, ecosystems, or the economy of the world region where they occurred. It is relevant, moreover, to mention that high-impact geophysical events may be qualified as being extreme by a society, although a similar event occurring in a different region or under different conditions would not have the same impact and thus would not be qualified as an extreme event by the same or a different society.

Taking into account the characteristics of geophysical extreme events, this book focuses on the aspects that are related to their observation and their modeling, as well as to estimating their socioeconomic impacts. The book brings together different communities of researchers and practitioners in the fields of the climate sciences and geophysics, mathematics and statistics, economy, and sociology; it gathers, in a unified setting, 21 representative related to extreme events research, many of which include applications to their impact on society or the environment.

Most of the 21 chapters included deal with novel methodologies and their applications for the study of extreme events and their impacts. The chapters are grouped into six themes. Part I is composed of five chapters on fundamentals and theory, one covering the statistical analysis of environmental and temperature data, two on dynamical system approaches to the analysis of extreme events, another one on climate tipping points, and the fifth one on a delay differential equation study of the El Niño–Southern Oscillation (ENSO). Part II has two chapters related to extreme events in Earth's space environment: one chapter analyzes extreme events in space weather, and the other the Chicxulub asteroid impact associated with the mass extinction at the K/T boundary.

Part III deals with climate and weather extremes, and it contains four chapters: one on extreme flooding in the midwest of the United States, the second one on the impacts of the 2005 Hurricane Wilma, the third on observations and modeling of damages caused by the 2004 Indian Ocean tsunami, and the fourth chapter on rogue wave events in a laboratory setting of capillary waves. Part IV is dedicated to extreme events in the solid

[1]*Instituto de Ingeniería, Universidad Nacional Autónoma de México (UNAM), México, DF, México*

[2]*Geosciences Department, Environmental Research & Teaching Institute (CERES-ERTI), and Laboratoire de Meteorologie Dynamique (CNRS and IPSL), Ecole Normale Supérieure, Paris, France*

[3]*Department of Atmospheric & Oceanic Sciences and Institute of Geophysics & Planetary Physics, University of California, Los Angeles, CA, USA*

[4]*Instituto de Geofísica, Universidad Nacional Autónoma de México (UNAM), México, DF, México*

Extreme Events: Observations, Modeling, and Economics, Geophysical Monograph 214, First Edition.
Edited by Mario Chavez, Michael Ghil, and Jaime Urrutia-Fucugauchi.
© 2016 American Geophysical Union. Published 2016 by John Wiley & Sons, Inc.

earth and it includes three chapters, the first on a multi-proxy approach for great magnitude earthquakes and tsunamis, the second on landslide risks in Italy, and the third one on an extreme event approach to volcanic eruptions.

Part V addresses, in four chapters, the socioeconomic impacts of extreme events: the first of these uses classical extreme value theory to study the economic impact of extreme events and in particular of hurricanes, the second chapter relies on a hybrid approach to assess the direct economic impacts of extreme-magnitude earthquakes, the third chapter is on tropical cyclones and their socioeconomic impacts, and the fourth one is on natural disasters and their impacts on a dynamic, nonequilibrium economy. Finally, in Part VI, three chapters deal with the very difficult and controversial issue of predicting extreme events and with the closely related one of preparedness: the first chapter treats extreme tsunami events in the Mediterranean region and their impact on the Algerian coasts, the second analyzes the complexity surrounding high-technology extreme events, in particular, the 2011 failure of the Fukushima nuclear power plant, while the third paper reviews a group effort on the predictive understanding of extreme events and its applications to disaster preparedness. We summarize here the main contributions of each of these chapters.

1.1. PART I: FUNDAMENTALS AND THEORY

In Chapter 2, G. Toulemonde and colleagues argue that the classical statistical assumption in analyzing extreme events, namely that of independence in space, time, or both, may not be valid in the geosciences in most cases. Furthermore, the statistical modeling of such dependences is complex and different modeling roads should be explored. First, the authors present some basic concepts of univariate and multivariate extreme value theory (EVT), followed by a series of examples on how this theory can help the practitioner to make inferences about extreme quantiles in a multivariate context.

In Chapter 3, C. Nicolis and G. Nicolis propose a deterministic dynamical systems approach to identify the principal signatures of the statistical properties of extremes. Then, the authors derive analytical expressions for n-fold cumulative distributions and their associated densities, for the exceedance probabilities and for the spatial propagation of extremes. Numerical simulations that exhibit substantial differences from classical EVT theory complement these analytical results. These differences are illustrated for dynamical systems giving rise to quasi-periodic behavior, intermittent chaos, and fully developed chaos, respectively.

In Chapter 4, S. Siegert and associates discuss the application of a physical weather model and a simple data-based model to probabilistic predictions of extreme temperature anomalies; the comparison between the two uses the concept of skill scores. The authors found that, although the result confirms the expectation that the computationally much more expensive weather model outperforms the simple data-based model, the performance of the latter is surprisingly good. Furthermore, they assert that over a certain parameter range, the simple data-based model is even better than the uncalibrated weather model. They propose the use of receiver operating characteristic (ROC) statistics to measure the performance of the predictors, and find that using this type of scoring, the conclusions about model performance partly change, which illustrates that predictive power depends on its exact definition.

In Chapter 5, T. Lenton and V. Livina apply concepts from dynamical systems theory to study extreme events in the climate system. In particular, they focus on "tipping points" or discontinuities, previously known as bifurcations in a system's large-scale behavior, and on the prospects for providing early warning for their imminent occurrence. The authors describe general methods for detecting and anticipating tipping points, for systems with a high level of internal variability that sample multiple states in time, as well as for systems with less variability that reside in a single state. They apply those methods to the ice-core record of abrupt climate changes in Greenland during the last ice age. Finally, they discuss the limitations of the general methods, and suggest combining them with system-specific vulnerability indicators and process-based models, to help assess the future vulnerability of different tipping elements in the climate system.

In Chapter 6, M. Ghil and I. Zaliapin study a delay differential equation (DDE) for ENSO in the relatively novel setting of non-autonomous dynamical systems and of their pullback attractors. This setting provides deeper insights into the variability of the sea surface temperature T in the Tropical Pacific. Their model includes three essential ENSO mechanisms: the seasonal forcing, the negative feedback due to the oceanic waves, and the delay caused by their propagation across the Tropical Pacific. Two regimes of model variability, stable and unstable, are analyzed. In the unstable regime and in the presence of a given, purely periodic, seasonal forcing, spontaneous transitions occur in the mean T, in the period, and in the extreme annual values. They conclude, among other findings, that the model's behavior exhibits phase locking to the seasonal cycle, namely the local maxima and minima of T tend to occur at the same time of year, which is a characteristic feature of the observed El Niño (warm) and La Niña (cold) events.

1.2. PART II: EXTREME EVENTS IN EARTH'S SPACE ENVIRONMENT

In Chapter 7, A. Ruzmaikin and co-authors apply the Max Spectrum statistical method, which is based on the scaling properties of speed maxima, to study the Sun's fast coronal mass ejections (CMEs). This kind of extreme space weather event is a disturbance in the space environment that presents hazards to the operation of spacecraft systems, instruments, or lives of astronauts. Empirical studies have shown that the speed distribution of CMEs is non-Gaussian. By applying the Max Spectrum technique to CMEs observations, the authors identified the range of speeds, of about 700–2000 km/s, that separates extreme CMEs from typical events. From their investigation of the temporal behavior of fast CMEs, it was concluded that they were not independent, but arrived in clusters and thus can be described by a compound Poisson process.

In Chapter 8, J. Urrutia-Fucugauchi and L. Pérez-Cruz analyzed the highly exceptional Chicxulub asteroid impact event at the Cretaceous/Paleogene boundary, and its effects on the Earth's climate, environment and life-support systems. This boundary marks one of the major extinction events in the Phanerozoic, which affected about 75% of species on Earth. First, the authors examined the impact event and the cratering in Mexico's Yucatán Peninsula and the waters off it, the timescales involved and the energy released. Then, they assessed the impact's regional and global effects, which involved major perturbations in the ocean and atmosphere. Finally, the authors discussed how and to what extent life-support systems are affected by extremely large impact events, and what the fossil record reveals about the extinction event and biotic turnover. In particular, they examined how sudden and extended the processes involved are, as well as the temporal records of extinction and recovery.

1.3. PART III: CLIMATE AND WEATHER EXTREMES

In Chapter 9, A. W. Robertson and colleagues studied Midwestern floods and, in particular, the April 2011 flooding event in the Ohio River Basin. The authors used a *K*-means clustering algorithm for daily circulation types during the March–May spring season to infer relationships between flooding events and circulation types, as well as relationships between these types and climate drivers; the drivers in this study included the interannual ENSO and the intraseasonal Madden-Julian oscillation (MJO). Their results suggest that anomalous southerly fluxes of moisture from the Gulf of Mexico are associated with weather types that occur in connection with the floods, while two of these circulation types are preferentially associated with La Niña. Statistically significant lagged relationships between the frequency of occurrence of these regimes and the MJO were also identified, and they are associated with convection propagating from the Indian Ocean to the Maritime Continent. Implications for prediction across timescales are also discussed.

In Chapter 10, E. Mendoza and associates analyze and model the observations of the record-breaking category 5 Hurricane Wilma of October 2005. This extreme meteorological event generated direct looses of about 2 billion USD in Cancún, Mexico. The authors assessed the hazards and vulnerability to tropical cyclones of this overdeveloped beach-lagoon system. Among other results, the authors showed that before tourist development started in the 1970s, the beach-lagoon system in Cancún functioned as a metastable beach, with erosion-accretion cycles and evidence of natural breaching in places. But the rapid, disorganized tourist development that has taken place, mainly in the last five decades, has degraded this system, increasing its vulnerability to extreme weather events and dramatically reducing its resilience. Hence the effects of Hurricane Wilma on Cancún beach cannot be ascribed only to climatic variability: they bear witness also to the anthropogenic activity that had already degraded the system over recent decades.

In Chapter 11, K. Goto and colleagues relied on field observations, satellite image analyses, and high-resolution numerical modeling to investigate details of local inundation due to the 2004 Indian Ocean tsunami; these multiple data sets also allowed them to make quantitative estimates of the damage generated by the tsunami that was generated by the Sumatra-Andaman earthquake. In particular, the authors investigated the damage to coastal morphology, marine ecosystems, and mangroves at Pakarang Cape, Thailand, and to structures, humans, and mangroves at Banda Aceh city, Indonesia. Their high-resolution numerical modeling of the tsunami hydrodynamics (i.e., inundation depth, hydraulic force, and current velocity) allowed them to generate fragility functions, which explained the observations of the local tsunami inundation and the damage generation, including the damage incurred to the coral communities. The authors suggest that their quantitative damage estimates represent an important step forward for tsunami risk assessment in high-risk, tsunami-prone countries worldwide.

In Chapter 12, M. G. Shats and co-authors argue that extreme wave events on small-scale water surfaces can be used as laboratory analogues of rogue or freak waves in the ocean. The latter ocean waves have heights and steepness much greater than expected from the sea state level and are responsible for a large number of maritime disasters. The authors also emphasize that the generation of rogue waves in the ocean is associated with a distinct tail in the probability density function (PDF) of wave heights. As observations of such rogue waves are rather scarce, the authors performed laboratory studies that consisted of periodically shaking the fluid container in the vertical direction. This shaking produces extreme wave events when capillary-gravity waves are excited at the frequency of the first subharmonic of the driving frequency. The latter laboratory waves appear to be unstable to amplitude modulation, and this instability leads to the decomposition of wave packets into ensembles of interacting oscillatory solitons called "oscillons." The wavefield dynamics is determined by the oscillon interactions, which include their merger, annihilation, and collision. Strikingly, collisions of same-phase oscillons lead to generation of extreme events that can be called "capillary rogue waves."

1.4. PART IV: EXTREME EVENTS IN THE SOLID EARTH

In Chapter 13, M.-T. Ramírez-Herrera and colleagues propose a multiproxy approach, which includes geological, microfossil, magnetic-property, geochemical, historical, ethnographic, instrumental data, and theoretical modeling analyses, to expand our knowledge about extreme-magnitude seismic events beyond the short instrumental record, and therewith to reduce the tsunami hazard to coastal communities. The authors focused their study on the coast of the Guerrero region, located in the Mexican subduction zone, where the occurrence of historical earthquakes and of the associated tsunamis is relatively well documented since the 16th century. Their main result shows that the Guerrero coast region has been exposed to large-magnitude destructive earthquakes and tsunamis, in addition to the AD 1979 and AD 1985 events, at least to a third one, in 3400 BP and that the latter reached 5 km inland. The authors highlight the need to carry out these types of studies in the Mexican subduction zone, to assess the hazard in this region to create resilient coastal communities.

In Chapter 14, P. Salvati and associates propose a new approach, based on the modeling of empirical distributions of landslide events with a Zipf distribution, to investigate landslide risk to the population of Italy over time. The authors present an updated version of an Italian historical catalog of landslide events with human consequences that cover the period 91 BC to AD 2011. Still, to overcome problems due to gaps in the updated catalog, they rely mainly on the information available for the 1861–2010 period. They studied the temporal and geographical variation of landslide risk in five subzones of the north, the center, and the south of Italy for three subintervals: 1861–1909, 1910–1959, and 1960–2010. The authors conclude that their new societal landslide risk level estimates are an important step for increasing

awareness of the problems posed by this type of extreme events among Italian administrators and citizens.

In Chapter 15, S. De la Cruz-Reyna and A. T. Mendoza-Rosas apply a three-step procedure to assess the volcanic hazard posed by potential extreme eruptive sequences of individual volcanoes or groups of volcanoes. The first step consists of expanding the, usually incomplete, historical eruptive series of a volcano by eruptive synthetic series constructed from any available geological-time eruption data. This step assumes a scaling, self-similar relationship between the eruption size and the occurrence rate of the latter. In the second step, a Weibull-model analysis of the distribution of quiescent times between successive eruptions is carried out to estimate their time dependence, if any. Finally, the eruption series are analyzed using EVT theory for a nonhomogeneous Poisson process with a generalized Pareto distribution as intensity function. From the results of this analysis, the probabilities of future eruptions can be estimated. Examples of the application of the proposed procedure to the Colima, El Chichon, and the Popocatepetl volcanoes of Mexico conclude the chapter.

1.5. PART V: SOCIOECONOMIC IMPACTS OF EXTREME EVENTS

In Chapter 16, R. Katz states that considerable effort has been dedicated to the statistics of extreme geophysical phenomena, while not much is known about the corresponding distribution of economic damage, due largely to the scarcity of data. He applies EVT to help explain the differences between upper-tail behavior of the economic-damage distribution and that of the underlying geophysical phenomenon. Based on physical considerations, the author proposes a damage function in the form of a power law, and concludes that a "penultimate" (or second-order) approximation of EVT is required to replace the standard asymptotic (or "ultimate") theory. This formulation implies, at least under a wide range of plausible conditions, that the distribution of economic damage can be heavy-tailed, even when the upper tail of storm intensity distribution, say, is bounded. These theoretical considerations are applied to the economic-damage distribution due to hurricanes and its relationship to storm intensity, as measured by maximum wind speed at landfall.

In Chapter 17, M. Chavez and co-authors formulate a hybrid approach to estimate the probability of exceedances of the intensities (PEIs) of extreme-magnitude earthquakes (EMEs) and the probability of exceedance of direct economic consequences (PEDECs) that arise from the damages to spatially distributed infrastructure within a site. The PEIs are obtained from samples of 3D-synthetic seismograms associated with EME scenarios by applying a machine learning technique. The PEDECs are computed by combining appropriate cadastral, direct economic costs and seismic vulnerability functions of the infrastructure and the spatial distribution of the intensities of the EME scenario. Truncated PDFs for the marginal distributions and copula models are applied to obtain the independent and joint probability distributions of the PEI and the PEDEC; these distributions, in turn, can be used to derive the associated return period for decision-making purposes. This hybrid approach is applied to obtain preliminary upper bounds on the probable maximum losses (PMLs) of the direct costs associated with the damage to the typical, one to three floor dwellings of Mexico City and Guadalajara, based on scenarios of an extreme, M_w 8.5 magnitude subduction earthquake. The preliminary PMLs obtained vary from 0.7 to 18 billion USD for Mexico City, and from 37 to 61 billion USD for Guadalajara. If ex-ante mitigation actions are taken to retrofit dwelling constructions and thus reduce their vulnerabilities, roughly 52,000 and 250,000 dwellings could be spared in Mexico City and Guadalajara, respectively, by investing ~0.8 and 6 billion USD, versus potential PMLs of 7 and 22 billion USD, in each city, respectively.

In Chapter 18, S. J. Camargo and S. M. Hsiang summarize the current knowledge on the link between tropical cyclones (TCs) and climate at various timescales, from subseasonal to anthropogenic warming, and on the quantitative modeling of the TCs' socioeconomic impact. They argue that the improvements in computational capabilities have enabled the representation of TCs in models of the global atmosphere and ocean to become much more realistic, especially by increasing the models' horizontal resolution; still, deficiencies remain in modeling storm intensity. With respect to the socioeconomic issues, the authors mention that the advancements in geospatial analysis have enabled researchers to link meteorological observations with socioeconomic data, and thus measure the effect that TC exposure has on numerous human outcomes. The authors conclude that the TCs' socioeconomic impact is larger than previously thought. Hence, the rational management of current and future TC risk must leverage policies and institutions, such as insurance coverage and infrastructure investments. The efficiency and value of the latter can only be determined through continued, systematic evaluation of the TCs' social cost.

In Chapter 19, A. Groth and colleagues combine the study of a dynamic, nonequilibrium model (NEDyM) of business cycles with that of time series of macroeconomic indicators to address the interactions between natural and socioeconomic phenomena. NEDyM simulates fairly realistic, endogenous business cycle, with an average periodicity of 5–6 years marked by slow expansions and rapid recessions. This model predicts that the macroeconomic response to natural disasters, under nonequilibrium conditions, is more severe during expansions than during recessions. This prediction contradicts the assessment of climate change damages or natural disaster losses that are based purely on long-term growth models, in which there is no asymmetry between expansions and contractions of the economy. To verify this NEDyM prediction, the authors analyze cyclic behavior in the U.S. economy, using nine aggregate indicators for the 1954–2005 interval. The analysis relies on multivariate singular spectrum analysis and finds that the behavior of the U.S. economy changes significantly between intervals of growth and recession, with higher volatility during expansions, as expected from the NEDyM model predictions.

1.6. PART VI: PREDICTION AND PREPAREDNESS

In Chapter 20, L. Amir and collaborators applied tsunami modeling to assess the hazard due to extreme-magnitude earthquakes and submarine slides causing tsunami events along the Mediterranean coasts of Algeria. Among other results, they found that tsunami water heights triggered by extreme, magnitude-7.5 earthquake scenarios with epicenters near the Oran and Algiers coasts are up to 2 m in height, while for submarine-slide sources the water heights can reach above 5 m along the western part of the Algerian coast. The authors discuss the challenges that Algeria would face due to the economic impact of such extreme tsunami and earthquake events on their coastal infrastructure. Finally, the chapter highlights the importance of the urgent and full implementation of the North-East Atlantic and Mediterranean Seas Tsunami Warning System (NEAMTWS) for the prevention and awareness of tsunami hazard and risk in the Mediterranean earthquake-prone region.

In Chapter 21, H. Castaños and C. Lomnitz analyze the aftermath of the extreme, M_w 9 magnitude Tohoku earthquake and its associated mega-tsunami, which led to the Fukushima nuclear catastrophe. Based on a detailed analysis of the available information on the old (~40 years) and current protocols applied worldwide for the design and operation of nuclear power plants, especially on those used for the Fukushima and Oyster Creek nuclear power plants, the authors argue that the Fukushima nuclear power plant was designed under a strategy known as "defense in depth," a military strategy consisting of delaying the progress of an enemy force by trading casualties for space. This strategy, when it is applied to the design of nuclear power plants, consists on adding subsystems construed as layers of redundant technology around the reactor core. This approach implies that nuclear safety is conditioned by a risky constellation of subordinated technologies, which combined with the occurrence of extreme geophysical events, such as the Tohoku megatsunami, results in a complex system whose behavior cannot be fully predicted. It is concluded that high-tech extreme events, such as the Fukushima, will continue to occur, mainly because of previously unforeseen weaknesses in their redundant subsystems.

In Chapter 22, V. Keilis-Borok and colleagues describe a uniform approach for predicting extreme events, also known as critical phenomena, disasters, or crises in a variety of fields. The basic assumption of the approach is that a pervasive class of hierarchical dissipative complex systems generates such events. This kind of system has the property that, after coarse-graining, it exhibits regular behavior patterns that include premonitory patterns signaling the approach of an extreme event. The authors also propose a methodology, based on optimal control theory, for assisting disaster management, in choosing an optimal set of disaster preparedness measures undertaken in response to a prediction. The chapter includes examples of the application of the uniform approach of premonitory patterns to the prediction of the occurrence of earthquakes, U.S. presidential elections, surges in unemployment, U.S. economic recessions, homicide surges, as well as examples related to disaster preparedness.

1.7. SUMMARY AND CONCLUSIONS

The 21 chapters discussed so far use a variety of mathematical, numerical, and statistical techniques to expand our understanding of extreme geophysical and climatic events, as well as the risks they impose on society. The physical and economic comprehension of these risks, as well as the current techniques to cope with them, has improved recently to a considerable extent. It appears that understanding, and hence predicting, extreme events might be possible in some cases. However, as shown in this book, the tools to estimate their probability distributions are already available in a number of areas of the geosciences. These recent advancements create a lot of opportunities and challenges for the researcher in and practioner of extremology, the science of extreme events, and their consequences.

Part I
Fundamentals and Theory

2

Applications of Extreme Value Theory to Environmental Data Analysis

Gwladys Toulemonde,[1] Pierre Ribereau,[1] and Philippe Naveau[2]

ABSTRACT

When analyzing extreme events, assuming independence in space and/or time may not correspond to a valid hypothesis in geosciences. The statistical modeling of such dependences is complex and different modeling roads can be explored. In this chapter, some basic concepts about univariate and multivariate extreme value theory will be first recalled. Then a series of examples will be treated to exemplify how this probability theory can help the practitioner to make inferences about extreme quantiles within a multivariate context.

2.1. INTRODUCTION: UNIVARIATE EXTREME VALUE THEORY

Extreme events are, almost by definition, rare and unexpected. Consequently, it is very difficult to deal with them. Examples include the study of record droughts, annual maxima of temperature, wind, and precipitation. Climate sciences is one of the main fields of applications of extreme value theory (EVT), but we can also mention hydrology [*Katz et al.*, 2002], finance, and assurance [*Embrechts et al.*, 1997], among others. Even if the probability of extreme events occurrence decreases rapidly, the damage caused increases rapidly and so does the cost of protection against them. The policymakers' summary of the 2007 Intergovernmental Panel on Climate Change clearly states that it *is very likely that hot extremes, heat waves, and heavy precipitation events will continue to become more frequent* and that *precipitation is highly variable spatially and temporally.*

From a probabilistic point of view, let us consider a sample of n independent and identically distributed (i.i.d.) random variables (r.v.) $X_1, X_2, ..., X_n$ from a distribution function F. In the same way that we have the central limit theorem (CLT) concerning the mean value of this sample, asymptotic results are available from EVT about the limit distribution of the rescaled sample's maximum value $X_{n,n} = \max_{i=1,...,n} X_i$ as the sample size n increases. Indeed, according to the classical EVT [*Embrechts et al.*, 1997; *Coles*, 2001; *Beirlant et al.*, 2004; *de Haan and Ferreira*, 2006], the correctly rescaled sample's maximum is, under suitable conditions, asymptotically distributed according to one of the three extreme value distributions named Gumbel, Fréchet, or Weibull.

More precisely if there exists sequences of constants $\{a_n\}$ and $\{b_n > 0\}$ and a nondegenerate distribution function G such that

$$\lim_{n \to +\infty} \mathbb{P}\left(\frac{X_{n,n} - a_n}{b_n} \leq x\right) = G(x)$$

[1]*Institut de Mathématiques et de Modélisation de Montpellier – UMR 5149, Montpellier, France*
[2]*Laboratoire des Sciences du Climat et de l'Environnement LSCE-IPSL-CNRS, Gif-sur-Yvette, France*

Extreme Events: Observations, Modeling, and Economics, Geophysical Monograph 214, First Edition.
Edited by Mario Chavez, Michael Ghil, and Jaime Urrutia-Fucugauchi.
© 2016 American Geophysical Union. Published 2016 by John Wiley & Sons, Inc.

then G belongs to one of the following families (with $\alpha > 0$):

1. Gumbel:

$$G(x) = \Lambda(x) = e^{-e^{-(x-a/b)}} \quad \text{with } x \in \mathbb{R}$$

2. Fréchet:

$$G(x) = \Phi_\alpha(x) = \begin{cases} 0 & \text{if } x \leq a \\ e^{-((x-a/b))^{-\alpha}} & \text{if } x > a \end{cases}$$

3. Weibull:

$$G(x) = \Psi_\alpha(x) = \begin{cases} e^{-(-(x-a/b))^{\alpha}} & \text{if } x \leq a \\ 1 & \text{if } x > a \end{cases}$$

A specificity of these three distributions is their max-stability property. Furthermore, they are the only max-stable distributions. A distribution G is max-stable if G is invariant, up to affine transformations, that is, up to location and scale parameters. In other words, we say that G is max-stable if there exists sequences $\{d_n\}$ and $\{c_n > 0\}$ such that, for all $n \geq 2$, the sample's maximum $X_{n,n}$ is equal in distribution to $c_n X + d_n$ with X following the same distribution G, what can be written as follows:

$$G^n(x) = G\left(\frac{x - d_n}{c_n}\right).$$

From a statistical point of view, the interest of this fundamental theorem is limited. Indeed each situation corresponds to different tail behavior of the underlying distribution F. The Fréchet distribution corresponds to the limit of maxima coming from heavy-tailed distributions like the Pareto distribution. The Weibull distribution is associated with distributions with a finite endpoint like the uniform distribution. The particular case of the Gumbel distribution has a special importance in EVT because it occurs as the limit of maxima from light-tailed distributions, for example, from the Gaussian distribution. Moreover, empirically, the Gumbel distribution fits particularly well in a wide range of applications especially in atmospheric sciences.

In practice we have to adopt one of the three families but we don't have any information about F. That's why a unified approach would be very appreciated in order to characterize the limit distribution of maxima.

The previous theorem could be reformulated in a unified way by using the generalized extreme value (GEV) distribution. If there exists sequences of constants $\{a_n\}$ and $\{b_n > 0\}$ and a nondegenerate distribution function G such that

$$\lim_{n \to +\infty} \mathbb{P}\left(\frac{X_{n,n} - a_n}{b_n} \leq x\right) = G_{\mu,\sigma,\gamma}(x)$$

then $G_{\mu,\sigma,\gamma}$ belongs to the GEV family

$$G_{\mu,\sigma,\gamma}(x) = \exp\left(-\left[1 + \gamma \frac{x - \mu}{\sigma}\right]^{-1/\gamma}\right)$$

with $x \in \left\{z : 1 + \gamma \frac{x - \mu}{\sigma} > 0\right\}$.

It is easy to remark that $G_{\mu,\sigma,\gamma}$ merges all univariate max-stable distributions previously introduced. It depends on an essential parameter γ characterizing the shape of the F-distribution tail. Since a strictly positive γ corresponds to the Fréchet family, this case corresponds to heavy-tailed distributions. Otherwise a strictly negative γ is associated with the Weibull family. For γ tends to 0, the function $G_{\mu,\sigma,\gamma}$ tends to the Gumbel one.

Practically, in order to assess and predict extreme events, one often works with the so-called block maxima, that is, with the maximum value of the data within a certain time interval including k observations. The maximum can be assumed to be GEV distributed in the case where k is large enough. If we obtain a sufficient number of maxima and if these maxima can be considered as an i.i.d. sample, estimation values for the GEV unknown parameters can be obtained with maximum likelihood procedure or probability weighted moments (PWM) for instance. The asymptotic behaviors of these estimators have been established [*Hosking et al.*, 1985; *Smith*, 1985; *Diebolt et al.*, 2008].

In the first considered example, we dispose of temperature daily maxima during 30 years in Colmar, a city in the east of France. We consider monthly maxima for the summer months: June, July, and August (see Figure 2.1). This way we avoid a seasonality in the data.

The choice of the block size denoted in the sequel by r, such as a year or a month, can be justified in many cases by geophysical considerations but this choice has actual consequences on estimation tools. In an environmental context, if we can often consider annual maxima as an i.i.d. sample, this hypothesis is stronger when we deal with monthly or weekly maxima for instance. Indeed in these latter cases we have typically a seasonality in the data so we are in a nonstationary context.

Coming back to our application, when the GEV distribution ($G_{\mu,\sigma,\gamma}$) is fitted by maximum likelihood directly on the sample of $k = 90$ monthly maxima on summer (3×30 years), we obtain $\hat{\mu} = 31.502$, $\hat{\sigma} = 2.456$, and $\hat{\gamma} = -0.256$. The corresponding 95%-confidence intervals are $[30.943; 32.060]$, $[2.058; 2.853]$, and $[-0.383; -0.128]$. The quantile plot in Figure 2.2 is close to the unit diagonal indicating a good fit of data (*Empirical*) by a GEV distribution

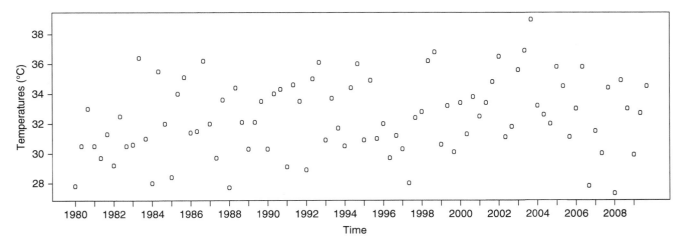

Figure 2.1 The y-axis corresponds to temperature maxima (in °C) for the months of June, July, and August from 1980 to 2009 (x-axis) recorded at Colmar (France).

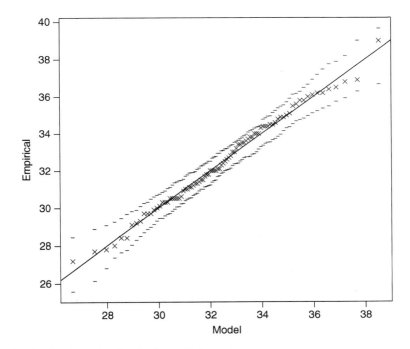

Figure 2.2 Quantile Plot for the GEV distribution—Colmar data.

(*Model*). The results on the GEV fitting must be taken with care. Indeed, taking the maxima only on 30 measures may lead to unexpected results [see *de Haan and Ferreira*, 2006]. Here, the limiting distribution of the maxima may be the Gumbel one even if the estimation of γ is negative (e.g., if the original variables are Gaussian distributed, the effective gamma is approximately $-1/(2\log k)$, where k is the block size).

A question of interest in this kind of application concerns the estimation of extreme quantiles of the maxima distribution on a period (a block). In other words, we are looking for $z_{1/p}$ such that $\mathbb{P}(X_{r,r} \leq z_{1/p}) = 1 - p$.

Since we have $\mathbb{P}(X_{k,k} \leq z_{1/p}) \approx G_{\mu,\sigma,\gamma}(z_{1/p})$, we obtain

$$z_{1/p} \approx \mu - \frac{\sigma}{\gamma}\left[1 - \left(-\log(1-p)\right)^{-\gamma}\right] \quad \text{if } \gamma \neq 0$$
$$\approx \mu - \sigma \log\left(-\log(1-p)\right) \quad \text{if } \gamma = 0.$$

The quantity z_T is called "return level" associated with a return period $T = (1/p)$. The level z_T is expected to be exceeded on average once every $T = (1/p)$ blocks (e.g., months).

We use the following estimator $\hat{z}_T$:

$$\hat{z}_T = \hat{\mu} - \frac{\hat{\sigma}}{\hat{\gamma}}\left[1 - \left(-\log(1-p)\right)^{-\hat{\gamma}}\right] \quad \text{if } \gamma \neq 0$$
$$= \hat{\mu} - \hat{\sigma}\log\left(-\log(1-p)\right) \quad \text{if } \gamma = 0.$$

Starting from the asymptotic behavior of the GEV parameters' vector estimator, it is possible to deduce, thanks to the δ-method [*Van der Vaart*, 1998], the asymptotic behavior of $\hat{z}_T$ leading us to associated confidence intervals.

Coming back to our example, we would like to compute the return level associated with the return period $T = 3 \times 50$ months corresponding to 50 years as we consider only 3 months a year. We easily obtain a return level $\hat{z}_{150} = 38.43$ and a 95%-confidence interval [37.107; 39.758]. This means that considering only summer periods, the temperature 38.43°C is expected to be exceeded on average once every 50 years. So thanks to EVT we are able to estimate a return level corresponding to 50 years, whereas we only consider data since 30 years.

We have supposed that maxima constitute an i.i.d. sample, which is reasonable with regard to Figure 2.1. A likelihood ratio test indicates no trend in our data. To support this aim we fit a GEV distribution with a linear trend in the localization parameter ($G_{\mu(t),\sigma,\gamma}$). We obtain

with the likelihood procedure $\hat{\mu}(t) = 30.635 + 0.059t$, $\hat{\sigma} = 2.439$, and $\hat{\gamma} = -0.281$. The corresponding likelihood ratio test statistic is $D = 2 \times (209.82 - 207.91) = 3.82$. This value is small when compared to the χ_1^2 distribution, suggesting that the simple model (without trend) is adequate for these data. Other estimation procedures have been developed in the nonstationary context. For example, *Maraun et al.* [2010] have proposed various models to describe the influence of covariates (possible nonlinearities in the covariates and seasonality) on UK daily precipitation extremes. In the same way, *Ribereau et al.* [2008] extend the PWM method in order to take into account temporal covariates and provide accurate GEV-based return levels. This technique is particularly adapted for small sample sizes and permits, for example, to consider seasonality in data.

If block sizes are sufficiently large and even if the stationary hypothesis is not always satisfied, the independence one remains very often valid. On the contrary, even if the series could be considered as stationary, the independence hypothesis is not always satisfied if we consider too small block size, like daily maxima.

As an example, Figure 2.3 represents a series of daily maxima of CO_2 (in part per million), a greenhouse gas recorded from 1981 to 2002 in Gif sur Yvette, a city of

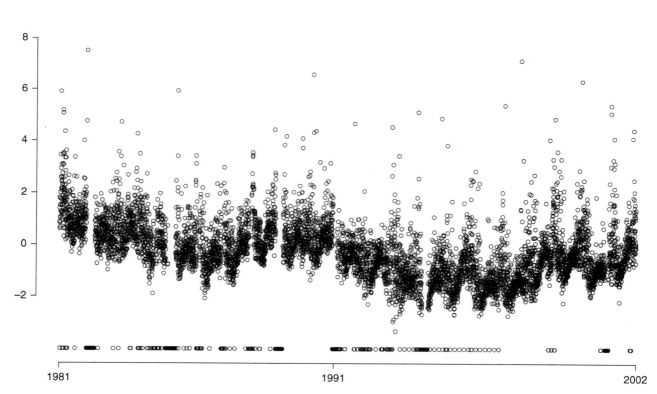

Figure 2.3 Series of daily maxima of carbon dioxide.

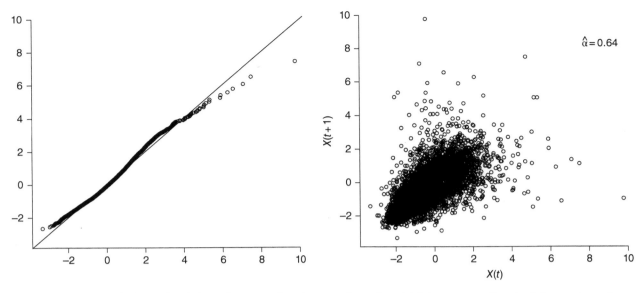

Figure 2.4 Gumbel QQplot (left) and scatter plot of successive values (right) corresponding to daily maxima of carbon dioxide.

France. The trend in the series has been removed in order to consider a stationary series.

This example illustrates the connection between light-tailed maxima and the Gumbel distribution. Indeed, if we fit a Gumbel distribution on the daily CO_2 maxima, we see on the Gumbel Quantile Quantile (QQ-)plot (see left part of Figure 2.4) that it is quite reasonable to suppose that these data are Gumbel distributed (with $\hat{\mu} = -0.44$ and $\hat{\sigma} = 0.76$). But in this practical case, the length of our observations is too short to study yearly maxima, or even monthly maxima. As a consequence, when studying daily maxima it is natural to observe some day-to-day memories. The scatter plot of successive values (see right part of Figure 2.4) confirms this short-term temporal dependence.

A very simple approach in the time series analysis would be to consider linear autoregressive (AR) models. Classical hypotheses are noise Gaussianity and model linearity. But in an extreme value context, if X_t is a maximum, then one expects X_t to follow a GEV distribution and it is impossible to satisfy this distributional constraint with a Gaussian additive AR process.

That's why *Toulemonde et al.* [2010] have proposed a linear AR process adapted to the Gumbel distribution. This model is based on an additive relationship between Gumbel and positive α-stable variables (A random variable S is said to be stable if for all non-negative real numbers c_1, c_2, there exists a positive real a and a real b such that $c_1 S_1 + c_2 S_2$ is equal in distribution to $aS + b$, where S_1, S_2 are i.i.d. copies of S.) [see *Hougaard*, 1986; *Crowder*, 1989; *Tawn*, 1990; *Fougères et al.*, 2009].

First, let us consider $S_{t,\alpha}$ being i.i.d. positive asymmetric α-stable r.v. defined by its Laplace transform for any $t \in \mathbb{Z}$

$$\mathbb{E}\left(\exp\left(-uS_{t,\alpha}\right)\right) = \exp\left(-u^{\alpha}\right), \text{ for all } u \geq 0 \text{ and for } \alpha \in \ ]0,1[. \tag{2.1}$$

Let $\{X_t, t \in \mathbb{Z}\}$ be a stochastic process defined by the recursive relationship

$$X_t = \alpha \ X_{t-1} + \alpha \ \sigma \ \log S_{t,\alpha} \tag{2.2}$$

where $\sigma > 0$. It has been proved first that Equation (2.2) has a unique strictly stationary solution,

$$X_t = \sigma \sum_{j=0}^{\infty} \alpha^{j+1} \log S_{t-j,\alpha} \tag{2.3}$$

and second that X_t follows a Gumbel distribution with parameters $(0, \sigma)$.

This model is a linear AR model and has consequently the associated advantages such that their conceptual simplicity and their flexibility for modeling quasi-periodic phenomena (e.g., sunspots time series) and short-term dependencies (e.g., day-to-day memories in weather systems). Whereas one drawback of current linear AR models is that they are unable to represent the distributional behavior of maxima, a key point of parameterization (2.2) is that X_t follows a Gumbel distribution. In other words this process is suitable for maxima data coming from light-tailed distributions. Even if our process is

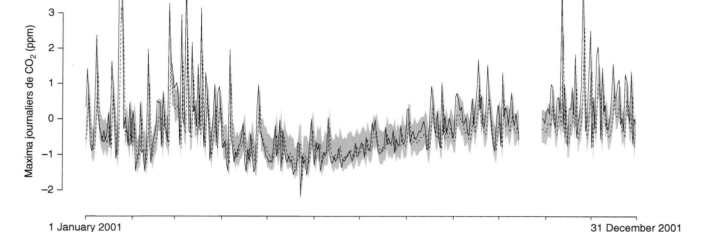

Figure 2.5 One-day previsions of daily maxima of CO_2 (y-axis) in the year 2001 (x-axis). The black line corresponds to the observed series and the dotted line corresponds to the estimated series (median). The gray area is delimited by the first and third empirical quartiles.

specific to the Gumbel distribution, it is possible to extend it for maxima coming from bounded or heavy-tailed distribution. Nevertheless this leads to a process which is not additive anymore.

Coming back to our example, identifying the temporal structure among the largest CO_2 measurements is of primary interest for the atmospheric chemist because this can help to predict future maxima of CO_2 at a specific location. As an illustration, Figure 2.5 presents one-step previsions of CO_2 daily maxima in the year 2001.

This method, presented in *Toulemonde et al.* [2010] is exemplified in their paper on daily maxima series of two other greenhouse gas, the methane (CH_4) and the oxide nitrous (N_2O) recorded at LSCE (Laboratoire des Sciences du Climat et de l'Environnement) in Gif-sur-Yvette (France). Since the beginning of 2007, the LSCE has proceeded to record daily maxima of CH_4 but has stopped the regular recordings of N_2O daily maxima. That's why in a recent paper, *Toulemonde et al.* [2013] proposed a method adapted to maxima from light-tailed distribution able to reconstruct a hidden series. In this state-space context, they take advantage of particle filtering methods. In an extreme adapted model, they compute optimal weights for the use of the auxiliary filter [*Pitt and Shepard*, 1999] and they denote this filter by APF-Opt. Based on observations of CH_4 and N_2O from 2002 to the middle of 2006, they obtained similar results than those presented in Figure 2.6 for the reconstruction of N_2O daily maxima.

Concerning inference procedure, as usually in the block maxima approach, only the maxima are used. To remove this drawback, another technique consists of modeling exceedances above a given threshold u. In the so-called Peaks-over-Threshold (PoT) approach, the distributions of these exceedances are also characterized by asymptotic results.

Let $X_1, \ldots, X_n$ a sample of n i.i.d. r.v. from a distribution function F. We consider the N_u of them which are over the threshold u. The exceedance Y_i corresponding to the variable X_i is defined by $X_i - u$ if $X_i > u$.

The distribution function F_u of an exceedance Y over a threshold u is given for $y > 0$ by

$$F_u(y) = \mathbb{P}(Y \leq y \mid X > u) = \mathbb{P}(X - u \leq y \mid X > u)$$
$$= \frac{\mathbb{P}(u < X \leq u + y)}{\mathbb{P}(X > u)} = \frac{F(u + y) - F(u)}{1 - F(u)}.$$

If the threshold is sufficiently high, we can approximate this quantity by the distribution function of the generalized Pareto distribution $H_{\gamma,\sigma}(y)$. We defined its survival function as follows

$$\bar{H}_{\gamma,\sigma}(y) = \left(1 + \gamma \frac{y}{\sigma}\right)^{-1/\gamma} \quad \text{if } \gamma \neq 0$$

$$= \exp\left(-\frac{y}{\sigma}\right) \quad \text{otherwise.}$$

This function is defined on $\mathbb{R}^+$ if $\gamma \geq 0$ or on $[0; -\sigma/\gamma[$ if $\gamma < 0$ where $\sigma > 0$ is a scale parameter and $\gamma \in \mathbb{R}$ a shape parameter.

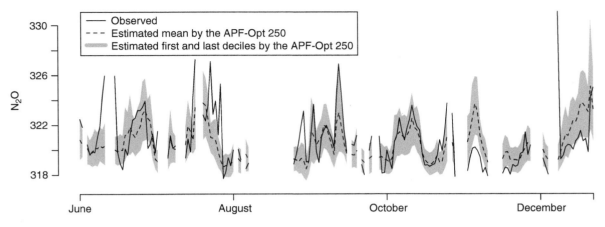

Figure 2.6 Mean values of particles from APF-Opt and punctual empirical CI 80% with 250 particles for the series of N_2O daily maxima in Gif-sur-Yvette from June to December 2006.

The famous theorem of *Pickands* [1975] establishes the following equivalence:

$$\lim_{n \to +\infty} \mathbb{P}\left(\frac{X_{n,n} - a_n}{b_n} \leq x\right) = G_{\mu,\sigma,\gamma}(x)$$

if and only if

$$\lim_{u \to x_F} \sup_{y \in [0; x_F - u]} \left|\bar{F}_u(y) - \bar{H}_{\gamma,\sigma(u)}(y)\right| = 0.$$

It is important to mention that the shape parameter in the block maxima approach coincides with the shape parameter in the PoT approach.

Coming back to extreme quantiles estimation, we have for $x_p \geq u$, the following approximation

$$p = \bar{F}(x_p) \approx \bar{F}(u)\left[1 + \gamma \frac{x_p - u}{\sigma}\right]^{-\frac{1}{\gamma}} \quad \text{if } \gamma \neq 0$$

$$\approx \bar{F}(u)\exp\left(-\frac{x_p - u}{\sigma}\right) \quad \text{if } \gamma = 0.$$

which implies

$$x_p = \bar{F}^{-1}(p) \approx u + \frac{\sigma}{\gamma}\left(\left[\frac{p}{\bar{F}(u)}\right]^{-\gamma} - 1\right) \quad \text{if } \gamma \neq 0$$

$$\approx u - \sigma \log\left(\frac{p}{\bar{F}(u)}\right) \quad \text{if } \gamma = 0.$$

By construction, x_p is the return level associated with the $1/p$-observation. In other words this level x_p is expected to be exceeded on average once every $1/p$-observations.

If we are interested on a return level associated with a return period T-blocks (e.g., months), denoted by z_T, and

suppose we have r observations per block (e.g., month), we will consider $p = (1/rT)$.

Finally, a PoT estimator $\hat{z}_T$ of the return level T-block with r observations per block is given by

$$\hat{z}_T = \hat{\bar{F}}^{-1}\left(\frac{1}{rT}\right) = u + \frac{\hat{\sigma}}{\hat{\gamma}}\left(\left[\frac{n}{rTN_u}\right]^{-\hat{\gamma}} - 1\right) \quad \text{if } \gamma \neq 0$$

$$= u - \hat{\sigma} \log\left(\frac{n}{rTN_u}\right) \quad \text{if } \gamma = 0.$$

The choice of the threshold is difficult and is clearly a question of trade-off between bias and variance for the estimation of the parameters (γ, σ). There is no perfect solution but only tools based, for example, on the mean excess function (MEF) which help us to make a choice. Again, as in the block maxima approach, the GPD approximation for excesses is asymptotic and results obtained on finite sample size should be considered carefully.

2.2. MULTIVARIATE APPROACH

The probabilistic foundations for the statistical study of multivariate extremes are well developed. Since the classical work of *Resnick* [1987], many books [see *Beirlant et al.*, 2004; *de Haan and Ferreira*, 2006; *Resnick*, 2007] have paid considerable attention to this particular case.

We will focus here on analog of block maxima results discussed in previous sections for univariate extremes. Suppose that $(X_1, Y_1), (X_2, Y_2), \ldots, (X_n, Y_n)$ is a sequence of i.i.d. random vectors with same common distribution function F. Examples of such variables are maximum and minimum temperatures or precipitations in two locations. As in the univariate case, the characterization of the behavior of extremes in a multivariate context is based on the block maxima. Denote

$$M_{x,n} = \max_{i=1,\dots,n}\{X_i\} \quad \text{and} \quad M_{y,n} = \max_{i=1,\dots,n}\{Y_i\}$$
$$M_n = \left(M_{x,n}, M_{y,n}\right).$$

M_n is the vector of component-wise maxima. Note that the maximum of the X_i can occur at a different time than the one of the Y_i, so M_n does not necessarily correspond to an observed vector. The multivariate EVT begins with the study of the M_n behavior. If $z = (z_1, z_2)$ and $M_n \leq z$, meaning that $M_{x,n} \leq z_1$ and $M_{y,n} \leq z_2$, we have

$$\mathbb{P}\left(M_n \leq z\right) = F(z)^n.$$

We assume that there exists two rescaling sequences of vector $\{a_n\}$ and $\{b_n\}$, where $a_{n,j} > 0$ and $b_{n,j} \in \mathbb{R}$ for $j = 1,2$ and G a distribution function with nondegenerate margins such that

$$F^n\left(a_n z + b_n\right) \to G(z)$$

where $a_n z + b_n = (a_{n,1} z_1 + b_{n,1}, a_{n,2} z_2 + b_{n,2})$. If such sequences exist, G is a bivariate extreme value distribution. With the same notations, another consequence is that

$$G^k\left(a_k z + b_k\right) = G(z)$$

that is G is max stable. The problem of the limiting distribution G is partially solved considering separately $(X_i)_i$ and $(Y_i)_i$ since the univariate EVT can be applied directly.

2.2.1. Characterization Theorem

As the margins of the limiting distribution are GEV distributed, that means we can get easier representation by assuming that the margins are known. Simple representations arise when assuming that both X_i and Y_i are unit Fréchet distributed with distribution function $G_{1,1,1}(z) = \exp(-1/z)$.

Once the margins transform to unit Fréchet, we should consider the re-scaled vector

$$M_n^* = \left(M_{x,n}^*, M_{y,n}^*\right) = \left(M_{x,n}/n, M_{y,n}/n\right),$$

in order to obtain standard univariate results for each margin.

Theorem 1 *Let (X_i, Y_i) be i.i.d. random vectors with unit Fréchet marginals and define $(M_{x,n}^*, M_{y,n}^*)$ as previous. If:*

$$\mathbb{P}\left(M_{x,n}^* \leq x, M_{y,n}^* \leq y\right) \to G(x,y)$$

where G is a nondegenerated distribution, then G is of the form:

$$G(x,y) = \exp\left(-V(x,y)\right), \quad x > 0, y > 0$$

where

$$V(x,y) = 2\int_0^1 \max\left(\frac{\omega}{x}, \frac{1-\omega}{y}\right) dH(\omega)$$

and H is a distribution on $[0,1]$ verifying the following mean constraint:

$$\int_0^1 \omega \, dH(\omega) = 1/2. \tag{2.4}$$

For example, if H is such that

$$H(\omega) = \begin{cases} 1/2 & \text{if } \omega = 0 \text{ or } 1 \\ 0 & \text{else} \end{cases}$$

the corresponding bivariate extreme value distribution is

$$G(x,y) = \exp\left\{-\left(x^{-1} + y^{-1}\right)\right\}$$

for $x > 0$ and $y > 0$. This distribution is a product of a function of x and another of y and therefore corresponds to the independence. Another interesting case of distribution H is a measure that place mass equal to 1 in 0.5. In that case, the bivariate extreme value distribution is

$$G(x,y) = \exp\left(-\max\left\{x^{-1}, y^{-1}\right\}\right)$$

for $x > 0$ and $y > 0$. It is the special case of variables X and Y which are unit Fréchet distributed and perfectly dependent, that is, $X = Y$ a.s.

As any function verifying the mean constraint defines a bivariate extreme distribution, there is a one-to-one relation between the set of bivariate extreme distributions with unit Fréchet margins and the set of distributions on $[0,1]$ satisfying (2.4). So any parametric family for H satisfying (2.4) defines a class of bivariate extreme value distribution.

One classical family is the logistic one. In that case, we have:

$$G(x,y) = \exp\left(-\left(x^{-1/\alpha} + y^{-1/\alpha}\right)^\alpha\right)$$

for $x > 0$ and $y > 0$ and for $\alpha \in (0,1)$. The popularity of this family is its simplicity and its flexibility. Indeed, as $\alpha \to 1$, it is easy to check that we get the independence. In contrast, if $\alpha \to 0$ we get the perfect dependence. So the logistic family covers all levels of dependence, but the model is limited since the variables x and y are exchangeable because of the symmetry of the density h. In order to avoid this limitation, there exists two generalizations of this model.

The first one is the asymmetric logistic family for which we have

$$G(x,y) = \exp\left\{-(1-t_1)x^{-1} - (1-t_2)y^{-1} - \left[\left(\frac{x}{t_1}\right)^{-1/\alpha} + \left(\frac{y}{t_2}\right)^{-1/\alpha}\right]^\alpha\right\}$$

where $0 < \alpha \leq 1$ and $0 \leq t_1, t_2 \leq 1$. The parameter α controls the dependence, while t_1 and t_2 control asymmetry. When $t_1 = t_2 = 1$, we get the logistic family.

As $\alpha \to 1$ or as t_1 or t_2 equal to 0, we get the independence, while if $\alpha \to 0$ and $t_1 = t_2 = 1$, we have the perfect dependence.

The second generalization is the bilogistic model defined by:

$$G(x,y) = \exp\left(-x^{-1}q^{1-\alpha} - y^{-1}(1-q)^{1-\beta}\right)$$

where $q = q(x,y,\alpha,\beta)$ is the solution of the following equation:

$$(1-\alpha)x^{-1}(1-q)^\beta - (1-\beta)y^{-1}q^\alpha = 0,$$

and $0 < \alpha, \beta < 1$. When $\alpha = \beta$, the bilogistic family reduces to the logistic class. The complete dependence arises when $\alpha = \beta$ tends to 0, while independence is obtained when $\alpha = \beta$ tends to 1 or when one of the two parameters is fixed and the other tends to 1.

2.2.2. Other Representations of Bivariate Extremes

We can obtain other kind of representations of bivariate extreme value distribution. For example, the following theorem presents a point-process approach. Let the set E denote here $E = [0,\infty]^2 \setminus \{0\}$, $\|.\|$ any norm of $\mathbb{R}^2$ and $B \subset E$ the associated unit sphere.

Theorem 2 *The following assertions are equivalent:*
- *G is a bivariate extreme value distribution with unit Fréchet margins as mentioned in Theorem 1.*
- *There exists a nonhomogeneous Poisson process on $[0,\infty) \times E$ with intensity Λ defined for $t > 0$ by $\Lambda([0,t] \times B) = t\mu^*(B)$, where for all $A \subset B$ and $r > 0$,*

$$\mu^*\left(\mathbf{x} \in E : \|\mathbf{x}\| > r; \frac{\mathbf{x}}{\|\mathbf{x}\|} \in A\right) = 2\frac{H(A)}{r}, \quad (2.5)$$

where $\mathbf{x} = (x_1, x_2)$ and H is a finite measure such that (2.4) holds and

$$G(\mathbf{x}) = \exp\left(-\mu^*\{(x_1,\infty) \times (x_2,\infty)\}\right).$$

This last representation gives an interesting interpretation of the distribution H. Let $\|\mathbf{x}\| = x_1 + x_2$, the transformation used in (2.5): $\mathbf{x} = (x_1, x_2) \to (x_1 + x_2, x_1/(x_1 + x_2)) = (r, \omega)$ is a transformation from Cartesian to pseudo-polar coordinates, in which r is a measure of distance from origin and ω measures angle on a $[0, 1]$ scale. It is easy to check that the case $\omega = 0$ corresponds to the case $x_1 = 0$ and $\omega = 1$ to the case $x_2 = 0$. Equation (2.5) implies that the measure μ^* is a product measure of a simple function of the radial component and a measure H of the angular component. In other words, the angular spread is determined by H and is independent of the radial distance.

Interpretation in the case that H is differentiable with density h is easier: since ω measures the direction of the extremes, $h(\omega)$ measures the relative frequency of extremes in this direction. With this representation, it is easy to understand what was previously mentioned: when $h(\omega)$ is large for values of ω close to 0 and 1, we tend to the independence because large values of x correspond to small values of y and vice versa. On the contrary, if the dependence is very strong, large values of x will correspond to large values of y, so $h(\omega)$ will be very large for values of ω close to 1/2 and small elsewhere.

In dimension 2, there exists a popular approach of the bivariate extreme value distribution based on the dependence function.

Theorem 3 (Representation using Pickands dependence function) *G is an extreme bivariate distribution with unit Fréchet marginals if and only if*

$$G(x,y) = \exp\left(-\left(\frac{1}{x} + \frac{1}{y}\right)A\left(\frac{x}{x+y}\right)\right)$$

where $A(.)$ is a convex function on $[0, 1]$ in $[1/2, 1]$ such that

$$\max(t, 1-t) \leq A(t) \leq 1$$

for all t in $[0, 1]$ and

$$A(0) = A(1) = 1$$
$$-1 \leq A'(0) \leq 0 \quad \text{and} \quad 0 \leq A'(1) \leq 1$$
$$A''(t) \geq 0.$$

The form of the Pickands function provides important information on the dependence between marginals:
- if $A(t) = 1$ we get the independence in the extremes,
- if $A(t) = \max(t, 1-t)$, we have the complete and perfect dependence.

Obviously, there is a link between the function A and the measure H:

$$A(u) = 2\int_0^1 \max\left(u(1-\omega), (1-u)\omega\right)dH(\omega).$$

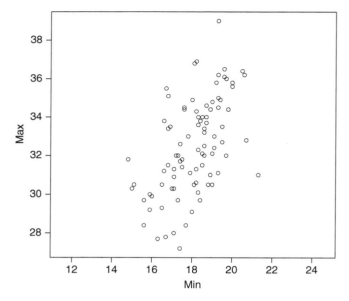

Figure 2.7 Summer maxima of minimum daily temperature (x) and maximum daily temperature (y) of the Colmar data.

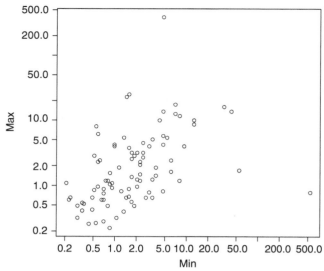

Figure 2.8 Summer monthly maxima of minimum daily temperature (x) and maximum daily temperature (y) with a Fréchet margins transformation (logarithm scale).

Other methods can be implemented to model the bivariate behavior between two consecutive maxima. The copula approaches [*Joe*, 1997; *Gudendorf and Segers*, 2010] allow to construct bivariate distributions under the assumption that all marginals are identified. We can also mention *Naveau et al.* [2009] and *Bacro et al.* [2010] who take advantage of bivariate EVT, that is, they choose and estimate a bivariate extremal dependence function.

2.2.3. Inference and Estimation

There exists a wide range of bivariate extreme distribution families. For example, in the R package evd [*Stephenson*, 2002], there are eight different classes.

The Figure 2.7 shows the summer maximum of minimum daily temperature against the corresponding maximum daily temperature. Obviously, there seems to be a trend for large values of the minimum temperature to correspond with large maximum temperature.

In order to better visualize the dependence in our data, it is possible to proceed to a transformation of the margins. A usual choice consists in transforming the two margins distributions into unit Fréchet distribution. If we fit a GEV distribution to the x_i, we get the following estimates:

$$\hat{\mu} = 17.62, \hat{\sigma} = 1.38, \hat{\gamma} = -0.33$$

while on the y_i the estimates are

$$\hat{\mu} = 31.59, \hat{\sigma} = 2.41, \hat{\gamma} = -0.25.$$

Here again, the approximation is made on a finite sample and may lead to errors on the dependence structure estimation of the model. This unit Fréchet margins transformation leads to the representation in Figure 2.8. The sample seems symmetric so a logistic model could be appropriated. Even if, for sake of simplicity, we have presented in Section 2.2.1 the logistic model with common unit Fréchet margins, practically, it is straightforward to estimate jointly the six GEV margins' parameters and the dependence parameter α using maximum likelihood. Table 2.1 represents the corresponding results.

The value of the dependence parameter α estimation is equal to 0.63 with an asymptotic confidence interval of $[0.51, 0.75]$ which corresponds to the first impression one can have looking at Figure 2.8: reasonably weak level of dependence but significantly different from independence. The maximized log-likelihood is equal to -344.27.

According to the Theorem 3, the Pickands dependence function is a convex function and their theoretical borders are represented with dotted lines in Figures 2.9 and 2.10. The Pickands dependence function corresponding to the fitted logistic model (Table 2.1) is represented in Figure 2.9 with the full line. A nonparametric estimate

Table 2.1 Results of Fitting a Logistic Bivariate Extreme Value Distribution to the Colmar Data

	μ_x	σ_x	γ_x	μ_y	σ_y	γ_y	α
Estimates standard error	17.59	1.37	−0.28	31.56	2.41	−0.21	0.63
	0.16	0.11	0.06	0.28	0.19	0.07	0.06

Values given are maximum likelihood estimates of the GEV parameters of both margins and maximum likelihood estimate of α.

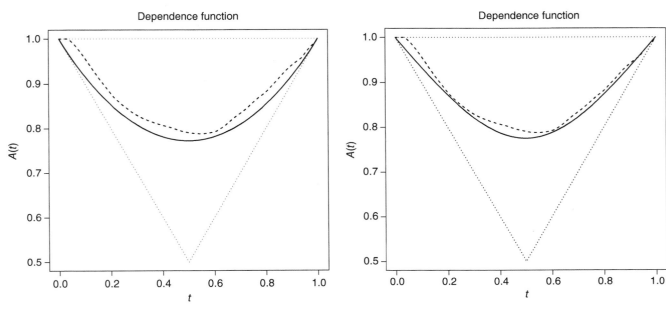

Figure 2.9 Nonparametric estimate of the Pickands dependence function for the Colmar data (dashed line) and the Pickands dependence function corresponding to the fitted logistic model (full line).

Figure 2.10 Nonparametric estimate of the Pickands dependence function for the Colmar data (dashed line) and the Pickands dependence function corresponding to the fitted bilogistic model (full line).

Table 2.2 Results of Fitting a Logistic Bivariate Extreme Value Distribution to the Colmar Data

	μ_x	σ_x	γ_x	μ_y	σ_y	γ_y	α	β
Estimates standard error	17.59	1.37	−0.28	31.54	2.40	−0.20	0.64	0.60
	0.14	0.10	0.05	0.23	0.17	0.06	0.09	0.09

Values given are maximum likelihood estimates of the GEV parameters of both margins and maximum likelihood estimates of α and β.

of the function is also presented with a dashed line. This figure seems to indicate that the fitting of the data may be improved by using a more complex model. That's why we represent in Figure 2.10 the Pickands dependence function corresponding to the fitted bilogistic model (Table 2.2).

Since the logistic model is a subset of the bilogistic model, we can apply a deviance test to choose the model.

For the bilogistic model the maximized log-likelihood is equal to −344.24. The Deviance statistics is then equal to 0.06, which is very small with respect to the 95% quantile of the χ_1^2 distribution. The benefit brought by the asymmetric logistic model is not sufficient. This is expected because of the estimation of α and β, the case $\alpha = \beta$ corresponding to the logistic model.

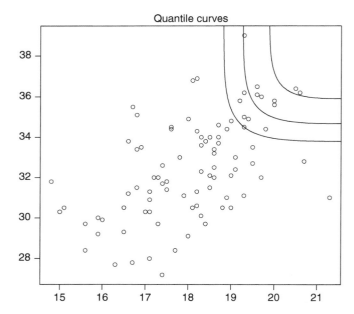

Figure 2.11 Quantile curves for the fitted logistic model for $q = 0.7$, 0.8, and 0.9 for the Colmar data.

Finally, Figure 2.11 represents the α quantile curves for the fitted logistic model for $q = 0.7$, 0.8, and 0.9 generalizing quantiles to the bivariate case.

2.3. CONCLUSION

Through a series of extreme data analysis, univariate and multivariate basic concepts in EVT have been presented in an environmental context. These concepts can be extended to the spatial case through max-stable fields, see for instance *de Haan* [1984] and *Smith* [1990]. Inference on such processes can be obtained using composite likelihood as described in *Lindsay* [1988] and *Varin* [2008] [see *Padoan et al.*, 2010] for an application in an extreme value context with an illustration on US precipitation extremes and [*Blanchet and Davison*, 2011] for an illustration on annual maximum snow depth.

ACKNOWLEDGMENT

The authors are grateful to the referee for their constructive comments from which the paper has benefitted a lot. Part of this work has been supported by the EU-FP7 "ACQWA" Project (www.acqwa.ch) under Contract Nr 212250, by the PEPER-GIS project, by the ANR-MOPERA project, by the ANR-McSim project, by the MIRACCLE-GICC project and by the *Chaire d'excellence "Generali – Actuariat responsable: gestion des risques naturels et changements climatiques."*

REFERENCES

Bacro, J. N., L. Bel, and C. Lantuéjoul (2010), Testing the independence of maxima: From bivariate vectors to spatial extreme fields, *Extreme*, *13*, 155–175.

Beirlant, J., Y. Goegebeur, J. Segers, and J. Teugels (2004), *Statistics of Extremes: Theory and Applications*, Wiley Series in Probability and Statistics, John Wiley & Sons, Inc., Hoboken, NJ.

Blanchet, J. and A. Davison (2011), Spatial Modelling of extreme snow depth, *The Annals of Applied Statistics*, *5*(3), 1699–1725.

Coles, S. (2001), *An Introduction to Statistical Modeling of Extreme Values*, Springer Series in Statistics, Springer-Verlag, London.

Crowder, M. J. (1989), A multivariate distribution with Weibull components, *J. Roy. Stat. Soc. B*, *51*, 93–108.

Diebolt, J., A. Guillou, P. Naveau, and P. Ribereau (2008), Improving probability weighted moment methods for the generalized extreme value distribution, *REVSTAT*, *6*, 33–50.

Embrechts, P., C. Klüppelberg, and T. Mikosch (1997), *Modelling Extremal Events for Insurance and Finance*, volume 33 of Applications of Mathematics, Springer-Verlag, Berlin.

Fougères, A.-L., J. P. Nolan, and H. Rootzén (2009), Models for dependent extremes using stable mixtures, *Scand. J. Statist.*, *36*, 42–59.

Gudendorf, G. and J. Segers (2010), Extreme-value copulas, in *Copula theory and its applications (Warsaw, 2009)*, Lecture Notes in Statistics—Proceedings, edited by P. Jaworski, pp. 127–146, Springer-Verlag, Berlin.

de Haan, L. (1984), A spectral representation for max-stable processes, *The Annals of Probability*, *12*, 1194–1204.

de Haan, L. and A. Ferreira (2006), *Extreme Value Theory: An Introduction*, Springer Series in Operations Research, Springer, New York.

Hosking, J. R. M., J. R. Wallis, and E. F. Wood (1985), Estimation of the generalized extreme-value distribution by the method of probability-weighted moments, *Technometrics*, *27*, 251–261.

Hougaard, P. (1986), A class of multivariate failure time distributions, *Biometrika*, *73*, 671–678.

Joe, H. (1997), *Multivariate Models and Dependence Concepts*, Monographs on Statistics and Applied Probability, 73, Chapman & Hall, London.

Katz, R., M. Parlange, and P. Naveau (2002), Extremes in hydrology, *Advances in Water Resource*, *25*, 1287–1304.

Lindsay, B. G. (1988), Composite likelihood methods, *Contemporary Mathematics*, *80*, 221–239.

Maraun, D., H. W. Rust, and T. J. Osborn (2010), Synoptic airflow and UK daily precipitation extremes. Development and validation of a vector generalized model, *Extremes*, *13*, 133–153.

Naveau, P., A. Guillou, D. Cooley, and J. Diebolt (2009), Modeling pairwise dependence of maxima in space, *Biometrika*, *96*, 1–17.

Padoan, S. A., M. Ribatet, and S. A. Sisson (2010), Likelihood-based inference for max-stable processes, *J. Am. Statist. Assoc.*, *105*, 263–277.

Pickands, J. (1975), Statistical inference using extreme order statistics, *Ann. Statist.*, *3*, 119–131.

Pitt, M. K. and N. Shepard (1999), Filtering via simulation: Auxiliary particle filters, *J. Am. Statis. Assoc.*, *94*, 590–599.

Resnick, S. I. (1987), *Extreme Values, Regular Variation and Point Processes*, Springer Verlag, New York.

Resnick, S. I. (2007), *Heavy-Tail Phenomena: Probabilistic and Statistical Modeling*, Operations Research and Financial Engineering, Springer, New York.

Ribereau, P., A. Guillou, and P. Naveau (2008), Estimating return levels from maxima of non-stationary random sequences using the Generalized PWM method, *Nonlin. Processes Geophys.*, *15*, 1033–1039.

Smith, R. L. (1985), Maximum likelihood estimation in a class of non-regular cases, *Biometrika*, *72*, 67–90.

Smith, RL. 1990. *Max-Stable Processes and Spatial Extremes.* Unpublished manuscript, University of North California.

Stephenson, A. G. (2002), evd: Extreme value distributions, *R News*, *2*, 31–32.

Tawn, J. A. (1990), Modelling multivariate extreme value distributions, *Biometrika*, *77*, 245–253.

Toulemonde, G., A. Guillou, P. Naveau, M. Vrac, and F. Chevallier (2010), Autoregressive models for maxima and their applications to CH_4 and N_2O, *Environmetrics*, *21*, 189–207.

Toulemonde, G., A. Guillou, and P. Naveau (2013), Particle filtering for Gumbel-distributed daily maxima of methane and nitrous oxide, *Environmetrics*, *24*, 51–62.

Van der Vaart, A. W. (1998), *Asymptotic Statistics*, Cambridge University Press, Cambridge.

Varin, C. (2008), On composite marginal likelihoods, *Advances in Statistical Analysis*, *92*, 1–28.

3

Dynamical Systems Approach to Extreme Events

Catherine Nicolis[1] and Gregoire Nicolis[2]

ABSTRACT

The principal signatures of deterministic dynamics in the probabilistic properties of extremes are identified in this chapter. Analytical expressions for n-fold cumulative distributions and their associated densities, for the exceedance probabilities and spatial propagation of extremes, are derived and complemented by numerical simulations. Substantial differences from the classical statistical theory are found and illustrated on generic classes of dynamical systems, giving rise to fully developed chaos, intermittent chaos, and quasi-periodic behavior.

3.1. INTRODUCTION

A typical record generated by a natural, technological, or societal system consists of periods, where a relevant variable undergoes small-scale fluctuations around a well-defined level provided by the long-term average of available values, interrupted by abrupt excursions to values that differ significantly from this level. Such *extreme events* are of great importance in a variety of contexts since they can signal phenomena, such as the breakdown of a mechanical structure, an earthquake, a severe thunderstorm, flooding, or a financial crisis. Information on the probability of their occurrence and the capability to predict the time and place at which this occurrence may be expected are thus of great value in, among others, the construction industry or the assessment of risks. While the probability of such events decreases with their magnitude, the damage that they may bring increases rapidly with the magnitude, as does the cost of protection against

them. These opposing trends make the task of prediction extremely challenging.

Extreme events are also of special relevance in fundamental research. In many respects, the ability of a complex system to adapt and to evolve is conditioned by the occurrence of exceptional events in, for instance, the form of transition between states or the exceedance of thresholds.

In general, extremes are considered to be governed by statistical laws in view of their unexpectedness and variability. There exists a powerful statistical theory of extremes, which in its most familiar version stipulates that the successive values $X_0,...,X_{n-1}$ of the variable recorded are independent and identically distributed random variables (i.i.d.r.v.'s). In the asymptotic limit of infinite observational window n, it leads, under suitable linear scaling, to three types of universal extreme value distributions (the Gumbel, Frechet, and Weibull distributions) that can be combined into a single generalized extreme value distribution (GEV) involving just three parameters [*Embrechts et al.*, 1997].

On the other hand, the fundamental laws of nature are deterministic. What is more, there is an increasing awareness that deterministic systems can generate complex behaviors in the form of abrupt transitions, a multiplicity

[1] *Institut Royal Météorologique de Belgique, Brussels, Belgium*
[2] *Interdisciplinary Center for Nonlinear Phenomena and Complex Systems, Université Libre de Bruxelles, Brussels, Belgium*

Extreme Events: Observations, Modeling, and Economics, Geophysical Monograph 214, First Edition.
Edited by Mario Chavez, Michael Ghil, and Jaime Urrutia-Fucugauchi.

of states, or spatiotemporal chaos, at the basis of a wide variety of phenomena encountered in everyday experience [*Nicolis and Nicolis, 2007b*].

A key point for our purpose is that under the aforementioned conditions, deterministic dynamics induces nontrivial probabilistic properties, such as the existence of invariant probability measures possessing certain regularity properties such as smoothness along at least certain directions in the phase space; or the stronger property of mixing that is, the irreversible approach to these invariant measures starting from sufficiently smooth initial probability distributions. These properties are at the origin of a "statistical physics of dynamical systems," an active field of research in the general area of nonequilibrium statistical mechanics [*Gaspard, 1998*].

The objective of this chapter is to bridge the gap between the stochastic character of extreme events, as perceived in our everyday experience, and the deterministic character of the laws of nature. To this end, deterministic dynamics will be embedded into a self-consistent probabilistic description, in which probabilities emerge as natural outcomes of underlying evolution laws. This will enable us to construct the principal quantities of interest in extreme value theory from first principles, free of phenomenological assumptions.

The general formulation is given in Section 3.2. Section 3.3 is devoted to the derivation of probability distributions of extreme values generated by one-dimensional maps in the interval, a generic class of models giving rise to complex behavior. Some further extreme value-related properties, such as exceedances and probabilistic properties of ranges of sums, are summarized in Section 3.4. Extreme events in spatially extended systems are considered in Section 3.5, and the main conclusions are summarized in Section 3.6.

3.2. EXTREME EVENTS AND DYNAMICAL COMPLEXITY: FORMULATION

The basic question asked in connection with extreme events is, given a sequence $X_0,\ldots,X_{n-1}$ constituted by successive values of an observable monitored at regularly spaced time intervals $0,\tau,\ldots,(n-1)\tau$, what is the probability distribution of the largest value x found in the sequence, $M_n = \max(X_0,\ldots,X_{n-1})$?

$$F_n(x) = \text{Prob}\left(X_0 \leq x,\ldots,X_{n-1} \leq x\right) \qquad (3.1)$$

Obviously, $F_n(a) = 0$ and $F_n(b) = 1$, a and b being the upper and lower limits (not necessarily finite) of the domain of variation of x. In actual fact, $F_n(x)$ is therefore a *cumulative probability* related to the probability density $\rho_n(x)$ (in so far as the latter exists) by

$$F_n(x) = \int_a^x dx' \rho_n(x') \qquad (3.2)$$

Clearly, as n increases $F_n(x)$ will shift toward increasing values of x, being practically zero in the remaining part of the domain of variation. The possibility to elaborate a systematic theory of extremes depends on the cumulative probability $F(x)$ of the underlying process ($F(x) = \text{Prob}(X \leq x)$). If the latter satisfies certain conditions, then one can zoom the vicinity of the upper limit of x through appropriate scaling transformations and explore the possibility of universal behaviors. On the contrary, taking the infinite n limit is at the expense of erasing information on the variability of extreme value-related properties, as captured by (finite time) fluctuations around the asymptotic averages. Accounting for such properties leads to nontrivial transient behaviors for certain ranges of observational time windows in the form of anomalous fluctuations, which are especially apparent in systems in which the probability density of the relevant variable is multihumped [*Nicolis and Nicolis, 2008*]. Furthermore, the n-fold probabilities such as $F_n(x)$ exhibit singularities, which are quite pronounced for small or even moderate n's in a wide range of threshold values x.

To evaluate the n-fold cumulative probability $F_n(x)$ in Equation 3.1, we start with the multivariate probability density $\rho_n(X_0,\ldots,X_{n-1})$ to realize the sequence $X_0,\ldots,X_{n-1}$ (not to be confused with $\rho_n(x)$ in Equation 3.2). We express this quantity as follows:

$$\rho_n(X_0,\ldots,X_{n-1}) = \left(\text{Prob to be in } X_0 \text{ in the first place}\right)$$
$$\times \prod_{k=1}^{n-1}(\text{Prob to be in } X_{k-1} \text{ given one was}$$
$$\text{in } X_0 \text{ } k \text{ time units before})$$

$$(3.3)$$

In both stochastic and deterministic systems, the first factor in Equation 3.3 is given by the invariant probability density, $\rho(X_0)$. In contrast, the two classes differ by the nature of conditional probabilities inside the n-fold product. In stochastic systems, these quantities are typically smooth. But in deterministic systems, the successive values of X are related by a set of evolution laws which we write schematically in the form

$$X_{k+1} = f(X_k) \qquad (3.4)$$

In a multivariate system, the time dependence of a given observable, such as the quantity monitored in an experimental record depends, typically, on the full set of variables present. In the following, we will assume that the conditions for a reduced description in which the observable of interest satisfies an autonomous dynamics are satisfied. As shown in dynamical systems theory [*Gaspard*, 1998], this may necessitate to project the dynamics on the most unstable direction, or to follow the traces of the full phase space trajectory on a Poincaré surface of section. As a result, the mapping $f(x)$ in Equation 3.4 will typically be noninvertible.

Be it as it may, Equation 3.3 will take the general form

$$\rho_n\left(X_0,...,X_{n-1}\right)=\rho\left(X_0\right)\prod_{k=1}^{n}\delta\left(X_k - f\left(X_{k-1}\right)\right) \quad (3.5)$$

By definition, the cumulative probability distribution $F_n(x)$ (the relevant quantity in a theory of extremes) is the n-fold integral of Equation 3.5 over $X_0,...,X_{n-1}$ from the lower bound a up to the level x of interest. This converts the delta functions into Heaviside theta functions, yielding

$$F_n\left(x\right)=\int_a^x dX_0\ \rho\left(X_0\right)\ \theta\left(x - f\left(X_0\right)\right)\cdots\theta\left(x - f^{(n-1)}\left(X_0\right)\right)$$

$$(3.6)$$

where the superscript k in f denotes the k-fold iterate of the mapping. In other words, $F_n(x)$ is obtained by integrating $\rho(X_0)$ over those ranges of X_0 in which $x \geq \left\{f(X_0),...,f^{(n-1)}(X_0)\right\}$. This structure, involving a product of step functions, is to be contrasted from the one obtained in the i.i.d.r.v. case, where $F_n(x)$ would simply be the nth power of $F(x)$.

Let x be moved upward now. New integration ranges will then be added, since the slopes of the successive iterates $f^{(k)}$ with respect to X_0 are, typically, both different from each other and X_0-dependent. Each of these ranges will open up past a threshold value, where either the values of two different iterates will cross, or an iterate will cross the manifold $x = X_0$. This latter type of crossing will occur at x values belonging to the set of periodic orbits of all periods up to $n-1$ of the dynamical system.

At the level of $F_n(x)$ and its associated probability density $\rho_n(x)$, these properties entail the following consequences [*Nicolis et al.*, 2006]. (1) Since a new integration range can only open up by increasing x, and the resulting contribution is necessarily nonnegative, $F_n(x)$ is a monotonically increasing function of x, as indeed expected. (2) More unexpectedly, the slope of $F_n(x)$ with respect to x will be subjected to abrupt changes at a discrete set of x values corresponding to successive crossing thresholds. At these values, it may increase or decrease, depending on the structure of branches $f^{(k)}(X_0)$ involved in the particular crossing configuration considered. (3) Being the derivative of $F_n(x)$ with respect to x, the probability density $\rho_n(x)$ will possess discontinuities at the points of nondifferentiability of $F_n(x)$ and will in general be nonmonotonic.

Properties (2) and (3) are fundamentally different from those from the statistical theory of extremes, where the corresponding distributions are smooth functions of x. In particular, the discontinuous nonmonotonic character of $\rho_n(x)$ complicates the already delicate issue of prediction of extreme events considerably.

3.3. ONE-DIMENSIONAL MAPS IN THE INTERVAL

Having identified some universal signatures of the deterministic character of the dynamics on the properties of extremes, we now turn to the derivation of analytic properties of $F_n(x)$ and $\rho_n(x)$ for some prototypical classes of dynamical systems.

3.3.1. Fully Developed Chaotic Maps in the Interval

A dynamical system exhibiting this kind of behavior possesses a mean expansion rate larger than unity, and an exponentially large number of points belonging to unstable periodic trajectories. Considering Equation 3.6, this will show up through the property that the set of points in which $F_n(x)$ changes slope and the set of discontinuity points of the associated probability density $\rho_n(x)$ become dense in some interval as n is increased. One may refer to this peculiar property as a "generalized devil's staircase." It follows that the first smooth segment of $F_n(x)$ will have a support of $O(1)$ and the last one an exponentially small support, delimited by the rightmost fixed point of the iterate $f^{(n-1)}$ and the right boundary b of the interval. Since $F_n(x)$ is monotonic and $F_n(b)=1$, the slopes will be exponentially small in the first segments and will gradually increase as x approaches b. These properties differ markedly from the structure found in the classical statistical theory of extremes [*Balakrishnan et al.*, 1995]. Figure 3.1a and b depicts (full lines) the functions $\rho_{20}(x)$ and $F_{20}(x)$, as deduced by direct numerical simulation of the tent map, an example of (3.4) defined by the iterative function

$$f\left(X\right)=1-\left|1-2X\right| \quad 0\leq X \leq 1 \quad (3.7)$$

The results confirm entirely the theoretical predictions. The dashed lines in the figure indicate the results of the statistical approach for the same system for which $\rho(x)$ happens to be a constant, leading to $F(x)=x$. One would think that this approach should be applicable since this system's correlation function happens to vanish from the very first time step. Yet we see substantial differences,

(a)

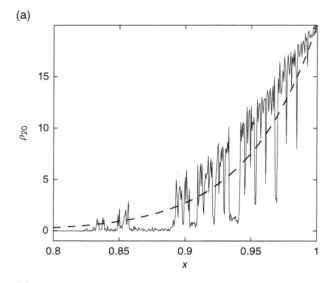

(b)

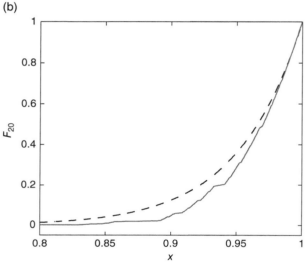

Figure 3.1 Probability density (a) and cumulative probability distribution (b) of extremes for the tent map, as obtained numerically using 10^6 realizations. Dashed curves represent the prediction of the classical statistical theory of extremes. The irregular succession of plateaus in $\rho_{20}(x)$ and the increase of the slope of $F_{20}(x)$ in the final part of the interval are in full agreement with the theory. The irregularity increases rapidly with the window and there is no saturation and convergence to a smooth behavior in the limit of infinite window.

both qualitative and quantitative, associated with considerable fluctuations, discontinuities, and a nonmonotonic behavior which persists for any value of window n. These differences underlie the fact that in a deterministic system, the condition of statistical independence is much more stringent than the rapid vanishing of the autocorrelation function.

3.3.2. Intermittent Chaotic Maps in the Interval

Intermittent systems are weakly chaotic systems in which the expansion rate in certain regions is close to unity. We take, without loss of generality, this region to be near the leftmost boundary a

$$f(X) \approx (X-a) + u|X-a|^z + \epsilon \quad a \le X \le b \quad (3.8)$$

where $z > 1$ and ϵ measures the distance from strict tangency of $f(X)$ with the $f(X) = X$ axis. As $\epsilon \to 0$, successive iterates $f^{(k)}(X)$ will follow the $f(X) = X$ axis closer and closer, and will thus become increasingly steep at their respective reinjection points where $f^{(k)}(X) = b$. As a result, the positions of these points (and hence of the (unstable) fixed points other than $X = a$ too, whose number is still exponentially large) will move much more slowly towards a and b compared to the fully chaotic case. Two new qualitative properties of $F_n(x)$ can be expected on these grounds, reflecting the presence of long tails of the correlation function in the system [*Balakrishnan et al.*, 1995]: the probability mass borne in the first smooth segment of this function near $X = a$ and the length of the last smooth segment near $X = b$ will no longer be exponentially small. This is fully confirmed by direct numerical simulation of Equation 3.8 for the symmetric cusp map,

$$f(X) = 1 - 2|X|^{1/2} \quad -1 \le X \le 1 \quad (3.9)$$

as seen in Figure 3.2. Using the explicit form of $f(X)$, one can check directly that $F_n(x) \approx 1 + x$ as $x \to -1$, $F_n(0) \approx n^{-1}$, a final segment of $F_n(x)$ of width $O(n^{-1})$ and $F_n(x) \approx 1 - n(1-x)^2/4$ as $x \to 1$ is.

3.3.3. Quasi-Periodic Behavior

The canonical form for this behavior is uniform quasi-periodic motion on an invariant set in the form of a two-dimensional torus, which is topologically equivalent to a square of side 2π subjected to periodic boundary conditions. It can be described by two angle variables ϕ_1 and ϕ_2 evolving according to the equations

$$\begin{aligned} \phi_1 - \phi_{10} &= \omega_1 t \\ \phi_2 - \phi_{20} &= \omega_2 t \quad \mathrm{mod}\, 2\pi \end{aligned} \quad (3.10a)$$

ω_1 and ω_2 being the two characteristic frequencies. If ω_1 and ω_2 are incommensurate, the evolution is ergodic, possessing a smooth invariant density equal to unity. Choosing a Poincaré surface of section transversal to ϕ_2, one is led to the circle map, a one-dimensional recurrence of the form

(a)

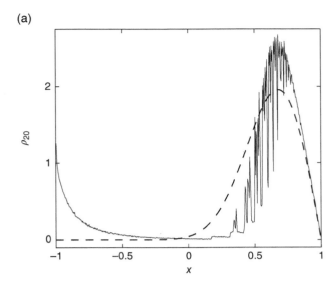

(b)

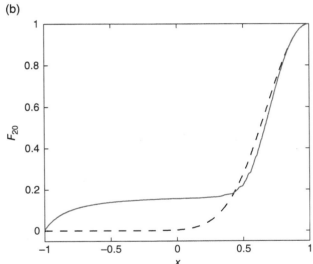

Figure 3.2 As in Figure 3.1, but for the cusp map. The irregularities pointed out in connection with Figure 3.1 subsist, the main new point being the presence of a more appreciable probability mass in the left part of the interval.

$$\phi_{n+1} = a + \phi_n \quad \mathrm{mod}\,1 \qquad (3.10b)$$

where $0 \le \phi_0 < 1$ and a is irrational. The fundamental difference with cases 3.3.1 and 3.3.2 is the breakdown of the mixing property and the absence of dynamical instability (all expansion rates are constant and equal to unity). Furthermore, there are neither fixed points nor periodic orbits. Yet the structure of $F_n(x)$, depicted in Figure 3.3, is similar to that of Figures 3.1b and 3.2b, displaying again slope breaks [*Nicolis et al.*, 2008]. These arise from the second mechanism invoked in Section 3.2, namely, intersections between different iterates of the

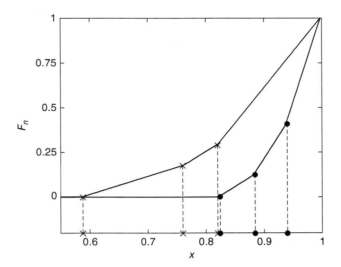

Figure 3.3 Cumulative probability distribution $F_n(x)$ of extremes for uniform quasi-periodic motion with $\omega_1/\omega_2 = (\sqrt{5} - 1)/3$. Upper curve corresponds to $n = 4$ and lower to $n = 10$. Note that in both cases the number of slope changes in $F_n(x)$, whose positions are indicated in the figure by vertical dashed lines, is equal to 3.

mapping functions. Remarkably, these intersections give rise to integration domains in the computation of $F_n(x)$ that can only have three sizes α, β, and $\alpha + \beta$, where α and β are determined by parameter a in Equation 3.10b.

3.4. SOME FURTHER EXTREME VALUE-RELATED PROPERTIES

3.4.1. Exceedances and Return Times

A key question for the purpose of prediction is: what are the waiting times between specific extreme events? To answer this requires us to evaluate, in addition to the quantities considered in the preceding section, the conditional probability $p_k(x)$ of the times, k of first exceedance of a certain level x starting from state X_0. Similar to what was discussed in Section 3.2, we may express this quantity as [*Nicolis and Nicolis*, 2007a]

$$p_k(x) = \frac{1}{F(x)} \int_a^x dX_0 \rho(X_0) \theta(x - f(X_0)) \cdots \\ \theta(x - f^{(k-1)}(X_0))(1 - \theta(x - f^{(k)}(X_0))) \qquad (3.11)$$

or, comparing with Equation 3.6,

$$p_k(x) = \frac{1}{F(x)}(F_k(x) - F_{k+1}(x)) \qquad (3.12)$$

It follows that for deterministic dynamical systems giving rise to complex behaviors, $p_k(x)$ will have a highly intricate structure with respect to both k and x, inherited from the nondifferentiability of the k-fold cumulative probability $F_k(x)$ of such systems (Figures 3.1, 3.2, and 3.3). This is to be contrasted from the i.i.d.r.v. expression, according to which p_k is an exponential distribution describing the probability of "success" $p = 1 - F(x)$ following $k - 1$ consecutive "failures" with probability $1 - p = F(x)$,

$$p_k(x) = F^{k-1}(x)(1 - F(x)) \qquad (3.13)$$

Note that even in the range of validity of this expression, the fluctuations of exceedance times around their mean are comparable to the mean itself, as one can check this by taking the first two moments of Equation 3.13:

$$\langle k \rangle = \frac{1}{1 - F(x)} \qquad \langle \delta k^2 \rangle = \frac{F^{1/2}(x)}{1 - F(x)} \qquad (3.14)$$

This makes the task of prediction—even in its most classical, purely statistical setting—quite hard given that, in addition, one deals with events occurring with low probability.

The limitations of the statistical approach and of the mean value-based predictions are illustrated in Figures 3.4 and 3.5. These figures depict the dependence of p_k on k for specific threshold values x and of p on x for specific window values k, for the three types of deterministic dynamical systems considered in Section 3.3, as obtained from Equations 3.11 and 3.12. The difference with the classical result of Equation 3.13, dashed line, is striking, reflecting the existence of strict selection rules underlying the dynamics. This is especially apparent in the case of intermittent systems (Figure 3.5a). As can be seen, the probability remains at quite appreciable levels for x values, far from the upper boundary of the domain of variation of x. For some range of k values, including the case $k = 10$ shown in the figure, this is manifested in the form of a bimodality, in full contrast with the predictions of classical statistical theory [*Nicolis and Nicolis*, 2007b].

3.4.2. Probabilistic Properties of Ranges of Sums

In many environmental recordings, especially in hydrology-related problems, such as the regime of river discharges, the variability is so pronounced that no underlying regularity seems to be present. An ingenious way to handle such records, suggested originally by *Hurst* [1951], is to monitor the distance r between the largest and the smallest value recorded in a certain time window τ and analyze its statistical properties as a function of τ.

(a)

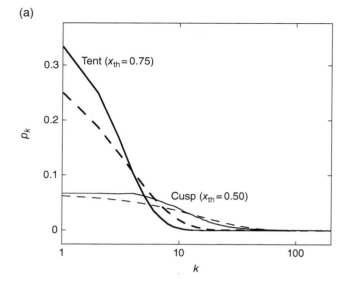

(b)

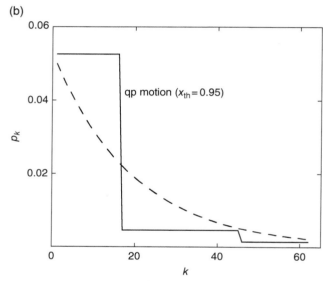

Figure 3.4 Probability distribution for the time of first exceedance of level x_{th} for the tent and cusp maps (full lines) as obtained numerically (a); and for the circle map (Eq. 3.10b) with $a = (\sqrt{5} - 1)/3$ as obtained analytically (full line) (b). Dashed lines correspond to the case of i.i.d.r.v.'s.

We start by deducing from the record $X_0, \ldots, X_{n-1}$ the sample mean $\overline{X}_n$ and the associated standard deviation C_n (assuming X_i's have a finite variance). Subtracting $\overline{X}_n$ from each of the values of the record leads then to a new sequence of variables that have by construction zero sample mean,

$$x_0 = X_0 - \overline{X}_n, \ldots, \quad x_{n-1} = X_{n-1} - \overline{X}_n \qquad (3.15)$$

Next, one introduces the cumulative sums of all x values up to x_k,

$$S_1 = x_0, \quad S_2 = x_0 + x_1, \ldots \qquad (3.16)$$

(a)

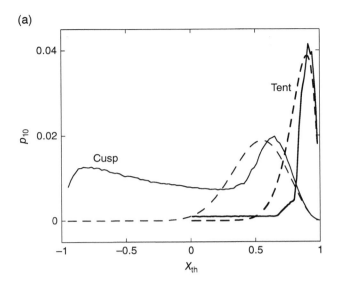

(b)

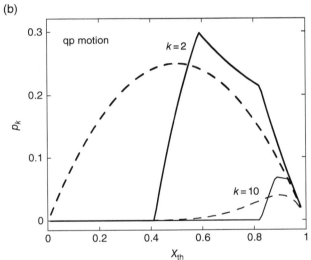

Figure 3.5 Probability distribution for the time $k = 10$ of first exceedance versus x_{th} for the tent and cusp maps (full lines) as obtained numerically (a); and for the circle map (Eq. 3.10b) for $k = 2$ and $k = 10$ as obtained analytically and numerically (b). Dashed lines correspond to the case of i.i.d.r.v.'s.

This set will have a maximum and a minimum value,

$$M_n = \max S_k, \quad m_n = \min S_k \qquad (3.17)$$

where the k's run up to n. The range r_n of the phenomenon described by the sequence is then quite naturally defined as

$$r_n = M_n - m_n \qquad (3.18a)$$

or, in rescaled form,

$$r_n^* = \frac{r_n}{C_n} \qquad (3.18b)$$

Since r_n is expected to display a high variability, one should evaluate its average value or variance to sort out systematic trends. The basic quantity involved in such an average is the (cumulative) probability distribution of the event

$$F(u,v,n) = \mathrm{Prob}(M_n \leq u, m_n \geq -v, n) \qquad (3.19)$$

where u and v are taken to be positive, $M_n > 0$, and $m_n < 0$. Since $r = M - m$, the probability density associated with $F(u,v,n)$ should be integrated over all values of u in the interval from 0 to r prior to the calculation of the moments of r:

$$P(r_n) = \int_0^{r_n} du\, f(u, r - v, n) \qquad (3.20a)$$

with

$$f(u,v,n) = \frac{\partial^2 F}{\partial u \partial v} \qquad (3.20b)$$

In a deterministic dynamical system, the quantity in Equation 3.19 is to be evaluated along the lines of Section 3.2. This task is complicated by the fact that contrary to Section 3.2 where the successive values X_k were related to the initial one X_0 by Equation 3.4, the dependence of the cumulative sums S_k on S_1 in the present case is much more involved [*Van de Vyver and Nicolis, 2010*]:

$$S_1 = X_0 - \bar{X}_n = X_0 - \frac{1}{n}\sum_{r=0}^{n-1} f^{(r)}(X_0) \equiv \Psi_n^{(1)}(X_0) \qquad (3.21a)$$

$$\vdots$$

$$S_k = k(S_1 - X_0) + \sum_{r=0}^{k-1} f^{(r)}(X_0) \equiv \Psi_n^{(k)}(X_0) \qquad (3.21b)$$

To express S_k entirely in terms of S_1 in (3.21b), one thus needs to express X_0 in terms of S_1 from (3.21a). Since f, and thus $\Psi_n^{(1)}$, is noninvertible, this latter dependence is not one-to-one,

$$X_{0,\alpha} = \left(\Psi_n^{(1)}\right)_\alpha^{-1}(S_1) \quad \text{and} \quad S_{k,\alpha} = \Psi_n^{(k)}(X_{0,\alpha}) \equiv g_\alpha^{(k-1)}(S_1) \qquad (3.22)$$

S_k is thus a multivalued function of S_1 depending on the domain I_α of X_0 values associated with branch α of the inverse of mapping $\Psi_n^{(1)}$. The procedure is, then, to partition domain I of map f into m subintervals, each containing one of the pre-images $X_{0,\alpha}$ of S_1, as S_1 runs over its interval of variation. The probability density of realizing the sequence $S_1,\ldots,S_n$ is then (cf. Eq. 3.5)

$$\rho_n(S_1,\ldots,S_n) = \sum_{\alpha=1}^{m} P(X_0 \in I_\alpha)\rho(S_1 \mid X_0 \in I_\alpha)$$
$$\times \prod_{j=1}^{n-1} \delta\left[S_{j+1} - g_\alpha^{(j)}(S_1)\right] \qquad (3.23)$$

and

$$F(u,v,n) = \sum_{\alpha=1}^{m} P(X_0 \in I_\alpha)\int_{-v}^{u} dS_1 \rho_\alpha(S_1)\int_{-v}^{u} dS_2$$
$$\cdots\int_{-v}^{u} dS_n \prod_{j=1}^{n-1} \delta\left[S_{j+1} - g_\alpha^{(j)}(S_1)\right] \qquad (3.24)$$

Figure 3.6 depicts the dependence of F, as obtained analytically from Equation 3.24 for the tent map (Eq. 3.7) as a function of v for u fixed and as a function of u for v fixed, for window $n = 3$. We observe again a broken line-like structure, much like the one found in Figure 3.1.

We next turn to the probability density of the range, Equation 3.20. The probability density of the nonnormalized range r for the tent map and for window $n = 3$, as obtained analytically from this equation is displayed in Figure 3.7. We observe a complex, stair-like structure, reminiscent of the one observed in Figure 3.1a. Figures 3.8a and b display the probability densities of normalized ranges r_n^* for the same dynamical system as obtained numerically from Equations 3.18b and 3.20a for windows $n = 3$ and $n = 100$. In addition to the jumps present in Figure 3.7, one observes the evidence of delta-like singularities, arising from the fact that the single integration over u in Equation 3.20a may not be sufficient to smooth the singularities arising when taking the second (mixed) derivative of $F(u,v,n)$ in Equation 3.20b. For comparison, in Figure 3.8b we plot the probability density associated with a case of i.i.d.r.v. possessing a uniform density as in the tent map originally evaluated by *Feller* [1951]. We observe that the actual probability density follows the main body of the i.i.d.r.v. density. Still, the irregular pronounced oscillations around the overall smooth envelope persist on small scales and remain present for much higher window values, for example, $n = 1000$.

Closely related to the foregoing is the Hurst phenomenon. Specifically, in a wide range of environmental records [*Hurst*, 1951], it turns out that the mean normalized range $\langle r_n^* \rangle$ varies with the window n as n^H, where H

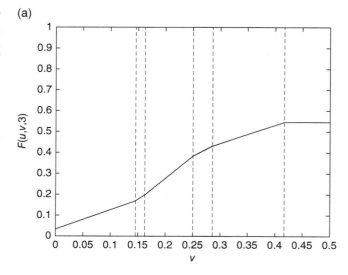

(a)

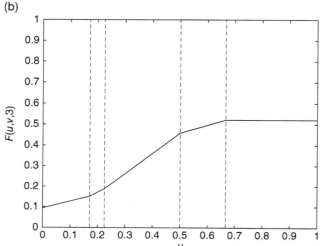

(b)

Figure 3.6 Cumulative probability distribution $F(u,v,3)$ (Eq. 3.19) for the tent map as a function of v with $u = 0.1$ (a); and as a function of u with $v = 0.1$ (b) as obtained numerically using 10^6 realizations and a mesh size equal to 0.01. Dashed lines indicate the nondifferentiable points.

(referred as Hurst exponent) is close to 0.7. To put this in perspective, *Feller* [1951] proved that for the reference case of i.i.d.r.v.'s H is bound to be 0.5. This implies in turn that S_k has somehow a persistent effect on X_k, that is, highs tend to be followed by highs, lows by lows. The question is, whether the kind of dynamical systems considered in this subsection give rise to this kind of behavior. There is as yet no satisfactory answer to it, owing to a slow drift of the exponent H deduced from numerical experiments with respect to the total length of the time series generated by the system.

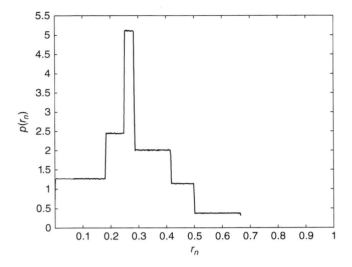

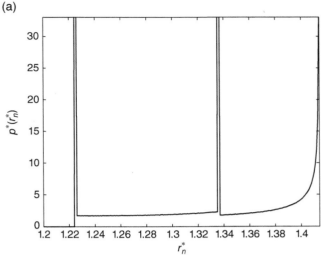

(a)

Figure 3.7 Probability density of the nonnormalized range for the tent map with $n = 3$ as obtained numerically. Number of realizations and mesh size as in Figure 3.6.

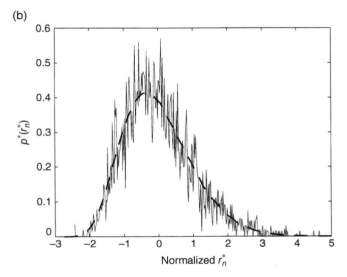

(b)

3.5. SPATIALLY EXTENDED SYSTEMS

So far we have been concerned with global properties such as statistics of the largest value encountered in a record within time windows n, or of the associated return times. Now, real-world systems are extended in space. The relevant issue is then not only whether an extreme event will or will not occur globally, but what is the particular spatial location that will witness at a given time interval the occurrence of such an event. This question can be mapped, in turn, into how extremes propagate in space. In this section, we summarize some results for a class of deterministic dynamical systems giving rise to chaotic behavior [*Nicolis and Nicolis*, 2009].

Consider a discrete one-dimensional lattice of N spatially coupled elements, each described by a continuous variable $x_n(j)$, where n is a discrete time and j is the lattice point. Let $f(x)$ be a function describing the local dynamics (Eq. 3.4) and D the coupling constant between a cell located on j with its first neighbors $j \pm 1$. The evolution of $x_n(j)$ is then given by the set of N coupled equations

$$x_{n+1}(j) = f(x_n(j))$$
$$+ \frac{D}{2}\left[g(x_n(j+1)) + g(x_n(j-1)) - 2g(x_n(j))\right] \tag{3.25}$$

where g is the coupling function. In the sequel, we will adopt the choice $g = f$ frequently made in the literature

Figure 3.8 Probability density of the normalized range for the tent map with $n = 3$ (a); and $n = 100$ (b) as obtained numerically. Dashed line in (b) stands for the i.i.d.r.v. case. Number of realizations and mesh size as in Figure 3.6.

[*Kaneko*, 1989] and choose an even number of cells, and write Equation 3.25 as follows:

$$x_{n+1}(j) = (1-D)f(x_n(j)) + \frac{D}{2}\Big[f(x_n(j+1))$$
$$+ f(x_n(j-1))\Big] - \frac{N}{2} \le j \le \frac{N}{2} \tag{3.26a}$$

Unless otherwise specified, periodic boundary conditions will be used throughout and the domain of variation of x and $f(x)$ will be limited to the interval $[a, b]$,

$$x_n(j) = x_n(j+N) \quad a \le x \le b, \quad a \le f(x) \le b \tag{3.26b}$$

Equations 3.26 are meant to be prototypical, encompassing large classes of dynamical systems giving rise to complex nonlinear behaviors. In this sense, the function $f(x)$ describing the local dynamics is, typically, a one-dimensional endomorphism, as obtained by mapping an underlying continuous time dynamics on a Poincaré surface of section, and by subsequently projecting this mapping along the most unstable direction of the motion. The choice of nearest-neighbor coupling is motivated by the fact that most of the continuous time models representing real-world physicochemical systems are in the form of partial differential equations involving the nabla or the Laplace operators which, once discretized in space, couple any given point to its first neighbors only. More involved couplings, including global ones, may be used for modeling networks such as neural nets, information systems, or social systems.

Among the different properties of the spatiotemporal dynamics generated by Equation 3.26, we are interested here in the instantaneous location of the largest value of $x_n(j)$ observed in the lattice, $M_n(i) = \max\{x_n(j)\}$. The question we address is how $M_n(i)$ will propagate in space, that is, how the lattice site i bearing initially ($n = 0$) the largest value observed instantaneously on the lattice will move time going on. We will proceed by mapping this question into a problem of generalized random walk [*Montroll and Weiss*, 1965], in which the main quantity of interest is the jump ΔR_m (in multiples of the lattice distance) accomplished at intermediate times $m = 1, 2, \ldots n$, the total displacement realized at the observation time n being

$$R_n = \sum_{m=1}^{n} \Delta R_m \qquad (3.27)$$

with

$$R_n^2 = \sum_{m=1}^{n} \Delta R_m^2 + \sum_{m \neq m'=1}^{n} \Delta R_m \Delta R_{m'}. \qquad (3.28)$$

Given the probability density $P(\Delta R)$ and other statistical properties of ΔR, the objective is then to derive the behavior of the displacement R_n as a function of the coupling constant and the parameters built in the iterative mapping $f(x)$.

As a first representative model, we consider a lattice of logistic maps. Consider the local dynamics in the absence of coupling,

$$x_{n+1} = 1 - \alpha x_n^2 \qquad -1 \leq x_n \leq 1 \qquad (3.29)$$

with $\alpha = 2$. Clearly, if set initially to a value close to 1 (its maximum value), the variable x is bound to evolve to a value close to -1 in the next iteration. The sojourn

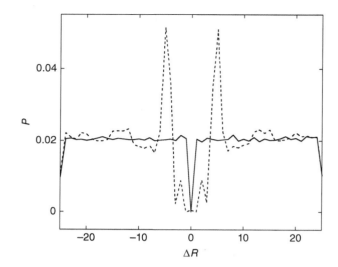

Figure 3.9 Probability of jumps ΔR from the cell containing initially the largest value of x as obtained numerically from Equation 3.26 with $N = 50$ and f given by Equation 3.29. The coupling constant D is $D = 0$ (full line) and $D = 0.95$ (dashed line). The number of realizations is 10^5.

probability of maximum in the cell $j = 0$ on which it initially occurred is thus zero and, starting from this cell, jumps of all possible magnitudes to the other cells are equally probable:

$$P(\Delta R) = 0 \qquad \Delta R = 0$$
$$= \frac{1}{N-1} \qquad \Delta R \neq 0 \qquad (3.30)$$

The variance of ΔR is given by

$$\langle \Delta R^2 \rangle = \frac{1}{N-1} \left[\sum_{j=1}^{N/2} j^2 + \sum_{j=1}^{(N/2)-1} j^2 \right]$$

Figure 3.9 depicts the probability density of the jumps ΔR, as obtained from the numerical solution of the full set of Equations 3.26s for $N = 50$ and f given by Equation 3.29. The full line represents the limiting case of uncoupled cells. The dashed line pertains to the opposite case of strong coupling. The distribution of ΔR develops an intricate structure reflected by strong selection rules whose expected overall result is to enhance the mobility of the maximum. This is confirmed by Figure 3.10, in which the behavior of the mean square distance as a function of time n, $\langle R_n^2 \rangle$, is summarized. The full line in the figure refers to the uncoupled case $D = 0$. It is a straight line whose slope, equal to ≈ 213, can be evaluated analytically. For reference, the result pertaining to 50 uncoupled cells, each undergoing a uniform noise process is also depicted (open circles) revealing a slope of ≈ 208.5.

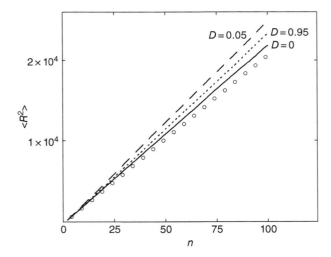

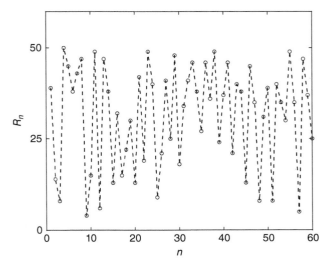

Figure 3.10 Time evolution of the mean square displacement of the largest value of x for the model of Figure 3.9 for different values of the coupling constant D. Empty circles represent the behavior of a uniform noise on the same interval.

Figure 3.11 Time evolution of the location R_n of the cell containing the maximum value of x for the model of Figure 3.9, with $D = 0.05$.

Switching on a nonzero coupling (dashed and dotted lines in the figure) keeps the behavior still diffusive since the corresponding curves are straight lines, but the overall mobility tends to be enhanced albeit in a nonmonotonic fashion, owing to the presence of intermediate synchronization windows.

The diffusive character of the propagation of the maximum is further confirmed by the computation of higher moments of R_n and of its probability distribution (not shown). As it turns out, the skewness is zero for all n's and the kurtosis tends rapidly to zero, whereupon the probability distribution becomes Gaussian.

Figure 3.11 shows a time series of successive values of the instantaneous position R_n of the maximum for weakly coupled logistic maps. As can be seen, the evolution is both quite irregular and far from a purely random process.

We close this section with some results pertaining to systems giving rise to intermittent chaos (cf. Section 3.3.2). Figure 3.12 displays the behavior of the mean square distance $\langle R_n^2 \rangle$ as a function of n for the symmetric cusp map (Eq. 3.9). The behavior is essentially diffusive, at least up to $n \approx 10^2$. The mobility of the maximum in the absence of coupling ($D = 0$, full line) is higher than the one obtained for an equal number of uncoupled cells undergoing a uniform noise process. This can be explained by the fact that for the map in Equation 3.9, the region of quiescent behavior is limited to the leftmost point of the interval. As a result, the sojourn time of the extreme (bound to be close to the rightmost point of the interval) in the cell in which it is initially observed will be very

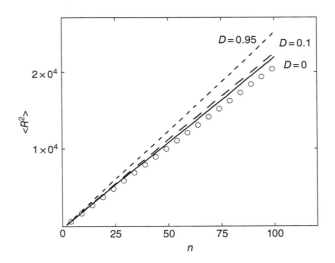

Figure 3.12 As in Figure 3.10 but for the cusp map.

small, entailing that its mobility will be large. As the coupling strength is increased, the mobility increases in a practically monotonic fashion, and in the limit of strong coupling the behavior is practically indistinguishable from the case of fully developed chaos.

3.6. CONCLUSIONS

The central theme of this chapter has been that the correlations and the selection rules inherent in deterministic dynamics are at the origin of distinct features of extreme value distributions, as compared to those derived in the classical statistical approach. Most prominent among them are the broken line-like structure of the n-fold cumulative distributions $F_n(x)$, the staircase-like structure of the associated probability densities $\rho_n(x)$ and their repercussions in the statistics of a number of relevant quantities, such as return times and ranges of sums. These features have potentially serious implications on the issue of prediction, beyond the fact that in view of the unexpectedness and variability of extremes, traditional predictors based on averages are bound to fail.

The dynamical systems approach to extreme events is still in its infancy. In contrast to classical statistical approach, the possibility that the extreme value distributions induced by deterministic dynamics lead to universal laws in the asymptotic limit of infinite observational window for the type of observables considered here is not guaranteed, at least under linear scaling. In this respect, it is worth noting that even within the framework of the classical theory, finite size corrections to the limiting distributions display some highly nontrivial properties [*Györgyi et al.*, 2008].

In a different line of approach, recently developed in the literature, the possibility that classical extreme value theory can be applied under certain conditions to specific classes of observables of dynamical systems other than those considered here has been established [*Freitas et al.*, 2008; *Lucarini et al.*, 2012].

Further open problems include the statistics of repeated crossings, memory effects, nonstationary systems, and finally, multivariate systems, where the intertwining between the unstable and stable directions tend to blur some of the trends put forward here for the prototypical class of one-dimensional mappings [*Nicolis and Nicolis*, 2012].

ACKNOWLEDGMENTS

We are pleased to acknowledge enlightening discussions over the years with our colleague V. Balakrishnan. This work is supported, in part, by the European Space Agency and the Belgian Federal Science Policy Office.

REFERENCES

Balakrishnan, V., C. Nicolis, and G. Nicolis (1995), Extreme value distributions in chaotic dynamics, *J. Stat. Phys.*, *80*, 307–336.

Embrechts, P., P. Klüppelberg, and T. Mikosch (1997), *Modelling Extremal Events*, Springer, New York.

Feller, W. (1951), The asymptotic distribution of the ranges of sums of independent random variables, *Ann. Math. Stat.*, *22*, 427–432.

Freitas, A. C. M., J. M. Freitas, and M. Todd (2008), Hitting time statistics and extreme value theory, *Probab. Theory Rel. Fields*, *147*, 675–710.

Gaspard, P. (1998), *Chaos, Scattering and Statistical Mechanics*, Cambridge University Press, Cambridge.

Györgyi, G., N. Maloney, K. Ozogány, and Z. Rácz (2008), Finite-size scaling in extreme statistics, *Phys. Rev. Lett.*, *100*, 210601.

Hurst, H. (1951), Long-term storage capacity of reservoirs, *Trans. Am. Soc. Civil Eng.*, *116*, 770–808.

Kaneko, K. (1989), Pattern Dynamics in spatiotemporal chaos: Pattern selection, diffusion of defect and pattern competition intermittency, *Phys. D*, *34*, 1–41.

Lucarini, V., D. Faranda, G. Turchetti, and S. Vaienti (2012), Extreme value theory for singular measures, *Chaos*, *22*, 023135.

Montroll, E. and G. Weiss (1965), Random walks on lattices. II, *J. Math. Phys.*, *6*, 167–181.

Nicolis, C., V. Balakrishnan, and G. Nicolis (2006), Extreme events in deterministic dynamical systems, *Phys. Rev. Lett.*, *97*, 210602.

Nicolis, C. and G. Nicolis (2012), Extreme events in multivariate deterministic systems, *Phys. Rev. E*, *85*, 056217.

Nicolis, C. and S. C. Nicolis (2007a), Return time statistics of extreme events in deterministic dynamical systems, *Europhys. Lett.*, *80*, 40003.

Nicolis, C. and S. C. Nicolis (2009), Propagation of extremes in space, *Phys. Rev. E*, *80*, 026201.

Nicolis, G. and C. Nicolis (2007b), *Foundations of Complex Systems*, World Scientific, Singapore.

Nicolis, G., V. Balakrishnan, and C. Nicolis (2008), Probabilistic aspects of extreme events generated by periodic and quasiperiodic deterministic dynamics, *Stochast. Dyn.*, *8*, 115–125.

Nicolis, S. C. and C. Nicolis (2008), Extreme events in bimodal systems, *Phys. Rev. E*, *78*, 036222.

Van de Vyver, H. and C. Nicolis (2010), Probabilistic properties of ranges of sums in dynamical systems, *Phys. Rev.*, *82*, 031107.

4

Skill of Data-based Predictions versus Dynamical Models: A Case Study on Extreme Temperature Anomalies

Stefan Siegert,[1,2] Jochen Bröcker,[1,3] and Holger Kantz[1]

ABSTRACT

We compare the probabilistic predictions of extreme temperature anomalies issued by two different forecast schemes. One is a dynamical physical weather model, and the other is a simple data model. We recall the concept of skill scores in order to assess the performance of these two predictors. Although the result confirms the expectation that the (computationally expensive) weather model outperforms the simple data model, the performance of the latter is surprisingly good. More specifically, for some parameter range, it is even better than the uncalibrated weather model. Since probabilistic predictions are not easily interpreted by the end user, we convert them into deterministic yes/no statements and measure the performance by receiver operating characteristic (ROC) statistics. Scored this way, conclusions about model performance partly vary, which illustrates that the predictive power depends on how it is quantified.

4.1. INTRODUCTION

In this chapter, extreme events are considered as short-lived large deviations from a system's normal state. More precisely, at least one relevant system variable or an order parameter (the latter being synonymous with "observation," which is a way to characterize a microstate of a system on macroscopic scales) assumes a numerical value, which is either much bigger or much smaller than "on average." Without being more specific, one might assume that such a value occurs in the tail of the probability distribution for this quantity, and that "extreme" means to observe a deviation from the mean which exceeds typical deviations. Hence, extreme events are inevitably also rare events.

For some phenomena, there are active debates on whether or not extremes occur more frequently than in a Gaussian distribution (e.g., for rogue waves [*Dysthe et al.*, 2008]). Indeed, for distributions with fat tails such as Lévy-stable distributions with $\alpha < 2$, power law tails lead to a much larger number of extremes and to a considerable percentage of extremes which are by orders of magnitude larger than normal events, as compared to Gaussian distributions. Since such distributions have diverging higher moments, this situation can robustly be detected in time series data by a lack of convergence of finite-time estimates of those moments. This can be nicely illustrated in the earthquake time series, when the released energy is considered instead of magnitude. The running mean of the energy per event increases with every major earthquake, and therefore does not converge at a finite value. This is in agreement with the fact that the probability distribution for released energy is observed to

[1]*Max Planck Institute for the Physics of Complex Systems, Dresden, Germany*

[2]*College of Engineering, Mathematics and Physical Sciences, University of Exeter, Exeter, UK*

[3]*Department of Mathematics and Statistics, University of Reading, Reading, UK*

Extreme Events: Observations, Modeling, and Economics, Geophysical Monograph 214, First Edition.
Edited by Mario Chavez, Michael Ghil, and Jaime Urrutia-Fucugauchi.
© 2016 American Geophysical Union. Published 2016 by John Wiley & Sons, Inc.

be a power law, $p(E) \propto E^{-\beta}$, with $\beta \approx 0.5$, which does not have a finite mean.

With the (trivial) observation that distributions and in particular the existence of higher moments is not a property which is invariant under nonlinear transformation of variables, it is not surprising that there are many natural phenomena where empirical magnitude-frequency distributions suggest that the underlying true distribution does not have diverging higher moments. We found that wind gusts even show exponential distributions, precipitation data do have some outliers in an otherwise exponential distribution, which cannot be easily interpreted, and river levels have a finite maximum. Nonetheless, phenomena such as wind gusts, precipitation, air pressure, and other atmospheric data can be studied under the aspect of extreme events. Moreover, passing over to a different macroscopic quantity, for example, the induced costs due to damage associated with a natural extreme event, evidently changes the nature of a magnitude distribution.

In summary, in this chapter we will consider events as being extreme whenever they are in the uppermost or lowermost range of values for a given quantity, regardless of how large the deviation from the mean value is. More specifically, we will discuss below extreme temperature anomalies, that is, large deviations of the surface temperature from its climatological average for the corresponding day of the year, which are to a good approximation Gaussian distributed. We consider the performance of predictors for the temperature anomaly to overcome a given threshold on the following day for all possible threshold values. Under this setting, one can speak of "prediction of extreme events" only in the limit of this threshold being very high, or, respectively, in the limit that the average event rate goes to zero. The unexpected result of this case study will be that the performance in this limit will differ when measured through different scoring schemes, and that it is therefore not evident how predictable such extremes really are in an abstract, nontechnical sense (for every precisely defined scoring scheme, there is certainly a precise number which characterizes predictability). The other aspect discussed in this chapter focuses on comparing sophisticated physical dynamical models with simple data-based predictors. Here, the conclusion is that physical dynamical models are usually better than data-based predictions. However, there are exceptions, and we present examples where a simple data-driven model outperforms a physical dynamical weather model.

4.2. FORECAST CONCEPTS

Prediction implies that we issue some statement about the future, based on information from the past, and that there is a time interval between the time when the prediction is issued and the time for which the prediction applies. In weather forecasting this is called the lead time, in other contexts it is called the "prediction horizon." The measurement against which the prediction is eventually compared is called the verification. Prediction targets can be either discrete or continuous. In the former case, the target variable can take on only a finite number of values. In the case of only two possibilities, we speak of a binary target. A continuous target can take on an infinite number of possible values. In the context of weather forecasting, the target event "above or below 30°C" is binary, "cold/mild/warm/hot" (defined by precise temperature ranges) is discrete, and predicting an exact temperature value is a continuous prediction target. For each of these targets, predictions can be either deterministic or probabilistic. Deterministic prediction involves a dogmatic statement about the target event, such as "it will be above 30°C tomorrow at noon" (binary), or "the temperature in two days at noon will be exactly 35°C" (continuous). Probabilistic predictions, on the contrary, assign probabilities to express degrees of (un-)certainty about the prediction target. A binary probabilistic prediction is, for example, "the probability of having above 30°C tomorrow at noon is 70%," and a continuous probabilistic prediction is "the probability distribution $p(T)$ assigned to tomorrow's temperature T at noon is a Gaussian with parameters $\mu = 32°C$ and $\sigma = 2°C$." Furthermore, prediction targets can refer to a given moment in time, or to a time interval, to a fixed location, or to a geographical region, etc. Another extension is to consider multivariate variables, such as wind velocity vectors or temperature fields. The actual realization of the target variable, the measurement against which the prediction is eventually compared, is referred to as verification. The above discussion highlights that in every prediction problem, a precise definition of the prediction target is crucial but not completely trivial, a point which might not be obvious at first sight.

Every forecasting algorithm is an input-output relation, where inputs are variables which characterize the knowledge about the system under concern at time t, and the output is one of the forecast products discussed above. For a given set of input data and the same prediction target, one can design very different ways to actually produce a specific value for the output. The simplest forecast is a constant value independent of any inputs. This can make sense, for example, in the case of continuous deterministic forecasts and probabilistic binary forecasts. For the deterministic forecast, it could be the mean value of the prediction target (or should it be its median?), and for the probabilistic forecast it could be the average frequency of occurrence of the target. But note that already for this very simple scheme the optimum specific value depends on the way the performance of a forecast is measured (e.g., whether to use the mean or the median depends on the performance measure). As a further complication, different forecast schemes for the very same target might use different sets of input variables.

There are many methods to detect and describe dependencies between input data and the target value on a training set. These include time series models, regression models, decision trees, or neural networks, just to name a few. In climate research, where physical models of the atmosphere-ocean systems are employed, the models differ not only in the way different physical processes are resolved and how the nonresolved processes are parametrized, but also in the spatial and temporal resolution of the models.

In this chapter, we will focus on two types of predictions, which we evaluate by two different types of performance measures. One prediction will be a probabilistic forecast for a binary event, which issues a probability p for "yes" and accordingly $1 - p$ for "no." The other will be a binary deterministic prediction which will either predict "yes" or "no," and it will be derived from the probabilistic forecast. These two types of predictions will be evaluated by proper skill scores and receiver operating characteristic (ROC) analysis, respectively.

Our target is the prediction of weather extremes. Since true weather extremes are rare and any statistical analysis of the performance of any predictor is strongly error prone, we will relax the requirement of "extreme" a bit and at the same time we will look at a quantity which exhibits "extremes" independent of season: We will study the fluctuations of temperature anomalies, and the prediction target is such that the anomaly will exceed a fixed threshold the next day, given that the anomaly of the present day is below the threshold. The latter restriction, prediction only if current temperature anomaly is "not extreme," takes into account the aspect of an "event." Even though a heat wave, say, typically lasts several days, prediction of its onset seems to be more interesting than the prediction that it will continue the next day. As said, we concentrate on temperature anomalies, which are the differences of the actual temperature and the climatological mean temperature at the given day of the year. Therefore, an extreme anomaly can occur at any season, and the event rate is independent of the current season.

We will use two types of models for performing predictions: Simple data models, where we predict the temperature anomaly of the next day based only on measurement data, with an interdependence structure that is extracted from a long dataset of historic recordings. The other model type relies on a global general circulation model, that is, a weather model which is fed with station data from the entire globe, and which contains a good portion of the physics of the atmosphere.

With these two types of models, we will predict the probability that the temperature anomaly will exceed a given threshold 24 hours ahead, if it is below that threshold at the time when the forecast is issued. Later, we will convert these predicted probabilities into binary deterministic forecasts. Given the fact that the weather model is by many orders of magnitude more complex and more costly than the data model, and it also contains a factor of (at least) 10^5 more input data which characterize the current state of the atmosphere, we expect that it will outperform the data model. But by how much? This case study will give some surprising results.

4.3. THE DATA

We consider a data set of temperature observations at 2 m height for Hannover, Germany. The data set is provided by the DWD climatological data base [*DWD*, 2011]. It consists of $N = 23,741$ daily temperature measurements T'_n taken at 12:00 UTC between 1946 and 2010. The time index n thus indicates "days since 1946/01/01." The mean and variance of the time series are $\overline{T'} = 12.06°C$ and $\overline{(T' - \overline{T'})^2} = (8.31°C)^2$, respectively.

Since the number of really extreme surface temperature events, that is, the number of exceptionally cold or exceptionally hot days per year, is rather small and clearly restricted to summer and winter season, we consider *anomalies*. The anomalies T_n are defined as the deviation of the actual temperature T'_n from a typical, expected temperature value c_n, called the *climatology*. A pragmatic approach to estimate the climatology for day n is to determine the average of observed temperature values on the same date over a number of previous years. However, the result even for 64 years (as they are available to us) is not a smooth function of n, as one would naively assume. We implement this smoothness assumption by modeling the climatology as a seasonal cycle which is composed of a constant component, a component proportional to $\sin(\omega n + \phi_1)$, and a component proportional to $\sin(2\omega n + \phi_2)$, where $\omega = 2\pi / (365.2425 \text{ days})$ is the rotational frequency of the Earth, and φ_1 and φ_2 are phases that have to be estimated along with the proportionality constants. Higher harmonics could be taken into account as well, but here we restrict the estimator to only the first two. The seasonal cycle c_n is estimated by choosing a coefficient vector $\beta = (\beta_0, ..., \beta_4)$ such that the sum of squared differences between the observed temperatures T'_n and

$$c_n = \beta_0 + \beta_1 \cos \omega n + \beta_2 \sin \omega n + \beta_3 \cos 2\omega n + \beta_4 \sin 2\omega n \tag{4.1}$$

is minimized. For the Hannover temperature time series, the least squares fit of β is given by $\hat{\beta} = (12.1, -2.9, -9.5, 0.2, -0.6)$. The temperature anomalies are then constructed from the observed data and the climatology by

$$T_n = T'_n - c_n. \tag{4.2}$$

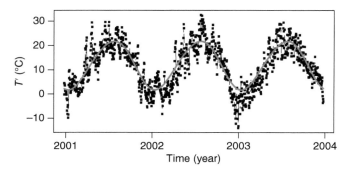

Figure 4.1 Black markers show a 3 year sample of the daily temperature data for Hannover (Germany), which we analyze in this study. The fitted climatology c_n is shown as a red line.

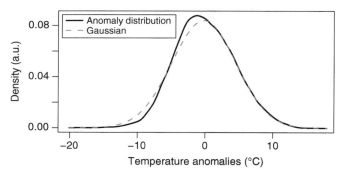

Figure 4.2 Temperature anomalies are calculated by subtracting the climatology from the temperature time series. The anomaly distribution reconstructed by kernel density estimation (black line) is approximately Gaussian (red line). Negative anomalies appear more concentrated toward zero than what would be expected in a Gaussian distribution.

A 3 year sample of the temperature data and the fitted seasonal cycle are shown in Figure 4.1. The anomaly T_n is what we consider as the nontrivial part of the temperature, the part that cannot be easily predicted since it is strongly fluctuating. Our goal will be to predict whether or not future anomalies exceed some (possibly high) threshold, given that the current anomaly is below that threshold.

The distribution of the temperature anomalies T_n is approximately Gaussian, as shown in Figure 4.2. The density was fit using Gaussian kernel density estimation with automatic bandwidth selection, as implemented by the R-function `density` provided by the `stats`-package [*R Development Core Team*, 2011; see also *Silverman*, 1998]. The distribution differs from a Gaussian in that it is slightly right-skewed, indicating that the negative anomalies are less variable than the positive ones. In a log-normal plot (not shown), the tails of the fitted distribution decay faster than that of the Gaussian distribution. This is an artifact of the density estimation procedure,

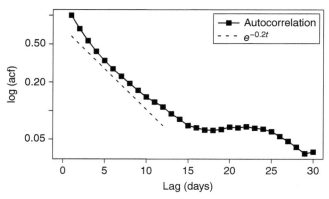

Figure 4.3 Autocorrelation function of the temperature anomalies T_n plotted in log-normal axes. It decays exponentially with a decay time of about five days.

where the tail behavior of the reconstructed distribution is governed by the tail of the kernel, which has a much smaller variance than the data whose distribution is estimated. We can thus not draw definite conclusions about the true tail behavior of our data.

The autocorrelation function of the temperature anomaly exhibits an approximately exponential decay with a decay time of about 5 days, as shown in Figure 4.3. The nonvanishing autocorrelation function for small lags indicates that the value of the anomaly at time n contains predictive information about the value of the anomaly at time $n+1$. So, evidently, temperature anomalies are not white noise.

4.4. THE FORECAST MODELS

In order to make forecasts about the future, we need models that can compute information about the future using information that is available at present. In the following section, we start from the simplest one-parameter model, then introduce a dynamical data-based model, and a complex weather model, together with an additional adjustment to observed data, so that we have a total of four models to be compared.

4.4.1. The Base Rate Model

A data model extracts details of dependencies between successive values of a time series which we can use for prediction. Many models coexist. In machine learning, rather general but parameterized input-output relations are used. Learn pairs of input and corresponding output are used to adapt the model parameters to the observed data. Alternatively, one can use well-established dynamical models, where the class of linear Gaussian models is the most prominent. In fact, in the following subsection, we will argue that a simple AR(1) process is an excellent compromise between model complexity and accuracy. Here, we start with an even simpler model.

A base rate model relies on the (known) average event rate r. It issues predictions which are independent of time and the present state of the true system; it simply predicts that the event will take place with probability r.

We want to predict whether the anomaly will exceed a certain threshold the next day. But we are only interested in such a prediction if the present anomaly is below that threshold. This latter complication takes into account that we are interested in the prediction of "events," that is, of something that is a change with respect to the current situation. Therefore, we will not make any prediction at time n at which the anomaly is already above the threshold, which means that for low thresholds we will have a strongly reduced number of prediction trials.

In this binary prediction, an event $X_{n+1} = 1$ is observed, whenever $T_{n+1} > \tau$ for a threshold value τ, but we make a prediction only if $T_n \leq \tau$, that is, if $X_n = 0$. Therefore, the event rate evaluated on N data is given by

$$r_\tau = \mathbb{P}(T_{n+1} > \tau \mid T_n \leq \tau) \approx \frac{\sum_{n=1}^{N-1}(1-X_n)X_{n+1}}{\sum_{n=1}^{N-1}(1-X_n)}. \quad (4.3)$$

This base rate model will now predict that, given $X_n = 0$ (i.e., $T_n \leq \tau$), the anomaly on the following day will exceed the threshold τ with a probability r_τ, independent of any information about the current weather. If $X_n = 1$ ($T_n > \tau$), no prediction will be made and the corresponding day is not considered a forecast instance. Therefore, we will refer to this model as the *conditional exceedance base rate* (CEBR) model.

The base rate model is the simplest model one can think of, and it will therefore serve as a benchmark. The only parameter of this model is the rate r_τ, which can be easily extracted from recorded data. In this sense, it is a purely data-driven model. Also, a sophisticated weather model creates weather predictions through modeling of physical processes, and there is no guarantee that such a model generates events with the correct base rate. Therefore, the benchmark provided by the base rate model is a serious one.

4.4.2. The AR(1) Model

A more reasonable model than the base rate model should consider our knowledge on the current weather state and thereby yield predictions which vary along the time axis. Based on the almost-Gaussianity of the temperature anomalies, and based on their almost-exponentially fast decay of autocorrelations, a reasonable model which makes use of current and past observations is a linear autoregressive (AR) process:

$$T_{n+1} = \mu + \sum_{i=1}^{p}\alpha_i T_{n+1-i} + \varepsilon_n, \quad (4.4)$$

where p is the order of the model, α_i are the constant AR parameters, and the residuals ϵ_n are white noise with zero mean and variance σ^2. We assume a mean $\mu = 0$, because we consider anomalies whose mean is zero by construction. Given the order p, the parameters could be adapted by minimization of the root mean squared prediction error with respect to α_i, or some modifications such as the Yule Walker equations. Different sophistications for the estimate of AR coefficients and also of the order of AR models exist [*Schelter et al.*, 2007].

We split the full dataset into a training and test set, that is, we fit the model coefficients on data from 1946 to 1978 (inclusive), and make predictions and compute their performance on the remaining data from 1979 onward. We use the R-function `ar` provided by the `stats`-package [*R Development Core Team*, 2011] to fit the AR parameters α_i and the variance of residuals σ^2 using maximum likelihood estimation. An optimal order of $p = 6$ is suggested by Akaike's information criterion [*Akaike*, 1974].

In Figure 4.4, it is shown that the parameters α_2 through α_6 of the optimal AR(6) are only of the order of 0.01, while the first parameter α_1 is almost identical to that of the AR(1) process. We use this as a motivation to override Akaike's suggestion and choose the AR(1) process as our best data-driven model of the temperature anomalies. That is, we model the temperature anomalies T_n by

$$T_{n+1} = \alpha T_n + \epsilon_n, \quad (4.5)$$

where $\alpha = 0.72$ and ϵ_n is the Gaussian white noise with variance $\sigma^2 = 3.06^2$.

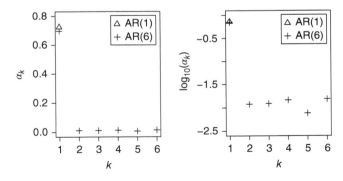

Figure 4.4 Coefficients of autoregressive models of order 1 (triangle) and of order 6 (crosses), plotted in normal (left) and logarithmic (right) ordinates. In the AR(6) model, which is suggested as the optimal model by AIC, the parameters α_2 through α_6 are of the order of 10^{-2} while the parameter α_1 is very close to that of the AR(1) model.

In an AR(1) process with zero mean, parameter α, and variance of residuals σ^2, it is straightforward to show that the marginal distribution has mean zero and variance $\sigma_C^2 = \mathbb{E}(T^2)$ equal to $\sigma^2/(1-\alpha^2)$. Using our parameter estimates of σ and α, we get $\sigma_C^2 = 4.42^2$, which is in agreement with the variance of the anomaly distribution shown in Figure 4.2.

From Equation 4.5, one can conclude that in an AR(1) process, the probability distribution of the state at time instance $n+1$, conditional on the state at instance n is a Gaussian with mean equal to αT_n and variance equal to σ^2, that is

$$(T_{n+1} \mid T_n) \sim \mathcal{N}(\alpha T_n, \sigma^2). \tag{4.6}$$

We denote the Gaussian probability distribution function and cumulative distribution function by

$$\varphi_{\mu,\sigma}(x) \equiv \frac{1}{\sqrt{2\pi}\sigma} \exp\left(-\frac{(x-\mu)^2}{2\sigma^2}\right), \tag{4.7}$$

and

$$\Phi_{\mu,\sigma}(x) \equiv \int_{-\infty}^{x} dt\, \varphi_{\mu,\sigma}(t), \tag{4.8}$$

respectively. If subscripts are missing, the conventions $\Phi \equiv \Phi_{0,1}$ and $\varphi \equiv \varphi_{0,1}$ apply. According to Equation 4.6, the probability of exceeding a threshold τ in an AR(1) process, conditional on the present value T_n, is given by

$$\mathbb{P}(T_{n+1} > \tau \mid T_n = t) = 1 - \Phi_{\alpha t,\sigma}(\tau) \tag{4.9}$$

If the true process that generates T_{n+1} is indeed an AR(1) process, Equation 4.9 provides the most complete information regarding the occurrence of an exceedance event.

4.4.3. The Weather Model

The physical processes in the atmosphere are pretty well understood, although not in full detail [*Holton*, 2004]. General circulation models (GCMs) are models based on the hydrodynamic transport equations for the wind field plus the thermodynamics of the transported air masses and their interaction through the temperature-dependent density of air. For more realism, further processes have to be included, such as the transport of different phases of atmospheric water and their transitions; the energy budget has to be adjusted, topography must be included, just to mention some. For detailed descriptions of state-of-the-art atmospheric models, see *ECMWF* [2009], *NOAA* [2011], or *DWD* [2012].

For the forecast of temperature anomaly exceedances, we use output from the NCEP reforecast project [*Hamill et al.*, 2005]. The reforecast project provides a dataset of global ensemble weather forecasts. In a long reforecast project, global temperature forecasts were issued using the same computational model for the period 1979 to present. That is, although this model was truly operational only for a few years, it has been employed a posteriori to perform predictions on past observations, and it has been used for predictions until today even though better models are available. This is an invaluable source of data, since serious statistical analysis of forecasts is possible if the same model is operated for several decades. Initialized daily at 0:00 UTC, the model output forecasts on a $2.5° \times 2.5°$ grid in 12 hourly interval up to 15 days into the future. An ensemble of 15 forecasts is produced by slightly varying the initial conditions using so-called Bred perturbations [*Toth and Kalnay*, 1997]. See *Leutbecher and Palmer* [2008] for a review of methods and applications of ensemble forecasting.

In order to issue temperature anomaly exceedance forecasts for Hannover, using the ensemble forecast, we proceed as follows. Hannover's geographical coordinates are 52.37°N, 9.73°E and the NCEP model has a grid point very close to these coordinates, namely at 52.5°N, 10.0°E. We use the values of the ensemble members at this grid point as an ensemble forecast for Hannover. We subtract from the ensemble members the climatology in order to transform the temperature forecast into an anomaly forecast. In the data-driven forecast, we used today's measurement to estimate the probability of occurrence of an exceedance event 24 hours in the future. Here, we use the 36 hours lead time model forecast, in order to account for the time lag between measuring the present state and actually having access to the model results.

In a first (naive) approach, we transform the ensemble into a predictive distribution function by Gaussian kernel density estimation, the same method that we used to estimate the anomaly distribution in Section 4.3. That is, we convert the discrete set of predicted temperature anomaly values into a continuous probability density function. Applied to ensemble forecasts, kernel density estimation is also referred to as ensemble dressing. Each ensemble member is dressed with a Gaussian kernel function with zero mean and width σ_k, which we calculate using Silverman's rule of thumb [*Silverman*, 1998]. For an ensemble of size K and standard deviation σ, this rule estimates the dressing kernel width σ_k as follows:

$$\sigma_k = \left(\frac{4\tilde{\sigma}^5}{3K}\right)^{1/5}. \tag{4.10}$$

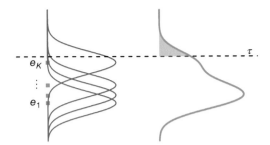

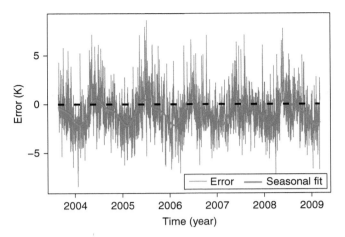

Figure 4.5 Illustration of ensemble dressing. Each ensemble member (red markers) is dressed with a Gaussian kernel of zero mean and width σ_k (blue lines). The superposition of all the dressing kernels provides the predictive distribution (red line). From this distribution, the exceedance probability of a threshold τ can be calculated (red shaded area).

Once the kernel width is estimated, the ensemble $\mathbf{e} = (e_1, \ldots, e_K)$ is transformed into a density for the temperature anomaly by

$$p(T \mid \mathbf{e}) = \frac{1}{K} \sum_{i=1}^{K} \varphi_{e_i, \sigma_k}(T). \quad (4.11)$$

Figure 4.5 illustrates this method, and the calculation of the exceedance probability of a threshold τ. We refer to the above method of obtaining the exceedance probabilities as the raw ensemble forecast.

4.4.4. Calibrated Weather Model

When using only the raw ensemble predictions, we ignore a very important point concerning physical dynamical forecast models, namely that past prediction errors can (and should) be used to improve future forecasts. With this insight, we enter the world of model output statistics [MOS; *Glahn and Lowry*, 1972; *Wilks and Hamill*, 2007].

The numerical model is only a sketch of the true atmosphere and thus model errors are inevitable. However, some of these model errors are systematic, such that they can be corrected. Two notorious systematic errors in weather models are seasonal bias and underdispersiveness. The bias is the average difference between ensemble mean and verification, which is nonzero and displays seasonality in the NCEP model (see Figure 4.6). Underdispersiveness means that the ensemble variance underestimates the mean square difference between ensemble members and verification. Both model errors are prevalent in the ensemble, and in the following we correct both of them.

Here we employ one of different possible calibration schemes. It shifts the values of every ensemble member by the same season-dependent value and corrects the ensemble dispersion by an adjustment of the width of the dressing kernels. More precisely, in order to fit the climatology to the temperature data in Section 4.3, we fit a second-order

Figure 4.6 The difference between the mean value of NCEP ensemble forecasts and observation varies systematically with season and its seasonal fit defines a bias which can be subtracted in order to improve forecast accuracy.

trigonometric polynomial to the time series of the bias. The ensemble is bias-corrected by shifting the ensemble mean according to the seasonal bias known from the 2 years preceding the year of forecast.

In order to correct for ensemble underdispersiveness, we inflate the width of the Gaussian kernels. In *Wang and Bishop* [2005], a method was proposed to estimate the kernel width for underdispersive ensembles under a second moment constraint. Denote by $\overline{d^2}$, the average squared difference between ensemble mean and verification, by $\overline{s^2}$ the average ensemble variance, and by K the number of ensemble members. The kernel width proposed by *Wang and Bishop* [2005] is then given by

$$\sigma_k^2 = \overline{d^2} - \left(1 + \frac{1}{K}\right)\overline{s^2}. \quad (4.12)$$

With these model corrections which require an archive of past observations and forecasts, we can perform improved temperature anomaly exceedance forecasts. Clearly, as in the AR(1)-model, we respect causality and we use only past data for our recalibration. The exceedance predictions are calculated as for the raw ensemble, but after correcting for the bias and inflating the dressing kernels. We refer to these predictions as the post-processed ensemble forecasts.

4.5. PROBABILISTIC PREDICTION OF EXTREME ANOMALIES

All of our four models can be used to issue forecasts of the probability that the temperature anomaly will exceed a predefined threshold the next day. Before we can compare the performances of these different models, we have to define how to measure the skill of a probabilistic forecast.

4.5.1. Scoring Rules and the Brier Skill Score

One way to evaluate probabilistic predictions is by means of strictly proper scoring rules [*Gneiting and Raftery*, 2007]. A scoring rule is a function $S(p, X)$ that combines a probabilistic forecast $p \in [0,1]$ and the corresponding event indicator $X \in \{0,1\}$, where $X = 1$ if the event happens and $X = 0$ otherwise. The scoring rule is proper if it forces the forecaster to issue his probability honestly. Take the Brier score [*Brier*, 1950], for example, which is given by

$$\text{Br}(p, X) = (X - p)^2. \qquad (4.13)$$

The Brier score is negatively oriented and 0 for a perfect forecast that assigns probability 1 to an event that actually occurs, and a probability 0 to an event that does not occur. A forecaster who thinks that the probability of occurrence of X is p can choose to issue a probability q as the forecast. One can calculate the subjective expectation value of the Brier score of the forecast q by

$$\mathbb{E}(X - q)^2 = p(1-q)^2 + (1-p)q^2, \qquad (4.14)$$

where one assumes that the true rate of occurrence is one's own estimate p. This expectation is minimized if and only if $q = p$ which makes the Brier score a strictly proper scoring rule, that is, the forecaster has no chance to improve the score by issuing a forecast q that is different from the best guess p. The same reasoning applies for the following scenario: Let p be the true rate of occurrence and let q be the best guess of the forecaster. Then the forecaster performs best whose estimate is closest to the true value. Let us stress that there are other, at first sight equivalent scoring rules, which lack this property: replacing, for example, $(X - q)^2$ by $|X - q|$ leads to an improper score, which can be improved by predicting $q = 1$ whenever $p > 1/2$ and $q = 0$ otherwise. Propriety of a scoring rule is thus a reasonable property to ask for. A further popular example of a strictly proper scoring rule is the ignorance score [*Roulston and Smith*, 2002], given by $-\log_2(p(X))$.

In the following, we will compare different probabilistic forecasting schemes by means of the Brier score. A common way to compare scores of different forecasts is by means of a skill score [*Wilks*, 2006]. Let $\bar{S}_1$ and $\bar{S}_2$ be the empirical averages of the Brier score of forecasting schemes 1 and 2, respectively. Then the Brier skill score (BSS) is defined by

$$\text{BSS} = 1 - \frac{\bar{S}_1}{\bar{S}_2}. \qquad (4.15)$$

The BSS indicates the fraction of improvement of forecasting scheme 1 over scheme 2 in terms of the Brier score. A BSS of 1 indicates that the forecasts issued by scheme 1 are perfect, that is, the forecast probability is unity each time the event happens and zero each time the event does not happen. A BSS of 0 indicates no improvement, and a negative BSS indicates that scheme 1 is inferior to scheme 2.

4.5.2. Theoretical Skill of the Base Rate Model

Before we test our models on the observed temperature anomalies, we compute the theoretical values of the performance measures for our data models, that is, the base rate model and the AR(1) model. Let us assume for a moment that the temperature anomalies are really generated by an AR(1) process with parameters α and σ. We define the exceedance threshold τ as the q-quantile of the climatological distribution of the temperature anomalies. As discussed before, this distribution has zero mean and variance $\sigma_C^2 = \sigma^2/(1 - \alpha^2)$. Thus, τ is defined such that

$$q = \Phi_{0,\sigma_C}(\tau) = \Phi\left(\frac{\tau}{\sigma_C}\right). \qquad (4.16)$$

Averaged over all observations, a fraction of $(1-q)$ of the temperature anomalies will be larger than τ. However, we only issue predictions on days when the temperature anomaly is below τ. Under this constraint, the average event rate r_τ is not equal to $(1-q)$, as the following calculations show. The event rate r_τ in our setting is given by

$$r_\tau = \mathbb{P}(T_{n+1} > \tau \mid T_n \leq \tau) \qquad (4.17)$$

which can be estimated from a dataset using Equation 4.3. In a true AR(1) process, we can calculate r_τ as a function of AR parameters as follows:

$$r_\tau = \mathbb{E}\left[\mathbb{P}(T_{n+1} > \tau \mid T_n = t) \mid t \leq \tau\right] \qquad (4.18)$$

$$= \mathbb{E}\left[1 - \Phi_{\alpha t, \sigma}(\tau) \mid t \leq \tau\right] \qquad (4.19)$$

$$= 1 - \left(\Phi_{0,\sigma_C}(\tau)\right)^{-1} \int_{-\infty}^{\tau} dt\, \Phi_{\alpha t, \sigma}(\tau)\varphi_{0,\sigma_C}(t), \qquad (4.20)$$

based on Equation 4.9 and the fact that T_n is marginally distributed according to the climatological Gaussian distribution with zero mean and variance σ_C^2. Note that Equation 4.20 is equal to $(1-q)$ only if $\alpha = 0$. The probability r_τ provides the CEBR forecast in this setting.

We numerically integrated the expressions in Equation 4.20 (using the R-function `integrate` provided by the `stats`-package, [*R Development Core Team*, 2011]) to produce the conditional exceedance rates in Figure 4.7. The threshold τ that defines the exceedance event is defined with respect to the climatological distribution which itself depends on the parameters of the process σ

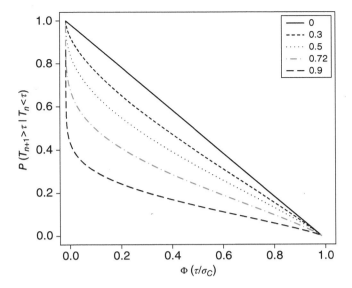

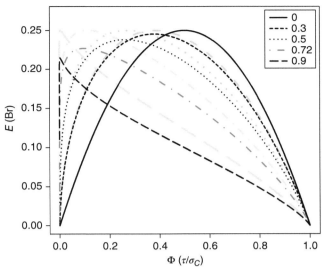

Figure 4.7 Conditional exceedance base rate r_τ for AR(1) data of a threshold τ at instance $n+1$, conditional on not exceeding τ at instance n, plotted over the q-value of τ in the climatological distribution. Different lines indicate different values of the AR parameter α. The line that corresponds to our temperature anomaly time series is shown red. Note that the climatological distribution is different for different values of α. As we define the threshold relative to the standard deviation of the climatological distribution, these curves are independent of σ.

Figure 4.8 Expected Brier scores of the CEBR forecast (gray thick lines) and the true conditional exceedance forecast (black and red lines) for AR(1) processes with different AR parameters α, as given by the legend.

correlations and where the conditional base rate is correspondingly smaller than one minus the quantile. We will compare all further forecasts with this benchmark in terms of the BSS.

The expected Brier scores given by Equation 4.22 are shown as gray lines in Figure 4.8. The maxima of all these curves assume the value 1/4, located at that quantile where the conditional rate $r_\tau = 1/2$.

We regard the CEBR as our null-model, the simplest possible prediction that a forecaster who has access to a historical dataset of temperature anomalies could issue. A more sophisticated forecasting scheme would always have to be compared to this simple null-model. We would only accept a more complicated forecasting scheme if it can beat the CEBR forecast.

4.5.3. Theoretical Skill of the AR(1) Model

One forecast that is definitely more sophisticated than the CEBR forecast can be obtained by issuing the true exceedance probability of the AR process at the present value of T_n, namely $1-\Phi_{\alpha T_n,\sigma}(\tau)$ as given by Equation 4.9. As was mentioned before, this is the most complete information as to the occurrence of an exceedance event in a true AR(1) process. The expected Brier score of this exceedance forecast is given by

and α. Its q-value is shown on the abscissa. Since in all functions in Equation 4.20, the arguments are scaled by σ, the curves of Figure 4.7 do not depend on σ.

Figure 4.7 shows that it might not be a good idea to issue $1-q$ as an exceedance forecast if τ is the climatological q-quantile. Due to the correlation of the process, the probability of hopping over the threshold, conditional on being below the threshold at forecast time is reduced compared to this probability in the uncorrelated process where $\alpha = 0$. The process has a tendency to stay below the threshold if it is already below the threshold. This tendency is more pronounced the higher the value of α, that is, the stronger the correlation. Since forecasts are only issued if the present state is below the threshold, forecasting $1-q$ would overestimate the CEBR if $\alpha > 0$.

The event $X : (T_{n+1} > \tau \mid T_n \leq \tau)$ occurs with a rate r_τ, given by Equation 4.20. The expectation value of the Brier score of a probabilistic forecast that constantly issues r_τ as a probability for X is readily calculated as follows:

$$\mathbb{E}\mathrm{Br}\left(r_\tau, X\right) = \left(1-r_\tau\right)^2 \mathbb{P}\left(X=1\right) + \left(0-r_\tau\right)^2 \mathbb{P}\left(X=0\right) \quad (4.21)$$

$$= r_\tau\left(1-r_\tau\right). \quad (4.22)$$

This is the expected Brier score of the CEBR forecast where the time series is assumed to possess AR(1)

$$\mathbb{E}\left[\mathrm{Br}\left(1-\Phi_{\alpha T_n,\sigma}(\tau), X_{n+1}\right) \mid T_n \leq \tau\right]$$
$$= \left[\Phi_{0,\sigma_C}(\tau)\right]^{-1} \int_{-\infty}^{\tau} dt\, \varphi_{0,\sigma_C}(t)\left\{\Phi_{\alpha t,\sigma}(\tau)\left[1-\Phi_{\alpha t,\sigma}(\tau)\right]\right\}.$$
$$(4.23)$$

The term in the curly brackets of Equation 4.23 is the expected Brier score at a fixed value of $T_n = t$ and this term is averaged over all values of $t \le \tau$, weighted by the marginal distribution.

We numerically integrate Equation 4.23 for different AR(1) parameters to produce Figure 4.8. In an uncorrelated process, where $\alpha = 0$, the expected Brier score of the true exceedance probability and that of the CEBR are identical, because the two forecast probabilities are identical. If the true process is uncorrelated, no prediction skill can be gained by assuming correlation. For processes with $\alpha > 0$, however, the expected Brier score of the CEBR is always higher (i.e., worse) than that of the true exceedance probability. Explicitly conditioning the forecast probability on the current state T_n leads to a significant gain in the forecast skill. This gain is monotonically increasing in the AR parameter α. The maxima of all curves occur at those points where the corresponding CEBR curves in Figure 4.7 cross the horizontal line $p = 0.5$. At this point, the uncertainty of the forecaster as to the occurrence or nonoccurrence of an exceedance event is maximum, thus leading to the Brier score being maximized. As τ approaches $+\infty$ or $-\infty$, all Brier scores tend to zero, that is, all forecasts become more and more perfect. This can be seen as a result of the growing certainty about the occurrence or nonoccurrence of an exceedance event if the threshold becomes ever smaller or larger.

Substituting Equations 4.22 and 4.23 in Equation 4.15, we compute the BSS that compares the Brier score of the AR(1) forecast to that of the constant CEBR forecast. Skill scores for different values of α are shown in Figure 4.9. In the range between these extremes, where τ is roughly between the 5- and the 95-percentile of the climatological distribution of the process, the BSS is approximately constant. In this range, the BSS is larger, the larger the AR parameter α is, that is, the more correlated the process is. While it is evident that the Brier score tends to 0 when the event rate tends to either 1 or 0, it is less evident that the BSS for the AR model does the same. The curves shown in Figure 4.9 are generated by the numerical integration, and seem to converge to zero for large and small τ, but we do not have any analytical estimates for the BSS in these limits.

In Figures 4.7, 4.8, and 4.9, the red lines report the theoretical results for that value of the AR parameter α which we obtain by a fit of an AR(1) model to our temperature anomaly data. Hence, we expect the empirical skill of the AR model on these data, to be discussed Section 4.5.4, to be similar.

4.5.4. Empirical Skill of the AR(1) Model

We now issue AR(1) model predictions for the Hannover temperature anomaly time series and compare these predictions with CEBR forecasts. We use the time period

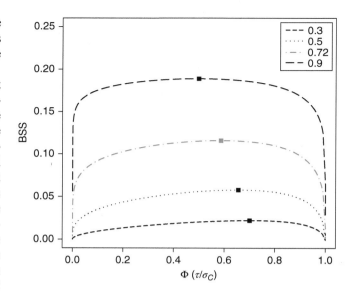

Figure 4.9 Brier skill score comparing the forecasting scheme, which forecasts the true exceedance probability to that forecasting only the CEBR for different AR(1) processes. The maxima are indicated by a marker.

between 1946 and 1978 (inclusive) to estimate the climatology, the AR(1) parameters α and σ, and the CEBR as a function of the threshold τ. Based on this information, we issue probabilistic predictions for the event that a threshold τ will be exceeded by the temperature anomaly, using the CEBR and the AR(1) model. We compare the probabilistic predictions to the actual outcomes of the events using the Brier score. Substituting the empirical averages of these scores in Equation 4.15 yields the BSS.

This BSS, comparing the predictions issued by the AR(1) model with those of the CEBR model, is shown in Figure 4.10 and compared with the analytical result provided by comparing Equations 4.22 and 4.23 for $\alpha = 0.72$, which is the empirical value of the AR parameter. Obviously, in the temperature anomaly time series, predictions can be issued regarding the occurrence of an exceedance event that are significantly more skilful than the CEBR. This result holds for a wide range of threshold values. Only for very large negative and positive anomalies does the confidence band overlap zero so that we cannot assume significant improvement of the AR forecast over the CEBR forecast. The analytical curve is fully contained in the confidence band, thus reassuring that the calculations above are correct, and that the temperature anomalies can indeed be modeled by an AR(1) process.

Regarding confidence intervals, note that in Figure 4.10, and in all other figures, the intervals are to be taken as pointwise confidence intervals, and not as confidence bands for the complete curve. If the confidence intervals are referred to the complete curve, they would be much

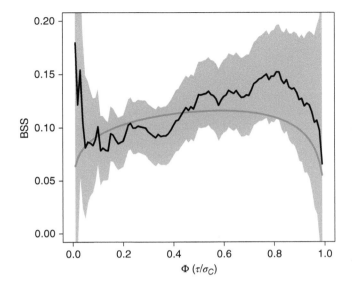

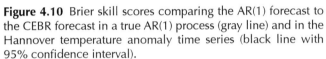

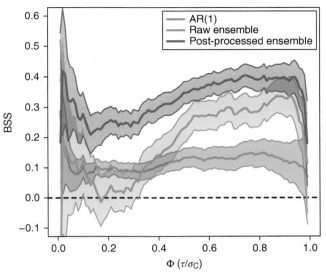

Figure 4.10 Brier skill scores comparing the AR(1) forecast to the CEBR forecast in a true AR(1) process (gray line) and in the Hannover temperature anomaly time series (black line with 95% confidence interval).

Figure 4.11 Brier skill scores of the raw ensemble, the post-processed ensemble, and the AR(1) forecast. 95% confidence intervals are included.

wider. This distinction is especially relevant if the points along the curve are not independent, which is clearly the case if they refer to predictive skill with respect to different threshold values. If the predictive skill is particularly good at a threshold value of, say 0.8, it is reasonable to assume that the predictive skill at a threshold value of 0.81 is also good.

4.5.5. Skill of the Raw and Post-Processed Ensemble Forecast Compared to the AR(1) Model

We evaluate the exceedance forecasts produced by the raw and post-processed ensemble, which are documented in Sections 4.4.3 and 4.4.4. Using the BSS, we compare their Brier score to the Brier score of the CEBR forecast. For reference and comparison, we include the BSS of the AR(1) forecast.

Figure 4.11 shows, as a function of the threshold, the BSS of the raw ensemble, of the post-processed ensemble, and of the AR(1) forecast. For thresholds with p-values around 0.2, the ensemble can hardly beat the CEBR, as indicated by a skill score close to zero. In this range, the AR(1) forecast clearly outperforms the raw ensemble. For larger thresholds, on the contrary, the raw ensemble outperforms the AR(1) predictions.

A valid question regarding Figure 4.11 is how can it be that a complex physical dynamical model is outperformed by the simple data-driven AR(1) model? A weakness of the atmospheric model is that, unlike the AR(1) model, it is not automatically calibrated to the observations.

Systematic model errors, for example, due to unresolved topography, or errors in the estimation of the initial model state can cause miscalibration of the ensemble-based exceedance forecasts, even though the weather model incorporates a thorough understanding of the physical processes in the atmosphere. However, as discussed in Section 4.4.4, observation data can be used to recalibrate the output of the ensemble predictions.

We rerun the ensemble-based exceedance forecasts after applying bias correction and variance inflation as described in Section 4.4.4. We model an operational forecasting scenario by using data from the past 2 years to apply corrections to forecast during a given year. That is, the seasonal bias and the width of the dressing kernel are calculated using ensemble output and observation data from the 2 years preceding the year of a given prediction. By this procedure, we account for the nonstationarity in the model output, for example, due to varying observation data.

Figure 4.11 shows the BSS of the post-processed ensemble forecast, taking the CEBR forecast as the reference forecast. The post-processed ensemble forecast is constantly better than the AR(1) forecast, as one would expect from a sophisticated physical dynamical model. The skill score of the AR(1) forecast is exceeded by up to 0.3 compared to that of the post-processed ensemble. Furthermore, the ensemble post-processing substantially improved the skill of the raw ensemble at all thresholds, most remarkably at values of around 0.2.

For very high and very low thresholds, the confidence intervals become very wide. The skill scores of the three forecasts do not differ significantly. All of them seem to tend to 0 for very large thresholds. In this respect, the ensemble forecasts share this property with the theoretical performance of the AR(1) model shown in Figure 4.9.

4.6. FROM PROBABILISTIC TO DETERMINISTIC PREDICTIONS OF EXTREME ANOMALIES

In certain situations, an end user might prefer a deterministic forecast over a probabilistic one. This is in particular the case if the specific action which the end user has to take in response to the forecast does not allow for a gradual adjustment, but consists of exactly two alternatives. Such a situation is typical of extreme weather: If, for example, a public event is sensitive to strong wind gusts, the two possible actions in response to the forecast "probability p for thunderstorm" are only to ignore this danger or to cancel the event.

If such a decision has to be made repeatedly under a constant cost/loss scenario, the end user will fix a certain threshold ζ, and will act as if the forecast was a deterministic "yes" if the predicted probability p_n is larger than ζ. If $p_n < \zeta$, the end user will act as if a "no" was predicted. A systematic way to evaluate such predictions for different values of ζ is ROC analysis.

4.6.1. The ROC Analysis

ROC analysis [*Egan*, 1975] is a performance analysis for evaluating binary predictions (0/1), unfortunately without a straightforward generalization to more than two classes. ROC analysis was originally introduced in signal processing: Assume that a binary signal (high/low) is sent over a noisy channel. The receiver has the task to reconstruct the alternation of high/low by using an adjustable threshold. The noisy channel leads to errors in this reconstruction.

Translated into prediction, we assume that the observations X are either "0" or "1," and that the predictions Y are as well either "0" or "1." If predicted value and observed value coincide, $X_n = Y_n$, this prediction was evidently successful. However, there are two different types of potential mis-prediction: The forecast can be (a) $Y_n = 1$ and the observation $X_n = 0$ or (b) vice versa. Skill scores, such as the root mean squared prediction error, would weight these two errors identically. In many applications, and in particular for extreme event prediction, and also in medical screening, this can be very misleading: The real world costs for a missed hit (case b) are usually very different from a false alarm (case a). Also, if the event rate is very small, optimization of the root mean squared prediction error might lead to assigning a better score to the trivial prediction which says "0" all of the time (no false alarms, only a few missed hits) than to one which makes

a fair attempt to predict some "1" and thus suffers from both types of errors.

In view of these complications, a commonly used performance measure for such binary prediction is the ROC curve. It assumes that the prediction scheme possesses a sensitivity parameter ζ, by which the relative number of $Y_n = 1$ predictions can be controlled. The ROC curve is a plot of the hit rate versus the false alarm rate parametrized by the sensitivity parameter ζ ranging from insensitive (no "1" predicted, i.e., no false alarms, no hits) to maximally sensitive (always "1" predicted, i.e., full record of hits, but also maximum number of false alarms). Formally, the hit rate $H(\zeta)$ is the probability of issuing alarms at sensitivity ζ, given that the event actually occurs:

$$H(\zeta) = \mathbb{P}(p_n > \zeta \mid X_n = 1) = \mathbb{P}(Y_n = 1 \mid X_n = 1) \approx \frac{\sum_n X_n Y_n}{\sum_n X_n},$$

(4.24)

and the false alarm rate $F(\zeta)$ is the probability of alarms given that no event occurs:

$$F(\zeta) = \mathbb{P}(p_n > \zeta \mid X_n = 0) = \mathbb{P}(Y_n = 1 \mid X_n = 0)$$
$$\approx \frac{\sum_n (1 - X_n) Y_n}{\sum_n (1 - X_n)}.$$

(4.25)

This scoring scheme has a number of advantages with respect to others:

1. a simple benchmark is a predictor, which at a given rate produces $Y_n = 1$, irrespective of any information, so that the pairs (X_n, Y_n) consist of two independent random variables. The ROC curve of this trivial predictor is the diagonal. Hence, the ROC curve of every nontrivial predictor has to be above the diagonal.

2. As the reasoning in (a) shows, there is no explicit dependence of the ROC curve on the event rate, in contrast to, for example, the Brier score. Therefore, ROC curves are suitable to compare predictive skills of different event classes, which also differ in their base rate.

3. If costs for individual false alarms and for missed hits can be quantified and are known, then one can determine the working point of a predictor, that is, the optimal sensitivity which minimizes the total costs.

A widely used summary index of a ROC curve is the area under the curve [AUC; *Egan*, 1975], defined as

$$\text{AUC} = \int_0^1 dF \, H(F).$$

(4.26)

Since the trivial ROC curve is the diagonal, the trivial AUC value, which should exceed the nontrivial predictor, is equal to 0.5. The perfect value of AUC equals unity and indicates a predictor that differentiates between events and nonevents perfectly. We apply ROC analysis in the following section to deterministic predictions of temperature anomaly exceedances.

4.6.2. Comparison of the Four Models by ROC

We now want to predict temperature anomaly exceedance events by deterministic predictions of the yes/no type. In other words, each day we want to predict either "yes, next day's anomaly will exceed the threshold τ" or "no, it will not." Evidently, there are many ways how one can arrive at such predictions. The most trivial and least useful one would be to simply toss a coin, in other words, to issue alarms randomly with a certain rate. However, this is not as useless as it seems, since this provides a benchmark for every serious prediction attempt: A predictor has to perform better than coin tossing in order to be useful. At a given exceedance threshold, the base rate model of Section 4.4.1 predefines the rate at which the coin should predict "yes." In the ROC analysis, we can try all possible rates. But since all these predictions are independent of the events, we create a diagonal line in the ROC plot, according to the arguments in Section 4.6.1.

For the three other models, we convert the predicted probabilities into deterministic yes/no predictions by the very simple rule mentioned earlier: Let the predicted probability by either the AR(1) forecast, or the raw ensemble, or the post-processed ensemble be p_n. We issue $Y_n = 1$ if $p_n > \zeta$ and $Y_n = 0$ otherwise. The threshold ζ adjusts the sensitivity: If ζ is close to 1, then very few Y_n will be set to 1, whereas for ζ close to 0 $Y_n = 1$ on many occasions. One might speculate that setting ζ such that the relative number of 1's among the Y_n is the same as among the verifications X_n is somehow optimal. Actually, in terms of calibration, this would be the best choice, but in practice different values of ζ might be preferred, as we will discuss later. In the following, we use the algorithm presented by *Fawcett* [2006] to calculate ROC curves. AUC's and their confidence intervals are calculated according to *DeLong et al.* [1988].

In Figure 4.12, we show two ROC curves for deterministic exceedance forecasts calculated from the probabilistic ones. For the first selected τ-value, the AR(1) model and the raw ensemble forecasts have about the same predictive skill in terms of BSS (Figure 4.11). Conversely, in terms of its ROC curve, the raw ensemble is closer to the post-processed ensemble than to the AR(1) forecast. Once again, the post-processed ensemble is superior to both. The second τ-value corresponds to exceedance events of very large thresholds. The ROC curves of the three non-trivial prediction schemes are closer to the optimal point $(0, 1)$ than at the smaller exceedance threshold τ. However, at this large threshold and at low values of the sensitivity parameter ζ, the ROC of the AR(1) forecast lies above that of the raw ensemble forecast. At high false alarm rates, the AR(1)-based forecast has a higher hit rate than the raw ensemble forecast.

The ROC plots in Figure 4.12 are typical of all other τ-values, the main variation being how closely the

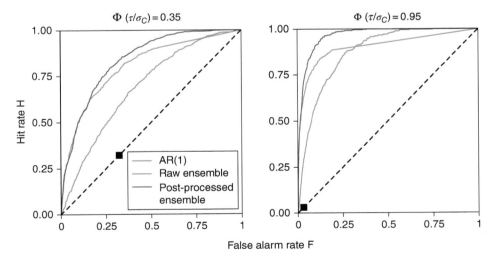

Figure 4.12 ROC curves for deterministic predictions of temperature anomaly exceedances, obtained by converting the probabilistic predictions issued by the AR(1) model and the two versions of the ensemble forecast. Two exceedance thresholds are shown: the 35-percentile, where the AR(1) model is superior to the raw ensemble forecast in terms of the Brier skill score (Figure 4.11) and the 95-percentile, which corresponds to exceedance events of very large thresholds. The black squares denote the hit rate and false alarm rate of a predictor, which randomly issues alarms with a rate equal to the corresponding CEBR.

individual curves approach the desired upper left corner ($H = 1, F = 0$). A coin-tossing model, generating $Y = 1$-predictions with any rate, will generate the diagonal. The black squares indicate the performance of such a model if the rate is taken as the true conditional exceedance base rate, Equation 4.3. One possible conclusion of this plot is: The base rate model causes a given percentage of false alarms. If we accept the same number of false alarms for the more sophisticated models, we have a much better hit rate. Or vice versa, the base rate model has a given fraction of hits. If our improved models are to be operated such that their hit rate is the same, then they would produce much less false alarms.

In Figure 4.13, we report the dependence of AUC on the threshold τ for the three nontrivial predictors. As for the BSS (Figure 11), we observe systematic differences for different exceedance thresholds τ and significant differences between the three prediction schemes. There are, however, a number of notable differences to the BSS. At low thresholds, where the AR(1) model outperforms the raw ensemble in terms of the BSS, the raw ensemble is much better in terms of the AUC, and even close to the post-processed ensemble. At very large thresholds, on the other side, the AR(1) model has a significantly higher AUC than the raw ensemble. This deficiency is eliminated by the post-processing. Another interesting behavior is the apparent increase of the AUC with increasing values of τ. This means that the more "extreme" the events get, the better they become predictable in the ROC sense. This effect has been previously observed for different prediction

targets in *Hallerberg et al.* [2007]. The BSS, on the contrary, tends to 0 for very large thresholds.

A possible explanation for these systematic differences between the evaluation criteria BSS and AUC is as follows: We have introduced an additional parameter, the sensitivity ζ, which is a kind of implicit recalibration. Assume a probabilistic model and a modification of that by simply dividing all predicted probabilities by two. The modified model would have exactly the same ROC curves and AUC as the original one because these measures are invariant with respect to monotonic transformations. On the contrary, the modified model would usually have a worse BSS because the Brier score is indeed sensitive to such a transformation. One could, therefore, argue that the ROC analysis only measures forecast resolution, which is higher, the better informed a forecaster is. The increase of performance of the weather model becomes thus more obvious. However, a formal connection between the AUC and forecast resolution in the sense of the reliability-resolution-uncertainty decomposition of the Brier score [*Murphy*, 1973] has yet to be established.

The fact that the ensemble post-processing improves the ROC measures shows that our ensemble post-processing is not the same as a simple linear recalibration of the forecast probabilities. As stated above, ROC measures are invariant under such a recalibration. But since we modify the raw ensemble and not the forecast probabilities, and since the seasonal bias correction alters the probabilities nonlinearly, we are able to significantly improve ROC curves and AUC of the exceedance forecasts by the ensemble post-processing.

4.7. DISCUSSION AND CONCLUSIONS

We gave an overview over different forecast products related to extreme events. The forecast itself, regardless of the specific forecast product, is an input-output relationship. Depending on the availability, one may use physical dynamical models, statistical learning algorithms, or data-based prediction schemes in order to make use of input data. The evaluation of such predictions, and hence the decision which forecast product is optimal for a given problem, requires the definition of a performance measure. Since there are many different possibilities for scoring, there might be several optimal predictors.

As a specific example, we discuss the prediction of temperature anomalies exceedance events. We compare two prediction schemes: One resulting from a dynamical weather model, the other a simple time series model fitted to past data of the measurement station under consideration. The difference in model complexity, computational effort, and dimensionality of input data is tremendous. Nonetheless, the performance of the time series model is not as bad as one might naively expect: The improvement

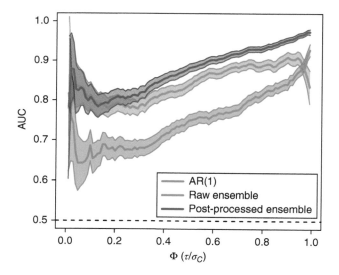

Figure 4.13 The area under curve, AUC, as a function of the exceedance threshold value, for the three models. 95% confidence intervals are included. The more the AUC-value exceeds 1/2, and the closer it is to the maximum of 1, the better the average performance.

over a benchmark predictor is in some sense of the same order of magnitude. Interestingly, there are even prediction tasks where the uncalibrated weather model performs worse than the time series model.

In weather forecasting, the calibration of a dynamical model to the local statistics is essential in order to provide good forecasts, because model errors introduce systematic biases. In situations where such calibration functions are unknown, such predictions may be systematically wrong and hence misleading. Such lack of calibration is evidently given in areas of the world where there are no measurement stations that might be used to calibrate the local forecasts. In view of climate change and extreme weather, this calibration issue leads to another problem: How the model post-processing has to be modified under changed climatic conditions can only be guessed. Unfortunately, for the estimate of the relative frequency of extreme anomalies, this calibration is essential, as can be seen in Figure 4.11. Since observation data for a climate different from the present one is unavailable, the probability of extreme weather events can only be estimated by dynamical models, even if they are not perfect. In settings where a dynamical model is unavailable due to lack of equations that describe the physics of the system, data-based modeling is a serious alternative; its performance might be better than the performance of an uncalibrated dynamical model.

By converting predicted probabilities into deterministic binary forecasts and evaluating these by ROC statistics, different properties of the forecast scheme are evaluated. A violation of calibration becomes irrelevant; hence, the raw ensemble performs almost as well as the post-processed ensemble. The last item confirms what we said in the introduction: We can only speak about the optimal predictor after we have decided how we wish to evaluate the skill of predictions.

Extreme event prediction is a rare event prediction, that is, prediction in the limit of the base rate tending to 0. Hence, we should compare the BSS and the AUC in the rightmost part of Figures 4.11 and 4.13, which compare a more sophisticated forecast to a base rate forecast. Whereas Figure 4.11 suggests that predictability tends to disappear (no improvement over the trivial base rate forecast), Figure 4.13 suggests the opposite: Events become the better predictable the higher we adjust the threshold of what we call extreme. This contradiction shows how relevant the choice of the performance measure, and related to that, the choice of the forecast product is.

The present study provides a number of directions for future studies: We have only considered forecasts 24 hours ahead. We expect the scores of all prediction models to decrease for higher lead times. Furthermore, the raw ensemble forecast should systematically outperform the AR(1) model at higher lead times. The reasons for the low BSS of the raw ensemble can be worked out more carefully by a decomposition of the Brier score into reliability, resolution, and uncertainty [*Murphy*, 1973]. We expect a bad reliability to be the primary reason for the lack of skill. The resolution term of the raw ensemble might be larger than that of the AR(1) forecast. We compared rather simple forecasting models both from the data-based and from the physical dynamical family of models. Neither the weather model nor the data-driven prediction model can be considered state-of-the-art. The performance of the NCEP reforecast model is surely not representative of state-of-the-art weather models. The conclusions might change if different prediction models are used.

REFERENCES

Akaike, H. (1974), A new look at the statistical model identification, *IEEE Trans. Autom. Control*, *19*(6), 716–723.

Brier, G. W. (1950), Verification of forecasts expressed in terms of probability, *Mon. Weather Rev.*, *78*(1), 1–3.

DeLong, E. R., D. M. DeLong, and D. L. Clarke-Pearson (1988), Comparing the areas under two or more correlated receiver operating characteristic curves: A nonparametric approach, *Biometrics*, *44*(3), 837–845.

DWD (Deutscher Wetterdienst) (2011), *Climatological Database*, www.dwd.de [accessed 13 April 2011].

DWD (Deutscher Wetterdienst) (2012), *Core Documentation of the COSMO-Model*, http://www.cosmo-model.org/content/model/documentation/core/ [accessed 5 July 2012].

Dysthe, K., H. E. Krogstad, and P. Müller (2008), Oceanic rogue waves, *Annu. Rev. Fluid Mech.*, *40*, 287–310.

ECMWF (European Centre for Medium-Range Weather Forecasting) (2009), *Integrated Forecast System Documentation CY33r1*, http://www.ecmwf.int/research/ifsdocs/CY33r1/index.html [accessed 5 July 2012].

Egan, J. P. (1975), *Signal Detection Theory and ROC Analysis*, Academic Press, New York.

Fawcett, T. (2006), An introduction to ROC analysis, *Pattern Recogn. Lett.*, *27*(8), 861–874.

Glahn, H. R., and D. A. Lowry (1972), The use of model output statistics (MOS) in objective weather forecasting, *J. Appl. Meteorol.*, *11*(8), 1203–1211.

Gneiting, T., F. Balabdaoui, and A. Raftery (2007), Probabilistic forecasts, calibration and sharpness, *J. R. Stat. Soc. Ser. B (Stat. Methodol.)*, *69*(2), 243–268.

Gneiting, T., and A. E. Raftery (2007), Strictly proper scoring rules, prediction, and estimation, *J. Am. Stat. Assoc.*, *102*(477), 359–378.

Hallerberg, S., E. G. Altmann, D. Holstein, and H. Kantz (2007), Precursors of extreme increments, *Phys. Rev. E*, *75*, 016706.

Hamill, T. M., J. S. Whitaker, and S. L. Mullen (2005), Reforecasts, an important data set for improving weather predictions, *Bull. Am. Meteorol. Soc.*, *87*(1), 33–46.

Holton, J. R. (2004), *An Introduction to Dynamic Meteorology*, Elsevier, Burlington, MA.

Leutbecher, M., and T. N. Palmer (2008), Ensemble forecasting, *J. Comput. Phys.*, *227*(7), 3515–3539.

Murphy, A. H. (1973), A new vector partition of the probability score, *J. Appl. Meteorol.*, *12*(4), 595–600.

NOAA (National Oceanic and Atmospheric Administration) (2011), *The Global Forecast System (GFS) – Global Spectral Model (GSM) Version 9.0.1*, http://www.emc.ncep.noaa.gov/GFS/doc.php [accessed 5 July 2012].

R Development Core Team (2011), *R A Language and Environment for Statistical Computing*, R Foundation for Statistical Computing, Vienna, Austria.

Roulston, M. S., and L. A. Smith (2002), Evaluating probabilistic forecasts using information theory, *Mon. Weather Rev.*, *130*(6), 1653–1660.

Schelter, B., M. Winterhalder, and J. Timmer (2007), *Handbook of Time Series Analysis: Recent Theoretical Developments and Applications*, Wiley-VCH, Weinheim.

Silverman, B. W. (1998), *Density Estimation for Statistics and Data Analysis*, Chapman Hall/CRC, London.

Toth, Z., and E. Kalnay (1997), Ensemble forecasting at NCEP and the breeding method, *Mon. Weather Rev.*, *125*(12), 3297–3319.

Wang, X., and C. H. Bishop (2005), Improvement of ensemble reliability with a new dressing kernel, *Q. J. Roy. Meteorol. Soc.*, *131*(607), 965–986.

Wilks, D. S. (2006), *Statistical Methods in the Atmospheric Sciences*, Academic Press, Amsterdam.

Wilks, D. S., and T. M. Hamill (2007), Comparison of ensemble-MOS methods using GFS reforecasts, *Mon. Weather Rev.*, *135*(6), 2379–2390.

5

Detecting and Anticipating Climate Tipping Points

Timothy M. Lenton[1] and Valerie N. Livina[2]

ABSTRACT

We focus on perhaps the most extreme events in the climate system; large-scale tipping points or "discontinuities" and the prospects for providing their early warning. Different types of climate tipping point are identified, in an idealized way, based on concepts from dynamical systems theory. Then generic methods for detecting and anticipating bifurcation-type tipping points are described, for systems with a high level of internal variability that are sampling multiple states, and for systems with less variability that reside in (but ultimately leave) a single state. The different methods are applied to the ice-core record of abrupt climate changes in Greenland during the last ice age, to help understand the underlying dynamics and to test for early warning signals prior to past tipping points. Limitations of the methods are discussed, and suggestions made to combine them with system-specific vulnerability indicators, and process-based models, to help assess the future vulnerability of different tipping elements in the climate system.

5.1. INTRODUCTION

Currently, striking changes in the climate system have added to the concern that human-induced climate change is unlikely to involve a smooth and entirely predictable transition into the future. The Arctic sea ice is retreating faster than forecast [*Stroeve et al.*, 2007], particularly in summer, reaching six of its lowest September minima in the satellite record during 2007–2012. The Greenland and West Antarctic ice sheets are losing mass at accelerating rates [*Rignot et al.*, 2008; *Pritchard et al.*, 2009]. Extreme droughts have afflicted the Amazon rainforest in the summers of 2005 and 2010 [*Phillips et al.*, 2009]. A massive, warming-encouraged insect outbreak had struck Canada's boreal forest [*Kurz et al.*, 2008]. The list goes on.

These large-scale components of the Earth system are among those that have been identified as potential "tipping elements" (Figure 5.1)—climate subsystems that could exhibit a "tipping point" where a small change in forcing (e.g., global temperature change) causes a qualitative change in their future state [*Lenton et al.*, 2008] (e.g., a change in the number or type of attractors of the system). The resulting transition may be either abrupt or irreversible or, in the worst cases, both. If such tipping point changes occur, they would surely result in dangerous climate changes [*Schellnhuber et al.*, 2006]. The Intergovernmental Panel on Climate Change (IPCC) refers to them as "large-scale discontinuities," and they are one among five "reasons for concern" about climate change [*Smith et al.*, 2009].

From a lay perspective, it would seem natural to describe climate tipping points as extreme events. However, in a scientific sense, the two are quite distinct. Extreme events are by definition rare events, that is,

[1]*Earth System Science, College of Life and Environmental Sciences, University of Exeter, Exeter, UK*
[2]*National Physical Laboratory, Teddington, Middlesex, UK*

Extreme Events: Observations, Modeling, and Economics, Geophysical Monograph 214, First Edition.
Edited by Mario Chavez, Michael Ghil, and Jaime Urrutia-Fucugauchi.

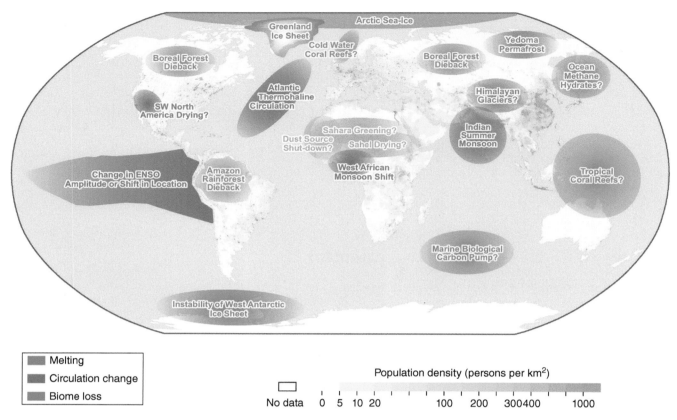

Figure 5.1 Map of potential policy-relevant tipping elements overlain on global population density, updated from *Lenton et al.* (2008). Question marks indicate systems whose status as policy-relevant tipping elements is particularly uncertain (Figure by Veronika Huber, Martin Wodinski, Timothy M. Lenton, and Hans-Joachim Schellnhuber).

outliers in a probability distribution of event sizes, where "events" are here understood as short-timescale behavior within an attractor. Tipping points, in contrast, represent a fundamental change in the attractors of a system, occurring over longer timescales. They can thus be visualized as shifting or reshaping the whole distribution of event sizes that a system exhibits. This distinction is recognized by, for example, the IPCC who consider the risk of extreme weather events as one of the four "reasons for concern" about climate change [*Smith et al.*, 2009]. That said tipping points and extreme events can be causally connected (in both directions).

Passing a tipping point can alter the risk of extreme events. For example, recent simulations suggest that if the Atlantic meridional overturning circulation (AMOC) weakens below a threshold strength (around 8 Sv), abrupt warming will occur in the Gulf of Guinea, causing a tipping point for the West African monsoon such that it fails to make its seasonal jump northward into the Sahel [*Chang et al.*, 2008]. This would be expected to reduce Sahel rainfall, including the frequency and intensity of extreme rainfall events, as well as reducing Atlantic hurricane activity [*Zhang and Delworth*, 2006].

Conversely, extreme events can sometimes tip a system from one attractor to another. For example, large areas of the tropics are thought to exhibit alternative attractors for vegetation state, with forest and savanna both being stable under the same mean annual rainfall regime [*Hirota et al.*, 2011; *Staver et al.*, 2011]. Wildfires can trigger the transition from forest to savanna, and are encouraged by extreme droughts, as seen recently in Amazonia [*Zeng et al.*, 2008].

Having faced the risk of approaching climate tipping points, it would be of considerable value if science could provide societies with some early warning about them. Of course high-impact extreme events, such as hurricanes or droughts, already have quite sophisticated early-warning systems in place, even though our ability to predict the origination of the events themselves is limited. Here we focus on the methods for detecting tipping points and providing early warning about them. The tantalizing possibility is that some climate tipping points are more predictable than many extreme events [*Lenton*, 2011].

We start by classifying tipping point phenomena, with a particular emphasis on how the type of underlying behavior affects their predictability. A generic method for detecting bifurcation-type tipping points in "noisy" systems is described, and applied to the ice-core record of abrupt climate changes in Greenland during the last ice age. Then a generic method for early warning of bifurcations is described, and again applied to the ice-core record. The limitations on early warning when applied to forecasting future climate tipping points are discussed, and suggestions made for how to combine the statistical methods with system-specific indicators and process-based models, to produce a vulnerability assessment of climate tipping points.

Readers interested in the scientific evidence for specific tipping elements identified on the map (Figure 5.1) are directed to other reviews [*Lenton et al.*, 2008; *Lenton*, 2012].

5.2. TYPES OF TIPPING POINT

In colloquial terms, the phrase "tipping point" captures the notion that "little things can make a big difference" [*Gladwell*, 2000]. In other words, at a particular moment in time, a small change can have large, long-term consequences for a system. This notion can be formalized and applied to the climate in a number of different ways. However, one general observation is that for a system to possess a tipping point, there must be strong positive feedback in its internal dynamics [*Levermann et al.*, 2012].

In earlier work, we defined a climate tipping point as follows [*Lenton et al.*, 2008]: identify a single forcing parameter (ρ), for which there exists a critical value (ρ_{crit}), from which a small perturbation ($\delta\rho > 0$) leads to a qualitative change in a crucial feature of a system (ΔF) after some observation time ($T > 0$). Here the critical threshold (ρ_{crit}) is the tipping point, beyond which a qualitative change occurs, and this change may occur immediately after the cause or much later. We introduced the term "tipping element" [*Lenton et al.*, 2008] to describe those large-scale subsystems (or components) of the Earth system that exhibit a tipping point (or tipping points), that is, they can be switched (under certain circumstances) into a qualitatively different state by small perturbations. To restrict the list we considered only components of the Earth system associated with a specific region or collection of regions, which are at least subcontinental in scale (length scale of order ~1000 km).

Many scientists (and mathematicians) intuitively take "tipping point" to be synonymous with a "bifurcation point" in the equilibrium solutions of a system, and these do indeed fit the definition above, as schematically illustrated (for a saddle-node-type bifurcation) in Figure 5.2a. Such bifurcations necessarily carry some irreversibility. However, other classes of nonlinear transition can meet the definition, and one schematic

example is given in Figure 5.2b. Again this shows the (time-independent) equilibrium solutions of a system, but here they are continuous (there is no bifurcation) and therefore the transition is reversible. Figure 5.2b is a special case, allowed by the choices of $\delta\rho$ and ΔF, but it is worth noting as some real systems, for example, Arctic sea ice cover, can exhibit large responses to small increases in forcing, yet rapidly and fully recover if the forcing is reduced again [*Tietsche et al.*, 2011]. For societal (rather than mathematical) purposes, the existence or nonexistence of a climate tipping point may be best considered in a time-dependent fashion (see the Supplementary Information of *Lenton et al.* [2008]).

A different type of tipping point is related to noise-induced transitions [*Horsthemke and Lefever*, 1984], as schematically illustrated in Figure 5.2c. In such transitions, internal variability causes a system to leave its current state (or attractor) and transition to a different state (or attractor). This does not require a bifurcation point to be passed; it can occur without any change in forcing (the parameter ρ). However, here it does require the coexistence of multiple states under a given forcing, which implies that the underlying system possesses bifurcation-type tipping points. As illustrated in Figure 5.2d, one can think of noise as pushing a system out of a valley (one stable steady state), up to the top of a hill (an unstable steady state), and it then comes rolling down the other side into a different valley (some new stable state). It is natural to describe perching on the top of the hill (at the unstable steady state) as a "tipping point," and it can be defined in terms of the corresponding value of the system feature (F_{crit}). However, the value of F_{crit} is a function of ρ (Figure 5.2c), so is not as well defined as ρ_{crit}. Noise-induced transitions do not strictly fit the tipping point definition given earlier [*Lenton et al.*, 2008], but they are related to it and can clearly occur in the climate system.

In general, noise-induced transitions become more likely to occur closer to a bifurcation point. Thus, given that the climate system has its own internally generated noise (familiar to us as the weather), we can expect that, if it is approaching a bifurcation point, it will leave its present state before the bifurcation point is reached [*Kleinen et al.*, 2003]. This means that abrupt climate changes are likely to involve a mixture of the idealized bifurcation and noise-induced mechanisms shown in Figure 5.2. A more general mathematical framework for tipping points in dynamical systems that combines these mechanisms [*Kuehn*, 2011], builds on the theory of fast-slow systems including stochastic dynamics [*Berglund and Gentz*, 2002, 2005].

Within this fast-slow systems framework, a third type of tipping point has recently been recognized [*Ashwin et al.*, 2012]; rate-dependent tipping, where a system undergoes a large and rapid change, but only when the

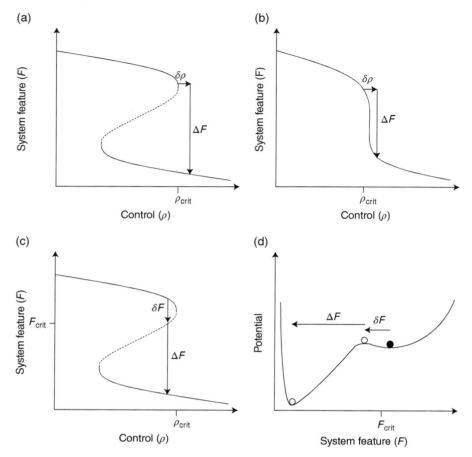

Figure 5.2 Schematic representations of different types of tipping point. (a) Bifurcation-type tipping: a bistable system passing a bifurcation point. (b) Non-bifurcation tipping: a mono-stable system exhibiting highly nonlinear change. (c) Noise-induced tipping: a bistable system undergoes a noise-induced transition between its two stable states, and (d) a representation of this transition within the system potential (y axis of (c) has become x axis of (d)). In (d), the wells represent stable steady states, the hilltop represents an unstable steady state, and the ball represents the actual state of the system (filled black is the initial state).

rate at which it is forced exceeds a critical value [*Levermann and Born*, 2007; *Wieczorek et al.*, 2011]. This has led to a recent categorization of three types of tipping mechanism [*Ashwin et al.*, 2012]: (1) bifurcation tipping, (2) noise-induced tipping, and (3) rate-dependent tipping. Here we focus on bifurcations and noise-induced tipping, because there is little work as yet on early warnings of rate-dependent tipping. In fact, our methods focus on detecting and (ideally) anticipating bifurcations, because purely noise-induced (i.e., stochastically driven) transitions are inherently unpredictable.

5.3. DETECTING BIFURCATIONS IN NOISY SYSTEMS

Although individual noise-induced transitions in the climate system are inherently unpredictable, if a system is experiencing a relatively high level of noise and sampling

several different attractors, then, in principle, one can deduce how many states it has, as well as their relative stability or instability. To do so successfully, it requires a sufficiently long time series for all available states that are being sampled. If the number of states and/or the stability of states changes over time, then, in principle, this can also be detected. However, to do so, it requires a long sliding window that is moving through an even longer time series. These ideas are at the heart of a recently developed method called "potential analysis" [*Livina et al.*, 2010, 2011].

Potential analysis assumes that the dynamics of a chosen climate variable can be described by a stochastic differential equation (i.e., one that includes a noise term), with an underlying potential (i.e., series of wells and hilltops) whose shape can be described by a polynomial equation. The chosen stochastic differential equation has a corresponding Fokker-Planck equation

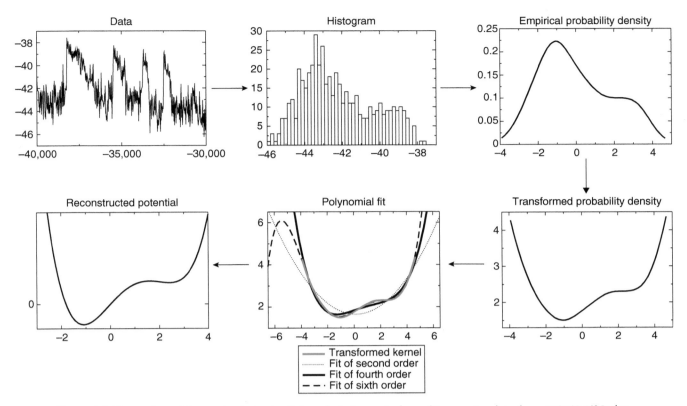

Figure 5.3 Illustration of the method of potential analysis for a window of time series data (here NGRIP δ^{18}O data 40–30 ka BP). The steps are: obtain histogram of the data; convert into empirical probability density (using a standard Gaussian kernel estimator); transform this distribution (take natural logarithm, invert and scale by noise level); least-squares fit the transformed distribution with polynomial functions of increasing even order and select the highest order before encountering a negative leading coefficient; accurately determine the coefficients using the Unscented Kalman Filter and reconstruct the potential.

describing the probability density function; crucially this has a stationary solution that depends only on the underlying potential function and the noise level. This gives a one-to-one correspondence between the potential and the stationary probability density of the system (the potential is directly proportional to the negative logarithm of the probability density, scaled by the square of the noise level). This allows the underlying potential to be reconstructed, given the probability density of a stretch of time series data and an estimate of the noise level.

The method is illustrated in Figure 5.3 (for the mathematics see *Livina et al.* [2011]). It starts by transforming a window of time series data into a histogram of the data. Next, this is converted into an empirical probability density of the data using a standard Gaussian kernel estimator. If the system has a single, stable state, the resulting distribution should have a single mode with smooth sides. Any deviations from this immediately provide a visual clue as to the existence of other states. In the example (which is of abrupt climate changes during the last ice age

recorded by the δ^{18}O proxy from the North Greenland Ice-core Project (NGRIP)), the probability density has a distinct "shoulder" suggesting the existence of a second state. Next, the probability density is inverted and log-transformed. The method then attempts to least-square fit the transformed distribution with polynomial functions of increasing, even order (starting with second order, i.e., a quadratic equation). At some point, the least-square fit returns a negative leading coefficient, which is not physically reasonable (this happens for a sixth-order fit in the example). So the polynomial of highest degree before this is encountered and considered the most appropriate representation of the probability density of the time series (fourth order in the example in Figure 5.3).

The number of states in the system is then determined from the number of inflection points in the fitted polynomial potential. The simplest potential has a single state with no inflection points. Each pair of inflection points corresponds to an additional state. This approach picks up real minima (wells) in the potential, or just flattening of the potential. The latter, importantly, are degenerate states corresponding to bifurcation points. In a final step, having determined its order, the coefficients of the potential can be accurately estimated using the Unscented Kalman Filter [*Kwasniok and Lohmann*, 2009]. For this to work well, the noise level must be accurately estimated, which can be done separately using a wavelet de-noising routine that separates the signal into the potential and the noise [*Livina et al.*, 2011]. The end result is a reconstructed potential.

5.4. TIPPING POINTS IN THE ICE-CORE RECORD

In principle, the method of potential analysis just described can detect bifurcations in a noisy climate system. Their timing can never be precisely tied down, because the method always has to work with a relatively long time window of data (typically of the order of 1000 data points). However, by moving a sliding window through a long time series, one should be able to detect changes in the number of climate states and their stability, over time.

To test this, potential analysis has been applied to a classic case study of abrupt climate change in Earth's recent past: the Dansgaard-Oeschger (DO) events [*Livina et al.*, 2010]. These rapid climate changes that occurred repeatedly during the last ice age were concentrated in the North Atlantic region but had widespread effects, and recorded most strikingly in Greenland ice cores. Figure 5.4 shows one such ice-core record: the GRIP [*Dansgaard et al.*, 1993] $\delta^{18}O$ stable water isotope record, which is a proxy for past air temperature at the ice-core site (and can also be influenced by changing water source temperatures and snowfall seasonality). The DO events result in abrupt increases in $\delta^{18}O$ (corresponding to warming).

What do these DO events reveal about the nature of past climate surprises? The precise mechanism for what was going on in the climate system continues to be debated [*Colin de Verdiere*, 2006; *Crucifix*, 2012], although most studies assign a key role to changes in the Atlantic thermohaline circulation, coupled with changes in sea ice cover. Regardless of the underlying mechanism, recent work has shown that the repeated transitions from cold "stadial" to warm "interstadial" states can be well described by a model of purely noise-induced transitions [*Ditlevsen et al.*, 2005] (Figure 5.2c and d). Recent analysis suggests that the cold stadial state remains stable during the last ice age and does not experience bifurcation [*Ditlevsen and Johnsen*, 2010]. However, when looking across the interval 70–20 ka BP, the warm state is characterized as being only marginally stable [*Kwasniok and Lohmann*, 2009] (e.g., Figure 5.3, which is for $\delta^{18}O$ over 40–30 ka BP from the NGRIP ice core).

On examining this more closely using the method of potential analysis (Figure 5.4c), the ice-core record is best characterized as having two states from 60 ka BP to about 25 ka BP, but only one state during the depths of the last glacial maximum (LGM) [*Livina et al.*, 2010]. It is inferred that a bifurcation occurred sometime before 25 ka BP, in which the warm interstadial state became unstable, and later it disappeared altogether. Reconstruction of the underlying potentials (Figure 5.4d) for the intervals (III) 40–30 ka BP and (IV) 30–20 ka BP confirms a corresponding switch from two to one stable state. It is reflected in the original record (Figure 5.4a) as the warm events becoming progressively shorter, until they are very short-lived indeed, and then they cease through the LGM. The warm climate state reappears during the interval of deglaciation (V) 20–10 ka BP, being sampled in the Bølling-Allerød warm interval (~14.7–12.7 ka BP). Then the cold climate state seemingly disappears around the start of the Holocene (VI) 10–0 ka BP (although an alternative interpretation is that it still exists, but it is never sampled because the noise level has dropped; Figure 5.4b). Consistent results have been obtained from analysis of the NGRIP ice-core record (from a site 325 km further North in Greenland) [*Livina et al.*, 2010].

In the case of a bifurcation that reduces the number of system states, detection (e.g., the switch from green to red around 25 ka BP in Figure 5.4c) typically occurs after the potential has degenerated and a bifurcation has occurred. That is because a system with a second state that has lost its stability but not disappeared altogether gives a "shoulder" in the probability density and is still best described by a fourth-order polynomial. However, this means that, conversely, in a system that is gaining an extra state, the method may pick this up before that state becomes stable (i.e., bifurcation occurs) and hence provide some early warning that a new climate state is appearing. Currently, observational time series data are being analyzed to search for such cases where potential analysis indicates that a new climate state is appearing.

The simple model of DO events just described does not account for all the features in the ice-core records, in particular, the gradual cooling that typically follows an abrupt warming (an asymmetrical response) (Figure 5.4a). Furthermore, although we adjust for the noise level in each interval when reconstructing the potential, the underlying model does not incorporate dependence of the noise level on the underlying climate state. Internal climate variability is considerably greater in the cold than in the warm state (Figure 5.4b) (i.e., the noise is multiplicative rather than additive). Future work can be expected to produce more advanced models. Still, to summarize our present understanding, the archetypal example of past abrupt climate changes illustrates that

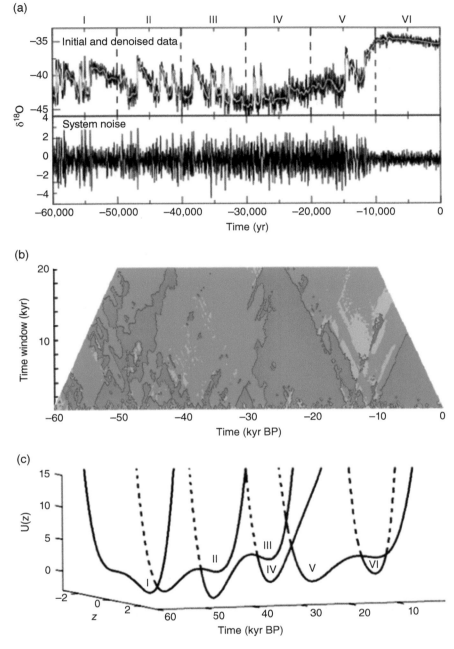

Figure 5.4 A test of bifurcation detection method in a noisy system. (a) GRIP ice-core δ¹⁸O proxy record of pale-otemperature over the past 60 ka at the summit in Greenland [*Dansgaard et al.*, 1993], at 20 year resolution and on the most recent GICC05 timescale [*Svensson et al.*, 2008], also showing the de-noised data and in the lower panel the corresponding noise level. (b) Contour plot of the number of detected states as a function of time and sliding window length (results plotted at the midpoints of the sliding windows), where red = 1 state, green = 2, cyan = 3, and purple = 4. This shows the loss of a second climate state (green to red transition across a wide range of window lengths) around 25 ka BP. (c) Reconstructed potential curves for the six 10 kyr intervals indicated in (a).

the climate system has undergone both noise-induced transitions and bifurcations in the past. These two underlying causes of climate tipping have very different implications as to whether individual events are predictable.

5.5. EARLY WARNING OF BIFURCATIONS

While purely noise-induced transitions (Figure 5.2c) are fundamentally unpredictable [*Ditlevsen and Johnsen*, 2010], bifurcation-type tipping points (Figure 5.2a) offer

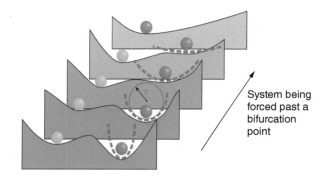

Figure 5.5 Schematic representation of a system being forced past a bifurcation point. The system's response time to small perturbations, τ, is related to the growing radius of the potential well (Figure by Hermann Held, from *Lenton et al.* [2008]).

encouraging prospects for early warning. Physical systems that are approaching bifurcation points show a nearly universal property of becoming more sluggish in response to a perturbation [*Wissel*, 1984; *Wiesenfeld and McNamara*, 1986; *Scheffer et al.*, 2009]. To visualize this, the present state of a system is pictured as a ball in a curved potential well (attractor) that is being nudged around by some stochastic noise process, for example, weather (Figure 5.5). The ball continually tends to roll back toward the bottom of the well (its lowest potential state) and the rate at which it rolls back is determined by the curvature of the potential well. As the system is forced toward a bifurcation point, the potential well becomes flatter. Hence, the ball will roll back ever more sluggishly. At the bifurcation point, the potential becomes flat and the ball is destined to roll off into some other state (alternative potential well). Mathematically speaking, the leading eigenvalue, which characterizes the rates of change around the present equilibrium state, tends to zero as the bifurcation point is approached.

So for those tipping elements that exhibit bifurcation tipping points (Figure 5.2a), an observed slowing down in time series data could provide a basis for early warning. This should be manifested as an increasing autocorrelation in the time series data (in simple terms, each data point becomes more like the surrounding ones). Following this rationale, a method of examining the decay rate to perturbations using a simple lag-1 autocorrelation function (ACF) was developed, averaging over short-term variability to isolate the dynamics of the longest immanent timescale of a system [*Held and Kleinen*, 2004]. The approach was subsequently modified by using detrended fluctuation analysis (DFA) to assess the proximity to a threshold from the power law exponent describing correlations in the time series data [*Livina and Lenton*, 2007]. At a critical threshold, the data become highly correlated across short- and middle-range timescales and the time

series behaves as a random walk with uncorrelated steps. Both methods need to span a sufficient time interval of data to capture what can be a very slow decay rate, and rapid forcing of a system could alter the dynamics and override any slowing down.

Model tests have shown that both early-warning methods work in principle, in simple [*Dakos et al.*, 2008], intermediate complexity [*Held and Kleinen*, 2004; *Livina and Lenton*, 2007], and fully three-dimensional [*Lenton et al.*, 2009] models. The challenge is to get the methods to work in practice, in the complex and noisy climate system. Initial tests found that the ending of the last ice age in a low-resolution Greenland ice-core record (GISP2 δ¹⁸O) is detected as a critical transition using the DFA method [*Livina and Lenton*, 2007]. Subsequent work showed increasing autocorrelation in eight paleoclimate time series approaching abrupt transitions, using the ACF method [*Dakos et al.*, 2008].

Recent work has emphasized that to get a reliable signal of an approaching bifurcation point, one should monitor changes in variance as well as autocorrelation in the data [*Ditlevsen and Johnsen*, 2010]. As a threshold is approached and the potential becomes flatter (Figure 5.5), one intuitively expects the variance to go up (i.e., the ball to make greater departures from the local stable state). If at the same time the system is slowing down, one must be careful to choose a long enough time window to accurately sample the variance. The resulting changes in variance may provide a statistically more robust and earlier warning signal than changes in autocorrelation [*Ditlevsen and Johnsen*, 2010].

5.6. EARLY WARNING OF THE END OF THE ICE AGE?

Having outlined the early warning methods, we now return to the Greenland ice-core record to see if there are any early-warning signals of past climate tipping points. Previous work has failed to find early-warning signals prior to any of the individual DO events, consistent with the view that they are noise-induced transitions [*Ditlevsen and Johnsen*, 2010]. However, potential analysis (Figure 5.4), and previous work with early-warning indicators, suggests there may be a bifurcation during the last deglaciation, in which the cold climate state lost its stability [*Livina and Lenton*, 2007; *Dakos et al.*, 2008]. Recently, we have reexamined this hypothesis in more detail, analyzing two different climate proxies from three different Greenland ice cores to see if there is a robust signal of critical slowing down [*Lenton et al.*, 2012].

Here, we show results for the GRIP ice core δ¹⁸O paleotemperature proxy across the interval 22–10 ka BP, from the LGM to the start of the Holocene (Figure 5.6a). This is a subset of the data set used for potential analysis

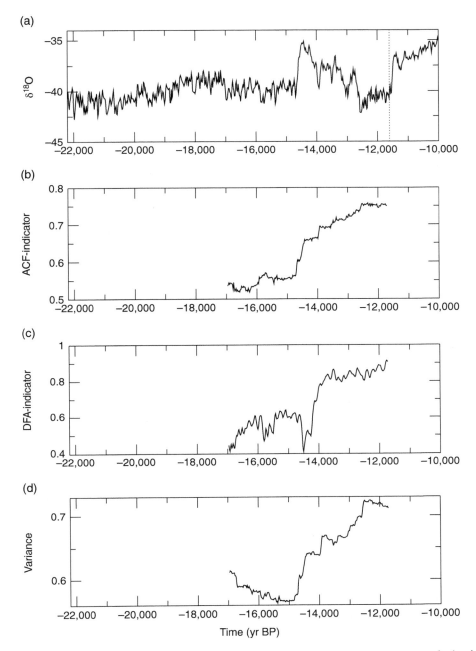

Figure 5.6 A test of tipping point early warning methods. (a) GRIP ice-core $\delta^{18}O$ proxy record of paleotempera-ture 22–10 ka [*Dansgaard et al.*, 1993], at 20 year resolution and on the most recent GICC05 timescale [*Svensson et al.*, 2008]. Vertical dashed line indicates where the analysis finishes, before exit from the Younger Dryas. Early warning indicators from (b) lag-1 autocorrelation, (c) detrended fluctuation analysis, and (d) variance. In (b) and (d), the data from (a) is first detrended using a filtering bandwidth of 25. In (b)–(d), a sliding window length of half the series is used to calculate the indicators.

(Figure 5.4). We apply both ACF and DFA methods to look for the signal of critical slowing down, and also look for any trend in variance. Both ACF and DFA indicators and variance show an increasing trend to the end of the Younger Dryas, consistent with approaching bifurcation (Figure 5.6b–d).

Neither ACF nor DFA indicators reach a critical value of 1. However, to correctly estimate the timing of critical behavior, one should in fact replot the indicators in the middle of each time window (rather than at the end) and extrapolate forward, which brings them close to (or in the case of the DFA indicator, in excess of) the critical value of 1 at the end of the Younger Dryas. Anyway, we expect that internal climate variability would have been sufficient to cause the abrupt warming into the Holocene warm state before a bifurcation was reached.

At face value, there seems to have been some early warning of an impending climate bifurcation on approaching the end of the Younger Dryas. In contrast, we find no robust early warning signal prior to the onset of the Bølling-Allerød [Figure 5.6; *Lenton et al.*, 2012], consistent with the hypothesis that (like the other DO events) this was a largely noise-induced transition. There are some technical issues with the analysis, in particular, that the abrupt transitions into or out of the Bølling-Allerød are not completely detrended and may thus be influencing the indicators. However, it can be seen visually that there is a slowing down in climate dynamics during the Bølling-Allerød compared to the preceding interval (Figure 5.6a). Furthermore, previous analysis of a tropical Atlantic data set has found a slowing down signal in the Younger Dryas [*Dakos et al.*, 2008]. The tantalizing suggestion is that were there Stone Age scientists in possession of the same methods and data sets, they may have had some warning of the impending abrupt transition into the Holocene!

5.7. LIMITATIONS ON EARLY-WARNING CAPABILITY

There appears to be some scope for early warning of an approaching bifurcation-type tipping point. However, there are still considerable practical limitations on whether a reliable early-warning signal could be detected before any future climate tipping point.

First, the early-warning method is based on changes in the slowest recovery rate of a system, and in the case of the ocean circulation or ice sheet dynamics, this timescale is in the order of a few thousand years. Therefore, one needs a long and relatively high-resolution paleorecord for the system in question, to get an accurate picture of its natural state of variability from which to detect changes. Often such records are lacking. However, some potential tipping points have much faster dynamics and relatively little internal memory, for example, sea ice or monsoons. For such systems, existing observational time series data may be sufficient.

Second, there is the problem that humans are forcing the climate system relatively rapidly. Hence, inherently "slow" tipping elements, such as ice sheets and the thermohaline circulation (THC) will be well out of equilibrium with the forcing. If a tipping element is forced slowly (keeping it in quasi-equilibrium), proximity to a threshold can be inferred in a model-independent way, but under rapid forcing, a dynamical model simulating transient behavior will also be needed.

Third, noise (stochastic internal variability) in a system may be such that it does not allow the detection of any trend toward slowing down. For example, there are now several years of direct observations showing that the strength of the THC exhibits high internal variability. Where internal variability is high, a tipping element could exit its present state well before a bifurcation point is reached. Clearly, the time it takes to discover proximity to a threshold must be shorter than the time in which noise would be expected to cause a system to change state—the "mean first exit time" [*Kleinen et al.*, 2003]—for an early warning to be achieved. However, the noise level for a particular tipping element can be measured and estimates of when future tipping could occur adjusted accordingly [*Thompson and Sieber*, 2011].

Finally, the most statistically robust signals are achieved when one has an ensemble of realizations of a system approaching a tipping point [*Kuehn*, 2011]. But this is clearly at odds with the objective of anticipating a future tipping point, which may never have occurred before.

5.8. DISCUSSION AND CONCLUSION

We have outlined some generic methods that can be used to detect and anticipate bifurcation-type tipping points in the climate system. These methods can help in understanding the underlying dynamics of known abrupt transitions in the paleoclimate record, and indeed the observational record. There are many caveats to the applicability of these methods, especially for early warning of future tipping points in the climate system. Still, existing real-world early-warning systems for natural hazards already have to cope with the generic problems of false alarms and missed alarms. Experience suggests the methods do not have to be perfect to be useful [*Basher*, 2006].

A less ambitious use of the methods described here would be to scan available climate data to sift out those systems where there are signals consistent with destabilization (which ecologists call declining resilience). This subset of systems could then be subject to more detailed analysis, combining process-based modeling and direct observation, to see if there is a mechanistic basis for thinking if any of them may be approaching a tipping point. For specific tipping elements, such as the THC, there are already leading indicators of vulnerability that are deducible from observational data [*Drijfhout et al.*, 2011]. The outstanding challenge is to combine the approaches we have described, which are rooted in dynamical systems theory and statistical modeling, with such observations and process-based simulation models.

There are several further suggestions for early-warning indicators of critical transitions in complex systems, many of which are being explored for ecological tipping points and could potentially be applied to the climate system. These include increasing skewness of responses [*Guttal and Jayaprakash*, 2008; *Biggs et al.*, 2009], spatial variance, and spatial skewnesses [*Guttal and Jayaprakash*, 2009]. Spatial indicators are of particular interest as there is rich, spatially explicit climate data, but indicators based on one-dimensional time series throw out all of this spatial information. Principal component analysis provides a widely used way of reducing the dimensionality of climate data without eliminating it altogether.

In climate science, there is much discussion over whether or not specific tipping points really exist; for example, is there a bifurcation-type threshold on the pathway to losing summer sea ice cover in the Arctic? Many recent studies argue "no" on the grounds that seasonal ice loss is readily reversible in models. The methods we describe can also be used to help resolve such debates [*Livina and Lenton*, 2013].

ACKNOWLEDGMENTS

We thank Michael Ghil for encouraging us to write this chapter, and to the Summer School on Biogeodynamics and Earth System Sciences in Venice, June 2011, for hosting fruitful discussions on the topics herein.

REFERENCES

Ashwin, P., S. Wieczorek, R. Vitolo, and P. M. Cox (2012), Tipping points in open systems: Bifurcation, noise-induced and rate-dependent examples in the climate system, *Philos. Trans. R. Soc. A Math. Phys. Eng. Sci.*, *370*(1962), 1166–1184.

Basher, R. (2006), Global early warning systems for natural hazards: Systematic and people-centred, *Philos. Trans. R. Soc. A Math. Phys. Eng. Sci.*, *364*(1845), 2167–2182.

Berglund, N. and B. Gentz (2002), Metastability in simple climate models: Pathwise analysis of slowly driven Langevin equations, *Stochastics Dyn.*, *2*(3), 327–356.

Berglund, N. and B. Gentz (2005), *Noise-Induced Phenomena in Slow-Fast Dynamical Systems: A Sample-Paths Approach*, Springer, Berlin.

Biggs, R., S. R. Carpenter, and W. A. Brock (2009), Turning back from the brink: Detecting an impending regime shift in time to avert it, *Proc. Natl. Acad. Sci. U. S. A.*, *106*(3), 826–831.

Chang, P., R. Zhang, W. Hazeleger, C. Wen, X. Wan, L. Ji, R. J. Haarsma, W.-P. Breugem, and H. Seidel (2008), Oceanic link between abrupt change in the North Atlantic Ocean and the African monsoon, *Nat. Geosci.*, *1*, 444–448.

Colin de Verdiere, A. (2006), Bifurcation structure of thermohaline millennial oscillations, *J. Clim.*, *19*, 5777–5795.

Crucifix, M. (2012), Oscillators and relaxation phenomena in Pleistocene climate theory, *Philos. Trans. R. Soc. A Math. Phys. Eng. Sci.*, *370*(1962), 1140–1165.

Dakos, V., M. Scheffer, E. H. van Nes, V. Brovkin, V. Petoukhov, and H. Held (2008), Slowing down as an early warning signal for abrupt climate change, *Proc. Natl. Acad. Sci. U. S. A.*, *105*(38), 14308–14312.

Dansgaard, W., S. J. Johnsen, H. B. Clausen, N. Dahl-Jensen, N. S. Gundestrup, C. U. Hammer, C. S. Hvidberg, J. P. Steffensen, A. E. Sveinbjornsdottir, J. Jouzel, and G. Bond (1993), Evidence for general instability of past climate from a 250-kyr ice-core record, *Nature*, *364*(6434), 218–220.

Ditlevsen, P. D., M. S. Kristensen, and K. K. Andersen (2005), The recurrence time of Dansgaard-Oeschger events and limits on the possible periodic component, *J. Clim.*, *18*(14), 2594–2603.

Ditlevsen, P. D. and S. J. Johnsen (2010), Tipping points: Early warning and wishful thinking, *Geophys. Res. Lett.*, *37*, L19703.

Drijfhout, S., S. Weber, and E. van der Swaluw (2011), The stability of the MOC as diagnosed from model projections for pre-industrial, present and future climates, *Clim. Dyn.*, *37*(7–8), 1575–1586.

Gladwell, M. (2000), *The Tipping Point: How Little Things Can Make a Big Difference*, pp. 304, Little Brown, New York.

Guttal, V. and C. Jayaprakash (2008), Changing skewness: An early warning signal of regime shifts in ecosystems, *Ecol. Lett.*, *11*, 450–460.

Guttal, V. and C. Jayaprakash (2009), Spatial variance and spatial skewness: Leading indicators of regime shifts in spatial ecological systems, *Theor. Ecol.*, *2*, 3–12.

Held, H. and T. Kleinen (2004), Detection of climate system bifurcations by degenerate fingerprinting, *Geophys. Res. Lett.*, *31*, L23207.

Hirota, M., M. Holmgren, E. H. Van Nes, and M. Scheffer (2011), Global resilience of tropical forest and savanna to critical transitions, *Science*, *334*(6053), 232–235.

Horsthemke, W. and R. Lefever (1984), *Noise-Induced Transitions: Theory and Applications in Physics, Chemistry, and Biology*, Springer-Verlag, New York.

Kleinen, T., H. Held, and G. Petschel-Held (2003), The potential role of spectral properties in detecting thresholds in the Earth system: Application to the thermohaline circulation, *Ocean Dyn.*, *53*, 53–63.

Kuehn, C. (2011), A mathematical framework for critical transitions: Bifurcations, fast-slow systems and stochastic dynamics, *Physica D*, *2010*(106), 1–20.

Kurz, W. A., C. C. Dymond, G. Stinson, G. J. Rampley, E. T. Neilson, A. L. Carroll, T. Ebata, and L. Safranyik (2008), Mountain pine beetle and forest carbon feedback to climate change, *Nature*, *452*, 987–990.

Kwasniok, F. and G. Lohmann (2009), Deriving dynamical models from paleoclimatic records: Application to glacial millennial-scale climate variability, *Phys. Rev. E*, *80*(6), 066104.

Lenton, T. M. (2011), Early warning of climate tipping points, *Nat. Clim. Change*, *1*, 201–209.

Lenton, T. M. (2012), Future Climate Surprises, in *The Future of the World's Climate*, edited by A. Henderson-Sellers and K. McGuffie, pp. 489–507, Elsevier, Oxford.

Lenton, T. M., H. Held, E. Kriegler, J. Hall, W. Lucht, S. Rahmstorf, and H. J. Schellnhuber (2008), Tipping elements in the Earth's climate system, *Proc. Natl. Acad. Sci. U. S. A.*, *105*(6), 1786–1793.

Lenton, T. M., R. J. Myerscough, R. Marsh, V. N. Livina, A. R. Price, S. J. Cox, and the GENIE team (2009), Using GENIE to study a tipping point in the climate system, *Philos. Trans. R. Soc. A Math. Phys. Eng. Sci.*, *367*(1890), 871–884.

Lenton, T. M., V. N. Livina, V. Dakos, and M. Scheffer (2012), Climate bifurcation during the last deglaciation?, *Clim. Past*, *8*, 1127–1139.

Levermann, A. and A. Born (2007), Bistability of the Atlantic subpolar gyre in a coarse-resolution climate model, *Geophys. Res. Lett.*, *34*, L24605.

Levermann, A., J. Bamber, S. Drijfhout, A. Ganopolski, W. Haeberli, N. R. P. Harris, M. Huss, K. Krüger, T. M. Lenton, R. W. Lindsay, D. Notz, P. Wadhams, and S. Weber (2012), Potential climatic transitions with profound impact on Europe: Review of the current state of six "tipping elements of the climate system", *Clim. Change*, *110*, 845–878.

Livina, V. N. and T. M. Lenton (2007), A modified method for detecting incipient bifurcations in a dynamical system, *Geophys. Res. Lett.*, *34*, L03712.

Livina, V. N., F. Kwasniok, and T. M. Lenton (2010), Potential analysis reveals changing number of climate states during the last 60 kyr, *Clim. Past*, *6*(1), 77–82.

Livina, V. N., F. Kwasniok, G. Lohmann, J. W. Kantelhardt, and T. M. Lenton (2011), Changing climate states and stability: From Pliocene to present, *Clim. Dyn.*, *37*(11–12), 2437–2453.

Livina, V. N. and T. M. Lenton (2013), A recent tipping point in the Arctic sea-ice cover: abrupt and persistent increase in the seasonal cycle since 2007, *The Cryosphere*, *7*, 275–286.

Phillips, O. L., L. E. O. C. Aragao, S. L. Lewis, J. B. Fisher, J. Lloyd, G. Lopez-Gonzalez, Y. Malhi, A. Monteagudo, J. Peacock, C. A. Quesada, G. van der Heijden, S. Almeida, I. Amaral, L. Arroyo, G. Aymard, T. R. Baker, O. Banki, L. Blanc, D. Bonal, P. Brando, J. Chave, A. C. A. de Oliveira, N. D. Cardozo, C. I. Czimczik, T. R. Feldpausch, M. A. Freitas, E. Gloor, N. Higuchi, E. Jimenez, G. Lloyd, P. Meir, C. Mendoza, A. Morel, D. A. Neill, D. Nepstad, S. Patino, M. C. Penuela, A. Prieto, F. Ramirez, M. Schwarz, J. Silva, M. Silveira, A. S. Thomas, H. t. Steege, J. Stropp, R. Vasquez, P. Zelazowski, E. A. Davila, S. Andelman, A. Andrade, K.-J. Chao, T. Erwin, A. Di Fiore, E. Honorio, H. Keeling, T. J. Killeen, W. F. Laurance, A. P. Cruz, N. C. A. Pitman, P. N. Vargas, H. Ramirez-Angulo, A. Rudas, R. Salamao, N. Silva, J. Terborgh, and A. Torres-Lezama (2009), Drought sensitivity of the Amazon rainforest, *Science*, *323*(5919), 1344–1347.

Pritchard, H. D., R. J. Arthern, D. G. Vaughan, and L. A. Edwards (2009), Extensive dynamic thinning on the margins of the Greenland and Antarctic ice sheets, *Nature*, *461*, 971–975.

Rignot, E., J. E. Box, E. Burgess, and E. Hanna (2008), Mass balance of the Greenland ice sheet from 1958 to 2007, *Geophys. Res. Lett.*, *35*, L20502.

Scheffer, M., J. Bacompte, W. A. Brock, V. Brovkin, S. R. Carpenter, V. Dakos, H. Held, E. H. van Nes, M. Rietkerk, and G. Sugihara (2009), Early warning signals for critical transitions, *Nature*, *461*, 53–59.

Schellnhuber, H. J., W. Cramer, N. Nakicenovic, T. Wigley, and G. Yohe (2006), *Avoiding Dangerous Climate Change*, Cambridge University Press, Cambridge.

Smith, J. B., S. H. Schneider, M. Oppenheimer, G. W. Yohe, W. Hare, M. D. Mastrandrea, A. Patwardhan, I. Burton, J. Corfee-Morlot, C. H. D. Magadza, H.-M. Fussel, A. B. Pittock, A. Rahman, A. Suarez, and J.-P. van Ypersele (2009), Assessing dangerous climate change through an update of the Intergovernmental Panel on Climate Change (IPCC) "reasons for concern", *Proc. Natl. Acad. Sci. U. S. A.*, *106*(11), 4133–4137.

Staver, A. C., S. Archibald, and S. A. Levin (2011), The global extent and determinants of savanna and forest as alternative biome states, *Science*, *334*(6053), 230–232.

Stroeve, J., M. M. Holland, W. Meier, T. Scambos, and M. Serreze (2007), Arctic sea ice decline: Faster than forecast, *Geophys. Res. Lett.*, *34*, L09501.

Svensson, A., K. K. Andersen, M. Bigler, H. B. Clausen, D. Dahl-Jensen, S. M. Davies, S. J. Johnsen, R. Muscheler, F. Parrenin, S. O. Rasmussen, R. Rathlisberger, I. Seierstad, J. P. Steffensen, and B. M. Vinther (2008), A 60 000 year Greenland stratigraphic ice core chronology, *Clim. Past*, *4*(1), 47–57.

Thompson, J. M. T. and J. Sieber (2011), Climate tipping as a noisy bifurcation: A predictive technique, *IMA J. Appl. Math.*, *76*(1), 27–46.

Tietsche, S., D. Notz, J. H. Jungclaus, and J. Marotzke (2011), Recovery mechanisms of Arctic summer sea ice, *Geophys. Res. Lett.*, *38*(2), L02707.

Wieczorek, S., P. Ashwin, C. M. Luke, and P. M. Cox (2011), Excitability in ramped systems: The compost-bomb instability, *Philos. Trans. R. Soc. A Math. Phys. Eng. Sci.*, *467*(2129), 1243–1269.

Wiesenfeld, K. and B. McNamara (1986), Small-signal amplification in bifurcating dynamical systems, *Phys. Rev. A*, *33*(1), 629–642.

Wissel, C. (1984), A universal law of the characteristic return time near thresholds, *Oecologia*, *65*(1), 101–107.

Zeng, N., J.-H. Yoon, J. A. Marengo, A. Subramaniam, C. A. Nobre, A. Mariotti, and J. D. Neelin (2008), Causes and impacts of the 2005 Amazon drought, *Environ. Res. Lett.*, *3*(1), 014002.

Zhang, R. and T. L. Delworth (2006), Impact of Atlantic multidecadal oscillations on India/Sahel rainfall and Atlantic hurricanes, *Geophys. Res. Lett.*, *33*, L17712.

6

Understanding ENSO Variability and Its Extrema: A Delay Differential Equation Approach

Michael Ghil[1,2] and Ilya Zaliapin[3]

ABSTRACT

We review and analyze in greater depth and detail a simple conceptual model of the sea surface temperature T in the Tropical Pacific. The model includes three essential mechanisms of El-Niño/Southern-Oscillation (ENSO) dynamics: the seasonal forcing, the negative feedback due to the oceanic waves, and the delay caused by their propagation across the Tropical Pacific. This model's rich behavior is studied via stability and bifurcation analysis in the three-dimensional (3D) space of its physically most relevant parameters: the strength b of the seasonal forcing, the atmosphere-ocean coupling parameter κ, and the characteristic propagation time τ of oceanic waves.

Two regimes of the model's parameter dependence, smooth and rough, are analyzed. They are separated by a sharp neutral curve in the (b, τ)-plane at constant κ. As the atmosphere-ocean coupling κ increases, the detailed structure of the neutral curve becomes very irregular and possibly fractal, while individual trajectories within the unstable region become quite complex and display multiple coexisting frequencies. In the unstable regime (and in the presence of given purely periodic, seasonal forcing) spontaneous transitions occur in the mean T of the solutions, in their period, and in their extreme annual values.

The model's behavior exhibits phase locking to the seasonal cycle, namely the local maxima and minima of T tend to occur at the same time of the year; this locking is a characteristic feature of the observed El Niño (warm) and La Niña (cold) events. Multiple model solutions coexist, and we describe their basins of attraction.

To shed further light on the parameter regimes in which the dynamics is quite complex, we introduce a key tool from the field of nonautonomous dynamical systems (NDS), namely pullback attractors. The study of the model's pullback attractor helps clarify the nature of the interaction between the seasonal forcing and the model's internal variability.

[1]*Geosciences Department, Environmental Research & Teaching Institute (CERES-ERTI), and Laboratoire de Meteorologie Dynamique (CNRS and IPSL), Ecole Normale Supérieure, Paris, France*

[2]*Department of Atmospheric & Oceanic Sciences and Institute of Geophysics & Planetary Physics, University of California, Los Angeles, CA, USA*

[3]*Department of Mathematics and Statistics, University of Nevada, Reno, NV, USA*

6.1. INTRODUCTION AND MOTIVATION

6.1.1. Key Ingredients of ENSO Theory

The El-Niño/Southern-Oscillation (ENSO) phenomenon is the most prominent signal of seasonal-to-interannual climate variability. It was known for centuries to fishermen along the west coast of South America, who witnessed a seemingly sporadic and abrupt warming of the cold,

Extreme Events: Observations, Modeling, and Economics, Geophysical Monograph 214, First Edition.
Edited by Mario Chavez, Michael Ghil, and Jaime Urrutia-Fucugauchi.

nutrient-rich waters that support the food chain in those regions; these warmings caused havoc to their fish harvests [*Philander*, 1990; *Diaz and Markgraf*, 1993; *Ghil and Zaliapin*, 2013]. The common occurrence of such warming shortly after Christmas inspired them to name it El Niño, after the "Christ child." Starting in the 1970s, researchers found that El Niño's climatic effects were far broader than just its manifestations off the shores of Peru [*Glantz et al.*, 1991; *Diaz and Markgraf*, 1993]. This realization led to a global awareness of ENSO's significance, and triggered an increased interest in modeling and forecasting exceptionally strong El Niño events [*Latif et al.*, 1994].

Nonlinear and complex phenomena like ENSO require a full hierarchy of models for their study, from "toy" models via intermediate ones to fully coupled general circulation models (GCMs) [*Neelin et al.*, 1998; *Ghil and Robertson*, 2000]. We focus here on a "toy" model, which captures a qualitative, conceptual picture of ENSO dynamics that includes a surprisingly full range of features. This approach allows one to achieve a rather comprehensive understanding of the model's, and maybe the phenomenon's, underlying mechanisms and their interplay.

The following conceptual elements have been shown to play a determining role in the dynamics of the ENSO phenomenon.

1. The Bjerknes hypothesis: *Bjerknes* [1969], who laid the foundation of modern ENSO research, suggested a *positive feedback* as a mechanism for the growth of an internal instability that could produce large positive anomalies of sea surface temperatures (SSTs) in the eastern Tropical Pacific. Recall that in the atmospheric, oceanic, and climate sciences, an *anomaly* is simply the difference between the instantaneous, or mean-monthly, value of a variable and its long-term "normal," that is, its climatological mean. Using observations from the International Geophysical Year (1957–1958), Bjerknes realized that this mechanism must involve *air-sea interaction* in the tropics.

The "chain reaction" starts with an initial warming of SSTs in the "cold tongue" that occupies the eastern part of the equatorial Pacific. This warming causes a weakening of the thermally direct Walker-cell circulation; this circulation involves air rising over the warmer SSTs near Indonesia and sinking over the colder SSTs near Peru. As the trade winds blowing from the east weaken and thus give way to westerly wind anomalies, the ensuing local changes in the ocean circulation encourage further SST increase. Thus, the feedback loop is closed and further amplification of the instability is triggered. A schematic diagram of the atmospheric and oceanic circulations in the Tropical Pacific under normal conditions (upper panel), and under El Niño (middle panel) and La Niña (lower panel) is shown in Figure 6.1.

2. Delayed oceanic wave adjustments: Compensating for Bjerknes's positive feedback is a *negative feedback* in the system that allows a return to colder conditions in the basin's eastern part [*Suarez and Schopf*, 1988]. During

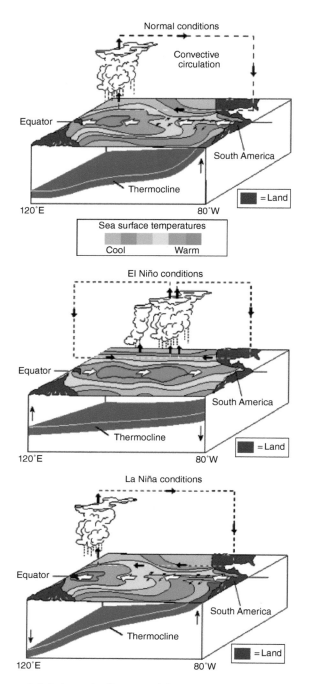

Figure 6.1 Schematic diagram of the atmospheric and oceanic circulation in the Tropical Pacific. Upper panel: climatological mean (normal), middle panel: El Niño (warm) phase, and lower panel: La Niña (cold) phase. The three-dimensional diagrams show the deepening of the seasonal thermocline (blue surface) near the coast of Peru during the warm phase, accompanied by anomalous surface winds (heavy white arrows), modified Walker circulation (lighter black arrows), and a displacement and broadening of the warmest SSTs from the "warm pool" in the western Tropical Pacific, near Indonesia, toward the east. The thermocline shallows during the warm phase and steepens during the cold phase, in response to the weakening and strengthening of the equatorial easterlies, respectively. Reproduced from *Spaulding and Namowitz* [2004].

the peak of the cold-tongue warming, called the *warm* or *El Niño* phase of ENSO, westerly wind anomalies prevail in the central part of the basin. As part of the ocean's adjustment to this atmospheric forcing, a Kelvin wave is set up in the tropical wave guide and carries a warming signal eastward; this signal deepens the eastern-basin thermocline, which separates the warmer, well-mixed surface waters from the colder waters below, and thus contributes to the positive feedback described above. Concurrently, slower Rossby waves propagate westward, and are reflected at the basin's western boundary, giving rise therewith to an eastward-propagating Kelvin wave that has a cooling, thermocline-shoaling effect. Over time, the arrival of this signal erodes the warm event, ultimately causing a switch to a *cold, La Niña* phase.

3. Seasonal forcing: A growing body of work [*Chang et al.*, 1994, 1995; *Jin et al.*, 1994, 1996; *Tziperman et al.*, 1994, 1995; *Ghil and Robertson*, 2000] points to resonances between the Pacific basin's intrinsic air-sea oscillator and the annual cycle as a possible cause for the tendency of warm events to peak in boreal winter, and for ENSO's intriguing mix of temporal regularities and irregularities. The mechanisms by which this interaction takes place are numerous and intricate, and their relative importance is not yet fully understood [*Battisti*, 1988; *Tziperman et al.*, 1995].

The past 30 years of research have shown that ENSO dynamics is governed, by and large, by the interplay of the nonlinear mechanisms, and that their simplest version can be studied in autonomous or forced delay differential equation (DDE) models [*Suarez and Schopf*, 1988; *Battisti and Hirst*, 1989; *Tziperman et al.*, 1994]. These DDE models follow their use in paleoclimate studies [*Bhattacharya et al.*, 1982; *Roques et al.*, 2013], provide a convenient paradigm for explaining interannual ENSO variability, and shed new light on its dynamical properties.

So far, though, the DDE model studies of ENSO have been limited to linear stability analysis of steady-state solutions, which are not typical in forced systems, case studies of particular trajectories, or one-dimensional (1D) scenarios of transition to chaos, where one varies a single parameter while the others are kept fixed. A major obstacle for the complete bifurcation and sensitivity analysis of DDE models lies in the complex nature of these models, whose numerical and analytical treatments are considerably harder than that of systems of ordinary differential equations (ODEs).

Ghil et al. [2008b] took several steps toward a comprehensive analysis, numerical and theoretical, of a DDE model relevant to ENSO phenomenology. In doing so, they also illustrated the complexity of phase-parameter-space structure for even a simple model of climate dynamics. Specifically, the authors formulated a toy DDE model for ENSO variability and focused on analysis of model solutions in a broad 3Ddomain of its physically relevant parameters. They showed that the model can reproduce many scenarios relevant to the ENSO phenomenology,

including prototypes of warm and cold events, interdecadal oscillations, and even intraseasonal activity reminiscent of Madden-Julian oscillations or westerly wind bursts.

The model was also able to provide a good justification for the observed quasi-biennial oscillation in Tropical Pacific SSTs and trade winds [*Philander*, 1990; *Diaz and Markgraf*, 1993; *Jiang et al.*, 1995; *Ghil et al.*, 2002]. The most important finding of *Ghil et al.* [2008b] was the existence of regions in the model's parameter space in which solution properties, like their mean or period, depend smoothly or sensitively on parameter values; these regions have a complex and possibly fractal geometric structure. Interestingly, the values of the model parameters that correspond to actual ENSO dynamics lie near the border between the smooth and "rough" regions in this space. Hence, if the dynamical phenomena found in the model have any relation to reality, SSTs in the Tropical Pacific are expected to have an intrinsically unstable behavior.

This chapter briefly reviews the results of *Ghil et al.* [2008b], *Zaliapin and Ghil* [2010], and *Ghil and Zaliapin* [2013] and pursues their DDE model analysis by focusing on multiple model solutions for the same parameter values and the dynamics of *local extrema*. Furthermore, we apply, for the first time, the concepts and tools of the theory of nonautonomous dynamical systems (NDS) and their pullback attractors to a better understanding of the interaction between the seasonal forcing and the internal variability of a relatively simple DDE model of ENSO.

The chapter is organized as follows. Section 6.2 introduces the DDE model of ENSO variability, reviews the main theoretical results concerning its solutions, and comments on the appropriate numerical integration methods. Our novel results on multiple solutions and their extrema are reported and illustrated in Section 6.3, while the model's pullback attractor is presented in Section 6.4. An overall discussion concludes the chapter in Section 6.5.

6.2. MODEL AND NUMERICAL INTEGRATION METHOD

6.2.1. Model Formulation and Parameters

Ghil et al. [2008b] studied the nonlinear DDE with additive, periodic forcing:

$$\frac{dh(t)}{dt} = -a\tanh\left[\kappa h(t-\tau)\right] + b\cos(2\pi\omega t). \quad (6.1)$$

Here $t \geq 0$ and the parameters a, κ, τ, b, and ω are all real and positive. Equation 6.1 mimics two mechanisms essential for ENSO variability: delayed negative feedback via the highly nonlinear function $\tanh(\kappa z)$ and periodic external forcing. It is inspired by, and further simplifies, earlier DDE models of ENSO [*Suarez and Schopf*, 1988; *Battisti and Hirst*, 1989; *Tziperman et al.*, 1994]; these

DDE models, in turn, were based on either fundamental physical considerations or simplifications of intermediate ENSO models [*Zebiak and Cane*, 1987].

The function $h(t)$ in (6.1) represents the thermocline depth anomalies, that is, its deviations from the annual mean in the Eastern Pacific. Accordingly, h can also be interpreted roughly as the regional SST anomaly, since a deeper thermocline corresponds to less upwelling of cold waters, and hence higher SST, and vice versa (Figure 6.1). The thermocline depth is affected by the wind-forced, eastward Kelvin and westward Rossby oceanic waves. The waves' delayed effects are modeled by the function $\tanh[\kappa h(t-\tau)]$; the delay τ is due to the finite wave velocity and corresponds roughly to the combined basin-transit time of the Kelvin and Rossby waves. The forcing term represents the seasonal cycle in the trade winds.

The model (6.1) is fully determined by its five parameters: feedback delay τ, atmosphere-ocean coupling strength κ, feedback amplitude a, forcing frequency ω, and forcing amplitude b. By an appropriate rescaling of time t and dependent variable h, we let $\omega = 1$ and $a = 1$. The other three parameters may vary, reflecting different physical conditions of ENSO evolution. We consider here the following ranges of these parameters: $0 \le \tau \le 2$ year, $0 < \kappa < \infty$, and $0 \le b < \infty$.

To completely specify the DDE model (6.1), we need to prescribe some initial "history," that is, the behavior of $h(t)$ on the interval $[-\tau, 0)$ [*Hale*, 1977]. Unless explicitly stated otherwise, we assume $h(t) \equiv 1$, $-\tau \le t < 0$, that is, we start with a warm year. Numerical experiments, with alternative specifications of the initial history, suggest that this choice does not affect our qualitative conclusions. In Section 6.3.4, though, we examine the multiplicity of solutions that arises from distinct initial histories.

6.2.2. Main Theoretical Result

Consider the function space $X = C([-\tau, 0), \mathbb{R})$ of continuous functions h from the initial interval $[-\tau, 0)$ to the real axis $\mathbb{R}$, $h: [-\tau, 0) \to \mathbb{R}$. This infinite-dimensional space X is equipped with the norm for $h \in X$ given by

$$\|h\| = \sup\{|h(t)|, t \in [-\tau, 0)\},$$

and becomes, therewith, a Banach space; here $|\cdot|$ denotes the absolute value in $\mathbb{R}$ [*Hale*, 1977; *Nussbaum*, 1998]. For convenience, we reformulate the DDE initial-value problem (IVP) in its rescaled form:

$$\frac{dh(t)}{dt} = -\tanh[\kappa h(t-\tau)] + b\cos(2\pi t), t \ge 0, \quad (6.2)$$

$$h(t) = \phi(t) \text{ for } t \in [-\tau, 0), \phi(t) \in X. \quad (6.3)$$

Ghil et al. [2008b] proved the following result.

> **Proposition 1**
> **(Existence, uniqueness, continuous dependence)** *For any fixed triplet of positive parameters* (τ, κ, b), *the IVP governed by Equations 6.2 and 6.3 has a unique solution* $h(t)$ *on* $[0, \infty)$. *This solution depends continuously on the initial data* $\varphi(t)$, *delay* τ, *and the right-hand side of (6.2) considered as a continuous map* $f: [0, T) \times X \to \mathbb{R}$, *for any finite time T.*

From Proposition 1, it follows, in particular, that the IVP (6.2) and (6.3) has a unique solution for all time, which depends continuously on the model parameters (τ, κ, b) and initial history $\varphi(t)$ for any finite time. This result implies that any discontinuity in the solution profile as a function of the model parameters or history indicates existence of an unstable solution that separates the attractor basins of two stable solutions [*Ghil et al.*, 2008b].

6.2.3. Numerical Integration

The results in this study are based on the numerical integration of DDE (6.2) with initial data (6.3). We emphasize that there are important differences between the numerical integration of DDEs and ODEs. These differences require development of special software for DDEs, often accompanied by the problem-specific modification of such software. We used here the Fortran 90/95 DDE solver of *Shampine and Thompson* [2006], available at http://www.radford.edu/~thompson/ffddes/. Technical details of dde solver, and a brief overview of other available DDE solvers are given by *Ghil et al.* [2008b].

6.3. PHASE-LOCKING OF EXTREMA AND MULTIPLE SOLUTIONS

For completeness, we review the earlier results [*Ghil et al.*, 2008b; *Zaliapin and Ghil*, 2010] in Sections 6.3.1 and 6.3.2, and emphasize recent ones in Sections 6.3.3, 6.3.4, and 6.4.

6.3.1. Examples of Model Dynamics

This subsection illustrates typical solutions of our DDE model and comments on physically relevant aspects of these solutions. Figure 6.2 shows six model trajectories, all of which correspond to $b = 1$. Panel (a) ($\kappa = 5$, $\tau = 0.65$) illustrates the occurrence of "low-h," or cold events every fourth seasonal cycle. Note that low values (i.e., negative anomalies) of h correspond to the boreal (Northern Hemisphere) winter, that is, to the upwelling season (December-January-February) in the eastern Tropical Pacific; in the present, highly idealized model, we can associate the extreme negative values with large-amplitude

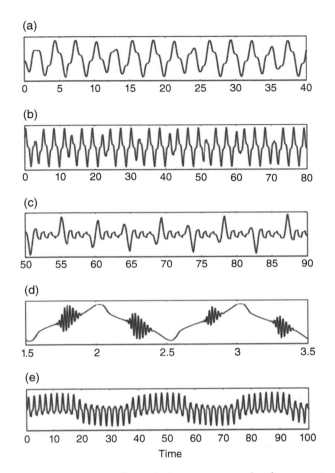

Figure 6.2 Noteworthy solution patterns of relevance to ENSO dynamics; seasonal forcing amplitude $b = 1$. (a) Regularly occurring cold (low-h) events, or La Niñas ($\kappa = 5$, $\tau = 0.65$); (b) irregular cold events ($\kappa = 100$, $\tau = 0.58$); (c) irregular alternations of warm (El Niño, high-h) and cold events ($\kappa = 50$, $\tau = 0.42$); (d) intraseasonal activity reminiscent of Madden-Julian oscillations or westerly wind bursts ($\kappa = 500$, $\tau = 0.005$); and (e) interdecadal variability in the annual mean and in the relative amplitude of warm and cold events ($\kappa = 50$, $\tau = 0.508$). Reproduced from *Ghil et al.* [2008b], with kind permission of Copernicus Publications on behalf of the European Geosciences Union (EGU).

cold events, or La Niñas. This solution pattern loses its regularity when the atmosphere-ocean coupling increases: Panel (b) ($\kappa = 100$, $\tau = 0.58$) shows irregular occurrence of large cold events with the inter-event time varying from three to seven cycles.

In panel (c) ($\kappa = 50$, $\tau = 0.42$), we observe alternately and irregularly occurring warm El Niño and cold La Niña events: the "high-h" events occur with a period of about 4 years and random magnitude. Panel (d) ($\kappa = 500$, $\tau = 0.005$) shows another interesting type of behavior: bursts of intraseasonal oscillations of random amplitude superimposed on regular, period-one dynamics. This pattern is

reminiscent of Madden-Julian oscillations [*Madden and Julian*, 1971, 1972, 1994] or of westerly wind bursts [*Harrison and Giese*, 1988; *Delcroix et al.*, 1993; *Verbickas*, 1998; *Boulanger et al.*, 2004; *Lengaigne et al.*, 2004; *Saynisch et al.*, 2006; *Gebbie et al.*, 2007]. Westerly wind bursts are physically related to atmospheric convection that is not a part of the current model. The somewhat surprising model result of high-frequency, intraseasonal variability suggests that realistic bursts might be excited in the atmosphere by, or interact synergistically with, the apparently slower mechanisms represented by this coupled model: they could be triggered by, rather than trigger, warm or cold ENSO episodes.

The solution in panel (e) ($\kappa = 50$, $\tau = 0.508$) demonstrates sustained interdecadal variability in the absence of any external source of such variability. The solution pattern illustrates spontaneous changes in the long-term annual mean, and in the distribution of positive and negative extremes, with respect to both time and amplitude.

6.3.2. Onset of Instabilities

Munnich et al. [1991] and *Tziperman et al.* [1994] reported that the onset of chaotic behavior in their ENSO models is associated with the increase of the atmosphere-ocean coupling κ. We explore parameter dependence in our model over its entire 3D parameter space. While this dependence is highly complex and apparently even fractal, we shall see at the end of Section 6.4.1 that, in the absence of destabilizing positive feedback, fairly irregular, quasi-periodic solutions are possible in our model, but truly chaotic ones are not.

First, we compute in the three panels of Figure 6.3 the trajectory maximum M as a function of the parameters b and τ for values of κ that increase from the top to the bottom panel. For small values of coupling (top panel), we have a smooth map, monotonously increasing in b and periodic with period 1 in τ. As the coupling increases, the map loses its monotonicity in b and periodicity in τ for large values of τ, but it is still smooth. For $\kappa \approx 2$ (middle panel), a neutral curve $f(b, \tau) = 0$ emerges that separates a smooth region (to the right of the curve), where we still observe monotonicity in b and periodicity in τ, from a region with rough behavior of M. The gradient of $M(b, \tau)$ is quite sharp across this neutral curve.

Further increase of the coupling results in a qualitative change in the maximum map. The neutral curve, which becomes sharp and rough, separates two regions with very different behavior of $M(b, \tau)$ (bottom panel). To the right of the curve, the map $M(b, \tau)$ is still smooth, periodic in τ, and monotonic in b. To the left, one sees discontinuities that produce rough and complicated patterns. The mean position of the neutral curve $f(b, \tau) = 0$ quickly converges to a fixed profile, although its detailed shape at

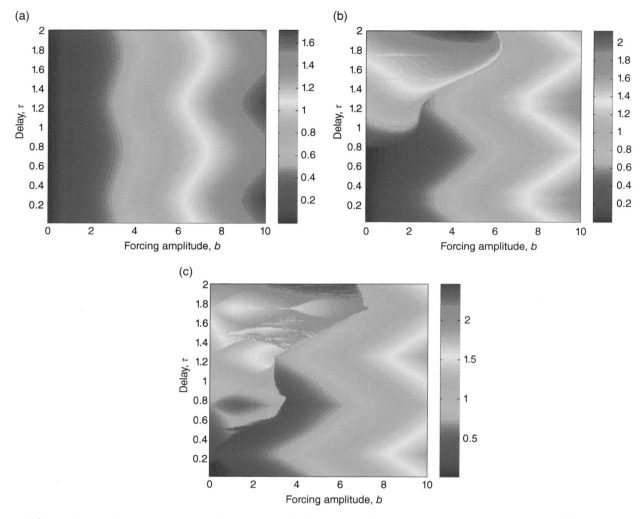

Figure 6.3 Maximum map $M = M(b, \tau)$. (a) $\kappa = 0.5$, (b) $\kappa = 2$, and (c) $\kappa = 11$. Note the onset of instabilities and emergence of a neutral curve $f(b, \tau) = 0$ that separates the smooth from the unstable regions. Reproduced from *Ghil et al.* [2008b], with kind permission of Copernicus Publications on behalf of the European Geosciences Union (EGU).

smaller scales continues to change with increasing κ. The limiting profile is close to the one observed for $\kappa = 11$ (bottom panel).

Figure 6.4 further shows the model instabilities. It shows the period P and maximal value M in 2D sections of the model parameter space.

6.3.3. Phase Locking of the Extrema

A distinctive feature of the warm ENSO phase, that is, of an El-Niño event, is its occurrence during a boreal winter. We study here the temporal location of the global maximum and global minimum of solutions, and their local extrema. The key result here is that practically all the extrema of our model solutions occur exclusively within a particular time interval of the seasonal cycle.

The positions of the local extrema (phases) were analyzed for tens of thousands of individual solutions of the model (6.2) and (6.3), spanning the entire parameter region $\{(b, \tau): 0 < b \leq 10, \ 0 < \tau \leq 2\}$, at different values of κ. This analysis was carried out (like that by *Ghil et al.* [2008b], as summarized in Figures 6.2, 6.3, and 6.4) when the solutions had settled into their asymptotic behavior, that is, after a sufficiently long transient. The representative results are summarized in Figure 6.5, where we used 10,000 individual solutions for each value of κ. The phase variable ϕ was normalized to lie between 0 and 1, with 0 at the time of year when the trade winds are strongest, that is, close to the first day of October.

The phenomenon of phase locking of the extrema is present for most combinations of the physically relevant model parameters. Moreover, the local maxima tend to

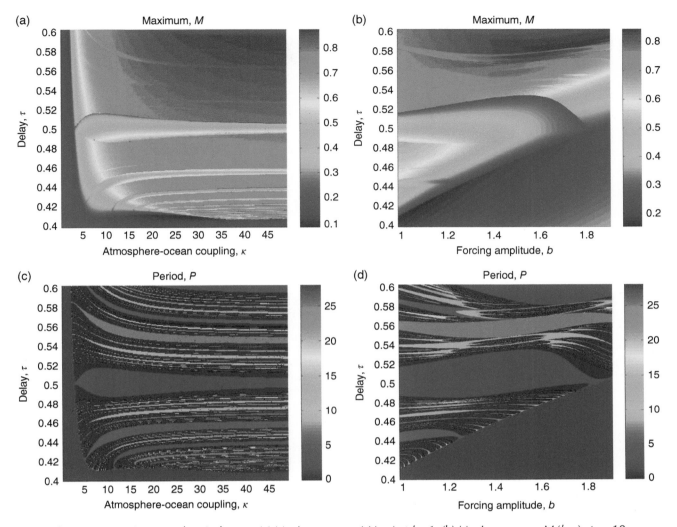

Figure 6.4 Maximum and period maps. (a) Maximum map, $M(\kappa, \tau)$ at $b = 1$; (b) Maximum map, $M(b, \tau)$ at $\kappa = 10$; (c) Period map, $P(\kappa, \tau)$ at $b = 1$; (d) Period map, $P(b, \tau)$ at $\kappa = 10$. Reproduced from *Ghil et al.* [2008b], with kind permission of Copernicus Publications on behalf of the European Geosciences Union (EGU).

occur, depending on the value of τ, at $\phi = 0.23$ (late December) or $\phi = 0.27$ (early January), while the local minima occur at $\phi = 0.73$ (late June) and $\phi = 0.77$ (early July).

We note that the seasonal forcing in our model vanishes at $\phi = 0.25$ (January 1) and $\phi = 0.75$ (July 1); hence the local maxima occur in the vicinity of zero forcing when the latter decreases, and the local mimina occur in the vicinity of zero forcing when the latter increases. This corresponds to the local maxima occurring in the model shortly after Christmas, like the observed El Niños, but the model La Niñas are in phase opposition, rather than close to the same season, as they are in the observations. The offset of the position of the extrema from the point of zero external forcing seems to be independent of the model parameters, and the double peaks in the histogram become sharper as the coupling parameter κ increases.

6.3.4. Multiple Solutions

The analysis so far [*Ghil et al.*, 2008b], and in the previous subsections of this chapter, has been done for the model governed by Equations 6.2 and 6.3 with fixed history, $\varphi(t) \equiv 1$. We now study the dependence of model solutions on distinct, yet still constant histories $\varphi(t) \equiv \varphi_0$.

Distinct values of the initial history result in distinct model solutions; this is shown in Figure 6.6 for the parameter values $b = 1$, $\tau = 0.5$, and $\kappa = 10$. To produce this figure, we used 20 distinct initial constant histories, uniformly distributed between $\varphi_0 = -2$ and $\varphi_0 = 2$; at time $t = 0$, there are thus 20 distinct trajectories. As time passes, these trajectories are attracted by several stable model solutions so that, by $t = 15$, there are only four distinct trajectories left.

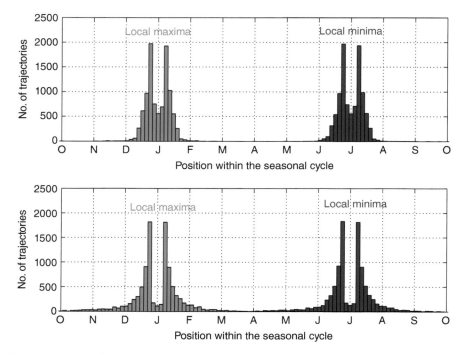

Figure 6.5 Phase locking of solution extrema: global results. Histogram of the position ϕ of the global maximum (red bars) and global minimum (blue bars) of solutions of Equation 6.2 with $\kappa = 2.0$ (top panel) and $\kappa = 11.0$ (bottom panel). Each panel uses 10,000 individual solutions with parameter values b and τ lying in the ranges $0 < b \leq 10$ and $0 < \tau \leq 2$, respectively.

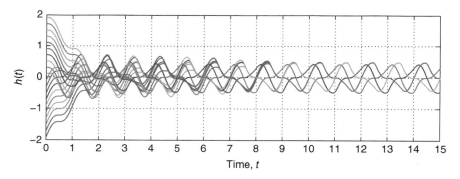

Figure 6.6 Multiple stable solutions. Twenty trajectories that correspond to as many distinct initial histories $\varphi(t) = \varphi_0$ collapse, after a transient, onto four stable solutions; these four solutions are indicated by four distinct colors (red, blue, purple, and green). Two of these solutions are *distinct*, and the other two can be obtained from the distinct ones by a time shift; notice that a given asymptotic solution, for example, the red one, attracts initial histories that can lie in different segments of the interval $\{\varphi_0 : -2 \leq \varphi_0 \leq 2\}$. Model parameters are $b = 1$, $\tau = 0.5$, and $\kappa = 10$; see also Figure 6.7.

We concentrate next on the stable solutions' domains of attraction. Figure 6.7 shows the model solutions, after the transient behavior has decayed, for $-10 \leq \varphi_0 \leq 10$, at two points in the model's parameter space: $A = (b = 2, \tau = 0.4, \kappa = 11)$ in the top panel, and $B = (b = 1, \tau = 0.5, \kappa = 10)$ in the bottom panel. Model solutions at point B are shown in Figure 6.6. At point A, the model has a unique stable solution, which attracts all initial trajectories as time evolves; thus the solution "profile" is constant along any vertical line in the figure's "Hovmoeller diagram."

At point B, the model has several distinct stable solutions. Recall from Section 6.2.2 that the solutions, and hence their basins of attraction, lie in the function space $X = C([-\tau, 0), \mathbb{R})$. The boundaries of these basins appear in Figure 6.7 as horizontal discontinuities in the solution profiles.

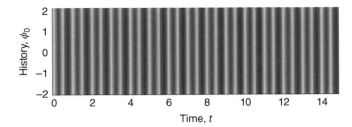

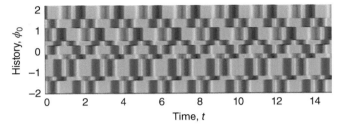

Figure 6.7 Solution profiles for different constant histories $\varphi(t) \equiv \varphi_0$. Top panel ($b=2$, $\tau=0.4$, $\kappa=11$): there exists a unique stable solution. Bottom panel ($b=1$, $\tau=0.5$, $\kappa=10$; same values as in Figure 6.6): there exist several stable solutions, and their basins of attraction are bounded by the horizontal discontinuity lines in the solution profiles; see text for details. The solutions in both panels are shown after a suitably long transient, and the time origin is shifted to start from zero.

There are eight horizontal discontinuities in the profiles, and so there appear to exist nine attraction basins; as seen in Figure 6.6, these nine basins correspond in fact to only four asymptotic solutions. Moreover, two of these four can, in turn, be obtained from the other two solutions by a time shift (not shown). The basins of attraction for these two solutions are unions of subintervals of different lengths of the interval $\{\varphi_0: -2 \le \varphi_0 \le 2\}$, at least when considering, as we have done here, only the subset of the function space X generated by constant initial histories.

Recall, moreover, that Proposition 1 implies that a discontinuity in the solution profile at φ_0 suggests that there exists an unstable solution at $\varphi(t) \equiv \varphi_0$. Hence, the boundaries of the domains of attraction correspond, in all likelihood, to unstable model solutions. Figure 6.7 suggests the existence of eight unstable solutions; the number of distinct unstable solutions may indeed be less than that. We return to the issue of the attractor basin boundaries at the end of Section 6.4.1.

6.4. PULLBACK ATTRACTORS AND QUASI-PERIODIC ORBITS

In this section, we report the new results regarding the DDE model governed by Equation 6.1. These results are discussed within the framework of NDS and their *pullback attractors*; see *Sell and You* [2002] and *Carvalho*

et al. [2013] for a general introduction on the topic, and see *Ghil et al.* [2008a] and *Chekroun et al.* [2011] for a presentation in the climate context.

6.4.1. Theoretical Considerations

To make good use of this theory, we need first to recast Equation 6.1 in its abstract functional form, namely

$$\frac{dh}{dt} = F\left(h_t\right) + g\left(t\right), h_t \in X := C([-\tau, 0), \mathbb{R}), \quad (6.4)$$

with X the Banach space of continuous functions from the half-open interval $[-\tau, 0)$ to the real axis $\mathbb{R}$, as defined in Section 6.2.2, and with

$$h_t\left(\theta\right) := h\left(t+\theta\right), -\tau \le \theta \le 0; \quad (6.5)$$

here $F\left(h_t\right) := -a \tanh [Dh_t]$, while the operator $D\varphi$ is defined by

$$D_\phi\left(\theta\right) := \kappa\phi\left(-\tau\right), \quad (6.6)$$

for any $\varphi \in X$, that is, D shifts the function φ on which it operates backward by τ and multiplies it by κ. The time-dependent forcing is, of course, the seasonal $g(t) = b \cos(2\pi \omega t)$ given in Equation 6.1.

Proposition 1 of Section 6.2.2 allows us then to show that Equation 6.4 generates, in the language of NDS theory [*Caraballo et al.*, 2005; *Carvalho et al.*, 2013], a *nonlinear process*, that is a solution map U defined by

$$(t,s,\phi) \mapsto U\left(t,s;\phi\right) := h_t \in X, t \ge s, \phi \in X, \quad (6.7)$$

where h_t is the unique solution of (6.4), such that $h_s = \varphi$ ($s \le t$). A key feature of such a process is the *process composition property*, which replaces the well-known semigroup property of autonomous differentiable dynamical systems (DDS). In the NDS setting, this property becomes

$$U\left(t,s\right) \circ U\left(s,r\right) = U\left(t,r\right), \ t \ge s \ge r. \quad (6.8)$$

The solution map U can be thus referred to as a two-parameter semigroup, with the two parameters t and s, that provides a two-time description of the dynamics associated with the DDE model given by (6.1), while in the autonomous case, a one-parameter semigroup, with the single parameter t, suffices to determine the dynamics [*Ghil et al.*, 2008a; *Chekroun et al.*, 2011].

It is possible to rigorously define a pullback attractor for the nonlinear process U in the infinite-dimensional Banach space X as follows [*Caraballo et al.*, 2005; *Carvalho et al.*, 2013]. A family of compact (Here, a compact set is understood in the sense of point set topology, for example [*Dugundji*, 1966]; for instance, the surface of a sphere or a bounded, closed interval in $\mathbb{R}$ are simple compact sets.) sets $\{\mathcal{A}(t)\}$ is said to be a (global) pullback attractor for U if, for all $s \in \mathbb{R}$, it satisfies the following two properties:

(i) (Invariance property) $U(t,s)\mathcal{A}(s) = \mathcal{A}(t)$ for all $t \geq s$; and

(ii) (Pullback attraction property) $\lim_{s\to\infty} \text{dist}_X(U(t,t-s)B, \mathcal{A}(t)) = 0$, for all bounded subsets of X.

The pullback attraction property (ii) considers the state of the system at time t at which we observe it, when the system was initialized in a distant past $t-s$, as $s \to \infty$ [*Ghil et al.*, 2008a; *Chekroun et al.*, 2011]. Here, dist$X$ (E, F) denotes the Hausdorff semi-distance between the subsets E and F of X,

$$d_X(E,F) := \sup_{x \in E} d_X(x,F) \text{ and } d_X(x,F) := \inf_{y \in F} d(x,y),$$

while d is the metric in X that is consistent with the norm on X that was defined in Section 6.2.2, $d(x,y) = \|x - y\|$.

The nonlinearity involved in (6.1) is sublinear at infinity, that is, $(\tanh x)/x \to 0$ as $|x| \to \infty$, and thus it can be shown that the process U generated by (6.4) possesses a global pullback attractor [*Caraballo et al.*, 2005]. We will illustrate certain geometrical features of this pullback attractor, in terms of the parameter values of Equation 6.1, in the next subsection, by means of numerical simulations. Before doing so, we note here some qualitative properties of the attractor that can be inferred directly from the nature of the negative feedback and the simple periodic forcing used.

We start our theoretical considerations by recalling some features associated with the global attractor of (6.4) when $g(t) \equiv 0$, that is, in the autonomous case. According to a Poincaré-Bendixson-type theorem [*Hartman*, 2008] for monotone cyclic feedback systems due to *Mallet-Paret and Sell* [1996], the negative feedback mechanism involved in (6.1) implies that the Ω-limit set [*Hale*, 1988] of any bounded solutions of (6.4) for $g(t) \equiv 0$, —that is, the set to which all such solutions tend as $t \to +\infty$—contains only periodic orbits or stationary points, along with their homoclinic or heteroclinic connections [*Krisztin*, 2008], if present.

Within this geometric context, when the periodic forcing is turned on, perturbation techniques based on Lyapunov-Perron methods strongly suggest that periodic orbits replace the stationary points in their neighborhoods, whereas doubly periodic, invariant tori replace the periodic ones [*Chekroun and Roques*, 2006, theorem 3.1; *Sell and You*, 2002, Section 7.6] for rigorous results in the context of partial differential equations. These mathematical considerations are entirely consistent

with the idea that a positive, Bjerknes-type feedback [*Philander*, 1990; *Diaz and Markgraf*, 1993; *Ghil and Zaliapin*, 2013; Section 6.1.1] is necessary to generate an instability, whose nonlinear saturation may then lead to chaos.

Returning now to the issue of the attractor basin boundaries suggested by Figure 6.7, the structure of the global attractor of a DDE like Equation 6.4 is "gradient-like," in the following sense: for actual gradient systems of the type $\dot{x} = -dV(x)/dx$, the global attractor is constituted by fixed points, some of which may be unstable and connected by heteroclinic orbits; whereas for our DDE, and in the absence of periodic forcing, the global attractor is constituted by limit cycles connected by heteroclinic orbits [*Krisztin*, 2008].

Once the periodic forcing is turned on, one can prove that these limit cycles become invariant tori, still possibly connected by heteroclinic orbits. Therefore, it is still true that locally stable attractors (i.e., in the present case, the locally attractive quasi-periodic orbits) are separated by unstable solutions, namely by unstable limit cycles or quasi-periodic solutions.

6.4.2. Numerical Results

As shown later, the numerical computation of pullback attractors constitutes a powerful tool for the closer examination of such theoretical conjectures. Figure 6.8 provides, in fact, a striking illustration of the qualitative properties of our ENSO model's pullback attractor. In the three panels of this figure, the attractors associated with Equation 6.4 are plotted in delay coordinates $(h(t), h(t + \Delta t))$, allowing one to characterize their nature.

These plots have been obtained by very long integrations of Equation 6.4 from $t - s = 19,000$ to $t = 20,000$, with $N = 500$ sets of initial data taken to be constant histories $\varphi(t)$ over $[-\tau, 0]$. The values of these histories are uniformly spaced within the interval $[-1, 1]$. The red curves represent the set of points obtained at the frozen time t, with initial data given at $t - s \simeq 19,000$, whereas each of the blue curves represents a standard forward integration of Equation 6.4, where all the points constituting the trajectory are displayed, after an initial transient (not shown) of length θ_0, with $\theta_0 \simeq 19,000$.

In all the cases reported here, we observe that the pullback attractor is a closed curve in the $(h(t), h(t + \Delta t))$-plane; this is a manifestation of the fact that the orbits tend toward an invariant torus for the set of parameters and of initial data used herein. Interestingly, each of these curves is a continuum of points: up to the numerical precision and the relatively small number of initial data used to generate these figures.

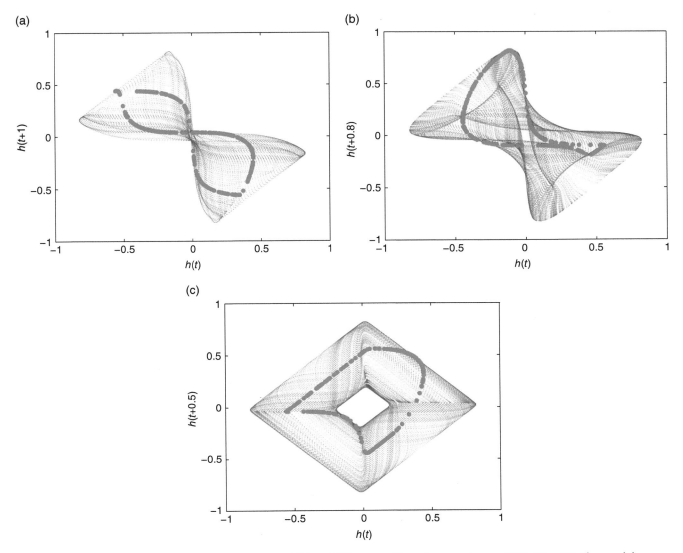

Figure 6.8 Pullback attractor of our DDE model for ENSO, plotted in delay coordinates $[h(t), h(t+\Delta t)]$. The model parameters are $b=1$, $\kappa=51$, and $\tau=0.52$. (a) $\Delta t=1$; (b) $\Delta t=0.8$; and (c) $\Delta t=0.5$. Forward trajectories in blue, pullback attractor in red. Animated version of these pullback attractors can be found at http://www.researchgate.net/publication/274718637.

This continuity indicates that, for the parameter regimes illustrated, the dynamics is attracted toward quasi-periodic orbits with incommensurable frequencies. Indeed, in the complementary case of commensurable frequencies, the pullback attractor would be constituted by a finite number of points lying on a closed curve. The latter case was illustrated in *Ghil et al.* [2008a] in the analogous situation of a noise-perturbed Arnold's map.

No pullback attractors with more complicated, fractal-like structures have been observed numerically to occur in the DDE model formulated by *Ghil et al.* [2008b] and analyzed herein. As already stated at the end of the previous subsection, this absence of chaotic solutions, notwith-standing the fractal boundaries between regimes noted in *Ghil et al.* [2008b] and *Zaliapin and Ghil* [2010], is entirely consistent with the model's lacking a positive, Bjerknes-like feedback.

Other DDE models of ENSO have both a positive and negative feedback, with two distinct delays, each of which acts upon one of the two feedbacks. Among these models, that of *Galanti and Tziperman* [2000] was studied by *Ghil* [2015], and Figure 6.9 shows the invariant measure associated with the model's pull-back attractor. Clearly, the situation is very different from the one found in Figure 6.8, and the pullback attractor in Figure 6.9 strongly suggests chaotic behavior.

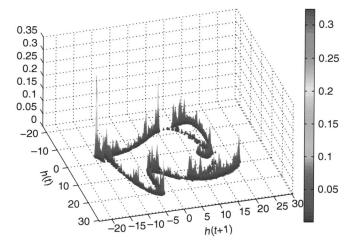

Figure 6.9 Time-dependent invariant measure of the *Galanti and Tziperman* [2000] model's pullback attractor, plotted in an isometric projection with the probability density on the perpendicular to the plane spanned by the coordinates [h(t), h(t + 1)]. The time here is in units of years, as in Figure 6.8, and the density is highly concentrated on a very "thin" support. From *Ghil* [2015], courtesy of M. D. Chekroun.

6.5. SUMMARY AND DISCUSSION

In this chapter, we reviewed and studied in greater depth a highly idealized model for ENSO variability that is governed by a DDE with a single, fixed delay, and additive periodic forcing [*Ghil et al.*, 2008b]. The use of DDE models to better understand basic ENSO mechanisms was pioneered by *Suarez and Schopf* [1988], *Battisti and Hirst* [1989], and *Tziperman et al.* [1994], following their application to paleoclimate studies by *Bhattacharya et al.* [1982; see *Neelin et al.*, 1998] for a comprehensive discussion. Such simple DDE models necessarily ignore a multitude of actual physical mechanisms and processes that might affect ENSO dynamics, as discussed in further detail by *Ghil et al.* [2008b]. Even so, these models have been shown to successfully capture complex phenomena found in much more detailed ENSO models, including fully coupled global climate models (GCMs), and observational data sets [*Ghil and Robertson*, 2000].

6.5.1. Phase Locking and Multiple Solutions

Given the obvious interest of these simple DDE models, we performed for the first time, to the best of our knowledge, an analysis of the model solutions' parameter dependence in a broad region of the 3D space of its physically relevant parameters: oceanic wave delay τ, ocean-atmosphere coupling strength κ, and seasonal forcing amplitude b [*Ghil et al.*, 2008b]. We found spontaneous transitions in the mean thermocline depth, and hence in

the SST, and the solutions' extreme annual values; these transitions occur for purely periodic, seasonal forcing. Our model, governed by Equations 6.2 and 6.3, generates intraseasonal oscillations of various periods and amplitudes, as well as interdecadal variability; see Figure 6.2.

A sharp neutral curve in the $(b - \tau)$ plane separates smooth parameter dependence in the model's map of "climate metrics" [*Taylor*, 2001; *Fuglestvedt et al.*, 2003] from the "rough" behavior; see Figures 6.3 and 6.4. We expect such separation between regions of smooth and rough dependence of solution metrics on parameters in much more detailed and realistic models, where it is hard to describe its causes completely [*Neelin et al.*, 2010; *Bracco et al.*, 2013; *Chekroun et al.*, 2014; *Ghil*, 2015].

The novelty of this chapter, with respect to earlier work on the DDE model of Equation 6.1 [*Ghil et al.*, 2008b; *Zaliapin and Ghil*, 2010], lies in part in its focus on multiple model solutions, as a function of initial data, and on the phase locking of local extrema with respect to the seasonal cycle. We found that our DDE model is characterized by the property of its solutions having *extrema* that lock to a particular *phase* ϕ of the seasonal cycle: the local maxima tend to occur one quarter cycle, that is, one season, after the most intense trade winds, that is, in boreal winter, while the local minima tend to occur one season after the least intense trades, that is, in boreal summer (see Figure 6.5).

As mentioned in Section 6.1, phase locking of warm events to boreal winter is a main feature of the observed El Niño events, to the point of having given them their name [*Philander*, 1990; *Diaz and Markgraf*, 1993; *Ghil and Zaliapin*, 2013]. At the same time, for small to intermediate seasonal forcing b, the position of the global maxima and minima appears to be highly sensitive to changes in parameter values: it may have significant jumps in response to vanishingly small changes in these values. Such sensitive dependence of model metrics on parameter values can also be observed in more detailed ENSO models [*Ghil*, 2015; Figure 6.7].

In reality, both warm (El Niño) and cold (La Niña) events lock to boreal winter, although the cold events are not only less intense [*Kondrashov et al.*, 2005], but also somewhat less sharply phase locked than the warm ones. It is not clear at this point which one of the lacking features of our DDE model gives rise to this unrealistic phase opposition, and we do mean to explore this matter further; especially so since even GCMs with many more detailed features may have their warm events in entirely the wrong season [*Ghil and Robertson*, 2000].

An additional interesting feature of our model, though, is the bimodality of the histogram for the phases of both warm and cold events; see again Figure 6.5. Similar bi- or multimodality of phase locking has been documented in both ODE models of ENSO and in much more realistic, so-called intermediate models [*Neelin et al.*, 2000]. A possible reason for such an effect may lie in the phase locking mechanism itself: as a model solution on the Devil's staircase [*Jin et al.*, 1994; *Tziperman et al.*, 1994] in parameter space "tries to adapt" to a particular integer multiple of the forcing period from below, it winds up short of the preferred phase, while it will wind up above that phase if its period is originally longer than the integer multiple it tries to achieve [*J. D. Neelin*, pers. commun., 2009].

Our simple model suggests that the multiple modes of the phase histogram in Figure 6.5 are separated by the phase at which the seasonal forcing disappears, and that the sharpness of each mode increases with the strength of the atmosphere-ocean coupling κ. It would be interesting to check whether similar behavior occurs in more detailed models, and in observations.

We found coexistence of multiple stable solutions for a wide range of model parameters; see Figures 6.6 and 6.7. Typically, each stable solution has its own basin of attraction, which we have explored in the subspace of solutions generated by constant initial histories $\varphi(t) \equiv \varphi_0$. In this subspace, we have found a finite and, actually, small number of stable solutions; some of these, in turn, could be simply obtained from others via a phase shift by an integer number of years. We will further analyze this property in a future study.

The boundaries of the attractor basins in Figure 6.7 suggest the existence of unstable solutions; their number is probably finite and comparable to the number of distinct stable solutions. We saw at the end of Section 6.4.1 that these unstable solutions are, in turn, unstable periodic or quasi-periodic solutions.

To summarize, the timing of global extrema (i.e., the hottest El Niños and coldest La Niñas) of our simple ENSO model is highly sensitive to the model's parameter values for a wide range of these values. But the local maxima and minima are locked to particular phases of the seasonal cycle. Multiple stable and unstable solutions exist, and the latter seem to play a key role in separating the attractor basins of the former.

Ghil et al. [2008a] and *McWilliams* [2007] have recently discussed the implications of *structural stability* [*Andronov and Pontryagin*, 1937] for climate models. The lack thereof is clearly a reason for difficulties in predicting extreme events, like the largest El Niños, sufficiently far in advance [see also *Ghil and Jiang*, 1998; *Held*, 2005]. *Ghil et al.* [2008a] showed that taking into account random perturbations can, in some simple models at least, lead to greater robustness of model behavior. We are planning to study such *stochastic structural stability* and *statistical stability* [*Chekroun et al.*, 2011; *Ghil*, 2015] effects in physically based but highly idealized ENSO models as well.

6.5.2. Pullback Attraction, Stability, and Parameter Dependence

It is increasingly clear that the proper mathematical formulation of climate problems is that of NDS and random dynamical systems (RDS) [*Ghil et al.*, 2008a; *Chekroun et al.*, 2011; *Dijkstra*, 2013; *Ghil*, 2015; *Moron et al.*, 2015]. On longer time scales, understanding the interplay between time-dependent forcing and internal variability becomes crucial. While autonomous DDS have served well the need of a mathematical framework for understanding weather dynamics on the relatively short time scale of days to weeks, this is no longer so once seasonal and anthropogenic effects become important.

In fact, ENSO dynamics are a perfect example for the interesting interaction between the seasonal cycle and intrinsic variability [*Chang et al.*, 1994, 1995; *Jin et al.*, 1994, 1996; *Tziperman et al.*, 1994, 1995; *Ghil and Robertson*, 2000; *Dijkstra*, 2005]. Hence, we introduced explicitly the NDS theory and pullback attraction in order to examine their usefulness in helping understand the effects of the seasonal forcing on ENSO model dynamics. Figure 6.8 clearly shows the simplicity of the pullback attractor (red curve) relative to the tangle of forward trajectories (blue curves). In fact, the traditional view of Ω-limit set as $t \to +\infty$ would just provide this set as the surface spanned by the blue trajectories, which is much less informative than the red curve.

We have seen (given the nature of the pullback attractor) that, for the parameter settings examined, this Ω-limit set is exclusively made up of quasi-periodic orbits with incommensurable frequencies and that no chaotic solutions are possible in our DDE model. On the contrary, the invariant measure supported on the pullback attractor in Figure 6.9 strongly suggests [cf. *Ghil*, 2015], that the ENSO model of *Galanti and Tziperman* [2000], among others, does give rise to chaotic behavior. These DDE models of ENSO, unlike that of *Ghil et al.* [2008b], do have both a positive, Bjerknes-type and a negative feedback, with two distinct delays, each of which acts upon one of the two feedbacks.

Hence, the topological structure of the pullback attractor, and the characteristics of the invariant measure it supports, can provide valuable clues to the nature of the dynamics, and its predictability [*Mukhin et al.*, 2014a, 2014b].

ACKNOWLEDGMENTS

We are grateful to our colleagues M. D. Chekroun, J. C. McWilliams, J. D. Neelin, and E. Simonnet for many useful discussions and their continuing interest in this work. In particular, M. D. Chekroun contributed the material for Section 6.4.1, which played a key role in our interpretation of Figures 6.8 and 6.9, as well as having produced the latter figure for *Ghil* [2015]. We thank Skip Thompson for his generous assistance and support in adapting the existing DDE integration software to our problem. This study was supported by NSF grants DMS-1049253 and OCE-1243175, and by ONR grant N00014-12-1-0911 from the Multidisciplinary University Research Initiative (MURI).

REFERENCES

Andronov, A. A. and L. S. Pontryagin (1937), Syst`emes grossiers, *Dokl. Akad. Nauk SSSR*, *14*(5), 247–250.

Battisti, D. S. (1988), The dynamics and thermodynamics of a warming event in a coupled tropical atmosphere/ocean model, *J. Atmos. Sci.*, *45*, 2889–2919.

Battisti, D. S. and A. C. Hirst (1989), Interannual variability in the tropical atmosphere-ocean system: Influence of the basic state and ocean geometry, *J. Atmos. Sci.*, *46*, 1687–1712.

Bhattacharya, K., M. Ghil, and I. Vulis (1982), Internal variability of an energy-balance model with delayed albedo effects, *J. Atmos. Sci.*, *39*, 1747–1773.

Bjerknes, J. (1969), Atmospheric teleconnections from the equatorial Pacific, *Mon. Weather Rev.*, *97*, 163–172.

Boulanger, J. P., C. Menkes, and M. Lengaigne (2004), Role of high- and low-frequency winds and wave reflection in the onset, growth and termination of the 1997-1998 El Niño, *Clim. Dyn.*, *22*(2–3), 267–280.

Bracco, A., J. D. Neelin, H. Luo, J. C. McWilliams, and J. E. Meyerson (2013), High-dimensional decision dilemmas in climate models, *Geosci. Model Dev. Discuss*, *6*, 2731–2767, doi:10.5194/gmdd-6-2731-2013.

Caraballo, T., P. Marin-Rubio, and J. Valero (2005), Autonomous and non-autonomous attractors for differential equations with delays, *J. Differ. Equ.*, *208*, 9–41.

Carvalho, A. N., J. A. Langa, and J. C. Robinson (2013), *Attractors for Infinite Dimensional Non-Autonomous Dynamical Systems*, Springer-Verlag, New York.

Chang, P., B. Wang, T. Li, and L. Ji (1994), Interactions between the seasonal cycle and the Southern Oscillation: Frequency entrainment and chaos in intermediate coupled ocean-atmosphere model, *Geophys. Res. Lett.*, *21*, 2817–2820.

Chang, P., L. Ji, B. Wang, and T. Li (1995), Interactions between the seasonal cycle and El Niño - Southern Oscillation in an intermediate coupled ocean-atmosphere model, *J. Atmos. Sci.*, *52*, 2353–2372.

Chekroun, M. D. and L. Roques (2006), Models of population dynamics under the influence of external perturbations: Mathematical results, *C. R. Acad. Sci. Paris, Ser. I*, *343*, 307–310.

Chekroun, M. D., E. Simonnet, and M. Ghil (2011), Stochastic climate dynamics: Random attractors and time-dependent invariant measures, *Phys. D*, *240*(21), 1685–1700.

Chekroun, J. D., D. Neelin, M. G. Kondrashov, and J. C. McWilliams (2014), Rough parameter dependence in climate models: The role of Ruelle-Pollicott resonances, *Proc. Natl. Acad. Sci. U. S. A.*, *111*(5), 1684–1690, doi:10.1073/pnas.1321816111.

Delcroix, T., G. Eldin, M. McPhaden, and A. Morli`ere (1993), Effects of westerly wind bursts upon the western equatorial Pacific Ocean, February-April 1991, *J. Geophys. Res.*, *98*(C9), 16379–16385.

Diaz, H. F. and V. Markgraf (Eds.) (1993), *El Niño: Historical and Paleoclimatic Aspects of the Southern Oscillation*, Cambridge University Press, New York.

Dijkstra, H. A. (2005), *Nonlinear Physical Oceanography: A Dynamical Systems Approach to the Large Scale Ocean Circulation and El Niño*, 2nd ed., Springer-Verlag, New York.

Dijkstra, H. A. (2013), *Nonlinear Climate Dynamics*, Cambridge University Press, New York.

Dugundji, J. (1966), *Topology*, Allyn and Bacon, Boston, MA.

Fuglestvedt, J. S., T. K. Berntsen, O. Godal, R. Sausen, K. P. Shine, and T. Skodvin (2003), Metrics of climate change: Assessing radioactive forcing and emission indices, *Clim. Change*, *58*, 267–331.

Galanti, E. and E. Tziperman (2000), ENSO's phase locking to the seasonal cycle in the fast-SST, fast-wave, and mixed-mode regimes, *J. Atmos. Sci.*, *57*, 2936–2950.

Gebbie, G., I. Eisenman, A. Wittenberg, and E. Tziperman (2007), Modulation of westerly wind bursts by sea surface temperature: A semistochastic feedback for ENSO, *J. Atmos. Sci.*, *64*, 3281–3295.

Ghil, M. and N. Jiang (1998), Recent forecast skill for the El Niño/Southern Oscillation, *Geophys. Res. Lett.*, *25*, 171–174.

Ghil, M. and A. W. Robertson (2000), Solving problems with GCMs: General circulation models and their role in the climate modeling hierarchy, in *General Circulation Model Development: Past, Present and Future*, edited by D. Randall, pp. 285–325, Academic Press, San Diego, CA.

Ghil, M., M. R. Allen, M. D. Dettinger, K. Ide, D. Kondrashov, M. E. Mann, A. W. Robertson, A. Saunders, Y. Tian, F. Varadi, and P. Yiou (2002), Advanced spectral methods for climatic time series, *Rev. Geophys.*, *40*(1 Art. No. 1003).

Ghil, M., M. D. Chekroun, and E. Simonnet (2008a), Climate dynamics and fluid mechanics: Natural variability and related uncertainties, *Phys. D*, *237*, 2111–2126, doi:10.1016/j.physd.2008.03.036.

Ghil, M., I. Zaliapin, and S. Thompson (2008b), A delay differential model of ENSO variability: Parametric instability and the distribution of extremes, *Nonlinear Process. Geophys.*, *15*, 417–433.

Ghil, M. and I. Zaliapin (2013), El-Niño/Southern Oscillation: Impacts, modeling, and forecasts, in *Encyclopedia of Natural Hazards*, edited by P. Bobrowski, pp. 250–262, Springer-Verlag, New York.

Ghil, M. (2015), A Mathematical theory of climate sensitivity or, How to deal with both anthropogenic forcing and natural variability?, in *Climate Change: Multidecadal and Beyond*, edited by C. P. Chang et al., pp. 31–51, World Scientific Publ. Co./Imperial College Press.

Glantz, M. H., R. W. Katz, and N. Nicholls (Eds.) (1991), *Teleconnections Linking World-wide Climate Anomalies*, pp. 545, Cambridge University Press, New York.

Hale, J. (1977), *Theory of Functional Differential Equations*, Springer-Verlag, New York.

Hale, J. (1988), *Asymptotic Behaviour of Dissipative Systems*, American Mathematical Society, Providence, RI.

Harrison, D. E. and B. Giese (1988), Remote westerly wind forcing of the eastern equatorial Pacific; some model results, *Geophys. Res. Lett.*, *15*, 804–807.

Hartman, P. (2008), *Ordinary Differential Equations (Classics in Applied Mathematics)*, 2nd ed., pp. 612, Society for Industrial and Applied Mathematics, Philadelphia, PA.

Held, I. M. (2005), The gap between simulation and understanding in climate modeling, *Bull. Am. Meteorol. Soc.*, *86*, 1609–1614.

Jiang, N., J. D. Neelin, and M. Ghil (1995), Quasi-quadrennial and quasi-biennial variability in the equatorial Pacific, *Clim. Dyn.*, *12*, 101–112.

Jin, F.-f., J. D. Neelin, and M. Ghil (1994), El Niño on the Devil's Staircase: Annual subharmonic steps to chaos, *Science*, *264*, 70–72.

Jin, F.-F., J. D. Neelin, and M. Ghil (1996), El Niño/Southern Oscillation and the annual cycle: Subharmonic frequency locking and aperiodicity, *Phys. D*, *98*, 442–465.

Kondrashov, D., S. Kravtsov, A. W. Robertson, and M. Ghil (2005), A hierarchy of data-based ENSO models, *J. Climate*, *18*, 4425–4444.

Krisztin, T. (2008), Global dynamics of delay differential equations, *Period. Math. Hung.*, *56*, 83–95.

Latif, M., T. P. Barnett, M. Flügel, N. E. Graham, J.-S. Xu, and S. E. Zebiak (1994), A review of ENSO prediction studies, *Clim. Dyn.*, *9*, 167–179.

Lengaigne, M., E. Guilyardi, J. P. Boulanger, C. Menkes, P. Delecluse, P. Inness, J. Cole, and J. Slingo (2004), Triggering of El Niño by westerly wind events in a coupled general circulation model, *Clim. Dyn.*, *23*(6), 601–620.

Madden, R. A., and P. R. Julian (1971), Description of a 40–50 day oscillation in the zonal wind in the tropical Pacific, *J. Atmos. Sci.*, *28*, 702–708.

Madden, R. A. and P. R. Julian (1972), Description of global-scale circulation cells in the tropics with a 40–50 day period, *J. Atmos. Sci.*, *29*, 1109–1123.

Madden, R. A. and P. R. Julian (1994), Observations of the 40–50-day tropical oscillation—A review, *Mon. Weather Rev.*, *122*(5), 814–837.

Mallet-Paret, J. and G. Sell (1996), The Poincaré-Bendixson theorem for monotone cyclic feedback systems with delay, *J. Differ. Equ.*, *125*, 441–489.

McWilliams, J. C. (2007), Irreducible imprecision in atmospheric and oceanic simulations, *Proc. Natl. Acad. Sci. U. S. A.*, *104*, 8709–8713.

Moron, V., A. W. Robertson, J.-H. Qian, and M. Ghil (2015), Weather types across the Maritime Continent: From the diurnal cycle to interannual variations, *Front. Environ. Sci.*, *2–65*, 19, doi:10.3389/fenvs.2014.00065.

Mukhin, D., E. Loskutov, A. Mukhina, A. Feigin, I. Zaliapin, and M. Ghil (2014a), Predicting critical transitions in ENSO models, Part I: Methodology and simple models with memory, *J. Climate*, doi:10.1175/JCLI-D-14-00239.1.

Mukhin, D., D. Kondrashov, E. Loskutov, A. Gavrilov, A. Feigin, and M. Ghil (2014b), Predicting critical transitions in ENSO models, Part II: Spatially dependent models, *J. Climate*, doi:10.1175/JCLI-D-14-00240.1.

Munnich, M., M. Cane, and S. E. Zebiak (1991), A study of self-excited oscillations of the tropical ocean-atmosphere system. Part II: Nonlinear cases, *J. Atmos. Sci.*, *48*(10), 1238–1248.

Neelin, J. D., D. S. Battisti, A. C. Hirst, F.-F. Jin, Y. Wakata, T. Yamagata, and S. E. Zebiak (1998), ENSO theory, *J. Geophys. Res. Oceans*, *103*(C7), 14261–14290.

Neelin, J. D., F. F. Jin, and H. H. Syu (2000), Variations in ENSO phase locking, *J. Climate*, *13*, 2570–2590.

Neelin, J. D., A. Bracco, H. Luo, J. C. McWilliams, and J. E. Meyerson (2010), Considerations for parameter optimization and sensitivity in climate models, *Proc. Natl. Acad. Sci. U. S. A.*, *107*(50), 21349–21354.

Nussbaum, R. D. (1998), Functional differential equations, http://citeseer.ist.psu.edu/437755.html (accessed 28 August 2015).

Philander, S. G. H. (1990), *El Niño, La Niña, and the Southern Oscillation*, Academic Press, San Diego, CA.

Roques, L., M. D. Chekroun, M. Cristofol, S. Soubeyrand, and M. Ghil (2013), Parameter estimation for energy balance models with memory, *Proc. R. Soc. A*, *470*, 20140349.

Saynisch, J., J. Kurths, and D. Maraun (2006), A conceptual ENSO model under realistic noise forcing, *Nonlinear Process. Geophys.*, *13*(3), 275–285.

Sell, G. and Y. You (2002), *Dynamics of Evolutionary Equations*, Springer-Verlag, New York.

Shampine, L. F. and S. Thompson (2006), A friendly Fortran 90 DDE solver, *Appl. Numer. Math.*, *56*(2–3), 503–516.

Spaulding, N. and S. Namowitz (2004), *Earth Science*, McDougal Littell, Evanston, IL.

Suarez, M. J. and P. S. Schopf (1988), A delayed action oscillator for ENSO, *J. Atmos. Sci.*, *45*, 3283–3287.

Taylor, K. E. (2001), Summarizing multiple aspects of model performance in a single diagram, *J. Geophys. Res.*, *106*, 7183–7192.

Tziperman, E., L. Stone, M. Cane, and H. Jarosh (1994), El Niño chaos: Overlapping of resonances between the seasonal cycle and the Pacific ocean-atmosphere oscillator, *Science*, *264*, 72–74.

Tziperman, E., M. A. Cane, and S. E. Zebiak (1995), Irregularity and locking to the seasonal cycle in an ENSO prediction model as explained by the quasi-periodicity route to chaos, *J. Atmos. Sci.*, *50*, 293–306.

Verbickas, S. (1998), Westerly wind bursts in the tropical Pacific, *Weather*, *53*, 282–284.

Zaliapin, I. and M. Ghil (2010), A delay differential model of ENSO variability, Part 2: Phase locking, multiple solutions and dynamics of extrema, *Nonlinear Process. Geophys.*, *17*, 123–135.

Zebiak, S. and M. A. Cane (1987), A model El-Niño Southern Oscillation, *Mon. Weather Rev.*, *115*, 2262–2278.

Part II
Extreme Events in Earth's Space Environment

7

Drivers of Extreme Space Weather Events: Fast Coronal Mass Ejections

Alexander Ruzmaikin,[1] Joan Feynman,[1] and Stilian Stoev[2]

ABSTRACT

An extreme Space Weather event is a disturbance in the space environment that presents hazards to the operation of spacecraft systems, instruments, or lives of astronauts. Space Weather events are driven by plasma ejections emitted from the solar corona. Many coronal mass ejections (CMEs) of varying speed are emitted, but only the high speed (fast) CMEs can cause hazardous (extreme) Space Weather events. Empirical studies have shown that the speed distribution of CMEs is non-Gaussian. Recent advances in statistical methods of analysis have made it possible to find the form of high-speed tail using approaches based on the properties of the data rather than curve-fitting skill. We apply the statistical method based on scaling properties of speed maxima, which is called the Max-Spectrum [*Stoev et al.*, 2011]. This approach allows the identification of the range of speeds that separates extreme CMEs from typical events, by identifying a power-law high-speed part of the spectrum from about 700 to 2000 km/s. This self-similar range of the speed distribution provides a meaningful definition of "fast" CMEs and indicates that these events are produced by a scale-invariant process. The investigation of the temporal behavior of fast CMEs indicates that they are not independent but arrive in clusters, and thus can be described by a generalized Poisson process. We characterize the fast CMEs clustering by the exponent called the extremal index. An independent correlation analysis of the extremes confirms and quantifies further the temporal dependence among the fast CME events.

7.1. INTRODUCTION

The term "Space Weather" refers to severe disturbances of the Earth's upper atmosphere and of the near-Earth space environment that are driven by solar activity [*Severe Space Weather Events*, 2008]. Space Weather events are seen in the beautiful natural extreme events: the auroras. Whether you see the aurora as moving white and green bands or a diffuse red light depends on your position on Earth. Within 20° of latitude of the equator, the sky during an aurora is red and seeing it would be a once in a lifetime experience. If you are near the magnetic poles of the Earth, the light is most likely to be green (Figure 7.1), and can be seen during most dark nights. If you are at mid-latitudes you may see the phenomena once or twice a year, and the moving light would be either whitish or greenish or a vivid red. Documentation of auroras in Europe and the Orient cover the time interval as far back as the 7th century BC [*Siscoe*, 1980]. These observations have been gathered in catalogs that have been used in scientific research on solar variability and its influence on Earth's climate.

Strong auroral currents can be hazardous when electric currents are induced on the Earth's surface. These currents

[1]*Jet Propulsion Laboratory, California Institute of Technology, Pasadena, CA, USA*
[2]*Department of Statistics, University of Michigan, Ann Arbor, MI, USA*

Extreme Events: Observations, Modeling, and Economics, Geophysical Monograph 214, First Edition.
Edited by Mario Chavez, Michael Ghil, and Jaime Urrutia-Fucugauchi.
© 2016 American Geophysical Union. Published 2016 by John Wiley & Sons, Inc.

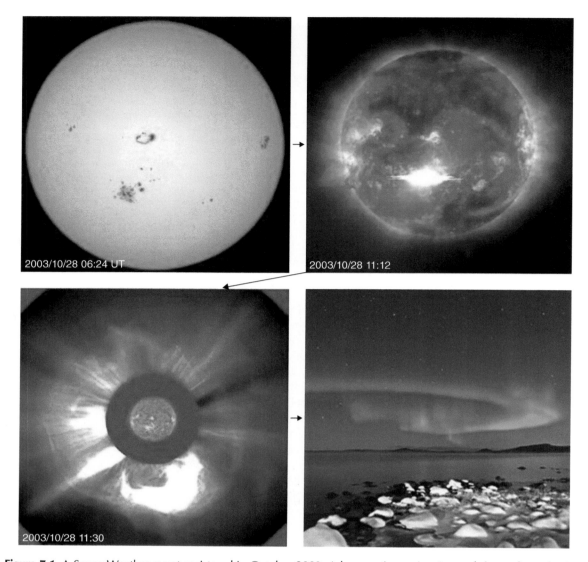

Figure 7.1 A Space Weather event registered in October 2003. A large active region (upper left panel) on the Sun erupted with a bright flare (upper right panel) followed within minutes by the coronal mass ejection (lower left panel), see http://sohowww.nascom.nasa.gov/hotshots/. Such events are usually accompanied by auroras. In the lower right corner, we show the aurora photographed by an aurora hunter (Andy Keen, http://www.aurorahunters.com).

can damage electric power grids as they did during the great geomagnetic storm of March 1989, when the collapse of northeastern Canadian Hydro-Quebec power grid left millions of people without electricity for up to 9 hours. Such currents also contribute to the corrosion of oil and gas pipelines. Space Weather-driven ionospheric density disturbances interfere with high-frequency radio communications along airplane routes, requiring aircraft to be diverted to lower latitudes, and affecting navigation signals from Global Positioning System (GPS) satellites [*Severe Space Weather Events*, 2008]. Bursts of energetic particles and radiation belt enhancements during strong Space Weather events can cause operational anomalies and damage electronics on spacecraft [*Feynman and*

Gabriel, 2000]. A key goal for Space Weather studies is to define severe and extreme conditions that might plausibly afflict human technology [*Baker et al.*, 2013]. Extreme Space Weather events are difficult to study, their rates of occurrence are difficult to estimate, and prediction of a specific future event is virtually impossible *Riley* [2012].

Severe Space Weather events are initiated by disturbances due to the sudden release of large amounts ($> 10^{16}$ g) of solar plasma into the solar wind from the solar corona. A dominant role in the formation of these events called coronal mass ejections (CMEs) is played by the magnetic field, which is generated by dynamo activity in the solar interior and permeates into the corona. A part of this field erupts as a result of an instability or loss-of-equilibrium process. Once a CME is underway, a whole host of additional processes are triggered including magnetic reconnection, shock formation, and particle acceleration [*Forbes et al.*, 2006; *Amari et al.*, 2011]. CMEs propagate from the Sun through the interplanetary space, some of them toward the Earth. They vary widely in their speeds. When viewed near the Sun, some are rather slow (< 200 km/s) and others have very high speeds exceeding 2500 km/s [*Kahler*, 1987]. The causes of these enormous differences in speeds have not been identified as yet, but the differences in speed are likely presaged by differences in the build-up phases of the CMEs [*Feynman*, 1997]. Among all CMEs, the most interesting in the context of Space Weather extremes are the high-speed CMEs. These fast CMEs and the shocks they generate in the solar wind are directly responsible for solar energetic particle (SEP) events [*Reames*, 1999; *Li et al.*, 2005]. The interaction of sufficiently strong southward magnetic field within fast CME (or induced by the compression of the solar wind behind the shock associated with the CME) with the Earth's magnetic field causes major geomagnetic storms [*Hirshberg and Colburn*, 1969; *Tsurutani and Gonzalez*, 1997; *Gopalswamy*, 2008]. Since the interaction is determined by the induced electric field (a product of speed and magnetic field), almost all fast (high-speed) CMEs are expected to be geoeffective.

CMEs are associated with active (sunspot) regions, which appear on the surface of the Sun. The frequency of occurrence of active regions is regulated by the solar cycle. Observations have shown that active regions have a tendency to cluster, that is, new active regions preferably emerge in the vicinity of old ones [*Gaizauskas et al.*, 1983; *Harvey and Zwaan*, 1993]. The clusters may live for as many as six solar rotations, and there are indications that the fastest CMEs originate mainly from them [*Ruzmaikin and Feynman*, 1998].

Historically, the cause of auroras was not known until 1869 when Richard Carrington observed a rare huge white light flare in a large group of sunspots on the Sun followed by an aurora the next night seen in New York, Havana, and Santiago, Chile. Carrington suggested that the aurora was somehow caused by the solar flare. It is now established that major solar flares are closely associated with fast CMEs that directly cause the aurora and hazardous Space Weather (Figure 7.1). For example, a cluster of activity near the active region AR 8210 observed in April–May 1998 produced six CMEs with speeds >1000 km/s [*Thompson et al.*, 2000]. During the famous Halloween period, October–November 2003, most of the 80 observed CMEs originated from a cluster of active regions [*Feynman and Ruzmaikin*, 2004; *Gopalswamy et al.*, 2005]. Over 30 of these CMEs had speeds between 1000 and 2000 km/s, and 7 had speeds exceeding 2000 km/s. They resulted in intense geomagnetic storms and large SEP events.

The plane of the sky CME speed propagation through the solar corona was measured by coronagraph carried on spacecraft. Here, we analyze the CMEs measured by the Large Angle and Spectrometric Coronagraph Experiment on board the Solar and Heliospheric Observatory (LASCO SOHO) and collected in the catalog developed in co-operation with the Naval Research Laboratory and the Solar Data Analysis Center at the Goddard Space Flight Center and at the Center for Solar Physics and Space Weather at the Catholic University of America [*Gopalswamy et al.*, 2009]. The entries begin in January 1996. Studies based on the dual spacecraft STEREO mission observations show that actual 3D speeds are well correlated with the speeds determined by LASCO [*Thernisien et al.*, 2009]. This justifies statistical analyses of the 2D LASCO catalog speeds.

Here, we discuss the scaling behavior of extreme (fast) CMEs [*Ruzmaikin et al.*, 2011] to find the tail of the probability distribution of CME speed and analyze the arrival times of the fast CMEs. Section 7.2 describes the data used for our statistical analysis. Section 7.3 introduces the method used to quantify the form of the high-speed tail and clustering of these extremes events. In Section 7.4, we investigate the distribution of times between occurrence of fast (extreme) CMEs, and introduce the quantities that characterize the clustering of extremes. In Section 7.5, we apply the techniques described in Sections 7.3 and 7.4 to characterize the distribution of speeds and clustering of observed fast CMEs. Section 7.6 summarizes the results and briefly discusses their possible implications for causes and consequences of fast CMEs.

7.2. A QUICK LOOK AT EXTREMES IN THE CME DATA

It is useful to infer some information about the extremes by looking directly at the data. The partial distribution function of the observed CME speeds listed in the LASCO catalog for the time period 1996–2009 is shown in Figure 7.2. The distribution function clearly has a non-Gaussian form, as first emphasized by *Yurchyshyn et al.* [2005], with the peak at 263 km/s and an extended high-speed tail. The mean speed is 472 km/s; about 18% (1746) of the CMEs have speeds exceeding 700 km/s, 6% (about 600 CMEs) have speeds exceeding 1000 km/s, and <0.5% CMEs have speeds exceeding 2000 km/s. But to separate extreme CMEs from the rest of the events with only this information would require an arbitrary choice of threshold for defining the high-speed tail of the distribution function.

It is also useful to look at the distribution of the observed time intervals between the CMEs with speeds exceeding a selected threshold. In Figure 7.3, we plot the distribution of the observed time intervals between events

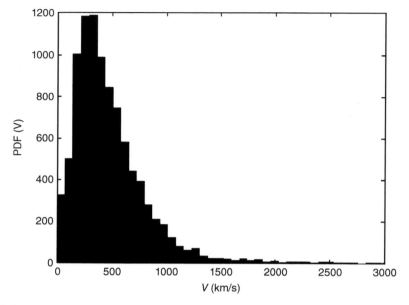

Figure 7.2 Partial distribution function (PDF) of the CME speeds from the LASCO catalog.

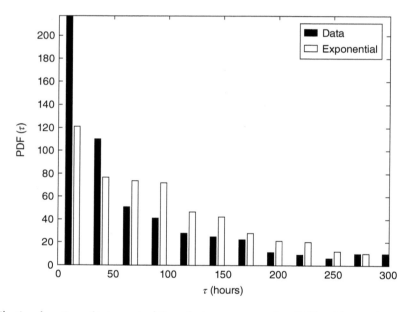

Figure 7.3 Distribution function of inter-arrival times between successive CMEs with speeds exceeding 1000 km/s (black) versus distribution function of inter-arrival times for a randomized data (white). The sample, with which the distributions are built, consists of 586 events. The exponential distribution has been generated by the operator log (1/r and (1,n)), where r and (1,n), are random numbers of length n of time intervals series, and are normalized using the mean value of the data time intervals. Both distributions have the same standard deviation, which is also a mean value for the randomized distribution. The peak near zero for the real CME data indicates the dominance of small inter-arrival times compared to the times from the random distribution (i.e., clustering of extremes).

for CMEs with speeds >1000 km/s. If these high-speed CMEs occurred independently of one another, one would expect this distribution to be exponential, which the figure clearly shows is not the case. There are about twice as many time intervals of duration less than about a day than would be expected for independent events. This means that many high-speed CMEs essentially arrive in clusters.

The problem is how to proceed with the analysis of extremes in a quantitative, mathematically justified manner. To avoid the obvious nonstationarity due to the solar cycle dependence, we limit the dataset to the high activity part of solar cycle 23 (January 1999 to December 2006, resulting in 9408 CMEs). The speed we use is given in the catalog as obtained by the second-order polynomial fit to the time-height measurements during the CME propagation through the solar corona. Note that even though we study the properties of extreme (fast) CMEs, the dataset input to the method includes all CMEs without preselection of those with high speeds. In particular, we will find the speed at which the tail of the distribution function begins without pre-identifying it.

7.3. MORE SOPHISTICATED APPROACHES TO STUDY EXTREMES

The main and widely used approach, which was pioneered by Leonard Tippett (1902–1985) during his work for the British Cotton Industry, is based on the fundamental theorem in extreme value theory [*Fisher and Tippett*, 1928; *Gnedenko*, 1943], which states that the distribution of a sample of maxima of independent random variables x converges to one of three forms: the Gumbel, Weibull, or Fréchet distribution. The three distributions can be combined into the generalized extreme value distribution:

$$G(x) = \exp\left\{-\left(1 + \gamma(x - \mu)/\sigma\right)^{-1/\gamma}\right\}, \quad 1 + \gamma(x - \mu)/\sigma > 0,$$

where $\sigma > 0$ is the scale, μ is the location, and γ is the shape parameter of the distribution. If $\gamma \to 0$, we obtain the Gumbel cumulative distribution: $\exp\{-e^{-(x-\mu)/\sigma}\}$. If $\gamma < 0$, then the right-side tail is bounded and G becomes the reversed Weibull law. Finally, when $\gamma > 0$ the right-side tail decays like a power law and G is called the Fréchet distribution.

The user of this approach tries to fit a data sample to one of these distributions. The quality of the fit is difficult to evaluate because of the scarcity of extreme events and a lack of precise mathematical technique to do the fitting. The curve fitting usually does not use specific data properties, it depends on the selected fraction of data, adjustable parameters, and the skill of the researcher. A modification of this approach is called "tail fitting." It refers only to the high-tail distribution of the random variable, with its full distribution remaining unknown, thus allowing the use of only the data above the selected threshold. The weakest point of this type of data analysis is the arbitrary selection of the threshold.

Here, we apply a different approach to determine a tail of the distribution. It employs the entire range of data to effectively estimate a threshold without any additional assumptions. The approach, called the Max-Spectrum

[*Stoev et al.*, 2011], is based on the use of scaling properties of the data maxima and does not involve a fit to an empirically determined distribution function. Its application produces two exponents: one defines the high-speed tail of the distribution function (i.e., the distribution of extreme CMEs) and the other characterizes the clustering of extremes in time. We briefly describe the application of Max-Spectrum method later to the CME speeds [*Ruzmaikin et al.*, 2011], referring the reader to the works by *Stoev et al.* [2011] and *Hamidieh et al.* [2009] for technical details and mathematical proofs. The method is based on investigating the data maxima in progressively expanding time scales. It employs the scaling of the data maxima observed at different time scales. The scaling approach, which was originally used in turbulence studies (recall the Kolmogorov's law for velocity increments) and now in many other applications, allows a natural extension of scaling when new data become available. It also allows an interpolation of the behavior of the variable beyond the limits of a given dataset if there is no indication of any preferred value that could break the scaling.

Consider the time series $X(i)$ of length N (in our case, it will be the CME speeds, $X(i) = V(i)$), where $1 < i < N$. For each time scale index j ($j = 1, 2, 3, \ldots, [\log_2 N]$), we form non-overlapping time blocks of length 2^j, that is, we progressively double the time scale. At each fixed scale, we calculate the maximum of the speed within each block:

$$D(j, k) = \max_{1 \leq i \leq 2^j} X\left(2^j(k-1) + i\right), \quad k = 1, 2, \ldots, b_j,$$

where $b_j = [N/2^j]$ is the number of blocks (of length 2^j) and i indexes the data points within the kth block on the time axis. The log-block-size plays the role of a time-scale parameter. Observe that the blocks of scale j are naturally nested in the blocks of scale $(j+1)$. Now, we average the logs of the block-maxima $D(j, k)$ over all blocks at the fixed scale j:

$$Y(j) = \frac{1}{b_j} \sum_{k=1}^{b_j} \log_2 D(j, k).$$

The function $Y(j)$, that is, a set of $[\log_2 N]$ numbers, is called the "Max-Spectrum" of the data. An important result, established by *Stoev et al.* [2011] is that if for a sufficiently large j

$$Y(j) \simeq j/\alpha + C, \tag{7.1}$$

where C is a constant and $\alpha > 0$, the tail of the data distribution follows a power law with exponent α. If the tail is not a power law, say exponential, Gaussian, or lognormal, the Max-Spectrum levels off at large scales.

Stoev et al. [2011] proved that the exponent α is the same for both independent and dependent data, provided that the time series are stationary and have the same distribution function. The dependence (related to the clustering of the times of extreme events) affects only the intercept in Equation 7.1. That is, if we have dependent data with the same distribution function, then with the same constant C, Equation 7.1 becomes:

$$Y(j) \simeq j/\alpha + C + \log_2(\theta)/\alpha, \qquad (7.2)$$

where the quantity $\theta(0 < \theta \leq 1)$ is called the extremal index.

The extremal index is widely used in statistical studies to characterize the temporal clustering of the extreme events [*Leadbetter et al.*, 1983]. It allows the distribution function of maxima of n *dependent* events to be presented as a distribution function of the maxima of roughly $n\theta$ *independent* events, that is, to group the n dependent events into $n\theta$ independent clusters. It allows a generalization of the fundamental Fisher-Tippett-Gnedenko theorem to the case of dependent (correlated) random events. Consider a stationary data time series X_t and let $M_n = \max_{1 \leq t \leq n} X_t$ be the maximum of n consecutive data points. The time series X_t has an extremal index θ, if for large n the probability

$$\mathcal{P}\left(\frac{M_n - d_n}{c_n} \leq x\right) = G^{\theta}(x), \text{ while } \mathcal{P}\left(\frac{M_n^* - d_n}{c_n} \leq x\right) = G(x),$$

where M_n^* is the maximum of n *independent* random variables X_t^* drawn from the same probability distribution as the original time series $X_t, c_n > 0$ and d_n are normalizing constants, and $G(x)$ is the cumulative extreme value distribution function introduced in the beginning of this section. The constants $c_n > 0$, d_n depend on the distribution function of the data. For example, if X_ts are distributed as a power law with exponent $\alpha > 0$, then $c_n = n^{1/\alpha}$ and $d_n = 0$. It is important that the constants $c_n > 0$, d_n are the same whether X_ts are *dependent* or *independent*.

Note that the extremal index refers only to the temporal dependence between *extreme* events, and not between all events. The smaller the index, the stronger the extreme events interdependence that is exhibited by clustering of time intervals between events. In the limiting case $\theta = 1$ (independent events), consider the onset times t_i of events exceeding a specified threshold U, which may be chosen as say 90-th or 95-th percentile of the CME speed distribution in our case, or from physical considerations. Then the distribution of times between two consecutive events $\tau_i = t_i - t_{i-1}, i = 1, 2, \ldots$ is simply $\mathcal{P}(\tau = k) = (1 - p)^{k-1} p$, where $k = 1, 2, 3, \ldots$, marks the time steps and $p = p(U)$ denotes

the probability of occurrence of one event in a unit of time. For large thresholds, p is small and this distribution is essentially exponential with the expectation value $1/p = 1/P(X_t > U)$. For a more detailed asymptotic treatment of the point process of exceedances, see *Hsing et al.* [1988].

Equations 7.1 and 7.2 suggest a method of estimating both α and θ [*Hamidieh et al.*, 2009; *Stoev et al.*, 2011]. The inverse exponent $1/\alpha$ is obtained as a slope of the line fitted to the Max-Spectrum of the data. The best linear fit outlines the self-similar part of the Max-Spectrum. We must take into account that in practice the larger the scale j, the fewer the block maxima $D(j, k)$ (indexed by k) and the greater the variability of the Max-Spectrum statistic $Y(j)$. The best way to deal with this problem is applying, as we do here, the method of generalized least squares, which accounts for the bias-variance trade-off [*Stoev et al.*, 2011].

Taking into account Equations 7.1 and 7.2, we can obtain estimates of the extremal index. By permuting the data with a substitute of data points (bootstrap) or by simply randomly permuting the original data time series, we obtain a time series V_i^*, $1 < i < N$, which has the same distribution function as the original dataset but the dependence (i.e., correlations between data points) has been destroyed. Carrying this out, we create a large set of pseudo-time series in which the original data dependence is destroyed and the events may be viewed as nearly independent of time. For each such time series, we compute a Max-Spectrum, $Y^*(j)$, $1 \leq j \leq [\log_2 N]$ that satisfies Equation 7.1. The Max-Spectrum of the original data $Y(j)$ satisfies Equation 7.2 with the same constant C, thus the difference between the two spectra yields an estimate of θ:

$$\hat{\theta}(j) = 2^{-\hat{\alpha}(Y^*(j) - Y(j))}, \qquad (7.3)$$

where $\hat{a}$ stands for an estimate of the tail exponent α, obtained from the slope of the Max-Spectrum. Since we have a large sample of pseudo-independent time series, we obtain many realizations of $\hat{\theta}(j)$ at each scale j. The median or the mean of these estimates can be taken as a point-estimator of θ at the scale j. The whole sample of estimates can be used to quantify the estimation error at each scale.

7.4. ON THE TIME BETWEEN OCCURRENCES OF EXTREMES

As shown in Section 7.2, the time intervals between the fast CMEs do not follow the standard exponential law for independent events but are correlated, thus indicating that extreme events occur in clusters. The standard tools of time series analyses, such as the autocorrelation function of a process under consideration, cannot provide information about clustering of extremes. Two basic ideas have been introduced to tackle the problem: the generalized Poisson process [*Hsing et al.*, 1988] and an asymptotic covariance function called "extremogram" [*Davis and Mikosch*, 2009].

The mean time interval between events within a cluster depends on the threshold defining extremes. It is known [*Hsing et al.*, 1988] that if one focuses on asymptotically larger thresholds, the time intervals τ_i between the extremes will converge (under time-rescaling) to a generalized (cluster) Poisson process, which is similar to a standard Poisson process, but with several (random number) events arriving clustered in time. The generalized Poisson process can be distinguished from the standard Poisson process by the extremal index $0 < \theta < 1$, the reciprocal of which is interpreted as the expected cluster size [*Leadbetter et al.*, 1983].

To obtain more detailed information about the clusters, we applied the statistical methodology called "de-clustering." The methodology employs a "de-clustering threshold time" τ_c defined by the extremal index [*Ferro and Segers*, 2003]. If the time interval between two extreme events is less than τ_c, then these events can be grouped into a cluster, that is, τ_c separates the intra-cluster time intervals from inter-cluster time intervals. To estimate the "de-clustering threshold time" we consider the sorted collection of all times between consecutive extreme events:

$$\tau_1 \geq \tau_2 \geq \cdots \geq \tau_{n-1} \qquad (7.4)$$

and take $\tau_c = \tau_{\theta \times n}$ as the $\theta \times n$ the largest among them [*Ferro and Segers*, 2003]. This choice of the de-clustering time is justified by the fact that the extremal index allows us to estimate the number of clusters. Indeed, if our time series consists of n extreme events (i.e., n fast CMEs with speeds exceeding a threshold U), they are on average grouped into $\theta \times n$ clusters. Now we consider the time intervals τ_i between extreme events as they occur in real-time sequence $i = 1, 2, 3, \ldots$. If m subsequent time intervals have $\tau_i < \tau_c$, the associated extreme events constitute a cluster of size m. If a time τ_k exceeds τ_c, the extreme events occurring at time step k and $k + 1$ belong to different clusters, which in particular can be size-one clusters, that is, single extreme events.

Note that de-clustering threshold time can be estimated in different ways. For example, one can use the observed distribution of time intervals between extremes in comparison with the exponential (see Figure 7.3) or the minimum time scale of the Max-Spectrum.

Another method of de-clustering, the extremogram generalizes the concept of the tail-dependence coefficient

$$\Lambda(\tau) = \lim_{x \to \infty} P(X(t) > x \mid X(t+\tau > x)), \qquad (7.5)$$

which describes a correlation between a pair of extreme data points shifted by a lag (τ). The collection of values of Λ contains information about the serial dependence between extremes in the time series X. The following limit is called the extremogram [*Davis and Mikosch*, 2009]

$$\rho_{AB}(\tau) = \lim_{n \to \infty} \frac{P\left(a_n^{-1} X(t) \in A, a_n^{-1} X(t+\tau) \in B\right)}{P\left(a_n^{-1} X(t) > A\right)}, \qquad (7.6)$$

where A, B are selected sets and a_n^{-1} is a sequence of increasing numbers so that $P(\mid X \mid > a_n) \propto n^{-1}$. If we choose $A = B = (1, \infty)$, the extremogram $\rho_{AB}(\tau)$ simply becomes the probability λ_k of observing another extreme event k time lags after an extreme event has already been observed, that is

$$\lambda_k = P(X_k > U \mid X_0 > U), \quad k = 1, 2, \ldots \qquad (7.7)$$

for a threshold U. If X_ks were time independent, this conditional probability would equal the unconditional probability $P(X_k > U)$. Therefore, X_ks are statistically dependent on time if λ_k is significantly different from $P(X_k > U)$. The parameter λ_k can be estimated with the following empirical statistics:

$$\hat{\lambda}_k = \left(\frac{\sum_{j=1}^{n-k} I\left(X_{j+k} > U, X_j > U\right)}{n-k}\right) \Big/ \left(\frac{\sum_{j=1}^{n} I\left(X_j > U\right)}{n}\right), \qquad (7.8)$$

where $I(A)$ equals 1 if the event A occurs and 0 otherwise.

7.5. THE DISTRIBUTION AND THE CLUSTERING OF FAST CMES

The CMEs in the LASCO catalog are listed according to the time of their first appearance above the C2 occulting disk, and hence are spaced unevenly in time. Since our method of data analysis requires evenly spaced records, we formed an hourly spaced time frame and assigned each CME to the hour of its first occurrence. Almost all CMEs are used, with no averaging or binning. The hours with no CMEs are assigned a zero speed. In a few cases when there is more than one CME in the same hour, we use the CME with the highest speed, which is well justified by our method based on the investigation of speed maxima. To avoid the obvious large nonstationarity due to solar cycle dependence, we limit the dataset to the high activity part of solar cycle 23 (from January 1999 to December 2006) resulting in 9408 CMEs. The speed used is given in the catalog, as obtained by the second-order polynomial fit to the time-height measurements during

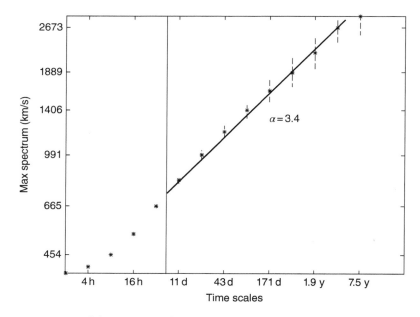

Figure 7.4 The Max-Spectrum of the CME speeds at progressively increasing time scales. The error bars are estimated using the generalized regression [*Stoev et al.*, 2011] and correspond to 95% confidence intervals. We converted the $\log_2$ units for $Y(j)$ into km/s and the scales j into time units 2^j. The vertical line segment at 16 hours ($j = 4$) indicates the starting scale selected for the evaluation of α. The speed (670 km/s) on this scale may be interpreted as the beginning of the distribution function tail, which defines the fast CMEs, and is shown on the right side of the vertical line.

the CME propagation through the solar corona. Note that even though we study properties of extreme (fast) CMEs, the data input to the method includes all CMEs without preselection of those with high speeds. In particular, the speed at which the tail of the distribution function begins is not preselected but estimated from the onset of the power tail.

Using the Max-Spectrum method described earlier, we calculated the values of the exponent α and of the extremal index θ for the CME speeds [*Ruzmaikin et al.*, 2011]. The resulting Max-Spectrum of the CME speeds is shown in Figure 7.4. Our best fit to the slope gives evidence that the cumulative distribution function of the CME speeds has a Fréchet type power-law tail, with the exponent $\alpha = 3.4$. The lower boundary of the linear portion of the Max-Spectrum identifies the onset of the power-law tail, that is, the corresponding speed threshold, and the self-similar range. This gives a meaningful definition of "the fast" CMEs. Specifically, we find that the Max-Spectrum above about 700 km/s is self-similar and the associated time scale is close to the de-cluster threshold time found by using the Ferro-Segers method. Bearing in mind the analogy with the standard, self-similar cascade process in turbulence, which is fully defined by a Kolmogorov-type spectral index, we conjecture that the physical process leading to the fast CMEs production is the same from about 700 km/s to the highest velocities in the dataset.

Figure 7.5 shows the extremal index estimated by the Max-Spectrum method. It does not work well for small speed thresholds. The deviations arise because the maxima taken in blocks of data in the Max-Spectrum method include both extreme ($\geq U$ km/s) and nonextreme ($< U$ km/s) speeds. Hence, the blocks of small sizes (small scales) are dominated by more numerous maxima having small speeds. The Max-Spectrum performs well when the size of blocks is larger, that is, at sufficiently large scales. It has the advantage of providing "confidence intervals" as illustrated with the histogram on the lower panel in Figure 7.5 plotted for the thresholds 1000–2300 km/s. The resulting empirical 95% confidence interval for θ is from 0.33 to 0.60 with a mid-point $\theta = 0.49 - 0.5$. The rapidly growing statistical error for the "most extreme" CMEs suggests that neither of the two methods should be used for speeds above 2300 km/s due to insufficient number of available data points. The θ in the range 0.3–0.6 with the mean 0.5 can be taken as an estimate of the extremal index. The inverse value of the index gives an estimate of an average cluster size 2–3, that is, *on average* an appearance of a fast CME will be followed by one or two other fast CMEs. These estimates can be further justified by the asymptotic statistical theory of *Hsing et al.* [1988].

Figure 7.6 shows the estimate of the tail-dependence parameter λ_k as a function of the lag k for the CME dataset with the threshold speed U corresponding to the 95-th

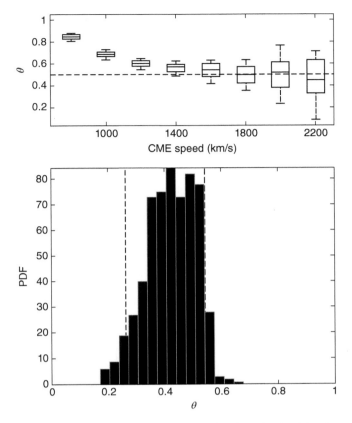

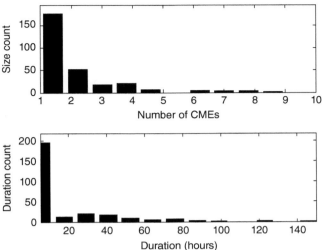

Figure 7.7 Distribution of cluster sizes and duration of CME clusters for fast CMEs with speeds exceeding 1000 km/s.

Figure 7.5 (Upper panel) The extremal index obtained by the Max-Spectrum method. The boxplots for each time scale are obtained from 100 independent realizations of the randomized $\hat{\theta}$, as explained in the text. The central mark in a box is the median, the box edges are the 10-th and 90-th percentiles, and whiskers extend to the most extreme data points. (Lower panel) The histogram of $\hat{\theta}$ for speed thresholds from 1000 to 2300 km/s.

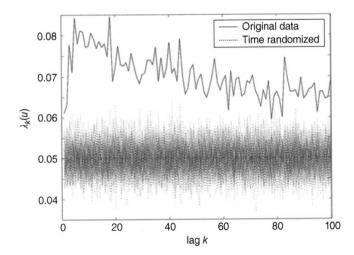

Figure 7.6 Tail correlation parameter for fast CMEs (> U = 534 km/s) as a function of the time lag (solid line). The dotted lines indicate 100 tail dependence estimates for randomly rearranged CMEs. The horizontal dashed line shows the 5% exceedance level.

percentile of the data (1000 km/s). To test the statistical significance of λ_k, we randomized the order of V_ks and calculated λ for these randomized (independent) in time data. This calculation was repeated independently 100 times, and the resulting λ_ks are shown by dots. One can see that λ is significantly larger than the unconditional probability $P(V_0 > U)$ (equal to 5% in this case) for lags less than at least 150 hours, thus confirming our conclusion that the fast CMEs are temporally dependent. This empirical estimate of λ_k may be used to predict the likelihood of a CME as fast or faster than U km/s k hours in the future.

Application of the de-clustering methodology allows us to find the number and content of clusters of fast CMEs. As an example, consider a threshold U = 1000 km/s and θ = 0.5. With this threshold, we have n = 586 fast CMEs with the "de-clustering time" τ_c = 42 hours. (A close de-clustering time can be obtained by comparing the distribution of observed time intervals with the exponential distribution, as has been shown in Figure 7.3.) By identifying the start and end times of intervals exceeding τ_c, we can count the number of clusters with 2, 3, ... and more members and the duration of these clusters (Figure 7.7). The maximum number of fast CMEs in a cluster found from the LASCO catalog used here is 9. The average duration time within a cluster is 18 hours with a standard error of 2 hours.

Table 7.1 provides more detailed information about the probability and the corresponding duration of clusters as a function of their size (number of CMEs in the cluster). We see that about 30% of the fast CMEs are single. The rest of the fast CMEs are in clusters of different sizes. There is a statistically significant portion of clusters (about 35%) with five or more members, which have an

Table 7.1 Example of Predictive Statistics for the Clusters of CMEs with Speed Exceeding 1000 km/s

Size	No. of Clusters	No. of CMEs in Clusters	Recording Probabilities	Mean Duration (hours)
1	177	177	0.61 (0.03)	—
2	53	106	0.18 (0.02)	20.1 (1.7)
3	18	54	0.06 (0.01)	39.7 (3.8)
4	20	80	0.07 (0.01)	56.8 (4.5)
5	7	35	0.02 (0.01)	70 (7.2)
>5	17	169	0.06 (0.01)	107.7 (10.6)

The first column (size) lists the number of CMEs in the cluster.
The second and third columns give the number of clusters of this size and total number of CMEs in these clusters.
The fourth column provides estimates and standard error (in parenthesis) of probabilities that a cluster of the corresponding size is recorded.
The last column lists the expected mean durations of the clusters (with standard error in parenthesis).

average duration of about 110 hours. This duration is in agreement with the estimate shown in Figure 7.6. These findings confirm and quantify the presence of temporal dependence of CMEs. Similar estimates can be made using different threshold speeds.

7.6. CONCLUSIONS

The Max-Spectrum method has allowed us to obtain a systematic statistical description of the fast CME speeds. We find by analyzing the data maxima that fast CME speeds have a Fréchet type self-similar distribution, that is, they asymptotically follow a power law with the power exponent 3.4 in the range of speeds from about 700–2000 km/s. Our tests show that the value of the exponent weakly depends on the size of the data sample, thus evidencing on non-stationary of the Max-Spectrum. For example, after splitting the studied time series into two parts we find $\alpha = 3.1$ for the first half and $\alpha = 3.2$ for the second half of the time series.

In statistics, the power-law tails are called "heavy." They are commonly observed in financial and internet traffic data. The fact that the CME speed has a heavy (power-law) tail means that the fast ones are produced with much larger probability than one would expect from the standard normal or exponential distribution. The lognormal distribution does not belong to the class of heavy-tailed distributions. Practically, for any large but finite data sample the lognormal distribution, which has two adjustable parameters (mean and standard deviation), approximates a power-law distribution rather well. And this is probably the reason why the lognormal distribution is often used. However, in contrast with the heavy-tailed distributions, the lognormal approximation needs reevaluation of the fitting parameters as new data become available.

The finding of the self-similar range of speed distribution provides a meaningful definition of "fast" CMEs and has an important consequence in our understanding of the physical process responsible for their generation. As indicated by observations [Feynman, 1997], fast CMEs apparently originate from the clusters of emerging magnetic flux on the solar surface. These powerful agglomerates of activity produce more energetic (fast) CMEs compared with single active regions. Thus, the clustering of active regions apparently simulates the clustering of fast CMEs. The existence of a self-similar range of scales and related speeds mean that the physical process responsible for producing the series of fast CMEs is the same over the range of scales and differs in some way from the process that generates slower CMEs. However, the connection between active regions and fast CMEs is not straightforward because not every active region produces a CME. Active regions are generated by solar dynamo process, and clustering of active regions is, at least conceptually understood in the context of the solar dynamo [Ruzmaikin, 1998]. But we do not yet know how and which cluster of solar activity produces a multiple set of fast CMEs.

Another finding from our study has a potential for developing the capability for statistical prediction of fast CMEs. We find that the onset times of fast CMEs are not independent, as would be expected according to a standard Poisson process, but they tend to cluster. This "clustering phenomenon" is described in the context of Extreme Value Theory by the extremal index [Leadbetter et al., 1983]. Using the extremal index, we estimated the critical time-scale that separates the time intervals between clusters from time intervals between CMEs within a cluster as a function of the speed threshold. Note that both exponents, α and θ, can be useful in statistical forecasting of fast CME. The exponent α gives us a range of fast CMEs speed thresholds, and θ is used to separate the time intervals between the clusters from the time intervals between CMEs within the clusters.

In the Space Weather context, clustering implies a serial impact of CMEs on interplanetary environments. For example, if a CME over 1000 km/s occurs one should expect with 60% probability another CME with the same speed or faster within the next two days (see Table 7.1 for more details). Lowering the speed threshold leads to more fast CMEs per cluster and longer duration of the clusters relative to the times between clusters. The clustering in time of fast CMEs also means that the process (mechanism) of their production must include the correlation (memory) between the subsequently launched CMEs. In other words, the process should not be simply additive (this type of process leads to normal, Gaussian distribution), but multiplicative, similar to the spread of forest fires or to the cascade process in the turbulent inertial range.

Associated with CMEs via acceleration process that takes place at the shock fronts produced by fast CMEs are high-flux SEP events [*Reames*, 1999; *Li et al.*, 2005]. A consequence of the CME clustering has in fact been used earlier in an empirical *definition of an SEP event* [*Feynman et al.*, 1993, 2002]. An SEP event was defined as a cluster of fluxes and fluences appearing over several days during which the proton fluence exceeds a selected threshold. A thus defined SEP event typically involves many successive increases in particle flux. The threshold was chosen in way that the cluster of CMEs would be assigned to a single SEP event. It has also been shown that the time between the thus defined SEP events is distributed according to the exponential law of the Poisson process, while the timing between all SEPs does not follow this distribution [*Jiggens and Gabriel*, 2011]. This definition of SEP events is widely used in space environment models employed for the designs of space missions [*Feynman et al.*, 1993]. The methods and results presented in this chapter provide a firm scientific basis for the definition of "extreme Space Weather events", including fast CME and extreme SEP events. Table 7.1 gives an example of statistical estimates that can be a useful guide in developing techniques for the prediction of fast CMEs and their related SEPs.

ACKNOWLEDGMENTS

This work was supported in part by the Jet Propulsion Laboratory of the California Institute of Technology, under a contract with the National Aeronautics and Space Administration. S. Stoev was partially supported by the NSF grant DMS-0806094.

REFERENCES

Amari, T., J. J. Aly, J. F. Luciani, Z. Mikic, and J. A. Linker (2011), Coronal mass ejection initiation by converging photospheric flows: Toward a realistic model, *Astrophys. J.*, *742*, L27, doi:10.1088/2041-8205/742/2/L27.

Baker, D. N., X. Li, A. Pulkkinen, C. M. Ngwira, M. L. Mays, A. B. Galvin, and K. D. C. Simunac (2013), A major solar eruptive event in July 2012: Defining extreme space weather scenarios, *Space Weather*, *11*, 585591, doi:10.1002/swe.20097.

Davis, R. A. and T. Mikosch (2009), The extremogram: A correlogram for extreme events, *Bernoulli*, *15*, 977–1009.

Ferro, C. A. T. and J. Segers (2003), Inference for clusters of extremes, *J. R. Statist. Soc. B*, *65*, 545–556.

Feynman, J. (1997), Evolving magnetic structures and their relationship to the coronal mass ejections, in *Coronal Mass Ejections*, Geophys. Monograph *99*, edited by N. Crooker, J. A. Joselyn, and J. Feynman, pp. 49–56, AGU, Washington, DC.

Feynman, J., G. Spitale, J. Wang, and S. Gabriel (1993), Interplanetary proton fluence model: JPL 1991, *J. Geophys. Res.*, *98*, 13281–13294.

Feynman, J. and S. Gabriel (2000), On space weather consequences and predictions, *J. Geophys. Res.*, *105*(A5), 10543–10564.

Feynman, J., A. Ruzmaikin, and V. Berdichevsky (2002), The JPL proton fluence model: An update, *J. Atmos. Sol. Terr. Phys.*, *64*, 1679–1686.

Feynman, J. and A. Ruzmaikin (2004), A high-speed erupting-prominence CME: A bridge between types, *Sol. Phys.*, *219*, 301–313.

Fisher, R. A. and L. H. Tippett (1928), Limiting forms of the frequency distribution of the largest and smallest member of a sample, *Proc. Camb. Philos. Soc.*, *24*, 180–190.

Forbes, T. G., J. A. Linker, J. Chen, C. Cid, J. Kta, M. A. Lee, G. Mann, Z. Miki, M. S. Potgieter, J. M. Schmidt, G. L. Siscoe, R. Vainio, S. K. Antiochos, and P. Riley (2006), CME theory and models, *Space Sci. Rev.*, *123*, 251–302.

Gaizauskas, V., K. L. Harvey, J. W. Harvey, and C. Zwaan (1983), Large-scale patterns formed by solar active regions during the ascending phase of cycle 21, *Astrophys. J.*, *265*, 1056–1065.

Gnedenko, B. (1943), Sur la distribution limite de terme maximum d'une série aléatoire, *Ann. Math.*, *44*, 423–453.

Gopalswamy, N. (2008), Solar connections of geoeffective magnetic structures, *J. Atmos. Sol. Terr. Phys.*, *70*, 2078–2100.

Gopalswamy, N., S. Yashiro, Y. Liu, G. Michalek, A. Vourlidas, M. L. Kaiser, and R. Howard (2005), Coronal mass ejections and other extreme characteristics of the 2003 October-November solar eruptions, *J. Geophys. Res.*, *110*, doi:10.1029/2004JA010958.

Gopalswamy, N., S. Yashiro, G. Michalek, G. Stenborg, A. Vourlidas, S. Freeland, and R. Howard (2009), The SOHO/LASCO CME Catalog, *Earth Moon Planet.*, *104*, 295–313.

Hamidieh, K., S. Stoev, and G. Michailidis (2009), On the estimation of the extremal index based on scaling and resampling, *J. Comput. Graph. Stat.*, *18*, 731–755, doi:10.1198/cgs.2009.08065.

Harvey, K. L. and C. Zwaan (1993), Properties and emergence patterns of bipolar active regions, *Sol. Phys.*, *148*, 85–118.

Hirshberg, J. and D. S. Colburn (1969), Interplanetary field and geomagnetic variations, a unified view, *Planet. Space Sci.*, *17*, 1183–1206.

Hsing, T., J. Hüsler, and M. R. Leadbetter (1988), On the exceedance point process for a stationary sequence, *Probab. Theory Relat. Fields*, *78*, 97–112.

Jiggens, P. T. A. and S. B. Gabriel (2011), Time distributions of solar energetic particle events: Are SEPEs really random?, *J. Geophys. Res.*, *114*, A10105, doi:10.1029/2009JA014291.

Kahler, S. (1987), Coronal mass ejections, *Rev. Geophys.*, *25*, 663–675, doi:10.1029/RG025i003p00663.

Leadbetter, M. R., G. Lindgren, and H. Rootzen (1983), *Extremes and Related Properties of Random Sequences and Processes*, Springer-Verlag, New York.

Li, G., G. P. Zank, and W. K. M. Rice (2005), Acceleration and transport of heavy ions at coronal mass ejection-driven shocks, *J. Geophys. Res.*, *110*, A06104, doi:10.1029/2004JA010600.

Reames, D. V. (1999), Particle acceleration at the Sun and in the heliosphere, *Space Sci. Rev.*, *90*, 413–491.

Riley, P. (2012), On the probability of occurrence of extreme space weather events, *Space Weather*, *10*, S02012, doi:10.1029/2011SW000734.

Ruzmaikin, A. (1998), Clustering of emerging flux, *Sol. Phys.*, *181*, 1–12.

Ruzmaikin, A. and J. Feynman (1998), Fast CMEs and their association with clustering of emerging flux, in *Journal of Physics of Space Plasmas*, edited by T. Cheng and J. R. Jasperse, pp. 295–300, MIT Center for Theoretical Geo/Cosmo Plasma Physics, Cambridge, MA.

Ruzmaikin, A., J. Feynman, and S. Stoev (2011), Distribution and clustering of fast coronal mass ejections, *J. Geophys. Res.*, *116*, doi:10.1029/2010JA016247.

Severe Space Weather Events–Understanding Societal and Economic Impacts Workshop Report (2008), The National Academies Press, http://www.nap.edu/catalog/12507.html (accessed 29 August 2015).

Siscoe, G. L. (1980), Evidence in the auroral record for secular solar variability, *Rev. Geophys. Space Phys.*, *18*, 647–658.

Stoev, S. A., G. Michailidis, and M. S. Taqqu (2011), Estimating heavy–tail exponents through max self–similarity, *IEEE Trans. Inf. Theory*, *57*(3), 1615–1635.

Thernisien, A., A. Vourlidas, and R. A. Howard (2009), Forward modeling of Coronal Mass Ejections using STEREO/SECCHI data, *Sol. Phys.*, *256*, 111–130, doi:10.1007/s11207-009-9346-5.

Thompson, B. E., E. W. Cliver, N. Nitta, C. Delannee, and J.-P. Delaboudiniere (2000), Coronal dimmings and energetic CMEs in April–May, 1998, *Geophys. Res. Lett.*, *27*, 1431–1435.

Tsurutani, B. T., and W. D. Gonzalez (1997), The interplanetary causes of magnetic storms, *AGU Monogr.*, *98*, 77–93.

Yurchyshyn, Y., S. Yashiro, V. Abramenko, H. Wang, and N. Gopalswamy (2005), Statistical distribution of speeds of coronal mass ejections, *Astrophys. J.*, *619*, 5099–6030.

8

Chicxulub Asteroid Impact: An Extreme Event at the Cretaceous/Paleogene Boundary

Jaime Urrutia-Fucugauchi[1] and Ligia Pérez-Cruz[2]

ABSTRACT

Crater-forming impacts represent a class of extreme events involving high-energy release and short time scales. Impacts constitute major geological processes shaping the surfaces and evolution of planetary bodies. The formation of large craters involves high pressures and temperatures resulting in intense deformation, fracturing, and melting. Impacts produce deep transient cavities, with excavation to deep levels in the crust, fragmentation, and removal of large volumes of rock. In this chapter, we analyze the Chicxulub impact and its effects on the Earth's climate, environment and life-support systems, in relation to the Cretaceous/Paleogene boundary. The boundary represents one of the major extinction events in the Phanerozoic, which affected about 75% of species. Effects of the impact have been intensely investigated, where the affectation in the evolution patterns was profound and long lasting. The disappearance of large numbers of species including complete groups severely affected the biodiversity and ecosystem composition in the marine and continental realms. There are several aspects involved in addressing the Chicxulub impact as an extreme event. First, we examine the impact event and cratering, time scales involved, and energy released. Next, we assess the impact's regional and global effects, which involve major perturbations in the ocean and atmosphere. From here, we discuss how and to what extent life-support systems are affected by large impacts, and what the fossil record tells about the extinction event and biotic turnover. In particular, how sudden or extended are the processes, extinction event and recovery temporal records.

8.1. INTRODUCTION

Over the past decades, study of extreme events has emerged as a major area in Earth sciences, across a wide range of disciplines with a strong inter- and multidisciplinary character and with implications into the social

[1] *Instituto de Geofísica, Universidad Nacional Autónoma de México (UNAM), México, DF, México*

[2] *Programa Universitario de Perforaciones en Océanos y Continentes, Departamento de Geomagnetismo y Exploración Geofísica, Instituto de Geofísica, Universidad Nacional Autónoma de México, México, DF, México*

and economic sciences. A major component is focused on studies of geological and geophysical processes with capacity to generate disasters [*Meyers*, 2010]. Examples of extreme events within this context include large earthquakes, explosive volcanic eruptions, crater-forming meteorite impacts, tsunamis, catastrophic landslides, and floods, which involve processes delivering large amounts of energy on short time scales at their extreme ends of process range [*Ghil et al.*, 2011].

In this chapter, we discuss the Chicxulub asteroid impact and the events at the Cretaceous/Paleogene (K/Pg) boundary in terms of a "geological extreme event." Large crater-forming events with capacity to

Extreme Events: Observations, Modeling, and Economics, Geophysical Monograph 214, First Edition.
Edited by Mario Chavez, Michael Ghil, and Jaime Urrutia-Fucugauchi.
© 2016 American Geophysical Union. Published 2016 by John Wiley & Sons, Inc.

Terrestrial impact crater record (~170–180 craters)

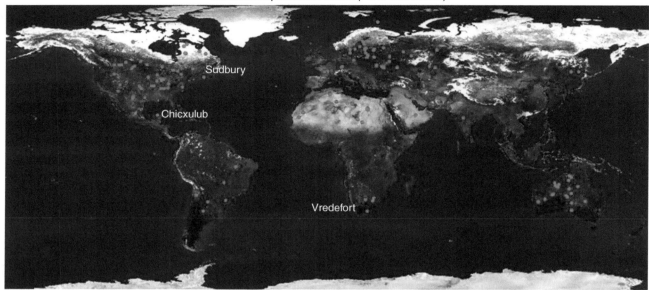

Three large complex multiring structures

Figure 8.1 Impact craters documented in the terrestrial record (Earth Impact Database, University of New Brunswick, http:www.unb.ca/passc/ImpactDatabase). The uneven distribution of craters (shown by red dots) correlates with the distribution of the most intensely mapped areas and Precambrian terrains. The three largest structures with multiring morphology are Vredefort, Sudbury, and Chicxulub.

produce severe regional and global effects, profoundly affecting the life-support systems on both short and long spatial and temporal scales represent a different type of extreme events—at the end of process range. Impact produced a large, ~200 km diameter structure with peak ring and multiring morphology. Chicxulub is the youngest and best preserved crater of only three multiring structures identified in the terrestrial record (Figure 8.1). Multiring craters are common features on the Moon and other bodies of the solar system. In contrast, on Earth the tectonic, magmatic, and erosional processes have erased the record of past large impacts. Crater-forming events deliver large amounts of energy in "seconds" time scales, resulting in deep excavation, fracturing, and deformation of the crust [*Melosh*, 1989]. In contrast, plate motions, sea-floor spreading, plate subduction, and mountain-building processes which involve intense deformation of Earth's lithosphere occur on longer time scales.

The K/Pg impact caused severe effects on the climate and environment on a global scale, which have been related to the mass extinction of organisms marking the K/Pg boundary [*Alvarez et al.*, 1980; *Schulte et al.*, 2010]. The end-Cretaceous extinction is one of the five major mass extinction events in the Phanerozoic, which affected about 40% of genera and 75% of species. The effects on life evolution are long lasting, affecting species on the marine and continental realms.

There are several different aspects involved in addressing the Chicxulub impact as an extreme event. First, we examine the impact and cratering process, with the energy release, deep excavation, mass removal, ejection of large amounts of fragmented rock, widespread crustal deformation, and crater formation. Time scales involved in the impact and cratering are short in seconds to thousands of seconds, with a large amount of energy released [*Melosh*, 1989; *Kenkemann*, 2002; *Collins et al.*, 2008]. Next, we assess the target deformation and local, regional, and global effects of the impact, cratering, and ejecta deposition, which involve crustal deformation and major perturbations in the ocean and atmosphere. From here, we discuss how and to what extent life-support systems are affected by large impacts, and what the fossil record tells about the extinction event and biotic turnover. Of particular interest is how sudden or extended are the processes and extinction records.

The study of *Alvarez et al.* [1980] introduced a sudden catastrophic explanation for the mass extinction of organisms involving the effects of an impact of a large asteroid or comet. *Alvarez et al.* [1980] presented geochemical data for the K/Pg boundary layer in the pelagic carbonate sequences from Italy, Denmark, and New Zealand. The boundary layer is enriched in iridium and other platinum group elements (PGEs) with

Figure 8.2 Distal Cretaceous/Paleogene boundary sections and K/Pg iridium anomaly. Views of the (a) Gubbio, Italy and (b) Caravaca, Spain Cretaceous/Paleogene (K/Pg) boundary sections, and (c) an example of the iridium anomaly for the Gubbio section.

concentrations of about 30, 160, and 20 times, respectively the background levels through the sections (e.g., Figure 8.2). The enrichments were associated with collision of an asteroid or a comet that injected large amounts of pulverized debris into the atmosphere, resulting in blockage of solar radiation, global cooling, and shut down of photosynthesis. The sizes of the bolide and resulting crater, estimated from various sets of assumptions, were in the range of 10 ± 4 km and ~200 km, respectively.

The impact hypothesis for the K/Pg boundary was met with opposition, mainly from within the paleontological community that considered the mass extinction occurring over an extended period. In the following years, evidence for an impact from analyses of the K/Pg boundary clay layer was confirmed by data from numerous marine boundary sections and eventually on continental sections [*Schulte et al.*, 2010]. The PGE anomaly is globally distributed, with K/Pg boundary sections showing a characteristic pattern with distance to the impact site (Figure 8.3). Studies have uncovered further impact indicators in the K/Pg boundary layer, in addition to the anomalous enrichment in iridium and PGEs, such as shocked quartz,

spinels, magnesioferrites, and cromites [e.g., *Claeys et al.*, 2002; *Morgan et al.*, 2006; *Villasante-Marcos et al.*, 2007].

Recognition of the ~200 km diameter Chicxulub crater as the K/Pg impact site in the Yucatan carbonate platform, southern Gulf of Mexico (Figure 8.4), provided strong support for the impact hypothesis [*Hildebrand et al.*, 1991; *Sharpton et al.*, 1992; *Schulte et al.*, 2010; *Urrutia-Fucugauchi et al.*, 2011a, 2011b]. The impact is the largest documented in the past 600 Ma, since multicellular organisms evolved. The two other multiring craters, Sudbury (Canada) and Vredefort (South Africa), were formed at 2000 and 1850 Ma in the Precambrian [*Grieve and Therriault*, 2000].

The nature and suddenness of the mass extinction of organisms and the impact of cause/effect relations and its role as the main sole extinction cause continue to be debated. This is largely due to the incompleteness and temporal resolution of the geological and fossil records, which even for the marine realm have limitations that hamper and preclude analyses of sharp discrete events. In the past three decades, studies have contributed to unravel the role of impacts in the evolution of Earth and other bodies of the solar system.

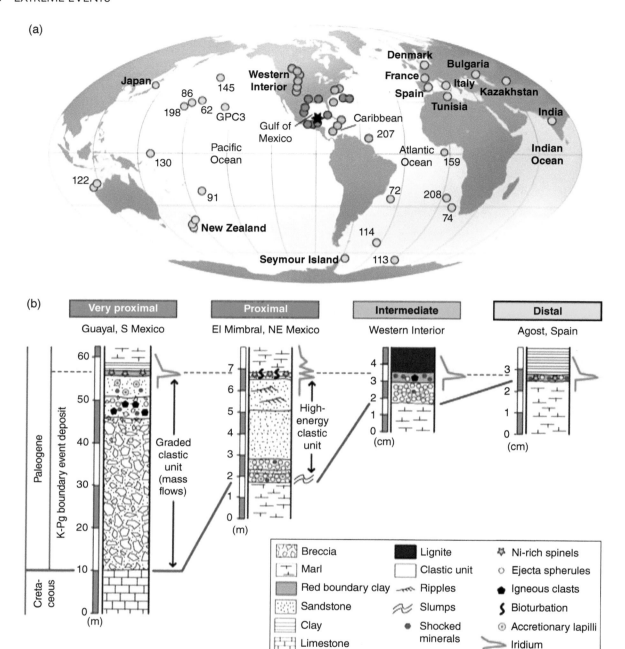

Figure 8.3 (a) Location of K/Pg boundary sites, separated into distal, intermediate, proximal, and very proximal sections [*Schulte et al.*, 2010]. Location of Chicxulub crater is indicated by the asterisk. Colors identify the distal, intermediate, proximal, and very proximal sections relative to distance from Chicxulub crater. Numbers in marine sections correspond to the Deep Sea Drilling Project and Ocean drilling Project Leg identifications. (b) Schematic stratigraphical columns for representative K/Pg sections at distal, intermediate, proximal, and very proximal locations [*Schulte et al.*, 2010].

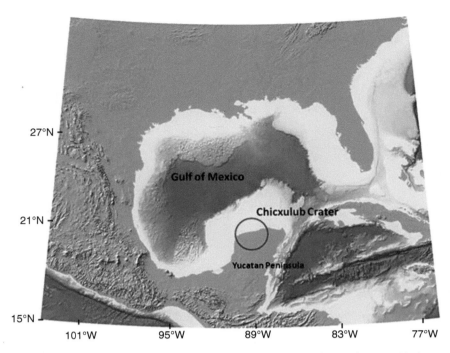

Figure 8.4 Location of the Chicxulub impact crater in the Yucatan Peninsula, southern Gulf of Mexico (base map is a digital terrain model of Gulf of Mexico-Caribbean Sea region). Note the extent of Yucatan carbonate platform shown in light blue.

8.2. EXTREME EVENTS IN THE GEOLOGICAL PAST

Study of extreme events in the geological records in the past has become more complex due to problems related to stratigraphical incompleteness and dating resolution of events. Analysis of the K/Pg boundary offers the possibility of exploring criteria for evaluating the geological record of an extreme event associated with a sudden catastrophic asteroidal impact, with reference to the K/Pg clay layer as a global stratigraphical marker of the Chicxulub impact.

The catastrophic nature of an impact explanation as cause of the K/Pg events and mass extinction was perceived as in contradiction to the uniformitarian view of geological processes. The impact theory posed a catastrophic explanation for one of the three major geological transitions in the geological time scale between the Mesozoic and Cenozoic eras. As such, the impact theory emerged central stage in a renewed debate about the role of catastrophism in the Earth's evolution.

Early on in the development and formulation of geological concepts and theories, a long-term debate occurred over what were considered competing frameworks or scientific paradigms. In the 18th and 19th centuries, debate was framed into the catastrophist and uniformitarian theories, with apparently opposite views of nature and geological processes. Eventually, uniformitarianism emerged to provide a framework for development of geological sciences, where present-day processes were held as key to understand the past. Stratigraphical principles such as the law of superposition provided the foundations for geological research.

Many geological processes were considered to occur in small incremental steps over relatively long time scales. Examples include erosion, sedimentation, mountain building, and motion of tectonic plates. Deep canyon systems are formed by removal of large amounts of material, usually by slow incremental erosion and transport processes. The formation of thick sedimentary sequences in large river deltas involves deposition of sediments for extended periods. Construction of mountain chains involves tectonic deformation with uplifting, folding, thrusting and faulting, and/or magmatic and volcanic activity. Opening and closing of ocean basins and formation and break up and drift of continental landmasses and supercontinents occur by plate motions at rates of a few centimeters per year. Their study has been partly based on observations of current processes and inferences and modeling of conceptual theories.

8.3. CHICXULUB IMPACT

The Chicxulub structure was first identified from oil exploration surveys, which discovered a large semicircular gravity anomaly in the northern sector of the Yucatan Peninsula (Figure 8.5). The anomaly pattern was interpreted as a buried volcanic center, which was apparently

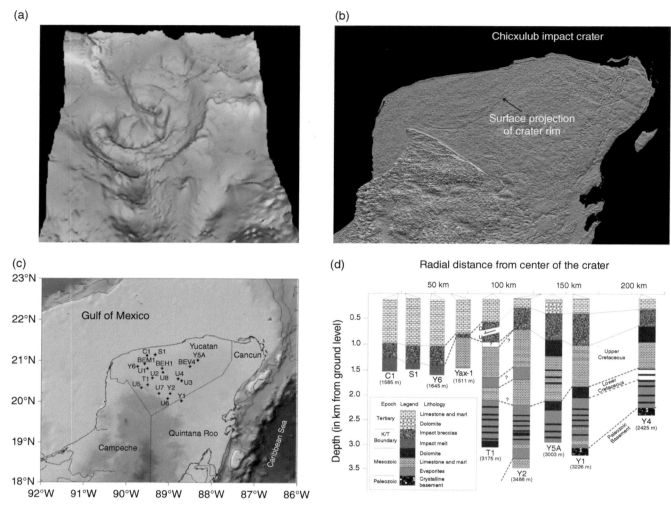

Figure 8.5 (a) Oblique three-dimensional view of Bouguer gravity anomaly map over the Chicxulub crater [from *Sharpton et al.*, 1993]. Observe the presence of a circular concentric anomaly with a semi-circular concentric anomaly that characterizes the multiring structure, with the gravity high in the central crater zone. (b) Interferometric radar satellite image for northern Yucatan Peninsula. The surface projection of the crater rim is marked by a semicircular topographic depression, which coincides with the cenote ring in the flat karstic terrain. Topographic depression is associated with differential compaction of impact breccias in side the crater in relation to the carbonate sequence. Note presence of fossil coastlines reflecting past sea-level changes [*Urrutia-Fucugauchi et al.*, 2008]. Base map from C-band interferometric radar image, Earth Shuttle Radar Topography Mission (Courtesy of NASA/JPL-Caltech). (c) Location of drilling sites in the northern Yucatan Peninsula from the PEMEX, UNAM, CSDP, and UNAM-CFE drilling programs [*Urrutia-Fucugauchi et al.*, 2011a, 2011b]. Schematic columns of the PEMEX boreholes, showing the major lithological units. The column for the Yaxcopoil-1 borehole is included.

confirmed by drilling within the central zone and recovering of andesitic rocks. In the late 1970s, aeromagnetic surveys documented a large magnetic anomaly pattern within the central zone of gravity anomalies (Figure 8.6). In 1981, the anomalies were alternatively interpreted in terms of an impact crater [*Penfield and Camargo-Zanoguera*, 1981]. In 1991, it was proposed that the crater was a possible K/Pg boundary impact [*Hildebrand et al.*, 1991], which was confirmed by radiometric dating and magnetic polarity stratigraphy [*Sharpton et al.*, 1992; *Urrutia-Fucugauchi et al.*, 1994].

In the last two decades, geophysical studies and drilling projects have investigated the structure and stratigraphy of the crater (Figure 8.5) [*Sharpton et al.*, 1993; *Kring*, 1995; *Hildebrand et al.*, 1998; *Morgan et al.*, 1997; *Morgan and Warner*, 1999; *Urrutia-Fucugauchi et al.*, 1996, 2004, 2008; *Gulick et al.*, 2008]. The geometric center of the geophysical anomalies lies at Chicxulub Puerto in the present coastline. The crater is part on land and part offshore. The Chicxulub crater is buried under about 1 km of Paleogene carbonate sediments. The flat relief of Yucatan permits to integrate the marine and terrestrial

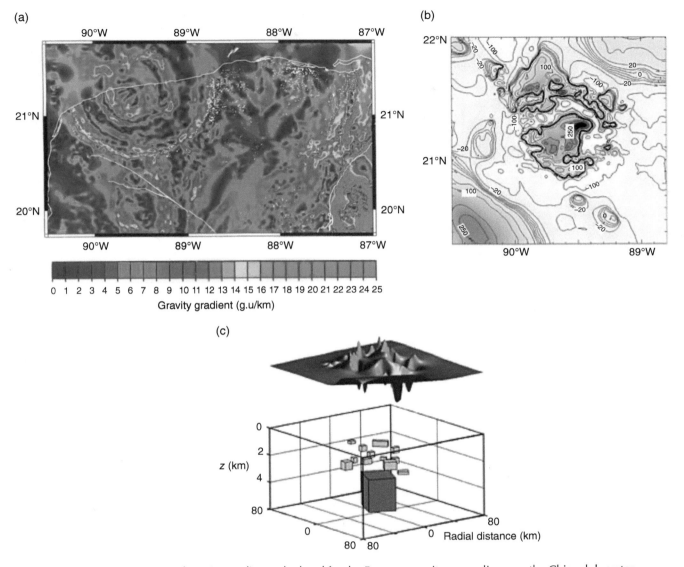

Figure 8.6 (a) Horizontal gravity gradient calculated for the Bouguer gravity anomalies over the Chicxulub crater [taken from *Connors et al.*, 1996]. The white dots represent location of the cenotes. Observe the correlation of the cenote ring with the gravity gradient anomaly. (b) Contour map of the aeromagnetic anomaly field over Chicxulub impact crater, in the northwestern sector of the Yucatan peninsula. Survey flight high over sea level is 500 m. Contour curves are given in nT. Observe the high-amplitude anomalies over the central sector of the Chicxulub crater. (c) 3D inversion model of magnetized source bodies [*Ortiz-Aleman and Urrutia-Fucugauchi*, 2010].

surveys with high resolution. Structural models derived from modeling the potential field anomalies, electromagnetic and seismic data define major crater features, including a central zone with the basement uplift, breccias and melt deposits, and terrace zones with radial faulting (Figure 8.7). Seismic reflection surveys have allowed mapping and imaging of crater morphology, Paleogene basin, and deep crustal deformation features [*Morgan et al.*, 1997; *Morgan and Warner*, 1999; *Gulick et al.*, 2008]. Joint modeling of geophysical and drilling data, particularly lithological columns and well-logging information

result in improved spatial resolution and structural characterization [*Hildebrand et al.*, 1998; *Urrutia-Fucugauchi and Pérez-Cruz*, 2008; *Urrutia-Fucugauchi et al.*, 2008, 2011a]. A marine seismic reflection survey provides a three-dimensional imaging of the structure with the peak ring, terrace zones, fractures, postimpact carbonates, impactites, and target Mesozoic sequence [*Gulick et al.*, 2008].

Aeromagnetic data show high-amplitude short wavelength anomalies in the central sector delimitated by the central gravity anomaly (Figure 8.6), which are associated with the basement uplift, breccias, and melt [*Pilkington*

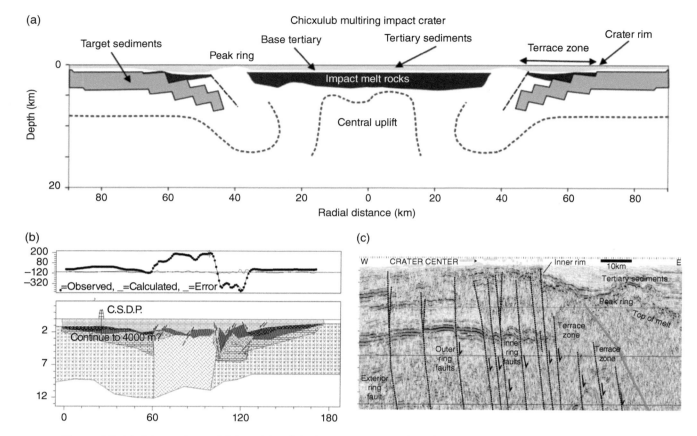

Figure 8.7 (a) Schematic model for Chicxulub deep structure (taken from *Collins et al.* [2008]). (b) Magnetic model for Chicxulub crater; observe the asymmetric crater structure documented in the models with respect to the central uplift and fault pattern [*Rebolledo-Vieyra et al.*, 2010]. (c) Marine seismic reflection Chicx-A profile of the western sector of the Chicxulub structure with structural interpretation added. Note the distribution and extent of the fault pattern [*Gulick et al.*, 2008].

and Hildebrand, 2000; *Ortiz-Aleman and Urrutia-Fucugauchi,* 2010; *Batista et al.,* 2013]. Aeromagnetic anomalies show three strong, well-defined concentric patterns, with a central high-amplitude 40 km diameter zone. Magnetic properties associated with the melt sheet, upper breccias, and central uplift present three to four orders of magnitude contrasts with the surrounding carbonate units. Models suggest sources extending to radial distances ~45 km from crater center, with average depths ranging between 2 and 4 km. Magnetic sources in central zone are located at about 3.5–8 km depth, with dominant contributions from the structural uplift [*Ortiz-Aleman and Urrutia-Fucugauchi,* 2010]. Low-amplitude magnetic anomalies associated with the impact breccias likely reflect effects of hydrothermal activity, with formation of secondary iron-titanium oxides [*Pilkington and Hildebrand,* 2000; *Urrutia-Fucugauchi et al.,* 2004: *Velasco-Villarreal et al.,* 2011]. Impact breccias show effects of hydrothermal activity related to fluid circulation in the fractured-porous formations [*Kring et al.,* 2004]. The hydrothermal system remained active for a long period in the Paleocene

[*Abramov and Kring,* 2007; *Escobar-Sanchez and Urrutia-Fucugauchi,* 2010].

Drilling projects conducted by Pemex, UNAM, UNAM-CFE, and CSDP have provided samples for laboratory analyses (Figure 8.5c and d). Pemex drilling incorporated intermittent core recovery, and there was need for detailed sampling through the lithological column [*Lopez Ramos,* 1976; *Urrutia-Fucugauchi et al.,* 2004, 2008]. The UNAM drilling program incorporated continuous coring in eight boreholes distributed within and immediately outside the crater rim, with three boreholes cutting the carbonate-impact breccia contact [*Urrutia-Fucugauchi et al.,* 1996]. Three boreholes in the southern sector at different radial distances from the crater center sampled the Paleogene carbonates and the impact breccia sequence, with the carbonate–breccia contact lying at varying depths between 222 and 332 m, below the surface. Impact breccias are characterized by clasts of carbonates, melt, and crystalline basement in a matrix characterized by carbonate-rich and melt-rich components. The breccia units, compared to the suevitic

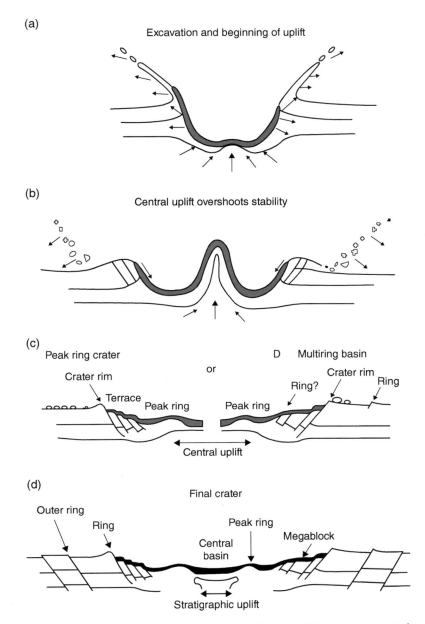

Figure 8.8 Schematic model for crater formation processes in large multiring structures (adapted from *Melosh* [1989]; *Collins et al.* [2008] and *Gulick et al.* [2008]). (a) Excavation of transient cavity and uplift. (b) Central uplift, ejecta emplacement with ejecta plume and lateral curtains, and crater modification. (c) Formation of peak ring and multiring basin morphologies. (d) Final crater morphology delimited by the crater ring and outer ring, with a central basin, basement uplift, melt sheet, megablock breccias, peak ring, and terrace zone.

and Bunte breccias in the Ries crater, have been cored in Chicxulub, with upper breccias rich in carbonate clasts and lower breccias rich in melt and basement clasts [*Urrutia-Fucugauchi et al.*, 1996]. Ejecta deposits are documented in these boreholes and in drilling in the eastern Merida-Valladolid area [*Urrutia-Fucugauchi et al.*, 2008]. Proximal deposits are exposed in areas to the south in Belize, Chetumal, and Campeche, which are part of the ejecta blanket covering the Yucatan Peninsula.

The geophysical and drilling data on Chicxulub have been reviewed in *Urrutia-Fucugauchi et al.* [2011a, 2011b], where additional details on the structure are discussed. A schematic model for the crater, showing the major elements of the crater rim, Tertiary basin, central uplift, terrace zone, melt sheet, and breccias is shown in Figure 8.7a. Models for the formation of large complex structures are being refined as further constraints from experiments and computer modeling are incorporated

(Figure 8.8). Final structure for complex craters forms in stages [*Melosh*, 1989; *Melosh and Ivanov*, 1999; *Pierazzo and Melosh*, 2000]. The structure develops after initial contact: excavation of a deep transient cavity, fragmentation of large volume of target rocks and formation of ejecta plume, uplift of lower crust basement and collapse. During this stage, the peak-ring structure formed. After crater formation, subsidence and faulting occurred due to differential compaction. The studies are providing insight on the various cratering stages from initial contact, excavation of transient cavity, fragmentation of target rocks, central uplift, plume and ejecta curtain collapse, melting, and formation of crater rings, terrace zone and postimpact deformation. The nature of the bolide has been investigated from geochemical and isotope analyses of the ejecta, which support an asteroid impact [*Mukhopadhyay et al.*, 2001; *Gelinas et al.*, 2004].

8.4. CHICXULUB IMPACT AND K/Pg BOUNDARY LAYER

One of the central issues in the impact hypothesis for the end-Cretaceous extinction of organisms has been the dating and correlation of events [*Kuiper et al.*, 2008; *Tohver et al.*, 2012]. This was addressed in the initial studies and has remained at the forefront of the discussions ever since. Crater-forming impacts deliver huge amounts of energy in very short time scales. Although they leave characteristic marks in the geological record, including the crater structure and ejecta deposits, resolving the spatial and temporal processes from the geological record and in particular the impact effects and relation to other induced or independent events presents a complex daunting problem. For the K/Pg boundary, problems relate to nature of the mass extinction, boundary events, fine-tuning connection of impact effects, and biotic recovery.

Studies have addressed the problem along different paths, examining the crater stratigraphy, ejecta deposits at proximal, intermediate and distal sections, and high-resolution stratigraphical correlations (Figure 8.3). Evidence on a causal relation comes from (1) coeval dates on Chicxulub impact melt and K/Pg tektites and glasses, (2) chemical fingerprinting of boundary layers and Yucatan target rocks, (3) dating of boundary-layer zircons in intermediate and distal sections, (4) distribution and characteristics of K/Pg sections in Gulf of Mexico-Caribbean Sea region, (5) distribution of shock quartz and other impact indicators, and (6) correlation of paleontological and stratigraphical records for the Maastrichtian and Danian sections. The studies provide strong support linking the K/Pg boundary clay with the Chicxulub impact [*Claeys et al.*, 2002; *Morgan et al.*, 2006; *Schulte et al.*, 2010; *Kamo et al.*, 2011].

Following the proposal that Chicxulub crater was the K/Pg impact site, several studies examined the links between the K/Pg layer and Chicxulub breccias and melt. Geochemical, mineralogical, and isotopic studies in different sections have documented the genetic links. Chemical compositions of impact glasses from Beloc, Haiti, and El Mimbral Mexico correlate with analyses for the Chicxulub melt and melt-rich breccias. 40Ar/39Ar dates for the Beloc impact glasses gave dates of 65.07 ± 0.1 Ma, similar to the dates on the Chicxulub melt rocks. U-Pb dates for shocked zircons from sections in Canada constrained the link to Chicxulub crater [*Krogh et al.*, 1993; *Kamo et al.*, 2011].

In proximal sections in the Gulf of Mexico and Caribbean, the ejecta are represented by a characteristic impact material-rich complex clastic unit. *Arenillas et al.* [2007] reported a detailed planktonic foraminifera record for the proximal sections of Bochil and Guayal in southern Mexico. The lowest Danian biozone P0 is documented in sediments on top of the complex clastic unit, consistent with a K/Pg boundary age. *Schulte et al.* [2010] analyzed the K/Pg boundary sections at varying distance from impact site (Figure 8.3) and relation to global effects. Very proximal ejecta deposits have been investigated by drilling, with boreholes in the southern crater sector showing >200 m thick sections of carbonate-rich and melt and basement-rich breccias, with an inverted stratigraphy [*Urrutia-Fucugauchi et al.*, 1996, 2011a, 2011b]. Sections in Belize and Chetumal areas record thick ejecta deposits with the basal spherule layer and diamictite unit [*Pope et al.*, 2005]. Proximal sites in southern Mexico and northern Central America show 1−80 m thick deposits. Sections in Cuba and the Caribbean Sea show occurrence of massive mass flow deposits hundred meters thick. Proximal sites in Gulf areas located ~500 to ~1000 km away show a basal spherule layer, high-energy sandstone deposits, fine-grained fireball, and clay layers. The fireball layer is characterized by enrichment of iridium and PGEs, shocked minerals, and showing evidence of heating to temperatures several hundred degrees high. Intermediate sites located some 1000−5000 km away record deposits with ~2−10 cm thick basal spherule layer and ~0.2−0.5 cm thick layer with shocked minerals, Ni-rich spinels, and granitic clasts. Distal sections more than 5000−7000 km away are characterized by basal spherule-rich and ~0.2–0.5 cm clay layers enriched in PGEs and Ni-rich spinels. *Schulte et al.* [2010] show that thickness of the ejecta layer decreases with increasing distance from Chicxulub, which is consistent with a single source of the K/Pg global ejecta layer.

Studies have investigated the strontium isotope anomaly at the K/Pg boundary sections [*Martin and MacDougall*, 1991; *Vonhof and Smit*, 1997]. Strontium isotope data have been related to the impact, including enhanced continental weathering by acid rain precipitation, impact ejecta, and soot from impact-induced fires [*MacDougall*, 1988]. Alternatively, sources such as the

Deccan Traps volcanic activity phases have been considered [*Vonhof and Smit*, 1997].

8.5. END-CRETACEOUS MASS EXTINCTION

Most of the species in the fossil record are extinct, with an estimate of 99%, which indicates that extinction is the norm in the evolution process. Extinction rates appear to vary, with times characterized by higher rates when the apparent ratios between extinction and speciation differ. From analyses of the fossil data, five periods of extinction known as the five mass extinction events are recognized. These extinctions occurred at Late Devonian, Late Ordovician, Permo-Triassic, Triassic and end-Cretaceous [*Raup and Sepkoski*, 1982; *Bambach*, 2006]. Estimates of the percentages of genera and species going extinct are difficult to estimate, but they may have affected about 75% of the species at the time.

The paleontological record has been examined searching for taxonomical, temporal and geographic patterns, numbers of groups and subgroups, and biodiversity [*Raup and Sepkoski*, 1982; *Straus and Sadler*, 1989; *Raup and Jablonski*, 1993]. Statistical analyses of fossil databases are used to defining trends and patterns of extinction and speciation. Records of continental organisms are less complete than marine records that allow greater resolution for analyzing trends and patterns of extinction and speciation. On the continents, one of the major groups going extinct was the non-avian dinosaurs. Dinosaurs arose in the Late Triassic and diversified reaching large sizes at a time when the major landmasses drifted apart after the supercontinent Pangea breakup [*Sereno*, 1999]. During the Cretaceous, major evolutionary changes took place, including the appearance of flowering plants.

An area that has been intensely surveyed for vertebrate fossil remains is the North American interior. Several studies on the dinosaur fossil record in the Hell Creek Formation in Montana and North Dakota have provided a fairly detailed record in the last stages of the Cretaceous. The K/Pg boundary layer is well exposed in the continental sedimentary exposures, which provides a stratigraphical marker. Studies in the 1970s identified a zone in the last meters of the Cretaceous with few fossil remains. This zone was later known as the 3 m gap and discussed in terms of the extinction of dinosaurs at the K/Pg [*Archibald*, 1996; *Sheehan et al.*, 2000]. The sedimentary sections continue to attract attention and recent surveys have uncovered dinosaur fossils within the zone below the K/Pg layer [*Lyson et al.*, 2011]. Discussions on the stratigraphical and fossil record and implications for gradual or sudden extinction at the boundary also highlight the issues of diversity of dinosaurs in the Cretaceous.

Recent studies have reexamined the diversity of dinosaur taxa during the Late Cretaceous. *Wang and Dodson* [2006] examined the diversity of non-avian dinosaurs, concluding that the genera documented for a small part of the diversity. They examined the decline in diversity for the last stages of the Cretaceous and concluded that diversity was steady, with no decline for the last 10 Ma of the Cretaceous. In contrast, *Barrett et al.* [2009] report based on the sauropodomorph record that dinosaur genus diversity declined during the last stages of the Cretaceous. *Brusalte et al.* [2012] analyzed the geographic and clade-specific patterns, finding a more heterogeneous distribution. They found that, while ceratopsids and hadrosaurs, and some North American groups reduced diversity in the two final stages of the Cretaceous, predator dinosaurs, mid-sized herbivores, and some groups in Asia showed stable diversity.

The K/Pg mass extinction had been associated to several different gradual incremental causes, including sea-level changes, climate change, ocean anoxia, and volcanic-induced environmental and climatic changes [*Hallam*, 1987; *Keller*, 2008]. In particular the association with the intense volcanic activity of the Deccan Traps in India has been investigated and proposed as a major cause of environmental changes. The chronology of Deccan Traps activity has been investigated in increasing detail [e.g., *Ravissa and Peuker-Ehrenbrink*, 2003; *Chenet et al.*, 2008; *Keller*, 2008], with emphasis on the correlation to K/Pg boundary events. The proposal by *Alvarez et al.* [1980] of the global effects of a large bolide impact introduced a cause involving short time scales. Distinguishing sudden from gradual extinction scenarios remains a difficult problem, mainly because of the incompleteness of the stratigraphical and paleontological records and the resolution of the dating and correlation methods [*Straus and Sadler*, 1989; *Springer*, 1990; *Marshall*, 1995; *Marshall and Ward*, 1996; *Payne*, 2003]. *Signor and Lipps* [1982] showed that due to the incomplete nature, stratigraphical distributions of last fossil appearances appear gradual even if the species became extinct at a given stratigraphical level. Several statistical methods have been developed to test sudden from gradual extinctions, which permit to place significance levels to the extinction patterns [*Wang et al.*, 2012].

The global environmental and climatic effects of the bolide impact have been examined in terms of effects on life-support systems. *Alvarez et al.* [1980] and studies that followed discussed impact effects related to the extinction of organisms. The impact-induced processes involve different time scales, from very short to long lasting [*Gilmour and Anders*, 1989; *Mukhopadhyay et al.*, 2001; *Keller et al.*, 2004, *Robertson et al.*, 2004; *Keller*, 2008]. Processes initially proposed include disruption of photosynthesis due to the fine-grained dust particles and sulfate aerosols in the upper atmosphere [*Alvarez et al.*, 1980]. The reduction of solar radiation resulted in freezing temperatures in continental regions and shut down of photosynthesis affecting the base of the global food chain in the marine and on land realms. Several studies have investigated the environmental effects of fine-grained ejecta particles and aerosols [*Toon et al.*, 1982, 1997; *Covey et al.*, 1990, 1994; *Pierazzo et al.*, 2003]. *Pope* [2002] analyzed the effects of dust and shutdown of photosynthesis, arguing that the dust-loading threshold for photosynthesis lies in the mass and distribution of the submicron-size dust. From theoretical calculations and coarse-dust fraction observations on the K/Pg boundary clay, *Pope* [2002] concluded that dust was not sufficient for globally blocking solar radiation and photosynthesis shutdown.

Robertson et al. [2004] proposed that the thermal pulse resulting from reentry of ejecta into the atmosphere was a major factor in the extinction event. They proposed that the intense infrared radiation affected organisms and ignited fires on a global scale. In their study, they analyzed the differential pattern of survival among nonmarine vertebrates, showing that the selectivity pattern was compatible with a sudden-killing mechanism. The effects of the infrared radiation pulse had been examined [*Melosh et al.*, 1990; *Toon et al.*, 1997], and associated with global wildfires [*Wolbach et al.*, 1988]. The magnitude of a thermal pulse propagating through the atmosphere associated with reentering ejecta was reexamined by *Goldin and Melosh* [2009], reassessing the self-shielding effects of infrared radiation.

Global wildfires ignited by the impact might have added to the environmental perturbation, injecting large amounts of smoke and carbon dioxide into the atmosphere. Studies on continental K/Pg boundary sections in interior North America identified occurrence of soot, interpreted as the remains of massive wildfires ignited by the thermal pulse generated by reentry of ejecta into the upper atmosphere [*Wolbach et al.*, 1988]. The global wildfire scenario has been challenged by *Belcher et al.* [2003] from studies of charcoal, soot, and pyrosynthetic polycyclic aromatic hydrocarbons, which show that they were not produced by vegetation fires but were the result of hydrocarbon combustion. *Belcher et al.* [2003, 2009] report that K/Pg boundary sections in interior North America contain less charcoal than the sequences above and below. The K/Pg layer is characterized by the lack of charred remains and instead shows abundance of non-charred plant material at interior North America sites. The soot morphological characteristics in marine sections appear inconsistent with biomass sources, supporting an origin from partial hydrocarbon combustion. Reports of carbon cenospheres formed from hydrocarbon combustion in marine and continental sections support observations against widespread global wildfires. The new evidence indicates combustion of organic material and hydrocarbons from the impact site in the Yucatan carbonate platform. Rough estimates of Gulf carbonate sequences suggest that organic matter may have been above global mean

values. Study by *Harvey et al.* [2008] shows that target carbonates with average abundances of organic matter appear compatible with concentrations estimated for carbon cenospheres and soot.

Impact was on the shallow Yucatan carbonate platform, as evidenced by the tsunami deposits in the areas around the Gulf of Mexico and elsewhere [*Bourgoise et al.*, 1988]. Impact affected the Yucatan sequence composed of limestones, evaporatites and dolomites, with release of large amounts of CO_2 and sulfur compounds in the atmosphere [*Brett*, 1992; *Pope et al.*, 1997]. Sulfur compounds may have resulted in acid rain, adding to the environmental perturbation. The injection of large quantities of CO_2 may have resulted in a greenhouse effect following the initial cooling episode [*Emiliani et al.*, 1981]. The deposition of silicate dust particles in the oceans affected the seawater chemistry causing a disruption in the carbonate-compensation level. Scenarios include the "Strangelove ocean" with primary productivity disrupted for a long time and suppression of flux of organic matter from the surface to the bottom. The effects on different parts of the oceans may have varied widely. The mass extinction affected groups of vertebrates, invertebrates, phytoplankton, and zooplankton, with entire groups disappearing. For instance, the planktonic foraminifera experienced losses of 90% of the species [*D'Hondt et al.*, 1996]. Estimates of recovery intervals for pelagic ecosystems involve several millions of years to be reestablished [*D'Hondt et al.*, 1996, 1998]. In contrast, continental margin ecosystems recovered relatively fast in short time scales.

Estimating the time represented by the K/Pg boundary layer, which was the initial motivation for the PGE geochemical study by *Alvarez et al* [1980], has been investigated using isotope studies. The boundary clay associated with the Chicxulub impact is globally distributed and relatively thin in distal sections. *Mukhopadhyay et al.* [2001] used helium-3 as a flux proxy of sedimentation rate in the clay layer and constrained the duration in less than about 10 kyr. In the study, they analyzed the Gubbio and Monte Conero sections in Italy and the Ain Settara section near El Kef in Tunisia. They report a near-constant flux of helium-3, which they use to rule out a comet shower and for the estimate of sedimentation rate. They conclude that there is not a long hiatus at the boundary, and that faunal turnover was relatively rapid. *Sepulveda et al.* [2009] examined the resurgence of marine primary productivity at the K/Pg boundary, which has been difficult to determine due to the lack of paleontological records tracing primary producers with no skeletons. They used stable carbon and nitrogen isotopes and abundances of algal steranes and bacterial hopanes in the K/Pg boundary Fish Clay in Denmark to quantify algal primary productivity. They conclude that there was a rapid resurgence of marine productivity with carbon fixation and ecological reorganization, after a short interval of possibly less than a century.

8.6. DISCUSSION

The formation of large complex craters involve high pressures and deformation, high temperatures and melting, excavation to deep crustal levels with fragmentation, and removal of large volumes of rock [*Melosh*, 1989]. Impacts constitute major geological processes shaping the surfaces of planetary bodies with implications for the composition and evolution of the crusts [*Neumann et al.*, 1996; *Mungall et al.*, 2004; *Urrutia-Fucugauchi and Pérez-Cruz*, 2009, 2011]. Large bolide impacts have deeper and long-lasting effects in planetary evolution [*Mohit and Phillips*, 2007]. Collisions of planetesimals and large asteroids were numerous in the early stages of evolution of the solar system. Remnants of such period are represented by the iron and differentiated meteorites which were once parts of differentiated bodies. Meteorite impacts spanning a wide range of compositions and sizes continue falling on Earth, most of them of small sizes, which provide unique and rich information on the early evolution of the Solar System, dynamic processes, effects on Earth systems and on potential hazards [e.g., *Covey et al.*, 1994; *Toon et al.*, 1997; *Lauretta and McSween*, 2006; *Urrutia-Fucugauchi et al.*, 2014]. An example of large collisions is the formation of the Earth-Moon system, with collision of a Mars-sized body with the early Earth, which resulted in partial melting of the Earth and formation of the Moon with bolide and Earth's components [*Canup and Asphaug*, 2001]. The ages for the Moon and Mars large impact basins record a period of heavy bombardment, which is documented in the inner solar system [*Frey*, 2006, 2008].

Mars is characterized by a hemispheric dichotomy, with the southern hemisphere with higher and abrupt topography and a northern hemisphere of lowlands and smooth relief [*McGill and Dimitriou*, 1990; *Watters et al.*, 2007]. The southern hemisphere is heavily cratered and includes the large impact basins [*Frey et al.*, 2002]. In contrast, the northern hemisphere has fewer craters and no large basins. The lowlands of the northern hemisphere present a thinner crust compared to the southern highlands that are 25 km thicker. Studies have proposed that the dichotomy was formed by a large impact, with the northern hemisphere being a very large impact basin [*Wilhelms and Squyres*, 1984; *Andrews-Hanna et al.*, 2008; *Marinova et al.*, 2008]. Impact may have occurred early in the solar system formation more than 4 Ga, producing a long-lasting effect on the evolution of Mars lithosphere with the hemispheric dichotomy.

Large crater-forming impacts occur in short time scales. The intense deformation at short time scales differs markedly from low stress rates that characterize geological processes of deformation and fracturing, which involve long time scales in a series of incremental steps [*Kenkemann*, 2002; *Lana et al.*, 2010]. Depending on pressure, rocks deform or fracture when a pressure limit is exceeded. In impact events the sudden large energy release with generation of shock waves on the target rocks imposing intense stresses, result in fracturing of a large rock volume. Transient pressures are large, producing high temperatures and strain rates, resulting in fracturing, shock mineral deformation, and melting [*Melosh*, 1989; *Cintala and Grieve*, 1998; *Pierazzo and Melosh*, 2000].

The end-Cretaceous mass extinction is part of the five big events documented in the fossil record for the Phanerozoic, being the second largest after the Permo-Triassic extinction [*Raup and Sepkoski*, 1982; *Bambach*, 2006]. The percentages of genera and species going extinct at any given time and extinction rates have been difficult to determine. The chronological control available does not permit to constraint adequately the duration of the extinction events. Detailed studies of stratigraphical sections provide better control on the timing, pattern, and synchronicity of extinctions, but even then sections are affected by hiatus and incompleteness problems. The duration of extinction events had been estimated in hundreds of thousands or millions of years [*Hallam*, 1987; *Archibald*, 1996]. The causation for the extinctions involves a range of mechanisms such as marine regressions and transgressions, global cooling or warming, ocean acidification, warming-induced calcification, ocean anoxia, and volcanic-induced climate perturbations [*Hallam*, 1987; *Archibald*, 1996; *Keller*, 2008]. These mechanisms affect the environment and climate at different spatial and temporal ranges, resulting in disappearing of genera and species. In this context, large bolide impacts introduced a drastically distinct scenario, involving an intense very short-lived perturbation with capacity for producing global changes and catastrophic affectation of organisms.

Mass extinctions are recognized from higher extinction rates as compared with background extinction patterns. Mass extinctions appear to involve and/or trigger additional processes, bringing qualitative and quantitative changes in extinction selectivity [*Jablonski*, 1994, 2005]. Mass extinctions result in macro-evolutionary changes, with empty ecological niches being filled involving complex dynamics in biota turnover. Studies of taxa extinction and survivorship, within the limitations on the incompleteness of fossil record, provide insight on inner structure and response for perturbations. Recovery patterns and trends of ecosystems portrait a complex dynamics with distinct spatial and temporal scales, which are beginning to be deciphered [*Jablonski*, 2008].

The effects of Chicxulub impact on the ecosystems extended for a long period of several millions of years.

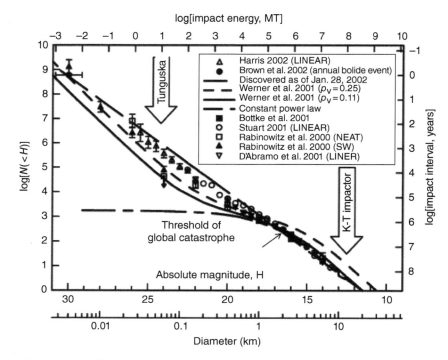

Figure 8.9 Logarithmic relationships among estimated impact interval (in years) and size distribution of cumulative number of NEAs as a function of impact energy release (in megatons MT), absolute magnitude of NEAs (H) and bolide diameter (in km) (taken from *Chapman* [2004]). The stellar magnitude H of an asteroid is estimated at 1 astronomical unit distance from Sun and Earth. Large impacts like Chicxulub with energy release of around 10 MT are characterized by long recurrence intervals, larger than 100 million years.

Disappearance of large numbers of species including complete groups severely affected the biodiversity and ecosystem composition in the marine and continental realms during the following periods. In the oceans, the K/Pg mass extinction affected groups of vertebrates, invertebrates, phytoplankton, and zooplankton, with entire groups disappearing, and long-term recovery time scales of several millions of years [*Sepkoski*, 1998; *Coxall et al.*, 2006]. The extinction was associated with a sharp decline in the flux of organic matter to the ocean deeps, with the suppression of pelagic marine productivity [*Zachos et al.*, 2008]. Recovery of the planktonic foraminifera involved diversification of new taxa during the Paleocene. The diversification patterns appear linked to recovery of the marine carbon cycle, with two stages recognized by *Coxall et al.* [2006] involving an extended period. Their study documents that time for reestablishment of integrated ecosystems in the deep ocean took several million years, following the collapse at the mass extinction event.

Effects of impacts in the environment and climate of the Earth have been intensely investigated, mainly in relation to the K/Pg boundary impact, where the affectation was profound and long lasting [*Pope et al.*, 1997; *Pierazzo et al.*, 2003; *Robertson et al.*, 2004]. The local and global

environmental effects depend on a number of factors, including the energy released, impact angle, latitude, oceanic or continental target, amount of dust and climate-active gases, etc. [*Toon et al.*, 1982, 1997; *Covey et al.*, 1990, 1994; *Wünnemann et al.*, 2010; *Schulte et al.*, 2010]. The energy released depends on the impactor mass and velocity, which permits to estimate the magnitude of the impact event. Approximate estimates of the energy released have been related to diameter of impactors. Large impacts like Chicxulub with energy release of around 10 MT are characterized by long recurrence intervals, larger than 100 million years, while smaller impacts tend to occur with short recurrence intervals. The frequency of impacts has also been related to the impactor size, giving a logarithmic plot that has been analyzed in terms of the hazard associated with impacts [*Chapman*, 2004; *Pierazzo and Artemieva*, 2012]. Hazard analyses posed by impacts have incorporated the size distribution of near-Earth asteroids (NEAs), which have been mapped in recent years (http://neo.jpl.nasa.gov/stats/). The relationships among estimated impact interval and size distribution for cumulative number of NEAs as a function of impact energy release and bolide diameter are plotted in Figure 8.9 (taken from *Chapman* [2004]). Large impacts have the capacity for global disruption of the ocean and atmosphere and affectation of the climate and life-support systems, with >10 km diameter impactors resulting on extinction events [*Schulte et al.*, 2010; *Pierazzo and Artemieva*, 2012].

8.7. CONCLUSIONS

In this chapter, we review the crater-forming impacts and their effects on the Earth's climate, environment, and life-supporting systems focusing on the K/Pg boundary and end-Cretaceous mass extinction of organisms. K/Pg boundary is marked by one of the major mass extinction events in the Phanerozoic, which affected about 40% of genera and 75% of species with whole groups disappearing, including the non-avian dinosaurs and ammonites.

Crater-forming impacts might be considered as a special class of extreme events with respect to other geological events, which are characterized by high energy release in "seconds" time scales. Impacts constitute major geological processes shaping the surfaces and evolution of planetary bodies. The formation of large complex craters with peak ring and multiring morphologies involves high pressures and temperatures resulting in intense deformation, fracturing and melting. Impacts produce deep transient cavities, with excavation to deep crustal levels, fragmentation, and removal of large volumes of rock.

The K/Pg boundary is marked by a clay layer globally distributed, which is characterized by anomalous contents of iridium, PGEs, and shocked minerals. The boundary clay marks the occurrence of a large bolide impact, which is traced by the Chicxulub crater. Chicxulub, located in the Yucatan Peninsula, southern Gulf of Mexico, is one of only three multiring basins in the terrestrial record. It is the only one with the ejecta preserved and the only multiring crater in the Phanerozoic. Studies examining the age, stratigraphical correlations, and composition of the K/Pg boundary layer have documented the genetic links to the Chicxulub crater. Impact resulted in deformation and shaking, which is recorded in the breccias and debris flow deposits in the Gulf of Mexico and Caribbean Sea area. Impact was on a shallow carbonate platform and resulted in huge tsunamis and in injection of carbon dioxide and sulfur components into the atmosphere.

Effects of impacts in the Earth's environment and climate are better understood, thanks mainly to studies of the K/Pg boundary impact. The affectation in the biota was profound and long lasting. Effects of the impact on the ecosystems extended for a long period of several millions of years. Disappearance of large numbers of species including complete groups severely affected the biodiversity and ecosystem composition in the marine and continental realms.

There are different aspects involved in addressing the Chicxulub impact as an extreme event. They include, examining the impact event and cratering, time scales involved and energy released and, assessing the local, regional and global effects, which involve major perturbations in the ocean and atmosphere modifying the climate and environment. We discuss how and to what extent life-support systems are affected by large impacts; and what the fossil record reveals about the extinction event and biotic turnover and how sudden or extended are the processes and extinction temporal records.

Studies of the K/Pg boundary events and mass extinction of organisms have focused increasing attention on the nature of sudden discrete events in the stratigraphical record. The impact hypothesis for the end-Cretaceous mass extinction reintroduced catastrophic scenarios for a discrete extreme event with long-lasting consequences. The impact produced a large crater in hundred of seconds time scales, generating severe effects on the Earth's atmosphere, oceans, and climate affecting life-support systems globally, causing a mass extinction.

Research on extreme events has over the past decades emerged as a major area in Earth and planetary sciences, across a wide range of disciplines, with a strong inter- and multidisciplinary character and with implications into the social and economical sciences. Extreme events within this context include large earthquakes, explosive volcanic eruptions, crater-forming impacts, tsunamis, catastrophic landslides and floods, which involve processes delivering huge amounts of energy on short time scales at their extreme ends of process range. Recognition and study of extreme events in the past geological records become more complex, due to problems related to stratigraphical and dating resolution of events. Stratigraphical analyses and recognition of sudden versus gradual processes remains a complex task, due to the incompleteness of the records, sampling resolution, biases, correlation, and dating. Analysis of the K/Pg boundary offers the possibility of exploring criteria for evaluating the geological record of an extreme event associated with a sudden catastrophic asteroidal impact.

ACKNOWLEDGMENTS

This study forms part of the UNAM Chicxulub Research Program and the Ocean and Continents Drilling Project. Partial support for the studies has been provided by UNAM PAPIIT project grants IN101112 and IG-101115.

REFERENCES

Abramov, O., and Kring, D. A., (2007), Numerical modelling of impact-induced hysdrothermal activity at Chicxulub crater. *Meteor. Planet. Sci.*, *42*, 93–112.

Alvarez, L. W., W. Alvarez, F. Asaro, and H. V. Michel (1980), Extraterrestrial cause for the Cretaceous–Tertiary extinction, *Science*, *208*, 1095–1108.

Andrews-Hanna, J. C., M. T. Zuber, and W. B. Banerdt (2008), The Borealis basin and the origin of the Martian crustal dichotomy, *Nature, 453,* doi:10.1038/nature07011.

Archibald, J. D. (1996), *Dinosaur extinction and the end of an area: What the fossil record say,* pp. 237, Columbia University Press, New York.

Arenillas, I., J. A. Arz, J. M. Grajales, G. Murillo, W. Alvarez, A. Camargo-Zanoguera, E. Molina, and A. Rosales (2007), Chicxulub impact event is Cretaceous/Paleogene boundary in age: New micropaleontological evidence, *Earth Planet. Sci. Lett., 249,* 241–257.

Bambach, R. K. (2006), Phanerozoic biodiversity mass extinctions, *Ann. Rev. Earth Planet. Sci., 34,* 127–155.

Barrett, P. M., A. J. McGowan, and V. Page (2009), Dinosaur diversity and the rock record, *Proc. R. Soc. B, 276,* doi:10.1098/rspb.2009.0352.

Batista, J., M. A. Pérez-Flores, and J. Urrutia-Fucugauchi (2013), Three-dimensional gravity modeling of Chicxulub Crater structure, constrained with marine seismic data and land boreholes, *Earth Planets Space, 65,* 973–983.

Belcher, C. M., M. E. Collinson, A. R. Sweet, A. R. Hildebrand, and A. C. Scott (2003), "Fireball passes and nothing burns"—The role of thermal radiation in the K-T event: Evidence from the charcoal record of North America, *Geology, 31,* 1061–1064.

Belcher, C. M., P. Finch, M. E. Collinson, A. C. Scott, and N. V. Grassineau (2009), Geochemical evidence for combustion of hydrocarbons during the K-T impact event, *Proc. Nat. Acad. Sci., 106,* 4112–4117.

Bourgeois, J., T. A. Hansen, P. L. Wiberg, and E. G. Kaufman (1988), A tsunami deposit at the Cretaceous-Tertiary boundary in Texas, *Science, 241,* 567–570.

Brett, R. (1992), The Cretaceous-Tertiary extinction: a lethal mechanism involving anhydrite target rocks, *Geoch. Cosmoch. Acta, 56,* 3603–3606.

Brusalte, S. P., R. J. Buttler, A. Prieto-Marquez, and M. A. Norell (2012), Dinosaur morphological diversity and the end-Cretaceous extinction, *Nature Comm., 3* Art. 804, doi:10.1038/natcomms/815.

Canup, R. M., and E. Asphaug (2001), Origin of the Moon in a giant impact near the end of the Earth's formation, *Nature, 412,* 708–712.

Chapman, C. R. (2004), The hazard of near-Earth asteroid impacts on Earth, *Earth Planet. Sci. Lett., 222,* 1–15.

Chenet, A. L., F. Fluteau, V. Courtillot, M. Gerard, and K. V. Subbarao (2008), Determination of rapid Deccan eruptions across the Cretaceous-Tertiary boundary using paleomagnetic secular variation: Results from a 1200-m-thick section in the Mahabaleshwar escarpment. *J. Geophys res., 113,* B04101.

Claeys, P., W. Kiessling, and W. Alvarez (2002), Distribution of Chicxulub ejecta at the Cretaceous-Tertiary boundary. In: Koeberl, C. and MacLeod, K.G. (Eds), Catastrophic Events and Mass Extinctions: Impacts and Beyond, *Geol. Soc. Am. Spec. Pap., 356,* 55–68.

Cintala, M., and R. Grieve (1998), Scaling impact melting and crater dimensions: Implications for the lunar cratering record, *Meteorit. Planet. Sci., 33,* 889–912.

Collins, G. S., J. Morgan, P. Barton, G. L. Christeson, S. Gulick, J. Urrutia-Fucugauchi, M. Warner, and K. Wünnemann (2008), Dynamic modeling suggests terrace zone asymmetry in the Chicxulub crater is caused by target heterogeneity, *Earth Planet. Sci. Lett.,* doi:10.1016/j.epsl.2008.03.032.

Connors, M., A. R. Hildebrand, M. Pilkington, C. Ortíz, R. E. Chávez, J. Urrutia-Fucugauchi, E. Graniel-Castro, A. Camara-Zi, J. Vasquez, and J. F. Halpenny (1996), Yucatan karst features and the size of Chicxulub crater, *Geophys. J. Int., 127,* F11–F14.

Covey, C., S. J. Ghan, J. J. Walton, and P. R. Weissman (1990), Global environmental effects of impact-generated aerosols: results from a general circulation model, in Sharpton, V.L. and Ward, P.D., eds, Global Catastrophes in Earth History, *Geol. Soc. Am. Spec. Pap., 247,* 263–270.

Covey, C., S. L. Thompson, P. R. Weissman, and M. C. MacCraken (1994), Global climatic effects of atmospheric dust from an asteroid or comet impact on Earth, *Global Planet. Change, 9,* 263–273.

Coxall, H. K., S. D'Hondt, and J. C. Zachos (2006), Pelagic evolution and environmental recovery after the Cretaceous-Paleogene mass extinction, *Geology, 34,* 297–300.

D'Hondt, S., J. King, and C. Gibson (1996), Oscillatory marine response to the Cretaceous-Tertiary impact, *Geology, 24,* 611–614.

D'Hondt, S., P. Donaghay, J. C. Zachos, D. Luttenberg, and M. Lindinger (1998), Organic carbon fluxes and ecological recovery from the Cretaceous-Tertiary mass extinction, *Science, 282,* 276–279.

Emiliani, C., E. B. Kraus, and E. M. Shoemaker (1981), Sudden death at the end of the Mesozoic, *Earth Plant. Sci. Lett., 55,* 317–334.

Escobar-Sanchez, J. E., and Urrutia-Fucugauchi, J., (2010), Chicxulub crater post-impact hydrothermal activity - evidence from Paleocene carbonates in the Santa Elena borehole. *Geofis. Int., 49,* 97–106.

Frey, H. V., J. H. Roark, K. M. Shockey, E. L. Frey, and S. E. H. Sakimoto (2002), Ancient lowlands on Mars, *Geophys. Res. Lett., 29,* 1384, doi:10.1029/2001/GL013832.

Frey, H. V. (2006), Impact constraints on, and a chronology for, major events in early Mars history, *J. Geophys. Res., 111,* E08S91, doi:10.1029/2005/JE002449.

Frey, H. V. (2008), Ages of very large impact basins on Mars: Implications for the Late Heavy Bombardment in the Inner Solar System, *Geophys. Res. Lett., 35,* L13203.

Gelinas, A., D. A. Kring, L. Zurcher, J. Urrutia-Fucugauchi, O. Morton, and R. J. Walker (2004), Osmium isotope constraints on the proportion of bolide component in Chicxulub impact melts, *Meteorit. Planet. Sci., 39,* 1003–1008.

Ghil, M., P. Yiou, S. Hallegatte, B. D. Malamud, P. Naveau, A. Soloviev, P. Friederichs, V. Keilis-Borok, D. Kondrashov, V. Kossobokov, O. Mestre, C. Nicolis, H. W. Rust, P. Shebalin, M. Vrac, A. Witt, and I. Zaliapin (2011), Extreme events: dynamics, statistics and prediction, *Nonlin. Process. Geophys., 18,* 295–350.

Gilmour, O., and E. Anders (1989), Cretaceous-Tertiary boundary event: Evidence for a short time scale, *Geochim. Cosmochim. Acta, 53,* 503–511.

Goldin, T. J., and H. J. Melosh (2009), Self-shielding of thermal radiation by Chicxulub impact ejecta: Firestorm or fizzle?, *Geology*, *37*, 1135–1138.

Grieve, R., and A. Therriault (2000), Vredefort, Sudbury, Chicxulub: Three of a kind?, *Ann. Rev. Earth Planet. Sci.*, *28*, 305–338.

Gulick, S., P. Barton, G. Christeson, J. Morgan, M. MacDonald, K. Mendoza, J. Urrutia-Fucugauchi, P. Vermeesch, and M. Warner (2008), Importance of pre-impact crustal structure for the asymmetry of the Chicxulub impact crater, *Nat. Geosci.*, *1*, 131–135.

Hallam, A. (1987), End-Cretaceous mass extinction event: Argument for terrestrial causation, *Science*, *238*, 1237–1242.

Harvey, M. C., S. C. Brassell, C. M. Belcher, and A. Montnari (2008), Combustion of fossil organic matter at the Cretaceous-Paleogene (K-P) boundary, *Geology*, *36*, 355–358.

Hildebrand, A. R., G. T. Penfield, D. A. Kring, M. Pilkington, A. Camargo-Zanoguera, S. B. Jacobsen, and W. V. Boynton (1991), Chicxulub Crater: A possible Cretaceous/Tertiary boundary impact crater on the Yucatan Peninsula, Mexico, *Geology*, *19*, 867–871.

Hildebrand, A., M. Pilkington, C. Ortiz-Aleman, R. E. Chavez, J. Urrutia-Fucugauchi, M. Connors, E. Graniel-Castro, A. Camara-Zi, J. F. Halpenny, and D. Niehaus (1998), Mapping Chicxulub crater structure with gravity and seismic data. In: Meteorites: Flux with Time and Impact Effects, Grady, R. *et al.* (Eds.), *Geol. Soc. Spec. Publ.*, *140*, 155–176.

Jablonski, D. (1994), Extinctions in the fossil record, *Phil. Trans. R. Soc. Lond. B*, *344*, 11–17.

Jablonski, D. (2005), Mass extinctions and macroevolution, *Paleontology*, *31*, 192–210.

Jablonski, D. (2008), Extinction and the spatial dynamics of biodiversity, *Proc. Natl Acad.Sci.*, *105*, 11528–11535.

Kamo, S. L., C. Lana, and J. V. Morgan (2011), U-Pb ages of shocked zircon grains link distal K-Pg boundary sites in Spain and Italy with the Chicxulub impact, *Earth Planet. Sci. Lett.*, *310*, 401–408.

Keller, G. (2008), Cretaceous climate, volcanism, impacts, and biotic effects, *Cretaceous. Res.*, *29*, 754–771.

Keller, G., T. Adatte, W. Stinnisbeck, M. Rebolledo-Vieyra, J. Urrutia-Fucugauchi, U. Kramar, and D. Stueben (2004), Chicxulub impact predates the K-T boundary mass extinction, *Proceed. Nat. Acad. Sci.*, *101*, 3753–3758.

Kenkemann, T. (2002), Folding within seconds, *Geology*, *30*, 231–234.

Kring, D. A. (1995), The dimensions of the Chicxulub impact crater and impact melt sheet, *J. Geophys. Res.*, *100*, 16979–16986.

Kring, D. A., L. Horz, L. Zurcher, and J. Urrutia-Fucugauchi (2004), Impact lithologies and their emplacement in the Chicxulub impact crater: Initial results from the Chicxulub scientific drilling project, Yaxcopoil, *Mexico. Meteorit. Planet. Sci.*, *39*, 879–897.

Krogh, T. E., S. L. Kamo, V. L. Sharpton, L. E. Marin, and A. R. Hildebrand (1993), U–Pb ages of single shocked zircons linking distal K/T ejecta to the Chicxulub crater, *Nature*, *366*, 731–733.

Kuiper, K. F., A. Deino, F. J. Hilgen, W. Krijsman, P. R. Renne, and J. R. Wijbrans (2008), Synchronizing rock clocks of Earth history, *Science*, *320*, 500–504.

Lana, C., C. R. Souza Filho, Y. R. Marangoni, E. Yokoyama, E. Trindade, E. Tohver, and W. U. Reimold (2010), Structural evolution of the 40 km wide Araguainha impact structure, central Brazil, *Meteorit. Planet. Sci.*, *43*, 701–716.

Lauretta, D. S., and H. Y. McSween (Eds) (2006), Meteorites and the Early Solar System II, Tucson, University of Arizona Press, 943 pp.

Lopez Ramos, E. (1976), Geological summary of the Yucatan peninsula, in *The Ocean Basins and Margins, vol. 3, The Gulf of Mexico and the Caribbean*, edited by A. E. M. Nairn and F. G. Stehli, pp. 257–282, Plenum, New York.

Lyson, T. R., A. Bercovici, S. G. B. Chester, E. J. Sargis, D. Pearson, and W. Joyce (2011), Dinosaur extinction: closing the "3 m gap", *Biol. Lett.*, doi:10.1098/rsbl.2011.0470.

MacDougall, J. D. (1988), Seawater strontium isotopes, acid rain, and the Cretaceous-Tertiary boundary, *Science*, *239*, 485–487.

Marinova, M. M., O. Aharonson, and E. Asphaug (2008), Mega-impact formation of the Mars hemispheric dichotomy, *Nature*, *453*, doi:10.1038/nature07070.

Marshall, C. R. (1995), Distinguishing between sudden and gradual extinctions in the fossil record: Predicting the position of the Cretaceous-Tertiary iridium anomaly using the ammonite fossil record on Seymour Island, Antarctica, *Geology*, *23*, 731–734.

Marshall, C. R., and P. D. Ward (1996), Sudden and gradual molluscan extinctions in the latest Cretaceous of Western European Tethys, *Science*, *274*, 1360–1363.

Martin, E. E., and J. D. MacDougall (1991), Seawater strontium isotopes at the Cretaceous/Tertiary boundary, *Earth Planet. Sci., Lett.*, *104*, 166–180.

McGill, G. E., and A. M. Dimitriou (1990), Origin of the Martian global dichotomy by crustal thinning in the Late Noachian or early Hesperian, *J. Geophys. Res.*, *95*, 12595–12605.

Melosh, H. J. (1989), *Impact Cratering: A Geologic Process*, pp. 245, Oxford University Press, New York.

Melosh, H. J., and B. A. Ivanov (1999), Impact crater collapse, *Ann. Rev. Earth Planet. Sci.*, *27*, 385–415.

Melosh, H. J., N. M. Schneider, K. J. Zahale, and D. Latham (1990), Ignition of global wildfires at the Cretaceous/Tertiary boundary, *Nature*, *343*, 251–254.

Meyers, R. A. (Ed.) (2010), *Extreme Environmental Events: Complexity in Forecasting and Early Warning*, pp. 1250, Springer, New York.

Mohit, P. S., and R. J. Phillips (2007), Viscous relaxation on early Mars: A study of ancient impact basins, *Geophys. Res. Lett.*, *34*, L21214, doi:10.1029/2007GL031252.

Morgan, J., M. Werner, and Chicxulub Group (1997), Size and morphology of the Chicxulub impact crater, *Nature*, *390*, 472–476.

Morgan, J., and M. Warner (1999), Chicxulub: The third dimension of a multi-ring basin, *Geology*, *27*, 407–410.

Morgan, J. V., C. Lana, A. Kearsley, B. Coles, C. Belcher, S. Montanari, E. Díaz-Martínez, A. Barbosa, and V. Neumann (2006), Analyses of shocked quartz at the global K-P boundary indicate an origin from a single, high-angle, oblique impact at Chicxulub, *Earth Planet. Sci. Lett.*, *251*, 264–279.

Mukhopadhyay, S., K. A. Farley, and A. Montanari (2001), A short duration of the Cretaceous-Tertiary boundary event : Evidence from extraterrestrial helium-3, *Science*, *291*, 1952–1955.

Mungall, J. E., D. E. Ames, and J. J. Hanley (2004), Geochemical evidence from the Sudbury structure for crustal redistribution by large bolides, *Nature*, *429*, 546–548.

Neumann, G. A., M. Zuber, D. E. Smith, and F. G. Lemoine (1996), The lunar crust: global structure and signature of major basins, *J. Geophys. Res.*, *101*, 16841–16863.

Ortiz-Aleman, C., and J. Urrutia-Fucugauchi (2010), Aeromagnetic anomaly modeling of central zone structure and magnetic sources in the Chicxulub crater, *Phys. Earth Planet. Int.*, *179*, 127–138, doi:10.1016/j.pepi.2010.01.007.

Payne, J. L. (2003), Applicability and resolving power of statistical tests for simultaneous extinction events in the fossil record, *Paleobiology*, *29*, 37–51.

Penfield, G. T., and A. Camargo-Zanoguera (1981), Definition of a major igneous zone in the central Yucatán platform with aeromagnetics and gravity, en Technical Program, Abstracts and Bibliographies, 51st Annual Meeting, Society of Exploration Geophysicists, Tulsa, OK, p. 37.

Pierazzo, E., and H. J. Melosh (2000), Understanding oblique impacts from experiments, observations, and modelling, *Ann. Rev. Earth Planet. Sci.*, *28*, 141–167.

Pierazzo, E., A. H. Hahamann, and L. C. Sloan (2003), Chicxulub and climate: Radiation perturbations of impact-produced S-bearing gases, *Astrobiology*, *3*, 99–118.

Pierazzo, E., and N. Artemieva (2012), Local and global environmental effects of impacts on Earth, *Elements*, *8*, 55–60.

Pilkington, M., and A. R. Hildebrand (2000), Three-dimensional magnetic imaging of the Chicxulub crater, *J. Geophys. Res.*, *105*, 23479–23491.

Pope, K. O. (2002), Impact dust not the cause of the Cretaceous-Tertiary mass extinction, *Geology*, *30*, 99–102.

Pope, K. O., K. H. Baines, A. C. Ocampo, and B. A. Ivanov (1997), Energy, volataile production and climatic effects of the Cretaceous/Tertiary impact, *J. Geophys. Res*, *102*, 21645–21664.

Pope, A. C., A. G. Ocampo, F. Fisher, D. E. Vega, D. T. Ames, B. King, R. J. Fouke, and G. K. Wachtman (2005), Chicxulub impact ejecta deposits in southern Quintana Roo, Mexico, and central Belize, *Geol. Soc. Am. Spec. Pap.*, *384*, 171–190.

Raup, D. M., and J. J. Sepkoski (1982), Mass extinctions in the marine fossil record, *Science*, *215*, 1501–1503.

Raup, D. M., and D. Jablonski (1993), Geography of end-Cretaceous marine bivalve extinctions, *Science*, *260*, 971–973.

Ravizza, G., and B. Peucker-Ehrenbrink (2003), Chemo-stratigraphic evidence of Deccan volcanism from the marine osmium isotope record, *Science*, *302*, 1392–1395.

Rebolledo-Vieyra, M., J. Urrutia-Fucugauchi, and H. Lopez-Loera (2010), Structural model of the Chicxulub impact crater derived from aeromagnetic anomaly and borehole data, *Rev. Mex. Ciencias Geol.*, *27*, 185–195.

Robertson, D. S., M. C. McKenna, O. B. Toon, S. Hope, and J. A. Lillegraven (2004), Survival in the first hours of the Cenozoic, *Geol. Soc. Am. Bull.*, *116*, 760–768.

Schulte, P., L. Alegret, I. Arenillas, J. A. Arz, P. J. Barton, P. R. Bown, T. J. Bralower, G. L. Christeson, P. Claeys, C. S. Cockell, G. S. Collins, A. Deutsch, T. J. Goldin, K. Goto, J. M. Grajales-Nishimura, R. A. Grieve, S. P. Gulick, K. R. Johnson, W. Kiessling, C. Koeberl, D. A. Kring, K. G. MacLeod, T. Matsui, J. Melosh, A. Montanari, J. V. Morgan, C. R. Neal, D. J. Nichols, R. D. Norris, E. Pierazzo, G. Ravizza, M. Rebolledo-Vieyra, W. U. Reimold, E. Robin, T. Salge, R. P. Speijer, A. R. Sweet, J. Urrutia-Fucugauchi, V. Vajda, M. T. Whalen, and P. S. Willumsen (2010), The Chicxulub asteroid impact and mass extinction at the Cretaceous-Paleogene boundary, *Science*, *327*, 1214–1218.

Sepkoski, J. J., Jr. (1998), Rates of speciation in the fossil record, *Phil. Trans. R. Soc. Lond. Ser. B*, *353*, 315–316.

Sepulveda, J., J. E. Wedler, R. E. Summons, and K.-U. Hinrichs (2009), Rapid resurgence of marine productivity after the Cretaceous-Paleogene mass extinction, *Science*, *326*, 129–132.

Sereno, P. (1999), The evolution of dinosaurs, *Science*, *284*, 2137–2147.

Sharpton, V. L., G. Dalrymple, L. Marin, G. Ryder, B. Schuraytz, and J. Urrutia-Fucugauchi (1992), New links between the Chicxulub impact structure and the Cretaceous/Tertiary boundary, *Nature*, *359*, 819–821.

Sharpton, V. L., K. Burke, A. Camargo-Zanoguera, S. A. Hall, D. S. Lee, L. E. Marín, G. Suáarez-Reynoso, J. M. Quezada-Muñeton, P. D. Spudis, and J. Urrutia-Fucugauchi (1993), Chicxulub multiring impact basin: Size and other characteristics derived from gravity analysis, *Science*, *261*, 1564–1567.

Sheehan, P. M., D. E. Fastovsky, C. Barreto, and P. G. Hoffman (2000), Dinosaur abundance was not declining in a "3 m gap" at the top of the Hell Creek formation, Montana and Dakota, *Geology*, *28*, 523–526.

Signor, P. W., and J. H. Lipps (1982), Sampling bias, gradual extinction patterns, and catastrophes in the fossil record. In: Silver, L.T. & Schultz, P.H. (Eds), Geological implications of large asteroids and comets on Earth, *Geol. Soc. Am. Spec. Pap.*, *190*, 291–296.

Springer, M. S. (1990), The effects of random range truncations on patterns of evolution in the fossil record, *Paleobiology*, *16*, 512–520.

Straus, D., and P. M. Sadler (1989), Classical confidence intervals and Bayesian probability estimates for ends of local taxon ranges, *Math Geol.*, *21*, 411–427.

Tohver, E., C. Lana, P. A. Cawood, I. R. Fletcher, F. Jourdan, S. Sherlock, B. Rasmussen, R. I. F. Trindade, E. Yokoyama, C. R. Souza Filho, and Y. Marangoni (2012), Geochronological constraints on a Permo-Triassic impact crater: U-Pb and [40]Ar/[39]Ar results from the 40km Araguainha crater of central Brazil, *Geochim. Cosmochim. Acta*, *86*, 214–227.

Toon, O. B., J. B. Pollack, T. P. Ackerman, R. P. Turco, C. P. McKay, and M. S. Liu (1982), Evolution of an impact-generated dust cloud and its effects on the atmosphere, *in* Silver, L.T., and Schultz, P.H., eds., Geological implications of impacts of large asteroids and comets on Earth, *Geol. Soc. Am. Spec. Pap.*, *190*, 187–200.

Toon, O. B., K. Zahale, D. Morrison, R. P. Turco, and C. Covey (1997), Environmental perturbations caused by the impacts of asteroids and comets, *Rev. Geophys.*, *35*, 41–78.

Urrutia-Fucugauchi, J., L. Marin, and V. L. Sharpton (1994), Reverse polarity magnetized melt rocks from the Cretaceous/Tertiary Chicxulub structure, Yucatan peninsula, Mexico, *Tectonophysics*, *237*, 105–112.

Urrutia-Fucugauchi, J., L. Marin, and A. Trejo (1996), UNAM scientific drilling program of Chicxulub impact structure—Evidence for a 300 kilometer crater diameter, *Geophys. Res. Lett.*, *23*, 1565–1568.

Urrutia-Fucugauchi, J., J. Morgan, D. Stoeffler, and P. Claeys (2004), The Chicxulub scientific drilling project (CSDP), *Meteorit. Planet. Sci.*, *39*, 787–790.

Urrutia-Fucugauchi, J., J. M. Chavez, L. Pérez-Cruz, and J. L. de la Rosa (2008), Impact ejecta and carbonate sequence in the eastern sector of Chicxulub Crater, *Comptes Rendus Geosciences*, *340*, 801–810, doi:10.1016/j.crte.2008.09.001.

Urrutia-Fucugauchi, J., and L. Pérez-Cruz (2008), Post-impact carbonate deposition in the Chicxulub impact crater region, Yucatan platform, Mexico, *Curr. Sci.*, *95*, 248–252.

Urrutia-Fucugauchi, J., and L. Pérez-Cruz (2009), Multiring-forming large bolide impacts and evolution of planetary surfaces, *Int. Geol. Rev.*, *51*, 1079–1102.

Urrutia-Fucugauchi, J., A. Camargo-Zanoguera, L. Pérez-Cruz, and G. Pérez-Cruz (2011a), The Chicxulub multiring impact crater, Yucatan carbonate platform, Mexico, *Geofis. Int.*, *50*, 99–127.

Urrutia-Fucugauchi, J., A. Camargo-Zanoguera, and L. Pérez-Cruz (2011b), Discovery and focused study of the Chicxulub impact crater, *EOS (Trans American Geophysical Union)*, *92*(25), 209–210.

Urrutia-Fucugauchi, J., and L. Pérez-Cruz (2011), Buried impact basins, the evolution of planetary surfaces and the Chicxulub multi-ring crater, *Geol. Today*, *27*, 222–227.

Urrutia-Fucugauchi, J., L. Pérez-Cruz, and D. Flores-Gutiérrez (2014), Meteorite paleomagnetism—From magnetic domains to planetary fields and core dynamos, *Geofis. Int.*, *53*, 343–363.

Velasco-Villarreal, M., J. Urrutia-Fucugauchi, M. Rebolledo, and L. Pérez-Cruz (2011), Paleomagnetism of impact breccias from the Chicxulub crater—Implications for ejecta emplacement and hydrothermal processes, *Phys. Earth Planet. Int.*, *186*, 154–171, doi:10.1016/j.pepi.2011.04.003.

Villasante-Marcos, Martinez, F., Osete, M., and Urrutia-Fucugauchi, J., (2007), Magnetic characterization of Cretaceous-Tertiary boundary sediments. *Meteor. Planet. Sci.*, *42*, 1505–1527.

Vonhof, H. B., and J. Smit (1997), High-resolution late Maastrichtian-early Danian oceanic Sr/Sr record: Implications for Cretaceous-Tertiary boundary events, *Geology*, *25*, 347–350.

Wang, S. C., and P. Dodson (2006), Estimating the diversity of dinosaurs, *Proc. Natl Acad. Sci. USA*, *103*, 13601–13605, doi:10.1073/pnas.0606028103.

Wang, S. C., A. E. Zimmerman, B. S. McVeigh, P. J. Everson, and H. Wong (2012), Confidence intervals for the duration of a mass extinction, *Paleobiology*, *38*, 265–277.

Watters, T. R., P. J. McGovern, and R. P. Irwin (2007), Hemispheres apart: The crustal dichotomy on Mars, *Annual Reviews Earth Planetary Sciences*, *35*, 621–652.

Wilhelms, D. E., and S. W. Squyres (1984), The Martian hemispheric dichotomy may be due to a giant impact, *Nature*, *309*, 138–140.

Wolbach, W. S., I. Gilmour, E. Anders, C. J. Orth, and R. R. Book (1988), Global fire at the Cretaceous–Tertiary boundary, *Nature*, *334*, 665–669.

Wünnemann, K., G. S. Collins, and B. Weiss (2010), Impact of a cosmic body into Earth's ocean and the generation of large tsunami waves: Insight from numerical modeling, *Rev. Geophys.*, *48*, RG4006.

Zachos, J. C., G. R. Dickens, and R. E. Zeebe (2008), An early Cenozoic perspective on greenhouse warming and carbon-cycle dynamics, *Nature*, *451*, 279–283, doi:10.1038/nature06588.

Part III
Climate and Weather Extremes

9

Weather and Climatic Drivers of Extreme Flooding Events over the Midwest of the United States

Andrew W. Robertson,[1] Yochanan Kushnir,[2] Upmanu Lall,[3] and Jennifer Nakamura[2]

ABSTRACT

The April 2011 floods in the Ohio River Basin and in the lower Mississippi River region were the latest of a set of major such flooding events recorded over the 20th century (defined in terms of a 10 year return maximum in stream flow). The questions of whether the recent 2011 event herald a return of more frequent flooding, and the degree of potential climate predictability of such events both require a better understanding of how the frequency and intensity of the synoptic weather events responsible for the floods vary on intra-seasonal-to-interdecadal timescales, and how these are influenced by large-scale modes of climate variability.

In this chapter, we present an analysis of daily circulation types (or regimes) derived from reanalysis wind data using a *K*-means cluster analysis for the March-May season, from which we infer relationships between flooding events and circulation types, and between these types and climate drivers, including the interannual El Niño-Southern Oscillation (ENSO) and the intra-seasonal Madden-Julian Oscillation (MJO). Anomalous southerly fluxes of moisture from the Gulf of Mexico are found to be pronounced in weather types that occur in connection with these floods. Two of these circulation types are preferentially associated with La Niña. Statistically significant lagged relationships between the frequency of occurrence of these regimes and the MJO are also identified, associated with convection propagating from the Indian Ocean to the Maritime Continent. Implications for prediction across timescales are also discussed.

9.1. INTRODUCTION

Extreme floods cause humanitarian disasters. They translate into higher averaged annual economic losses than any other natural disaster, and account for approximately half of all losses due to natural hazards globally

[*Kron*, 2005]. Consequently, there is significant concern as to how the frequency and intensity of extreme floods may change with climate. In tandem, there is an urgent need to better understand how partly predictable modes of climate variability impact the probability of flood events, in order to manage climate-related risks across multiple timescales, from weekly to interannual and beyond. The seminal work of *Hirschboeck* [1988] defines floods as an intersection between dynamic hydrometeorological variability and geographically fixed geomorphological features. Hirschboek hypothesized that climate-induced variations in the intensity and frequency of atmospheric moisture transports, and their

[1]*International Research Institute for Climate and Society (IRI), Columbia University, New York, USA*

[2]*Lamont-Doherty Earth Observatory, Columbia University, New York, USA*

[3]*Department of Earth and Environmental Engineering, Columbia University, New York, USA*

Extreme Events: Observations, Modeling, and Economics, Geophysical Monograph 214, First Edition.
Edited by Mario Chavez, Michael Ghil, and Jaime Urrutia-Fucugauchi.

intersection with river basin dynamics could in turn be responsible for epochal variations in the frequency, severity, location, and distribution of floods. Climate undergoes natural fluctuations through persistent and oscillatory regimes at intra-seasonal (e.g., the 30–60 day Madden-Julian Oscillation, MJO), interannual (e.g., the El Niño-Southern Oscillation, ENSO) timescales, as well as decadal and longer (e.g., the Pacific Decadal Oscillation or PDO), and as a function of anthropogenic changes of the atmosphere and land surface. This multi-timescale evolution changes the "odds" of occurrence of heavy local precipitation events, and hence of floods [*Sankarasubramanian and Lall*, 2003], and it has been argued that flood frequency is quite sensitive to modest changes in climate [*Knox*, 1993].

Flood events may last minutes with a spatial scale of a few km^2 (flash floods) or months with a spatial scale in excess of $10^6 km^2$ (e.g., the 1993 Mississippi flood). Here, we are primarily concerned with extreme floods over large areas, and correspondingly longer durations. The flood dynamics are more complicated when drainage basins larger than $10^4 km^2$ are considered : (1) the potential for high heterogeneity in the initial soil moisture field is greater and (2) the direction and location of the storm moving through the basin lends a significant heterogeneity to the rainfall distribution as well.

The literature on the scaling properties of floods with drainage area suggests that the precipitation input type (e.g., convective dominated vs. snowmelt vs. frontal) and drainage network attributes, jointly determine different scaling behaviors of discharge with area [e.g., *Farquharson et al.*, 1992; *Gupta et al.*, 1994; *Pandey et al.*, 1998; *Gupta*, 2004]. There is evidence that these scaling exponents for floods may vary across events or types of events in the same location, likely because of differences in storm tracks and drainage area precipitation coverage. As the drainage area increases (e.g., upper + lower Mississippi basins), it is not clear whether these scaling relationships will hold since a mix of mechanisms may be at play in generating such large floods. As the relevant atmospheric spatial scales increase, phenomena such as tropical and extra-tropical cyclones, and their associated fronts become important for large-area rainfall production and subsequent flooding potential. These features are directly related to large-scale circulation patterns, and have well-defined moisture tracks, that is, organized fluxes of moisture over a deep atmospheric layer.

Konrad [2001] attempted to identify the most extreme precipitation events as a function of averaging area over the eastern United States (1950–1996 period, 2 day $10 km \times 10 km$ gridded rainfall over 10 overlapping circular regions from 2500 to $500,000 km^2$) and the associated hydroclimatic mechanisms. The heaviest events, extending across the greatest range of spatial scales in the Midwest, occurred during the 1968 and 1973 fall seasons over Kansas, and were associated with strong transport of Gulf of Mexico moisture by an interacting system of slow moving cyclones. In the Northeast and Southeast, the most significant rainfall events at all spatial scales were found to be associated with tropical storms and hurricanes. Tropical cyclones were also prominent in the South-Central region at all scales. Thus, in almost all cases for the regions considered, large-scale flow systems dominate intense rainfall with large-area coverage, and also down to smaller scales.

Mechanistic connections between the probabilities of extreme floods and climate necessarily involve daily weather timescales, and relationships between local weather and the larger, slower modes of climate variability and change mentioned before. Mid-latitude atmospheric intra-seasonal variability is known to be characterized by certain large-scale flow patterns that appear repeatedly at fixed geographical locations, and persist beyond the lifetime of individual synoptic-scale storms. These patterns were termed *Grosswetterlagen* (large-scale weather situations) by *Bauer* [1951], and were later systematized in terms of teleconnection patterns [*Wallace and Gutzler*, 1981], or persistent anomalies [*Dole and Gordon*, 1983] in mid-tropospheric geopotential height fields, and more recently in terms of circulation types (or "weather regimes") that typically persist for several days to 2 weeks, with rapid transitions between them associated with the nonlinearity of atmospheric dynamics [*Vautard*, 1990; *Kimoto and Ghil*, 1993a, 1993b]. Weather regimes are known to organize mid-latitude storms [e.g., *Robertson and Metz*, 1990] and associated with significant temperature anomalies [*Michelangeli et al.*, 1995]. In addition, there is evidence from observations and general circulation model (GCM) experiments that external forcings on the mid-latitudes, associated with ENSO or anthropogenic effects, may affect systematically the probability distribution function (PDF) of weather regimes [*Ghil and Childress*, 1987; *Molteni et al.*, 1993]. Building on these concepts, *Robertson and Ghil* [1999] identified weather regimes using a *K*-means analysis of daily $700 hPa$ geopotential height maps to link the daily temperature and rainfall statistics at synoptic stations over the western United States with ENSO.

The April 2011 flood event in the Ohio River Basin, and the related lower Mississippi River floods was the latest of a set of major such flooding events recorded over the 20th century (defined in terms of a 10 year return maximum in stream flow). Composite analysis of these events reveals an anomalous northward moisture transport in a "moist conveyor belt" from the Gulf of Mexico and the tropical Atlantic, with convergence associated with the "Bermuda High" subtropical anticyclone to the east, and the synoptic events impinging on it from the west [*Nakamura et al.*, 2013]. The questions of whether the recent 2011 event heralds a return of more frequent flooding, and the degree of potential climate predictability of such events both require a better understanding of how the frequency and intensity of the synoptic events responsible for the floods vary on intra-seasonal to inter-decadal timescales, and are thus potentially influenced by large-scale modes of low-frequency climate variability.

Here, we present an analysis of daily circulation types derived from the reanalysis geopotential data over the Midwest of the United States using a *K*-means cluster analysis for the March-May season, over the time period 1961–2011 (Section 9.3). The data sets used and methodological considerations are presented in Section 9.2, including the definition of flood events. In Section 9.4, we infer relationships between flooding events and circulation regimes, and between these regimes and climate drivers, including ENSO and the MJO. The chapter concludes with a discussion and concluding remarks (Section 9.5).

9.2. DATASETS, METHODOLOGY, AND FLOOD EVENTS

Ten year flood events were estimated from daily river discharge data at seven gauging stations in sub-basins of the Ohio River based on the Hydro-Climatic Data Network (HCDN) of the United States Geological Survey, as described in detail by *Nakamura et al.* [2013]. In all, 20 historical flood events were identified over the 1901–2008 period as shown in Figure 9.1; the events were quite unevenly distributed over the period with groupings around 1900, the 1930s–1940s, and in the 1960s. In this

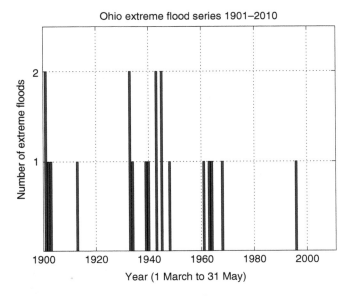

Figure 9.1 Number of extreme floods per spring season.

chapter, we will focus on the post-1960 events, in order to examine relationships with synoptic conditions from reanalysis data.

We employ an analysis of daily circulation variability over central North America [30–50°N, 105–75°W], derived from the National Centers for Environmental Prediction (NCEP)-National Center for Atmospheric Research (NCAR) reanalysis 700 hPa geopotential height data on a 2.5-degree latitude-longitude grid [*Kalnay et al.*, 1996] using a *K*-means analysis [*Robertson and Ghil*, 1999] for the March-May (MAM) season, 1961–2011. *K*-means is a partitioning method that classifies all days into a predefined number of clusters, so as to minimize the sum of squared distances within the set of clusters. The daily geopotential height data was firstly projected onto its three leading empirical orthogonal functions (EOFs) to obtain three principal component (PC) time series accounting for 86% of the variance, for analysis with *K*-means. The data were not filtered in time prior to the analysis, so as to retain the synoptic weather timescales that may be connected with flood events. The *K*-means clusters of 700 hPa geopotential height data are referred to broadly as *circulation types* (*CT*) in the following.

Figure 9.2 shows composite anomalies one day prior to the flood peak of vertically integrated moisture flux and its divergence (panel a), together with 850 hPa temperature (colors) and mean sea level pressure (MSLP, panel b), taken from the study of *Nakamura et al.* [2013] for the entire 20th century (and constructed from the extended reanalysis data of *Compo et al.* [2011]). The composite event is characterized by a strong northward flux of moisture over the eastern half of North America, and anomalously warm temperatures to the east of the flood region, accompanied by an east-west dipole of MSLP. The surface pressure pattern is notably phase shifted to the east, with the largest zonal gradient (and warm temperatures) over the eastern seaboard, rather than over the Ohio River Basin, which lies approximately [34–42°N, 89–78°W].

9.3. DAILY CIRCULATION TYPES

The *K*-means 7-cluster solution was found to yield a near-maximum classifiability index (CI) [*Michelangeli et al.*, 1995], within the range of $K = 4-10$, as shown in Figure 9.3, and was selected for further analysis. The CI measures the similarity of partitions of the data, obtained from 100 different initial random seeds of the algorithm. The single partition that matches most closely the remaining 99 is then selected. This partition (i.e., set of clusters) can be interpreted as a set of geopotential height patterns that typify the daily variability. Other choices of domain or algorithmic details lead to patterns differing in details, but we have verified that the general features of the

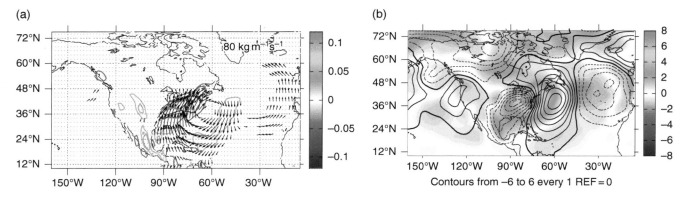

Figure 9.2 Anomaly composite of 20 extreme flood events (1901–2008) observed in large drainage basins (size > 10^3 km^2) within the Ohio Valley (basin outlines in hot pink) one day prior to start of 10 year flood [*Nakamura et al.*, 2013]. (a) Vertically integrated 600 hPa: surface moisture flux in kg m^{-1} s^{-1} (strongest 20% of values shown as arrows) and moisture divergence in g m^{-2} s^{-1} (contours) (b) 850 hPa temperature (colors, °C), and mean sea level pressure (contours, hPa).

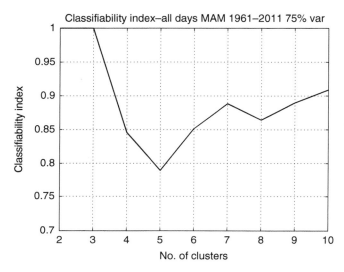

Figure 9.3 Classifiability index of K-means solution for partitions of the data comprising $K = 2-10$ clusters.

circulation patterns presented below are robust. Partitions with $K = 2-3$ have perfect classifiability, but were found not to yield circulation patterns related to flooding events.

Anomaly composite maps of the 7 clusters are shown in Figure 9.4, plotted over a larger region to highlight larger-scale aspects, and with the vertically integrated moisture flux anomaly composites superimposed. Anomalies are taken relative to the long-term (1961–2011) MAM average. The circulation types (CTs) are characterized by both synoptic-scale meridionally elongated dipolar wave patterns (CT 1, 3, 4), and monopole patterns with larger longitudinal scales (CT 2, 5, 7). The number of days falling into each CT is given in each panel of Figure 9.4, and range from 391 days for CT 2 (~ 8 days/season) to 961 days for CT 4 (~ 19 days/season).

The matrix of transitions between the CTs is given in Table 9.1. All the CTs exhibit moderate persistence with self-transition probabilities ranging from 0.49 (CT 4) to 0.73 (CT 6). The strongest off-diagonal transitions suggest the circuit $4/5 \rightarrow 1 \rightarrow 4/5$, and $4 \rightarrow 2 \rightarrow 7$. In terms of the seasonality of CT occurrence frequency, shown in Figure 9.5, the frequency of CT 6 and 7 increases through the MAM transition season, with CT 4 peaking in late April/early May; the other clusters characterize late winter conditions, and decrease in prevalence through the season.

The CTs 1, 2, and 4 are associated with enhanced southerly moisture fluxes from the Gulf of Mexico, with differing longitudinal locations of the main moisture path, according to the phase of the geopotential height pattern. The transitions in Table 9.1 suggest eastward propagation of these paths, $1 \rightarrow 4 \rightarrow 2$. The anomalous moisture fluxes can be split (linearized) into contributions due to (a) anomalies in circulation acting on mean gradients of moisture, (b) the impact of the time-averaged winds on transient moisture anomalies, or (c) a nonlinear product of circulation anomalies advecting moisture anomalies. Visual inspection of composite maps of these terms (not shown) indicated the term (a) to be dominant, such that the moisture flux anomalies in Figure 9.4 were largely a product of circulation anomalies.

9.4. ASSOCIATIONS BETWEEN CIRCULATION TYPES AND FLOOD EVENTS

The extent to which these circulation types were active during the five identified extreme flooding events in the Ohio River Basin is shown in Figure 9.6, in terms of the frequency of occurrence of each CT during the 10 day period preceding (and including) each event. There is a statistically significant greater chance for the days

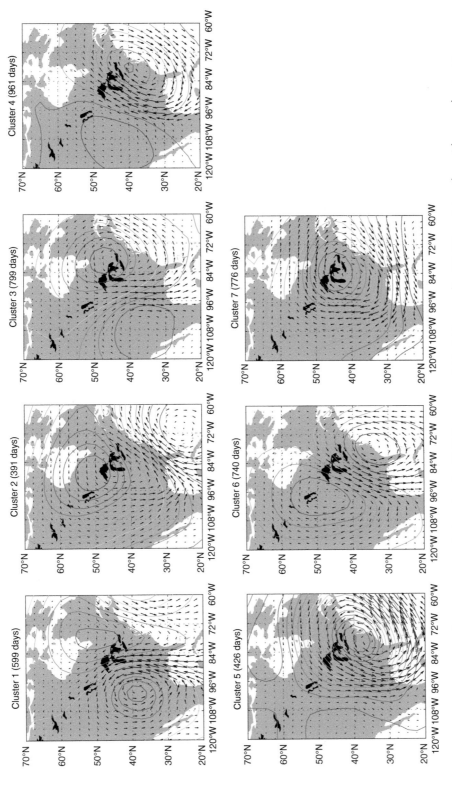

Figure 9.4 Seven-cluster *K*-means solution, showing 700 hPa geopotential height anomalies (CI: 20 gpm), together with anomaly composites of vertically integrated moisture fluxes (arrows). Panel titles give the number of MAM days assigned to each cluster.

Table 9.1 Matrix of Daily Transition Probabilities between the Clusters (in %)

From Cluster		To Cluster						
		1	2	3	4	5	6	7
	1	52	5	9	13	20	0	1
	2	2	53	11	11	1	9	13
	3	9	11	57	9	6	1	6
	4	14	16	7	49	1	1	12
	5	20	4	16	0	59	0	0
	6	2	7	2	0	1	73	16
	7	1	10	5	12	1	14	57

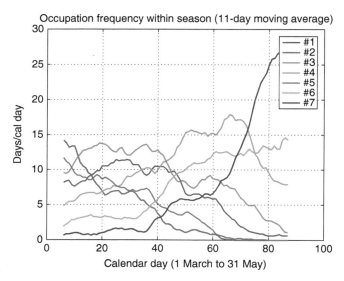

Figure 9.5 Mean seasonal evolution of cluster (CT) frequency, averaged across the 51 MAM seasons, and then smoothed with an 11 day moving average.

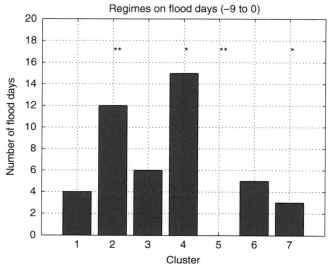

Figure 9.6 Frequency of occurrence of each cluster (CT) during the 10 day period preceding five 10 year MAM flood events: 13 May 1961, 5 March 1963, 10 March 1964, 25 May 1968, and 4 May 1996. In the case of 5 March 1963, only 5 days were selected (1–5 March). One (two) asterisk denotes statistical significance at the two-sided 90% (95%) confidence level, calculated using a bootstrap resampling method in which the set of days is sampled randomly 1000 times with replacement from the 51 MAM seasons.

preceding flood events to belong (especially) to CT 2, a deep trough centered north of the Great Lakes, and with CT 4, an anomalous ridge centered over the eastern seaboard. Taken together, CTs 2 and 4 bear some resemblance to the east-west dipolar MSLP flood-event composite pattern in Figure 9.2b. To examine these two key regimes in more detail, Figure 9.7 shows composite anomalies of isentropic potential vorticity (IPV) [*Hoskins et al.*, 1985] on the 315 K isentrope. The two regimes are seen to be highly contrasting in terms of IPV, with very large positive anomalous values accompanying the deep trough in CT 2, but rather weak anomalies in CT 4. However, the composite average may mask the transient IPV signature of CT 4, which is the least persistent of the 7 CTs. The enhanced meridional gradient of IPV in CT 2 is indicative of enhanced baroclinicity, conducive to cyclogenesis. CT 2 is a winter pattern (Figure 9.5), and occurrences of CT 2 later in the transition season, or when conditions to the south are anomalously warm, are likely to yield particularly strong fluxes of moisture into the Ohio River Basin.

Figure 9.8 shows the daily evolution of rainfall and cluster membership during April 2011, when extreme floods were recorded on the Ohio River, peaking on 27 April. This event was not included in the calculation shown in Figure 9.6, and thus provides a test case. Much of the month was characterized by CT 4, with CT 2 associated with the large rainfall spike on 4–5 April, both consistent with Figure 9.6. However, the largest rainfall spike that precipitated the flooding lags CT 4, and is accompanied by CT 1, an intense low over the SW United States, and strong northward moisture fluxes over the Mississippi valley. The daily transition probabilities, shown in Table 9.1, indicate that CT 4 is on average the least persistent, with preferred transitions into CTs 1 and 2, both interpretable in terms of eastward wave propagation.

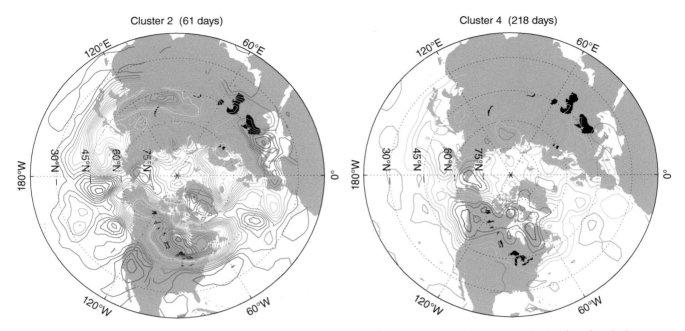

Figure 9.7 Potential vorticity on the 315 K isentrope for CTs 2 and 4. Contour interval: 0.2 PV Units ($10^{-6}\,K\,m^2\,kg^{-1}\,s^{-1}$), warm colors positive.

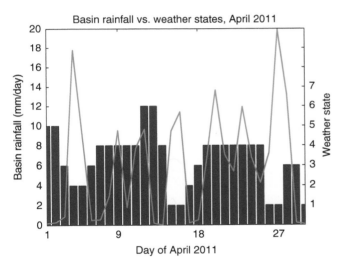

Figure 9.8 Daily rainfall averaged over the Ohio River Basin (red curve), together with cluster membership (bars), during April 2011.

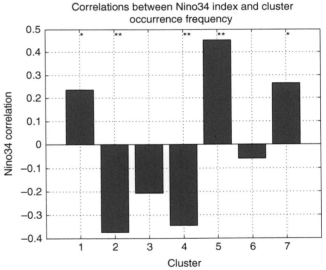

Figure 9.9 Anomaly correlation between the number of days in each cluster (CT) in each MAM season and the value of the Niño 3.4 index. One (two) asterisk denotes statistical significance at the two-sided 90% (95%) confidence level, calculated using a bootstrap resampling method in which the 51-year Niño 3.4 index time series was randomized 1000 times.

9.5. ASSOCIATIONS BETWEEN CIRCULATION TYPES AND ENSO OR THE MJO

The association between cluster frequency and the ENSO is plotted in Figure 9.9, in terms of the anomaly correlation between the Niño 3.4 sea surface temperature (SST) index of ENSO, averaged over each MAM season, 1961–2011, and the frequency of occurrence of each circulation type. Both CTs 2 and 4 are preferentially associated with La Niña events, statistically significant at the 95% confidence level, while CT 5 (no flood days) is the most strongly associated with El Niño. Since there is an inverse relationship between these CTs and the five extreme flood events (flooding with more CTs 4 and 2, and less CT 5), La Niña translates to a higher probability of floods and El Niño to a lower probability. This can be compared with the study of *Higgins et al.* [2007] who found more heavy precipitation days over the Ohio valley during La Niña, compared to El Niño, during January-March, though no relationship was found during April-June.

To determine the association between cluster frequency and the MJO, Figure 9.10 shows counts of cluster occurrence days during the eight phases of the MJO (lead 0) as defined by *Wheeler and Hendon* [2004], as well as the analogous cluster daily counts 1–14 days after the given MJO phase. Most notably CT 4, which is most strongly

associated with the five flood events since 1961, is found to be significantly more common when the MJO is in phase 5 during the previous two weeks, corresponding to convection located over the Maritime Continent and western Pacific. When the MJO leads CT 4 by 10–14 days, the strongest relationship is with MJO phase 3 (convection over the Indian Ocean), indicative of a potentially predictable component. During the winter season, *Becker et al.* [2011] found a large response in the precipitation rate anomaly over the eastern United States during MJO phases 5–7, that is, when MJO-related enhanced tropical convection is moving through the far western to central Pacific, broadly consistent with our

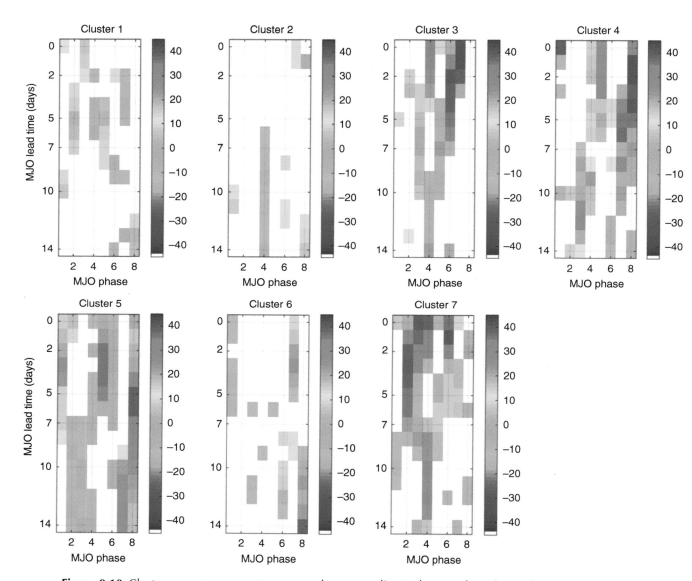

Figure 9.10 Cluster occurrence counts expressed as anomalies (colors, in days) for each phase of the MJO, 1979–2010 (MAM). The ordinate gives the number of days that the MJO phase precedes the North American circulation types, from 0 (simultaneous) to 14 days. Colored tiles are significant at the 90% confidence level, obtained using a bootstrapping method.

result. This wintertime location is slightly further east compared to our CT 4 for MAM, and bears similarity with CT 7 where the strongest lead-0 relationship is with MJO phase 6, which is characterized by a northward moisture flux over the Great Plains.

9.6. DISCUSSION AND CONCLUDING REMARKS

The work reported here demonstrates clear association between synoptic circulation types and historical extreme ("10 year") flood events on the Ohio River Basin. Anomalous northward fluxes of moisture from the Gulf of Mexico are pronounced in two circulation types (CTs 2, 4) that occurred preferentially in the 10 day periods preceding five flood events since 1961. These two circulation types were both found to be preferentially associated with La Niña, providing one causal mechanism for the recent flooding during April of 2011. In addition, CT 4 was found to be significantly more common during phase 5 of the MJO cycle, when convection is located over the Maritime Continent and western Pacific; this provides a second potentially predictable linkage because this MJO association can be traced back 10–14 days before the flood event.

The results of this work illustrate how typical and recurrent synoptic daily circulation patterns are preferentially associated with extreme floods over the U.S. Midwest during the spring season, and how these same geopotential height patterns tend to occur more frequently during the La Niña phase of ENSO and phase 5 of the MJO. The April 2011 event was characterized by 13 days of CT 4 and La Niña conditions. However, the MJO convection was located in the western Pacific sector (phase 6–7) until 9 April, after which its amplitude became weak, and the role of the MJO in the April 2011 event is not clear.

The main caveat of the current study is the small sample size of five flood events. While statistically significant, the relationships between the circulation types and ENSO or the MJO are only modest in strength. Clearly, ENSO and the MJO are not the only ingredients, and further work is required to identify other factors that may influence the probability of extreme flood events, through the intermediaries of the circulation types identified here or otherwise. The interdecadal modulation in frequency of flood events is intriguing. By piecing together different influences acting on different timescales, it may become possible, particularly during certain "windows of opportunity" when ENSO and MJO amplitudes are high, to issue useful flood-risk estimates at seasonal lead times, that are updated as forecasts with shorter lead times become in range of the target date. *Jones et al.* [2011] report that the skill of weather forecasts of extreme precipitation in the contiguous United States during winter is higher when the MJO is active, and has enhanced convection over the Western Hemisphere, Africa, and/or the western Indian Ocean.

In the context of climate change, *Min et al.* [2011] have recently reported substantial upward trends in observed daily extreme precipitation over the United States, 1951–1999. These, however, are not reflected in the Ohio Valley extreme floods time series in Figure 9.1. Flood frequency may change due to changes in the frequency of occurrence of certain circulation types, or due to changes in the rainfall extremes associated with a given circulation type: thus the number of storms may change, or the storms themselves may become more intense, or some combination of the two. Of the two circulation types associated preferentially with flooding, CT 2, the wintertime deep trough has become less prevalent in recent years, while CT 4 was more prevalent in the 1960s. Further work with longer circulation data records, such as using the recently developed extended reanalysis for the 20th century [*Compo et al.*, 2011] will be required to investigate these longer time scales.

ACKNOWLEDGMENTS

This work was supported by an NOAA Climate Prediction Program for the Americas (CPPA) grant, and under a cooperative agreement between NOAA and IRI. We would like to thank the Editors, and one anonymous reviewer for his/her constructive comments.

REFERENCES

Bauer, F. (1951), Extended range weather forecasting, in *Compendium of Meteorology*, American Meteorological Society, Boston, MA. pp. 814–833.

Becker, E. J., E. H. Berbery, and R. W. Higgins (2011), Modulation of cold-season U.S. daily precipitation by the Madden-Julian oscillation, *J. Climate*, 24(19), 5157–5166, doi:10.1175/2011JCLI4018.1.

Compo, G. P., J. S. Whitaker, P. D. Sardeshmukh, N. Matsui, R. J. Allan, X. Yin, B. E. Gleason, R. S. Vose, G. Rutledge, P. Bessemoulin, S. Brönnimann, M. Brunet, R. I. Crouthamel, A. N. Grant, P. Y. Groisman, P. D. Jones, M. C. Kruk, A. C. Kruger, G. J. Marshall, M. Maugeri, H. Y. Mok, Ø. Nordli, T. F. Ross, R. M. Trigo, X. L. Wang, S. D. Woodruff, and S. J. Worley (2011), The twentieth century reanalysis project, *Q. J. Roy. Meteorol. Soc.*, 137(654), 1–28.

Dole, R. M., and N. D. Gordon (1983), Persistent anomalies of the extratropical Northern Hemisphere wintertime circulation: Geographical distribution and regional persistence characteristics, *Mon. Weather Rev.*, 111(8), 1567–1586.

Farquharson, F. A. K., J. R. Meigh, and J. V. Sutcliffe (1992), Regional flood frequency-analysis in arid and semiarid areas, *J. Hydrol.*, 138, 487–501.

Ghil, M., and S. Childress (1987), *Topics in Geophysical Fluid Dynamics: Atmospheric Dynamics, Dynamo Theory and Climate Dynamics*, Springer-Verlag, New York.

Gupta, V. K. (2004), Emergence of statistical scaling in floods on channel networks from complex runoff dynamics, *Chaos Solitons Fractals*, *19*, 357–365.

Gupta, V. K., O. J. Mesa, and D. R. Dawdy (1994), Multiscaling theory of flood peaks—regional quantile analysis, *Water Resour. Res.*, *30*, 3405–3421.

Higgins, R. W., V. B. S. Silva, W. Shi, and J. Larson (2007), Relationships between climate variability and fluctuations in daily precipitation over the United States, *J. Climate*, *20*(14), 3561–3579, doi:10.1175/JCLI4196.1.

Hirschboeck, K. (1988), Flood hydroclimatology, in *Flood Geomorphology*, edited by V. Baker, R. Kochel, and P. Patton, pp. 27–49, John Wiley & Sons, Inc., New York.

Hoskins, B. J., M. E. McIntyre, and A. W. Robertson (1985), On the use and significance of isentropic potential vorticity maps, *Q. J. Roy. Meteorol. Soc.*, *111*(470), 877–946.

Jones, C., L. M. V. Carvalho, J. Gottschalck, and W. Higgins (2011), The Madden–Julian oscillation and the relative value of deterministic forecasts of extreme precipitation in the contiguous United States, *J. Climate*, *24*(10), 2421–2428, doi:10.1175/2011JCLI-D-10-05002.1.

Kalnay, E., M. Kanamitsu, R. Kistler, W. Collins, D. Deaven, L. Gandin, M. Iredell, S. Saha, G. White, J. Woollen, Y. Zhu, M. Chelliah, W. Ebisuzaki, W. Higgins, J. Janowiak, K. C. Mo, C. Ropelewski, J. Wang, A. Leetmaa, R. Reynolds, R. Jenne, and D. Joseph (1996), The NCEP/NCAR 40-year reanalysis project, *Bull. Am. Meteorol. Soc.*, *77*(3), 437–471.

Kimoto, M., and M. Ghil (1993a), Multiple flow regimes in the northern hemisphere winter. Part I: Methodology and hemispheric regimes, *J. Atmos. Sci.*, *50*(16), 2625–2644.

Kimoto, M., and M. Ghil (1993b), Multiple flow regimes in the northern hemisphere winter. Part II: Sectorial regimes and preferred transitions, *J. Atmos. Sci.*, *50*(16), 2645–2673.

Knox, J. C. (1993), Large increases in flood magnitude in response to modest changes in climate, *Nature*, *361*, 430–432.

Konrad, C. E. (2001), The most extreme precipitation events over the eastern United States from 1950 to 1996: Considerations of scale, *J. Hydrometeorol.*, *2*, 309–325.

Kron, W. (2005), Flood risk = hazard x values x vulnerability, *Water Int.*, *30*(1), 58–68.

Michelangeli, P.-A., R. Vautard, and B. Legras (1995), Weather regimes: Recurrence and quasi stationarity, *J. Atmos. Sci.*, *52*(8), 1237–1256.

Min, S.-K., X. Zhang, F. W. Zwiers, and G. C. Hegerl (2011), Human contribution to more-intense precipitation extremes, *Nature*, *470*(7334), 378–381.

Molteni, F., L. Ferranti, T. N. Palmer, and P. Viterbo (1993), A dynamical interpretation of the global response to equatorial Pacific SST anomalies, *J. Climate*, *6*(5), 777–795.

Nakamura, J., U. Lall, Y. Kushnir, A. Robertson, and R. Seager (2013), Dynamical structure of extreme floods in U.S. Midwest and the UK, *J. Hydrometeorol.*, *14*, 485–504.

Pandey, G., S. Lovejoy, and D. Schertzer (1998), Multifractal analysis of daily river flows including extremes for basins of five to two million square kilometres, one day to 75 years, *J. Hydrol.*, *208*, 62–81.

Robertson, A. W., and M. Ghil (1999), Large-scale weather regimes and local climate over the western United States, *J. Climate*, *12*, 1796–1813.

Robertson, A. W., and W. Metz (1990), Transient-eddy feedbacks derived from linear theory and observations, *J. Atmos. Sci.*, *47*(23), 2743–2764.

Sankarasubramanian, A., and U. Lall (2003), Flood quantiles in a changing climate: Seasonal forecasts and causal relations, *Water Resour. Res.*, *39*, 1134.

Vautard, R. (1990), Multiple weather regimes over the North Atlantic: Analysis of precursors and successors, *Mon. Weather Rev.*, *118*(10), 2056–2081.

Wallace, J. M., and D. S. Gutzler (1981), Teleconnections in the geopotential height field during the Northern Hemisphere winter, *Mon. Weather Rev.*, *109*(4), 784–812.

Wheeler, M. C., and H. H. Hendon (2004), An all-season real-time multivariate MJO index: Development of an index for monitoring and prediction, *Mon. Weather Rev.*, *132*(8), 1917–1932.

10

Analysis of the Hazards and Vulnerability of the Cancun Beach System: The Case of Hurricane Wilma

Edgar Mendoza,[1] Rodolfo Silva,[1] Cecilia Enriquez-Ortiz,[1]
Ismael Mariño-Tapia,[2] and Angélica Felix[1]

ABSTRACT

This chapter assesses the hazards and vulnerability to tropical cyclones of the overdeveloped beach-lagoon system at Cancun in Mexico. Urbanization began in the late 1960s and has continued at a growing pace ever since. Before tourist development started, the beach-lagoon system functioned as a metastable beach, with erosion-accretion cycles and evidence of natural breaching in places. In this chapter, it is shown that the rapid, disorganized tourist development that has taken place has degraded the coastal beach-lagoon system, increasing its vulnerability to extreme weather events and dramatically reducing its resilience (destroying the high-beach sand reserves and impeding the possibility of breaching). The historical occurrence of tropical storms is also revised as some studies indicate that the average intensity of tropical cyclones is increasing; no definite trends pointing to an increase in storm frequency were found. However, the need to avoid storm-induced coastal damage (erosion and flooding) is reflected in the numerous projects that aim to improve the management of the area and reduce its vulnerability to hurricanes. The consequences seen today lead the authors to suggest that the effects of Hurricane Wilma on Cancun beach cannot be ascribed only to climatic variability since the anthropogenic activity had already degraded the system over recent decades. Nevertheless, it is recognized that Hurricane Wilma was a record-breaking extreme meteorological event.

10.1. INTRODUCTION

Cancun beach is the most important tourist destination in Mexico; it offers a long, straight coastline of white, medium-fine sand and clear turquoise sea. Cancun is the largest tourist development in the country with 148 hotels of 4 and 5 stars and more than 28,000 hotel rooms where 45% of all international visitors to Mexico stay. Tourist expenditure of between 2 and 3 billion USD [*SEDETUR*, 2008] provides 35% of Mexico's annual tourist income.

Exploitation of destinations such as Cancun seems to be paradoxical; on the one hand, they are highly valuable because of their natural beauty, but on the other, they have proven to be very vulnerable to almost any natural and/or artificial perturbation. Nevertheless, several sites have been highly developed in Mexico, disregarding ecological and environmental costs. It is therefore not surprising that the value of these beaches decreases with time, as well as the quality and number of visitors; for example, from 2008 to 2009 the total hotel mean occupation rate fell from 71% to 60% while the tariffs of 3 star hotels also fell, revealing an increasing demand for cheaper facilities [*Balderas*, 2009]. The case of Cancun is that of a complex morphology combining a barrier island and a lagoon system. The Yucatan Peninsula is a large limestone shelf, lying beneath a layer of carbonate rocks

[1]*Instituto de Ingeniería, Universidad Nacional Autónoma de México, México, DF, México*
[2]*Departamento de Recursos del Mar, CINVESTAV-Mérida, Yucatán, México*

Extreme Events: Observations, Modeling, and Economics, Geophysical Monograph 214, First Edition.
Edited by Mario Chavez, Michael Ghil, and Jaime Urrutia-Fucugauchi.

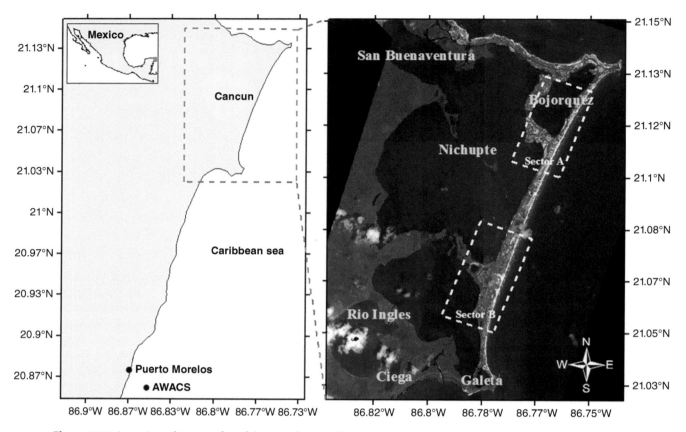

Figure 10.1 Location of Cancun beachfront and coastal lagoon system. The position of the AWACS and the detail sectors are also shown.

and sediments. The high sea level reached during the Pleistocene period accreted a series of beach ridges along the mainland coast. Later the sea level fell leaving the carbonate dune ridges exposed and between these ridges, carbonate mud deposits were laid during the Holocene [*Ward et al.*, 1985] and tombolos developed at both ends of the barrier island.

The lagoon system contains seven water bodies: Bojorquez and Nichupte lagoons being the largest (see Figure 10.1). The island is ~17 km long and <700 m wide, composed of fine- to medium-grained oolitic sands blown into dunes as high as 17 m. Before the tourist resort was developed the geomorphology of the area would have allowed a metastable beach (i.e., a relatively stable beach), highly and rapidly modified by the frequent extreme meteorological events it faced, for example, tropical storms and hurricanes. The water exchange between the lagoon and the sea would have increased under extreme meteorological conditions when the sea level rose and barrier breaching was possible [*Pedrozo*, 2008].

The anthropogenic impact in the region started in the late 1960s and was not properly planned and controlled; massive infrastructure destroyed vast wetland and dune areas, modifying the native biomass and bringing in foreign species with high maintenance costs. Extensive development was in place by the late 1970s [*Felix et al.*, 2008] with numerous solid buildings seriously affecting the beach dynamics, disrupting the sediment balance and therefore inducing a chronic erosion problem, which was obviously aggravated by extreme meteorological events [*Diez et al.*, 2009]. The erosion events that occurred from the mid-1970s to mid-1980s were barely noticed until 1988 when the erosion caused by Hurricane Gilbert left the beach in a critical condition and even damaged some buildings. This prompted the first studies of the region, which aimed to give the authorities some understanding of the problem; beach monitoring also started in the late 1980s. Unfortunately, no permanent program was established and Hurricanes Ivan (2004), Emily (2005), and Wilma (2005) eroded the beach still further, until there was no dry part left and the waves began to hit the buildings themselves. Hurricane Wilma alone is estimated to have cost more than 3000 million USD in infrastructure losses (www.cenapred.unam.mx), neither considering the natural, social, and cultural losses, nor considering the costs involved in recovering tourist activity. After this devastation, more studies and monitoring took place [*Felix et al.*, 2008; *Diez et al.*, 2009; *Gonzalez*, 2009], which have provided better understanding of the mistakes made in the tourist development programs as well as the response of the beach through time. However a clearer panorama, characterization of the hazards involved and a thorough vulnerability analysis are still needed.

This study is aimed to describe the degree of vulnerability of Cancun beach and, looking at historical data, to discuss the hazards that should be taken into account if a successful and sustainable resort is seen as the future for Cancun.

10.2. PHYSICAL CHARACTERISTICS OF THE STUDY SITE

Wind patterns. Cancun is subject to the dominant trade winds (NE-E-SE), interrupted for some days when pulses of strong (>15 m/s) northerly winds from winter cold fronts cross the area.

Wave climate. The wave climate obtained via numerical modeling over a 60 year period [*Ruiz et al.*, 2009] consists of waves arriving from the East and East-South-East under normal conditions (68% of the time) and less frequent events of waves from the East-North-East occurring during the summer. The range of modeled significant wave heights is 0.5–3 m with wave periods of 4–10 s.

The region is influenced by a dominant offshore current traveling to the North (the Yucatan Current) derived from a low frequency sea-level change [*Coronado et al.*, 2007]. The tidal regime is semidiurnal microtidal (<0.30 m).

Sediment dynamics. The wave behavior supports the initial hypothesis describing persistent sediment transport toward the north, suggested by several studies carried out in Cancun prior to the first beach nourishment in 2006 [*CFE*, 2001, 2003]. Nevertheless, there is almost no evidence of significant sand accumulation at the northern end of the system [*Felix et al.*, 2008]; on the contrary, sand loss is predominant there. Recent studies, including morphological data analysis and wave propagation models [*Gonzalez*, 2009], show that refraction and diffraction processes generate divergence of sediment transport from the middle part to the northern and southern ends of Cancun [*Felix et al.*, 2008; *Ruiz*, 2010]. This means that the sand traveling to the North is somehow leaving the system.

To understand the interaction between the Cancun beach front and its potential marine hazards, the long-term evolution of both the morphological array and the local hydrodynamics needs to be studied. The coastline evolution was analyzed through a series of historical aerial photographs to compare the beach characteristics before and after urbanization took place. Recent monitoring activities (since the 1990s) provide sparse quantitative beach evolution data. The hydrodynamics were

inferred from analysis of long-term (60 years) wave characteristics, identifying storms and hurricanes and obtaining their main characteristics. This was achieved using the hybrid wave model WAM-HURAC [*Ruiz et al.*, 2009] input with wind reanalysis data (NCEP/NCAR). The hybrid model couples the parametric model HURAC and a third-generation wave model WAM [*WAMDI-Group*, 1988] to get long-term continuous databases for waves in mean, storm, and extreme regimes (see ANNEX). The results were validated and tested using the records of seven buoys located in the Gulf of Mexico and Caribbean Sea [*Ruiz et al.*, 2009].

One of the most relevant particularities of the Cancun beachfront is the periodical occurrence of hurricanes. These phenomena are known to cause great morphological evolution and to be the most serious hazard affecting coastal areas; thus it is important to understand their effects and to elucidate future trends to achieve proper coastal management and risk assessment. *Knutson et al.* [2010] stated that it remains uncertain whether past changes in any tropical cyclone activity (frequency, intensity, rainfall, etc.) exceed the variability expected through natural causes. It is not clear if the global frequency of tropical cyclones will either decrease or remain essentially unchanged. *Knutson et al.* [2010] also show low confidence in the projected changes if individual basins are seen. In all tropical regions the frequency of the most intense (rare/high-impact) storms may not increase by a substantially larger percentage. On the other hand, the vulnerability of coastal regions to storm-surge flooding is expected to increase with or without future sea level rise if coastal development continues to disregard long-term natural processes.

In any case, given the damage and relevance of Hurricane Wilma, we consider it important to present its characteristics and offer some recorded data as an example of the hazards that have to be considered in future coastal planning.

10.3. HURRICANE WILMA

Hurricane Wilma was undoubtedly the most devastating storm to hit Cancun, far exceeding any other recorded in the last 60 years. However, Wilma was not the most intense storm to have hit Cancun; Hurricane Gilbert (1988) exceeded records for category, wind velocity, and minimum central pressure at the time it reached the coast.

Notwithstanding, Wilma was a record-breaking hurricane in various aspects: (1) It developed extremely quickly, intensifying from a 30 m/s (108 km/h) tropical storm to a 77 m/s (277 km/h) category 5 (H5) hurricane in the span of just 24 hours, and in only 8 hours changed from H1 to H5, an unprecedented event for an Atlantic tropical cyclone. (2) Given its intensity, it came late in the

Figure 10.2 Effects of the erosion caused by hurricane Wilma.

season, being the first category 5 hurricane to develop in October. (3) It had the lowest central barometric pressure (882 mb) ever registered in North Atlantic storms. (4) Wilma had the smallest eye ever known in the basin, which contracted to a diameter of 3.2 km. (5) Finally, it moved extremely slowly across the Mexican Caribbean, staying for over 48 hours in the region. According to the Wave Climate Atlas for the Mexican Atlantic [*Silva et al.*, 2008], storms with significant wave heights of 12–13 m, like Hurricane Wilma, show a return period of around hundred years.

This combination of characteristics had disastrous consequences on the coastal zone of Cancun. More than 7 million cubic meters of sand were removed from the beach system, leaving 68% of subaerial beach as bedrock and the rest considerably eroded (Figure 10.2). Practically, the whole barrier suffered extreme erosion, though the southern region of the beach was largely accreted [*Silva et al.*, 2006].

However, environmentally speaking, an exceptional natural cleaning process took place in the lagoon system behind the beach, probably enhanced by breaching, and several square meters of old mangrove died and gave place to younger trees. This means that an extreme meteorological event like Hurricane Wilma brings many natural benefits; it is the poorly planned infrastructure which is incompatible with the natural cycles and processes.

Probably, the worst effects left by Hurricane Wilma were those related to social and economic activities, which were virtually halted for several weeks. Furthermore, many indirect costs were not known until months later, that is, the tourist industry returned to operations very quickly, while the community in general took longer and needed far more resources to recover completely. The total cost attributed to Hurricane Wilma was around 1800 million USD; obviously the main damage (more than 90%) was registered by tourist infrastructure, but other sectors were also severely damaged. Table 10.1, taken from *García et al.* [2006], shows a summary of the costs, divided into economic sectors, of the damage left by Hurricane Wilma.

The effects of Hurricane Wilma on the Cancun beachfront were also assessed by combining "in situ" measurements and numerical modeling. Direct wave measurements were collected with an acoustic Doppler current meter (AWACS) moored 20 m deep, off Puerto Morelos (Figure 10.1). The statistics of waves and currents during the passage of Hurricane Wilma are presented in Figure 10.3. For a full description, the reader is referred to *Escalante et al.* [2009] and *Silva et al.* [2009].

10.4. RESULTS

The only source of information to compare the Cancun system before and after urbanization took place are the historical aerial photographs. This material shows evidence of beach persistence in time, even though it is known that intense storms frequently hit the site before the tourist infrastructure was developed on the barrier. The permanent presence of the beach denotes a system sufficiently able to restore itself after storm-induced damage. Since the 1970s, intense urbanization is evident in the photographs. This development transformed the flexible sand bar into a rigid structure of solid buildings and highways, preventing the free sediment dynamics, the breaching of the dune, and the underground flows. When the system was undeveloped and extreme storm events occurred, the dune would provide enough material for the beach to change its profile to a more dissipative one, capable of wave energy attenuation; additionally the

Table 10.1 Cost of Direct and Indirect Damage Caused by Hurricane Wilma (in Million USD)

Concept	Direct damage	Indirect damage	Total	Percent
Dwellings	49.9	9.5	59.5	3.3
Education	10.1	0.0	10.1	0.6
Health	0.9	0.0	0.9	0.1
Hydraulic infrastructure	2.9	0.7	3.6	0.2
Social infrastructure subtotal	63.9	10.3	74.3	4.2
Transport and communications	9.9	4.8	14.8	0.8
Electricity sector	25.7	5.4	31.1	1.7
Economic infrastructure subtotal	35.7	10.3	46.0	2.6
Fishing and agriculture	3.1	13.2	16.3	0.9
Tourist industry	349.6	1287.2	1636.9	91.6
Environmental services	4.8	NA	4.8	0.3
Emergency response	NA	9.4	9.4	0.5
Production and environment subtotal	357.5	1309.9	1667.5	93.3
GENERAL TOTAL	457.26	1330.6	1787.8	100.0

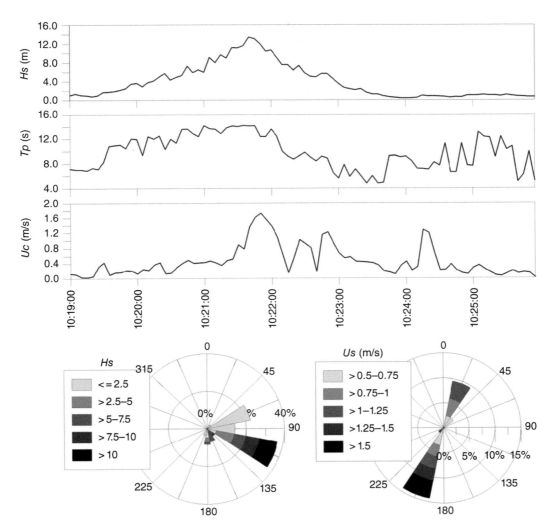

Figure 10.3 Wave and current statistics from measurements recorded during the passage of Hurricane Wilma (19–25 October 2005) in Cancun, Mexico.

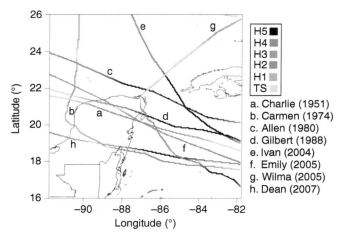

Figure 10.4 The most intense hurricanes to have affected the beachfront of Cancun from 1948 to 2010.

Table 10.2 Number of Tropical Storms Occurring in the North Atlantic and Cancun Region Since 1948

Tropical storms (number of)	Category of storms (Saffir-Simpson)				
	H5	H4	H3	H2	H1
North Atlantic	26	69	78	70	156
Cancun region	11	12	16	11	20

flexible sand bar would allow natural breaching, considerably improving the water quality in the lagoon through temporarily increased water exchange with the sea. The intense urbanization altered the natural dynamics leaving a constrained lagoon system known to be polluted and stagnant [*Leon et al.*, 2009] and a narrow, high, vulnerable sand beach with high erosion potential on the ocean side of the barrier [*Bodegom*, 2004].

During the last 60 years, a large number of storms and hurricanes have affected Cancun, as revealed by the analysis of the wave characteristics from 1948 to 2011; the most intense being Hurricanes Charlie (1951), Carmen (1974), Allen (1980), Gilbert (1988), Ivan (2004), Emily (2005), Wilma (2005), and Dean (2007). See Figure 10.4. According to the National Hurricane Center (NOAA) database, during the years 1948–2010, a total of 688 tropical storms were identified in the North Atlantic basin and from those, 152 crossed the Cancun region (Table 10.2).

Since the 1960s, scientists around the world have been warning about possible climate changes and how they would affect the planet [*Mann and Emanuel*, 2006]. Recently, the increase in the number and the magnitude of hurricanes has been related to global warming [*Mann and Emanuel*, 2006]. However, *Kossin et al.* [2007] stated that "the time-dependent differences between the University of Wisconsin-Madison/National Climatic Data Center (UW/NCDC) record and the Joint Typhoon Warning Center (JTWC) best track records underscore the potential for data inconsistencies to introduce spurious (or spuriously large) upward trends in longer-term measures of hurricane activity. Using a homogeneous record, we were not able to corroborate the presence of upward trends."

In this sense, the database of more than 60 years of hurricanes gathered at the National University of Mexico allows us to perform a historical, simple, but revealing,

analysis of tropical storm occurrence. Considering only hurricanes of category H1–H5, Figure 10.1 shows yearly the average number of hurricanes by intensity, N (avg), the average duration of each category in hours, and the number of hurricanes in the North Atlantic basin. The average values were evaluated as the weighted mean:

$$N(\text{avg}) = \frac{1}{W_i} \sum_{j=i-4}^{j=i+4} N_i w_i \qquad (10.1)$$

$$w_i = 1 - \frac{|i-j|}{5}; \quad i-4 < j < i+4 \qquad (10.2)$$

$$W_i = \sum_{j=i-4}^{j=i+4} w_j \qquad (10.3)$$

where, i is the year and N is the number of the events of each category. If i is <1948 or >2010, then those values were not considered. Figure 10.1 does not show any trend regarding the number, intensity, or duration of the hurricanes; an irregular behavior with recurrent peaks seems to be a better description of the time series shown in Figure 10.5. It is convenient to note that the years in which the most destructive hurricanes occurred correspond to the years with the highest recorded durations.

Figure 10.6 (drawn along the same criteria as Figure 10.1) was created considering the H1–H5 hurricanes that passed closer than 5° from Cancun beachfront. The figure shows, contrary to what was said referring to Figure 10.1, an apparent local, increasing trend in frequency, intensity, and persistence of hurricanes beginning around 2002 and with a peak in 2005. Obviously, the effect of Hurricanes Ivan (2004), Emily, Wilma (2005), and Dean (2006) is clearly governing the trend. The figure also shows that the intensity and persistence of the storms that have hit Cancun in the last 15 years is higher than in the previous 40 years.

As a result of the analysis of the full database, Figure 10.7 shows a comparison between the most relevant parameters related to hurricane occurrence, that is, significant maximum wave height, H_{smax}; significant mean wave height, H_{smed}; maximum wind velocity, V_{max}; mean wind velocity, V_{med}; and normalized energy, E_{nor}. The normalized energy was estimated as the ratio of the

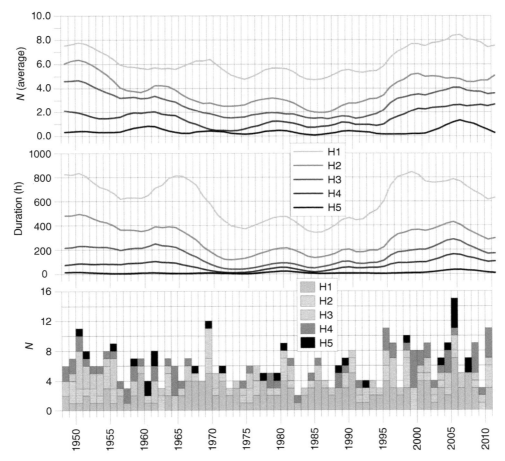

Figure 10.5 Annual average number of hurricanes by intensity, number of hours registered for each category, and number of hurricanes in the North Atlantic basin from 1948 to 2011.

energy of the hurricane and the energy of a sea state persisting for 24 hours with wind velocity higher than 100 km/h (standard storm). This parameter allows an energetic comparison between the different hurricanes and could be interpreted as a quantification of how many standard storms a given region has experienced; as the normalized energy involves time, it is also representative of the duration or persistence of a storm or hurricane.

It can be seen from Figure 10.7 that no single hurricane is the worst scenario for all the parameters involved; meteorological events cannot be characterized by one single parameter (e.g., intensity), but by a combination of as many as possible. For example, Hurricane Wilma (2005) is by far the most energetic hurricane to hit the Cancun coastal area, but the storm that generated the highest maximum waves and wind velocities was Gilbert (1988), due mainly to the duration of the hurricane (Wilma's displacement speed was quite slow; 9 km/h on average and just 3 km/h in its slowest stage). However, the highest mean wind velocities registered belonged, again, to Wilma (2005), but the ones reported for Dean (2006) are

very similar; finally, the greatest mean wave heights are reported for Wilma (2005) and both Gilbert (1988) and Dean (2006) registered lower and very similar values.

10.5. DISCUSSION

Although several studies have been carried out to investigate climatic variability and its effects on coastal systems, uncertainty remains high, revealing the need for further study. Particularly when dealing with extreme events such as hurricanes, which are almost unpredictable, the models, management policies, and protection plans need to incorporate more variables (e.g., trajectory, displacement speed, and duration) because, as has been shown in this work, knowing the wind velocity is not sufficient to evaluate the destructive potential of this kind of storm.

When we consider the last 60 years, except for Gilbert in 1988, the most destructive hurricanes have occurred in recent times (15 years). A clear, high intensity time period with several energetic storm strikes occurring during the early 2000s included Hurricane Isidore (2002), Ivan (2004),

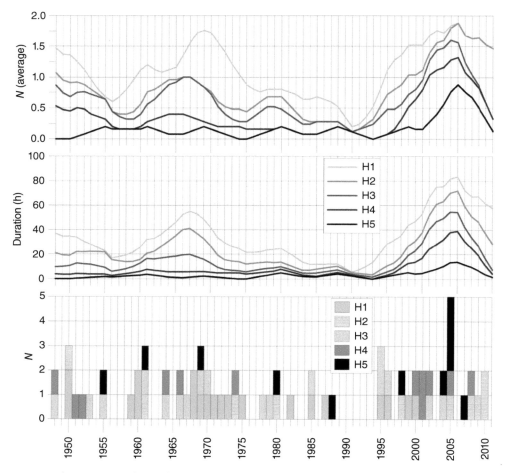

Figure 10.6 Annual average number of hurricanes by intensity, number of hours registered for each category, and number of hurricanes that passed 5° or closer to Cancun from 1948 to 2011.

Emily and Wilma (both in 2005). Both, Emily and Wilma, developed significant wave heights above 12 m (storms with 100 year return periods). Nowadays, it is generally recognized that there is no evidence of an increase in the number of storms related to climate change, but the majority of studies coincide in a general but local increase in storm intensity and duration (Figure 10.2) that can be seen historically and in the projections [*Ranger and Niehorster*, 2011].

In the Cancun system during intense storms, huge amounts of sand are removed by waves and littoral currents and usually deposited offshore on a long shore bar and trough. These modifications create a local natural defense, by increasing the energy dissipation generated by storm waves traveling through the shallow coastal environment; the sand on the higher beach and dunes being the essential source for this natural process to take place. When tourist infrastructure was built on top of the dunes, the whole cycle was broken, the beach sand was no longer sufficient to remain stable, and even the infrastructure that caused the imbalance was seriously damaged. Since the region was developed, Cancun has

exhibited a permanent erosion problem that becomes critical after high intensity storms occur; naturally Cancun was a metastable beach, but the combination of hurricanes and the poorly planned infrastructure are responsible for the irreversible damage to the beach. The increased vulnerability of Cancun beach was evidenced by Hurricane Wilma and can be seen in Figure 10.8, where a comparison has been drawn between the coastline positions in October 2005 and April 2006 for sectors A and B, shown in Figure 10.1; the eroded area (zone in red color) demonstrates that the beach almost disappeared. In the same figure some small, dry beach remnants can be seen, which coincide with places where beach dunes were left untouched. Even though *Gonzalez* [2009] reported accretion at the south of the beachfront, far from recovering, the beach is found to be unstable due to its decreased resilience. It is clear to the authors that this loss of resilience cannot be attributed only, not even mainly, to natural events. To corroborate the latter, Figure 10.9 shows the land use changes between 1960 and 1983 in panels 1 and 3 and from 1983 to 2006 in panels 2 and 4 for

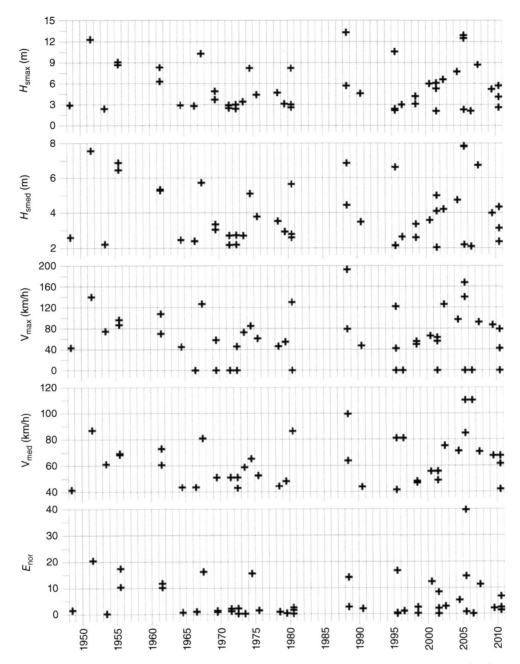

Figure 10.7 Maximum significant wave height, mean significant wave height, maximum wind velocity, mean wind velocity, and normalized wave energy for each year (1948–2010) close to Cancun.

sectors A and B in Figure 10.1, respectively. In panel 1 of Figure 10.9, the introduction of nonnative vegetation in large areas is the main characteristic, not only some tourist infrastructure was built, but also native vegetation was planted. The beachfront seems to be unchanged, but the beach dune has begun to be invaded; panel 3, sector B, shows vast unchanged land, but alterations to the morphology of the lagoon were made (marked as artificial

water bodies). Up to 2006, panel 2 shows almost all the areas of sector A given to tourist infrastructure or under construction, a very small dry beach can be detected, but the rigidization of the bar is evident; panel 4 presents a very similar pattern with most of the areas covered by tourist infrastructure or under construction and also large areas of nonnative vegetation (golf courses). The massive introduction of rigid structures minimized the

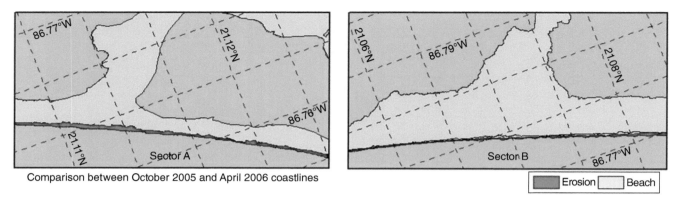

Comparison between October 2005 and April 2006 coastlines

Erosion ☐ Beach

Figure 10.8 Dry beach losses due to Hurricane Wilma in the selected detail sectors of Cancun beachfront.

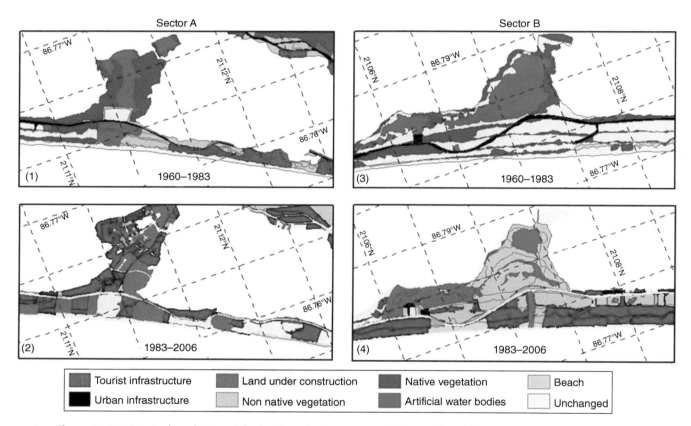

Figure 10.9 Historical evolution of the land use in two sectors of Cancun beachfront.

flexibility of the system reducing the resilience and leaving an area of high vulnerability, with little dry beach and virtually no beach dune.

Grave mistakes like this should be avoided in future by adhering to policies of commitment to the promotion of a responsible use of the coastal regions, which aim to keep the natural healthy balance in the environment. This can be achieved through long-term studies including all the natural processes affecting a region as well as the modifications imposed or planned.

Finally, looking at Table 10.1 again, it can be seen that apart from tourism, severe damage was reported to dwellings, electricity infrastructure, and fishing and agriculture; this means that basic human needs were strongly degraded for some months, and even though the costs of these sectors look low compared to those of tourist infrastructure, it is important to point out that almost all the damage to the latter was covered by insurance companies. In this sense it is undeniable that the tourist industry shows high vulnerability, but if its economic possibilities are taken into account, it is able to recover quickly, while community activities are more vulnerable and they need much more time to normalize. As a result, the infrastructure that has altered the natural cycles permanently increases not only its own vulnerability, but also that of the community around it. For Cancun and probably for many other places in the short term, the human modifications to the coast are currently the biggest threat, inducing greater risk than long-term climatic processes.

ANNEX HURAC MODEL

The cyclone parametric model HURAC is based on the Hydromet-Rankin Vortex from Holland (1980) and Bretschneider (1990) models. The HURAC model substantially improves the estimation of the wind and wave fields. It also simplifies the methodologies presented by *Silva et al.* [2000, 2002] and *Ruiz et al.* [2009]. The HURAC model comprises three sub-models as described:
1. Atmospheric pressure module

$$P_r = P_0 + (P_N - P_0)\exp\left(-\frac{R}{r}\right)$$

where, P_0 is pressure at the hurricane center ("eye"), in mb, P_r is atmospheric pressure to r radial distance, in mb

and km, respectively, P_N is normal pressure, in mb, and R is cyclostrophic wind radii, in km.
2. Wind module
To determine the maximum wind gradient and the wind velocity 10 m above the mean water level:

$$U_R = 21.8\sqrt{P_N - P_0} - 0.5fR$$
$$W = 0.886\left(F_v U_R + 0.5V_F\cos(\theta + \beta)\right)$$

where, U_R is the maximum wind gradient by a stationary hurricane, in km/h, W is the wind velocity 10 m above the mean water level by a hurricane which is moving, in km/h, V_F is the transfer velocity, in km/h, F_v is the velocity decreased parameter, in km/h, and $(\theta + \beta)$ is the total angle between the transfer velocity and the maximum wind gradient, in degrees.
3. Wave module

$$H_s = 0.2887F_h\left(1 - \frac{6.69N_C}{1 + 10.3N_C - 3.25N_C^2}\right)$$
$$\sqrt{R(P_N - P_0)}\left(1 + \frac{V_F\cos(\theta + \beta)}{2U_R F_V}\right)^2$$

where, H_s is the wave significant height, in m, F_h is the wave height decreased parameter, in m, and N_c is the cyclostrophic Coriolis factor, in rad/h.

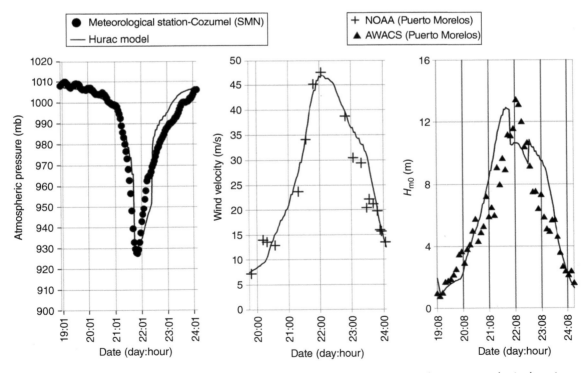

Figure 10.10 Physical characteristics of Hurricane Wilma: barometric pressure from meteorological station at Cozumel Island (National Meteorological System, SMN), wind reanalysis data from the Hurricane Research Division (HRD, NOAA), and significant wave height calculated from in situ measurements at 20 m depth opposite Puerto Morelos, Quintana Roo. The continuous line represents the modeled data (HURAC) for all the variables.

The validation of the HURAC model was made with recorded data for Hurricane Wilma. Figure 10.10 shows the results of atmospheric pressure, wind, and wave heights computed with the HURAC model and measured data from (1) the meteorologic station of the SMN (Servicio Meteorológico Nacional de la CONAGUA, Mexico http://smn.cna.gob.mx/) at Cozumel Island, (2) the superficial wind reanalysis system from the NOAA (Hurricane Research Division of the National Oceanic and Atmospheric Administration, www.nhc.noaa.gov/), and (3) an acoustic Doppler profiler deployed by the Engineering Institute of the National University of Mexico [*Silva et al.*, 2009]. A good correlation is found between the computed and measured data.

REFERENCES

Balderas, O. (2009), Barómetro Turístico Cancún, Quintana Roo Diciembre 2009. Asociación de Hoteles de Cancún/ ACTI, México, http://www.acticonsultores.com (accessed 4 September 2015).

Bodegom, M. (2004), Beach Nourishment. An evaluation of equilibration design methods, Cancun beach rehabilitation project, M.Sc. thesis, Delft University of Technology, 149 pp.

CFE (2001), Estudios y Modelos de Simulacion y Proyecto Ejecutivo para la rehabilitacion Integral de las playas en el tramo entre Punta Cancun y Punta Nizuc.

CFE (2003), Presentacion y mantenimiento de la zona federal maritimo terrestre entre Punta Cancun y Punta Nizuc.

Coronado, C., J. Candela, R. Iglesias-Prieto, J. Sheinbaum, M. Lopez, and F. J. Ocampo-Torres (2007), On the circulation in the Puerto Morelos fringing reef lagoon, *Coral Reefs*, 26(1), 149–163.

Diez, J. J., M. D. Esteban, and R. M. Paz (2009), Cancun-Nizuc coastal barrier, *J. Coast. Res.*, 25(1), 57–68.

Escalante, E., C. Silva, E. Mendoza, I. Marino-Tapia, and F. Ruiz (2009), Análisis de la variación del nivel del mar y de las corrientes inducidas por el huracán Wilma frente a Puerto Morelos, Quintana Roo, méxico, *Ing. Hidrául. México*, XXIV(2), 111–126.

Felix, A., E. Mendoza, R. Silva, E. Rivera Arriaga, and F. Palacio (2008), Analysis of the natural and anthropogenic evolution of Cancun beach, México, as a contribution to its sustainable management, *The First proCoast Seminar on Coastal Research*, Portugal.

García, N., Marin, R., Méndez, K., and Bitrán, D. (2006). Características e impacto socioeconómico de los huracanes Stan y Wilma en la República Mexicana en el 2005, Centro Nacional de Prevención de Desastres/Comisión Económica para América Latina y el Caribe de las Naciones Unidas, México, 325 pp.

Gonzalez, M. (2009), Analisis de las variaciones morfodinamicas en la playa de Cancun, Quintana Roo: Herramientas para el manejo costero, M.Sc. thesis, Universidad Autonoma de Campeche, 99 pp.

Knutson, T., J. McBride, J. Chan, K. Emanuel, G. Holland, C. Landsea, I. Held, J. Kossin, A. Srivastava, and M. Sugi (2010), Tropical cyclones and climate change, *Nat. Geosci.*, 3, 157–164.

Kossin, J., K. Knapp, D. Vimont, R. Murnane, and B. Harper (2007), A globally consistent reanalysis of hurricane variability and trends, *Geophys. Res. Lett.*, 34(L04815), 1–6.

Leon, F., N. Carbajal, T. Frickey, and L. Santos (2009), Microbial identification of the Nichupte-Bojorquez coastal lagoon in Cancun, Mexico, *Aquat. Ecol.*, 43(2), 197–205.

Mann, M. and K. Emanuel (2006), Atlantic hurricane trends linked to climate change, *Eos Trans. Am. Geophys. Union,*, 87(24), 233.

Pedrozo, D. (2008), Respuesta Hidrodinámica del Sistema Lagunar Nichupte, Cancun, Mexico, M.Sc. thesis, UNAM, 139 pp.

Ranger, N. and Niehorster, F. (2011). Deep uncertainty in long-term hurricane risk: Scenario generation and implications for future climate experiments, Working Paper No. 61, Centre for Climate Change Economics and Policy, 26 pp.

Ruiz, G. (2010), Determinación del estado morfodinámico de segmentos de playa que poseen obstáculos sumergidos y emergidos, Ph.D. thesis, Universidad Nacional Autonoma de Mexico, 195 pp.

Ruiz, G., R. Silva, D. Pérez, G. Posada, and G. Bautista (2009), Modelo híbrido para la caracterización del oleaje, *Tecnol. Cienc. Agua*, XXIV(3), 5–22.

SEDETUR (2008). Tourism statistics, http://sedetur.qroo.gob. mx/estadisticas/estadisticas.php (accessed 19 August 2015).

Silva, R., G. Díaz, A. Contreras, G. Bautista, and C. Sánchez (2000), Determination of oceanographic risks from hurricanes on Mexican Coast, *6th International Workshop on Wave Hindcasting and Forecasting*, Monterrey, CA, pp. 137–151.

Silva, R., G. Govaere, P. Salles, G. Bautista, and G. Díaz (2002), Oceanographic vulnerability to hurricanes on the Mexican coast, *International Conference on Coastal Engineering*, ASCE, Cardiff, pp. 39–51.

Silva, R., I. Mariño-Tapia, C. Enriquez-Ortiz, E. Mendoza, and P. Wong (2006), Monitoring shoreline changes at Cancun Beach, Mexico, *International Conference for Coastal Engineering (ICCE)*, World Scientific, San Diego, CA, pp. 1013–1022.

Silva, R., G. Ruiz, G. Posada, D. Perez, and G. Rivillas (2008), Atlas de Clima Maritimo de la Vertiente Atlantica Mexicana.

Silva, R., E. Mendoza, E. Escalante, I. Mariño-Tapia, and F. Ruiz (2009), Oleaje inducidopor el huracán Wilma en Puerto Morelos, Quintana Roo, México, *Ing. Hidrául. México*, XXIV(2), 93–109.

WAMDI-Group (1988), The WAM model-a third generation ocean wave prediction model, *J. Phys. Oceanogr.*, 18, 1775–1810.

Ward, W. C., A. E. Weidie, and W. Black (1985), Recent carbonate sediments of the inner shelf, in *Geology and Hydrogeology of the Yucatan and Quaternary Geology of Northeastern Yucatan Peninsula*, edited by W. C. Ward, A. E. Weidie, and W. Back, pp. 274, New Orleans Geological Society, New Orleans, LA.

11

Observations and Modeling of Environmental and Human Damage Caused by the 2004 Indian Ocean Tsunami

Kazuhisa Goto,* Fumihiko Imamura,* Shunichi Koshimura,* and Hideaki Yanagisawa**

ABSTRACT

This chapter have specifically introduced our studies of local inundation of the 2004 Indian Ocean tsunami and show how to quantitatively estimate tsunami damage based on field observations, satellite image analyses, and high-resolution numerical modeling results. We investigated damage to coastal morphology, marine ecosystems, and mangroves at Pakarang Cape, Thailand, and to structures, humans, and mangroves at Banda Aceh city, Indonesia. We produced 17 and 23 m grid digital bathymetric/topographic datasets, respectively for those areas, with grid cell resolutions sufficiently fine for comparison with field observation data. From these datasets, we produced a nested grid system spanning the Indian Ocean to the Pakarang Cape coast and Banda Aceh city and calculated tsunami inundation. Such high-resolution numerical modeling is useful to elucidate processes of (1) local tsunami inundation, (2) damage generation, and (3) quantitative damage associated with tsunami hydrodynamics: flow depth, hydraulic force, and current velocity. We clarified that the occurrence of substantial morphological change, especially the deposition of huge boulders, was dependent upon the initial wave form and coastal profile. This fundamental idea is also applicable to the damage incurred by the coral communities. Fragility functions of mangroves, structures, and tsunami casualties estimated in our studies enable us to express the relation between the damage and hydrodynamic features of the tsunami inundation flow, quantitatively. Such quantitative damage estimation based on lessons from the 2004 Indian Ocean tsunami is an important step for tsunami-risk assessment for high-risk countries.

11.1. INTRODUCTION

On 26 December 2004, a huge earthquake (Mw 9.0–9.3) occurred northwest of Sumatra Island, Indonesia. Following this earthquake, one of the largest tsunamis (the 2004 Indian Ocean tsunami) in human history struck coastal areas of more than 10 countries skirting the Indian Ocean. The tsunami killed nearly 230,000 people, causing severe property damage and economic losses [*Imamura et al.*, 2006; *Satake et al.*, 2007]. The general public throughout world was impacted by the tsunami, as were various scientific communities. Figure 11.1a depicts the variation over time of the number of published papers with a keyword of "tsunami." Although several large tsunami events occurred during the 1990s, the number of papers varied gradually at those times. In contrast, the number of papers drastically increased—by approximately four times—immediately after the 2004 Indian Ocean tsunami (year 2005). More than two thirds of the

Disaster Control Research Center, Graduate School of Engineering, Tohoku University, Sendai, Japan

* Present address: International Research Institute of Disaster Science, Tohoku University, Sendai, Japan

** Present address: Faculty of Liberal Arts, Tohoku Gakuin University, Sendai, Japan

Extreme Events: Observations, Modeling, and Economics, Geophysical Monograph 214, First Edition.
Edited by Mario Chavez, Michael Ghil, and Jaime Urrutia-Fucugauchi.

(a)

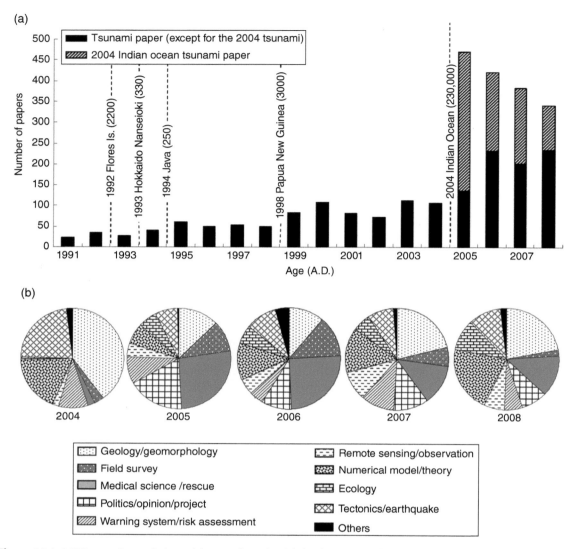

(b)

Figure 11.1 (a) Time series variation of the number of published papers with the keyword "tsunami," sought using the ISI Web of Science (modified after *Goto and Fujino* [2008]). The year and number of casualties of each major tsunami event are also shown in this figure. (b) The annual change of the approximate percentage of published papers from different research fields with the keyword "tsunami."

papers described and discussed this tsunami event, implying the degree to which this tsunami was viewed as a devastating event by scientific communities.

Before the 2004 Indian Ocean tsunami, papers categorized under Geology, Tectonics, and numerical modeling were generally dominant (Figure 11.1b). In contrast, in 2005 and 2006, papers that discussed politics, medical science (including rescue activity), and field surveys drastically increased, reflecting high demands for emergency activities from such research fields immediately following the tsunami event. Moreover, the topics of discussions of recent papers in 2007–2008 throughout the world have gradually shifted to development of tsunami warning systems and tsunami-risk assessment (Figure 11.1b).

Researchers in tsunami in high-risk countries have again realized the degree to which the tsunami impact is fearful and the extent to which urgent improvements of countermeasures against tsunami disasters are highly required in their own countries.

To conduct a proper tsunami-risk assessment and to produce a disaster prevention plan based on a lesson from the 2004 Indian Ocean tsunami, the relation between the hydrodynamic features of the tsunami (e.g., flow depth, hydraulic force, and current velocity) and damage to humans, structures (houses and buildings), ecosystems, and coastal morphology must be clarified quantitatively. Such investigations have mainly been conducted based on field observation data. In fact, several studies have undertaken damage estimation based on the observed wave height or inundation area [*Fernando et al.*, 2005; *Marchand*, 2006; *Matsutomi et al.*, 2006; *Szczuciński et al.*, 2006; *Thanawood et al.*, 2006; *Tomita et al.*, 2006; *Kelletat et al.*, 2007; *Umitsu et al.* 2007]. Although such approaches are important, it is difficult to estimate quantitative damage solely from field observation data. For example, *Imamura et al.* [2008] noted that the degree of damage caused by the tsunami is related to the hydrodynamic force, which is mainly a function of the current velocity of the tsunami, rather than inundation area or wave height [*Noji et al.*, 1993]. Current velocity can sometimes be estimated based on information from aerial photographs [*Takahashi et al.*, 1993], from differences in flow depth between the front and rear of structures [*Matsutomi et al.*, 2005, 2006; *Matsutomi and Okamoto*, 2010], and from video recordings [*Borrero*, 2005; *Matsutomi et al.*, 2005; *Fritz et al.*, 2006]. However, hydrodynamic force and current velocity are difficult to estimate solely from field observation data [*Imamura et al.*, 2008].

Moreover, *Goto and Imamura* [2009] mentioned that the degree of damage caused by the tsunami on land does not necessarily correspond to the damage on a shallow sea environment. *Goto et al.* [2009] reported, based on numerical modeling results, that the distributions of the maximum current velocities at the shallow sea environment differed considerably depending on the initial wave form (wave crest or trough that arrives first) and the coastal profile, even though the wave heights and current velocities at the shoreline were almost identical. Therefore, the tsunami wave height and inundation area measured on land are not necessarily useful to evaluate damage to the shallow sea environment, such as damage to coral communities and other marine ecosystems [*Goto and Imamura*, 2009; *Goto et al.*, 2009].

In this context, high-resolution numerical modeling, which has resolution of over several meters to several tens of meters in grid cells and which is directly comparable to field observation data, is a necessary complement to field observation data. Quantitative comparison between the damage attributable to the 2004 Indian Ocean tsunami observed at the field and numerical modeling results is an important step that must be made in producing a future tsunami disaster prevention plan. Nevertheless, major objectives of previous numerical modeling for the 2004 Indian Ocean tsunami are investigation of the rupture process of the fault [*Fujii and Satake*, 2007] and assessment of the global reach of the tsunami [*Titov et al.*, 2005]. These studies didn't evaluate local damage. Very few high-resolution calculations of tsunami inundation are conducted.

At the Disaster Control Research Center, Tohoku University, we have specifically pursued quantitative investigation of the tsunami inundation process and

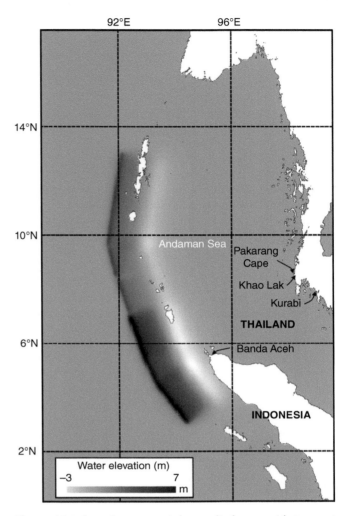

Figure 11.2 Location map of the studied area with tsunami source model proposed by *Koshimura et al.* [2009a].

exploration of the relation between the damage and the hydrodynamic features of the tsunami based on high-resolution numerical modeling results. Especially, we have investigated damage to coastal morphology [*Goto et al.*, 2007, 2008, 2009, 2010], marine ecosystems [*Goto and Imamura*, 2009; *Sugawara et al.*, 2009], and mangroves [*Yanagisawa et al.*, 2006, 2009a, 2009b] at Pakarang Cape (Figure 11.2), Thailand. We have also examined damage to structures [*Koshimura et al.*, 2009a, 2009b], humans [*Oie et al.*, 2006; *Koshimura et al.*, 2009a], and mangroves [*Yanagisawa et al.*, 2007, 2010] at Banda Aceh city, Indonesia (Figure 11.2). As reviewed in these papers herein, we describe our studies, which have integrated field observations and high-resolution numerical modeling to conduct quantitative damage estimation in Thailand and Indonesia.

11.2. NUMERICAL MODEL

11.2.1. Generation and Propagation of the 2004 Indian Ocean Tsunami

According to the review by *Imamura et al.* [2006], the tsunami occurred due to impulsive disturbances of water surface offshore from northwestern Sumatra Island to the Andaman Sea near Myanmar. The fault length is ~1000 km. None had exceeded Mw = 9.0 in the past although several earthquakes with ensuing tsunamis Mw = 8–8.5 have occurred in this region [*Imamura et al.*, 2006]. The 2004 earthquake was therefore the first that exceeded Mw = 9.0 in the Indian Ocean in history. Because of the directivity of the wave energy along the short axis of the tsunami source, the tsunami propagated mainly toward the east and west [*Imamura et al.*, 2006]. When the eastbound tsunami reached to Thailand and Malaysia, westbound tsunami were propagating over the Indian Ocean and reached the coast of India and Sri Lanka and Maldives [*Imamura et al.*, 2006]. Although the Andaman Sea is shallow, the Indian Ocean is quite deep. Consequently, the tsunamis traveled at different speeds [*Imamura et al.*, 2006]. The trough of the first tsunami wave arrived at Thailand's coast; while the crest of the wave arrived first at Sri Lanka [*Imamura et al.*, 2006]. The tsunami propagated continuously across the Indian Ocean and reached the Atlantic and Pacific Oceans [*Titov et al.*, 2005]. Maximum tsunami run-ups were 10–48 m on the western shore of Sumatra, 5–18 m in Thailand, and 10–15 m in Sri Lanka [after *Imamura et al.*, 2006].

11.2.2. Numerical Methods

As like described by *Goto et al.* [2007], we usually used a linear equation to describe a shallow-water wave on the spherical earth to simulate tsunami propagation in the open sea [*Imamura* 1995; *Goto et al.* 1997]. Furthermore, we made allowances for the Coriolis force. Then, we used a nonlinear equation in a Cartesian coordinate system for a shallow water wave to simulate tsunami propagation in the coastal zone and the inundation area [*Goto et al.* 1997), with allowance made for bottom friction. The governing equations are described as follows:

$$\frac{\partial \eta}{\partial t} + \frac{\partial M}{\partial x} + \frac{\partial N}{\partial y} = 0 \tag{11.1}$$

$$\frac{\partial M}{\partial t} + \frac{\partial}{\partial x}\left(\frac{M^2}{D}\right) + \frac{\partial}{\partial y}\left(\frac{MN}{D}\right) + gD\frac{\partial \eta}{\partial x} \\ + \frac{gn^2}{D^{7/3}} M\sqrt{M^2 + N^2} = 0 \tag{11.2}$$

$$\frac{\partial N}{\partial t} + \frac{\partial}{\partial x}\left(\frac{MN}{D}\right) + \frac{\partial}{\partial y}\left(\frac{N^2}{D}\right) + gD\frac{\partial \eta}{\partial y} \\ + \frac{gn^2}{D^{7/3}} N\sqrt{M^2 + N^2} = 0 \tag{11.3}$$

Therein, η is a vertical displacement of water surface above the still water surface, M and N, respectively, signify discharge fluxes in the x- and y-directions, D is the total water depth ($=h+\eta$), g signifies gravitational acceleration, and n is Manning's roughness. The staggered leapfrog method (a finite-difference method) is used to solve these equations [*Goto et al.* 1997]. The bore front condition is based on *Kotani et al.* [1998].

We used the constant coefficient n in the form of Manning's formula for bottom friction, depending on land conditions: 0.02 for bare ground and grass, 0.025 for sea and rivers, 0.06 for buildings, and 0.03 for vegetation area and 0.045 for populated area [*Yanagisawa et al.*, 2009a; *Koshimura et al.*, 2009a]. *Yanagisawa et al.* [2009a] used the variable roughness coefficient based on the equivalent roughness model [*Harada and Kawata*, 2005] for friction in mangrove forests:

$$n' = \sqrt{\frac{D^{4/3}}{2gV}(C_D A) + n_0^2} \tag{11.4}$$

where n' is the variable roughness coefficient, D is the tsunami flow depth (water level from ground), V is the volume of water per unit area on the bottom floor (m^{-2}), n_0 is the bottom roughness coefficient without trees, C_D is the drag coefficient, and A is the projected vertical sectional area of trees per unit area on the bottom floor (m^{-2}). Land conditions were investigated using satellite imagery before the tsunami and field observations (Figure 11.3a). The bottom friction was referred from earlier reports [*Yanagisawa et al.*, 2009a].

For friction in densely populated areas at Banda Aceh city, *Koshimura et al.* [2009a] used the variable roughness coefficient estimated using the following equivalent roughness model [*Kotani et al.*, 1998; *Aburaya and Imamura*, 2002; *Dutta et al.*, 2007]:

$$n' = \sqrt{\frac{D^{4/3}}{2gd} \times C_D \times \frac{\theta}{100-\theta} + n_0^2} \tag{11.5}$$

In the given equation, d is the horizontal scale of houses and θ is the building/house occupancy ratio in the computational grid.

Figure 11.4 depicts study areas in Thailand and Indonesia, each of which is subdivided into five regions. The transoceanic propagation model is connected to the model of nearshore propagation and coastal inundation,

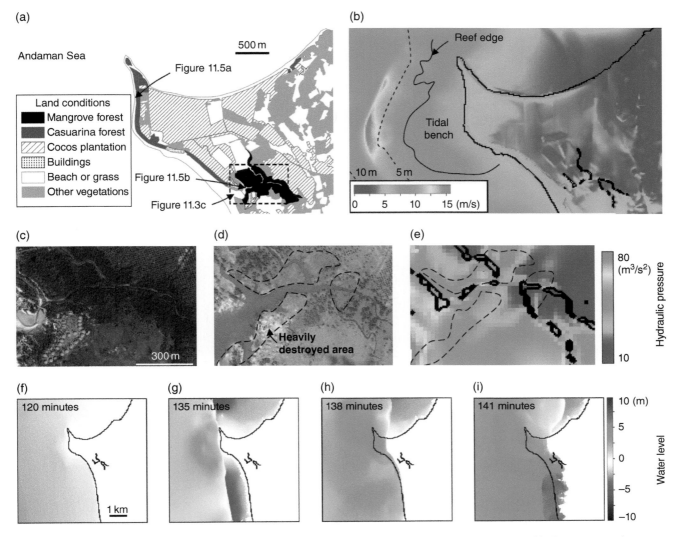

Figure 11.3 (a) Land conditions at Pakarang Cape determined using satellite imagery and field observations. (b) Numerical result for the maximum tsunami current velocity (m/s) around the cape (modified after *Goto et al.* [2007]). The scale is the same as that of (a). Close-up satellite images of the mangrove forest around the Cape (c) before the tsunami (13 January 2003) and (d) after the tsunami (29 December 2004). The mangrove trees along the river were severely destroyed by the tsunami. These satellite images were provided by Space Imaging/CRISP-Singapore. (e) A distribution of modeled hydraulic pressure (m³/s²). High hydraulic pressure is observed along the river. The scales for (d) and (e) are the same as that of (c). Snapshots of computed tsunami water levels at (f) 120, (g) 135, (h) 138, and (i) 141 minutes after generation of the tsunami waves. The scales for (g)–(i) are the same as that of (f).

which has finer spatial resolution, according to the nonlinear shallow-water theory. We used a 1-arc-minute grid (about 1860 m) with digital bathymetric and topographic data for transoceanic propagation (region 1 in Figure 11.4a), and much finer spatial resolution data for coastal areas. We also measured the topography around the Pakarang Cape and Banda Aceh city and respectively created 17 m (region 5a in Figure 11.4c) and 23 m (region 5b in Figure 11.4e) grid digital datasets [*Oie et al.*, 2006; *Yanagisawa et al.*, 2006, 2007, 2009a, 2009b; *Goto et al.*, 2007; *Koshimura et al.*, 2009a]. These resolutions of grid

cells are sufficiently fine for comparison with the field observation data. Using these topographic/bathymetric data, we constructed a nested grid system across the Indian Ocean to the coast of Pakarang Cape and Banda Aceh city.

Development of the source model of the 2004 Indian Ocean tsunami is problematic [*Koshimura et al.*, 2009a] because the fault rupture area is considerably extensive (~1000 km) and its rupture process is complex [*Fujii and Satake*, 2007]. For example, the rupture velocity of the fault remains controversial [*Ammon et al.*, 2005; *Ishii*

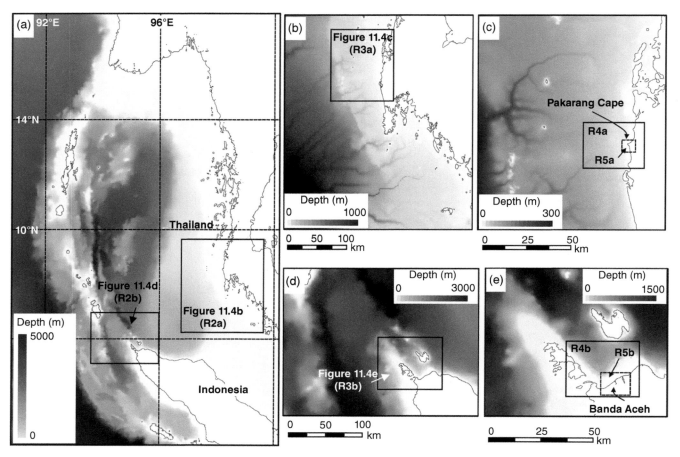

Figure 11.4 The computational domain for the model of tsunami propagation and run-up to Pakarang Cape and Banda Aceh city (after *Koshimura et al.* [2009a]; *Yanagisawa et al.* [2009a]). Figures portray (a) region 1, (b) region2a (R2a), (c) region 3a (R3a), (d) region 2b (R2b), and (e) region 3b (R3b). Water depths in respective regions are shown by the gray scale.

et al., 2005; *Tanioka et al.*, 2006; *Fujii and Satake*, 2007]. Moreover, a tsunami source model that explains all tidal records and field observations in the tsunami-affected countries has not yet been proposed. Our major objectives are local tsunami inundation at Pakarang Cape and Banda Aceh city. We adopted tsunami source models that explain well the tidal record and field observations in each studied region. For the Pakarang Cape, we assumed a composite fault model proposed by *Koshimura et al.* [2005] and *Takashima et al.* [2005] as the tsunami source [*Goto et al.*, 2007; *Yanagisawa et al.*, 2009a]. At Banda Aceh city, we assumed the model proposed by *Koshimura et al.* [2009a] (Figure 11.2). These models reproduce the sea surface height of mid-ocean tsunami as measured from a satellite (Jason 1) [*Gower*, 2007; *Hayashi*, 2008] as well as records of measurements taken at tidal observatories in Thailand and Indonesia.

Validities of the numerical model results were confirmed by our series of papers [see *Goto et al.*, 2007; *Koshimura et al.*, 2009a; *Yanagisawa et al.*, 2009a, 2009b,

2010]. These models well reproduced the observed inundation depth, inundation area, and the current velocity at each studied area.

11.3. IMPACT OF THE TSUNAMI AT PAKARANG CAPE, THAILAND

Pakarang Cape, an area damaged severely by the 2004 Indian Ocean tsunami, is located ~10 km north of Khao Lak, Thailand (Figure 11.2). The tsunami wave height along the shore at Pakarang Cape was <9 m (averagely 4–7 m) [*Matsutomi et al.*, 2005; *Goto et al.*, 2008]; the inundation area was estimated as <2.5 km² [*Goto et al.*, 2007]. *Matsutomi et al.* [2006] also estimated the current velocity as 6–8 m/s at severely damaged buildings near the coast of Khao Lak.

Pakarang Cape was a well-studied area by international survey teams after the 2004 Indian Ocean tsunami [*Goto et al.*, 2007, 2008, 2009, 2010; *Di Geronimo et al.*, 2009; *Feldens et al.*, 2009; *Sugawara et al.*, 2009] because

Figure 11.5 (a) A photograph showing the coastal erosion at western part of Pakarang Cape, Thailand (March 2005). Abundant boulders were deposited on the tidal bench. (b) A photograph showing the mangrove forest at the Cape. Most mangrove trees were destroyed; only a few *Rhizophora* sp. survived (August 2006). Some young trees have started to grow among the surviving trees.

the tsunami severely damaged the environment there. Furthermore, extensive data even before the tsunami, including high-resolution satellite images, were available. Here, we review the tsunami impact against the coastal morphology, marine ecosystem (foraminifera and corals), and mangroves at Pakarang Cape and their recovery processes based on field observations.

11.3.1. Coastal Morphology

The coastal morphology at Pakarang Cape was altered considerably by the 2004 Indian Ocean tsunami. As portrayed in Figure 11.5a, great amounts of coastal sediments were eroded and the coastal trees were felled by erosion [*Goto et al.*, 2008]. Megaripples, with wavelength of ~1 m

at the shore and with height of <20 cm, were observed in a coastal forest [*Goto et al.*, 2008]. *Goto et al.* [2008] inferred that the megaripples were formed by eastward-flowing currents based on the observation that they had the form of concentric semicircles that were concave toward the sea. No report of sandy tsunami deposits were made around Pakarang Cape, but *Hori et al.* [2007] and *Fujino et al.* [2008] reported that the sandy tsunami deposits, with thickness of up to 21 cm, extended beyond 1 km from the shoreline at Khao Lak.

At Pakarang Cape, many large boulders, which were fragments of reef rocks with sizes estimated as <14 m^3 (22.7 t), are scattered along its western shore (Figure 11.5a), where up to 600 m offshore the sea floor is a flat and shallow tidal bench composed of reef rocks [Figure 11.3b;

Goto et al., 2007]. *Goto et al.* [2007] described that corals accreted on these boulders were species that lived at depths shallower than 10 m. Moreover, several boulders were of microatolls, suggesting that they were located originally in the intertidal zone. Subsequently, these boulders were transported from the reef slope to the reef flat, which in turn indicates that the horizontal displacement distance of boulders might have been up to 1 km [*Goto et al.*, 2007]. Boulders were also observed offshore of Pakarang Cape (4–5 m water depth) and their concentration decreases toward the deeper zone (~10 m) [*Goto et al.*, 2007, 2009]. *Feldens et al.* [2009] further suggested that the source of these boulders might be stone ridges that were visible in their side scanning sonar data at water depths between 30 and 40 m.

It is particularly interesting that no boulders were found on land, indicating that the hydraulic force of the tsunami wave dissipated rapidly on reaching the land because of the higher bottom friction due to the steep slope [*Goto et al.*, 2007, 2010].

The coastal sediments eroded by the tsunami waves around the cape have almost been restored now by natural processes of sediment redistribution [*Di Geronimo et al.*, 2009], although boulders on the tidal bench have not been displaced some 2 years after the tsunami [*Goto et al.*, 2007]. *Choowong et al.* [2009] also investigated the recovery process of the beach profile near Khao Lak based on satellite images and field observations. Their results show that the present situation of the beach zone has almost completed its reversion to an equilibrium stage and this has occurred within the 2 years following the tsunami event [*Choowong et al.*, 2009].

11.3.2. Marine Ecosystem

11.3.2.1. Foraminifera

The influence of the tsunami on marine ecosystems was investigated by *Sugawara et al.* [2009] based on micropaleontological analysis of nearshore to offshore sediments at Pakarang Cape and Kurabi (Figure 11.2). They reported that agglutinated foraminifers, which are characteristic of intertidal brackish environments, were observed in post-tsunami sediments from foreshore to offshore zones. Their result suggests that original sediments distributed in foreshore to nearshore zones were transported seaward by the tsunami backwash [*Sugawara et al.*, 2009]. *Sugawara et al.* [2009] suggested that landward redistribution of sediments by the tsunami run up was ineffective compared with the backwash of the study area because the distribution pattern of planktonic and benthic species living in offshore zones showed minor landward migration by the tsunami. Based on these observations, *Sugawara et al.* [2009] concluded that the tsunami backwash-induced sediment flows transported larger amounts of coastal sediments to offshore.

Evidence also suggests that shallow-sea species (*Ammobaculites*, *Ammonia*, *Elphidium*, and *Rosalina* genera) were transported toward the deep zone by backwash [*Sugawara et al.*, 2009]. Two years after the tsunami, however, species of these genera recovered their original environments [*Sugawara et al.*, 2009].

11.3.2.2. Corals

Damage to Thailand's coral communities by the tsunami varied greatly among locations: up to 13–40% of all corals were damaged [*Chavanich et al.*, 2005, 2008; *Comley et al.*, 2005; *Pennisi*, 2005]. The characteristics of coral and coastal profiles and initial tsunami waveform might be important factors underlying the variation of damage caused by the 2004 tsunami [*Chavanich et al.*, 2008; *Goto et al.*, 2009; *Goto and Imamura*, 2009]. Nevertheless, because of the absence of an appropriate model, quantitative analyses for exploring the relations of these factors have not been conducted yet [*Goto and Imamura*, 2009].

Corals around Pakarang Cape were not healthy even before the 2004 Indian Ocean tsunami, although coral reefs had developed at western part [*Goto et al.*, 2007]. Most had probably died before the tsunami because the seawater around the cape is not conducive to coral growth [*Department of Fishery, Thailand*, 1999; *Benzoni et al.*, 2006; *Goto et al.*, 2007]. Nevertheless, small coral growths were observed on submarine boulders at 4–10 m water depth 2 years after the tsunami. They were only ~4–5 cm in diameter, suggesting that live coral was recruited after the 2004 Indian Ocean tsunami [*Goto et al.*, 2007].

11.3.3. Mangroves

At the southern part of Pakarang Cape, a mangrove forest surrounded a small river (Figure 11.3a and c). The forest was composed of *Rhizophora* sp. with minor quantities of *Bruguiera* sp., *Excoecaria agallocha*, and *Avicennia* sp. near the river mouth [*Yanagisawa et al.*, 2009a]. *Yanagisawa et al.* [2009a], through analyses of satellite images, found that the tsunami destroyed > 70% of the mangrove forest (Figures 11.3c, d, and 11.5b).

Yanagisawa et al. [2009a] further investigated the position and size of 287 mangrove trees. They clarified that the survival rate of *Rhizophora* sp. increased concomitantly with increasing stem diameter at the top of the prop roots: the survival rate was 72% with a 25–30 cm stem diameter, 50% with a 20–25 cm stem diameter, and 19% with a 15–20 cm stem diameter. Because *Rhizophora* trees have prop roots sufficiently thick to resist the tsunami hydrodynamic force, they were probably severed at the stem or prop roots while they were rarely uprooted [*Yanagisawa et al.*, 2009a].

The survival rate of *Bruguiera* trees was <10% and uprooted trees accounted for 42% of all *Bruguiera* trees: they were probably uprooted easily by the tsunami since they didn't have thick prop roots [*Yanagisawa et al.*, 2009a]. The *Avicennia* sp. survival rate was almost 0% because they had no thick prop roots and their stem diameter was less than that of other species [*Yanagisawa et al.*, 2009a].

Previous papers that have presented discussion related to the mitigation effect of mangrove forest on the 2004 Indian Ocean tsunami [*Danielsen et al.*, 2005; *Kathiresan and Rajendran*, 2005] suggest that areas with mangroves were substantially less damage. However, other researchers have questioned whether mangroves can contribute to tsunami disaster mitigation [*Kerr et al.*, 2006; *Wolanski*, 2007]. Results by *Yanagisawa et al.* [2009a] imply that mitigation effects of mangroves on a tsunami are highly variable depending on various factors such as mangrove species, size, topography, and hydrodynamic features of the tsunami. The relation between the damage to mangroves and the hydrodynamic features of the tsunami demands further clarification to quantify the mitigation effect of mangroves on the tsunami impact (see Section 11.6.2).

Some surviving mangrove trees have reproduced and young trees started to grow around the surviving trees at ~1.5 years after the tsunami (Figure 11.5b). However, our field observations revealed that most surviving mangrove trees at the cape were dead after the tsunami for reasons that remain unclear. Moreover, other grasses and trees have grown to replace the mangrove trees. Therefore, it remains uncertain whether the mangrove forest at the cape will recover. Even if they recover in the future, it will probably require many years.

11.4. IMPACT OF THE TSUNAMI AT BANDA ACEH CITY, INDONESIA

Banda Aceh city, located at northern end of Sumatra Island (Figure 11.2), has an area of ~61 km², in which 260,000 people resided before the tsunami. *Koshimura et al.* [2009a] investigated satellite images taken before the tsunami and found that the land use of the city was mainly subdivided into (1) wetland or swamps, which were partly used for aquaculture (up to 2 km inland from the coastline), and (2) populated regions (2–2.5 km from the coastline). Dense mangrove forests had been distributed in the coastal area in the past (Figure 11.6), but most were cut down to make aquaculture ponds for shrimp [*Yanagisawa et al.*, 2007]. Consequently, several patchy mangrove forests were distributed along the coastline. At the city, international tsunami survey teams extensively investigated the inundation depth or height, and the inundation area [*Borrero*, 2005; *Matsutomi et al.*, 2006;

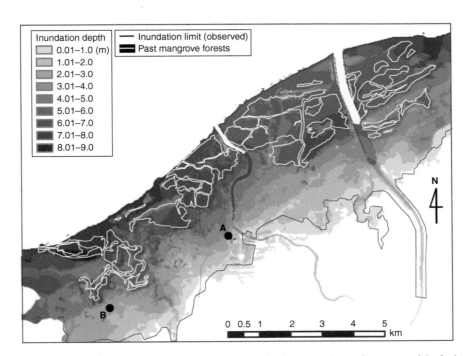

Figure 11.6 Spatial distribution of modeled inundation flow depth at Banda Aceh city (modified after *Koshimura et al.* [2009a]). The black solid line represents the observed inundation limit; the white solid line shows approximate region of the past mangrove forests (modified after *Yanagisawa et al.* [2007] and *Koshimura et al.* [2009a]). Points A and B show locations where the velocities were measured [*Fritz et al.*, 2006].

Tsuji et al., 2006; see also the summary by *Koshimura et al.*, 2009a]. According to the survey results, tsunami heights were up to 12 m along the western coast. The height decreases slightly toward the northeast. The tsunami inundated 3–4 km inland throughout the city and inundated areas of more than 10 km inland along the river (Figure 11.6).

The current velocities in the city were estimated from video recordings [*Borrero*, 2005; *Matsutomi et al.*, 2005; *Fritz et al.*, 2006]: ranging from 2–4 m/s at point A to 3.3–4.5 m/s at point B in Figure 11.6 [*Fritz et al.*, 2006].

11.4.1. Structural and Human Damage

Koshimura et al. [2009a] studied structural and human damage at Banda Aceh city as described further. Houses and structures in Banda Aceh city consist mainly of low-rise wooden houses, timber construction, and non-engineered RC construction [*Saatcioglu et al.*, 2006]. Reportedly, the numerous houses and structures survived the strong ground vibration by earthquake, but they were later destroyed by the tsunami [*Saatcioglu et al.*, 2006]. The Japan International Cooperation Agency [*JICA*, 2005] investigated 1000 cases of structural damage based on visual interpretations of the pre- and post-tsunami satellite images. According to these data, most structures within ~2–3 km from the shoreline, where the tsunami flow depth was >3–4 m, were destroyed by the tsunami [*Koshimura et al.*, 2009a]. A boundary between surviving and destroyed structures was clearly apparent [*Koshimura et al.*, 2009a], implying that a kind of threshold of structural damage in the city was likely to be related to hydrodynamic features of the tsunami, as discussed next (see Section 11.6.3).

Actually, *JICA* [2005] also investigated the number of tsunami casualties in each Desa (village) of the city. According to those data, the total number of dead or missing persons was ~70,000 (27% of the pre-tsunami population) [*Koshimura et al.*, 2009a]. It is noteworthy that it remains uncertain where the residents affected by the tsunami exactly migrated because the residents might have been aware of tsunami arrival and they might have evacuated [*Koshimura et al.*, 2009a]. Despite great uncertainty, the overall trend shows that the number of dead or missing persons was very high near the shoreline (in some Desa, the death/missing rate was almost 100%), decreasing inland [*Koshimura et al.*, 2009a].

11.4.2. Damage to Mangrove Forests

Yanagisawa et al. [2007] investigated 789 mangrove trees (*Rhizophora* sp.) in all at the coast of Banda Aceh. As with those at Pakarang Cape, the survival rate of *Rhizophora* sp. increased concomitantly with increasing stem diameter at the top of the prop roots. The survival rate was higher than 50% for mangroves with a 20–25 cm stem diameter. This observation is consistent with that at Pakarang Cape. Based on this finding, *Yanagisawa et al.* [2007] described that *Rhizophora* sp. with a 20–25 cm stem diameter would resist the tsunami inundation flow of several meters in depth. In contrast, almost all mangroves, including those with 35–40 cm stem diameter, were destroyed at the western end of the city, where the tsunami inundation height (~12 m) was greatest in the city.

11.5. MODELED TSUNAMI INUNDATION PROCESSES AT EACH STUDIED AREA

In the previous section, we summarized field observations of tsunami damage at Pakarang Cape and Banda Aceh city. Field observation data are useful to understand what types of damage were caused by the tsunami and the extent to which the damaged environments have recovered. Nevertheless, it remains difficult to identify the relation between the damage and hydrodynamic features of the tsunami solely from field observation data quantitatively because the data of flow depth and inundation area measured at the field are too scarce to enable comparison with the enormous quantity of data of tsunami damage. For example, we have data of approximately 1000 structures at Banda Aceh city [*JICA*, 2005; *Koshimura et al.*, 2009a], although the measured inundation depths and heights were only ~116 points [*Koshimura et al.*, 2009a]. Therefore, we cannot exploit the field observation data much for damage estimations. Moreover, tsunami flow depths and inundation areas measured at the field do not inform us about the tsunami inundation process. For these reasons, it is difficult to discuss the processes that caused the damage. High-resolution numerical modeling result can be a very strong tool to complement the observed hydrodynamic features of the tsunami. In this section, we briefly review the tsunami inundation processes calculated by our numerical models [*Goto et al.*, 2007; *Koshimura et al.*, 2009a; *Yanagisawa et al.*, 2009a].

11.5.1. Pakarang Cape

According to calculations by *Goto et al.* [2007] and *Yanagisawa et al.* [2009a, 2009b], the sea receded before the arrival of the first tsunami wave (Figure 11.3f), and a major part of the tidal bench and seafloor was exposed above the sea surface. The first tsunami wave arrived at the Cape at ~130–135 min after the tsunami generation; then it inundated the river and inland areas (Figure 11.3g, h, and i).

Because the ground is lower around the river than in surrounding areas, tsunami waves reached inland deeper along the river near the mangrove forest [*Goto et al.*,

2007]. The tsunami inundation from the river reached the maximum inundation distance (2.5 km inland from the shoreline). However, the first wave at the bench reached only ~1 km inland from the shoreline.

The maximum current velocity was estimated as 8–15 m/s between the reef edge and ~500 m offshore and <5 m/s on land (Figure 11.3b) [*Goto et al.*, 2007], and up to 5 m/s along the entire river channel in the mangrove forest [*Yanagisawa et al.*, 2009a].

11.5.2. Banda Aceh

The first tsunami wave arrived at the city at ~40 minutes after the tsunami generation; it then inundated inlands almost perpendicularly to the shoreline [*Oie et al.*, 2006; *Yanagisawa et al.*, 2007, 2010; *Koshimura et al.*, 2009a]. The modeled tsunami flow depth is up to 7–9 m along the western coast of Banda Aceh and 3–4 m in flow depth at the most densely populated area [*Koshimura et al.*, 2009a]. The tsunami deeply inundated areas from the river in the northeast of the city are up to 10 km from the shoreline but overall, the tsunami inundated ~3–4 km from the shoreline [*Koshimura et al.*, 2009a]. Figure 11.6 shows that the modeled inundation limit is well consistent with the field observation [*Koshimura et al.*, 2009a].

The maximum current velocity of the first tsunami wave was estimated as 9 m/s at the western coast of the city and up to 4 m/s in the densely populated area [*Koshimura et al.*, 2009a].

11.6. INTEGRATED ANALYSES OF THE DAMAGE ATTRIBUTABLE TO THE TSUNAMI

We conducted detailed field surveys, analyses of satellite images, and high-resolution numerical modeling at Pakarang Cape and Banda Aceh city. What can we do using these different types of data? First, high-resolution numerical modeling results are useful for understanding environmental changes and damage to humans. Moreover, numerical modeling results support quantitative comparison between the hydrodynamic features of the tsunami and various types of damage that occurred in the studied area. In this section, we review the damage generation processes and quantitative damage estimations using high-resolution numerical modeling results.

11.6.1. Displacement Process of Boulders at Pakarang Cape and Implications for Damage to Marine Ecosystems

As described earlier, coastal morphology and marine ecosystems around Pakarang Cape were heavily damaged by the tsunami, but most recovered within 2 years after the tsunami [*Choowong et al.*, 2009; *Di Geronimo et al.*,

2009]. On the other hand, huge boulders deposited on the tidal bench were not displaced by usual waves after the tsunami. Such boulders will greatly modify the coastal morphology in the future. Consequently, the displacement process of these boulders and their effect on morphological change along the coast must be clarified.

As depicted in Figure 11.3b, the current velocities of the tsunami were considerably high (8–15 m/s) between the reef edge and 500 m offshore—the possible source area of boulders now deposited on the tidal bench [*Goto et al.*, 2007]—because the wave height became highest around this region as a result of the considerable receding tidal level immediately before the arrival of the first wave crest [*Goto et al.*, 2009]. Current velocities around this region were much higher than the critical velocities necessary to displace the boulders at the cape (<3.2 m/s) [*Goto et al.*, 2007], suggesting that the tsunami had sufficient hydrodynamic force to have moved and deposited these boulders on the tidal bench.

As explained by *Goto et al.* [2007], all boulders at Pakarang Cape were stopped at the shoreline, irrespective of their size, even though the tsunami inundation areas were >2.5 km from the shoreline. Because of the steep beach slope and high bottom friction (Figure 11.3b), our numerical results suggest that the current velocity becomes much lower along the shoreline and thus these boulders were probably stopped at the shoreline because of the drastic reduction of the wave velocity [*Goto et al.*, 2007, 2010]. This feature in turn suggests that the spatial distribution of boulders well reflected the tsunami inundation process and spatial and temporal variations of the tsunami's hydraulic force.

Several reports have described the displacement of boulders by historically large tsunamis striking along the coast [*Simkin and Fiske*, 1983; *Nakata and Kawana*, 1995; *Goff et al.*, 2006; *Suzuki et al.*, 2008]. Our results suggest that these boulders can be useful to estimate the hydrodynamic features of the historical tsunamis. For example, *Imamura et al.* [2008] developed a numerical model for the transport of a boulder by a tsunami. Using the model, the time series of the hydrodynamic force and current velocity acting on the boulder as well as their maximum values can be estimated. Such information is useful to elucidate the power of paleotsunamis, which can support disaster mitigation efforts [*Imamura et al.*, 2008].

Transportation of large boulders by the 2004 Indian Ocean tsunami has been rarely observed; such boulders were reported at Phi Phi Don Island, Thailand [*Kelletat et al.*, 2007] and northwestern parts of Sumatra Island, Indonesia [*Baird et al.*, 2005; *Paris et al.*, 2009]. *Goto et al.* [2009], based on their cross-sectional numerical analyses, reported that initial waveform (trough or crest arrives first), the original setting of boulders (attached to the reef rock or scattered), and coastal topography (steep or gentle) are important to determine whether many boulders were transported and deposited by the tsunami. *Goto et al.* [2009] concluded that the following factors affected to form spectacular tsunami boulder field at Pakarang Cape: (1) pre-tsunami sources of boulders offshore of the reef edge, (2) gentle reef slope inclination (~1/100), and (3) arrival of the trough-start wave at the Cape.

These observations are also applicable for damage estimation of marine ecosystems [*Goto et al.*, 2009]. For example, *Chavanich et al.* [2008] described, based on field observations at the Mu Ko Similan Marine National Park in Thailand, that severe coral damage occurred where the reef slope dropped gradually away to the offshore. Numerical results show that a higher current velocity is generated at a gentle slope than at a steep slope [*Goto and Imamura*, 2009; *Goto et al.*, 2009]. Therefore, *Goto and Imamura* [2009] concluded that a stronger and longer tsunami influence can be generated at gentle slopes, supporting *Chavanich et al.* [2008].

11.6.2. Tsunami Mitigation Effect of Mangroves at Pakarang Cape and Banda Aceh

According to *Yanagisawa et al.* [2009a], damage to mangroves was most severe along the river (Figure 11.3d). Figure 11.3e depicts the modeled hydraulic pressure (=Du^2, where u is the current velocity) at each grid cell. As the figure portrays, the tsunami hydraulic pressure is very strong along the river. The result is well consistent with field observations. Such a direct comparison is useful for understanding the relation between the mangrove forest destruction and hydrodynamic features of the tsunami.

More quantitatively, *Yanagisawa et al.* [2009a] calculated the bending stress σ_t of each tree to clarify the damage probability of a *Rhizophora* tree. The bending stress is useful as a representative factor of the strength of a mangrove tree against a tsunami flow [*Yanagisawa et al.*, 2009a] and the relation to the maximum bending moment M can be estimated using the following equation based on linear elastic theory:

$$M = \sigma_t W \qquad (11.6)$$

Therein, W is a section modulus of a circle. To estimate the destruction rate (damage probability) against bending stress, *Yanagisawa et al.* [2009a] grouped 20 data points of survived and destroyed trees and defined the destruction rate as the number of destroyed trees divided by the group size (Figure 11.7a). They further proposed a fragility function (regression curve) for mangroves to describe the relation between the destruction rate P of *Rhizophora* trees and bending stress using a probit model by a

log-normal distribution function as follows [*Yamaguchi and Yamazaki*, 2001]:

$$P(x) = \Phi\left[\frac{\ln x - \mu}{\sigma}\right] \qquad (11.7)$$

In Equation 11.7, x is the hydrodynamic feature of the tsunami (σ_t is the bending stress resulting from the hydrodynamic force); μ and σ, respectively, signify the mean and standard deviations of $\ln x$; and Φ is the standardized normal distribution function. From Figure 11.7a, it is readily apparent that the mangrove trees survived the tsunami impact with bending stress up to 5 (Nmm^{-2}), although they were largely destroyed by bending stress higher than 50 (Nmm^{-2}) [*Yanagisawa et al.*, 2009a].

The fragility function (Figure 11.7a) enables us to produce a model including the damage probability of mangrove forests to investigate the tsunami reduction effect of mangrove forest. *Yanagisawa et al.* [2009a] further conducted a cross-sectional calculation and found that a mangrove forest of *Rhizophora* sp. with a density of 0.2 trees per square meter and 15 cm stem diameter in a 400 m wide area can reduce tsunami flow depth by 30% when the incident wave is assumed to have a 3.0 m flow depth and a wave period of 30 minutes at the shoreline [see figure 8 of *Yanagisawa et al.*, 2009a]. These hydraulic values resemble those at the shoreline of Pakarang Cape. On the other hand, most of the mangrove forests are destroyed by a tsunami flow depth >6 m [*Yanagisawa et al.*, 2009a]. In their calculation, the reduction effect of tsunami flow depth decreased when the depth became >3 m [*Yanagisawa et al.*, 2009a].

Yanagisawa et al. [2007] conducted similar analyses for the mangroves at Banda Aceh city. Using the damage probability at the city, they clarified that a mangrove forest of *Rhizophora* sp., with a density of 0.25 trees per square meter and a 20 cm stem diameter in a region where mangrove forests had been before they were cut down for making shrimp ponds (Figure 11.6), could have reduced the flow depth by up to 73% and tsunami inundation area by up to 25%. Such analyses are critically important for making afforestation plans for mangroves as natural barriers against tsunami impact [*Yanagisawa et al.*, 2007].

11.6.3. Evaluation of Damage to Structures and Humans at Banda Aceh City

Koshimura et al. [2009a] analyzed the relation between the number of destroyed and surviving structures and the modeled tsunami at Banda Aceh city. They further explored the relation between the damage probabilities and hydrodynamic features of the tsunami using the following equation:

$$P(x) = \Phi\left[\frac{x - \mu}{\sigma}\right] \qquad (11.8)$$

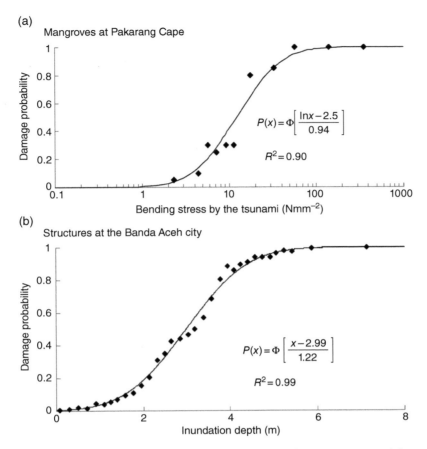

Figure 11.7 Fragility functions (a) for the mangrove (*Rhizophora* tree) damage in terms of the modeled bending stress by the tsunami (modified after *Yanagisawa et al.* [2009a]), and (b) for structural damage in terms of the modeled inundation (flow) depth (modified after *Koshimura et al.* [2009a]). Rhombi signify the distribution of damage probabilities. The solid lines show best-fitted curves of the plot.

Therein, *x* represents the hydrodynamic features of the tsunami (here we adopted flow depth). Results show that the structures at the city were markedly vulnerable when the local flow depth was >2–3 m, although almost all structures were destroyed when the flow depth was 6 m or higher (Figure 11.7b) [*Koshimura et al.*, 2009a].

It is noteworthy that the tsunami damage to structures resulted from both hydrodynamic force and the impact of floating debris [*Koshimura et al.*, 2009a]. These facts are included on the damage probabilities, but not on the numerical model results [*Koshimura et al.*, 2009a]. Therefore, as *Koshimura et al.* [2009a] described, the proposed fragility function might be overestimated in terms of damage probabilities to the hydrodynamic features of tsunami.

Koshimura et al. [2009a] also proposed a fragility function of the mortality ratio with regard to the flow depth using data provided by *JICA* [2005]. Although the plot is highly dispersed because of many uncertainties involved, in general, tsunami casualties increase when the flow depth exceeds 2 m, and almost no survivors were expected at a depth of 8 m [*Koshimura et al.*, 2009a].

Fragility functions were developed using data of structural damage and tsunami casualties at Banda Aceh city. These incorporate multiple uncertainties such as regionality. In fact, the mortality rate in terms of the tsunami inundation depth at Banda Aceh city is known to be considerably higher than the Japanese historical tsunami cases [*Oie et al.*, 2006]. Consequently, applicability of each proposed fragility function to other areas should be evaluated in future studies [*Koshimura et al.*, 2009a].

11.7. CONCLUDING REMARKS

As described in this chapter, we reviewed summary of our studies that integrated field observation data, analyses of satellite images, and high-resolution numerical modeling, the latter of which has several meters to several tens of meters in grid cells. High-resolution numerical modeling results enable us to elucidate the generation processes of damage and to explore the relation between field-observed damage and hydrodynamic features of the tsunami. For example, we clarified that the occurrence of substantial morphological change, especially the deposition of huge boulders, was dependent upon the initial wave form and coastal topography. This fundamental idea is also applicable to damage incurred by the marine ecosystems. However, quantitative estimations of damage on coastal morphology and marine ecosystems have been conducted poorly. Development or improvement of numerical models for changes of morphology and marine ecosystems by the tsunami must be conducted for proper damage estimation. On the other hand, fragility functions of mangroves, structures, and tsunami casualties have been proposed by *Yanagisawa et al.* [2009a, 2010] and *Koshimura et al.* [2009a]. These fragility functions enable us to express the relation between the damage and hydrodynamic features of the tsunami inundation flow, quantitatively. Such evaluation is a critically important step for future tsunami-risk assessment. As described by the authors, however, more field data of damage at different research locations must be collected to elucidate the universality of the proposed fragility functions.

ACKNOWLEDGMENTS

Our researches were supported by a Grant-in-Aid from MEXT (K. Goto, no: 20740292), JSPS (F. Imamura, no: 18201033), and Industrial Technology Research Grant Program in 2008 (S. Koshimura, Project ID: 08E52010a) from New Energy and Industrial Technology Development Organization (NEDO).

REFERENCES

Aburaya, T. and F. Imamura (2002), The proposal of a tsunami run up simulation using combined equivalent roughness, *Ann. J. Coastal Eng.*, *49*, 276–280(in Japanese).

Ammon, C. J., C. Ji, H. Thio, D. Robinson, S. Ni, V. Hjorleifsdottir, H. Kanamori, T. Lay, S. Das, D. Helmberger, G. Ichinose, J. Palet, and D. Wald (2005), Rupture process of the 2004 Sumatra–Andaman earthquake, *Science*, *308*, 1133–1139.

Baird, A. H., S. J. Campbell, A. W. Anggoro, R. L. Aediwijaya, N. Fadi, Y. Herdiana, T. Kartawijaya, D. Mahyddin, A. Mukminin, S. T. Paedede, M. S. Pratchett, E. Rudi, and A. M. Siregar (2005), Achenese reef in the wake of the Asian tsunami, *Curr. Biol.*, *15*, 1926–1930.

Benzoni, F., D. Basso, T. Giaccone, D. Pessani, F. S. Cappelletti, R. Leonardi, P. Galli, M. Choowong, S. Di Geronimo, and E. Robba (2006), Post-tsunami condition of a coral reef in Leam Pakarang (Andaman Sea, Thailand), *Proceedings, International Society for Reef Studies European Meeting*, 19–22 September, Bremen, pp. 194.

Borrero, J. C. (2005), Field survey of northern Sumatra and Banda Aceh, Indonesia after the tsunami and earthquake of 26 December 2004, *Seismol. Res. Lett.*, *76*, 309–317.

Chavanich, S., A. Siripong, P. Sojisuporn, and P. Menasveta (2005), Impact of tsunami on the seafloor and corals in Thailand, *Coral Reefs*, *24*, 535.

Chavanich, S., V. Viyakarn, P. Sojisuporn, A. Siripong, and P. Menasveta (2008), Patterns of coral damage associated with the 2004 Indian Ocean tsunami at Mu Ko Similan Marine National Park, Thailand, *J. Nat. Hist.*, *42*, 177–187.

Choowong, M., S. Phantuwongraj, T. Charoentitirat, B. Chutakositkano, S. Yumuang, and P. Charusiri (2009), Beach recovery after 2004 Indian Ocean tsunami from Phang-nga, Thailand, *Geomorphology*, *104*, 134–142.

Comley, J., S. O'Farrell, S. Hamylton, C. Ingwersen, and P. Walker (2005), The impact of the December 2004 Indian Ocean tsunami on the coral reef resources of Mu Ko Surin Marine National Park, Thailand, Report of Coral Cay Conservation, London, 26 pp.

Danielsen, F., M. K. Sorensen, M. F. Olwig, V. Selvam, F. Parish, N. D. Burgess, T. Hiraishi, V. M. Karunagaran, M. S. Rasmussen, L. B. Hansen, A. Quarto, and N. Suryadiputra (2005), The Asian tsunami: A protective role for coastal vegetation, *Science*, *310*, 643.

Department of Fishery, Thailand (1999), Map of coral reefs in Thai waters: Andaman Sea, *Coral Reef Management Project*, Department of Fishery Thailand, 198 p.

Di Geronimo, I., M. Choowong, and S. Phantuwongraj (2009), Geomorphology and superficial bottom sediments of Khao Lak coastal area (SW Thailand), *Pol. J. Environ. Stud.*, *18*, 111–121.

Dutta, D., J. Alam, K. Umeda, and M. Hayashi (2007), A two-dimensional hydrodynamic model for flood inundation simulation: A case study in the lower Mekong River Basin, *Hydrol. Process.*, *21*, 1223–1237.

Feldens, P., K. Schwarzer, W. Szuczucinski, K. Stattegger, and D. Sakuna (2009), Impact of 2004 tsunami on seafloor morphology and offshore sediments, Pakarang Cape, Thailand, *Pol. J. Environ. Stud.*, *18*, 63–68.

Fernando, H. J. S., J. L. McCulley, S. G. Mendis, and K. Perera (2005), Coral poaching worsens tsunami destruction in Sri Lanka, *EOS Trans.*, 301–304.

Fritz, H. M., J. C. Borrero, C. E. Synolakis, and J. Yoo (2006), 2004 Indian Ocean tsunami flow velocity measurements from survivor videos, *Geophys. Res. Lett.*, *33*, L24605.

Fujii, Y. and K. Satake (2007), Tsunami source of the 2004 Sumatra–Andaman earthquake inferred from tide Gauge and satellite data, *Bull. Seismol. Soc. Am.*, *97*, S192–S207.

Fujino, S., H. Naruse, A. Suphawajruksakul, T. Jarupongsakul, M. Murayama, and N. Ichihara (2008), Thickness and grain size distribution of Indian Ocean tsunami deposits at Khao Lak and Phra Thong Island, southwestern Thailand, in *Tsunamiites—Features and Implication*, edited by T. Shiki et al., pp. 123–132, Elsevier, Berlin.

Goff, J., W. C. Dudley, M. J. de Maintenon, G. Cain, and J. P. Coney (2006), The largest local tsunami in 20th century Hawaii, *Mar. Geol.*, *226*, 65–79.

Goto, C., Y. Ogawa, N. Shuto, and F. Imamura (1997), IUGG/IOC time project, numerical method of tsunami simulation with the leap-frog scheme. *IOC Manuals and Guides*, UNESCO, Paris, no. 35, 130 p.

Goto, K., S. A. Chavanich, F. Imamura, P. Kunthasap, T. Matsui, K. Minoura, D. Sugawara, and H. Yanagisawa (2007), Distribution, origin and transport process of boulders deposited by the 2004 Indian Ocean tsunami at Pakarang Cape, Thailand, *Sediment. Geol.*, *202*, 821–837.

Goto, K. and S. Fujino (2008), Problems and perspectives of the tsunami deposits after the 2004 Indian Ocean tsunami, *J. Geol. Soc. Jpn*, *114*, 599–617 (in Japanese).

Goto, K., F. Imamura, N. Keerthi, P. Kunthasap, T. Matsui, K. Minoura, A. Ruangrassamee, D. Sugawara, and S. Supharatid (2008), Distributions and Significances of the 2004 Indian Ocean tsunami deposits—Initial results from Thailand and Sri Lanka, in *Tsunamiites – Features and Implication*, edited by T. Shiki et al., pp. 105–122, Elsevier, Berlin.

Goto, K. and F. Imamura (2009), A simple numerical model for the damage of corals by tsunami, in *Coral Reefs: Biology, Threats and Restoration*, edited by T. B. Davin and A. P. Barnnet, pp. 239–249, NOVA Publisher, Hauppauge, NY.

Goto, K., K. Okada, and F. Imamura (2009), Importance of the initial waveform and coastal profile for tsunami transport o boulders, *Pol. J. Environ. Stud*, *18*, 53–61.

Goto, K., K. Okada, and F. Imamura (2010), Numerical analysis of boulder transport by the 2004 Indian Ocean tsunami at Pakarang Cape, Thailand, *Mar. Geol.*, *268*, 97–105.

Gower, J. (2007), The 26 December 2004 tsunami measured by satellite altimetry, *Int. J. Remote Sens.*, *28*, 2897–2913.

Harada, K. and Y. Kawata (2005), Study on tsunami reduction effect of coastal forest due to forest growth, *Ann. Disas. Prev. Inst. Kyoto Univ.*, *48C*, 161–166 (in Japanese).

Hayashi, Y. (2008), Extracting the 2004 Indian Ocean tsunami signals from sea surface height data observed by satellite altimetry, *J. Geophys. Res. Oceans*, *113*, C01001, doi:10.1029/2007JC004177.

Hori, K., R. Kuzumoto, D. Hirouchi, M. Umitsu, N. Janjirawuttikul, and B. Patanakanog (2007), Horizontal and vertical variation of 2004 Indian tsunami deposits: An example of two transects along the western coast of Thailand, *Mar. Geol.*, *239*, 163–172.

Imamura, F. (1995), Review of tsunami simulation with a finite difference method, in *Long-Wave Runup Models*, edited by H. Yeh, P. Liu, and C. Synolakis, pp. 25–42, World Scientific, Singapore.

Imamura, F., S. Koshimura, K. Goto, H. Yanagisawa, and Y. Iwabuchi (2006), Global disaster: The 2004 Indian Ocean tsunami, *J. Disaster Res.*, *1*, 131–135.

Imamura, F., K. Goto, and S. Ohkubo (2008), A numerical model for the transport of a boulder by tsunami, *J. Geophys. Res. Ocean*, *113*, C01008, doi:10.1029/2007JC004170.

Ishii, M., P. M. Shearer, H. Houston, and J. E. Vidale (2005), Extent, duration and speed of the 2004 Sumatra–Andaman earthquake imaged by Hi-Net array, *Nature*, *435*, 933–936.

Japan International Cooperation Agency (JICA) (2005), The study on the urgent rehabilitation and reconstruction support program for Aceh province and affected areas in north Sumatra, Final Report 1, JICA, Tokyo.

Kathiresan, K. and N. Rajendran (2005), Coastal mangrove forests mitigated tsunami, *Estuar. Coast. Shelf Sci.*, *65*, 601–606.

Kelletat, D., S. R. Scheffers, and A. Scheffers (2007), Field Signatures of the SE-Asian mega-tsunami along the west coast of Thailand compared to Holocene Paleo-tsunami from the Atlantic region, *Pure Appl. Geophys.*, *164*, 413–431.

Kerr, A. M., A. H. Baird, and S. J. Campbell (2006), Comments on "Coastal mangrove forests mitigated tsunami" by K. Kathiresan and N. Rajendran, *Estuar. Coast. Shelf Sci.*, *67*, 539–541.

Koshimura, S., M. Takashima, S. Suzuki, H. Hayashi, F. Imamura, and Y. Kawata (2005), Estimation of the possible tsunami disaster potential within the Indian Ocean, *Ann. J. Coast. Eng.*, *52*, 1416–1420 (in Japanese).

Koshimura, S., T. Oie, H. Yanagisawa, and F. Imamura (2009a), Developing fragility functions for tsunami damage estimation using numerical model and post-tsunami data from Banda Aceh, Indonesia, *Coast. Eng. J.*, *51*, 243–273.

Koshimura, S., Y. Namegaya, and H. Yanagisawa (2009b), Tsunami Fragility—A new measure to assess tsunami damage, *J. Disaster Res.*, *4*, 479–488.

Kotani, M., F. Imamura, and N. Shuto (1998), Tsunami run-up simulation and damage estimation by using GIS, *Proc. Coast. Eng.*, *45*, 356–360 (in Japanese).

Marchand, H. (2006), Impacts of the tsunami on a Marine National Park area—Case study of Lanta Islands (Thailand), *Ocean Coast. Manag.*, *49*, 923–946.

Matsutomi, H., T. Sakakiyama, S. Nugroho, Y. Tsuji, Y. Tanioka, Y. Nishimura, T. Kamataki, Y. Murakami, M. Matsuyama, and K. Kurizuka (2005), The 2004 Indian Ocean tsunami at Banda Ache and the environs and problems from a viewpoint of damage estimation, *Ann. J. Coast. Eng.*, *52*, 1366–1370 (in Japanese).

Matsutomi, H., T. Sakakiyama, S. Nugroho, and M. Matsuyama (2006), Aspects of Inundated flow due to the 2004 Indian Ocean tsunami, *Coast. Eng. J.*, *48*, 167–195.

Matsutomi, H. and K. Okamoto (2010), Inundation flow velocity of tsunami on land, *Isl. Arc*, *19*, 443–457.

Nakata, T. and T. Kawana (1995), Historical and prehistorical large tsunamis in the southern Ryukyus, Japan, in *Tsunami: Progress in Prediction, Disaster Prevention and Warning*, edited by Y. Tsuchiya and N. Shuto, pp. 211–222, Kluwer Academic Publishers, Netherlands.

Noji, M., F. Imamura, and N. Shuto (1993), Numerical simulation of movement of large rocks transported by tsunamis, *Proceedings of the IUGG/IOC International Tsunami Symposium*, 23–27 August, Wakayama, pp. 189–197.

Oie, T., S. Koshimura, H. Yanagisawa, and F. Imamura (2006), Numerical modeling of the 2004 Indian Ocean tsunami and damage assessment in Banda Aceh, Indonesia, *Proc. Coast. Eng.*, *53*, 221–225 (in Japanese).

Paris, R., P. Wassmer, J. Sartohadi, F. Lavigne, B. Barthomeuf, E. Desgages, D. Grancher, P. Baumert, F. Vautier, D. Brunstein, and C. Gomez (2009), Tsunamis as geomorphic crises: Lessons from the December 26, 2004 tsunami in Lhok Nga, West Banda Aceh (Sumatra, Indonesia), *Geomorphology*, *104*, 59–72.

Pennisi, E. (2005), Powerful tsunami's impact on coral reefs was hit and miss, *Science*, *307*, 657.

Saatcioglu, M., A. Ghobarah, and I. Nistor (2006), Performance of structures in Indonesia during the December 2004 great Sumatra earthquake and Indian Ocean tsunami, *Earthq. Spectra*, *22*, S295–S317.

Satake, K., E. A. Okal, and J. C. Borrero (2007), Tsunami and its hazard in the Indian and Pacific Oceans: Introduction, *Pure Appl. Geophys.*, *164*, 249–259.

Simkin, T. and R. S. Fiske (1983), *Krakatau, 1883: The Volcanic Eruption and Its Effects*, pp. 464, Washington, DC, Smithsonian Institution Press.

Sugawara, D., K. Minoura, N. Nemoto, S. Tsukawaki, K. Goto, and F. Imamura (2009), Foraminiferal evidence of submarine sediment transport and deposition by backwash during the 2004 Indian Ocean tsunami, *Isl. Arc*, doi:10.1111/j.1440-1738.2009.00677.x.

Suzuki, A., Y. Yokoyama, H. Kan, K. Minoshima, H. Matsuzaki, N. Hamanaka, and H. Kawahata (2008), Identification of 1771 Meiwa tsunami deposits using a combination of radiocarbon dating and oxygen isotope microprofiling of emerged massive *Porites* boulders, *Quat. Geochronol.*, *3*, 226–234.

Szczuciński, W., N. Chaimanee, P. Niedzielski, G. Rachlewicz, D. Saisuttichai, T. Tepsuwan, S. Lorenc, and J. Siepak (2006), Environmental and geological impacts of the 26 December 2004 tsunami in coastal zone of Thailand—overview of short and long-term effects, *Pol. J. Environ. Stud.*, *15*, 793–810.

Takahashi, T., F. Imamura, and N. Shuto (1993), Numerical simulation of topography change due to tsunamis, *Proceedings of the IUGG/IOC International Tsunami Symposium*, 23–27 August, Wakayama, pp. 243–255.

Takashima, M., S. Koshimura, and K. Meguro (2005), Development of possible tsunami exposure estimation module for tsunami disaster response, *Proceedings of the 4th International Symposium on New Technologies for Urban Safety of Mega Cities in Asia*, 18–19 October, Singapore, pp. 481–488.

Tanioka, Y., Yudhicara, T. Kusunose, S. Kathiroli, Y. Nishimura, S. Iwasaki, and K. Satake (2006), Rupture process of the 2004 great Sumatra–Andaman earthquake estimated from tsunami waveforms, *Earth Planets Space*, *58*, 203–209.

Thanawood, C., C. Yongchalermxhai, and O. Densrisereekul (2006), Effects of the December 2004 tsunami and disaster management in southern Thailand, *Sci. Tsunami Haz.*, *24*, 206–217.

Titov, V., A. B. Rabinovich, H. O. Mofjeld, R. E. Thomson, and F. I. Gonzalez (2005), The global reach of the 26 December 2004 Sumatra tsunami, *Science*, *309*, 2045–2048.

Tomita, T., F. Imamura, T. Arikawa, T. Yasuda, and Y. Kawata (2006), Damage caused by the 2004 Indian Ocean tsunami on the southwestern coast of Sri Lanka, *Coast. Eng. J.*, *48*, 99–116.

Tsuji, Y., Y. Namegaya, H. Matsumoto, S. Iwasaki, W. Kanbua, M. Sriwichai, and V. Meesuk (2006), The 2004 Indian tsunami in Thailand: Surveyed runup heights and tide gauge records, *Earth Planets Space*, *58*, 223–232.

Umitsu, M., C. Tanavud, and B. Patanakanog (2007), Effects of landforms on tsunami flow in the plains of Banda Aceh, Indonesia, and Nam Khem, Thailand, *Mar. Geol.*, *242*, 141–153.

Wolanski, E. (2007), Protective functions of coastal forests and trees against natural hazards, in *Coastal Protection in the Aftermath of the Indian Ocean Tsunami. What Role for Forests and Trees?*, pp. 157–179, FAO, Bangkok.

Yamaguchi, N. and F. Yamazaki (2001), Estimation of strong motion distribution in the 1995 Kobe earthquake based on building damage data, *Earthq. Eng. Struct. Dyn.*, *30*, 787–801.

Yanagisawa, H., S. Koshimura, K. Goto, F. Imamura, T. Miyagi, and K. Hayashi (2006), Tsunami inundation flow in the mangrove forest and criteria of tree damages—Field survey of the 2004 Indian Ocean Tsunami in Khao Lak, Thailand, *Ann. J. Coast. Eng.*, *53*, 231–235 (in Japanese).

Yanagisawa, H., S. Koshimura, T. Miyagi, T. Oie, and F. Imamura (2007), The potential role of mitigating effects of mangrove forest against the 2004 Indian Ocean tsunami in Banda Aceh, *Proc. Coast. Eng.*, *54*, 246–250 (in Japanese).

Yanagisawa, H., S. Koshimura, K. Goto, T. Miyagi, F. Imamura, A. Ruangrassamee, and C. Tanavud (2009a), The mitigating effects of mangrove forest on a tsunami flow based on field surveys and numerical analysis at Pakarang Cape, Thailand, *Estuar. Coast. Shelf Sci.*, *81*, 27–37.

Yanagisawa, H., S. Koshimura, K. Goto, T. Miyagi, and F. Imamura (2009b), Damage of mangroves by the 2004 Indian Ocean tsunami at Pakarang Cape and Namkem, Thailand, *Pol. J. Environ. Stud*, *18*, 35–42.

Yanagisawa, H., S. Koshimura, T. Miyagi, and F. Imamura (2010), Tsunami damage-reduction performance of a mangrove forest in Banda Aceh, Indonesia inferred from field data and a numerical model, *J. Geophys. Res.*, *115*, C06032, doi:10.1029/2009JC005587.

12

Extreme Capillary Wave Events Under Parametric Excitation

Michael G. Shats, Hua Xia, and Horst Punzmann

ABSTRACT

Extreme wave events have recently been discovered in the parametrically excited surface ripples. When a fluid container is periodically shaken in the vertical direction, capillary-gravity waves are excited at the frequency of the first subharmonic of the driving frequency. Such waves appear to be unstable to the amplitude modulation. The modulation instability leads to the destruction of waves into ensembles of interacting oscillating solitons. Presented laboratory studies suggest a quasi-particle nature of the parametrically driven surface ripples. The wave field dynamics is determined by the oscillon interactions, including their merger, annihilation, and collisions. Collisions of the same phase oscillons lead to generation of the extreme events, or capillary rogue waves.

12.1. INTRODUCTION

Extreme wave events on the water surface usually bring to mind rogue or freak waves in the ocean. These waves, which have heights and steepness much greater than expected from the sea state, are responsible for a large number of maritime disasters, as reviewed by *Slunyaev et al.* [2009]. Large wave events have also been found in other systems, for example, in optical rogue waves studied by *Solli et al.* [2007] and in superfluid helium, found by *Ganshin et al.* [2008].

Systematic studies of rogue waves in the ocean are severely restricted by the rarity of these events, as well as by obvious difficulties in their characterization in rough oceanic environment. Nevertheless, extreme wave events on the water surface can be systematically studied in laboratory experiments. It has been recently found by *Shats et al.* [2010] that parametrically excited capillary-gravity waves are modulationally unstable and tend to

nonlinearly evolve into ensembles of oscillons whose interaction is probably responsible for the generation of capillary rogue waves. Generation of such relatively high amplitude waves (amplitudes are in excess of 5 rms of the wave background) is manifested as the onset of a distinct tail in the probability density function (PDF) of the wave heights.

Here we review results of recent studies into the nature of nonlinear capillary wave fields and analyze possible mechanisms of extreme wave events. It should be noted that capillary waves, which belong to a short wave branch of surface waves, are heavily damped compared to their long wavelength counterparts, the gravity waves. As a result of strong damping, the nonlinear effects are most clearly observed in constantly driven systems, such as vertically vibrated containers, where high wave steepness can be achieved.

12.2. PARAMETRIC WAVE EXCITATION

Michael Faraday pioneered experimental studies of the liquid surface ripple over 180 years ago by performing experiments with vertically vibrated containers [*Faraday,*

Research School of Physics and Engineering, The Australian National University, Canberra, Australian Capital Territory, Australia

Extreme Events: Observations, Modeling, and Economics, Geophysical Monograph 214, First Edition.
Edited by Mario Chavez, Michael Ghil, and Jaime Urrutia-Fucugauchi.

1831]. Since then, parametric wave excitation has become a standard laboratory tool for generating constantly driven (as opposed to decaying, or propagating) surface ripples in the gravity-capillary range of frequencies [see, *Douady*, 1990; *Gluckman et al.*, 1995; *Wright et al.*, 1996; *Henry et al.*, 2000; *Brazhnikov et al.*, 2002; *Lommer and Levinsen*, 2002; *Falcon et al.*, 2009; *Punzmann et al.*, 2009; *Snouck et al.*, 2009]. For reviews on the early studies of nonlinear surface interactions under parametric excitation, see reviews by *Miles and Henderson* [1990] and *Perlin and Schultz* [2000].

When a liquid is vibrated as a whole at the frequency ω_0, a standing wave at the frequency of the first subharmonic $\omega_1 = \omega_0/2$ is excited above some critical level of acceleration. This process can be described as a decay of the infinitely long wave $(\omega_0, \vec{k}_0)$ into two oppositely propagating subharmonic waves:

$$\omega_0 = \omega_1 + \omega_2 = 2\omega_1 \qquad (12.1)$$

$$\vec{k}_0 = \vec{k}_1 + \vec{k}_2 \approx 0, \qquad (12.2)$$

where $\vec{k}_1 = -\vec{k}_2$, and

$$\omega_1 = \omega_2 = \left(gk + \frac{\alpha}{\rho} k^3 \right)^{1/2}. \qquad (12.3)$$

Here g is the acceleration of gravity, α is the surface tension coefficient, and ρ is the fluid density. Such a decay leads to the generation of waves at the frequency $\omega_1 = \omega_0/2$, often referred to as the Faraday waves.

Apart from the decay of the $\vec{k}_0 = 0$ wave, three wave interactions are severely restricted for capillary waves and are forbidden for gravity waves. For capillary waves, simultaneous satisfaction of energy and momentum conservation,

$$\omega\left(\vec{k}_1 + \vec{k}_2 \right) = \omega\left(k_1 \right) + \omega\left(k_2 \right) \qquad (12.4)$$

is only possible for some wave triads, $\vec{k}_1$, $\vec{k}_2$, and $\vec{k}_0 = \vec{k}_1 + \vec{k}_2$.

The proof of this is as follows [*Bazhanov*, private communication, 2010]. The components of three two-dimensional vectors satisfying $\vec{k}_0 = \vec{k}_1 + \vec{k}_2$ can be expressed as follows:

$$\vec{k}_1 = (a, 0, 0)$$
$$\vec{k}_2 = (b, c, 0)$$
$$\vec{k}_0 = (a + b, c, 0)$$

For the dispersion relation of $\omega \sim k^\alpha$ the synchronism condition (12.4) will read:

$$a^\alpha + \left(b^2 + c^2 \right)^{\alpha/2} = \left((a + b)^2 + c \right)^{\alpha/2}.$$

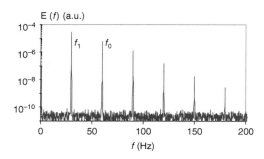

Figure 12.1 Frequency spectrum of parametrically excited capillary waves at low forcing. Shaker frequency is $f_0 = 60$ Hz, vertical acceleration is $\Delta a = a - a_{\text{th}} = 0.5g$ above the parametric threshold a_{th}.

By dividing this equation by a and after substituting $b/a = x$, $c/a = y$, $(a + b)/a = 1 + x$, the following equation can be obtained:

$$1 + \left(x^2 + y^2 \right)^{\alpha/2} = \left((1 + x)^2 + y^2 \right)^{\alpha/2},$$

which for capillary waves $(\omega \sim k^{3/2})$ should be solved numerically:

$$1 + \left(x^2 + y^2 \right)^{3/4} - \left((1 + x)^2 + y^2 \right)^{3/4} = 0.$$

The solution of this equation gives the result which is similar to that obtained by *McGoldrick* [1965]. The resonant conditions (12.4) are severely restricted for capillary and capillary-gravity waves. The selection rules favor interacting triads with disparate wave vectors, for example, those with $k_0 \ll k_1, k_2$, and the angles between interacting wave vectors in a narrow band between 75° and 82°. This means, contrary to common belief, that the capillary wave dispersion *does not* universally satisfy the synchronism condition (12.4). For example, three-wave interactions cannot be taken for granted in the systems characterized by discrete frequency and wave number spectra. The majority of experiments on parametrically excited waves driven by monochromatic excitation show discrete frequency spectra dominated by the first subharmonic and a large number of its harmonics, such as the one shown in Figure 12.1. In this case, condition (12.4) is not satisfied and three-wave interactions are forbidden. This means that the quadratic nonlinearity plays no role in the nonlinear evolution of parametrically excited surface waves.

12.3. MODULATION INSTABILITY OF CAPILLARY WAVES

Four-wave interactions are allowed for surface waves regardless of the wave dispersion. Moreover, both gravity and capillary waves are unstable to small amplitude

(a)

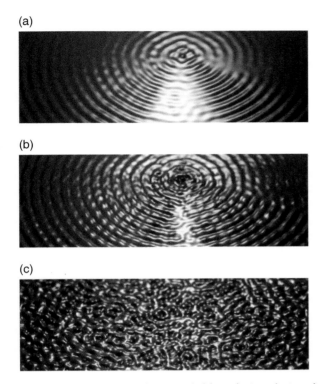

(b)

(c)

Figure 12.2 Snapshots of the wavefield evolution during the startup: (a) $t = 0.125$ s, (b) $t = 0.25$ s, (c) $t = 0.625$ s. Surface ripple is excited parametrically at $f_0 = 60$ Hz.

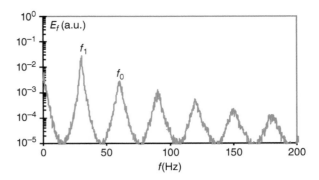

Figure 12.3 Frequency spectrum of parametrically excited capillary waves at higher forcing. Shaker frequency is $f_0 = 60$ Hz, vertical acceleration is $\Delta a = 1.15g$.

modulations. This modulation instability, for gravity waves is known as the Benjamin-Feir instability [1967], develops when the Lighthill criterion is satisfied:

$$\left(\partial \omega / \partial |a|^2 \right)\left(\partial^2 \omega_k / \partial k^2 \right) < 0 \qquad (12.5)$$

This criterion, with the parameter a being the wave amplitude, is satisfied for both branches of surface waves since nonlinear frequency corrections have different signs: $\omega = \omega_k [1 + (ka)^2 / 2]$ for gravity waves, and $\omega \approx [(k^3 T / \rho)(1 + k^2 a^2 / 16)^{-1/2}]^{1/2}$ for capillary waves [*Crapper*, 1957]. Though $\partial^2 \omega_k / \partial k^2$ is negative for gravity waves and positive for capillary waves, the Lighthill criterion is satisfied for both branches.

Modulation instability of capillary waves was identified by *Punzmann et al.* [2009] and *Xia et al.* [2010]. Figure 12.2 illustrates the dynamics of the wave excitation captured using fast video camera. The images show the surface of a fluid container filled with water. The container is mounted on a shaker which accelerates the container in the direction normal to the fluid surface at the frequency of 60 Hz. Initially, 0.125 s after the forcing is switched on, Figure 12.2a, the wave fronts of the excited wave are concentric circles, reflecting the shape of the container wall. However, very soon these wave fronts become azimuthally modulated (Figure 12.2b), and after about 0.6 s the wave field appears

to be severely disordered (see Figure 12.2c). Similar evolutions are observed for all excitation frequencies.

The transverse (azimuthal) modulation of plane waves occurs not only in parametrically excited systems in vertically shaken containers, but also similar effect is found when one uses a planar wave-maker in a tank, or a plunger. When a wave-maker is driven at the frequency f_0, perturbations at the subharmonic frequency $f_1 = f_0 / 2$, or cross waves, modulate the initially planar wave fronts and, at higher forcing level, dominate the wave spectrum [*Garrett*, 1970; *Barnard and Pritchard*, 1972; *Lichter and Shemer*, 1986].

As the instability develops, frequency harmonics spectrally broaden in a characteristic, self-similar shape, as shown in Figure 12.3. The broadened harmonics can be approximated by same secant hyperbolic shape in a broad range of accelerations: $E_f \sim \text{sech}^2[b(f - f_n)]$. The spectral width increases approximately proportionally with the drive, as was shown by *Punzmann et al.* [2009]. The origin of the "triangular" shape of the frequency spectra and mechanisms of the line broadening will be discussed in Section 12.5.

A characteristic signature of modulation instability is the presence of four-wave interactions of the carrier wave with its sidebands: $\omega_{n-} + \omega_{n+} = 2\omega_n$, $k_1 + k_2 = 2k_n$, or in another form, $\omega_{n-,n+} = \omega_n \pm \Omega$, $k_{1,2} = k_n \pm K$, where Ω is the modulation frequency [*Zakharov and Ostrovsky*, 2009]. To identify modulation instability in experiments, one needs to detect these interactions.

The first evidence in support of the four-wave interaction process in capillary waves was presented by *Shats et al.* [2010]. The degree of the four-wave coupling can be characterized by tricoherence, or a normalized trispectrum, defined as follows:

$$t^2\left(\omega_1, \omega_2, \omega_3\right) = \frac{\left| \left\langle F_1 F_2 F_3^* F_{1+2-3}^* \right\rangle \right|^2}{\left\langle \left| F_1 F_2 F_3^* \right|^2 \right\rangle \left\langle \left| F_{1+2-3}^* \right|^2 \right\rangle}, \qquad (12.6)$$

where, F_i is the Fourier component of the surface elevation $\eta(t)$ at the frequency ω_i and F_{1+2-3}^* is the complex conjugate at the frequency $\omega_1 + \omega_2 - \omega_3$. If tricoherence is zero, it is indicative of no coherent phase coupling between the wave quartets, while $t^2 = 1$ corresponds to coherent phase coupling.

The level of the tricoherence in parametrically excited ripples was found to be high, $t^2 > 0.5$ [*Shats et al.*, 2010], indicating strong phase coupling in four-wave interactions. Such high levels of tricoherence confirmed the significance of the underlying four-wave interactions indicating that the four-wave process (cubic nonlinearity) is at work in the conditions when the three-wave interactions (quadratic nonlinearity) are forbidden.

12.4. CAPILLARY ROGUE WAVES

Extreme events on the water surface in the capillary wave range were first reported by *Shats et al.* [2010]. Following the definition of a rogue wave in the context of oceanic waves [see *Dysthe et al.*, 2008], we define rogue waves as events whose peaks exceed the standard deviation of the wave background, σ, by a factor of more than five $\eta > 5\sigma$. Figure 12.4a shows a time trace of the surface elevation at the strongest forcing, just below the threshold of the droplet formation. This trace illustrates an extreme wave event (> 6 mm wave crest height). A horizontal gray line in Figure 12.4a corresponds to $\eta = 5\sigma$. Two movie frames show the waveforms: before the peak, Figure 12.4b, and during the large event, Figure 12.4c. The rogue wave is characterized by an almost vertical wave front. The

gradient in the light intensity on the photograph of Figure 12.4c is due to the refraction of the laser light at a very steep wave. A PDF of the normalized wave crest heights, $x = \eta_c / \sigma$, for this regime is illustrated in Figure 12.5. Up to the crest heights of $x = 5$, the PDF is approximately exponential, $\sim e^{-2x}$. For the strongest waves, $x > 5$, this probability is substantially higher that expected from the e^{-2x} trend.

An important question related to the high probability of large events, seen in Figure 12.5, is whether there is a threshold for the occurrence of rogue waves. The fast video technique does not provide sufficient spatial resolution to resolve wave heights at low forcing. To characterize the onset of rogue waves, a more sensitive technique is used, based on the measurement of the intensity of light transmitted through a layer of diffusing liquid, whereby the intensity is proportional to the surface height. This technique is very sensitive to small surface perturbations and it complements fast video imaging required at large wave amplitudes.

Figure 12.6 shows spectra of parametrically excited waves at 30 Hz ($f_0 = 60$ Hz) along with the corresponding PDFs for three levels of forcing. As the forcing is gradually increased, gradual broadening of the spectrum showing exponential tails is observed. The shape of these spectra ("triangular" when plotted in log-linear scale) can be approximated by the hyperbolic secant function [*Punzmann et al.*, 2009]. Above a certain forcing threshold, a strongly increased probability of the large wave events is observed, as seen in Figure 12.6f. The onset of the tails in the PDF of the waves with the crest heights in excess of

(a)

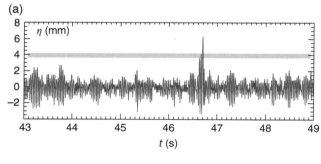

(b)

(c)

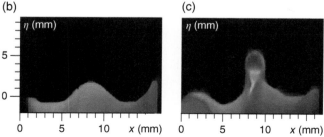

Figure 12.4 Phenomenology of capillary rogue waves at high level of forcing. (a) Time trace of the surface elevation showing an extreme wave event. Video frames show waveforms (b) four periods before the large event, and (c) during the large event.

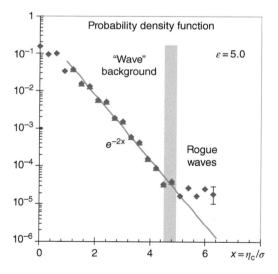

Figure 12.5 Probability density function of the wave crests versus normalized crest height at high forcing (data corresponds to Figure 12.4. $\epsilon = a / a_{th} - 1$ is the supercriticality, which characterizes forcing above the threshold of parametric excitation.

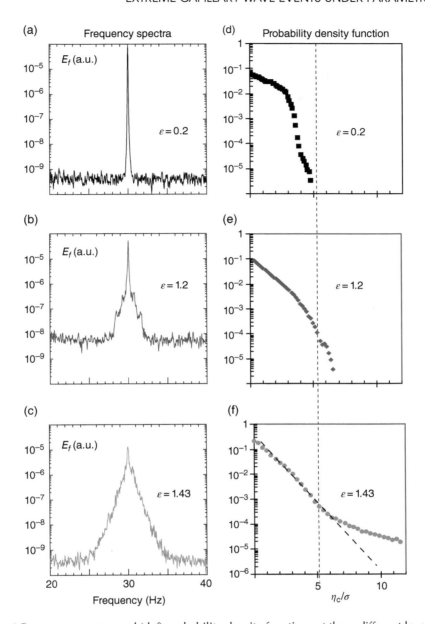

Figure 12.6 (a–c) Frequency spectra and (d–f) probability density functions at three different levels of forcing.

5σ correlates with the formation of broad exponential spectra. This high probability of rogue waves is then sustained up to the highest levels of forcing, up to the droplet generation threshold.

The rogue wave generation probably results from a process, similar to the collision of breathers, as proposed by *Akhmediev et al.* [2009], or it is due to the envelope soliton interactions observed in nonlinear numerical models by *Clamond et al.* [2006].

In the next section, we discuss the nature of the parametrically excited gravity-capillary ripple and possible mechanisms of the rogue wave formation.

12.5. SOLITONIC NATURE OF CAPILLARY RIPPLE

As has been discussed in Section 12.3, capillary waves are modulationally unstable. Modulation instability leads to the transverse modulation of the wave fronts. A later stage of this process is known as the cross-wave instability. To illustrate this process, we first investigate how modulation instability affects an initially linear wave.

Figure 12.7 shows a surface wave envelope (60 Hz carrier wave frequency) measured using thin laser transmission technique at two different levels of forcing. At low forcing, Figure 12.7a, a wave is modulated relatively smoothly,

(a)

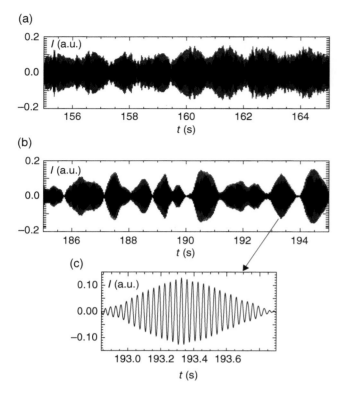

(b)

(c)

Figure 12.7 Temporal evolution of the wave height at (a) $\epsilon = 0.6$, and (b) $\epsilon = 1.43$. The inset (c) shows zoom into one of the envelope solitons.

while at higher forcing level, Figure 12.7b, this wave appears to be broken into bursts of different duration and different lengths. The shape of the envelopes of individual bursts, or wavelets, however, stays the same. Individual wavelets are well approximated by the secant hyperbolic function,

$$s(t) = (\pi/b) \, \text{sech}\left[\pi^2/(bt)\right] e^{if_0 t},$$

which is a well-known solution of the nonlinear Schrödinger equation by *Zakharov and Rubenchik* [1973] describing envelope solitons. This shape of the wavelets is in agreement with the hyperbolic secant spectra of the capillary ripple shown in Figure 12.3. Thus, in the time domain, localized measurements of the surface perturbation suggest that the initially continuous waves become broken into ensembles of envelope solitons as a result of modulation instability.

What remains unclear is how these envelope solitons are realized in physical space. Figure 12.8 shows a photograph of the surface ripple in water, forced at $f_0 = 60$ Hz at an acceleration of $a = 1.2g$. The wavefield looks random; it is dominated by oscillating "blobs," ~4 mm in diameter. Blobs move randomly on the surface; they merge and collide with other blobs. The frequency spectrum of the

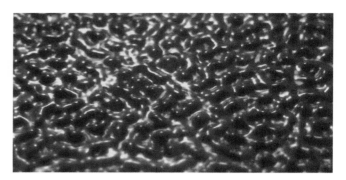

Figure 12.8 A photograph of the parametrically excited surface ripple at $f_0 = 60$ Hz and acceleration $\Delta a = 1.2g$ in water.

surface gradient, measured using reflection of a very thin (0.5 mm) laser beam off the surface, is not random. It consists of spectrally broadened harmonics, $f_n = nf_0/2$, similar to that of Figure 12.3.

It has been shown by *Shats et al.* [2012] that such surface ripples consisting of oscillating blobs, seen in Figure 12.8, are made of oscillating solitons, or oscillons. Such localized oscillatory perturbations of the liquid surface have been studied since 1984 in various parametrically driven systems, but only recently have been identified in deep monochromatically vibrated water [*Shats et al.*, 2012]. The first parametrically driven stationary solitonic structures were discovered on the water surface in a resonator by *Wu et al.* [1984]. Later oscillons were found in granular layers by *Umbanhowar et al.* [1986], in thin layers of highly dissipative fluids by *Lioubashevski et al.* [1996], in non-Newtonian fluids by *Lioubashevski et al.* [1999], in strongly dissipative liquids vibrated at two frequencies by *Arbell and Fineberg* [1998] and, recently in a very narrow vertically vibrated cell by *Rajchenbach et al.* [2011].

To prove that oscillons exist in deep Newtonian fluids which are driven monochromatically, we first illustrate observations in highly viscous water solution of glycerine. Figure 12.9 shows snapshots of a fast video. Frames of Figure 12.9a and c are $T_0 = 1/f_0$ apart, where f_0 is the shaker frequency. In this case an oscillon does not propagate. It is observed as a peak, Figure 12.9a, which after time T_0 turns into a crater, Figure 12.9b. The oscillon frequency is thus $f_1 = f_0/2$. This is a stable (non-decaying) so-called subcritical oscillon, which can be triggered externally (e.g., by a falling droplet) while vibrating the fluid very close to but still below the threshold of the parametric excitation.

The shape of a subcritical oscillon has been studied by illuminating it using a thin vertical laser sheet, as shown in Figure 12.10a. In this case, a fluorescent dye was added to the water-glycerine solution (which fluoresces in orange light when illuminated by green laser sheet). The shape of the oscillon peak is well approximated by the secant hyperbolic fit as shown in Figure 12.10b. The

(a)

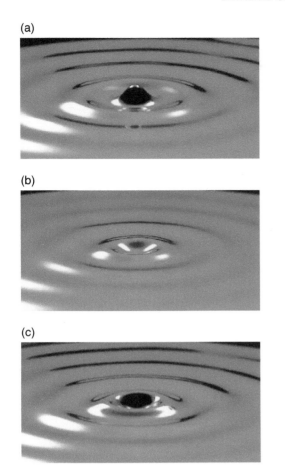

(b)

(c)

Figure 12.9 A single subcritical oscillon excited by external perturbation at $a = 3.1g$ at $f_0 = 30$ Hz in viscous water solution of glycerine. Photos are frames of a fast video (300 fps). Photos (a–c) are taken with a 0.03 s delay between the frames corresponding to three consecutive periods of the shaker oscillations.

frequency spectrum of the surface gradient was measured using the reflection of a thin laser beam off the liquid surface. The spectrum consists of the dominant first subharmonic of the driving frequency (here $f_1 = 30$ Hz) and its multiple harmonics, Figure 12.10c. This is a very interesting observation since the origin of multiple harmonics in parametrically excited systems is not well understood in the literature. It is often attributed to nonlinear wave interactions, or even to the turbulent energy cascade, as, for example, discussed by *Snouck et al.* [2009]. The result of Figure 12.10c suggests that multiple harmonics do not result from the interaction of plane waves, but they are intrinsic to individual oscillons.

When the water-glycerine solution is driven above the parametric threshold, a regular oscillon matrix is observed, as seen in Figure 12.10d. In this case, similarly to other systems (e.g., those reported in the granular medium by *Umbanhowar et al.* [1986]), there are two types of oscillons differing from each other by the $1/f_1$ phase

(a)

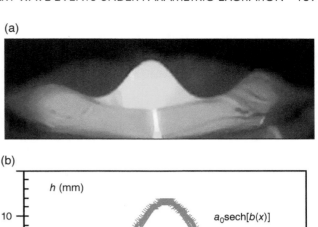

(b)

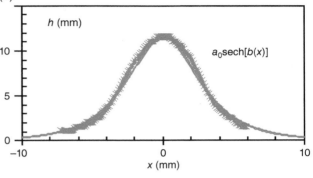

(c)

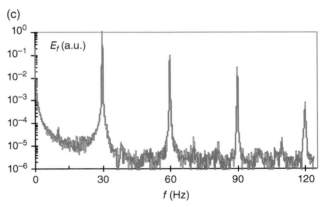

(d)

Figure 12.10 (a) A snapshot of the oscillon profile illuminated by a vertical laser sheet (fluorescent dye was added to the water-glycerine solution). (b) Surface elevation of the oscillon is well approximated by the secant hyperbolic fit. (c) Frequency spectrum of the surface gradient of a single subcritical oscillon. (d) Surface ripple on the glycerine-water solution above critical excitation ($a = 3.3g$). The excitation frequency is 60 Hz.

shift in time. They may be referred to as "positive" and "negative" oscillons. As has been found in granular layers by *Umbanhowar et al.* [1986], oscillons of like phase show a short-range, repulsive interaction, whereas oscillons of the opposite phase attract and bind. A similar behavior is observed in our experiments with liquids: oscillons behave somewhat similar to charged particles. This oscillon interaction leads to a variety of effects, including the formation of complex patterns on the liquid surface.

As has been shown recently by *Shats et al.* [2012], strong dissipation is not necessary for the oscillon formation. They are probably formed universally as a result of nonlinear stages of modulation instability. It is just easier to isolate and visualize them in highly viscous, strongly dampened, or non-Newtonian liquids. As has been shown by *Shats et al.* [2012], very stable matrices of oscillons can be easily generated in distilled water by adding microscopic amounts of proteins to water. Typically, 0.2–1 ppm (in weight) concentration of proteins do not noticeably change the surface tension or viscosity of water. However, such a minute amount is sufficient to greatly reduce horizontal mobility of oscillons, regardless of the nature of proteins. Small additions of either bovine serum albumin, gelatine, or skim milk (casein proteins) dramatically change a disordered ripple, such as that in Figure 12.8b, into an ideal matrix, similar to that in Figure 12.10d.

It should be noted that such small quantities of proteins, or natural polymers are probably present in many natural water reservoirs. Our laboratory results in distilled water with added proteins have also been reproduced when using water taken from a local lake.

Now let us return to the relationship between the temporal and spatial features of oscillons. We hypothesize that a difference in horizontal mobility of oscillons determines the spectral widths of the frequency harmonics. The shape of an oscillon in physical space is given by the hyperbolic secant, $h(x) \sim \mathrm{sech}(ax)$, Figure 12.10b. Its slow (compared with the period of oscillation) movement about the observation point should lead to a modulation envelope $h(t) \sim \mathrm{sech}[\pi/(at)]$ in the time domain. This, in turn, should lead to a spectral line shape in a frequency spectrum given by the squared hyperbolic secant function of frequency, $E(f) \sim \mathrm{sech}^2[b(f - f_0)]$ [*Punzmann et al.*, 2009].

The analysis of the surface ripples confirms these expectations. Figure 12.11a shows shapes of the spectral lines (first subharmonic) in pure water and in the water-albumin solution. A higher mobility of oscillons in water leads to the line shape $E(f) \mathrm{sech}^2[b(f - f_0)]$. The addition of albumin reduces the line width to the instrumental limit determined by the measurement time. In the time domain, the higher oscillon mobility in water leads to the observation of the envelope solitons reported by *Punzmann et al.* [2009] and *Xia et al.* [2010]. These results

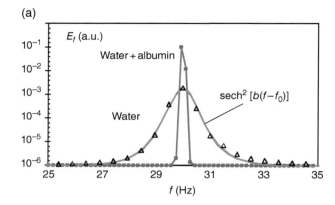

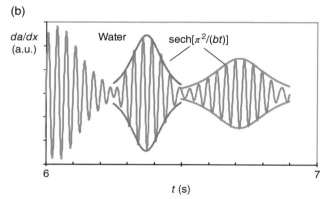

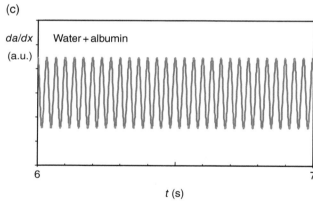

Figure 12.11 Shapes of the spectral lines on the water surface illustrated in Figure 12.1. (a) Frequency spectral line of the first subharmonic (30 Hz) in water (triangles) and in water-albumin solution (squares). Solid red line shows sech^2 fit. (b) A waveform of the surface gradient da/dx at the fixed point on the surface of water. Red lines show sech fit. (c) A waveform of the surface gradient da/dx in the water-albumin solution.

reveal that the hyperbolic secant envelopes result from the shape of individual oscillons in physical space. The sech analytic fit to the time-domain signal is illustrated in Figure 12.11b. In contrast to this, and consistent with the narrow spectrum, stationary solitons within the matrix (Figure 12.10d) generate non-modulated harmonic signals seen in Figure 12.11c.

12.6. DISCUSSION AND CONCLUSIONS

As described earlier, recent studies of parametrically excited capillary waves offer new interpretation of the nature of the surface ripples. In this new picture, one deals with ensembles of quasi-particles, or oscillons, rather than with weakly interacting plane waves. Oscillons are formed as the result of modulation instability of parametrically excited waves. Since both gravity and capillary waves are modulationally unstable, the formation of oscillons occurs in a broad range of frequencies.

Spatially localized solitons oscillate at the frequency of the first subharmonic $f_1 = f_0/2$ of the forcing frequency f_0. Their frequency spectra also show multiple harmonics of f_1. Their spatial profiles are well approximated by the hyperbolic secant fit. When an oscillon moves horizontally about the observation point, its frequency spectrum becomes broadened and the line shape reproduces the sech spatial profile. In distilled water, high oscillon mobility leads to their collisions, merger, and annihilation. These processes are similar to those found in numerical studies of the damped nonlinear Schrödinger equation by *Wang* [2001]. The process of the coalescence of dissipative solitons in parametrically driven spatially extended system has been recently studied by *Clerc et al.* [2011].

In the water-glycerine solution, or in water with microscopic additions of proteins, the mobility of oscillons is much reduced. This promotes the formation of regular patterns which do not facilitate the generation of extreme events.

The discovery of the oscillonic nature of the parametrically excited surface ripples can help better understanding mechanisms of the capillary rogue wave formation. The PDFs of capillary ripples shown in Figures 12.5 and 12.6f are exponential, which is consistent with the shape of oscillons in physical space. Extreme events occur above a certain threshold in forcing, as seen in Figure 12.6. The existence of the threshold probably has to do with the threshold of the like-phase oscillon collisions. The increase in the drive leads to the increase in the horizontal mobility of oscillons, which helps overcoming repulsion forces between same phase oscillons and increases their collision probability.

ACKNOWLEDGMENTS

This work was supported by the Australian Research Council's Discovery Projects funding scheme (DP110101525).

REFERENCES

Akhmediev, N., J. M. Soto-Crespo, and A. Ankiewicz (2009), How to excite a rogue wave?, *Phys. Rev. A*, *80*, 043818.

Arbell, H. and J. Fineberg (1998), Spatial and temporal dynamics of two interacting modes in parametrically driven surface waves, *Phys. Rev. Lett.*, *81*, 4384.

Barnard, B. J. S. and W. G. Pritchard (1972), Cross-waves. Part 2. Experiments, *J. Fluid Mech*, *55*, 245–255.

Benjamin, T. B. and J. E. Feir (1967), The disintegration of wave trains on deep water, *J. Fluid Mech.*, *27*, 417–430.

Brazhnikov, M. Y., G. V. Kolmakov, A. A. Levchenko, and L. P. Mezhov-Deglin (2002), Observation of capillary turbulence on the water surface in a wide range of frequencies, *Europhys. Lett.*, *58*, 510–516.

Clamond, D., M. Francius, J. Grue, and C. Kharif (2006), Long time interaction of envelope solitons and freak wave formations, *Eur. J. Mech. B/Fluids*, *25*, 536–553.

Clerc, M. G., S. Coulibaly, L. Gordillo, N. Mujica, and R. Navarro (2011), Coalescence cascade of dissipative solitons in parametrically driven systems, *Phys. Rev. E*, *84*, 036205.

Crapper, G. D. (1957), An exact solution for progressive capillary waves of arbitrary amplitude, *J. Fluid Mech.*, *2*, 532–540.

Douady, S. (1990), Experimental study of the Faraday instability, *J. Fluid Mech.*, *221*, 383–409.

Dysthe, K., H. E. Krogstad, and P. Müller (2008), Oceanic rogue waves, *Annu. Rev. Fluid Mech.*, *40*, 287–310.

Falcon, C., E. Falcon, U. Bortolozzo, and S. Fauve (2009), Capillary wave turbulence on a spherical fluid surface in low gravity, *Europhys. Lett.*, *86*, 14002.

Faraday, M. (1831), On the forms and states assumed by fluids in contact with vibrating elastic surfaces, *Philos. Trans. R. Soc. Lond.*, *121*, 319–340.

Ganshin, A. N., V. B. Efimov, G. V. Kolmakov, L. P. Mezhov-Deglin, and P. V. E. McClintock (2008), Observation of an inverse energy cascade in developed acoustic turbulence in superfluid helium, *Phys. Rev. Lett.*, *101*, 065303.

Garrett, C. J. R. (1970), On cross-waves, *J. Fluid Mech.*, *41*, 837–849.

Gluckman, B. J., C. B. Arnold, and J. P. Gollub (1995), Statistical studies of chaotic wave patterns, *Phys. Rev. E*, *51*, 1128–1147.

Henry, E., P. Alstrom, and M. T. Levinsen (2000), Prevalence of weak turbulence in strongly driven surface ripples, *Europhys. Lett.*, *52*, 27–32.

Lichter, S. and L. Shemer (1986), Experiments on nonlinear cross waves, *Phys. Fluids*, *29*, 3971–3975.

Lioubashevski, O., H. Arbell, and J. Fineberg (1996), Dissipative solitary states in driven surface waves, *Phys. Rev. Lett.*, *76*, 3959.

Lioubashevski, O., Y. Hamiel, A. Agnon, Z. Reches, and J. Fineberg (1999), Oscillons and propagating solitary waves in a vertically vibrated colloidal suspension, *Phys. Rev. Lett.*, *83*, 3190.

Lommer, M. and M. T. Levinsen (2002), Using laser-induced fluorescence in the study of surface wave turbulence, *J. Fluoresc.*, *12*, 45–50.

McGoldrick, L. F. (1965), On the rippling of small waves: a harmonic nonlinear nearly resonant interaction, *J. Fluid Mech.*, *52*, 725–751.

Miles, J. and D. Henderson (1990), Parametrically forced surface waves, *Annu. Rev. Fluid Mech.*, *22*, 143–165.

Perlin, M. and W. W. Schultz (2000), Capillary effects on surface waves, *Annu. Rev. Fluid Mech.*, *32*, 241–274.

Punzmann, H., H. Xia, and M. Shats (2009), Phase randomization of three-wave interactions in capillary waves, *Phys. Rev. Lett.*, *103*, 064502.

Rajchenbach, J., A. Leroux, and D. Clamond (2011), New standing solitary waves in water, *Phys. Rev. Lett.*, *107*, 024502.

Shats, M., H. Punzmann, and H. Xia (2010), Capillary rogue waves, *Phys. Rev. Lett.*, *104*, 104503.

Shats, M., H. Xia, and H. Punzmann (2012), Parametrically excited water surface ripples as ensembles of oscillons, *Phys. Rev. Lett.*, *108*, 034502.

Slunyaev, A., C. Kharif, and E. Pelinovsky (2009), *Rogue Waves in the Ocean*, Springer, Berlin.

Snouck, D., M.-T. Westra, and W. van de Water (2009), Turbulent parametric surface waves, *Phys. Fluids*, *21*, 025102.

Solli, D. R., C. Ropers, P. Koonath, and B. Jalali (2007), Optical rogue waves, *Nature*, *450*, 1054–1057.

Umbanhowar, P. B., F. Melo, and H. L. Swinney (1986), Localized excitations in a vertically vibrated granular layer, *Nature*, *382*, 793–796.

Wang, X. (2001), Parametrically excited nonlinear waves and their localizations, *Phys. D*, *154*, 337–359.

Wright, W. B., R. Budakian, and S. J. Putterman (1996), Diffusing light photography of fully developed isotropic ripple turbulence, *Phys. Rev. Lett.*, *76*, 4528–4531.

Wu, J., R. Keolian, and I. Rudnick (1984), Observation of a nonpropagating hydrodynamic soliton, *Phys. Rev. Lett.*, *52*, 1421–1424.

Xia, H., M. Shats, and H. Punzmann (2010), Modulation instability and capillary wave turbulence, *Europhys. Lett.*, *91*, 14002.

Zakharov, V. E. and A. M. Rubenchik (1973), Instability of waveguides and solitons in nonlinear media, *Sov. Phys. JETP*, *38*, 494–500. [(1973), *Zh. Eksp. Teor. Fiz.*, **65**, 997–1002].

Zakharov, V. E. and L. A. Ostrovsky (2009), Modulation instability: the beginning, *Phys. D*, *238*, 540–548.

Part IV
Extreme Events in the Solid Earth

13

A Review of Great Magnitude Earthquakes and Associated Tsunamis along the Guerrero, Mexico Pacific Coast: A Multiproxy Approach

María-Teresa Ramírez-Herrera,[1] Néstor Corona,[2] and Gerardo Suárez[3]

ABSTRACT

The recent occurrence of great earthquakes and their associated tsunamis in the Pacific and Indian oceans have raised awareness on the need of historical and geological data to expand our knowledge of extreme events beyond the short instrumental record and to reduce the hazard to coastal communities. The coast of Guerrero parallels the active Mexican subduction zone, where some of the largest earthquakes are known to have triggered tsunamis. The occurrence of historical earthquakes and their tsunamis in this region is relatively well documented since the 16th century. Nevertheless, information about geological evidence of earthquakes and their associated tsunamis is scarcely documented. This study reviews data from published sources with two objectives: first, to highlight the usefulness of a multiproxy approach on the tropical Guerrero coast, where the probability of preservation of the geological evidence is lower due to the intrinsic characteristic of the tropics; and second, to outline our current understanding of prehistorical and historical earthquakes and their tsunamis in this area. The multiproxy approach adopted (including geological, microfossils, magnetic properties, geochemical, historical, ethnographical, theoretical modeling analyses, and instrumental data) shows that the coast of Guerrero has been exposed to destructive great earthquakes and tsunamis for the past 3500 BP years: the AD 1979 and AD 1985 events, and a great event occurring in 3400 BP. Geological evidence for the great event of 3400 BP indicates that this tsunami reached 5 km inland on the Guerrero coast. This study shows the need to investigate further the geological record of the tropical coast parallel to the Mexican subduction zone to assess the hazard in this region to create resilient coastal communities.

[1]Laboratorio Universitario de Geofísica Ambiental (LUGA) and Instituto de Geografía, Universidad Nacional Autónoma de México, México, DF, México

[2]Centro de Estudios en Geografía Humana, El Colegio de Michoacán, Michoacán, México

[3]Instituto de Geofísica, Universidad Nacional Autónoma de México, México, DF, México

13.1. INTRODUCTION

The great earthquakes and tsunamis of 2011 in Tohoku, Japan, 2010 in Maule, Chile, and 2004 in Sumatra, Indonesia, have raised awareness on the need for historical and geological studies to help in the assessment of earthquake and tsunami hazards to coastal

Extreme Events: Observations, Modeling, and Economics, Geophysical Monograph 214, First Edition.
Edited by Mario Chavez, Michael Ghil, and Jaime Urrutia-Fucugauchi.
© 2016 American Geophysical Union. Published 2016 by John Wiley & Sons, Inc.

communities. The Indian Ocean tsunami of 2004 killed over 226,000 people. This disaster led to the development of new research aimed at better understanding the origin and behavior of tsunamis [*Kanamori*, 2006; *Stein*, 2006; *Satake and Atwater*, 2007; *Lagos and Cisternas*, 2008]. It demonstrated clearly the high cost of ignoring previous earthquakes and tsunamis [*Lagos and Cisternas*, 2008]. Moreover, these most recent great earthquakes and tsunamis have a documented history that indicates the presence of similar events in the past, which should have been considered in any hazard assessment analysis [*Goto et al.*, 2011]. Historical records provide information in the order of centuries; geological data, on the other hand, can add millennia of data to the short instrumental record, and may help in understanding the occurrence and recurrence of large earthquakes and their tsunamis [*Orfanogiannaki and Papadopoulos*, 2007; *Satake and Atwater*, 2007; *Yanagisawa et al.*, 2007]. This information is fundamental for an adequate earthquake and tsunami hazard assessment [*González et al.*, 2009].

Geological studies using a multiproxy approach are particularly valuable in areas where there is limited instrumental record of previous earthquakes and tsunamis. Whereas there is abundant literature on the historical records of these phenomena [*Ambraseys*, 1979, 1995; *Ambraseys and Finkel*, 1990; *Ambraseys and Adams*, 1996; *García-Acosta and Suárez*, 1996; *Glade et al.*, 2001; *Gianfreda et al.*, 2001; *Frechet et al.*, 2008; *Suárez and Albini*, 2009; *Papadopoulos*, 2011; *Strunz et al.*, 2011; *Corona and Ramírez-Herrera*, 2012], there are relatively few geological studies of past events [*Atwater and Moore*, 1992; *Atwater et al.*, 1995, 2004; *Nanayama et al.*, 2003; *Sawai et al.*, 2004, 2008; *Cisternas et al.*, 2005; *Natawidjaja et al.*, 2006]. Neither are common in Mexico [*Curray et al.*, 1969; *González-Quintero*, 1980; *Bodin and Klinger*, 1986; *Ramírez-Herrera et al.*, 1998, 2004; *Ramírez-Herrera and Urrutia-Fucugauchi*, 1999; *Ramírez-Herrera and Zamorano-Orozco*, 2002].

Nevertheless, an increasing number of publications concerning paleoearthquakes and paleotsunamis in subduction zones have seen the light during the last decades [*Cisternas et al.*, 2005; *Morton et al.*, 2007; *Jankaew et al.*, 2008; *Monecke et al.*, 2008; *Goto et al.*, 2011; *Horton et al.*, 2011]. Historically documented events have been used as a guide to perform paleoseismic and paleotsunami studies. Unfortunately, the geological signature of these earthquakes and the stratigraphical evidence of tsunamis are not always preserved. The reasons may be that the tsunami left no deposit onshore or that the tsunami deposits were destroyed due to post-depositional changes, bioturbation, preexisting topography, erosion, and other factors.

13.1.1. Earthquake and Tsunami Record: A Multiproxy Approach

The study of preinstrumental earthquakes and tsunamis requires a multidisciplinary approach and involves several techniques: historical studies, interviews with the local population with knowledge about past earthquakes and tsunamis, geomorphological and geological studies (e.g., coring and trenching, grain size analysis, organic content, stratigraphy, micropaleontology, geochemistry, magnetic susceptibility, rock magnetic properties, radiometric dating, and numerical modeling) [*Morton et al.*, 2007; *Ramírez-Herrera et al.*, 2007, 2012; *Font et al.*, 2010]. As this field evolves, new proxies continue to be developed, such as the anisotropy of the magnetic susceptibility of tsunami deposits [*Wassmer et al.*, 2010; *Wassmer and Gómez*, 2011; *Ramírez-Herrera et al.*, 2012; *Goguitchaichvili et al.*, 2013].

This study reviews the results of a multiproxy approach used in tropical environments, where the probability of preserving the geological evidence is lower than in more temperate environments, due to physical, biological, and chemical processes intrinsic to these regions, such as mangrove ecosystems and associated bioturbation, accelerated chemical weathering, frequency and intensity of storms, among others. This study also presents the results of evidence found of past earthquakes and their tsunamis in the Guerrero, Pacific coast of Mexico.

13.2. EARTHQUAKE AND TSUNAMI HISTORICAL DATA OF THE MEXICAN PACIFIC COAST

The Mexican Pacific coast is parallel to the subduction zone of the Rivera and Cocos plates under the North American plate (Figure 13.1). Several large subduction earthquakes of $M_w > 7$ have occurred over the last century [*Kostoglodov and Ponce*, 1994]. Although infrequent, a few large magnitude, $M_w \geq 8$, events have been generated in the Mexican subduction zone (MSZ). Examples of these large earthquakes during last century are the Jalisco 1932 earthquake (M_w 8.2), the Colima 1995 earthquake (M_w 8.0), and the Michoacán earthquake of 1985 (M_w 8.1); the last one devastated parts of Mexico City, causing great human and economic losses, estimated in the range of billions of dollars.

The search for historical tsunami data is a more recent development, which has taken place in the last two decades [*Sánchez*, 1982; *Sánchez and Farreras*, 1993; *Farreras*, 1997]. However, research on the geological evidence of earthquakes and their tsunamis on the MSZ started only in the last decade [*Ramírez-Herrera et al.*, 2005, 2007, 2009, 2012].

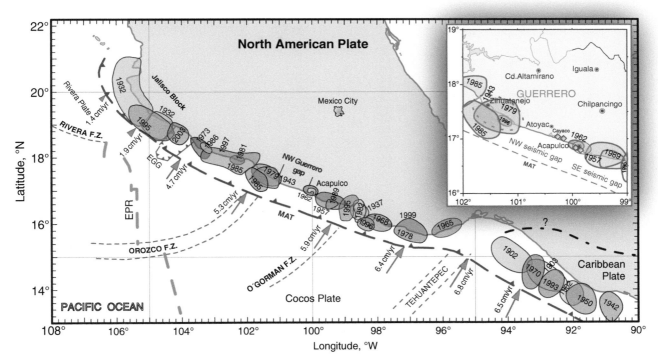

Figure 13.1 Tectonic and seismic setting of the Pacific Coast of Mexico. Abbreviations: MAT = Middle American Trench, F.Z. = Fracture zones, EPR = East Pacific Rise, EGG = El Gordo Graben. Symbols: Shaded circles indicate rupture areas and numbers the years of most important subduction seismic events of last century. Small dashed lines indicate fracture zones; thick dash with arrowheads show subduction zone. Thick dash shows location of EPR. Plate convergence rates are shown in cm/yr. Arrows indicate direction of convergence. Insert shows close-up to the Guerrero seismic gap. Rhombus in insert indicates GPS station and leveling sites [*Ramírez-Herrera et al.*, 1999].

13.2.1. Historical Earthquake Data

Reports of historical earthquakes along the MSZ spans only the last 500 years [*García-Acosta and Suárez*, 1996]. Although Mexico was already populated and indigenous codices provide some insight into the seismic record, the more reliable records date back to only the 16th century [*García-Acosta and Suárez*, 1996]. The historical evidence of earthquakes in Mexico stems from a variety of sources: governmental and church reports of damage, travelers' logs and books, archival data describing the cost of repairs, private letters, among others.

In particular, the Guerrero coast has experienced large historical earthquakes. However, no earthquakes with magnitude >7 have occurred since 1911 on the Guerrero seismic gap [*Lowry et al.*, 2001; *Larson et al.*, 2004]. It is possible that a major interplate earthquake with magnitude M_w 8.1–8.4 may occur along this segment of the coast [*Suárez et al.*, 1990]. Evidently, the probability of

tsunami occurrence associated with an earthquake of this size is potentially very high.

Four large earthquakes $M_w > 7$ occurred at the turn of the century: 14 January 1900, 20 January 1900, 15 April 1907, and 16 December 1911 (Figure 13.2). However, a tsunami is associated with only the first one [*Milne*, 1911; *Soloviev and Go*, 1975; *Sánchez and Farreras*, 1993; *García-Acosta and Suárez*, 1996].

13.2.2. Tsunami Historical Data

The Pacific Coast of Mexico shows 70 tsunamis from 1732 to 2011. The most destructive tsunamis during the last 100 years are those of 16 November 1925 in Zihutanejo and 22 June 1932 in Cuyutlán, Colima [*Sánchez and Farreras*, 1993; *Farreras*, 1997]. Documentary records show that for both of these events, 11 m high tsunami waves were recorded hitting the coasts near the city of Zihuatanejo, Guerrero state, and city of Cuyutlán in

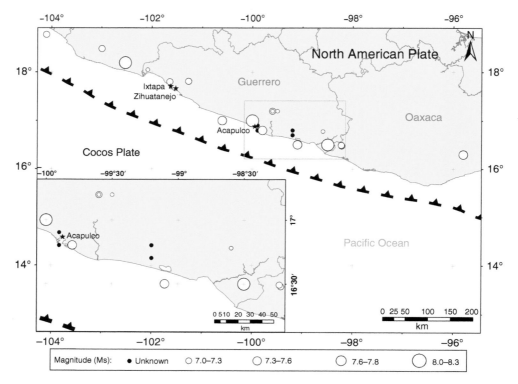

Figure 13.2 Earthquakes with $M_w \geq 6.9$ in the Guerrero area. White circles indicate the location of epicenters of the earthquakes along the coast of Guerrero. The black dots are the location of epicenters with no defined magnitude (*NOAA* [2012]).

Colima, respectively [*Sánchez and Farreras*, 1993; *Farreras*, 1997]. Nevertheless, a recent review of the historical data suggests that the source for the Zihuatanejo and Cuyutlán tsunamis may not be subduction earthquakes, but submarine landslides [*Singh et al.*, 1998; *Corona and Ramírez-Herrera*, 2012].

The largest tsunami in the history of Mexico took place on 28 March 1787, produced by an earthquake on the Oaxaca coast, which ruptured ~450 km of the MSZ with an equivalent magnitude of about 8.6 [*Suárez and Albini*, 2009]. The tsunami is reported to have reached 6.5 km inland [*García-Acosta and Suárez*, 1996; *Nuñez-Cornú et al.*, 2008; *Suárez and Albini*, 2009]. This event raises the question of whether events as large as this one or even larger may take place in other segments of the MSZ.

More recently, tsunami records in Mexico for earthquakes occurring after 1952 come from tide-gauges and, to a lesser degree, from post-tsunami measurements or visual observations. *Farreras* [1997] and *Sánchez and Farreras* [1993] report 34 tsunamis generated by earthquakes in the MSZ. The maximum wave height recorded at the tide-gauge stations is 3.0 m. Historical data for the last three centuries suggest that the tsunami wave heights on the Mexican Pacific coast may be much larger than what is being recorded during the past 60 years using tide-gauges.

Only a few post-tsunami field surveys have been carried out in Mexico. Post-tsunami field data were reported after the 19 and 20 September 1985 Michoacán earthquakes [*Abe et al.*, 1986] and the 9 October 1995 Colima-Jalisco earthquake M_w 8 [*Borrero et al.*, 1997; *Ortiz et al.*, 1998].

A total of 31 tsunamis have been reported along the coast of Guerrero between 1537 and 2012 (Table 13.1). In the majority of cases, the information is sparse because population density has been historically low along the Pacific Coast of Mexico. Except for the events listed as numbers 18, 27, and 28 on Table 13.1, which were reported as affecting Zihuatanejo and Ixtapa coast with different maximum water heights than in Acapulco, the effects of the other tsunamis have been reported only for the city of Acapulco, which is the oldest and more populated locality along the coast of Guerrero since colonial times (Table 13.1).

The parameter most commonly reported in a tsunami is the height of the tsunami wave. This parameter can only be measured accurately if tide-gauge data are available. Otherwise, this is a qualitative observation made by local observers and subject to errors and exaggerations. A more useful parameter is the inundation height of the tsunami wave. Unfortunately, this observation is seldom reported in the case of Mexican tsunamis. Tsunami heights reported in Mexico range from 0.2 to 11 m.

Table 13.1 Historical Record of Tsunamis Recorded in Acapulco, Guerrero State

Event	Date	Maximum Water Height (m)	Seismic Magnitude (Ms)	Event	Date	Maximum Water Height (m)	Seismic Magnitude (Ms)
1	1537	a	a	18	1925-11-16	11[b]	7
2	1732-02-25	3	a	19	1950-12-14	0.3	7.5
3	1754-09-01	4	a	20	1957-07-28	1.3	7.9
4	1784-03-28	3	a	21	1962-05-11	0.81	7
5	1787-03-28	4	8.6	22	1962-05-19	0.34	7.2
6	1820-05-04	4	7.6	23	1965-08-23	0.4	7.8
7	1833-03-10	a	a	24	1973-01-30	0.43	7.5
8	1834-03-14	a	7	25	1979-03-14	1.3	7.6
9	1845-04-07	a	8	26	1981-10-25	0.09	7.3
10	1852-12-04	a	7	27	1985-09-19	1.15	8.1
11	1854-12-04	a	a			1.5[c]	
12	1860-03-17	a	a			3[b]	
13	1868-05-25	a	a	28	1985-09-21	1.2	7.6
14	1868-08-12	a	a			1.2[b]	
15	1903-07-16	a	a	29	1995-09-14	a	7.2
16	1907-04-14	2	8.3	30	2003-01-22	0.35	7.6
17	1909-07-30	9	7.8	31	2012-03-20	0.2	7.6

Source: *NGDC-NOAA* [2012].
[a]Undefined measures.
[b]Recorded in Zihuatanejo.
[c]Recorded in Ixtapa.

Without a doubt, the largest tsunami recorded in historical times in Mexico is the 28 March 1787 tsunami. The historical reports of the tsunami produced by this earthquake indicate that it extended from the southern part of the coast of Guerrero to the Isthmus of Tehuantepec; this is a distance of ~600 km along the coast. The reports available describe an inundation area that extended over 6 km inland, both in southern Guerrero and near the Isthmus of Tehuantepec [*García-Acosta and Suárez*, 1996; *Suárez and Albini*, 2009].

13.3. GEOLOGICAL DATA

In what follows, we summarize results of geological data for three earthquakes and their tsunamis in Guerrero, Mexico, which are derived from a multiple proxy analysis [*Ramírez-Herrera et al.*, 2005, 2007, 2009, 2012]. We distinguish the term "historical" referring to data pertaining to the period of written records; "paleoearthquake" and "paleotsunami" refer to those events that occurred prior to written records.

13.3.1. 3400 BP

A catastrophic paleotsunami appears to be associated with a great local earthquake, which occurred at ca. 3400 BP on the Guerrero coast [*Ramírez-Herrera et al.*, 2007, 2009]. Land-level changes after ca. 6000–5200 yr BP observed in sediment cores from Laguna Mitla

(Figure 13.3) suggest local vertical displacements in coastal elevation caused by seismotectonic movements at the MSZ [*Ramírez-Herrera et al.*, 2007, 2009]. The stratigraphy at Laguna Mitla indicates a rapid shift from freshwater/brackish to marine conditions ca. 3400 yr BP. In addition, discrete sand layers above a brackish mangrove peat are associated with a sudden marine inundation, which is suspected of tsunami origin. The sand deposit characteristics (e.g., fining-up sands, internal mud laminations, a sharp-erosional lower contact, and incorporated rip-up mud clasts) and the geochemical evidence (increases in Na and Sr concentrations) suggest an apparently catastrophic marine flooding by ca. 3400 yr BP (extrapolated age, from ^{14}C 3043 Cal BP at 300 cm depth). Similar Sr-, Br-, and Ca-enriched sand layers, indicative of a marine setting, have been present at the nearby Laguna Coyuca [*Ramírez-Herrera et al.*, 2005].

A sand unit reflects a transient marine flooding event and the overlying marine blue clay level suggest an apparent coastal submergence at ca. 3400 BP (Figure 13.4). This coastal submergence is also corroborated by the presence of local submerged shell-middens, associated with past human occupation, at Laguna Coyuca [*Ramírez-Herrera et al.*, 2007, 2009]. Also paleoclimate data derived from pollen, diatoms, and marine plankton at the adjacent Laguna Tetitlan suggest a coastal submergence by 3170±280 yr BP [*González-Quintero*, 1980]. Today, the distance of the coring site to the coastline is ~5 km and the current sand barrier was already present

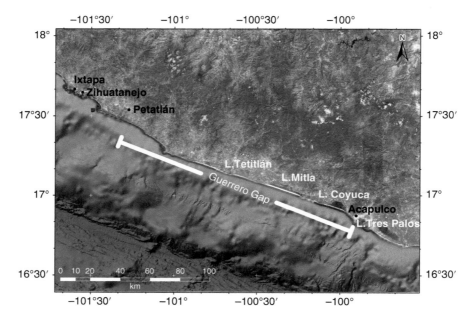

Figure 13.3 Location map: the Laguna Mitla, and adjacent Laguna Coyuca and Laguna Tetitlan. Red dot indicate study site and location of coring (modified from *Ramírez-Herrera et al.* [2005, 2007, 2009, 2012]).

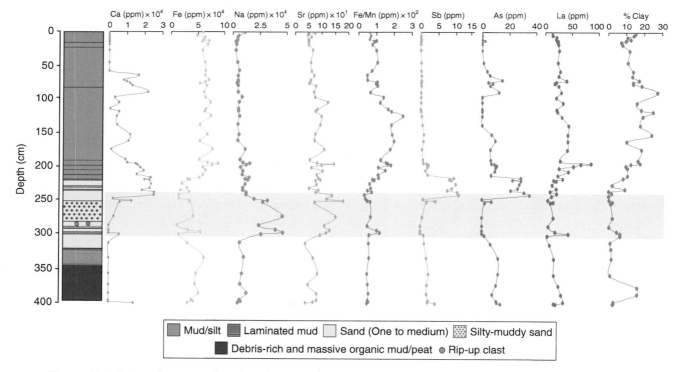

Figure 13.4 Selected trace and major element concentrations (Ca, Fe, Na, Sr, Fe/Mn, Sb, As, La) for core ACA-04-06, Mitla lagoon, Guerrero. Detail of core stratigraphy and percent clay data are also shown. Shaded bar shows position of tsunami event by 3400 yr BP (modified from *Ramírez-Herrera et al.* [2007]).

by 3400 BP [*Ramírez-Herrera et al.*, 2007]. Thus considering the distance of the site to the sand barrier, a great tsunami would be a plausible explanation for the marine inundation.

13.3.2. Two Modern Events (AD 1979 and AD 1985)

Data collected at the Ixtapa, Guerrero estuary sites provide evidence for the first geological record of two marine inundations (IXT-01 and IXT-02) that occurred during the last 60 years. The characteristics of these deposits are consistent with a tsunami, and not to storm inundation [*Morton et al.*, 2007]. Such characteristics include the presence of mud rip-up clasts, fine-upward grain size, deposit distance from the shoreline, abrupt basal contact, and buried soils [*Ramírez-Herrera et al.*, 2012].

A sand layer (sand bed IXT-01) is observed in all cores, pits, and trenches, which is presumably associated with the 14 March 1979 earthquake. The sand layer is a relatively thin (~2 cm), massive sand unit with an abrupt erosional basal contact. This sand unit contains both mud rip-up clasts and organic debris in the lower part of the deposit, indicating high-energy flow, perhaps caused by an overwash event. Of note are distinct geochemical (Sr, Ba, and Ca) and marine foraminifera signals, together with rare broken, brackish-tolerant diatoms. The scarcity of diatoms in tropical environments has been noted elsewhere [*Kamatani*, 1982; *Jankaew et al.*, 2008; *Monecke et al.*, 2008]. The presence of *Amphora coffeaeformis*, *Diploneis finnica*, and *Nitzschia scalpelliformis* in sediments immediately below sand bed IXT-01

and of *N. scalpelliformis* below IXT-02 might represent a diatom bloom (Figure 13.5). Such a diatom bloom is inferred to have been triggered by the influx of saltwater and by the mobilization of nutrients into the water column at the time of the catastrophic saltwater inundation [*Ramírez-Herrera et al.*, 2012]. Radiocarbon data indicate a date of 131.2 ± 0.5 pMC (percent modern carbon). Therefore, this event is most likely associated with a relatively recent tsunami that occurred along the Ixtapa-Zihutanejo coastline. Tentatively, this sand unit appears to be related to the March 1979 earthquake and tsunami.

A series of proxy data from a sand unit in the Ixtapa estuary (IXT-02) is consistent with a marine inundation [*Morton et al.*, 2007; *Ramírez-Herrera et al.*, 2012]. This sand unit is a relatively thin (~8 cm), massive, structureless sequence, fining-upward with an abrupt basal contact. It also contains mud rip-up clasts, organic debris, and a distinct geochemical signature representative of marine inundation (Sr, Ba, and Ca). The sedimentological and geochemical characteristics of IXT-02 suggest that it may well be the result of tsunami deposition. Moreover, the presence of intertidal foraminifera to shallow marine foraminifera (*Haplophragmoides columbiensis*) and marine diatoms (*A. coffeaeformis* and *D. finnica*) in the sediments immediately overlying IXT-02 are indicative of a short-lived change from a fresh-brackish to a marine environment (Figure 13.5). This environmental change is interpreted as the result of possible coseismic deformation caused by local earthquake-induced subsidence at the site [*Ramírez-Herrera et al.*, 2012].

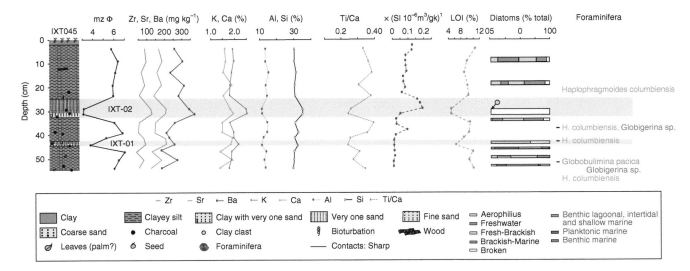

Figure 13.5 Detail of Ixtapa site showing stratigraphy, mean grain size (mz), elemental concentrations (Zr, Sr, Ba, Ca, K, Al, Si, and Ti/Ca index), magnetic susceptibility, lost on ignition (LOI), diatom and foraminifera data. Light gray shading shows Events 1 and 2; Note *1*—MS samples were collected from trench Ixt-045 where Event 1 is between 38–40 cm depth (modified from *Ramírez-Herrera et al.* [2012]).

13.4. HISTORICAL AND INSTRUMENTAL DATA IN SUPPORT OF GEOLOGICAL EVIDENCE OF EARTHQUAKES AND TSUNAMIS IN GUERRERO

The two modern events observed in the geological record, IXT-01 and IXT-02, produced modern radiocarbon dates. Historical and instrumental data were examined to correlate these events with registered events in this area.

The 14 March 1979 tsunami was generated by an earthquake source that occurred near Ixtapa-Zihuatanejo at 5:07 am local time (17.3″N, 101.3″W: Figure 13.1) [*Meyer et al.*, 1980; *Valdés et al.*, 1982; *Hsu et al.*, 1983; *Mendoza*, 1993]. The M_w 7.6 earthquake had a rupture area of ~1200 km², located entirely offshore [*Sánchez and Farreras*, 1993]. The nearest tidal-gauge station to the epicenter is located about 80 km to the southeast, near the city of Acapulco. The observed tsunami wave height was 1.3 m [*Soloviev et al.*, 1992; *Sánchez and Farreras*, 1993; *NGDC*, 2011]. Tsunamis can increase in amplitude when entering estuaries and overflow their banks, as has been observed during the most recent tsunami events in Chile, 2010 and in Japan, 2011. The surrounding areas of the Ixtapa estuary are scarcely populated. However, a testimony given by local witness described that the area was flooded after the 1979 and 1985 earthquakes [*Ramírez-Herrera et al.*, 2012]. Therefore, it is most likely that the event IXT-01 correlates with the 1979 earthquake and tsunami.

It is not possible to determine geologically which of the two 1985 earthquakes, September 19 or 21, deposited the observed sand unit IXT-02. We hypothesize that the 21 September event (M_w 7.6), which was located closer to the Ixtapa-Zihuatanejo area, was the most likely source of

this deposit. Despite the fact that the 19 September 1985 earthquake had a larger magnitude (M_w 8.1), most of the rupture area of this event was located inland, while the 21 September 1985 earthquake had its entire rupture area offshore, that is, an earthquake potentially capable of producing a larger tsunami. Moreover, the observed land-level change interpreted from environmental indicators distinguished in the stratigraphical and microfossil record agrees with our coseismic deformation model using *Mendoza*'s [1993] coseismic slip data for the 21 September 1985 earthquake and our model for vertical coseismic displacement (Figure 13.6).

13.5. DISCUSSION AND CONCLUSIONS

Three earthquakes and their probable tsunamis have been identified in the Guerrero area using a multiproxy approach [*Ramírez-Herrera et al.*, 2007, 2009, 2012]. Additional possible paleotsunamis [*Ramírez-Herrera et al.*, 2005] have been tentatively proposed, based on geological evidence found elsewhere on the Guerrero coast of the Mexican Pacific.

A great event in the late Holocene (3400 yr BP) on the Guerrero coast was identified by a shift in environments and a relative sea-level rise, indicating tectonic subsidence, preceded by a marine inundation of 5 km inland. The spatial distribution along shore and the extent to which this tsunami inundated different sites needs further testing. The seismogenic nature of this event, however, is evident in the stratigraphy, which indicates a rapid change from a marginal lagoon to a marine environment by ca. 3400 yr BP, with a gradual return to more terrestrial conditions.

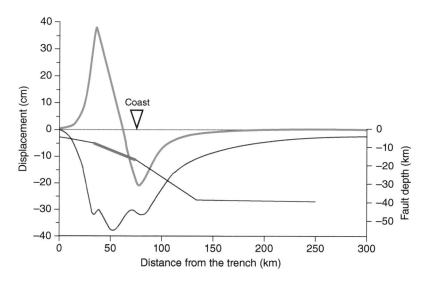

Figure 13.6 Model of tectonic subsidence (dislocation in a homogeneous elastic half-space: *Savage*, 1983) (modified from *Ramírez-Herrera et al.* [2012]).

Multiproxy data from sediments in the Zihuatanejo-Ixtapa area show evidence for two 20th-century tsunamis in Ixtapa estuary. The two tsunami deposits found at the Ixtapa site are associated with local earthquakes: sand unit IXT-01 is probably associated with the 1979 event and IXT-02 with the 1985 event. Coseismic deformation associated with the 1985 event is also inferred from the sedimentary record. Additional evidence to support the tsunami origin of the sand layers IXT-01 and IXT-02 is the distance of the anomalous layers from the shoreline, about 250 m and about 90 m from the current estuary [*Ramírez-Herrera et al.*, 2012].

Historically documented evidence also suggests that the site is sufficiently landward to avoid substantial inundation by storms. Another consideration that strengthens a potential tsunami origin for these deposits is the frequency of such extreme events. Between 1951 and 2008, a total of 19 hurricanes occurred along Mexico's Pacific coast [*NOAA*, 2012]. If this area was regularly inundated by such large events it would be expected to see numerous storm deposits in the cores—they are not. Finally, age range estimates for the inundation events support a tsunami origin hypothesis [*Ramírez-Herrera et al.*, 2012].

Geological evidence for modern, historical, and paleotsunamis has been widely described in the literature [*Atwater et al.*, 1995; *Hutchinson and McMillan*, 1997; *Goff et al.*, 2001; 2010; *Pinegina and Bourgeois*, 2001; *Chagué-Goff et al.*, 2002; 2011; *Kortekaas and Dawson*, 2007; *Morton et al.*, 2007; *Jankaew et al.*, 2008; *Monecke et al.*, 2008]. These descriptions agree with the characteristics described for the deposits found on the Guerrero coast.

The results summarized in this review are intended to create a comprehensive overview of historically and geologically recorded great events in Mexico. Multiproxy data have proven to be an invaluable tool in determining the origin of the geological evidence of earthquakes and tsunamis in this tropical environment. A wider range of proxies [*Ramírez-Herrera et al.*, 2007] instead of the conventional suite of sediment grain size and microfossils (diatoms and/or foraminifera), most often used in temperate environments where these basic indicators tend to be well preserved, help to demonstrate the occurrence earthquake and tsunamis. The correlation of proxy data with historical records, interviews, numerical modeling, and a post-tsunami survey [*Abe et al.*, 1986] has further enhanced these interpretations.

Moreover, the application of this multiproxy approach to the Guerrero coast allowed revealing the potential hazard by great earthquakes and their tsunamis to the population on the Guerrero coast. The identification of a possibly extreme earthquake and tsunami in 3400 BP suggests the hazard posed to the highly populated coastal area of Guerrero.

In summary, we consider that the historical record together with the identification and the characterization of geological evidence of earthquakes and their tsunamis in a given area may provide a unique opportunity to obtain realistic, average earthquake-tsunami recurrence intervals, coseismic deformation data, minimum inundation distances, and the elapsed time since the last event. This information is crucial for constraining the earthquake and tsunami hazard. The ability to distinguish the geological evidence produced by past tsunamis from other meteorological events will greatly enhance our knowledge of the magnitude and frequency of these events. This, in turn, will greatly enhance our understanding of regional earthquake and tsunami hazard in countries such as Mexico.

ACKNOWLEDGMENTS

Ramírez-Herrera received financial support from PAPPIIT-UNAM grant No. IN123609, PASPA-DGAPA 2015, UNAM, and SEP-CONACYT grant No. 129456. Gerardo Suárez acknowledges support from a SEP-CONACYT grant No. 82821.

REFERENCES

Abe, K., M. Hakuno, M. Takeuchi, and T. Katada (1986), Survey report on the tsunami of the Michoacan, México earthquake of September 19, 1985, *Bull. Earthquake Res. Inst.*, *61*, 475–481.

Ambraseys, N. N. (1979), A test case of historical seismicity: Is-fahan and Chahar Mahal, Iran, *Geogr. J.*, *145*, 56–71.

Ambraseys, N. N. (1995), Magnitudes of Central American earthquakes 1898–1930, *Geophys. J. Int.*, *121*, 545–556.

Ambraseys, N. N. and C. F. Finkel (1990), The Marmara Sea earthquake of 1509, *Terra Nova*, *2*, 167–174.

Ambraseys, N. N. and R. D. Adams (1996), Large-magnitude Central American earthquakes, 1898–1994, *Geophys. J. Int.*, *127*, 665–692.

Atwater, B. F. and A. L. Moore (1992), A tsunami about 1000 years ago in Puget Sound, Washington, *Science*, *258*, 1614–1617.

Atwater, B. F., A. R. Nelson, J. J. Clague, G. A. Carver, D. K. Yamaguchi, P. T. Bobrowsky, J. Bourgeois, M. E. Darienzo, W. C. Grant, E. Hemphill-Haley, H. M. Kelsey, G. C. Jacoby, S. P. Nishenko, S. P. Palmer, C. D. Peterson, and M. A. Reinhart (1995), Summary of coastal geologic evidence for past great earthquakes at the Cascadia subduction zone, *Earthq. Spectra*, *11*, 1–18.

Atwater, B. F., R. Furukawa, E. Hemphill-Haley, Y. Ikeda, and K. Kashima (2004), Seventeenth-century uplift in Eastern Hokkaido, Japan, *Holocene*, *14*, 487–501.

Bodin, P. and T. Klinger (1986), Coastal uplift and mortality of intertidal organisms caused by the September 1985 Mexico earthquakes, *Science*, *233*, 1071–1073.

Borrero, J., M. Ortiz, V. V. Titov, and C. E. Synolakis (1997), Field survey of Mexican tsunami, *Eos Trans. AGU*, *78*(8), 85, 87–88.

Chagué-Goff, C., S. Dawson, J. R. Zachariasen, K. R. Berryman, D. L. Garnett, H. M. Waldron, and D. C. Mildenhall (2002), A tsunami (ca. 6300 years BP) and other environmental changes, northern Hawke's Bay, New Zealand, *Sediment. Geol.*, *150*, 89–102.

Chagué-Goff, C., J. L. Schneider, J. R. Goff, D. Dominey-Howes, and L. Strotz (2011), Expanding the proxy toolkit to help identify past events—Lessons from the 2004 Indian Ocean Tsunami and the 2009 South Pacific Tsunami, *Earth Sci. Rev.*, *107*, 107–122.

Cisternas, M., B. F. Atwater, F. Torrejon, Y. Sawai, G. Machuca, M. Lagos, A. Eipert, C. Youlton, I. Salgado, T. Kamataki, M. Shishikura, C. P. Rajendran, J. K. Malik, Y. Rizal, and M. Husni (2005), Predecessors of the giant 1960 Chile earthquake, *Nature*, *437*, 404–407.

Corona, N. and M. T. Ramírez-Herrera (2012), Mapping and historical reconstruction of the great Mexican 22 June 1932 tsunami, *Nat. Hazards Earth Syst. Sci.*, *12*(5), 1337–1352.

Curray, J. R., F. J. Emmel, and P. J. S. Crampton (1969), Holocene history of a strand plain lagoonal coast, Nayarit, Mexico, in *Memorias Simposio Internacional, Lagunas costeras*, pp. 63–100, UNAM-UNESCO, Mexico, D.F.

Farreras, S. (1997), Tsunamis en Mexico, in *Contribuciones a la Oceanografia Fisica en Mexico*, Monografia No.3, edited by M. F. Lavin, pp. 73–96, Union Geofisica Mexicana, Ensenada.

Font, E., C. Nascimento, R. Omira, M. A. Baptista, and P. F. Silva (2010), Identification of tsunami-induced deposits using numerical modeling and rock magnetism techniques: A study case of the 1755 Lisbon tsunami in Algarve, Portugal, *Phys. Earth Planet. In.*, *182*, 187–198.

Frechet, J., M. Meghraoui, and M. Stucchi (Eds.) (2008), *Historical Seismology: Interdisciplinary Studies of Past and Recent Earthquakes, Modern Approaches in Solid Earth Sciences*, Springer-Verlag, New York.

García-Acosta, V. and G. Suárez (1996), *Los Sismos de la Historia de México*, Fondo de Cultura Económica/Universidad Nacional Autonoma de México/Centro de Investigaciones y Estudios Superiores en Antropologia Social, México.

Gianfreda, F., G. Mastronuzzi, and P. Sans'o (2001), Impact of historical tsunamis on a sandy coastal barrier: An example from the northern Gargano coast, southern Italy, *Nat. Hazards Earth Syst. Sci.*, *1*, 213–219.

Glade, T., P. Albini, and F. Frances (Eds.) (2001), *The Use of Historical Data in Natural Hazards Assessment*, Kluwer Academic Publishers, Dordrecht.

Goff, J., C. Chagué-Goff, and S. Nichol (2001), Palaeotsunami deposits: A New Zealand perspective, *Sediment. Geol.*, *143*, 1–6.

Goff, J., S. Pearce, S. L. Nichol, C. Chagué-Goff, M. Horrocks, and L. Strotz (2010), Multi-proxy records of regionally-sourced tsunamis, New Zealand, *Geomorphology*, *118*, 369–382.

Goguitchaichvili, A., M. T. Ramírez-Herrera, M. Calvo-Rathert, B. Aguilar Reyes, A. Carrancho, C. Caballero, F. Bautista, and J. M. Contreras (2013), Magnetic fingerprint of tsunami-induced deposits in the Ixtapa–Zihuatanejo Area, Western Mexico, *Int. Geol. Rev.*, doi:10.1080/00206814.2013.779781.

González, F. I., E. Geist, B. Jaffe, U. Kânoğlu, H. Mofjeld, C. E. Synolakis, V. V. Titov, D. Arcas, D. Bellomo, D. Carlton, T. Horning, J. Johnson, J. Newman, T. Parsons, R. Peters, C. Peterson, G. Priest, A. Venturato, J. Weber, F. Wong, and A. Yalciner (2009), Probabilistic tsunami hazard assessment at seaside, Oregon, for near- and far-field seismic sources, *J. Geophys. Res.*, *114*, C11.

González-Quintero, L. (1980), Paleoecologia de un sector costero de Guerrero, Mexico (3000 años), in *Coloquio sobre paleo-botanica y palinologia*, edited by INAH, pp. 133–157 Coleccion Cientifica Prehistoria.

Goto, K., C. Chagué-Goff, S. Fujino, J. Goff, B. Jaffe, Y. Nishimura, B. Richmond, D. Sugawara, W. Szczuciński, D. R. Tappin, R. C. Witter, and E. Yulianto (2011), New insights into tsunami risk from the 2011 Tohoku-oki event, *Mar. Geol.*, *290*, 46–50.

Horton, B. P., Y. Sawai, A. D. Hawkes, and R. C. Witter (2011), Sedimentology and paleontology of a tsunami deposit accompanying the great Chilean earthquake of February 2010, *Mar. Micropaleontol.*, *79*, 32–138.

Hsu, V., J. F. Gettrust, C. E. Helsley, and E. Berg (1983), Local seismicity preceding the March 14, 1979, Petatlan, Mexico Earthquake (Ms= 7.6), *J. Geophys. Res.*, *88*(B5), 4247S–4262S.

Hutchinson, I. and A. D. McMillan (1997), Archaeological evidence for village abandonmentassociated with late Holocene earthquakes at the northern Cascadia SubductionZone, *Quatern. Res.*, *48*, 79–87.

Jankaew, K., B. F. Atwater, Y. Sawai, M. Choowong, T. Charoentitirat, M. E. Martin, and A. Prendergas (2008), Medieval forewarning of the 2004 Indian Ocean tsunami in Thailand, *Nature*, *455*, 1228–1231.

Kamatani, A. (1982), Dissolution rates of silica from diatoms decomposing at various temperatures, *Mar. Biol.*, *68*, 91–96.

Kanamori, H. (2006), Lessons from the 2004 Sumatra-Andaman earthquake, *Phil. Trans. R. Soc. A*, *364*, 1927–1945.

Kortekaas, S. and A. G. Dawson (2007), Distinguishing tsunami and storm deposits: An example from Martinhal, SW Portugal, *Sediment. Geol.*, *200*, 208–221.

Kostoglodov, V. and L. Ponce (1994), Relationship between subduction and seismicity in the Mexican part of the Middle America trench, *J. Geophys. Res.*, *99*, 729–742.

Lagos, M. and Cisternas, M. (2008), El Nuevo Riesgo de Tsunami Considerando el Peor Escenario, *Actas del X Coloquio Internacional de Geografía: Diez años de cambios en el mundo, en la geografia y en las ciencias sociales*, Barcelona.

Larson, K. M., A. Lowry, V. Kostoglodov, W. Hutton, O. Sánchez, W. Hudnut, and G. Suárez (2004), Crustal deformation measurements in Guerrero, Mexico, *J. Geophys. Res.*, *109*(B4), doi:10.1029/2003JB002843.

Lowry, A. R., K. M. Larson, V. Kostoglodov, and R. Bilham (2001), Transient slip on the subduction interface in Guerrero, southern Mexico, *Geophys. Res. Lett.*, *28*, 3753–3756.

Mendoza, C. (1993), Coseismic slip of two large Mexican earthquakes from teleseismicbody waveforms: Implications for asperity interaction in the Michoacan plateboundary segment, *J. Geophys. Res.*, *98*(B5), 8197–8210.

Meyer, R. P., W. D. Pennington, L. A. Powell, W. L. Unger, M. Guzmán, J. Havskov, S. K. Singh, C. Valdés, and J. Yamamoto (1980), A first report on the Petatlan, Guerrero, Mexico Earthquake of 14 March 1979, *Geophys. J. Int.*, *7*, 97–100.

Milne, J. (1911), Catalogue of destructive earthquakes [7 to 1899 A.D.], paper presented at *81st Meeting of the British Association for the Advancement of Science*, Portsmouth, London.

Monecke, K., W. Finger, D. Klarer, W. Kongko, B. C. McAdoo, A. L. Moore, and S. M. Sudrajat (2008), A 1,000-year sediment record of tsunami recurrence in northern Sumatra, *Nature*, *455*, 1232–1234.

Morton, R. A., G. Gelfenbaum, and B. E. Jaffe (2007), Physical criteria for distinguishing sandy tsunami and storm deposits using modern examples, *Sediment. Geol.*, *200*, 184–207.

Nanayama, F., K. Satake, R. Furukawa, K. Shimokawa, and B. F. Atwater (2003), Unusually large earthquakes inferred from tsunami deposits along the Kuril trench, *Nature*, *424*, 660–663.

Natawidjaja, D. H., K. Sieh, M. Chlieh, J. Galetzka, B. Suwargadi, H. Cheng, R. L. Edwards, J. P. Avouac, and S. Ward (2006), Source parameters of the great Sumatran megathrust earthquake of 1797 and 1833 inferred from coral microatolls, *J. Geophys. Res.*, *111*, B06403, doi:10.1029/2005JB004025.

National Geophysical Data Center (2011), Historical Tsunami Database, National Geodata Base Center.

National Geophysical Data Center-National Oceanic and Atmospheric Administration (2012), NOAA/WTC Tsunami Event Database, Boulder, CO.

Núñez-Cornú, F., M. Ortíz, and J. J. Sánchez (2008), The Great 1787 Mexican Tsunami, *Nat. Hazards*, *47*, 569–576.

Orfanogiannaki, K. and G. A. Papadopoulos (2007), Conditional probability approach of the assessment of tsunami potential: Application in three tsunamigenic regions of the Pacific Ocean, *Pure Appl. Geophys.*, *164*, 593–603.

Ortíz, M., S. K. Singh, J. Pacheco, and V. Kostoglodov (1998), Rupture length of October 9, 1995 Colima-Jalisco earthquake (Mw 8) estimated from tsunami data, *Geophys. Res. Lett.*, *25*(15), 2857–2860.

Papadopoulos, G. A. (2011), *A Seismic History of Crete—The Hellenic Arc Trench, Earthquakes and Tsunamis: 2000 BC–2011 AD*, pp. 415, Ocelotos Publications, Athens.

Pinegina, T. K. and J. Bourgeois (2001), Historical and paleo-tsunami deposits on Kamchatka, Russia: Long-term chronologies and long-distance correlations, *Nat. Hazards Earth Syst. Sci.*, *1*, 177–185.

Ramírez-Herrera, M. T., J. J. Zamorano Orozco, P. M. Ortiz, J. Urrutia-Fucugauchi, R. Reyna, R. Gutierrez, E. León, and J. S. Marshall (1998), Quaternary tectonic uplift along the Pacific coast of Jalisco, Southwest Mexico, *EOS Trans. AGU*, *11*(10Abstract T31E-01).

Ramírez-Herrera, M. T., V. Kostoglodov, M. A. Summerfield, J. Urrutia-Fucugauchi, and J. J. Zamorano (1999), A reconnaissance study of the morphotectonics of the Mexican subduction zone, *Ann. Geomorphol.*, *118*, 207–226.

Ramírez-Herrera, M. T. and J. Urrutia-Fucugauchi (1999), Morphotectonic zones along the coast of the Pacific continental margin, southern Mexico, *Geomorphology*, *28*, 237–250.

Ramírez-Herrera, M. T. and J. J. Zamorano-Orozco (2002), Coastal uplift and mortality of coralline algae caused by a 6.3 M_w earthquake, Oaxaca, Mexico, *J. Coast. Res.*, *18*(1), 75–81.

Ramírez-Herrera, M. T., V. Kostoglodov, and J. Urrutia-Fucugauchi (2004), Holocene-emerged notches and tectonic uplift along the Jalisco coast, Southwest Mexico, *Geomorphology*, *58*, 291–304.

Ramírez-Herrera, M. T., A. Cundy, and V. Kostoglodov (2005), Probables sismos y tsunamis prehistóricos durante los últimos 5000 años en la costa de la brecha sísmica de Guerrero México, Mexico, in *XV Congreso Nacional de Ingenieria Sísmica, I-07*, pp. 1–17, Sociedad Mexicana de Ingenieria Sísmica México, México, D.F.

Ramírez-Herrera, M. T., A. Cundy, V. Kostoglodov, A. Carranza-Edwards, E. Morales, and S. Metcalfe (2007), Sedimentary record of late-Holocene relative sea-level change and tectonic deformation from the Guerrero Seismic Gap, Mexican Pacific coast, *Holocene*, *17*(8), 1211–1220.

Ramírez-Herrera, M. T., A. B. Cundy, V. Kostoglodov, and M. Ortiz (2009), Late Holocene tectonic land-level changes and tsunamis at Mitla lagoon, Guerrero, Mexico, *Geofis. Int.*, *48*(2), 195–209.

Ramírez-Herrera, M. T., M. Lagos, I. Hutchinson, V. Kostoglodov, M. L. Machain, M. Caballero, A. Gogichaisvili, B. Aguilar, C. Chagué-Goff, J. Goff, A. C. Ruiz-Fernández, M. Ortiz, H. Nava, F. Bautista, G. I. Lopez, and P. Quintana (2012), Extreme wave deposits on the Pacific coast of Mexico: Tsunamis or storms?—a multiproxy approach, *Geomorphology*, *139–140*, 360–371.

Sánchez, A. J. and S. F. Farreras (1993), *Catalog of Tsunamis on the Western Coast of Mexico*, pp. 79, U.S. Department of Commerce, National Oceanic and Atmospheric Administration, National Environmental Satellite, Data, and Information Service, National Geophysical Data Center, Boulder, CO.

Sánchez, E. (1982), *Lista cronológica de sismos históricos mexicanos*, edited by T. IIMAS, UNAM, México, D.F.

Satake, K. and B. Atwater (2007), Long-term perspectives on giant earthquakes and tsunamis at subduction zones, *Annu. Rev. Earth Planet. Sci.*, *35*, 349–374.

Savage, J. C. (1983), A dislocation model of strain accumulation and release at a subduction zone, *J. Geophys. Res.*, *88*(B6), 4984–4996, doi:10.1029/JB088iB06p04984.

Sawai, Y., K. Satake, T. Kamataki, H. Nasu, and M. Shishikura (2004), Transient uplift after a seventeenth-century earthquake along the Kuril subduction zone, *Science*, *306*, 1918–1920.

Sawai, Y., Y. Fujii, O. Fujiwara, T. Kamataki, J. Komatsubara, Y. Okamura, K. Satake, and M. Shishikura (2008), Marine incursions of the past 1500 years and evidence of tsunamis at Suijin-numa, a coastal lake facing the Japan Trench, *Holocene*, *18*(4), 517–528.

Singh, S. K., J. F. Pacheco, and N. Shapiro (1998), The earthquake of 16 November, 1925 (Ms=7.0) and the reported tsunami in Zihuatanejo, México, *Geofis. Int.*, *37*(1).

Soloviev, S.L. and Go, C.N. (1975) Catalogue of tsunamis on the eastern shore of the Pacific Ocean, Canadian Translation of Fisheries and Aquatic Sciences No. 5078, edited by Canada Institute for Scientific and Technical Information National Research Council, Ottawa, Nauka Publishing House, Moscow.

Soloviev, S. L., C. N. Go, and K. S. Kim (1992), *A Catalog of Tsunamis in the Pacific, 1969–1982*, edited by N. D. Academy of Sciences of the USSR (translated from Russian to English by Amerind Publishing Co. Pvt. Ltd., 1988), pp. 80, Soviet Geophysical Committee, Moscow.

Stein, S. (2006), Limitations of a young science, *Seismol. Res. Lett.*, *77*, 351–353.

Strunz, G., J. Post, K. Zosseder, and S. Wegscheider (2011), Tsunami risk assessment in Indonesia, *Nat. Hazards Earth Syst. Sci.*, *11*, 67–82.

Suárez, G., T. Monfret, G. Wittlinger, and C. David (1990), Geometry of subduction and depth of the seismogenic zone in the Guerrero Gap, Mexico, *Nature*, *345*, 336–338.

Suárez, G. and P. Albini (2009), Evidence for Great Tsunamigenic Earthquakes (M 8.6) along the Mexican Subduction Zone, *Bull. Seismol. Soc. Am.*, *99*, 892–896.

Valdés, C., R. P. Meyer, R. Zdfiiga, J. Havskov, and S. K. Singh (1982), Analysis of the Petatlan aftershocks: Number, energy release and asperities, *J. Geophys. Res.*, *87*, 8519–8527.

Wassmer, P., J.-L. Schneider, A.-V. Fonfrège, F. Lavigne, R. Paris, and C. Gomez (2010), Use of Anisotropy of Magnetic Susceptibility (AMS) in the study of tsunami deposits: Application to the 2004 deposits on the eastern coast of Banda Aceh, North Sumatra, Indonesia, *Mar. Geol.*, *275*, 255–272.

Wassmer, P. and C. Gómez (2011), Development of the AMS method for unconsolidated sediments. Application to tsunami deposits, *Géomorphologie*, *3*, 279–290.

Yanagisawa, K., F. Imamura, T. Sakakiyama, T. Annaka, T. Takeda, and N. Shuto (2007), Tsunami assessment for risk management at nuclear power facilities in Japan, *Pure Appl. Geophys.*, *164*, 565–576.

14

Landslide Risk to the Population of Italy and Its Geographical and Temporal Variations

Paola Salvati,[1] Mauro Rossi,[1,2] Cinzia Bianchi,[1] and Fausto Guzzetti[1]

ABSTRACT

Landslides cause damage to the population in Italy every year. Using an updated version of a historical catalog of landslide events with human consequences, we employed a new approach to investigate landslide risk to the population in Italy over time. We studied the temporal and geographical variation of risk on the basis of two classifications of the Italian territory. We used (1) the five zones based on the average terrain elevation and the distance to the seacoast of the Italian municipalities and (2) the topographical areas based on a semi-quantitative, stepwise approach of derivatives of altitude. We estimated individual landslide risk levels in the five zones for the north, center, and south of Italy and for three different periods between 1861 and 2010. To determine new societal landslide risk levels, we established the probability of experiencing severe landslide events in the eight topographical areas by modeling the empirical distributions of events with a Zipf distribution. The catalog used covers the period 91 BC to 2011; the number of events in the catalog increased with time. The reduced number of events in the early part of the catalog is attributed to incompleteness, a known bias in non-instrumental records of natural events. To overcome problems of incompleteness in carrying out the risk analysis, we used the recent portion of the catalog between 1861 and 2010. We believe that the quantification of the risk posed by landslides to the population is an important step for increasing awareness of the problem among Italian administrators and citizens.

14.1. INTRODUCTION

During the 20th century and the first decade of the 21st century, landslides in Italy have killed or injured 8077 people in at least 1398 events at 1239 different sites. In the same period, the number of homeless and evacuees caused by landslides exceeded 211,000. These figures indicate that landslide risk to the population in Italy is severe and widespread and that establishing landslide risk levels to the population is therefore a problem of both scientific and societal interest.

Even though landslides are common in Italy and they cause damage to the population every year, little interest has been shown in this problem at both the scientific and political levels. A great deal of work has been done to evaluate and map the landslide risk for specific areas in Italy, but fewer studies have been carried out to assess landslide risk levels to the population.

Latter [1969] suggested that the number of deaths caused by landslides can be used as a measure of the magnitude of a landslide disaster, and *Morgan* [1991, 1997], *Cruden and Fell* [1997], *Fell and Hartford* [1997], and *Evans* [1997] attempted to establish landslide risk

[1]*Istituto di Ricerca per la Protezione Idrogeologica, Consiglio Nazionale delle Ricerche, Perugia, Italy*

[2]*Dipartimento di Scienze della Terra, Università degli Studi di Perugia, Perugia, Italy*

Extreme Events: Observations, Modeling, and Economics, Geophysical Monograph 214, First Edition.
Edited by Mario Chavez, Michael Ghil, and Jaime Urrutia-Fucugauchi.

levels, and related definition criteria, on the basis of the number of people killed by slope failures. According to these authors, when we refer to the population, quantitative landslide risk analyses are aimed at defining individual and societal (collective) risk levels. Generally, the risk analyses require a catalog of landslides and their human consequences, that is, deaths, missing persons, injured people, evacuees, and homeless. Using the historical information on damage to the population of Italy, estimates of individual and societal risk levels at national scale were first determined by *Salvati et al.* [2003], and were revised by *Guzzetti et al.* [2005a, 2005b]. *Cascini et al.*, in 2008, established individual and societal risk owing to landslides in the Campania region (southern Italy) and *Salvati et al.* [2010] estimated societal landslide risk levels in the 20 Italian regions. Most of these previous findings are based on administrative classifications of the Italian territory that do not properly correspond with the morphological assets. Furthermore, for some Italian regions, there were not enough data to calculate correct regional estimates [*Salvati et al.*, 2010].

As in our previous works, we start with a very detailed description of the temporal and geographical distribution of harmful landslide events and landslide casualties for which there is information in the historical catalog. We then describe the new risk analyses: we established individual risk levels in the five elevation zones; we analyzed the variation of these risk levels in the north, center, and south of Italy; and for each elevation zone, we investigated their variation throughout the period 1861–2010. To establish societal landslide risk we calculated new frequency/density curves of harmful landslide events for each of the eight topographical areas into which the Italian territory was divided by *Guzzetti and Reichenbach* [1994]. The new results were compared with those of our previous regional study, and the density curves we have calculated for other natural hazards, such as floods, earthquakes, and volcanic activity were compared with the new ones for landslides, calculated at a national scale. We also analyzed possible connections between landslide events with casualties and other natural harmful events.

14.2. GLOSSARY

We use the term "fatalities" to indicate the sum of the deaths and the missing persons due to a harmful landslide event. Casualties indicate the sum of fatalities and injured people. Evacuees were people forced to abandon their homes temporarily, while the homeless were people that lost their homes. Human consequences encompass casualties, homeless people, and the evacuees. A fatal landslide event is an event that resulted in fatalities. Individual risk is the risk posed by a hazard (e.g., a landslide) to any unidentified individual. Societal (or collective) risk is the risk posed by a hazard (e.g., a landslide) on society as a whole. Intensity and severity are used as synonyms to measure the number of fatalities or casualties. For clarity, intensity is used to analyze and discuss individual risk, and severity for societal risk.

14.3. RECORD OF HARMFUL LANDSLIDE EVENTS IN ITALY

Using different sources of information, including archives, chronicles, newspapers, scientific journals, technical reports, and other bibliographical sources, *Salvati et al.* [2003]; *Guzzetti et al.* [2005b]; and *Salvati et al.* [2010] compiled a comprehensive historical catalog of landslide events with direct human consequences to the population of Italy. Details on the sources of information used, and on the problems encountered in compiling the historical record are given in *Guzzetti et al.* [2005b] and in *Salvati et al.* [2010]. For this work, we have updated the record of harmful landslide events in Italy to cover the 2102 year period 91 BC to 2011 (Table 14.1). We performed the update by: (1) searching systematically national newspapers available online and, where available, their digital databases, (2) obtaining daily information from Google Alert (http://www.google.com/alerts) using pre defined keywords, (3) searching blogs and other Internet resources for specific events, (4) searching digital newspaper libraries and digital catalogs of archive documents, and (5) reading chronicles and recently published local history books.

Table 14.1 Statistics of Landslides Events with Deaths, Missing Persons, Injured People, Evacuees, and Homeless in Italy for Different Periods

Parameter	91 BC to 2011	1861–1909	1910–1959	1960–2011
Length of period (yr)	2,102	49	50	52
Deaths (d)	14,779	595	1,792	3,416
Missing persons (m)	40	1	24	15
Injured people (i)	2,752	83	720	1,940
Fatalities (d+m)	14,819	596	1,816	3,431
Casualties (d+m+i)	17,571	679	2,536	5,371
Evacuees and homeless people	217,400	5,750	51,470	156,220
Largest number of casualties in an event	1,917	79	220	1,917

The updated record lists 3545 landslide events that have resulted in deaths, missing persons, injured people, evacuees, and homeless in Italy, from 91 BC to 2011 (2102 years). In the record, quantitative information on the number of the human consequences caused by harmful landslides is available for 3089 historical events, 87.1% of the total number of the events. These events resulted in at least 17,571 casualties and in at least 218,000 homeless and evacuated people. For 456 events in the catalog (12.9%) information exists that landslide events have caused direct damage to the population, but the exact or approximate extent of the damage remains unknown [*Salvati et al.*, 2010]. Qualitative information on the number of casualties is abundant in the oldest portion of the catalog, and quantitative information on the homeless and the evacuees is most abundant after 1900.

14.3.1. Temporal Distribution of Landslide Events

The historical record lists 3545 harmful landslides, 53 of which (1.5%) are undated. The oldest landslide in the record that probably resulted in deaths was caused by an earthquake that occurred in the Modena province, Northern Italy, in 91 BC. During this event, landslides destroyed rural settlements [*Boschi et al.*, 1995], but the number and type of the human consequences remain uncertain. Since then, for 60 landslides in the historical record only qualitative information on the consequences is available (open squares in Figure 14.1). The first event in the catalog with a known number of fatalities (24 deaths) occurred in 843 AD at Ceppo Morelli, in the Piedmont region, Northern Italy.

Inspection of the Figure 14.1 shows that the number of reported events has increased significantly after 1700,

and considerably after 1900. The severity of the recorded events, measured by the number of casualties, has also changed with time. The few landslide events recorded in the oldest portion of the catalog caused a large number of casualties, although the largest disaster due to a single landslide occurred on 9 October 1963, when 1917 people were killed by the Vajont rockslide.

During the 1018 year period 843–1860, 131 landslide events have caused at least 8979 casualties, with an average of 68.5 casualties per event. The figure decreased to 4.7 casualties per event in the 100 year period 1861–1960, the result of 698 events with 3286 total casualties. In the most recent period 1961–2011, the average number of casualties per event has increased to 7.0. Differences in the average number of casualties per event indicate that the oldest events reported in the historical record were mainly catastrophic, but also that the first part of the record is incomplete for the medium- and the low-severity events [*Guzzetti*, 2000]. In the record, lack of occurrences in any given period may be due either to incompleteness or to variations in the conditions that led to slope failures, including climate anomalies, rainfall events, land-use changes, and human actions [*Glade et al.*, 2001; *Guzzetti et al.*, 2005b].

Figure 14.2a shows the monthly distribution of landslide events with casualties, and the number of landslide casualties in Italy, in the 151 year period 1861–2011. In this period, damaging landslides were common in all seasons, with a peak in the autumn when 436 harmful events (30.2%) have resulted in 4429 landslide casualties (51.8%). The majority of the landslide events (192) occurred in November, and the largest number of casualties were recorded in October (3441). To investigate possible variations in time of the monthly distribution of landslide

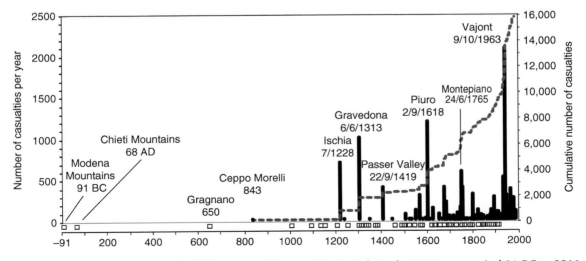

Figure 14.1 Historical record of landslide events with casualties in Italy in the 2102 year period 91 BC to 2011. Open squares show landslide events for which casualties occurred in unknown numbers. Dashed line shows the cumulative number of landslide casualties.

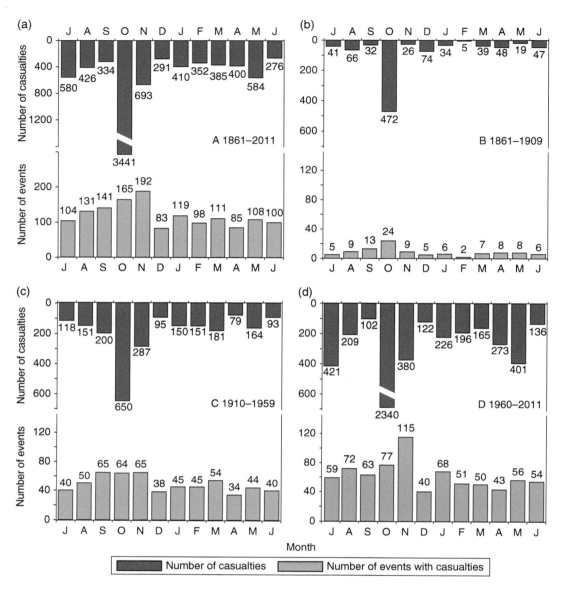

Figure 14.2 Monthly distribution of landslide events with casualties in Italy in the 151 year period 1861–2011 (a) and for three periods 1861–1909 (b), 1910–1959 (c), and 1960–2011 (d).

events with casualties, we segmented the historical catalog in three 50 year periods, that is, 1861–1909, 1910–1959, and 1960–2011 (Figure 14.2b–d).

Inspection of the bar charts reveals the strong increase in the number of casualties in October due to the Vajont catastrophe (broken columns in Figure 14.2a and d). It is also possible to see a slight variation in the monthly distribution of the landslide events with the peak value shifting from October to November. We explain the differences with possible variations in the distribution of the precipitation in the considered periods, possibly driven by climate changes.

14.3.2. Geographical Analysis

Information on the precise or approximate location of landslides with human consequences in Italy is available for most of the events listed in the historical record (97.6%). Figure 14.3 portrays the location of 3021 sites that have experienced one or more landslide events with human consequences. Harmful landslide events occurred in all of the 20 Italian regions, and in 1761 of the 8102 Italian municipalities (21.7%). As we described in previous investigations, the sites affected by harmful landslides are not distributed equally in Italy. Harmful landslides in the

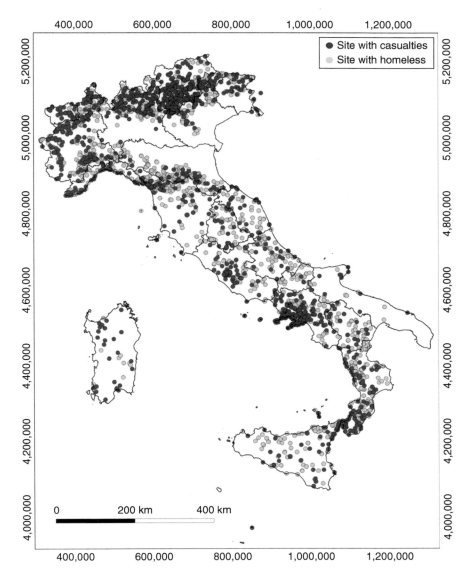

Figure 14.3 Map showing the location of 3021 sites affected by landslide events with direct consequences to the population in Italy in the 2102 year period 91 BC to 2011. Coordinate Reference System EPGS: 23032. Black dots show location of sites with landslide casualties (deaths, missing persons, injured people). Gray dots show location of sites with homeless and evacuated people.

historical record were more common in the Alps, in the Piedmont, and Liguria regions in Northern Italy, and in the Campania and Calabria regions in Southern Italy. Harmful landslide events occurred at many sites, but only at few sites human consequences were frequent [*Salvati et al.*, 2003; *Guzzetti et al.*, 2005b]. Using order statistics [*David and Nagaraja*, 2003], we find that of the 3021 landslide sites in the historical record, 2710 were affected once, 310 sites were affected 2 or more times, 8 sites were affected 5 or more times, and only 2 sites were affected 10 or more times. This indicates not only that landslide risk to the population is widespread in Italy but also that there are few sites where harmful events are frequent.

The geographical persistence of landslides is highest in Campania, the region that experienced the largest number of landslide casualties (4105) in Southern Italy.

In our previous study, we analyzed the distribution of the number of landslide casualties in the 20 Italian regions for different periods (Figure 14.4). We used this temporal analysis to describe the most catastrophic and relevant landslide events that occurred in Italy. In the period 843–1860, a period for which we consider the historical catalog to be incomplete, the region that experienced the largest number of landslide casualties was Lombardy (2498; Figure 14.4c). In this region, the first catastrophic event occurred in June 1313 when a debris

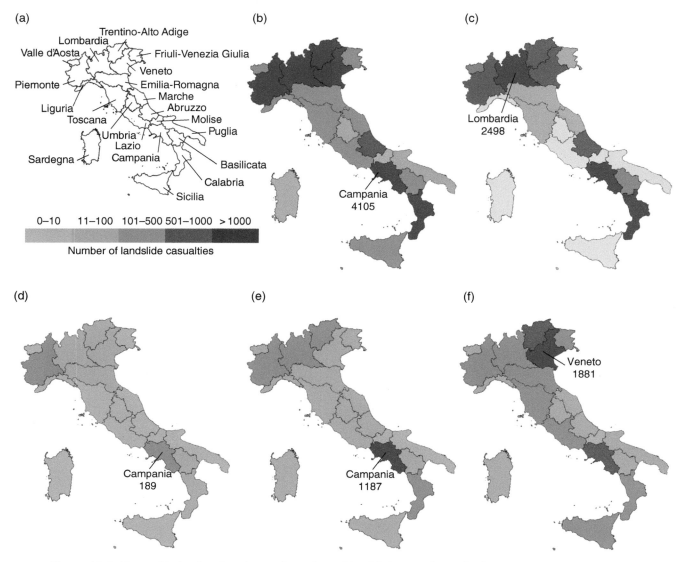

Figure 14.4 Maps of Italy showing the total number of landslide casualties (deaths, missing persons, injured people) in the 20 Italian regions for five periods. (a) Index map showing location and names of the 20 Italian regions. (b) Period 843–2011, (c) Period 843–1860, (d) Period 1861–1909, (e) Period 1910–1959, and (f) Period 1960–2011. Increasing shades of gray show increasing number of casualties.

flow destroyed the village of Gravedona, on the northern shore of Lake Como, completely submerging the village and killing ~1000 residents. The second catastrophic event occurred during the night of 4 September 1618 at Piuro, when 1200 people were buried by a rock avalanche that destroyed the village [*Guzzetti et al.*, 2005a]. Between 1861 and 1959, the Campania region suffered the largest number of casualties (Figure 14.4d and e), the result of destructive events which occurred chiefly in the Salerno area. In the most recent part of the record (1960–2011), the Veneto region, Northern Italy, experienced the largest number of casualties (1881; Figure 14.4f), most of which was caused by the 9 October 1963 Vajont rockslide. In the

same period, the Campania region suffered the second largest number of casualties (792). The large number of casualties in Campania, historically and in the recent period, is the result of soil slips, debris flows, and mud flows in areas where a cover of volcanic ash overlies limestone on steep slopes, a highly hazardous geological setting typical of the area surrounding the Vesuvius volcano [*Vallario*, 2001; *Aceto et al.*, 2003; *Guzzetti et al.*, 2005b].

For this work, we have studied the geographical variation in the number of landslide events, and in the number of landslide casualties, in the five subdivisions established by the Italian National Institute of Statistics (ISTAT, web site: www.istat.it): 1, mountain; 2, coastal mountain; 3, hill;

Table 14.2 Number of Landslide Events with Casualties and Number of Landslide Casualties for Each Physiographical Subdivision in Three Main Geographical Areas (North, Center, and South) in Italy in the 151 Year Period 1861–2011

	ISTAT Physiographical Subdivisions	Area		Events		Casualties	
		km²	%	#	#/100 km²	#	#/100 km²
North	1: Mountain	54,958	18.24	550	1.001	3947	7.182
	2: Coastal Mountain	481	0.16	8	1.662	39	8.104
	3: Hill	21,257	7.50	96	0.452	449	2.112
	4: Coastal Hill	1682	0.56	24	1.427	44	2.616
	5: Plain	41,882	13.90	9	0.021	14	0.033
Center	1: Mountain	22,368	7.42	43	0.192	133	0.595
	2: Coastal Mountain	302	0.11	16	5.295	51	16.88
	3: Hill	30,595	10.15	54	0.176	180	0.588
	4: Coastal Hill	10,171	3.38	32	0.315	160	1.573
	5: Plain	5379	1.78	51	0.948	106	1.971
South	1: Mountain	24,087	18.24	56	0.232	235	0.976
	2: Coastal Mountain	3914	1.30	41	1.048	228	5.825
	3: Hill	39,464	13.1	80	0.203	373	0.945
	4: Coastal Hill	22,250	7.38	276	1.240	1972	8.863
	5: Plain	22,547	7.48	55	0.244	249	1.104

4, coastal hill; and 5, plain. The five subdivisions are the result of the aggregation of adjacent municipalities, based on average terrain elevation values, and distance to the seacoast. The subdivisions are therefore based on administrative limits and physiographical conditions. We analyzed the distribution separately in the north, center, and south of Italy. Northern Italy (120×10^3 km², 39.9%) encompasses the Italian Alps, the Po, and Veneto plains, and part of the northern Apennines; Central Italy (69×10^3 km², 22.9%) comprises the central Apennines, the northern and central Tyrrhenian coast, and the central Adriatic coas; and Southern Italy (112×10^3 km², 37.2%) consists of the southern Apennines, the southern Tyrrhenian and Adriatic coasts, the Ionian coast, Sicily, and Sardinia. Table 14.2 shows that the largest number of landslide events with casualties (550) in the record was reported in the mountain subdivision of Northern Italy. In this physiographical subdivision, which includes the Alps, high intensity and prolonged rainfall events, combined with the availability of debris on steep slopes, have resulted in several destructive debris flows. The presence of large relative relief and hard rocks (e.g., granite, metamorphic rocks, massive limestone, and dolomite) has further facilitated the occurrence of rock falls, rock slides, and rock avalanches [*Guzzetti*, 2000], which are particularly hazardous landslide types due to their high mobility [*Cruden and Varnes*, 1996]. In Central Italy, the number of landslide events and landslide casualties is low, with the exception of the coastal mountain zone corresponding to the Apuane Alps in Tuscany. This area, which consists of five coastal mountain municipalities, is characterized by cumulated mean annual rainfall exceeding 3000 mm [*D'Amato Avanzi et al.*, 2004], and exhibits the largest spatial density of landslide casualties

(16.9 casualties/100 km²). In Southern Italy, landslide casualties are most abundant in the coastal hills (1972). In these areas, slopes are steep, relative relief is high, catchments are small, and rocks are highly tectonized and easily erodible [*Esposito et al.*, 2003; *Porfido et al.*, 2009].

We further studied the distribution and the frequency of harmful landslide events in each physiographical subdivision within the 20 Italian regions and results are shown in Tables 14.3 and 14.4. First, for each region, we calculated the percentage of the municipalities that experienced at least one harmful landslide event in each physiographical subdivision (Table 14.3). In the five subdivisions, less than half of the municipalities suffered landslide events, with the exception of the Apuane Alps, where all the municipalities have experienced at least one harmful landslide event. Next, we calculated the density of the harmful landslide events in each physiographical subdivision, and for each region. The density of the harmful events was calculated as the ratio between the total number of events in the considered area, and the total extent of the considered area in square kilometers (Table 14.4). The largest spatial density of events was measured in the coastal hills of Campania (0.18 events per square kilometer).

14.4. RISK EVALUATION

To study the temporal and geographical variations of landslide risk in Italy, we investigated the number of fatalities in relation to the size of the population, and we analyzed the frequency of the damaging events and the severity of the consequences, measured by the number of casualties. We used the former to determine individual

Table 14.3 Percentage of the Italian Municipalities, for Each Region, that Suffered Harmful Landslide Events, in the Five ISTAT Physiographical Subdivisions, for the Period 91 BC to 2011

		Percentage of Municipalities				
		1—Mountain	2—Coastal Mountain	3—Hill	4—Coastal Hill	5—Plain
North	Piemonte	36.89	—	17.21	—	4.32
	Valle d'Aosta	40.54	—	—	—	—
	Lombardia	32.70	—	6.85	—	0.53
	Trentino-Alto Adige	47.45	—	—	—	—
	Veneto	48.72	—	14.17	—	0.58
	Friuli-Venezia Giulia	41.38	—	25.00	—	1.82
	Liguria	14.14	63.64	7.14	32.53	—
	Emilia-Romagna	55.07	—	28.85	10.00	1.21
Center	Toscana	30.26	100.00	20.00	12.50	24.00
	Umbria	58.33	—	27.94	—	—
	Marche	23.25	—	10.75	11.65	—
	Lazio	10.00	—	15.94	38.23	23.53
	Abruzzo	19.28	—	18.18	16.44	—
South	Molise	11.90	—	19.51	18.18	—
	Campania	26.56	—	22.32	58.54	24.07
	Puglia	—	—	21.57	15.79	2.78
	Basilicata	29.33	33.33	34.04	—	66.67
	Calabria	29.79	47.46	25.47	32.81	27.27
	Sicilia	28.81	25.64	20.77	25.81	20.51
	Sardegna	11.76	—	6.14	14.46	3.70

Table 14.4 Density of Harmful Landslide Events for Each Region

		Number of Events/km^2				
		1—Mountain	2—Coastal Mountain	3—Hill	4—Coastal Hill	5—Plain
North	Piemonte	0.0201	—	0.0184	—	0.0025
	Valle d'Aosta	0.0129	—	—	—	—
	Lombardia	0.0288	—	0.0081	—	0.0003
	Trentino-Alto Adige	0.0262	—	—	—	—
	Veneto	0.0233	—	0.0105	—	0.0002
	Friuli-Venezia Giulia	0.0114	—	0.0138	0.0094	0.0007
	Liguria	0.0056	0.0727	0.0048	0.0332	—
	Emilia-Romagna	0.0139	—	0.0117	0.0048	0.0002
Center	Toscana	0.0090	0.0927	0.0033	0.0020	0.0098
	Umbria	0.0093	—	0.0080		—
	Marche	0.0045	—	0.0051	0.0069	—
	Lazio	0.0031	—	0.0059	0.0173	0.0197
	Abruzzo	0.0061	—	0.0145	0.0106	—
South	Molise	0.0061	—	0.0091	0.0036	—
	Campania	0.0117	—	0.0164	0.1837	0.0261
	Puglia	—	—	0.0024	0.0023	0.0005
	Basilicata	0.0075	0.0057	0.0073	—	0.0236
	Calabria	0.0123	0.0273	0.0128	0.0203	0.0066
	Sicilia	0.0043	0.0200	0.0044	0.0077	0.0033
	Sardegna	0.0012	—	0.0015	0.0020	0.0020

Density computed as the ratio of the total number of events in each subdivisions and the total area of the subdivision, in square kilometers, in the five ISTAT physiographical subdivisions, for the period 91 BC to 2011.

risk criteria, and the latter to determine societal risk levels [*Fell and Hartford*, 1997; *Guzzetti et al.*, 2005b; *Salvati et al.*, 2010]. To ascertain the individual and the societal landslide risk levels in Italy, we used the newly updated record of landslide events with casualties in Italy in the 150 year period 1861–2010.

14.4.1. Individual Landslide Risk

Individual risk levels are measured by mortality (or death) rates, which are given by the number of fatalities in a population, scaled to the size of the population, per unit time. In Italy, individual risk levels were first defined by *Guzzetti* [2000], and revised by *Salvati et al.* [2003] and *Guzzetti et al.* [2005b]. To calculate mortality, information on the number of fatalities and on the size of the population per year is required. We obtained (1) the number of landslide fatalities per year from the historical catalog of landslides with human consequences in Italy, and (2) information on the size of the population from general censuses data collected every 10 years by ISTAT, since 1861. For compatibility with previous studies [*Salvati et al.*, 2003, 2010; *Guzzetti et al.*, 2005a, 2005b], in this work mortality is the number of landslide fatalities per 100,000 people in a period of 1 year.

First, we investigated the distribution and the variation of the Italian population in the period 1861–2010. In this 150 year period, the population almost tripled, from 22.2 to 60.3 million. The increase was largest in the plains, moderate in the hills, and lowest in the mountains. From the 1920s, and increasingly in the second half of the 20th century, there was migration from mountainous areas to urban areas, which are generally located in the plains or lowland hills. Consequently, the increase in the size of the population in urban areas was larger than in the rural areas, and some of the hills and the mountains suffered net losses in the number of inhabitants [*Guzzetti et al.*, 2005a]. Analysis of Figure 14.5 reveals that in the ISTAT physiographical subdivisions the largest increase in population occurred in the plains, with a maximum increase of about 13 million in the Po and Veneto plains, in Northern Italy. Minor increases were observed in the hills, more precisely in the inland hills of Northern and Central Italy, and in the coastal hills of Southern Italy.

Using yearly information on the population of each physiographical subdivision, for the three main geographical subdivisions (North, Center, South), we calculated the yearly landslide mortality rates (LMR), and the corresponding average values, in the period 1861–2010 as shown in Figure 14.6. The largest average LMR was

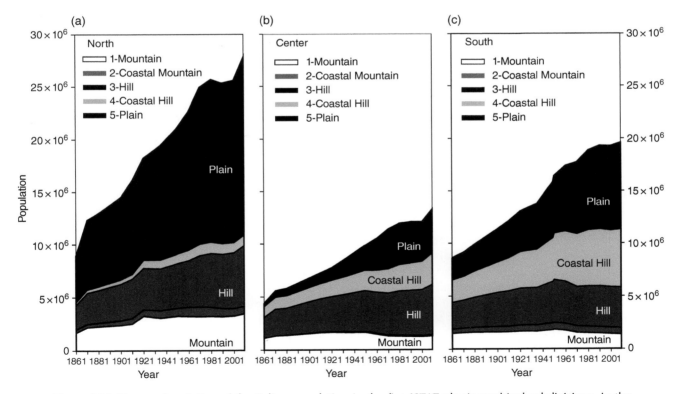

Figure 14.5 Temporal variation of the Italian population in the five ISTAT physiographical subdivisions, in the 150 year period 1861–2010, for the north (a), center (b), and south (c) areas of Italy. Shades of gray show different physiographical subdivisions: 1, mountain; 2, coastal mountain; 3, hill; 4, coastal hill; 5, plain.

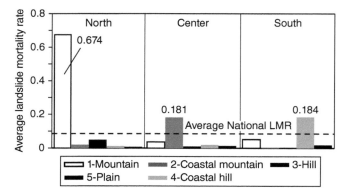

Figure 14.6 Average LMR in the five ISTAT physiographical subdivisions, and in the north, center, and south of Italy, for the 150 year period 1861–2010. Black dashed line shows average LMR for the whole of Italy.

Table 14.5 Average LMR in the Five ISTAT Physiographical Subdivisions, and in the North, Centre, and South of Italy, for Three 50 Year Periods: 1861–1909, 1910–1959, and 1960–2010

		1861–1909	1910–1959	1960–2010
North	1: Mountain	0.222	0.208	1.567
	2: Coastal Mountain	0.005	0.003	0.051
	3: Hill	0.060	0.054	0.032
	4: Coastal Hill	—	0.016	0.021
	5: Plain	$8.2E^{-4}$	$3.9E^{-4}$	$6.4E^{-4}$
Center	1: Mountain	0.014	0.051	0.042
	2: Coastal Mountain	0.067	0.103	0.369
	3: Hill	$7.3E^{-4}$	0.023	0.014
	4: Coastal Hill	—	0.049	0.009
	5: Plain	—	0.027	0.014
South	1: Mountain	0.012	0.090	0.052
	2: Coastal Mountain	0.004	0.350	0.139
	3: Hill	0.028	0.020	0.034
	4: Coastal Hill	0.048	0.452	0.048
	5: Plain	—	0.010	0.045

recorded in the mountains of Northern Italy (0.674), followed by the coastal hills of Southern Italy (0.184), and by the coastal mountains of Central Italy (0.181). The smallest LMRs, in the range 0.0006–0.002, were measured in the plains. Overall, the national LMR in the observation period was 0.084.

To investigate the temporal variation of landslide mortality, we calculated the average LMR for three subsequent periods: 1861–1909, 1910–1959, and 1960–2010. Results are shown in Table 14.5. In the most recent period (1960–2010), mortality increased in the mountains of Northern Italy and in the coastal mountains of Central Italy. In Southern Italy, mortality decreased slightly in the mountains, and significantly in the coastal hills. The marked increase of mortality in the mountains of the Northern Italy was primarily the result of two high-impact events: (1) the 9 October 1963 Vajont rockslide with 1917 casualties, and (2) the 19 July 1985 Stava mudslide, caused by embankment failure at the Prestavel mine, with 268 casualties. The two disasters are both related to the presence or the failure of man-made structures. Excluding the two events from the analysis, the average landslide mortality in the mountains of Northern Italy in the period 1960–2010 was very similar to the mortality measured in the same area for the previous periods. We conclude that, in Italy, individual landslide risk has not increased significantly in the last 150 years, with the exception of the coastal mountains of Central Italy, corresponding chiefly to the Apuane Alps.

We have further investigated the variation of the LMRs for events of increasing intensity (i.e., an increasing number of fatalities per event), and we have analyzed their temporal variation for the three considered periods 1861–1909, 1910– 1959, and 1960–2010. For the

purpose, we divided the historical record into three intensity classes: (1) low intensity (1–5 fatalities), (2) medium intensity (6–50 fatalities), and (3) high intensity (>50 fatalities). We then calculated the average LMR for each intensity class, for the five physiographical subdivisions, in Northern, Central, and Southern Italy, and for the three considered periods. Results are shown in Figure 14.7; since the scarcity of high-intensity data, in the histograms, the high-intensity class are considered together with the medium class. Figure 14.7 allows for the following general considerations: (1) the largest LMR (0.349) was measured in the coastal hills of Southern Italy in the period 1910–1959, and was the result of high-intensity events that each caused more than 50 fatalities; (2) high-intensity events (>50 fatalities) are rare in the record, and those that occurred in the most recent period in the mountains (i.e., the 1963 Vajont rockslide and the 1985 Stava mudflow) were related to the presence or the failure of man-made structures; (3) for medium-intensity events (causing 6–50 fatalities), landslide mortality remained substantially constant in the mountains and the coastal mountains, decreased slightly in the hills of Northern Italy, in the 150 year observation period; and (4) in the most recent period 1960–2010, the risk posed by low-intensity events (causing 1–5 fatalities) increased slightly in the mountains of Central and Southern Italy, in the coastal mountains of Northern and Central Italy, and in the coastal hills.

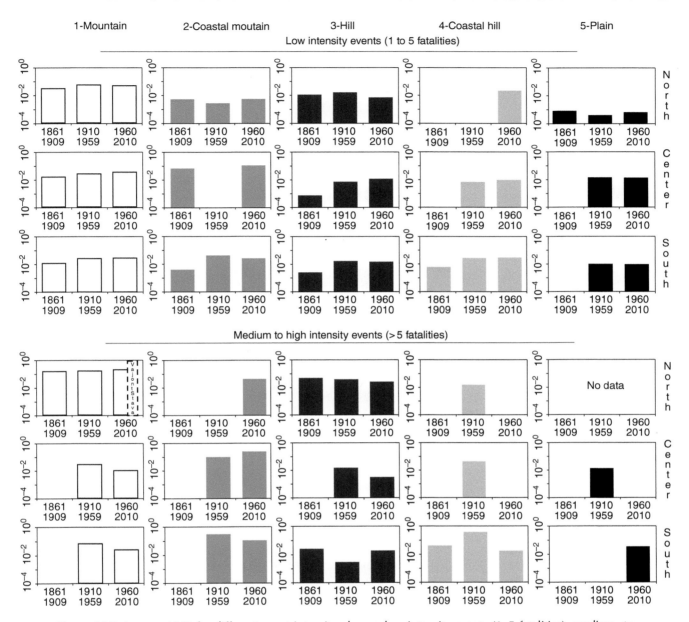

Figure 14.7 Average LMR for different event intensity classes: low-intensity events (1–5 fatalities), medium- to high-intensity events (>5 fatalities) in the five ISTAT physiographical subdivisions, and in the north, center, and south of Italy, for three periods: 1861–1909, 1910–1959, and 1960–2010.

14.4.2. Societal Landslide Risk

To determine societal landslide risk in Italy, we constructed frequency-consequences plots, and we used the plots to investigate the relationships between the (noncumulative) probability of the events and the severity of the consequences, measured by the number of the casualties. To establish societal risk, we adopted the method proposed by *Guzzetti et al.* [2005b], and modified by *Salvati et al.* [2010]. In this method, the empirical probability distribution of the landslide casualties is modeled by a Zipf

distribution. The Zipf distribution, defined for a population of finite size, prescribes a power-law probability for the size of an event, given that the size can take an integer value of at least one [*Reed*, 2001; *Newman*, 2005; *Rossi et al.*, 2010]. For a Zipf distribution, the probability mass function (PMF) is given by

$$\text{PMF}(c;c,N) = \left(c^s H_{N,s}\right)^{-1} \quad (14.1)$$

where c is the number of casualties per event, s is the scaling exponent for the Zipf distribution that measures the proportion of small versus large events, N is the largest number of casualties in a single event in the dataset, and

$$H_{N,s} = \sum_{c=1}^{N} C^{-s}$$

with $S \in \mathbb{R}^+$; $c \in \{1, 2, \ldots, N\}$.

To determine the PMF of the landslide events with casualties from the empirical data, we adopted a maximum likelihood estimation approach [*White et al.*, 2008]. We further adopted a "bootstrapping" re-sampling procedure [*Efron*, 1979; *Davison and Hinkley*, 2006] to estimate the mean value of the Zipf parameter ($s_{\text{mean-boot}}$), and the associated variability (σ_s).

Salvati et al. [2010] used the scaling exponent s of the Zipf distribution to compare societal landside risk at the regional scale in Italy. Regions that exhibited the largest risk levels (largest $s = 2.33$) were Trentino-Alto Adige (Northern Italy) and Campania (Southern Italy), whereas the Emilia Romagna had the lowest value of $s = 1.30$. Interpretation of the geographical variation of the s values was somewhat uncertain, because the analysis of societal risk was based on administrative subdivisions with little relation to the physical settings, and because the standard error ε associated with the estimation of the s value was high for some of the regions, a result of the reduced number of events in the catalog for these regions.

To overcome these limitations, we have performed a new analysis using a topographical (morphometric) subdivision of Italy based on a semi-quantitative, stepwise approach that combined a cluster analysis of four derivatives of altitude, visual interpretation of morphometric maps, and comparative inspection of small-scale geological and structural maps [*Guzzetti and Reichenbach*, 1994]. The classification has divided Italy into eight major physiographical provinces from the aggregation of 30 minor divisions that reflect physical, geological, and structural

differences in the Italian landscape (Table 14.6). We used these major physiographical provinces to calculate new landslide societal risk levels. For each physiographical province, the s Zipf parameter was determined for the period 1861–2010. We excluded from the analysis the North Italian Plain province, because of the lack of sufficient data in the historical record. To evaluate the performance of the Zipf model plots [*Wilk and Gnanadesikan*, 1968], we performed 2-sample Kolmogorov–Smirnov tests [*Kolmogorov*, 1933; *Smirnov*, 1933]. In Table 14.7 low values of the ks statistic, and large values of the p-value, indicate a better model fit.

The Zipf models (Figure 14.8 and Table 14.7) give the expected relative proportion of small, medium, and large events, with the total number of casualties in an event measuring the severity of the event. The scaling exponent s (the slope of the Zipf distribution) can be used to compare the proportion of events characterized by different levels of severity in the various provinces. The provinces that exhibit steep Zipf curves (large-scaling exponents s) have a smaller probability of experiencing severe events when compared to those that have less steep curves (small exponents s) and for which the relative proportion of severe events is larger. Table 14.7 shows that, in the considered provinces, s varies between 1.48 and 1.97 (mean, $\mu = 1.71$, standard deviation, $\sigma = 0.15$). We argue that the large variation depends on (1) the physiographical and climatic settings that determine the local susceptibility to harmful landslide events in the different provinces; (2) the frequency and intensity of the triggers, including intense or prolonged rainfall, in the different provinces; (3) the size of the physiographical provinces; and (4) the distribution of the population at risk in the different provinces.

Societal landslide risk depends on the relative proportion of small, medium, and large severity events, which controls the slope of the Zipf distribution, and on the temporal frequency of the events, that is, on the number

Table 14.6 Major Physiographical Provinces in Italy, Obtained from the Topographical Divisions of Italy Proposed by *Guzzetti and Reichenbach* [1994]

	Physiographical Provinces	Abbreviation	Minor Divisions
1	Alpine Mountain System	Alps	Western Alps, Central-Eastern Alps, Carso, Alpine Foothills
2	North Italian Plain	PoPl	Po Plain, Veneto Plain
3	Alpine-Apennines Transition Zone	AlAp	Monferrato Hills, Ligurian Upland
4	Apennines Mountain System	Apen	Northern Apennines, Central Apennines, Molise Apennines, Molise-Lucanian Hills, Lucanian Apennines, Sila, Aspromonte, Sicilian Apennines
5	Tyrrhenian Lowland	Tyrr	Central Italian Hills, Tosco-Laziale Section, Lazio- Campanian Section
6	Adriatic Lowland	Adri	Central Apennine Slope, Murge-Apulia Section, Gargano Upland
7	Sicily	Sici	Marsala Lowland, Sicilian Hills, Iblei Plateau, Etna
8	Sardinia	Sard	Sardinian Hills, Gennargentu Highland, Campidano Plain, Iglesiente Hills

Table 14.7 Societal Landslide Risk in Italy

Parameter	Alps	AlAp	Apen	Tyrr	Adri	Sici	Sard
Number of events (n)	624	50	356	300	36	25	30
Largest number of casualties per event (N)	1917	19	20	30	33	100	14
Zipf parameter (s)	1.972	1.483	1.593	1.729	1.683	1.708	1.796
Standard error s (ε)	0.042	0.159	0.042	0.065	0.181	0.187	0.251
KS D-statistic (ks)	0.045	0.120	0.070	0.157	0.083	0.120	0.133
KS —-value (p)	0.556	0.864	0.344	0.001	1.000	0.994	0.952
Mean s bootstrap ($s_{mean\text{-}boot}$)	1.965	1.476	1.582	1.721	1.716	1.700	1.823
Standard deviation s bootstrap (σ_s)	0.022	0.093	0.019	0.035	0.086	0.080	0.117
N samples bootstrap (n_{boot})	16	200	28	33	278	400	333

Scaling exponent (s) and associated standard error (ε) for Zipf models obtained through maximum likelihood estimation of empirical casualty data for the period 1861–2010. KS D-statistic (ks) and KS p-value (p) measure the performance of the Zipf models. Mean s bootstrap ($s_{mean\text{-}boot}$) and the standard deviation s bootstrap (σ_s) obtained using a bootstrapping resampling procedure.

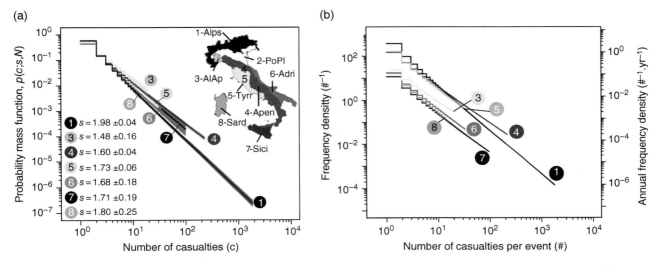

Figure 14.8 Societal landslide risk in the physiographical provinces. For the 150 year period 1861–2010, the plot on the left shows the PMF of landslide events with casualties (a). Map shows location of the physiographical provinces in Italy. Different shades of gray used for different provinces (Table 14.6). The plot on the right (b) shows the frequency density (left y-axis) and the annual frequency density (right y-axis) of landslide events with casualties in the Italian physiographical provinces against the severity of the landslide events (x-axis) measured by the total number of casualties in the 150 year period 1861–2010.

of events in a period, or per unit time (e.g., a year). For each physiographical province, we normalized the PMF to the total number of events with casualties in the province (Figure 14.8b). A close inspection of the plot allows us to comment on the risk levels in the different physiographical provinces, as a function of the severity of the events, measured by the number of casualties. Based on the visual inspection of Figure 14.8b, we have selected three severity classes: low-severity events (landslides that can result in 10 casualties or less), medium-severity events (from 11 to 20 casualties), and high-severity events (more than 20 casualties). The Alpine Mountain System has the highest probability of experiencing low-severity events.

The trend changes with the increase in the landslide severity. For medium-severity events, the Apennines Mountain System has nearly the same probability as the Alpine Mountain System of experiencing events. Finally, the Apennines Mountain System has the largest probability of causing high-severity events.

14.5. COMPARISON TO OTHER NATURAL HAZARDS

In Italy, landslides are not the only natural hazard that poses a threat to the population. Floods, earthquakes, and volcanic activity are other types of hazards with

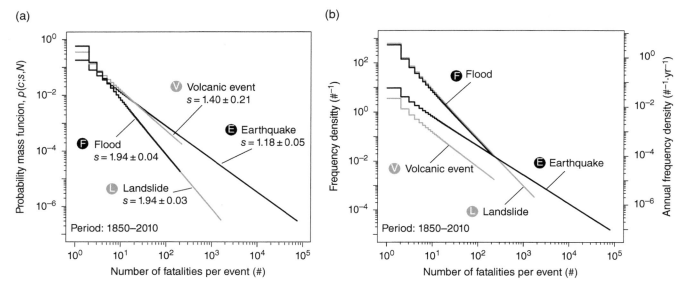

Figure 14.9 Comparison of societal risk levels to the population of Italy posed by earthquakes (E), floods (F), landslides (L), and volcanic events (V) with fatalities (deaths and missing persons) in the period 1861–2010. (a) PMF of events with fatalities (y-axis) against the severity of the events (x-axis), measured by the total number of fatalities. (b) Frequency density (left y-axis) and annual frequency density (right y-axis) of events against the severity of the events (x-axis), measured by the total number of fatalities.

human consequences in Italy [*Guzzetti*, 2000; *Salvati et al.*, 2003, 2012; *Guzzetti et al.*, 2005a]. In this section, using the results of our previous findings [*Salvati et al.*, 2012], we compare levels of societal landslide risk to the risk posed by floods, earthquakes, and volcanic activity in Italy. For the purpose, we used the catalog of floods with human consequences in Italy compiled by *Salvati et al.* [2010], and the catalogs of earthquakes and of volcanic events with human consequences in Italy prepared by *Guzzetti et al.* [2005a]. The updated catalogs cover the periods: (1) AD 589 to 2010 for floods (40,572 fatalities in 1068 events in 1422 years), (2) AD 51 to 2010 for earthquakes (331,560 fatalities in 135 events, in 1960 years), and (3) AD 79 to 2010 for volcanic events (35,340 fatalities in 17 events, in 1932 years).

Details on the approach used for the analysis are given in *Salvati et al.* [2012]. The analysis was performed using the fatalities data (deaths and missing persons), and not casualty data, because for earthquakes and for volcanic events systematic information on injured people was not available. The analysis cover the period 1850–2010.

The slope of the distributions shown in Figure 14.9 allows for a quantitative comparison of the different societal risk posed by floods (F), landslides (L), earthquakes (E), and volcanic events (V). The scaling exponents s for landslides and floods are identical ($s = 1.94$), and the uncertainty in the estimation of the scaling parameter, measured by the standard errors ($\varepsilon = 0.04$ for floods and $\varepsilon = 0.03$ for landslides), indicates that the two distributions are

statistically indistinguishable. As *Salvati et al.*, in 2012 found, the relative proportion of large versus small fatal events is the same in Italy for floods and landslides. Further inspection of Figure 14.9a reveals that the scaling exponents of the Zipf distributions for earthquakes ($s = .18$) and volcanic events ($s = 1.40$) are significantly smaller than those obtained for floods and landslides ($s = 1.94$). Even considering the uncertainty associated with the estimates of the scaling parameter s ($\varepsilon = 0.05$ for earthquakes and $\varepsilon = 0.21$ for volcanic events), the proportion of large versus small fatal events caused by geological triggers (i.e., earthquake and volcanic events) is significantly larger than the proportion of fatal events caused by meteorological triggers (floods and for landslides).

To consider the severity (measured by the number of fatalities) and the temporal frequency of the different hazards, we scaled the PMF shown in Figure 14.9a to the total number of harmful events, for the different hazards (Figure 14.9b). Visual analysis of Figure 14.9b allows for the following considerations. For the events with <100 fatalities, the frequency of landslides and floods is significantly larger than the frequency of earthquakes, which is larger than the frequency of volcanic events. In the same period, for events with more than 100 fatalities, harmful earthquakes were more frequent than any of the other hazards. We maintain that the observed differences measure the different ways in which floods, landslides, earthquakes, and volcanic events interact with the built-up environment and the population.

14.6. CONNECTIONS BETWEEN LANDSLIDES AND OTHER HAZARDS

Landslides can be triggered or can cause other hazards. Landslides are triggered by earthquakes [*Keefer*, 1984, 2013; *Fortunato et al.*, 2012] and by primary or secondary volcanic activity [*Moore et al.*, 1994; *Masson et al.*, 2002; *Frattini et al.*, 2004; *McMurtry et al.*, 2004; *De Vita et al.*, 2006]. Landslides can cause tsunamis [*Moore et al.*, 1994; *Locat and Lee*, 2009], and the failure of landslide dams can result in catastrophic flash floods and inundations [*Schuster*, 1986; *Costa and Schuster*, 1988; *Ermini and Casagli*, 2002]. We searched the historical record of harmful landslides in Italy for failures related to (i.e., triggered by or causing) other hazards, and particularly (1) for harmful landslides caused by earthquakes or volcanic activity and (2) for destructive flash floods caused by the collapse of landslide dams.

Although earthquake-induced landslides are one of the most hazardous secondary effects of earthquakes [*Prestininzi and Romeo*, 2000; *Carro et al.*, 2003], the number of events with human consequences in the Italian historical record is limited. The catalog lists 15 earthquake-induced landslides with human consequences, of which 11 landslides caused deaths or injured people and 5 landslides caused evacuees and homeless (Figure 14.10 and Table 14.8). Two of the listed earthquake-induced landslide caused many fatalities as a consequence of landslide tsunamis. On 6 February 1783, the 5.8 M Calabria earthquake triggered a landslide of about $V_L = 5 \times 10^6\, m^3$ (ID 5 in Table 14.8 and Figure 14.10). The rock avalanche fell from Monte Paci, near the village of Scilla, Southern Calabria, in the Tyrrhenian Sea and produced a tsunami with a 16 m high run-up. The landslide-generated tsunami killed about 1500 people [*Mazzanti and Bozzano*, 2011]. On 28 December 1908, the 7.1 M Messina earthquake produced a large tsunami that killed at least 60,000 people. *Billi et al.* [2008] argued that a submarine landslide (ID 8 in Table 14.8 and Figure 14.10) might have caused the tsunami.

The historical catalog lists eight damaging flash floods related to the failure of landslide dams (Figure 14.8, Table 14.8). The number of fatalities caused by these

Figure 14.10 Location of harmful historical landslides caused by earthquakes (black dots), and of harmful flash floods produced by the collapse of landslide dams (gray dots) in Italy. See Table 14.8 for further information on the events.

Table 14.8 Harmful Landslide Events Triggered by or Causing Other Hazards, Particularly Harmful Landslides Caused by Earthquakes and Destructive Flash Floods Caused by the Collapse of Landslide Dams

ID	Related Hazard	Location	Date	Damage to the Population
1	Earthquake	Emilia-Romagna	91 BC	Undetermined fatalities
2	Earthquake	Veneto	07/01/1117	Undetermined fatalities and homeless
3	Earthquake	Marche	30/04/1279	Undetermined fatalities
4	Earthquake	Emilia-Romagna	24/12/1779	Undetermined homeless
5	Earthquake	Calabria	06/02/1783	1300 fatalities
6	Earthquake	Campania	09/04/1853	Undetermined fatalities
7	Earthquake	Basilicata	17/12/1857	Tens of fatalities
8	Earthquake	Sicilia	28/12/1908	Undetermined fatalities
9	Earthquake	Friuli-Venezia Giulia	06/05/1976	1 dead
10	Earthquake	Basilicata	09/09/1998	1 dead
11	Earthquake	Trentino-Alto Adige	17/07/2001	2 deaths and 2 injured people
12	Earthquake	Trentino-Alto Adige	17/07/2001	1 dead
13	Earthquake	Molise	31/10/2002	Undetermined homeless
14	Earthquake	Lombardia	25/11/2004	Undetermined homeless
15	Earthquake	Umbria	15/12/2009	Undetermined homeless
16	Landslide dams	Trentino-Alto Adige	22/09/1419	400 deaths
17	Landslide dams	Piemonte	17/10/1610	13 deaths
18	Landslide dams	Emilia-Romagna	11/04/1690	10 deaths
19	Landslide dams	Friuli-Venezia Giulia	15/08/1692	Undetermined fatalities and homeless
20	Landslide dams	Trentino-Alto Adige	31/05/1826	52 deaths and 238 homeless
21	Landslide dams	Valle d'Aosta	31/10/1840	80 deaths
22	Landslide dams	Lombardia	1855	Undetermined homeless
23	Landslide dams	Piemonte	23/08/1900	7 deaths

events varies from a few tens to a few hundreds, confirming that these types of landslide-induced hazards are extremely dangerous to the population.

14.7. CONCLUSIONS

We used a unique historical record of landslide events with human consequences to update the estimates of the individual and the societal landslide risk in Italy [*Salvati et al.*, 2003, 2010; *Guzzetti et al.*, 2005a, 2005b]. Analysis of the geographical distribution of the sites where landslide have caused damage to people, between 91 BC and 2011, has confirmed that landslides with human consequences are most abundant in the mountain zone of Northern Italy, and in the coastal hill of Southern Italy. In Italy, landslide mortality depends on the physiographical setting and the intensity of the events. In the recent period 1960–2010, landslide mortality has increased in the mountains of Northern Italy and in the coastal mountains of Central Italy. In Southern Italy, mortality has decreased slightly in the mountains, and significantly in the coastal hills. In the same period, the individual risk posed by low-intensity events has increased slightly in several areas in Italy.

Studying the frequency and the severity of the landslide events with casualties, we updated the measures of societal landslide risk in Italy. We modeled the historical landslide casualty data in seven physiographical provinces, and we showed that the Alps has the largest probability of experiencing low-severity landslide events. The behavior changes with increasing event intensity, with the Apennines exhibiting the largest probability of experiencing high-severity events.

A comparative analysis of the societal risk posed by landslides, floods, earthquakes, and volcanic events in Italy, confirmed that the frequency and severity of the geological events (earthquakes and volcanic activity) and of the meteorologically induced events (floods and landslides) are different [*Guzzetti et al.*, 2005a]. For the less severe events, the frequency of harmful landslides and floods is larger than the frequency of harmful earthquakes and volcanic events. For catastrophic events (with more than 100 fatalities), earthquakes are more frequent than all the other hazards.

We expect the results of our study to improve the understanding of the risk posed by landslides and the other natural hazards to the population of Italy. The study provides information for comparing the risk levels posed by natural hazards with the risk posed by other societal and technological hazards, and the leading medical causes of death in Italy [*Salvati et al.*, 2003], and with the levels of risk perceived and accepted by society in Italy. Further, the study provides the rationale for establishing insurance, and the design of national and regional landslide risk reduction strategies.

ACKNOWLEDGMENTS

This Research is supported by the Italian National Department for Civil Protection (DPC). We are grateful to two referees and the editor for their constructive comments that improved the quality of the manuscript.

REFERENCES

Aceto, L., L. Antronico, G. Gullà, D. Niceforo, A. Scalzo, M. Sorriso-Valvo, and P. G. Nicoletti (2003), *Suscettibilità alle colate rapide di fango in alcune aree della Campania*, Rubettino Industrie Grafiche ed Editoriali, Soveria Mannelli.

Billi, A., R. Funiciello, L. Minelli, C. Faccenna, G. Neri, B. Orecchio, and D. Presti (2008), On the cause of the 1908 Messina tsunami, southern Italy, *Geophys. Res. Lett.*, *35*, L06301, doi:10.1029/2008GL033251.

Boschi, E., G. Ferrari, P. Gasperini, E. Guidoboni, G. Smirglio, and G. Valensise (Eds.) (1995), *Catalogo dei forti terremoti in Italia dal 41 a.C. al 1980*, ING-SGA, Bologna.

Carro, M., M. De Amicis, L. Luzi, and S. Marzorati (2003), The application of predictive modeling techniques to landslides induced by earthquakes: The case study of 26 September 1997 Umbria-Marche earthquake (Italy), *Eng. Geol.*, *36*, 139–159.

Cascini, L., S. Ferlisi, and E. Vitolo (2008), Individual and societal risk owing to landslides in the Campania region (southern Italy), *Georisk*, *2*(3), 125–140, doi:10.1080/17499510802291310.

Costa, J. E. and R. L. Schuster (1988), The formation and failure of natural dams, *Geol. Soc. Am. Bull.*, *100*, 1054–1068.

Cruden, D. M. and D. J. Varnes (1996), Landslide types and processes, in *Landslides, Investigation and Mitigation*, Transportation Research Board Special Report 247, edited by A. K. Turner and R. L. Schuster, pp. 36–75, Transportation Research Board, Washington D.C.

Cruden, D.M. and R. Fell (Eds.) (1997), Landslide risk assessment, *Proceedings International Workshop on Landslide Risk Assessment*, Honolulu, 19–21 February *1997*, A.A. Balkema Publisher, Rotterdam.

D'Amato Avanzi, G., R. Giannecchini, and A. Puccinelli (2004), The influence of the geomorphological settings on shallow landslides. An example in a temperate climate environment: The June 19, 1996 event in northwestern Tuscany (Italy), *Eng. Geol.*, *73*, 215–228.

David, H. A. and H. N. Nagaraja (2003), *Order Statistics*, 3rd ed., John Wiley & Sons, Inc., Hoboken, NJ.

Davison, A. C. and D. Hinkley (2006), *Bootstrap Methods and Their Applications*, Cambridge Series in Statistical and Probabilistic Mathematics, 8th ed., Cambridge University Press, Cambridge.

De Vita, P., D. Agrello, and F. Ambrosino (2006), Landslide susceptibility assessment in ash-fall pyroclastic deposits surrounding Mount Somma-Vesuvius: Application of geophysical surveys for soil thickness mapping, *J. Appl. Geophys.*, *59*(2), 126–139, doi:10.1016/j.jappgeo.2005.09.001.

Efron, B. (1979), Bootstrap methods: Another look at the jackknife, *Ann. Stat.*, *7*, 1–26.

Ermini, L. and N. Casagli (2002), Prediction of the behaviour of landslide dams using a geomorphological dimensionless index, *Earth Surf. Processes Landforms*, *28*, 31–47.

Esposito, E., S. Porfido, C. Violante, and F. Alaia (2003), Disaster induced by historical floods in a selected coastal area (Southern Italy), paper presented at *the Workshop PHEFRA, Paleofloods, Historical Data and Climatic Variability*.

Evans, S. G. (1997), Fatal landslides and landslides risk in Canada, in *Landslide Risk Assessment*, edited by D. M. Cruden and R. Fell, pp. 185–196, Balkema, Rotterdam.

Fell, R. and D. Hartford (1997), Landslide risk management, in *Landslide Risk Assessment*, edited by D. M. Cruden and R. Fell, pp. 51–109, Balkema, Rotterdam.

Fortunato, C., S. Martino, A. Prestininzi, and R. W. Romeo (2012), New release of the Italian catalogue of earthquake-induced ground failures (CEDIT), *Ital. J. Eng. Geol. Environ.*, *2*, 63–74, doi:10.4408/IJEGE.2012-02.O-05.

Frattini, P., G. B. Crosta, N. Fusi, and P. Dal Negro (2004), Shallow landslides in pyroclastic soils: A distributed modelling approach for hazard assessment, *Eng. Geol.*, *73*(3-4), 277–295, doi:10.1016/j.enggeo.2004.01.009.

Glade, T., P. Albini, and F. Frances (Eds.) (2001), *The Use of Historical Data in Natural Hazard Assessments*, Kluwer Academic Publisher, Dordrecht.

Guzzetti, F. (2000), Landslide fatalities and evaluation of landslide risk in Italy, *Eng. Geol.*, *58*, 89–107.

Guzzetti, F. and P. Reichenbach (1994), Towards a definition of topographic divisions for Italy, *Geomorphology*, *11*, 57–74.

Guzzetti, F., P. Salvati, and C. P. Stark (2005a), Evaluation of risk to the population posed by natural hazards in Italy, in *Landslide Risk Management*, edited by O. Hungr, R. Fell, R. Couture, and E. Eberhardt, pp. 381–389, Taylor & Francis Group, London.

Guzzetti, F., C. P. Stark, and P. Salvati (2005b), Evaluation of flood and landslide risk to the population of Italy, *Environ. Manage.*, *36*(1), 15–36.

Keefer, D. K. (1984), Landslides caused by earthquakes, *Geol. Soc. Am. Bull.*, *45*, 406–421.

Keefer, D. K. (2013), Landslides generated by earthquakes: Immediate and long-term effects, in *Treatise on Geomorphology*, vol. 5, pp. 250–266, Elsevier, Amsterdam.

Kolmogorov, A. (1933), *Grundbegriffe der Wahrscheinlichkeitsrechnung*, Julius Springer, Berlin.

Latter, J. H. (1969), Natural disasters, *Adv. Sci.*, *25*, 362–380.

Locat, J. and H. Lee (2009), Submarine mass movements and their consequences: An overview, in *Landslides—Disaster Risk Reduction*, edited by K. Sassa and P. Canuti, pp. 115–142, Sperling-Verlag, Berlin Heidelberg.

Masson, D. G., A. B. Watts, M. Gee, R. Urgeles, N. C. Mitchell, T. P. Le Bas, and M. Canals (2002), Slope failures on the flanks of the western Canary Islands, *Earth Sci. Rev.*, *57*(1–2), 1–35.

Mazzanti, P. and F. Bozzano (2011), Revisiting the February 6th 1783 Scilla (Calabria, Italy) landslide and tsunami by numerical simulation, *Mar. Geophys. Res.*, *32*, 273–286.

McMurtry, G. M., P. Watts, G. J. Fryer, J. R. Smith, and F. Imamura (2004), Giant landslides, mega-tsunamis, and paleo-sea level in the Hawaiian Islands, *Mar. Geol.*, *203*(3-4), 219–233, doi:10.1016/S0025-3227(03)00306-2.

Moore, J. G., W. R. Normark, and R. T. Holcomb (1994), Giant Hawaiian landslides, *Annu. Rev. Ecol. Syst.*, *22*, 119–144.

Morgan, G.C. (1991), Quantification of Risks from Slope Hazards, Open File Report 1992-15, Geological Survey of Canada.

Morgan, G. C. (1997), A regulatory perspective on slope hazards and associated risks to LIFE, in *Landslide Risk Assessment*, edited by D. M. Cruden and R. Fell, pp. 285–295, Balkema, Rotterdam.

Newman, M. E. J. (2005), Power laws, Pareto distributions and Zipf's law, *Contemp. Phys.*, *46*(5), 323–351.

Porfido, S., E. Esposito, F. Alaia, F. Molisso, and M. Sacchi (2009), The use of documentary sources for reconstructing flood chronologies on the Amalfi rocky coast (southern Italy), in *Geohazard in Rocky Coastal Area*, edited by C. Violante, pp. 173–187, The Geological Society, London.

Prestininzi, A., and R. W. Romeo (2000), Earthquake-induced ground failures in Italy, *Eng. Geol.*, *58*(3-4), 387–397, doi:10.1016/S0013-7952(00)00044-2.

Reed, W. J. (2001), The Pareto, Zipf and other power laws, *Econ. Lett.*, *74*(1), 15–19.

Rossi, M., A. Witt, F. Guzzetti, B. D. Malamud, and S. Peruccacci (2010), Analysis of historical landslide time series in the Emilia-Romagna region, northern Italy, *Earth Surf. Processes Landforms*, *35*, 1123–1137, doi:10.1002/esp.1858.

Salvati, P., F. Guzzetti, P. Reichenbach, M. Cardinali, and C.P. Stark (2003), Map of landslides and floods with human consequences in Italy, scale 1:1,200,000, CNR Gruppo Nazionale per la Difesa dalle Catastrofi Idrogeologiche Publication no. 2822.

Salvati, P., C. Bianchi, M. Rossi, and F. Guzzetti (2010), Societal landslide and flood risk in Italy, *Nat. Hazards Earth Syst. Sci.*, *10*, 465–483, doi:10.5194/nhess-10-465-2010.

Salvati, P., C. Bianchi, M. Rossi, and F. Guzzetti (2012), Flood risk in Italy, in *Changes in Flood Risk in Europe*, edited by Z. W. Kundzewicz, pp. 277–292, Taylor & Francis Group.

Schuster, R. L. (Ed.) (1986), *Landslide Dams: Processes, Risk, and Mitigation*, ASCE Geotechnical Special Publication no. 3, ASCE, New York.

Smirnov, N. (1933), Estimate of deviation between empirical distribution functions in two independent samples, *Bull. Moscow State Univ.*, *2*(2), 3–16.

Vallario, A. (2001), *Il dissesto idrogeologico in Campania*, Cuen, Napoli.

White, E. P., B. J. Enquist, and J. L. Green (2008), On estimating the exponent of power-law frequency distributions, *Ecology*, *89*(4), 905–912, doi:10.1890/07-1288.1.

Wilk, M. B. and R. Gnanadesikan (1968), Probability plotting methods for the analysis for the analysis of data, *Biometrika*, *55*(1), 1–17.

15

An Extreme Event Approach to Volcanic Hazard Assessment

Servando De la Cruz-Reyna and Ana Teresa Mendoza-Rosas

ABSTRACT

The statistical analysis of size-qualified volcanic eruption time series is an essential step for the assessment of volcanic hazard. Such series generally describe complex processes that may be time dependent, involving different types of eruptions over a wide range of timescales. The hazard assessment thus requires a characterization of the eruptions that reflects their destructive potential, that is, an appropriate measure of their "size." However, available data to size qualify eruptions are frequently unknown and incomplete, as often are their times of occurrence. This is particularly true for "rare," uncommon eruptions exceeding the "normal" activity, which may be regarded as extreme events. Here, we describe statistical methods that have proven useful to deal with such difficulties, and describe a procedure to analyze eruptive sequences of individual volcanoes or groups of volcanoes, as illustrated with several examples of hazard estimates. The procedure involves three steps: First, the historical eruptive series is complemented with a series constructed from any available geological-time eruption data. Either series may contain extreme events, but it is more likely that such extreme eruptions belong to the geological record. Both series are then linked assuming a scaling, self-similarity relationship between the eruption size and the occurrence rate of each magnitude class. Second, a Weibull analysis of the distribution of repose times between successive eruptions manifests the time dependence, if any, through its shape parameter. Finally, the linked eruption series are analyzed using extreme value theory as a nonhomogeneous Poisson process with a generalized Pareto distribution as intensity function, from which the probabilities of future eruptions may be estimated.

15.1. INTRODUCTION

Measuring volcanic eruptions is a problem that has not been completely solved, particularly, when such measurement is intended to assess the hazards and risks related to eruptions. Unlike earthquakes, in which dimensioning parameters such as magnitude and intensity are well defined, the nature of volcanic activity makes the problem much more difficult. An eruption is a very complex phenomenon in which energy is released in many different ways and in variable proportions. Even "similar"

eruptions of the same volcano (say eruptions releasing the same amount of magmatic mass, that is, of the same mass magnitude) may have different energy partitions and may affect the environment around the volcano in widely different ways, making it difficult to assign a size to both, an eruption and to its effects.

In contrast, the problem of measuring earthquakes over a wide range of sizes has been solved through the use of scales that are based not only on the amplitude of recorded seismic waves but also on the whole spectrum that instruments allow to record, greatly increasing the dynamic range over which earthquakes can be measured. Additionally, the seismic magnitude scales (body and surface waves, seismic moment) have been constructed to

Instituto de Geofísica, Universidad Nacional Autónoma de México, México, DF, México

Extreme Events: Observations, Modeling, and Economics, Geophysical Monograph 214, First Edition.
Edited by Mario Chavez, Michael Ghil, and Jaime Urrutia-Fucugauchi.
© 2016 American Geophysical Union. Published 2016 by John Wiley & Sons, Inc.

be as self-consistent as possible, and produce a suitably linear scale of the logarithm of the energy release as a function of magnitude over at least 10 orders of magnitude. Therefore, the energy released at the source may be directly estimated from an earthquake magnitude, and consistently a measure of the energy arriving to a certain point of the Earth's surface is represented by the earthquake intensity. Defining seismic hazard in terms of the probability that a certain amount of seismic energy arrives at a certain rate to a given site as a result of an earthquake occurring in a determined region is thus a problem that is being solved with the limitations imposed by a limited amount of high-quality data, but without showing inherent difficulties related to posing of the problem. Is it possible to do something similar to assess the volcanic hazard posed by a volcano or by a group of volcanoes? Answering this question would first require adopting an appropriate measurement of the "size" of eruptions that describes their destructive power as effectively as possible. Second, a suitable scale relating such size scale with a parameter relevant to the probability of occurrence such as the mean recurrence time, or its inverse, the rate of occurrence over a wide dynamic range is needed. Next, we propose a statistical procedure that attempts to fulfill these requirements.

15.2. ERUPTION SIZE AND IMPACT

Although the conceptual framework of volcanic hazard and risk assessment has an evident advantage over the seismic problem, which is the fact that seismic hazard is a function of both spatial and temporal coordinates in the sense that both site and time of a large earthquake are unknowns, at least the position of the volcano in question is known. The hazard assessment problem is thus to determine the probability that an eruption of certain characteristics may occur in a given volcano (or group of volcanoes) over a given time span. Notwithstanding this apparent advantage, attempting to address volcanic hazard in a similar way to seismic hazard faces some inherent problems that has not yet been solved. One of such problems is measuring the size of volcanic activity in a way that has a maximum relevance to the concepts of hazard and risk. Perhaps one of the clearest statements of this difficulty was offered by *Walker* [1980]: "Explosive volcanic eruptions show several different kinds of "bigness," and five may be considered, namely *magnitude, intensity, dispersive power, violence,* and *destructive potential.*" "Magnitude" refers to the total amount of material emitted by an eruption. *Tsuya* [1955] defined a 10-level magnitude scale based on the volume of each of three types of erupted materials (lavas, pyroclastics, and lithics) that results appropriate to compare among different types of materials after converting the measured volume into a dense rock equivalent (DRE) volume in which the volume contribution of cavities has been removed. *Yokoyama* [1957] suggested extending Tsuya's scale by volume to one by energy, considering the different types of released energy (seismic, elastic, thermal, kinetic, acoustic), concluding that thermal energy is frequently the dominant term, and therefore, a scale based on energy is proportional to a juvenile mass-release scale. *Hédérvari* [1963] defined an energy magnitude scale accounting for different forms of energy release during eruptions based on the same formula used in seismology to calculate the eruption magnitude.

"Intensity" is the rate of magma discharge, which may as well be calculated as the rate of energy release. Intensity may be estimated from the maximum height of an eruptive column, and from the dispersal of lithics and pyroclastics [*Settle*, 1978; *Fedotov*, 1985; *Carey and Sigurdsson*, 1989]. The latter authors have found a positive correlation between magnitude and intensity for several major eruptions. "Dispersive Power" is closely related to intensity and refers to the extent over which the erupted materials are dispersed, and dependent on the eruptive style. "Violence" was defined by *Walker* [1980] as a measure of bigness to volcanic events in which the distribution of the volcanic products is determined mainly by their momentum, as is the case of fast-moving pyroclastic flows or surges. Similarly, "Destructive Potential" was defined as the extent of devastation, actual or potential, caused by an eruption. Walker proposed the areal extent of building vegetation and farmland destruction as a measure of that parameter, which tends to increase with magnitude, but which is also very sensitive to the style and intensity of the eruption. It is thus clear that in general, dispersive power and destructive potential are proportional to magnitude and intensity.

A composite estimate of those parameters (depending on the available data) was defined in 1982 by Newhall and Self as the volcanic explosivity index (VEI), and the largest catalogs of eruption sizes has been compiled based on that scale [*Simkin et al.*, 1981; *McClelland et al.*, 1989; *Simkin and Siebert*, 1994; *Siebert and Simkin*, 2002]. The VEI is thus a general indicator of the explosive character of an eruption. It is thus not adequate for nonexplosive effusive eruptions. Eruptions are assigned a scale from 0 to 8, which is claimed to be the maximum number of categories that can be realistically distinguished. The VEI scale may be consulted in any of the aforementioned references.

Recently, other dimensioning scales have been proposed. *Pyle* [1995] defined two volume magnitude scales based on a measure of an eruption bulk volume $A \times 10^i \mathrm{m}^3$: a discrete scale $k = i - 4$, majorly coincident with the VEI, and a similar continuous scale $M = i - 4.0 + \log A$. More recently, another mass magnitude scale [*Pyle*, 2000] was proposed as $M_m = \log(\text{erupted mass, kg}) - 7$, and an intensity scale as $I_m = \log(\text{mass eruption rate, kg/s}) + 3$.

Since the largest available volcanic activity catalogs are based on the VEI, and this scale contains in its definition parameters that are directly related to the measure of an eruption impact, and considering that other scales such as the mass-magnitude scales referred in the previous paragraph are largely compatible with the VEI, it is just natural that many of the hazard analyses published since the VEI scale have been based on this parameter, as we do in the following sections. Further considerations about the adequacy of this parameter as a measure of the impact of eruptions are discussed in depth by *Scandone et al.* [1993a], particularly through their analysis of the relevance of the magma discharge rate, calculated mostly from the eruption column height, as a true measure of the intensity, and thus of the eruption power and destructive power of the volcanic activity.

15.3. EXTREME VALUE THEORY APPROACH TO MODELING OCCURRENCES OF VERY LARGE ERUPTIONS IN GROUPS OF VOLCANOES

Extreme value methods are increasingly being used in the study of diverse natural phenomena, for example, rainfall [*Beguería*, 2005; *Villarini et al.*, 2011], floods [*Claps and Laio*, 2003], atmospheric pollution [*Anderson et al.*, 1997], wind speeds and gusts [*Brabson and Palutikof*, 2000; *Cheng and Yeung*, 2002; *Lin*, 2003], and hurricane winds [*Elsner et al.*, 2006; *Jagger and Elsner*, 2006]. Extreme value theory is a statistical discipline with a rich mathematical content that deals with the stochastic behavior of the maximum or minimum values of events in stochastic processes, which are distributed at the tail of the occurrences distribution. Large magnitude or intensity phenomena, though rare, may provide potential underlying information to gain a better understanding of the physical processes governing the events. Since some of the catastrophes that have impacted human kind have resulted from unexpectedly large natural phenomena, the application of extreme value theory has lately acquired great interest in the Earth sciences, as it allows modeling the unusual and infrequent extreme events, rather than the common and frequent ones as the more commonly used statistic does.

Extreme value theory has been applied to large groups of volcanoes. Such analyses have been made using predominantly the mass magnitude defined by *Pyle* [2000], as described at the end of the previous section to characterize the size of the eruptions. *Mason et al.* [2004] considered that such scale had an upper limit and set the "largest" explosive events as the Fish Canyon tuff eruption with a mass magnitude M_m about 9.2. They developed a preliminary analysis of the recurrence rate of such eruptions applying the extreme value theory, by compiling a database of the largest explosive eruptions occurring

since the Ordovician, and used a Weibull distribution to fit the tail of the distribution. They also compared the energy released by volcanic eruptions with the energy released by asteroid impacts, concluding that explosive volcanic eruptions are more frequent than impacts with a similar energy yield. Following a similar line, *Coles and Sparks* [2006] applied a maximum likelihood framework and the extreme value techniques to obtain estimates of the worldwide probability for future extreme eruptions at different levels of magnitude, using the Hakayawa Catalog (Y. Hayakawa, Hayakawa's 2000-year eruption catalog, 1997, http://www.edu.gunma-u.ac.jp/~hayakawa/catalog/2000W), a database of large volcanic eruptions in the last 2000 years. They analyzed the eruptions exceeding a mass magnitude M_m 4 using a Poisson process model for extremes [*Pickands*, 1971; *Smith*, 1989], considering the magnitudes of the events and the times of their occurrences as points in a two-dimensional space. Since the record showed a significant underreporting of low-magnitude events that increased with the age of eruptions, they used a censored intensity function that took into account such bias of the recording.

Deligne et al. [2010] expanded the work of *Coles and Sparks* [2006] and applied again extreme value theory to the record of explosive volcanic eruptions with magnitude (using VEI and M_m) larger or equal to 4 of the global Holocene explosive volcanism, based mostly on the Smithsonian Global Volcanism Program Database [*Siebert and Simkin*, 2002]. As Coles and Sparks do, each eruptive event is characterized as a point above a threshold on a magnitude-time (M-t) space, and assumed to be a two-dimensional Poisson process. Models presumed to be almost complete, or complete; one of the eruptions from AD 1750 to the present and a second from AD 1900 to the present were applied to datasets. They then applied a model taking underreporting into consideration to the entire Holocene database. Results in all cases predicted eruption size limits significantly smaller than actual extreme eruptions, and those limits depended on the chosen threshold. To explain this, they suggested that their models predicted smaller limits of eruption sizes than those reported in the geologic record due to a sampling bias attributed to a different nature between "ordinary" eruptions and extreme, caldera forming events.

Furlan [2010] proposed an alternative step intensity function, based on a change-point model to improve the fit to the process of *Coles and Sparks* [2006] and reduce the bias from the under-recording. The change-point model assumes that changes in the worldwide eruption rate over the last two millennia may be attributed to discrete changes of the eruption recording capabilities through time. If a change is detected at time k, the proposed intensity function is constructed from a step function with respect to those times in such a way that the under-recording is absent after the time k, while before time k, the probability of recording an eruption is proportional to its magnitude. The distribution parameters were refined using Bayesian techniques as an alternative to the maximum likelihood method of Coles and Sparks. The posterior distribution resulting from the Bayesian analysis allowed to estimate models with more complex parametric structures that fit better to the observed data and provide less-biased estimates of the probability of future events with extreme levels.

15.4. SCALING LAWS AND EXTREME VALUE METHODS: APPLICATIONS TO INDIVIDUAL AND GROUPS OF VOLCANOES

When dealing with individual volcanoes, in which the extent and quality of the eruption databases (VEI and/or ejected mass of each dated eruption) is scarce and usually incomplete, the assessment of hazard commonly requires an additional tool, which may be an appropriate scaling law to estimate the sizes of eruptions that have been dated but have little or no additional information on their magnitudes.

Mulargia et al. [1985] used extreme value statistics to estimate the probability of major eruption analyzing sequences of Etna volcano flank eruptions occurring between 1600 and 1980, and characterizing the magnitude of the eruptions using a scaling law linearly relating the erupted mass to the duration of the eruption, a parameter that was well reported in most cases. Then, using the duration as dependent variable, and a type I Gumbel distribution, the probabilities of occurrence of major eruptions were estimated. Although this was objected by *Chester* [1986], on the basis that such scaling law assumes essentially constant effusion rates, Mulargia *et al.* replied that the correlation between erupted volume and duration had an acceptable 0.81 correlation coefficient.

15.4.1. Large Group of Volcanoes

A different scaling law based on global data has been proposed by *De la Cruz-Reyna* [1991, 1996]. Analyzing the VEI catalogs of the time, *Simkin et al.* [1981], *Newhall and Self* [1982] found a high correlation between the logarithm of the global occurrence rate of explosive eruptions in a given VEI category log λ_{VEI}, and the VEI. Figure 15.1 shows the correlation between the occurrence rates of the global available data for the period 1500–1970 and the corresponding VEI values in the range 3–6. The line is well fit by:

$$\log \lambda_{VEI} = a - b(VEI) \qquad (15.1)$$

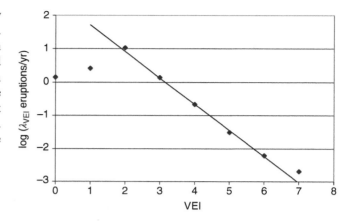

Figure 15.1 Linear relationship between the logarithm of the occurrence rate of eruptions in a given VEI category, and the VEI. The line is fitted to the points in the VEI range 3–6 only.

with $a = 2.5$, and $b = 0.79$, when the explosive eruption rate is measured in eruptions per year, with a correlation coefficient -0.999 in that range [*De la Cruz-Reyna*, 1991]. These values have been later tested and confirmed with more recent, updated catalogs [*McClelland et al.*, 1989; *Simkin and Siebert*, 2000]. The significant departure of this line form VEI values 0 and 1 have two possible explanations: Eruptions in this range have a different nature and do not follow the same distribution of the higher magnitudes, and/or these VEI values are significantly underreported, even considering that the abovementioned catalogs assign a default value VEI 2 to eruptions in which the available information is poor or doubtful. Possibly both causes contribute, since low-VEI eruptions are frequently long-duration effusive episodes, and the underreporting of minor eruptions has been a persistent issue in the studies referred in previous sections. Either way, those low VEI values should not be considered for the statistical analysis of explosive eruptions. The deviation of VEI 7 class from the line is discussed below.

Similarly, using published total (thermal and mechanical, in Joules) energy release data from 21 well-documented eruptions, plotted in Figure 15.2 [*De la Cruz-Reyna*, 1991 and references therein: table 6], a correlation between the energy released in each VEI category E_{VEI} and the VEI was found as follows:

$$\log E_{VEI} = 14(\pm 1.13) + 0.79 VEI \qquad (15.2)$$

where E_{VEI} is expressed in Joules. The error range in the constant accounts for the scatter in the VEI versus log E_{VEI} regression represented by the thin lines in Figure 15.2. The correlation coefficient in this case is 0.71.

Combining Equations 15.1 and 15.2, the dependence on VEI vanishes, and an interesting result is obtained: the quantity $\lambda_{VEI} E_{VEI}$, that is, the total yearly energy release of

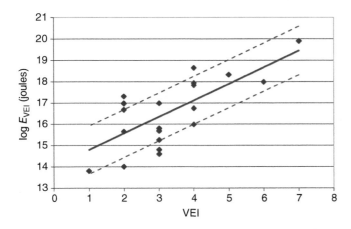

Figure 15.2 The solid line shows the regression between the total energy release of 21 well-studied eruptions [*Yokoyama*, 1957; *Macdonald*, 1972; *De la Cruz-Reyna*, 1991: (table 6)] and the VEI values reported by *Simkin et al.* [1981]. The dashed lines are each separated one standard deviation from the regression solid line.

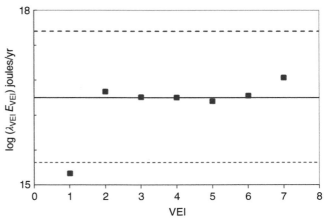

Figure 15.3 Mean yearly energy release of eruptions in different VEI categories. The thick horizontal line represents the total yearly energy release of eruptions in each VEI category, seemingly constant in the VEI range 3–6, and the dashed lines represent the range shown in relation 3, as calculated from Equation 15.2.

eruptions in each VEI category seems to be essentially constant, at least for the last 500 yr time span and the VEI range 3–6, indicating that the worldwide activity is distributed in such a way that given a time interval, about the same energy is released by the total number of eruptions in each given VEI category in that range.

$$\lambda_{VEI} E_{VEI} \sim 2.4 \times 10^{15} \sim 4.4 \times 10^{17} \text{ J/yr worldwide} \quad (15.3)$$

with a mean value of 3.16×10^{16} J/yr. For this estimate to be appropriate, the sampled time interval must be longer than the return period of the highest VEI category considered in the analysis, otherwise under-sampling may occur for that level, causing a higher than expected energy for that VEI category, if an eruption of that size occurs in the interval, as is the case of the VEI 7 Tambora, 1815 eruption shown in Figure 15.3. For this reason, the VEI 7 category with a mean return time of about 1000 yr according to Equation 15.1 was not used in the estimate of the regression line slope in Figure 15.1.

It is important to emphasize that these results hold for the relationship between eruption energy releases estimated from the VEI, as expressed by Equation 15.2, but may differ if other measure of the eruption size is used. For example, *Pyle* [1995] finds that a dependence of energy rates on magnitude appears when the tephra volume scale is used.

The scaling properties expressed by Equations 15.1–15.3 may be very useful for estimating the volcanic hazard, as it reveals an averaging property of a large group of volcanoes to release in a given time interval about the same amount of energy in each VEI category, meaning that

while some volcanoes tend to release energy in large, high-intensity eruptions, others do it in more frequent minor or moderate eruptions. Although this is an unsurprising result, as most natural phenomena occur in that way, the surprising issue is the capability of the VEI to average this characteristic in such a way that the VEI categories release about the same energy worldwide when a sufficiently long period is considered. Scaling law (15.1) is constructed from the most reliable (in terms of sampling) VEI range. Using a self-similarity approach we base our analysis on the assumption that this law may be extrapolated to most of the VEI range. In addition, it allows redefining the discrete VEI scale as a continuous scale based on the rate of occurrence of eruptions releasing a given energy.

Since the destructive potential of an eruption depends on both, the total ejected mass (and, therefore, on the total released energy), and the intensity (the mass eruption rate, and thus the energy release rate or power), the VEI values that consider magnitude and intensity seem to be an adequate scale to measure the hazard of eruptions as it reflects well the aforementioned averaging property.

15.4.2. Applications of the Scaling Criteria to Individual Volcanoes

Equation 15.1 may thus be a used as a general scaling law in such a way that the abovementioned averaging property yield the given $a = 2.5$, and $b = 0.79$ coefficients for the worldwide volcano dataset, meaning that although individual volcanoes may have scaling relations as in Equation 15.1, they should have their own, specific coefficients that may at times coincide with the global average. This was carefully tested by *Scandone et al.* [1993b] in their hazard and risk analysis of the Vesuvius and Campi Flegrei areas.

To address the problem of hazard assessment of a particular single volcano, we then should use the available information about all the recognizable events, small or large, of its past eruptive history, even when it is clear that they may represent an incomplete catalog, and try to take advantage of the abovementioned scaling properties to determine the probabilities of future eruptions of any size that may cause damage. This is particularly important when evaluating the hazard derived from major eruptions that are likely to be under-sampled (since its mean recurrence time may be longer than the sampled interval) or even absent in the eruption record. For this we capitalize on the scaling law (15.1) assuming that eruptions may be regarded as different size manifestations of the same type of phenomena, and that they comprise the occurrence of the under-sampled high-intensity categories. This scaling law unifies a broad range of eruption sizes and may lead to a relatively simple assessment of the volcanic hazard over a wide spectrum of explosive eruption styles.

Physically, this corresponds to considering a volcano as a thermodynamic system in long-term dynamic equilibrium that will erupt when its energy level exceeds certain threshold. Then, a fraction of that energy is released by an eruption [*De la Cruz-Reyna*, 1991]. Although the released fraction of energy and the way this energy is partitioned during an eruption are random variables, an appropriate statistical approach supported on the scaling laws may provide reliable estimates of the hazard, that is, the probabilities of futures eruptions in a given VEI category.

As an example, Figures 15.4, 15.5, and 15.6 illustrate applications of the scaling law (15.1) to individual volcanoes in Mexico [*Mendoza-Rosas and De la Cruz-Reyna*, 2008, 2010]. To evaluate the hazard of those volcanoes, they proposed a method to estimate the probabilities of occurrence of at least one volcanic eruption exceeding a VEI magnitude over different time periods. This method involves using the scaling relationship (15.1) to estimate the most likely VEI values of important, but poorly documented past eruptions in terms of the eruption occurrence rate λ of each class magnitude VEI, linking the (assumed complete) historical and the geological records to obtain robust volcanic eruption histories as VEI-characterized time series. *Mendoza-Rosas and De la Cruz-Reyna* [2008, 2010] constructed different models of the distribution of large events using the available geological information, and selected the model which best fitted the eruption rates obtained from Equation (15.1). From those estimates of the large-eruption rates, they inferred the number of eruptions that exceeded a specific

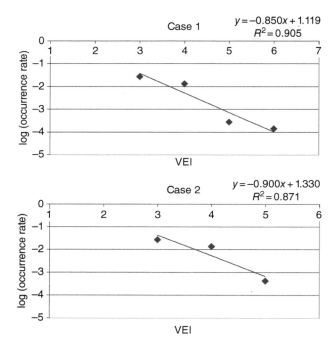

Figure 15.4 Best fits of Equation 15.1 for two possible eruptive histories of Colima volcano (from *Mendoza-Rosas and De la Cruz-Reyna* [2008]).

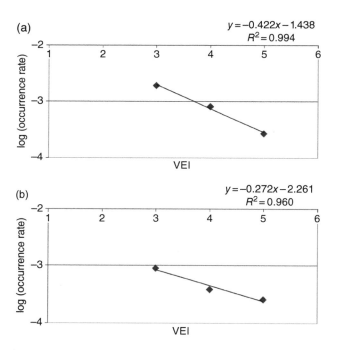

Figure 15.5 Best fits of Equation 15.1 for two possible eruptive histories of El Chichón volcano considering eruptions with VEI ≥ 3 in two sampling periods: (a) From an event dated at 3707 yr BP, and including 7 VEI 3 eruptions, 3 VEI 4 eruptions, and 1 VEI 5 eruption. (b) From a major event in the past dated at 7772 yr BP; includes 7 VEI 3 eruptions, 3 VEI 4 eruptions, and 2 VEI 5 eruptions (from *Mendoza-Rosas and De la Cruz-Reyna* [2010]).

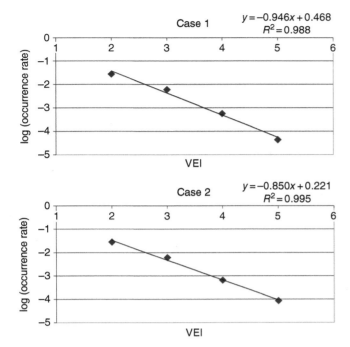

Figure 15.6 Best fits of Equation 15.1 for the most likely eruption histories of Popocatépetl volcano. Case 1 counts 14 VEI 2 eruptions and 3 VEI 3 eruptions in the historical period of 496 yr, and 8 VEI 4 eruptions, and 1 VEI 5 eruption since a major eruption dated at 23,000 yr BP. Case 2 counts the same historical record, and 7 VEI 4, and 2 VEI 5 eruptions since the 23,000-yr BP event (from *Mendoza-Rosas and De la Cruz-Reyna* [2008]).

threshold magnitude. Figure 15.4 illustrates two possible eruptive histories of Colima volcano, in which the vague information available about Holocene eruptions made it difficult to estimate their dates and magnitudes, and in some cases, the overlapping of dating errors allowed the possibility of counting twice a single event. The first possible eruptive history (Case 1) considers 12 VEI 3 eruptions and 6 VEI 4 eruptions during the historical period of 446 yr, and 2 VEI 5 eruptions and 1 VEI 6 eruption since a major event dated at 7040 yr BP, while Case 2 counts 12 VEI 3 eruptions and 6 VEI 4 eruptions in the historical period, and 3 VEI 5 eruptions in 7040 yr. Case 1 was adopted as the best model of eruption history for the probability calculation of future eruptions.

El Chichón volcano, which caused the worst volcanic disaster in the history of Mexico in 1982 is a difficult case due to the scarce information of dates and sizes of past eruptions, since it only began to be systematically studied after the event. A similar analysis for that volcano is illustrated in Figure 15.5, where two possible eruptive histories are constructed considering eruptions with VEI≥3 in two sampling periods [*Mendoza-Rosas and De*

la Cruz-Reyna, 2010]. The better fitting case (a) was preferred to estimate the hazard.

Popocatépetl volcano, located in a region with the highest population density of Mexico started erupting in December 1994, and the activity continues to the time of this submission. Its eruptive history includes major eruptions that may cause important tephra falls affecting over 20 million people. An assessment of the hazards posed by this volcano requires knowing the best estimate of the size of past major events. Figure 15.6 [*Mendoza-Rosas and De la Cruz-Reyna*, 2008] illustrates two possible distributions of the VEI-characterized eruption time series of that volcano. The better fitting of Case 2 made it preferred for the hazard estimations.

To gain additional information about the eruptive sequence, *Mendoza-Rosas and De la Cruz-Reyna* [2008, 2010] applied a Weibull distribution to analyze the repose periods, which allowed a quantitative description of the nonstationary quality of the time series through the distribution's shape parameter. The stationarity and independence properties were prechecked by a moving average method and a serial correlation diagram of successive repose intervals, respectively. To assess the volcanic hazard that considers the historical, usually complete, and the geological, probably incomplete eruptive series they proposed as the best estimate of the volcanic hazard from the integrated time series, a procedure based on the use of a nonhomogenous generalized Pareto distribution (GDP) [*Davison and Smith*, 1990; *Coles*, 2001; *Reiss and Thomas*, 2001] as intensity function describing the exceedances (eruption magnitudes exceeding an established threshold). Such GDP is an essential piece of the extreme value theory [*Pickands*, 1971; *Smith*, 1989], described by a shape parameter k, a scale parameter σ, and a location parameter u (threshold). This GDP has the cumulative distribution function:

$$G_{k,a}(y) = 1 - \left(1 - \frac{ky}{\sigma}\right)^{1/k} \quad \text{for } k \neq 0$$
$$1 - e^{-y/\sigma} \quad \text{for } k = 0$$

where $y = x - u$ is the realization of an excess, x is the exceedance, and u is the established threshold.

This GPD is less sensitive to the possible time dependence of the large-magnitude eruption sequence, since it only considers the number of exceedances over a threshold of a series that may be stationary or not. *Mendoza-Rosas and De la Cruz-Reyna* [2008, 2010] referred to this GPD as the intensity function of a nonhomogeneous generalized Pareto–Poisson process (NHGPPP), and used it to calculate the probability of occurrence of large-magnitude eruptions exceeding a threshold (volcanic hazard) of five Mexican volcanoes, three of which were used as examples above. One difficulty resulting from this method is that it implies that an exceedance only requires that an eruption exceeds a given VEI. However, since the VEI scale is not an open scale, for it ends in 8, the GDP probabilities of eruptions exceeding VEI 8 must be subtracted from the calculated probabilities, otherwise the hazard may be overestimated.

15.5. CONCLUDING REMARKS

In this conceptual approach about the integration of some extreme event methods to the evaluation of volcanic hazard, we examined some formulations that have been applied to studying and modeling the statistical characteristics and recurrence rates of the global volcanic activity. A challenge common to all formulations is the age-dependent loss of information on the dates and sizes of past eruptions, challenge that has been confronted in diverse ways. Here, we focus in a course based on a self-similarity scaling law derived from a property of the worldwide explosive volcanic activity to release energy at about the same rate in each VEI category over a given time interval, provided that the mean recurrence time of the largest VEI category under consideration does not exceeds the sampled interval. This effect is assumed here to be a consequence of the averaging effect of superposing the eruptive histories of many individual volcanoes, each having its own VEI-dependent log-linear distribution of the eruption rate. The main hypothesis is thus that, as seismic regions have characteristic Gutenberg-Richter b-values, volcanoes may be characterized by similar log-linear distributions, as expressed by Equation 15.1. Such self-similarity property allows assigning or adjusting the missing or incomplete size–rate data of the eruptive time series to fit the scaling criterion. Probabilities of future eruptions are then estimated using an NHGPPP, which incorporates the effect of scarce data of major past eruptions, and is less sensitive to dating errors since only the number of exceedances above a threshold are relevant. Applications of these methods and comparisons with other statistical distributions are discussed in *Mendoza-Rosas and De la Cruz-Reyna* [2008, 2010]. *Sobradelo et al.* [2011] applied this methodology to estimate volcanic hazards in the Canary Islands.

ACKNOWLEDGMENTS

The authors wish to thank two anonymous reviewers whose comments and suggestions helped to improve the quality of the manuscript. This work was carried out with support from DGAPA-PAPIIT UNAM grant IN106312.

REFERENCES

Anderson, C. W., N. Mole, and S. Nadarajah (1997), A switching Poisson process model for high concentrations in short-range atmospheric dispersion, *Atmos. Environ.*, *31*(6), 813–824.

Beguería, S. (2005), Uncertainties in partial duration series modelling of extremes related of the choice of the threshold value, *Journal of Hydrology*, *303*, 215–230.

Brabson, B. B. and J. P. Palutikof (2000), Test of the generalized Pareto distribution for predicting extreme wind speeds, *J. Appl. Meteorol.*, *39*, 1627–1640.

Carey, S. and H. Sigurdsson (1989), The intensity of plinian eruptions, *Bull. Volcanol.*, *51*, 28–40.

Cheng, E. and C. Yeung (2002), Generalized extreme gust wind speeds distributions, *J. Wind Eng. Ind. Aerodyn.*, *90*, 1657–1669.

Chester, D. K. (1986), Comments on "A Statistical Analysis of Flank Eruptions on Etna volcano" by F. Mulargia, S. Tinti and E. Boschi, *J. Volcanol. Geotherm. Res.*, *28*, 385–395.

Claps, P. and F. Laio (2003), Can continuous streamflow data support flood frequency analysis? An alternative to the Partial Duration Series approach, *Water Resour. Res.*, *39*(8), 1216, doi:10.1029/2002WR001868.

Coles, S. (2001), *An Introduction to Statistical Modeling of Extreme Values*, pp. 224, Springer-Verlag, London.

Coles, S. G. and R. S. J. Sparks (2006), Extreme value methods for modelling historical series of large volcanic magnitudes, in *Statistics in Volcanology*, Special Publications of the International Association of Volcanology and Chemistry of the Earth's Interior, vol. *1*, edited by H. Mader, S. Cole, and C. B. Connor, pp. 47–56, Geological Society of London.

Davison, A. C. and R. L. Smith (1990), Models for exceedances over high thresholds, *J. R. Stat. Soc.*, *52*(B), 393–442.

De la Cruz-Reyna, S. (1991), Poisson-distributed patterns of explosive eruptive activity, *Bull. Volcanol.*, *54*, 57–67.

De la Cruz-Reyna, S. (1996), Probabilistic analysis of future explosive eruptions, in *Monitoring and Mitigation of Volcanic Hazards*, edited by R. Scarpa and R. I. Tilling, pp. 599–629, Springer, Berlin.

Deligne, N. I., S. G. Coles, and R. S. J. Sparks (2010), Recurrence rates of large explosive volcanic eruptions, *J. Geophys. Res.*, *115*, B06203, doi:10.1029/2009JB006554.

Elsner, J. B., T. H. Jagger, and A. A. Tsonis (2006), Estimated return periods for Hurricane Katrina, *Geophys. Res. Lett.*, *33*, L08704, doi:10.1029/2005GL025452.

Fedotov, S. A. (1985), Estimates of heat and pyroclast discharge by volcanic eruptions based upon the eruption cloud and steady plume observations, *J. Geodyn.*, *3*, 275–302.

Furlan, C. (2010), Extreme value methods for modelling historical series of large volcanic magnitudes, *Stat. Model.*, *10*(2), 113–132.

Hédérvari, P. (1963), On the energy and magnitude of volcanic eruptions, *Bull. Volcanol.*, *25*, 373–385.

Jagger, T. H. and J. B. Elsner (2006), Climatology models for extreme Hurricane winds near the United States, *J. Climate*, *19*, 3220–3236.

Lin, X. G. (2003), Statistical modelling of severe wind gust, *International Congress on Modelling and Simulation*, 14–17 July, Townsville, vol. *2*, pp. 620–625.

Macdonald, G. A. (1972), *Volcanoes*, pp. 510, Prentice-Hall, Englewood Cliffs, NJ.

Mason, B. G., D. M. Pyle, and C. Oppenheimer (2004), The size and frequency of the largest explosive eruptions, *Bull. Volcanol.*, *66*, 735–748, doi:10.1007/s00445-004-0355-9.

McClelland, L., T. Simkin, M. Summers, E. Nielsen, and T. Stein (1989), *Global volcanism 1975-1985*, pp. 655, Smithsonian Institution, Washington, DC.

Mendoza-Rosas, A. T. and S. De la Cruz-Reyna (2008), A statistical method linking geological and historical eruption time series for volcanic hazard estimations: Applications to active polygenetic volcanoes, *J. Volcanol. Geotherm. Res.*, *176*, 277–290.

Mendoza-Rosas, A. T. and S. De la Cruz-Reyna (2010), Hazard estimates for El Chichón volcano, Chiapas, Mexico: A statistical approach for complex eruptive histories, *Nat. Hazards Earth Syst. Sci.*, *10*, 1159–1170, doi:10.5194/nhess-10-1159-2010.

Mulargia, F., S. Tinti, and E. Boschi (1985), A statistical analysis of flank eruptions on Etna volcano, *J. Volcanol. Geotherm. Res.*, *23*, 263–272.

Newhall, C. G. and S. Self (1982), The Volcanic Explosivity Index (VEI): An estimate of explosive magnitude for historical volcanism, *J. Geophys. Res.*, *87C2*, 1231–1238.

Pickands, J. (1971), The two-dimensional Poisson process and extremal processes, *J. Appl. Probab.*, *8*, 745–756.

Pyle, D. M. (1995), Mass and energy budgets of explosive volcanic eruptions, *Geophys. Res. Lett.*, *22*(5), 563–566.

Pyle, D. M. (2000), Sizes of volcanic eruptions, in *Encyclopedia of Volcanoes*, edited by H. Sigurdsson, B. Hughton, S. R. McNutt, H. Rymer, and J. Stix, pp. 263–269, Academic Press, San Diego, CA.

Reiss, R. D. and M. Thomas (2001), *Statistical Analysis of Extreme Values*, 2nd ed., pp. 316, Birkhauser, Basel.

Scandone, R., L. Giacomelli, F. Fattori-Speranza, and W. Plastino (1993a), Classification and quantification of volcanic eruptions, *Boll. Geofis. Teor. Appl.*, *50*, 103–116.

Scandone, R., G. Arganese, and F. Galdi (1993b), The evaluation of volcanic risk in the Vesuvian area, *J. Volcanol. Geotherm. Res.*, *58*, 263–271.

Settle, M. (1978), Volcanic eruption clouds and the thermal power output of explosive eruptions, *J. Volcanol. Geotherm. Res.*, *3*, 309–324.

Siebert, L. and T. Simkin (2002), Volcanoes of the world: An illustrated catalog of Holocene volcanoes and their eruptions, Smithsonian Institution, Global Volcanism Program Digital Information Series, GVP-3, http://www.volcano.si.edu/world/ (accessed 20 August 2015).

Simkin, T., L. Siebert, L. McClelland, D. Bridge, C. Newhall, and J. H. Latter (1981), *Smithsonian Institution*, pp. 233, Washington, DC.

Simkin, T. and L. Siebert (1994), *Volcanoes of the World*, 2nd ed., Geoscience Press, Tucson, AZ.

Simkin, T. and L. Siebert (2000), Earth's volcanoes and eruptions: An overview, in *Encyclopedia of Volcanoes*, edited by H. Sigurdsson, B. Hughton, S. R. McNutt, H. Rymer, and J. Stix, pp. 249–262, Academic Press, San Diego, CA.

Smith, R. L. (1989), Extreme value analysis of environmental time series: An application to trend detection in ground-level ozone (with discussion), *Stat. Sci.*, *4*, 367–393.

Sobradelo, R., J. Martí, A. T. Mendoza-Rosas, and G. Gómez (2011), Volcanic hazard assessment for the Canary Islands (Spain) using Extreme value theory, *Nat. Hazards Earth Syst. Sci.*, *11*, 2741–2753.

Tsuya, H. (1955), Geological and petrological studies of Volcano Fuji, 5, *Bull. Earthq. Res. Inst., Univ. Tokyo*, *33*, 341–384.

Villarini, G., J. A. Smith, M. L. Baeck, R. Vitolo, D. B. Stephenson, and W. F. Krajewski (2011), On the frequency of heavy rainfall for the Midwest of the United States, *J. Hydrol.*, *400*, 103–120.

Walker, G. P. L. (1980), The Taupo pumice: Product of the most powerful known (Ultraplinian) eruption?, *J. Volcanol. Geotherm. Res.*, *8*, 69–94.

Yokoyama, L. (1957), Energetics in active Volcanoes (2nd paper), *Bull. Earthq. Res. Inst., Univ. Tokyo*, *35*, 75–97.

Part V
Socioeconomic Impacts
of Extreme Events

16

Economic Impact of Extreme Events:
An Approach Based on Extreme Value Theory

Richard W. Katz

ABSTRACT

Much attention has been devoted to the statistics of extreme geophysical phenomena. However, at least in part because of a dearth of data, not much is known about the corresponding distribution of economic damage caused by extreme events. In this chapter, the statistical theory of extreme values is applied to provide an explanation for how the apparent upper tail behavior of the distribution of economic damage is possibly consistent with that for the underlying geophysical phenomenon. Rather than standard asymptotic (or "ultimate") theory, it turns out that a "penultimate" (or second-order) approximation is required. If this relationship (or damage function) is in the form of a power transformation as suggested by physical considerations, then penultimate extreme value theory would imply, at least under a wide range of plausible conditions, that the distribution of economic damage would have an apparent heavy tail, even if storm intensity has an apparent bounded upper tail. The focus is on an example of the economic damage from hurricanes and its relationship to storm intensity, as measured by maximum wind speed at landfall.

16.1. INTRODUCTION

Much of the economic impact of meteorological, as well as of other geophysical phenomena, is realized through extremes. For example, during the time period 1900 through 2005, 20% of the 160 damaging hurricanes making landfall along the Gulf and Atlantic coasts of the United States caused about 82% of the total economic damage (Figure 16.1, based on a dataset adjusted not only for inflation but also for shifts in societal vulnerability; see Section 16.4.1 and *Pielke et al.* [2008]). This percentage is in close agreement with the value of 80% predicted by the so-called Pareto Principle [*Defeo and Juran*, 2010], and quite inconsistent with a bell-shaped curve or an upper tail that decays at an exponential rate. As such, it is only this extreme upper tail of the probability distribution

of the economic impact of geophysical phenomena that is of utmost concern, particularly to the insurance and reinsurance industries [*Embrechts et al.*, 1997; *Murnane*, 2004].

For various reasons, there is a dearth of high-quality data concerning the economic impact of extreme geophysical events, even potentially catastrophic ones such as floods [*Pielke and Downton*, 2000]. Besides the inherent difficulties in quantifying damage, these reasons include inconsistent reporting standards. As such, the best damage data are limited primarily to those recorded by insurance companies for insured properties. An alternative approach has been to indirectly derive the economic impact of extreme geophysical events through what is sometimes called a "damage function" [*Pielke*, 2007] or "loss function" [*Watson and Johnson*, 2004]. Such damage functions have typically been in the form of a power transformation [*Nordhaus*, 2010].

The shape of the distribution of many geophysical variables in the extreme upper tail is fairly well understood.

National Center for Atmospheric Research, Boulder, CO, USA

Extreme Events: Observations, Modeling, and Economics, Geophysical Monograph 214, First Edition.
Edited by Mario Chavez, Michael Ghil, and Jaime Urrutia-Fucugauchi.

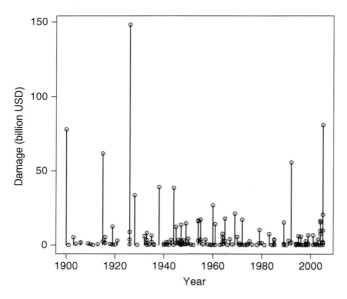

Figure 16.1 Time series of adjusted economic damage caused by hurricanes, 1900–2005. For multiple events during the same year, the points are superimposed.

For example, variables such as precipitation totaled over short time periods (e.g., an hour or a day) and stream flow typically possess an apparent "heavy" tail (i.e., the probability of exceeding a high threshold decays as an approximate power law as the threshold increases *Katz et al.* [2002]; *Koutsoyiannis* [2004]). It might be anticipated that, depending on the form of damage function, the upper tail behavior of economic damage is inherited from that of the corresponding underlying geophysical phenomenon.

To study the characteristics of the distribution of the economic impact of extreme geophysical events, it would be natural to make use of the statistical theory of extreme values [*Gumbel*, 1958; *Coles*, 2001]. Nevertheless, the majority of the statistical analyses so far have not made explicit use of this theory. Rather, they have relied on parametric distributions, such as the lognormal [*Katz*, 2002; *Nordhaus*, 2010], whose properties are not necessarily flexible enough for the extreme upper tail. Exceptions include *Jagger et al.* [2008, 2011], *Katz* [2010], and *Katz et al.* [2002].

First, a brief review of basic extreme value theory is provided, along with a more refined version involving "penultimate" approximations (Section 16.2). Next, the approximate upper tail behavior of economic damage is related to that of the underlying geophysical variable through a damage function, in the form of a power transformation, in combination with a penultimate approximation (Section 16.3). As an example, these theoretical considerations are then applied to the economic damage caused by hurricanes (Section 16.4). Finally, Section 16.5 consists of a discussion.

16.2. EXTREME VALUE THEORY

16.2.1. Ultimate Approximations

16.2.1.1. Block Maxima

The fundamental result in the classical statistical theory of extreme values is the Extremal Types Theorem [*Gumbel*, 1958; *Coles*, 2001]. Let $\{X_1, X_2,...\}$ denote a strictly stationary time series (i.e., any finite-dimensional joint distribution of the X_t's is invariant under shifts in time). Consider the maximum value of the first n observations of this time series, denoted by $M_n = \max\{X_1, X_2,...,X_n\}$. The Extremal Types Theorem concerns the possible forms of limiting distribution of the maximum, suitably normalized. It states that if there exists normalizing constants, $a_n > 0$ and b_n, such that

$$\Pr\{(M_n - b_n)/a_n \leq x\} \to G(x) \text{ as } n \to \infty, \quad (16.1)$$

where G is a cumulative distribution function (CDF), then G must be in the form of the generalized extreme value (GEV) distribution. That is,

$$G(x;\mu,\sigma,\xi) = \exp\left\{-\left[1 + \frac{\xi(x-\mu)}{\sigma}\right]^{-1/\xi}\right\}, \quad (16.2)$$

$1 + \xi(x-\mu)/\sigma > 0$. Here μ, $\sigma > 0$, and ξ denote the location, scale, and shape parameters, respectively. The GEV distribution includes three types: (1) the Weibull, with a bounded upper tail, if $\xi < 0$; (2) the Fréchet, with a heavy tail, if $\xi > 0$; and (3) the Gumbel if $\xi = 0$, formally obtained by taking the limit as $\xi \to 0$ in (16.2).

The Extremal Types Theorem does not require that the time series necessarily be temporally independent. Rather, it still holds for a wide range of forms of temporal dependence, including clustering at high levels for observations close together in time and for temporal dependence that becomes weak for observations far apart in time [*Leadbetter et al.*, 1983]. In particular, it even holds for long-memory time series in which the temporal dependence decays at a relatively slow rate; for example, if the autocorrelation function of a Gaussian time series decays at faster than a logarithmic rate. Further, an analogous extreme value theory can be established for a wide class of dynamical systems [*Freitas and Freitas*, 2008; *Freitas et al.*, 2010; *Faranda et al.*, 2011; *Lucarini et al.*, 2012].

By the assumption of stationarity, the time series is identically distributed, say with a common CDF $F(x) = \Pr\{X_t \leq x\}, t = 1, 2, \dots$. For simplicity, further assume that F has an unbounded upper tail (i.e., $F(x) < 1$ for all x). Then F (sometimes referred to as the "parent" distribution) is said to be in the *domain of attraction* of the Gumbel if

(16.2) holds with $\xi = 0$ (similarly for the other two types of GEV). For instance, it turns out that the exponential, gamma, normal, and lognormal distributions are all in the domain of attraction of the Gumbel.

One way to determine the domain of attraction is based on a concept known as the "hazard rate" (or "hazard function" or "failure rate"). The *hazard rate* of a CDF F is defined as follows:

$$h_F(x) = \frac{F'(x)}{1 - F(x)}, \qquad (16.3)$$

where F' (i.e., the derivative of F) denotes the corresponding probability density function (PDF) [*Reiss and Thomas*, 2007]. In the context of reliability theory or survival analysis, the hazard rate can be thought of as the instantaneous rate of "failure."

In extreme value theory, only the behavior of $h_F(x)$ for large x is relevant. A sufficient condition for the CDF F to be in the domain of attraction of the Gumbel distribution (known as the von Mises condition [*Reiss and Thomas*, 2007]) can be expressed in terms of the limiting behavior of the derivative of the reciprocal of the hazard rate as follows:

$$(1 / h_F)'(x) \to 0 \text{ as } x \to \infty. \qquad (16.4)$$

It is fairly straightforward to verify that this condition holds for the specific CDFs mentioned earlier in this subsection. For example, the hazard rate of an exponential distribution is constant (consistent with its "memoryless" property), so it follows that (16.4) is satisfied.

16.2.1.2. Peaks over Threshold

More modern extreme value theory has focused on the limiting behavior of the upper tails of distributions. Intuitively, it is only the upper tail that determines the limiting distribution of the maximum (e.g., as in (16.4)). The motivation for this alternative approach is that more of the inherently limited information about extremes can be used. For instance, if the second highest value over the entire record happened to occur within the same time block (i.e., a season or year) as the highest one, then it would be discarded in the block maxima approach.

Consider a high threshold u and suppose that this threshold is exceeded at time t (i.e., $X_t > u$). Denote the "excess" over the threshold by $Y_t = X_t - u$. Analogous to the Extremal Types Theorem, for sufficiently high threshold u, the excess has an approximate generalized Pareto (GP) distribution [*Coles*, 2001]. The CDF of the GP is given by

$$H[y; \sigma(u), \xi] = 1 - \left\{ 1 + \xi \left[\frac{y}{\sigma(u)} \right] \right\}^{-1/\xi}, \ y > 0, \quad (16.5)$$

$1 + \xi [y/\sigma(u)] > 0$. Here $\sigma(u) > 0$ and ξ denote the scale and shape parameters, respectively. The interpretation of the shape parameter is identical to that for the GEV distribution. As the notation suggests, the scale parameter depends on the threshold u, with the excess over a higher threshold having an approximate GP distribution with the same shape parameter, but requiring an adjustment to the scale parameter.

Not only the excess over a high threshold needs to be statistically modeled, but also the rate at which the threshold is exceeded. Given that exceeding a high threshold is a rare event, it is natural to model this rate as a Poisson process, say with rate parameter $\lambda > 0$. Consequently, the total number of threshold exceedances within a time interval of length T would have a Poisson distribution with rate parameter (or mean) λT.

The combination of these two components is sometimes called a Poisson-GP model or peaks over threshold (POT) approach [*Katz et al.*, 2002]. Because the maximum of a sequence falls below a specified value if and only if there are no exceedances of that same value, a natural connection exists between the block maxima and POT techniques. In particular, the POT approach can be used to more efficiently estimate the parameters of the GEV distribution for block maxima.

In this regard, the two-dimensional point process approach to modeling extremes can be thought of as an extension of the Poisson-GP model, but parameterized instead in terms of the GEV distribution for block maxima [*Smith*, 1989; *Davison and Smith*, 1990]. This approach is especially convenient for introducing covariates (e.g., trends) into the statistical model for extremes [*Coles*, 2001].

16.2.2. Penultimate Approximations

The extreme value theory approximations just described can be thought of as "ultimate" (or first order), in the sense of only holding in the limit (i.e., as the block size n or the threshold u trends to infinity). More refined (second order or penultimate) approximations are also available, with potentially increased accuracy in practice. The rationale for considering such approximations is not at all new, dating from the very beginning of the development of extreme value theory. In case of the parent distribution being normal, *Fisher and Tippett* [1928] pointed out that the rate of convergence of the distribution of the maxima to the limiting Gumbel distribution was relatively slow. As an alternative, they suggested that the Weibull type of GEV distribution would actually provide a more accurate "penultimate" approximation in this situation.

For simplicity, only the case in which the parent CDF F is in the domain of attraction of the Gumbel is considered, with it further being assumed that the von Mises condition (16.4) holds. The basic idea is to make use of the approximate behavior of the quantity (i.e., derivative of the reciprocal of the hazard rate) on the left-hand side of (16.4) for large x, rather than simply taking the limit as $x \to \infty$. Instead of the Gumbel, the GEV distribution is used with shape parameter ξ_n depending on the block size n as follows [Reiss and Thomas, 2007; Furrer and Katz, 2008]:

$$\xi_n \approx (1/h_F)'(x)\big|_{x=u(n)} \qquad (16.6)$$

Here,

$$u(n) = F^{-1}(1-1/n) \qquad (16.7)$$

denotes the $(1-1/n)$th quantile of the parent CDF F (sometimes called the "characteristic largest value"). An approximation symbol still appears in (16.6) because $u(n)$ for large n, or $h_F(x)$ for large x, may need to be approximated. By (16.4), $\xi_n \to 0$ as $n \to \infty$, so this penultimate approximation converges toward the ultimate approximation as the block size increases.

16.2.2.1. Stretched Exponential Distribution

As an example to be used later in the application to hurricane damage, it is assumed that the parent CDF F is the "stretched exponential" (i.e., a "reflected" or "reverse" version of the Weibull type of GEV). That is,

$$F(x;\sigma,c) = 1 - \exp\left[-\left(\frac{x}{\sigma}\right)^c\right], \quad x > 0, \qquad (16.8)$$

where $\sigma > 0$ and $c > 0$ denote the scale and shape parameters, respectively.

For this particular form of parent distribution (16.8), the hazard rate and the characteristic largest value can be expressed in closed form as follows:

$$h_F(x;\sigma,c) = \left(\frac{c}{\sigma}\right)\left(\frac{x}{\sigma}\right)^{c-1}, \quad u(n) = \sigma(\ln n)^{1/c}. \qquad (16.9)$$

So making use of (16.6) and (16.9), the shape parameter of the penultimate GEV distribution is given by [Furrer and Katz, 2008]

$$\xi_n = \frac{1-c}{c \ln n}. \qquad (16.10)$$

Note that this penultimate shape parameter (16.10) does converge to zero as the block size n increases, consistent with the stretched exponential being in the domain of attraction of the Gumbel as mentioned earlier. Nevertheless, for finite block size n, (16.10) implies that $\xi_n < 0$ (i.e., Weibull type of GEV) for $c > 1$; sometimes

termed a "superexponential" distribution [Embrechts et al., 1997] and exploited in engineering design for wind extremes [Cook and Harris, 2004]. On the other hand, (16.10) implies that $\xi_n > 0$ (i.e., Fréchet type of GEV) for $c < 1$; sometimes termed a "subexponential" distribution [Embrechts et al., 1997] and used for precipitation extremes [Wilson and Toumi, 2005; Furrer and Katz, 2008]. Only in the special case of an exponential distribution (i.e., $c = 1$) does $\xi_n = 0$, so there is no benefit to the penultimate approximation.

16.2.2.2. Simulation Study

Table 16.1 summarizes the results of a limited simulation study to illustrate the benefits of penultimate approximations. The simulations are all based on the parent distribution being the stretched exponential distribution (16.8). Using the parameter estimation technique of maximum likelihood (ML) [Coles, 2001], the GEV distribution (16.2) was fitted to a sample of 40,000 maxima for block sizes of $n = 50$, 100, and 200 from the simulated stretched exponential distributions with shape parameter $c = 0.25$, 1/3, 0.5, 2/3, 2, and 3 and scale parameter $\sigma = 1$. From the same simulated stretched exponential distribution, the GP distribution (16.5) was also fitted by ML to approximately 80,000 excesses over a high threshold (designed to achieve roughly the same standard errors as for the block maxima). Because of the penultimate approximation (16.10) being expressed in terms of the block size n for the GEV distribution, it is not completely clear what the corresponding threshold for the GP should be.

Table 16.1 Estimated Shape Parameters (Denoted by $\hat{\xi}$) of GEV and GP Distributions for Simulations from Stretched Exponential Distribution

n	c	$\hat{\xi}$ for GEV[a]	$\hat{\xi}$ for GP[a]	ξ_n
50	0.25	0.713 (0.006)	0.563 (0.006)	0.767
100	0.25	0.608 (0.006)	0.497 (0.005)	0.651
200	0.25	0.526 (0.005)	0.441 (0.005)	0.566
50	1/3	0.477 (0.005)	0.367 (0.005)	0.511
100	1/3	0.392 (0.005)	0.328 (0.005)	0.434
200	1/3	0.346 (0.005)	0.288 (0.005)	0.377
50	0.5	0.228 (0.004)	0.179 (0.004)	0.256
100	0.5	0.192 (0.004)	0.163 (0.004)	0.217
200	0.5	0.171 (0.004)	0.148 (0.004)	0.189
50	2/3	0.119 (0.004)	0.089 (0.004)	0.128
100	2/3	0.097 (0.004)	0.078 (0.004)	0.109
200	2/3	0.087 (0.004)	0.076 (0.004)	0.094
50	2	−0.094 (0.003)	−0.086 (0.003)	−0.128
100	2	−0.094 (0.003)	−0.082 (0.003)	−0.109
200	2	−0.078 (0.003)	−0.073 (0.003)	−0.094
50	3	−0.135 (0.003)	−0.108 (0.003)	−0.170
100	3	−0.112 (0.003)	−0.104 (0.003)	−0.145
200	3	−0.108 (0.003)	−0.093 (0.003)	−0.126

[a] Standard error given in parentheses.

Given that the derivation of (16.10) makes use of the characteristic largest value $u(n)$, this particular threshold (i.e., the $(1 - 1/n)$th quantile of the stretched exponential distribution) was used as a heuristic choice.

For these various parameter combinations, Table 16.1 gives the estimated shape parameters for both the GEV and GP distributions, along with the corresponding value of ξ_n for the penultimate approximation (16.10). As compared to the shape parameter of the GEV distribution fitted directly to the sample of simulated maxima, the penultimate approximation produces a value slightly too far from zero. Still this refined approximation constitutes a substantial improvement over the ultimate approximation of $\xi = 0$. Especially when c is relatively far from one, the shape parameter of the GP distribution fitted directly to the sample of simulated excesses over a high threshold is somewhat closer to zero than that for the corresponding fitted GEV. But this discrepancy may be, at least partially, an artifact of the choice of threshold.

16.3. DAMAGE FUNCTIONS

16.3.1. Power Transformation

It is common to assume that the function converting the intensity of the geophysical event into the corresponding economic damage is in the form of a power transformation [Prahl et al., 2012]. This functional form is justified on the basis of physical principles, empirical evidence, or mathematical convenience.

Suppose that the geophysical variable is denoted by V and the corresponding economic damage (or loss) by L. Then it is assumed that L is related to V by the power transformation:

$$L_t = aV_t^b, \quad a > 0, \quad b > 0, \tag{16.11}$$

where the pair of observations (V_t, L_t) corresponds to an event occurring at time t. In the case of hurricanes where V is the maximum wind speed at landfall, it has been argued on a physical basis that the exponent $b = 3$ in (16.11), as consistent with the hurricane power dissipation index used by Emanuel [2005] [also see Emanuel, 2011]. Otherwise, both the parameters a and b in (16.11) are estimated.

The power transformation (16.11) implies log–log linearity for the relationship between the damage L and the intensity V of the geophysical event. So it is straightforward to estimate the exponent b as the slope in the regression of $\ln L$ versus $\ln V$. That is, applying the logarithmic transformation to both sides of (16.11) gives

$$\ln L_t = \ln a + b \ln V_t. \tag{16.12}$$

Some empirical evidence obtained from such regression analyses indicates that $b > 3$ for hurricane damage [Pielke, 2007; Nordhaus, 2010].

16.3.2. Tail Behavior of Damage

A natural question concerns the implications of the form of damage function for the upper tail behavior of the distribution of damage. In fact, it has even been argued that the form of damage function could be inferred by comparing the upper tail behavior of the intensity of the geophysical event with that of the corresponding damage.

Unfortunately, such an "inverse" problem turns out to be ill-posed, even under ultimate extreme value theory. On the one hand, if the intensity V of the geophysical event has a normal distribution (i.e., a light-tailed distribution in the domain of attraction of the Gumbel), then the loss L determined by (16.11) would also be in the domain of attraction of the Gumbel [Leadbetter et al., 1983]. Further, the lognormal distribution sometimes fitted to economic damage (i.e., corresponding to the damage function being the exponential instead of a power transformation) is also light-tailed in the sense of ultimate extreme value theory, a property not always recognized in the literature on hurricanes [Saunders and Lea, 2005]. So, this is an example in which a nonlinear transformation preserves the upper tail being light in the sense of ultimate extreme value theory.

On the other hand, if the geophysical variable V has an exponential distribution and the damage function is the exponential, then the damage L would have a Pareto distribution [Reiss and Thomas, 2007]. So, this is an example in which a nonlinear transformation changes the upper tail behavior from light to heavy in the sense of ultimate extreme value theory. If penultimate extreme value theory is taken into account, then the situation becomes even more complex.

It might be argued that treating a sequence of damages caused by an environmental hazard as independent and identically distributed (IID) would be physically unrealistic. For instance, a major landslide would effectively change the landscape forever. Yet, at least for the application to hurricanes, it appears that the IID assumption is reasonable. In particular, it is quite rare for more than one hurricane to cause catastrophic damage at the same location without sufficient time for rebuilding.

16.3.2.1. Stretched Exponential Distribution

Suppose that the geophysical variable V has a stretched exponential distribution; that is, with CDF given by (16.8). Then (16.11) implies that the damage L also has a stretched exponential distribution, but with different scale and shape parameters, σ^* and c^*, related to the original scale and shape parameters, σ and c, by [*Johnson and Kotz*, 1970]

$$c* = \frac{c}{b}, \quad \sigma* = a\sigma^b. \tag{16.13}$$

Thus, in the sense of penultimate extreme value theory, (16.10) implies that the upper tail of the underlying geophysical phenomenon V can be apparently bounded (i.e., if $c > 1$), yet that of the corresponding economic damage L can be apparently heavy (i.e., if $b > c$).

16.4. ECONOMIC DAMAGE CAUSED BY HURRICANES

16.4.1. Hurricane Data

The economic damage caused by hurricanes striking the U.S. coast along the Gulf of Mexico and Atlantic Ocean exhibits a rapid increase over the past century, even if corrected for inflation. Yet most, if not all of this increase, is attributable to shifts in societal vulnerability, as opposed to any change in climate. As a remedy to this problem, *Pielke et al.* [2008] developed a hurricane damage dataset (called "PL05") adjusted for wealth and population in addition to inflation.

To construct a damage function, a measure of hurricane intensity is needed as well. Following *Chavas et al.* [2013], the maximum wind speed at landfall was obtained from the NOAA Atlantic basin hurricane database (HURDAT). Hurricanes that made multiple landfalls were treated as separate events. Because of the ambiguity about landfall, a few events were eliminated. Although other characteristics such as storm size also have an effect, wind speed has the advantage of being the best single indicator. Further, wind speed data are available for the entire period of record for damage. It should be noted that the dataset actually includes some tropical storms that caused damage despite not attaining hurricane status, with smallest intensity value being 30 kt.

It has recently been argued that it would be more informative to create an index, expressing damage as a proportion of the maximum possible [*Neumayer and Barthel*, 2011; *Chavas et al.*, 2013]. The motivation for such an index is to try to eliminate variations in damage due the location of landfall. Nevertheless, the original adjusted damage data will be analyzed here to facilitate the interpretation of upper tail behavior based on extreme value theory.

To avoid bias against relatively low damage events early in the record, only storms causing greater than 0.1 billion USD are analyzed, reducing the number of events from 208 to 160 over the available time period of 1900–2005. Figure 16.1 shows the time series of adjusted economic damage from hurricanes (in USD for the year 2005). The highest adjusted damage, about 150 billion USD, is associated with the Great Miami hurricane in 1926. In other words, the hypothetical damage caused by this storm if it had occurred in 2005 instead of 1926, would be considerably higher than that for Hurricane Andrew (if it had occurred in 2005 instead of 1992) or that for Hurricane Katrina in 2005.

16.4.2. Tail Behavior of Hurricane Damage

It is clear from Figure 16.1 that the distribution of hurricane damage is highly positively skewed, if not heavy tailed. It is common to fit the lognormal distribution to such damage data (i.e., equivalent to assuming that the log-transformed damage data have a normal distribution). For the present hurricane damage dataset, a quantile-quantile (Q-Q) plot of the log-transformed data indicates that the normal distribution does indeed provide a reasonably good fit (results not shown, but see *Katz* [2002]).

As mentioned earlier, the lognormal distribution has a light tail in the sense of ultimate extreme value theory. Yet, similar to the stretched exponential distribution, this distribution can be either bounded or heavy tailed in the sense of penultimate extreme value theory. Nevertheless, a GP distribution will be fitted to the upper tail of the distribution of damage, instead of relying on the lognormal fit to all of the data.

Part (i) of Table 16.2 includes the parameter estimates and standard errors based on ML for the GP distribution fit to the excess in damage $Y_t = L_t - u$, conditional on $L_t > u$ at time t. The value of the threshold, $u = 7.5$ billion USD, was obtained by trial and error giving a total of 31 excesses. There is substantial evidence of a heavy tail, with the estimated shape parameter being 0.477 or roughly consistent with other analyses [*Jagger et al.*, 2008, 2011; *Katz*, 2010; *Chavas et al.*, 2013]. Nevertheless, it is quite difficult to estimate the shape parameter precisely, with a 50% confidence interval of $0.308 < \xi < 0.681$ being obtained based on the method of profile likelihood [*Coles*, 2001].

For some purposes, an estimated shape parameter based on only the excess damages for which the maximum wind speed at landfall V exceeds a threshold of 82.5 kt will be needed, a smaller dataset of only 25 excesses. Part (ii) of Table 16.2 gives the results of fitting the GP distribution to this reduced dataset, obtaining a slightly higher estimated shape parameter of 0.495 and a somewhat wider 50% confidence interval of $0.302 < \xi < 0.733$.

To assess the fit of the GP distribution to excess damage, it is convenient to consider the "survival function" (i.e., the complement of the CDF). From (16.5), it follows that

$$\ln\{1 - H[y; \sigma(u), \xi]\} = -\left(\frac{1}{\xi}\right)\ln\left\{1 + \xi\left[\frac{y}{\sigma(u)}\right]\right\}. \tag{16.14}$$

Table 16.2 Parameter Estimates and Standard Errors for GP Distribution Fit to Excess in Damage Over Threshold of 7.5 Billion USD

Model	Parameter	Estimate[a]
(i) All data	$\sigma(u)$	11.598 (3.675)
($n = 31$)	ξ	0.477 (0.275)
(ii) $V > 82.5$ kt	$\sigma(u)$	12.803 (4.620)
($n = 25$)	ξ	0.495 (0.316)
(iii) Covariate V	σ_0	1.256 (1.060)
($n = 31$)	σ_1	0.011 (0.009)[b]
	ξ	0.452 (0.286)

[a] Standard error given in parentheses.
[b] P-value ≈ 0.228 for likelihood ratio test of $\sigma_1 = 0$.

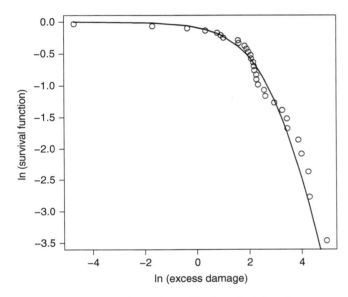

Figure 16.2 Log-transformed empirical survival function versus log-transformed excess in hurricane damage over 7.5 billion USD, along with survival function for fitted GP distribution (solid line).

In other words, survival function of the GP distribution is approximately linear for large excesses on a log-log scale. Further, the slope of the approximate straight line is negative for a heavy-tailed distribution (i.e., $\xi > 0$).

Figure 16.2 shows a plot of the log-transformed survival function versus the log-transformed excess damage for both the empirical and fitted GP distributions. It indicates that the GP distribution provides a reasonable fit, with the approximate linearity of the empirical survival function for high excesses being evident.

16.4.3. Hurricane Damage Function

Figure 16.3 shows a scatter plot of log-transformed hurricane damage versus log-transformed wind speed, along with a smoothed curve based on loess [*Venables and*

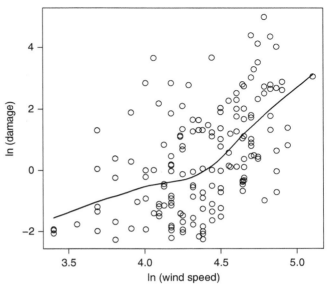

Figure 16.3 Scatter plot of log-transformed hurricane damage versus log-transformed maximum wind speed at landfall, along with smoother based on loess (solid line).

Ripley, 2002]. The loess curve appears somewhat nonlinear, but roughly piecewise linear with a steeper slope for high wind speeds (say, $V > 82.5$ kt). So, the scatter plot suggests that, at least for high wind speeds, the damage function may be approximately in the form of a power transformation (16.11). It should be noted that *Murnane and Elsner* [2012] also pointed out this apparent lack of log-log linearity.

Table 16.3 gives the estimated parameters, standard errors, and residual standard error (RSE) from the regression of log-transformed damage on log-transformed wind speed, both for all the data and for only the subset with wind speed $V > 82.5$ kt (reducing the size of the dataset from 160 to 78). By (16.12), this slope can be viewed as an estimate of the exponent of the power transformation. For all the data, the estimated slope is about 2.6 or roughly one standard error below the physically based value of $b = 3$; for only the data with high wind speed, the estimated slope is about 4.2 or roughly one standard error above $b = 3$. In both cases, a t-test of $b = 0$ gives overwhelming statistical significance. As already mentioned, a few recent studies have found estimates of b considerably higher than three. For instance, *Nordhaus* [2010] concluded that $b \approx 9$ and *Bouwer and Botzen* [2011] that $b \approx 8$. In a sensitivity analysis, *Pielke* [2007] set $b = 3, 6$, or 9.

An alternative approach to obtaining a hurricane damage function would be based on extreme value theory, considering only the relationship with wind speed for the most damaging hurricanes [*Chavas et al.*, 2013]. Instead of fitting an unconditional GP distribution to the excess in damage above a high threshold u (as in Section 16.4.2),

Table 16.3 Parameter Estimates, Standard Errors, and RSE for Power Transform Damage Function

Model	Parameter	Estimate[a]
(i) All data	ln a	−11.153 (1.503)
($n = 160$)	b	2.635 (0.342)[b]
	RSE	1.474
(ii) $V > 82.5$ kt	ln a	−18.509 (5.045)
($n = 78$)	b	4.239 (1.082)[c]
	RSE	1.418

[a] Standard error given in parentheses.
[b] P-value virtually zero for t-test of $b = 0$.
[c] P-value ≈ 0.0002 for t-test of $b = 0$.

Table 16.4 Parameter Estimates and Standard Errors for Stretched Exponential and GP Distributions Fit to Wind Speed

Distribution (Data)	Parameter	Estimate[a]
(i) Stretched exponential	σ	63.920 (2.391)
($V > 27.5$ kt, $n = 160$)	c	2.214 (0.141)
(ii) Stretched exponential	σ	26.956 (2.214)
($V > 82.5$ kt, $n = 78$)	c	1.444 (0.133)
(iii) GP	$\sigma(u)$	17.203 (3.702)
($V > 107.5$ kt, $n = 34$)	ξ	−0.188 (0.133)

[a] Standard error given in parentheses.

one or more of the parameters of the GP could depend on wind speed. Given $L_t > u$ and conditional on the covariate V_t at time t, assume that the scale parameter of the GP can be modeled as follows:

$$\ln \sigma_t(u) = \sigma_0 + \sigma_1 V_t, \qquad (16.15)$$

with the shape parameter ξ being held constant. Here the scale parameter is log-transformed to preserve $\sigma_t(u) > 0$.

Part (iii) of Table 16.2 includes the results of fitting such a conditional GP distribution with the same threshold of $u = 7.5$ billion USD, again using ML to estimate the parameters. A likelihood ratio test can be used to compare the fit of this conditional GP distribution to that of the unconditional GP [part (i) of Table 16.2; *Coles*, 2001]. This test of the slope parameter $\sigma_1 = 0$ in (16.15) is not statistically significant, with a *P*-value about 0.23. Most likely, this lack of statistical significance is attributable to the relatively small sample size involved (i.e., only 31 excesses). In fact, if a lower threshold of $u = 5$ billion USD is used instead as in *Chavas et al.* [2013], a *P*-value of about 0.05 is obtained or at least borderline statistical significance.

16.4.4. Distribution of Hurricane Wind Speed

Table 16.4 gives the ML parameter estimates and standard errors of distributions fit to the maximum wind speed at landfall. Fitting a continuous distribution to this dataset is somewhat problematic, because most of the observations are only available at a resolution of 5 kt resulting in a considerable number of ties. Nevertheless, the stretched exponential distribution fit to all of the data, using a lower bound of 27.5 kt, yields an estimate of the shape parameter c of about 2.2 (part (i) of table); to only the data with $V > 82.5$ kt (i.e., the same threshold used in part (ii) of Table 16.3) an estimate of about 1.4. These estimates are reasonably consistent with the typical values of about $c = 2$ or 3 for wind speeds in general [*Cook and Harris*, 2004].

An alternative approach would be based on extreme value theory, only fitting the GP distribution to excess wind speed over a high threshold. Part (iii) of Table 16.4 includes the results for a threshold of $u = 107.5$ kt, again obtained by trial and error, resulting in 34 excesses. The ML estimate of the shape parameter ξ is about −0.19, or an apparent bounded upper tail. Taking into account the standard error of about 0.13, this estimate is reasonably consistent with the penultimate approximation (16.10), based on the stretched exponential distribution with a shape parameter of $c = 2$ or 3.

16.4.5. Inferred Tail Behavior of Hurricane Damage

16.4.5.1. Penultimate Approximation
With the results from Sections 16.4.2 to 16.4.4 in hand, inferences about the upper tail behavior of the distribution of economic damage caused by hurricanes can now be made. Suppose it is assumed that

1. the wind speed has a stretched exponential distribution (16.8) with shape parameter c; and that

2. the damage function is in the form of a power transformation (16.11) with exponent b.

Then (16.13) implies that hurricane damage has a stretched exponential distribution with a shape parameter given by $c^* = c/b$. Consequently, the penultimate approximation (16.10) for the shape parameter of the upper tail of the distribution of damage is given by

$$\xi_n = \frac{1 - (c/b)}{(c/b) \ln n}. \qquad (16.16)$$

The estimates of c and b are based on only the data for which the wind speed $V > 82.5$ kt with the block size n remaining somewhat ambiguous as discussed earlier. Substituting the estimates of $b = 4.239$ from Table 16.3 and of $c = 1.444$ from Table 16.4 into (16.16) gives a shape parameter ξ_n for the GP distribution of about 0.495 for $n = 50$, 0.420 for $n = 100$, and 0.365 for $n = 200$. Note that the value of the shape parameter for $n = 50$ is quite close to the actual estimates of 0.477 and 0.495 from parts

(i) and (ii) of Table 16.2. If the uncertainty in the estimates of c and b is taken into account as well, a considerably wider range of possible values of the shape parameter of the GP distribution would be obtained.

16.4.5.2. Simulation Study

As a final test of the plausibility of the proposed chance mechanism for the distribution of hurricane damage having an apparent heavy tail, a simulation study is performed. This simulation is designed to minimize the sensitivity of the results to the assumptions involved, even at the risk of producing a conservative estimate of the degree of heaviness of the upper tail. It entails a combination of nonparametric resampling and parametric stochastic simulation.

The simulation algorithm consists of the following steps:

(i) Resample with replacement [i.e., the bootstrap technique, *Venables and Ripley*, 2002] from the 78 observed wind speeds $V > 82.5$ kt to produce a new pseudo-sample of the same length, say $V_1^*, V_2^*, \ldots, V_{78}^*$.

(ii) For each of these 78 pseudo-wind speeds, generate a log-transformed hurricane damage value by

$$\ln L_t^* = \ln a + b \ln V_t^* + \varepsilon_t. \qquad (16.17)$$

Here (16.17) consists of (16.12) plus an error term ε_t, assumed normally distribution with zero mean and standard deviation denoted by σ_ε, to reflect the imperfect relationship between wind speed and damage. The estimates of $\ln a$ and b from part (ii) of Table 16.3 are substituted into (16.17), along with the corresponding RSE as an estimate of σ_ε. Finally, the exponential function is applied to convert $\ln L_t^*$ into the untransformed damage L_t^*.

(iii) Fit the GP distribution to the simulated excesses in damage $L_t^* - u$, given $L_t^* > u$, using the same threshold of $u = 7.5$ billion USD, and record the estimated shape parameter.

This simulation algorithm is conservative for two reasons. First, rather than using the stretched exponential distribution (in particular, with an unbounded upper tail) to simulate wind speed, the largest value generated by the bootstrap cannot exceed the highest observed value (i.e., 165 kt). Second, the error term in (16.17) is generated by a normal distribution (i.e., a light-tailed distribution), whereas the actual residuals might well have a heavier upper tail.

Steps (i–iii) were repeated 1000 times, with the estimated shape parameters of the GP distribution averaging about 0.515, with a lower quartile of 0.279, a median of 0.523, and an upper quartile of 0.748. Despite the conservative nature of this simulation study, it still produces shape parameter estimates entirely consistent with the actual estimates listed in parts (i) and (ii) of Table 16.2. Further, the simulated interquartile range (i.e., the difference between the upper and lower quartiles) is only slightly wider than the actual 50% confidence interval based on part (ii) of Table 16.2.

16.5. DISCUSSION

One plausible chance mechanism has been provided concerning how the distribution of maximum wind speed at landfall, a measure of hurricane intensity, could have an apparent finite upper bound, yet the distribution of economic damage from hurricanes could have an apparent heavy upper tail. This chance mechanism is based on penultimate extreme value theory. Strictly speaking, the upper tail of the distribution of damage need not be heavy-tailed in the sense of ultimate extreme value theory. Still, in practice this pre-asymptotic effect would be indistinguishable from genuine asymptotic behavior. As such, it would need to be taken seriously in the context of risk assessment for insurance or reinsurance.

Nevertheless, there are other possible explanations for the apparent heavy upper tail of the distribution of hurricane damage. It may be that this heavy tail arises, at least in part, as a consequence of damage being aggregated over a population, irrespective of the underlying geophysical phenomenon. In fact, Vilfredo Pareto originally derived the Pareto distribution (or "Pareto's law") as a model for how income or capital should be distributed over a population [*Arnold*, 1983].

Only the economic damage from hurricanes has been analyzed in the present chapter. Damage data for other geophysical phenomena including floods, tornadoes, and earthquakes do exist [*Smith and Katz*, 2013]. Unfortunately, the quality of such datasets tends to be even lower than for hurricanes. In the case of floods, there is much evidence that streamflow and precipitation themselves possess a heavy tail as already mentioned in the Introduction. So the economic damage from floods should naturally be anticipated to have a heavy-tailed distribution, even without any resort to penultimate extreme value theory [*Katz et al.*, 2002].

Increased attention to the statistical characteristics of economic damage from extreme geophysical phenomena has arisen in recent years because of concerns about climate change, especially in the insurance and reinsurance sectors. The heavy-tailed behavior of damage makes the detection of trends quite challenging [*Bouwer*, 2011; *Crompton et al.*, 2011]. Nevertheless, some trends in hurricane damage achieving at least borderline statistical significance have been detected in recent years [*Nordhaus*, 2010; *Barthel and Neumayer*, 2012]. Trends in the frequency of occurrence of damaging hurricanes are also starting to emerge [*Katz*, 2010]. The methods proposed in the present chapter could be readily extended to incorporate a projected shift in the distribution of the maximum wind speed of hurricanes at landfall. Finally, it would be natural to incorporate other covariates, including indices of large-scale atmospheric or oceanic circulation such as the El Niño-Southern Oscillation phenomena, into extremal models for damage [*Jagger et al.*, 2008, 2011; *Mestre and Hallegatte*, 2009].

ACKNOWLEDGMENTS

I thank Nicholas Cavanaugh, Daniel Chavas, Christina Karamperidou, Katherine Serafin, and Emmi Yonekura for inspiring me to revisit this topic, and for providing me with the maximum wind speed data extracted from HURDAT (www.aoml.noaa.gov/hrd/hurdat). I also thank two anonymous reviewers for their helpful comments. The adjusted hurricane damage data set (PL05) is available at:

sciencepolicy.colorado.edu/publications/special/
normalized_hurricane_damages.htm

The statistical analysis made use of the extRemes and ismev packages in the open source statistical programming language R (www.r-project.org). Research was partially supported by NCAR's Weather and Climate Assessment Science Program. The National Center for Atmospheric Research is sponsored by the National Science Foundation.

REFERENCES

Arnold, B. C. (1983), *Pareto Distributions*, International Co-operative Publishing House, Burtonsville, MD.

Barthel, F. and E. Neumayer (2012), A trend analysis of normalized insured damage from natural disasters, *Clim. Change*, *113*, 215–237.

Bouwer, L. M. (2011), Have disaster losses increased due to anthropogenic climate change?, *Bull. Am. Meteorol. Soc.*, *92*, 39–46.

Bouwer, L. M. and W. J. W. Botzen (2011), How sensitive are US hurricane damages to climate? Comment on a paper by W.D. Nordhaus, *Clim. Change Econ.*, *2*, 1–7.

Chavas, D., E. Yonekura, C. Karamperidou, N. Cavanaugh and K. Serafin (2013), U.S. hurricanes and economic damage: Extreme value perspective, *Nat. Hazard. Rev.*, *14*, 237–246.

Coles, S. (2001), *An Introduction to Statistical Modeling of Extreme Values*, Springer, London.

Cook, N. J. and R. I. Harris (2004), Exact and general FT1 penultimate distributions of extreme wind speeds drawn from tail-equivalent Weibull parents, *Struct. Saf.*, *26*, 391–420.

Crompton, R. P., R. A. Pielke Jr. and K. J. McAneney (2011), Emergent timescales for detection of anthropogenic climate change in US tropical cyclone loss data, *Environ. Res. Lett.*, *6*, doi:10.1088/1748-9326/6/1/014003.

Davison, A. C. and R. L. Smith (1990), Model for exceedances over high thresholds, *J. R. Stat. Soc. Ser. B*, *52*, 393–442.

Defeo, J. and J. M. Juran (2010), *Juran's Quality Handbook: The Complete Guide to Performance Excellence*, sixth ed., McGraw-Hill, New York.

Emanuel, K. (2005), Increasing destructiveness of tropical cyclones over the past 30 years, *Nature*, *436*, 686–688.

Emanuel, K. (2011), Global warming effects on U.S. hurricane damage, *Weather Clim. Soc.*, *3*, 261–268.

Embrechts, P., C. Klüppelberg and T. Mikosch (1997), *Modelling Extremal Events for Insurance and Finance*, Springer, Berlin.

Faranda, D., V. Lucarini, G. Turchetti and S. Vaienti (2011), Numerical convergence of the block-maxima approach to the generalized extreme value distribution, *J. Stat. Phys.*, *145*, 1156–1180.

Fisher, R. A. and L. H. C. Tippett (1928), Limiting forms of the frequency distribution of the largest or smallest member of a sample, *Proc. Camb. Philos. Soc.*, *24*, 180–190.

Freitas, A. C. M. and J. M. Freitas (2008), On the link between dependence and independence in extreme value theory for dynamical systems, *Stat. Probab. Lett.*, *78*, 1088–1093.

Freitas, A. C. M., J. M. Freitas and M. Todd (2010), Hitting time statistics and extreme value theory, *Probab. Theory Relat. Fields*, *147*, 675–710.

Furrer, E. M. and R. W. Katz (2008), Improving the simulation of extreme precipitation events by stochastic weather generators, *Water Resour. Res.*, *44*, W12439, doi:10.1029/2008WR007316.

Gumbel, E. J. (1958), *Statistics of Extremes*, Columbia University Press, New York.

Jagger, T. H., J. B. Elsner and M. A. Saunders (2008), Forecasting US insured hurricane losses, in *Climate Extremes and Society*, edited by H. F. Diaz and R. J. Murnane, pp. 189–208, Cambridge University Press, Cambridge.

Jagger, T. H., J. B. Elsner and R. K. Burch (2011), Climate and solar signals in property damage losses from hurricanes affecting the United States, *Nat. Hazards*, *58*, 541–557.

Johnson, N. L. and S. Kotz (1970), *Continuous Univariate Distributions-1*, Houghton Mifflin, Boston, MA.

Katz, R. W. (2002), Stochastic modeling of hurricane damage, *J. Appl. Meteorol.*, *41*, 754–762.

Katz, R. W. (2010), Discussion on "Predicting losses of residential structures in the state of Florida by the public hurricane loss evaluation model" by S. Hamid et al., *Stat. Methodol.*, *7*, 592–595.

Katz, R. W., M. B. Parlange and P. Naveau (2002), Statistics of extremes in hydrology, *Adv. Water Resour.*, *25*, 1287–1304.

Koutsoyiannis, D. (2004), Statistics of extremes and estimation of extreme rainfall: II Empirical investigation of long rainfall records, *Hydrol. Sci. J.*, *49*, 591–610.

Leadbetter, M. R., G. Lindgren and H. Rootzén (1983), *Extremes and Related Properties of Random Sequences and Processes*, Springer, New York.

Lucarini, V., D. Faranda and J. Wouters (2012), Universal behaviour of extreme value statistics for selected observables of dynamical systems, *J. Stat. Phys.*, *147*, 63–73.

Mestre, O. and S. Hallegatte (2009), Predictors of tropical cyclone numbers and extreme hurricane intensities over the North Atlantic using generalized additive and linear models, *J. Climate*, *22*, 633–648.

Murnane, R. J. (2004), Climate research and reinsurance, *Bull. Am. Meteorol. Soc.*, *85*, 697–707.

Murnane, R. J. and J. B. Elsner (2012), Maximum wind speeds and US hurricane losses, *Geophys. Res. Lett.*, *39*, L16707, doi:10.1029/2012GL052740.

Neumayer, E. and F. Barthel (2011), Normalizing economic loss from natural disasters: A global analysis, *Glob. Environ. Chang.*, *21*, 13–24.

Nordhaus, W. D. (2010), The economics of hurricanes and implications of global warming, *Clim. Change Econ.*, *1*, 1–20.

Pielke, R. A., Jr. (2007), Future economic damage from tropical cyclones: Sensitivities to societal and climate changes, *Philos Trans R Soc A*, *365*, 2717–2729.

Pielke, R. A., Jr. and M. W. Downton (2000), Precipitation and damaging floods: Trends in the United States, 1932–97, *J. Climate*, *13*, 3625–3637.

Pielke, R. A., Jr., J. Gratz, C. W. Landsea, D. Collins, M. A. Saunders and R. Musulin (2008), Normalized hurricane damage in the United States: 1900–2005, *Nat. Hazard. Rev.*, *9*, 29–42.

Prahl, B. F., D. Rybski, J. P. Kropp, O. Burghoff and H. Held (2012), Applying stochastic small-scale damage functions in German winter storms, *Geophys. Res. Lett.*, *39*, L06806, doi:10.1029/2012GL050961.

Reiss, R.-D. and M. Thomas (2007), *Statistical Analysis of Extreme Values with Applications to Insurance, Finance, Hydrology and Other Fields*, third ed., Birkhäuser, Basel.

Saunders, M. A. and A. S. Lea (2005), Seasonal prediction of hurricane activity reaching the coast of the United States, *Nature*, *434*, 1005–1008.

Smith, A. B. and R. W. Katz (2013), US billion-dollar weather and climate disasters: Data sources, trends, accuracy and biases, *Nat. Hazards*, *67*, 387–410.

Smith, R. L. (1989), Extreme value analysis of environmental time series: An application to trend detection in ground-level ozone (with discussion), *Stat. Sci.*, *4*, 367–393.

Venables, W. N. and B. D. Ripley (2002), *Modern Applied Statistics with S*, fourth ed., Springer, New York.

Watson, C. C., Jr. and M. E. Johnson (2004), Hurricane loss estimation models, *Bull. Am. Meteorol. Soc.*, *85*, 1713–1726.

Wilson, P. S. and R. Toumi (2005), A fundamental probability distribution for heavy rainfall, *Geophys. Res. Lett.*, *32*, L14812, doi:10.1029/2005GL022465.

17

Extreme Magnitude Earthquakes and Their Direct Economic Impacts: A Hybrid Approach

Mario Chavez,[1] Eduardo Cabrera,[2] Silvia Garcia,[1] Erik Chavez,[3] Mike Ashworth,[4] Narciso Perea,[1] and Alejandro Salazar[5]

ABSTRACT

The occurrences of extreme magnitude earthquakes (EME), such as the 11 March 2011 Mw 9 Tohoku, Japan, the 9 May 2008 Mw 7.9 Wenchuan, China, and the 19 September 1985 Mw 8.01 Michoacan, Mexico, which led to a large number of casualties and huge economic losses, have shown that the seismic hazard and risk estimations in these seismotectonic regions were grossly underestimated. Hence, a hybrid approach, which uses both observations and modeling of the earthquake phenomena and its effects on the built environment, is proposed to estimate the probabilities of exceedances of intensities (PEI) of an EME and of their direct economic consequences (PEDEC) due to the damages of spatially distributed infrastructure within the site. The PEIs are obtained by using a modeling procedure, which combines long-period 3D finite difference and high-frequency simulations, to generate samples of 3D synthetic seismograms at a site associated with a given EME scenario. The stochastic and fractal character of the seismic source of the EME are included in the modeling. A machine learning procedure is applied to obtain small-scale spatial distribution of ground intensities at the site due to the EME. The PEDECs are computed by combining cadastral, direct economic costs, and seismic vulnerability functions of the infrastructure of interest, and the spatial distribution of intensities of the EME scenario. Marginals' probability density functions and Copula models are applied to obtain independent and joint probability distributions of the PEI and PEDEC, from which their associated return period () probabilities can be derived for decision-making purposes. The uncertainties (and future updates) of the information required to estimate the PEI and PEDEC can be cascaded throughout the end-to-end computation of the hybrid approach. As recent studies suggest that most of the circum-Pacific subduction zones (which includes the Mexican subduction region) can generate EMEs with Mw ≥ 8.5, two examples of the application of the proposed hybrid approach to obtain preliminary estimates of PEIs, PEDECs, and probable maximum losses (PMLs) of the direct costs of the damage to one- to three-floor dwelling constructions in Mexico City and Guadalajara due to the potential occurrence of extreme Mw 8.5 subduction magnitude with epicenters in the Mexican Pacific Ocean Coast are presented. The importance of estimating the PEI and PEDEC using bounded (truncated) marginal probability distributions, and considering their stochastic

[1]Instituto de Ingenieria, Universidad Nacional Autónoma de México (UNAM), Mexico, DF, Mexico

[2]Institute of Advanced Research Computing, School of Engineering and Computing Sciences, Durham University, Durham, UK

[3]Centre for Environmental Policy, Imperial College London, London, UK

[4]Scientific Computing Department, STFC Daresbury Laboratory, Sci-Tech Daresbury, Warrington, UK

[5]Instituto de Geofisica, Universidad Nacional Autónoma de México (UNAM), Mexico, DF, Mexico

Extreme Events: Observations, Modeling, and Economics, Geophysical Monograph 214, First Edition.
Edited by Mario Chavez, Michael Ghil, and Jaime Urrutia-Fucugauchi.

dependence is highlighted. The preliminary PMLs for the extreme Mw 8.5 magnitude scenarios varies from 0.7 to 18 billion USD for Mexico City, and from 37 to 61 billion USD for Guadalajara. The convenience of implementing mitigation policies, such as increasing the seismic strength of the existing (or planned) infrastructure, in combination with taxes and insurance incentives to increase risk mitigation ex-ante event investments are also analyzed. If ex-ante mitigation retrofitting actions are taken to reduce the vulnerabilities of the one- to three-floor dwelling constructions of Mexico City and Guadalajara, ~52,000 and ~250,000 dwellings could be saved by investing ~0.8 and ~6 billion USD, versus potential PMLs (due to the extreme Mw 8.5 magnitude scenarios) of ~7 and ~22 billion USD, respectively.

17.1. INTRODUCTION

The crucial observations reported for extreme magnitude earthquakes (EME) such as the 11 March 2011 Mw 9 Tohoku, Japan earthquake (Mw, the moment magnitude, is an objective measure of the energy released by an earthquake), the 9 May 2008 Mw 7.9 Wenchuan, China earthquake, and the 19 September 1985 Mw 8.01 Michoacan, Mexico earthquake, whose estimated frequency of occurrence varied from hundreds or thousands (the Tohoku and Wenchuan events), to tens or hundreds (the Michoacan event) of years, have shown that the seismic hazard estimates (i.e., the probability that the ground motion intensity at a site due to the occurrence of earthquakes would exceed for a lapse of time) for their respective regions were grossly underestimated [*Aguilar et al.*, 1996; *EERI*, 2008; *Tajima et al.*, 2013]. As a consequence, the seismic risk (i.e., the probability that humans will incur loss or damage to their built environment if they are exposed to a seismic hazard) observed for these EME were very important and unexpected, both in terms of casualties and economic losses.

With reference to the Tohoku 2011 earthquake (Figure 17.D1), a maximum Mw 8.6 was expected for the region, while the recorded event reached Mw 9. Incidentally, the tsunami barriers located in the Tohoku region were built for tsunamis generated by earthquakes of up to Mw 7.5 magnitude. Therefore, the assumption for the maximum possible earthquake scenario derived from historical observations recorded in the region resulted in the major underestimation of the maximum possible event for the region [*Tajima et al.*, 2013]. The 2011 Tohoku earthquake and associated tsunami caused about 19,000 casualties, nuclear accidents (most notably the level 7 meltdowns of three reactors in the Fukushima Daiichi Nuclear Power Plant complex, which were decommissioned), and destruction of ~200,000 buildings. The estimated earthquake and tsunami-related direct losses were of 125–158 billion USD and 112–145 billion USD, which are 42% and 39% of the total direct losses, respectively. In comparison, the average insured losses were of 37.2 billion USD [*Vervaeck and Daniell*, 2012].

In the case of the Wenchuan 2008 earthquake (see Figure 17.C1), the basic seismic design levels were established in its epicentral region (under which the earthquake started) for a Mercalli Modified Intensity (a subjective scale of the effects of an earthquake reported at a site) MMI VII (i.e., negligible damage in buildings of good design and construction, considerable damage in poorly built or badly designed structures; *Stein and Wysession*, 2003) versus the MMI XI observed (i.e., few, if any masonry structures remained standing, bridges were destroyed); *EERI* [2008]. A total of ~70,000 casualties and ~7,000,000 constructions damaged or totally destroyed were reported [*NCDR*, 2008] in this earthquake. The direct economic losses incurred were ~160 billion USD and the total insured payouts amounted to only 0.266 billion USD *CIRC* [2013].

In the Michoacan 1985 earthquake (see Figure 17.A1), a maximum ground motion acceleration (A_{max}) of 169 cm/s^2 was recorded on the so-called Mexico City compressible soil zone [*Seed et al.*, 1988], about three times the seismic design, A_{max} of 60 cm/s^2, recommended in the 1976 Mexico City construction code (enforced until the 1985 event) for this soil zone. A recommendation which, as it was shown before this earthquake by *Chavez and de León* [1983, 1984], for EME would lead to large probabilities of failure for reinforced concrete infrastructure located on the mentioned Mexico City soil zone. This was confirmed by the construction damages observed in the 1985 Michoacan Mw 8.01 earthquake [*Aguilar et al.*, 1996]. For the 1985 Michoacan EME, the official figures of casualties or missing and injured were 9500 and 40,000, respectively [*Swiss Re*, 2006]. Three thousand constructions in Mexico City were destroyed and 100,000 suffered serious damages [*NIST*, 2014]. Estimates put the direct economic loss due to this earthquake at 4 billion USD (8 USD billion in 2010 prices according to *Da Victoria Lobo* [2010], or 11 billion USD according to *OECD* [2013] estimates). In contrast, the losses insured were 0.6 billion USD [*Da Victoria Lobo*, 2010].

The seismological, engineering, and economic observations for the 2011 Tohoku, the 2008 Wenchuan, and the 1985 Michoacan EMEs call for the development of new paradigms to generate better estimates, both of the seismic hazard and the consequences associated with the seismic risk. Ideally, these estimates should be expressed in terms of probability density distributions of the ground (motion) intensities and the direct and indirect economic impacts. This would enable us to analyze plausible scenarios of EME risk management through implementation of technological and/or economic policies. Among other instruments to achieve these objectives, the reliable estimation of the potential earthquake loss exposure to EME, including the PML is crucial. Also, the convenience of implementing risk mitigation policies, such as increasing the seismic resistance of the existing (or planned) infrastructure by ex-ante event investments toward this aim should be considered.

A hybrid approach has been proposed to estimate the probabilities of exceeding the intensities of an EME, PEI, at a specific site, and its direct economic consequences, PEDEC, due to the damages to existing or planned infrastructure. The proposed hybrid approach allows using the information available on the earthquake phenomenon both at large and small spatial and temporal scales, and the information of its effects on the seismic behavior of the infrastructure of interest in previous large magnitude events (occurred in the region, or other seismic zones of the world). The seismic information is used in the realistic modeling of the wave propagation of the EME from its seismic source up to the specific site, from which their maximum ground motion intensity parameters and PEI can be obtained. These parameters are used in combination with the cadastral, seismic vulnerability, and economic information available on the infrastructure of interest, in order to obtain their associated PEDEC and PML. Univariate PDF and Copula probabilistic models are used to obtain independent and joint probability distributions of the PEI and PEDEC, from which their associated return periods can be derived for decision-making purposes. The latter can be used to analyze and eventually facilitate the implementation of different scenarios of seismic risk mitigation policies for stakeholders of the specific site/region. With the proposed hybrid approach, the uncertainties (and future updates) of the information required to estimate the PEI and PEDEC can be cascaded through the end-to-end computation.

The proposed hybrid approach is applied to obtain preliminary estimates of the PEIs and PEDECs for Mexico City and Guadalajara, corresponding to their dwelling construction stock (of one- to three-floor), due to the plausible occurrence of extreme Mw 8.5 magnitude earthquake scenarios with different epicenters in the Pacific Ocean Coast of Mexico. The preliminary estimates of the corresponding PMLs associated with these earthquake scenarios are also obtained, and the impact of seismic risk mitigation policies on the PMLs addressed.

This chapter is divided into eight sections. The proposed hybrid approach to obtain the PEI, PEDEC and PML due to the occurrence of an EME is presented in Section 17.2. Discussions about the maximum magnitudes and the frequency of occurrence of subduction EMEs worldwide and in Mexico, and the plausible occurrence in the latter in case of extreme Mw 8.5 magnitude earthquake scenarios are addressed in Section 17.3. In Sections 17.4 and 17.5, the preliminary results of the application of the hybrid approach to obtain the preliminary PEIs, PEDECs, and PMLs for the one- to three-floor dwelling constructions of Mexico City are presented; and in Sections 17.6 and 17.7, similar results corresponding to the City of Guadalajara, due to EMEs Mw 8.5 scenario earthquakes are presented. The analysis of the impact of seismic mitigation policies on the preliminary expected PMLs on Mexico City and Guadalajara are presented in Sections 17.5 and 17.7, respectively. Finally the main conclusions of the chapter are presented.

17.2. HYBRID APPROACH FOR THE ESTIMATION OF DIRECT ECONOMIC IMPACTS OF EXTREME MAGNITUDE EARTHQUAKES

17.2.1. The Proposed Hybrid Approach

In this section the hybrid approach proposed to estimate the PEI associated with an EME, and its PEDEC, due to the (potential) damage of existing or planned infrastructure located at a specific site, in a region where the EME might occur is presented.

The PEI for the specific site can be obtained by using a modeling procedure that includes:

(a) The generation of samples of synthetics ground motion at the site of interest for the EME scenario, by applying the seismic wave propagation methodology suggested by *Chavez et al.* [2010, 2011].

(b) The computation of the spatial distribution of maximum intensities of these synthetics by using a new recurrent neural network technique (RNN) [*Chavez et al.*, 2014], or an amplification factor (AF) procedure described in subsequent section.

(c) The computation of histogram of the results of (b) and its corresponding fitted PDF, and from the latter obtain the associated PEI for the EME scenario.

The modeling procedure described earlier allows us to incorporate:

1. The large, spatial (tens or hundreds of kilometers) and temporal (tens, hundreds, or thousands of years) scale characteristics of the EME scenario, that is, its seismic source dimension (from which the magnitude Mw of the EME depends) and its frequency of occurrence, respectively.

2. Its corresponding small-scale characteristics, such as the random fractal spatial (of tens to hundreds of meters) and time (from few seconds to minutes) distribution of the rupture of the EME seismic source.

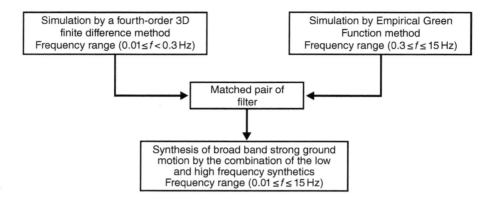

Figure 17.1 Hybrid procedure combining long period and high-frequency simulations [*Chavez et al.*, 2011].

3. The influence of the geological layers (seismic properties) found from the latter up to the specific site (tens or hundreds of kilometers) on the EME seismic wave propagation path.

4. The effect of the local (layers) geology underneath the site (of tens or hundreds of meters), on the seismic waves arriving at cells (of tens/hundreds of square meter) in which the surface occupied by the infrastructure of interest can be discretized.

5. The use of actual ground motion records (at the specific site) of earthquakes of smaller magnitudes than the EME scenario.

The PEDEC associated with the PEI computed in (c) can be obtained by:

(d) Identifying the seismic vulnerability and monetary costs for the infrastructure layout (or planned) on each of the cells mentioned in 4.

(e) Calculating for each of the cells the surface of the infrastructure expected to be damaged due to the EME scenario, by combining the samples of the maximum intensities of (strong ground motions) synthetics obtained in step (b) with the seismic vulnerability functions of the infrastructure of interest identified in (d).

(f) Obtaining the sample of the direct economic cost of the damage to infrastructure by combining the results of (e) with the information about the cost of infrastructure.

(g) Computing the histograms and their fitted PDF of the direct costs of the infrastructure obtained in step (f), and of its corresponding PEDEC and PML.

(h) Carrying out the computation of joint probabilities of the PEI and PEDEC using a copula model framework with the results of (c) and (g).

It is relevant to mention that in the proposed hybrid approach, the uncertainties and future updates of the information required to accomplish steps (a)–(c) for the PEI, and (d)–(f) for the PEDEC can and should be considered, and therefore the uncertainties can be cascaded up to the final PEI and PEDEC results.

This uncertainty cascading will be discussed in Sections 17.5 and 17.7. In the following sections, the main methodologies mentioned in each step are presented in brief.

17.2.2. Procedure to Generate 3D Strong Ground Motion Synthetics for an Extreme Magnitude Earthquake Scenario at the Site of Interest

The methodology to generate samples of synthetic ground motion at a site of interest for an EME scenario combines low- and high-frequency simulations as shown schematically in Figure 17.1 [*Chavez et al.*, 2011]. The low-frequency simulations are obtained by using a staggered finite difference solution of the 3D elastodynamic formulation of the seismic wave propagation. The high-frequency synthetics are generated with the Empirical Green Function (EGF) method. In the EGF, the ground motion from a large event can be obtained through the superposition of the ground motions of small events. A brief synthesis of the theoretical bases of both methods is presented in the following sections.

17.2.2.1. Low-Frequency Simulations

For the velocity-stress formulation of the elastic wave equation in a 3D medium occupying a volume Vol and boundary S, the medium can be described using the Lamé parameters $\lambda(\bar{x})$ and $\mu(\bar{x})$ and mass density $\rho(\bar{x})$, where $(\bar{x}) \in R^3$ [*Minkoff*, 2002]. The velocity-stress form of the elastic wave equation consists of nine coupled, first-order partial differential equations for the three-particle velocity vector components $v_i(\bar{x},t)$ and six independent stress tensor components, $\sigma_{ij}(\bar{x},t)$ where $i, j = 1, 2, 3$, and assuming that $\sigma_{ij}(\bar{x},t) = \sigma_{ji}(\bar{x},t)$,

$$\frac{\partial v_i(\bar{x},t)}{\partial t} - b(\bar{x})\frac{\partial \sigma_{ij}(\bar{x},t)}{\partial x_j} = b(\bar{x})\left[f_i(\bar{x},t) + \frac{\partial m_{ij}^a(\bar{x},t)}{\partial x_j}\right]$$

(17.1)

and

$$\frac{\partial \sigma_{ij}(\bar{x},t)}{\partial t} - \lambda(\bar{x})\frac{\partial \upsilon_k(\bar{x},t)}{\partial x_k}\delta_{ij} -$$
$$\mu(\bar{x})\left[\frac{\partial \upsilon_i(\bar{x},t)}{\partial x_j} + \frac{\partial \upsilon_j(\bar{x},t)}{\partial x_i}\right] = \frac{\partial m_{ij}^s(\bar{x},t)}{\partial t} \quad (17.2)$$

Where $b(\bar{x}) = 1/\rho(\bar{x})$, $f(\bar{x},t)$ is the force source tensor, $m_{ij}^a(\bar{x},t) = \frac{1}{2}[m_{ij}(\bar{x},t) - m_{ji}(\bar{x},t)]$ and $m_{ij}^s(\bar{x},t) = \frac{1}{2}[m_{ij}(\bar{x},t) + m_{ji}(\bar{x},t)]$ are the anti-symmetric and symmetric source moment tensors, and δ_{ij} is the Kronecker delta function. The traction boundary condition (normal component of stress) must satisfy

$$\sigma_{ij}(\bar{x},t)n_j(\bar{x}) = t_i(\bar{x},t) \quad (17.3)$$

For $\bar{x}$ on S, where $t_i(\bar{x},t)$ are the components of the time-varying surface traction vector and $n_j(\bar{x})$ are the components of the outward unit normal to S. The initial conditions on the dependent variables are specified at Vol and S at time $t = t_0$ by

$$\upsilon_i(\bar{x},t) = \upsilon_i^0(\bar{x}), \quad \sigma_{ij}(\bar{x},t) = \sigma_{ij}^0(\bar{x}) \quad (17.4)$$

If the orientation of interest is on a particular axis defined by the dimensionless unit vector e, then the particle velocity seismogram is given by

$$\upsilon_e(\bar{x}_r,t) = e_k v_k(\bar{x}_r,t)$$
$$= e_1 v_1(\bar{x}_r,t) + e_2 v_2(\bar{x}_r,t) + e_3 v_3(\bar{x}_r,t) \quad (17.5)$$

In our simulations, the source was assumed to have zero resultant force and moment such that $f_i(\bar{x},t) = 0$ and $m_{ij}^a(\bar{x},t) = 0$. The symmetric moment tensor density is defined as $m = \mu(\bar{x})D(\bar{x})$, where D is the kinematic slip. For a general fault shape, we project the moment density into the closest points on the grid [Olsen et al., 1997].

The low-frequency ($0.01 \leq f < 0.3$ Hz) seismic wave field is simulated by using a recently optimized 3D seismic wave propagation parallel finite difference code (3DWPFD). This code is the implementation of a 3D staggered-grid finite difference method to solve the system of Equations 17.1–17.4 [Madariaga, 1976; Cabrera et al., 2007; Chavez et al., 2008, 2010; Moczo et al., 2014] by using an explicit scheme that is second-order accurate in time and fourth-order accurate in space. The code uses the absorbing boundary conditions by Cerjan et al. [1985] on the sides and bottom of the 3D model and free-surface boundary condition FS2 by Gottschaemmer and Olsen [2001], and the wave attenuation is expressed as a function of V_p and V_s velocities of the layered media [Chavez et al., 2011].

The main input for the 3DWPFD code are:
(i) The 3D geometry and mechanical properties of the finite physical domain used to model the seismic region where the EME might occur.
(ii) The kinematic slip of the finite (planar) seismic source of the EME.
(iii) The time and spatial discretization values adopted for the finite volume Vol and the seismic source.

Further details about the implementation, tests, and benchmark studies performed on different supercomputer platforms of the developed 3DWPFD optimized code can be found in Cabrera et al. [2007] and Chavez et al. [2008]).

17.2.2.2. High-Frequency Simulations

The high-frequency ($0.3 \leq f \leq 15$ Hz) synthetics can be generated using EGF method [Hartzell, 1978; Irikura, 1986]. This method uses the strong ground motions associated with the rupture of a finite seismic source $U(t)$, which can be made up of several asperities (or subevents) of a large-magnitude earthquake by the superposition of the ground motions of small magnitude events, $u(t)$, produced by ruptures of a finite number of elementary sources or sub-faults located in the asperities or subevents of the large magnitude event. As suggested by Irikura [1986, 1998] and Kamae et al. [1998], $U(t)$ can be obtained by applying Equation 17.6:

$$U(t) = C\sum_{i=1}^{N}\sum_{j=1}^{N}\frac{r}{r_{ij}}F(t - t_{ij})\cdot u(t) \quad (17.6)$$

where C is the stress drop ratio of the large and small events, N is the number of elementary sources, r and r_{ij} are the distances from the site to the hypocenter of the small event to the ijth subfault, respectively, and $F(t)$ is a filtering function. The number of elementary sources, N, is computed by the scaling relation between the ratio of the seismic moment of the large (M_o) and small (m_o) earthquakes:

$$\frac{M_o}{m_o} = CN^3. \quad (17.7)$$

Finally, the broadband ground motion of the EME of interest can be obtained from the low- and high-frequency synthetics by using matched filters (see Figure 17.1) [Chavez et al., 2011].

Examples of the results obtained with the hybrid methodology to generate synthetic ground motions for several EME events in different seismotectonic environments are presented in Appendices 17.A–17.D. The detailed application of the methodology to the wave propagation of the 1985 Mw 8.01 Michoacan, Mexico earthquake and its results are presented in Appendix 17.A. In Appendices 17.B, 17.C, and 17.D the main results obtained for the 1995 Mw 8 Colima-Jalisco, Mexico, the 2008 Mw 7.9 Wenchuan, China, and the 2011 Mw 9 Tohoku, Japan, earthquakes, respectively, are included.

We notice that for all the results presented in Appendices 17.A–17.D, the agreement between the observations and the modeling results for the four EME are acceptable for seismic hazard and risk evaluation purposes.

17.2.3. Recurrent Neural Network Method

The procedure described in Section 17.2.2 allows us to generate synthetic strong ground motions at M locations on the surface of the site of interest, which can be discretized in N cells, with $M < N$ (see Appendix 17.B). In order to obtain the maximum intensity parameter of these synthetics (such as their peak ground acceleration, PGA) at the $(N–M)$ locations of the site's discretized surface, an RNN was proposed.

The heuristic and theoretical basis of the proposed RNN method, which is synthesized in Figure 17.2, is based on the first law of geography *"everything is related to everything else, but near things are more related than distant things"* [*Tobler*, 1970]. This conceptual observation is essentially connected to the so-called spatial analysis. In spatial analysis, the focus is on specific types of mathematical spaces (a mathematical space exists whenever a set of observations and quantitative measures of their attributes are available), namely, a geographic space, where the observations correspond to locations in a spatial measurement framework that captures their proximity in the real world (see Figure 17.2a sites A–D). For instance, the PGAs recorded at certain locations on the surface of the site of interest due to the occurrence of an EME.

The step-by-step procedure applied to PGA observations with the proposed RNN, within the geographic space of interest, is as follows:

(i) Build a neural interpolator for estimating the descriptor values at points different from the locations with known PGA.

(ii) Select points close enough located at k distances from the recording PGA stations; k is very small so they can be called "nearest neighbors" (see Figure 17.2b).

(iii) Estimate the PGA values at the latter points. The interrelation with the "real" recording values, to those from near and distant locations, is assured by the neural procedure.

(iv) These neuro-calculated values become training examples in the next iteration through the recurrent connection between the output and input layer.

(v) The closer points are, in the following iteration, the "virtual" recording stations, and a new set of estimations in sites located at k distances are estimated (see Figure 17.2c, d, and e), and

(vi) The recurrences are stopped when the PGA values in all the locations on the surface have been estimated (see Figure 17.2f).

It is important to point out that the proposed RNN is not used here merely as a spatial interpolator for estimating the PGA values at unobserved locations. The neural tool is a spatial regression method that captures spatial dependency in a kind of multidimensional regression analysis, providing information on 2D relationships among the PGA involved. As the PGAs are estimated for the whole set of "real" observations and they are *re-used* as training examples in the next network operation (temporal/spatial dependency), the neuro-spatial relationships are massively enhanced in subsequent iterations, taking into account the proximity and remoteness of the PGA values.

17.2.3.1. Architecture of the Recurrent Neural Network

The standard feedforward neural network, or multi-layer perceptron (MLP), is the best-known member of the family of many types of neural networks [*Haykin*, 1999]. Feedforward neural networks have been applied in tasks of prediction and classification of data for many years [*Egmont-Petersen et al.*, 2002; *Theodoridis and Koutroumbas*, 2008]. The dynamic NN, or neural networks for temporal processing, extend the feedforward networks with the capability of dynamic operation. This means that the NN behavior depends not only on the current input as in feedforward networks but also on previous operations of the network.

The RNN, as networks for temporal processing, gains knowledge through recurrent connections where the neuron outputs are fed back into the network as additional inputs [*Graves et al.*, 2009]. The fundamental feature of a RNN is that the network contains at least one feedback connection, so that activation can flow around in a loop. This enables the networks to perform temporal processing and learn sequences (e.g., perform sequence recognition/reproduction or temporal association/prediction). The learning capability of the network can be achieved by gradient descent procedures, similar to those used to derive the backpropagation algorithm for feedforward networks [*Hinton et al.*, 2006].

The network consists of a static layer, which generally has a higher number of neurons compared to the number of state variables of the system, from which the output is directed to an adder, where it is subtracted from the previous value of the variable Z_i, identified by the system. From this operation, the derivatives of each of the i state variables identified by the system are generated.

The dynamic recurrent multilayer network described in Equation 17.8 can identify the behavior of an autonomous system [$u = 0$, Equation 17.9]:

$$\frac{d}{dt}z = \overline{f}(z) = Ax + \varpi\sigma(Tz) \qquad (17.8)$$

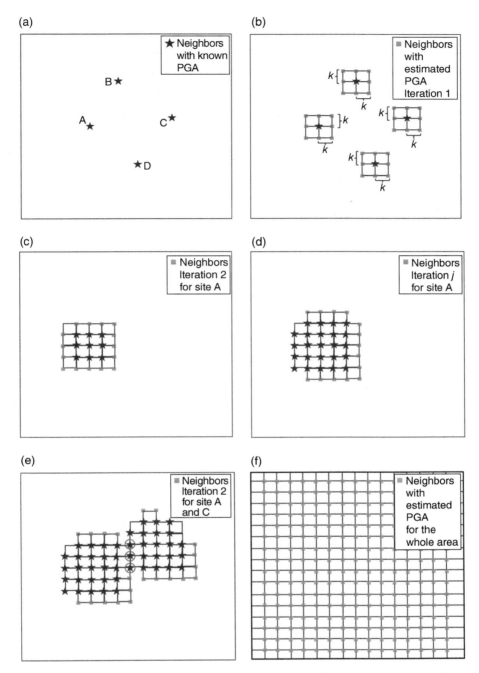

Figure 17.2 Schematic representation of the proposed recurrent neural network (RNN) procedure. k is the distance between the stations where the observed/estimated peak ground accelerations (PGAs) are known/estimated. (a) Sites A–D with observed PGAs (identified by a star), (b) results of the first iteration of the RNN procedure in which the estimated PGAs (identified by small gray squares) are obtained, (c) results of the second iteration of the RNN procedure for site A, (d) results of the jth iteration of the RNN procedure for site A, (e) results of an iteration of the RNN procedure for sites A and C, and (f) final results of the RNN procedure [*Chavez et al.*, 2014].

$$\frac{d}{dt}x = f(x) = Ax + f_o(x) \qquad (17.9)$$

Here $x, z \in R^n, A \in R^{n \times n}, f(x): R^n \to R^n, \bar{f}(z): R^n \to R^n,$ $w \in R^{n \times N}, T \in R^{n \times n}, \sigma(z) = [\sigma(z_1), \sigma(z_2), ..., \sigma(z_n)]$, the transfer function $\sigma(\theta) = \text{tansig}(\theta)$, n is the number of state variables of the system, N is the number of neurons in the hidden layer, and $f_o(x)$ is the estimated $f(x)$. According to *Haykin* [1999], without loss of generality, if the source is assumed to be an equilibrium point, the system

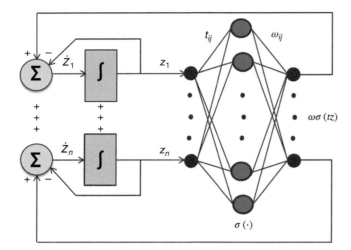

Figure 17.3 Dynamic multilayer networks. z_i is the output of the static layer i, $\dot{Z}_i$ is the derivative with respect to time of Z_i, t_{ij} is the expected value, ω_{ij} is the weight and σ is the transfer function [*Chavez et al.*, 2014].

(Equation 17.9) will be identified with the network (Equation 17.8) about its attraction region and guarantees that the error in the approximation $e(t)$ is limited. Mathematical and algorithm details of the proposed procedure are included in Chavez et al. [2014].

Learning rules. The static stage of the dynamic recurrent multilayer network is usually trained with a back-propagation algorithm. These algorithms are widely described in the vast literature, for example in *Hochreiter et al.* [2001] and *Serrano et al.* [2009]. The training patterns of the static layer are different combinations of values of the state variables, and the target patterns are given by the sum of each state variable with their corresponding derivative, as shown in the same Figure 17.3. The network is trained after the structure of Equation 17.10:

$$\frac{d}{dt}\begin{bmatrix} z_1 \\ z_2 \\ \vdots \\ z_n \end{bmatrix} = \begin{bmatrix} -z_1 \\ -z_2 \\ \vdots \\ -z_n \end{bmatrix} + \begin{bmatrix} w_{11} & w_{12} & \cdots & w_{1n} \\ w_{21} & w_{22} & \cdots & w_{2n} \\ w_{n1} & w_{n2} & \cdots & w_{nn} \end{bmatrix}$$

$$\times \begin{bmatrix} \sigma\left(t_{11}z_1 + t_{12}z_2 + \cdots + t_{1n}z_n\right) \\ \sigma\left(t_{21}z_2 + t_{22}z_2 + \cdots + t_{2n}z_n\right) \\ \vdots \\ \sigma\left(t_{n1}z_1 + t_{n2}z_2 + \cdots + t_{nn}z_n\right) \end{bmatrix} \quad (17.10)$$

Here t_{ij} are expected values of the variable.

To ensure that the network has identified the system dynamics, the Jacobian of the network at the source (Equation 17.11) should have values very close to those of the system that has been approximated.

$$J_M = -I_n + WT \quad (17.11)$$

where J_M is the Jacobian, I_n is the identity matrix of dimension n, W is the weights matrix, and $T = \sigma(t_{ij}z_j)$. The dynamic multilayer network of Figure 17.3 can be transformed into a dynamic network (Hopfield type) by means of the following linear transformation:

$$X = Tz \text{ and } \frac{dx}{dt} = T\frac{dz}{dt} \quad (17.12)$$

Generally, the T matrix is square, but if it is not, the transformation is performed by means of the generalized inverse. The transformed network will have the structure

$$\frac{d}{dt}x = -INX + TW\sigma(x) \quad (17.13)$$

Here, the new state vector $\chi \in R^n$, $\{TW\} \in R^{N \times N}$, IN is the identity matrix of dimension N, and the transformation (Equation 17.12) extends the dynamic multilayer network (Equation 17.10) into the dynamic recurrent Hopfield network (Equation 17.13). In the Hopfield network, the number of states is greater than or equal to the number of states of the multilayer network $N \geq n$. After transformation, the network has the structure of Equation 17.14.

$$\frac{d}{dt}\begin{bmatrix} x_1 \\ x_2 \\ \vdots \\ x_N \end{bmatrix} = \begin{bmatrix} -x_1 \\ -x_2 \\ \vdots \\ -x_N \end{bmatrix} + [TW] \times \begin{bmatrix} \sigma(x_1) \\ \sigma(x_2) \\ \vdots \\ \sigma(x_N) \end{bmatrix} \quad (17.14)$$

The Jacobian of the network described in Equation 17.13 should have values close to those of the system that has been approximated and should be equal to those of the multilayer network.

$$J_H = -I_N + WT \quad (17.15)$$

Here, J_H is the Hopfield Jacobian given in Equation 17.16.

$$\frac{d}{dt}\begin{bmatrix} z_1 \\ z_2 \\ \vdots \\ z_n \end{bmatrix} = \begin{bmatrix} -z_1 \\ -z_2 \\ \vdots \\ -z_n \end{bmatrix} + \begin{bmatrix} w_{11} & w_{12} & \cdots & w_{1n} \\ w_{21} & w_{22} & \cdots & w_{2n} \\ w_{n1} & w_{n2} & \cdots & w_{nn} \end{bmatrix}$$

$$\times \begin{bmatrix} \sigma\left(t_{11}z_1 + t_{12}z_2 + \cdots + t_{1n}z_n\right) \\ \sigma\left(t_{21}z_2 + t_{22}z_2 + \cdots + t_{2n}z_n\right) \\ \vdots \\ \sigma\left(t_{n1}z_1 + t_{n2}z_2 + \cdots + t_{nn}z_n\right) \end{bmatrix} \quad (17.16)$$

An algorithm of the proposed RNN procedure, which includes the steps implicit in Equations 17.8–17.16 was developed using the tools of the Mathworks website. The RNN method was validated in a numerical experiment, by using the 3D finite difference wave propagation code 3DWPFD described in Section 17.2.2, to obtain the 3D low-frequency synthetic wave velocity propagation field for the 28 September 2004 Mw 6 Parkfield, California, earthquake, and then it was successfully applied to the 1995 Mw Colima-Jalisco, Mexico, earthquake [*Chavez et al.*, 2014].

17.2.4. Copula Probability Distributions

In order to characterize the interdependence between PEI and PEDEC, the use of the copula-based multivariate probability distribution theory provides a suitable framework. Copulas allow characterization of the stochastic dependence of uniform transforms of marginal (univariate) probability distributions [*Sklar*, 1959]. In the following section, a brief synthesis of Copula theory is presented, with emphasis on the Gumbel-Hoogard Arquimidean copula used in this study. The application of the latter to describe the dependence between the PEI and PEDEC for EME are presented in Sections 17.5 and 17.7.

Sklar's theorem states that any multivariate joint distribution can be formulated using univariate transforms of the marginal distribution functions and a copula which describes the dependence between the variables [*Sklar*, 1959]:

Definition 1

A k-dimensional copula ($k \geq 2$) is a k-variate distribution function on $I^k = [0; 1]^k$ whose univariate marginals are distributed uniformly on $I = [0, 1]$.

Consequently, a given k-dimensional copula is associated with a random variable of the form $U_{d \in [|1,k|]} \sim F_U(I)$ where $F_U(I)$ is a uniform cumulative distribution on I. A k-dimensional copula function is defined as:

$$C(u_1, \ldots, u_n) = P(U_1 \leq u_1, \ldots, U_k \leq u_k) \quad (17.17)$$

According to this definition, multivariate distributions whose marginals are uniform can be modeled with copulas following Sklar's theorems 2 and 3 [*Sklar*, 1959]:

Theorem 2

If X and Y are two random variables and F and G are, respectively, X and Y's cumulative distribution functions continuous in $\mathbb{R}$ and $H(x, y) : \mathbb{R} \to \mathbb{R}$ is the joint distribution of F and G, then, there exists a unique copula function on Range (F) × Range (G) such that:

$$\forall (x,y) \in \mathbb{R} \times \mathbb{R} \to H(x,y) = C(F(x), G(y))$$

Conversely, if C is a copula, then the function $H : \mathbb{R} \times \mathbb{R} \to I$ defined by $H(x,y) = C(F(x),G(y))$ is a joint distribution with G and F marginals.

Theorem 3

A copula function $C : I^k \to I$ is a copula if the following conditions hold:

- $\forall_i \in [|1, k|]; C(u_1, \ldots, u_i, \ldots, u_k) = u_i$ when all except u_i are equal to 1
- C is isotonic; that is, if $\forall (u, v) \in I^2 : u < v$ then $C(u) < C(v)$
- C is k-increasing

From these two theorems, it follows that a copula C exists for any k-variate distribution function. The copula C, when all functions F_i are continuous can be obtained as:

$$C(u_1, \ldots, u_k) = F\left(F^{-1}(u_1), \ldots, F^{-1}(u_k)\right) \quad (17.18)$$

17.2.4.1. Archimedean Copulas

The family of Archimedean copulas is based on a common generator function. The generator function provides a flexible framework for fixing different degrees of marginals' dependence, based on the tuning of one or two parameter values [*McNeil and Neslehova*, 2009]. On the k-dimensional space, with $u = (u_1, u_2, \ldots, u_n)$, an Archimedean copula function is, from $I^k \to I$, defined as follows:

$$C(u) = \Psi\left(\Psi^{-1}(u_1) + \Psi^{-1}(u_2) + \cdots + \Psi^{-1}(u_k)\right) \quad (17.19)$$

The Archimedean copula generator Ψ has three main properties:

1. $\Psi : [0, \infty] \to I$ is continuous and strictly decreasing on the interval $[0, \infty]$
2. $\Psi(0) = 1$ and $\Psi^{-1}(0+) = \infty$, where Ψ^{-1} is the pseudo inverse of Ψ
3. $\lim_{t \to \infty}(\Psi(t)) = 0$

In addition to the above, Ψ has to be k-monotone on the $[0, \infty]$ interval for C(u) to be a copula function [*McNeil and Neslehova*, 2009].

Among the Archimedean copulas which have been proposed [*Nelsen*, 2006], the Gumbel-Hoogard copula offers interesting characteristics in the context of extreme events, which is the framework of the hazard and risk assessment application in this study.

The Gumbel-Hoogard copula is an asymmetric Archimedean copula and allows characterization of dependence both in the upper and lower tail of its joint distribution. It is expressed as follows [*Nelsen*, 2006; *McNeil and Neslehova*, 2009]:

$$C(u,v) = \exp\left(-\left[(-\ln(u))^\alpha + (-\ln(v))^\alpha\right]^{1/\alpha}\right) \quad (17.20)$$

And its generator is:

$$\varphi(t) = \left(-\ln(t)\right)^{\alpha} \quad \text{where } \alpha \in [1,\infty] \quad (17.21)$$

The Gumbel-Hoogard copula is also an extreme value copula because it satisfies the max-stable property, which can be interpreted in the following manner [*Nelsen*, 2006]:

Let $(X_1, ..., X_n)$ and $(Y_1, ..., Y_n)$ be identically distributed random vectors such that the couples (X_i, Y_i) are bound by the same copula C.

Let C_{max} be the copula of the couple $(X_{(n)}, Y_{(n)}) = (\max(X_i),\max(Y_i))$, which according to *Nelsen* [2006] leads to:

$$C_{max}(u,v) = C\left(u^{1/n},v^{1/n}\right)^n = C(u,v) \quad (17.22)$$

This means that for the Gumbel-Hoogard copula, the couple (X_i, Y_i) is bound by the same copula, as the couple $(X_{(n)}, Y_{(n)})$. Therefore, the Gumbel-Hoogard copula is appropriate to model dependence between extreme (random) events.

Thus, it follows that the copula-based multivariate modeling and in particular the Gumbel-Hoogard copula provides a convenient framework for modeling the joint probability distribution in the context of this study. Hence the Gumbel-Hoogard copula modeling is adopted in the present study to assess the joint probabilistic risk associated with the occurrence of EME's intensities and of their direct economic consequences.

17.2.4.2. Joint Probabilities

Based on the copula density function $C(F_X(x), F_Y(y))$, with $F_X(x)$ and $F_Y(y)$ the cumulative probability distributions of the stochastic variables X and Y, the following joint probabilities can be obtained Shiau (2006):

The probabilities of X and Y surpassing x and y values are:

$$P(X \geq x, Y \geq y) = 1 - F_X(x) - F_Y(y) + F_{X,Y}(x,y) \quad (17.23)$$

$$P(X \geq x, Y \geq y) = 1 - F_X(x) - F_Y(y) + C\left(F_X(x), F_Y(y)\right) \quad (17.24)$$

The probabilities of X or Y surpassing x and y values are:

$$P(X \geq x) \cup P(Y \geq y) = 1 - F_{X,Y}(x,y) \quad (17.25)$$

$$P(X \geq x) \cup P(Y \geq y) = 1 - C\left(F_X(x), F_Y(y)\right) \quad (17.26)$$

The probability distributions of X knowing that Y exceeds a threshold y are:

$$P(X \leq x | Y \geq y) = P(Y \geq y, X \leq x)/P(Y \geq y)$$
$$= F_X(x) - F_{X,Y}(y,x)/\left[1 - F_Y(y)\right] \quad (17.27)$$

$$P(X \leq x | Y \geq y) = \left[F_X(x) - C\left(F_Y(y), F_X(x)\right)\right]/\left[1 - F_Y(y)\right] \quad (17.28)$$

17.2.4.3. Return Periods

17.2.4.3.1. Return Periods for Univariate Distributions

Instead of using the probability of exceedance results for extreme events, their corresponding return periods are used, which is defined as the inverse of the probability of exceedance of those events and allows displaying the output of risk assessments in simple metrics suitable for decision making. Considering an expected time interval $E(L)$ between the occurrence of two extreme events, the return period T_X of an event following a (univariate) distribution $F_X(x)$ which exceeds a threshold x, can be expressed as follows:

$$T_X = \frac{E(L)}{1 - F_X(x)} \quad (17.29)$$

17.2.4.3.2. Return Periods for Bivariate Distributions

In the case of bivariate distributions with probability of exceedance expressed by Equations 17.23–17.28, their corresponding return periods can be expressed as follows. From Equation 17.24, the return period of X and Y exceeding x and y values, is respectively:

$$T_{X,Y} = \frac{E(L)}{1 - F_X(x) - F_Y(y) + C\left(F_X(x), F_Y(y)\right)} \quad (17.30)$$

Similarly, based on Equation 17.26, the return period of X or Y exceeding x and y values, respectively is:

$$T_{X,Y} = \frac{E(L)}{1 - C\left(F_X(x), F_Y(y)\right)} \quad (17.31)$$

Also, from Equation 17.28, the return period of X exceeding a threshold value x knowing that Y is higher than the threshold y, can be expressed as follows:

$$T_{X|Y \geq y} = \frac{T_Y}{P(X \geq x, Y \geq y)}$$
$$= \frac{E(L)}{\left(\left[1 - F_Y(y)\right]\left[1 - F_X(x) - F_Y(y) + C\left(F_X(x), F_Y(y)\right)\right]\right)} \quad (17.32)$$

17.2.5. Application of the Hybrid Approach

In order to illustrate the application of the hybrid approach for the estimation of the direct economic impacts of EME on the infrastructure located at a specific site, the results for the estimation of the PEIs, PEDECs and PMLs of Mexico City and Guadalajara one- to three-floor dwelling construction stock due to the probable occurrence of extreme Mw 8.5 subduction earthquakes with epicenters in the Mexican Pacific Ocean Coasts are presented in Sections 17.4–17.5 and 17.6–17.7, respectively. Also, the impact of seismic risk mitigation policies, such as increasing the seismic strength of the constructions by retrofitting (i.e., by reducing their seismic vulnerability) on their respective PMLs, is addressed in Sections 17.5 and 17.7.

17.3. EXTREME MAGNITUDE SUBDUCTION EARTHQUAKES WORLDWIDE AND IN MEXICO

17.3.1. Spatial Distributions of Extreme Magnitude Subduction Earthquakes Worldwide

The detailed analysis and estimation of the spatial location and occurrence time of EME in the world has been the subject of recent studies, especially after the occurrence of the 2004 Mw 9.1 Andaman, Indonesia [*Ammon et al.*, 2005], the 2010 Mw 8.8 Maule, Chile [*Vigny et al.*, 2011], the 2011 Mw 9 Tohoku, Japan, and the 2008 Mw 7.9 Wenchuan, China, earthquakes. These studies aimed to answer two questions which are crucial

for the assessment of the seismic hazard and risk due to the occurrence of extreme magnitude events in the world, and especially of those occurring in the seismic circum-Pacific belt: that is (1) which are the maximum magnitudes Mw of the EME and (2) what are their time of recurrence (their return period) in each of the different seismic zones indicated in Figure 17.4.

For example, *McCaffrey* [2007, 2008], by using data of magnitude $M \geq 7.5$ subduction zone (zones of the world in which two tectonic plates interact, moving in different directions and velocities, and one of them bends and descends beneath the other plate, producing the so-called interplate earthquakes [*Stein and Wysession*, 2003]) thrust earthquakes that occurred (mainly) from 1900 to 2006 (and few historical ones from 1700 to 1900), and based on theoretical seismotectonic and statistical considerations, as well as by using Monte Carlo simulation techniques, concluded that with respect to the recurrence times and taking into account the short history of observation, the probable occurrence of an (extreme) Mw ≥ 9 earthquake at any of the subduction zones included in Figure 17.4 cannot be ruled out. Furthermore, another conclusion is that from one to three of those EME would occur in the world per century [*McCaffrey*, 2008]. In another recent study carried out by *Goldfinger et al.* [2013], apart from seismological data, paleoseismic information was also

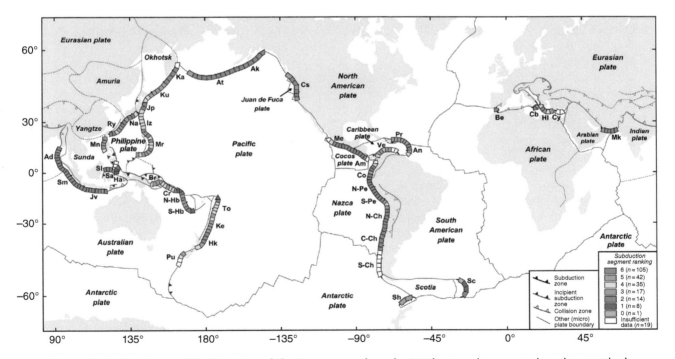

Figure 17.4 Global map of the 24 active subduction zones, where the 200 km trench segments have been ranked from $S = 0$–6, in terms of their predicted capability of generating extreme magnitude earthquakes with Mw > 8.5. For the highest possible score ($S = 6$) and the lowest possible score ($S = 0$), the values of S of a particular trench segment imply a high and a low risk of producing an Mw > 8.5 earthquake, respectively. Abbreviations for the subduction zone segments in the figure are included in figure 1 of *Schellart and Rawlinson* [2013].

used to enlarge the observational period of the regions where the 2011 Tohoku earthquake occurred. Similar data from the Cascadia region located in the western border between the United States and Canada, where historical large magnitude subduction earthquakes have occurred was also used. The results obtained by *Goldfinger et al.* [2013], suggested, as in *McCaffrey* [2007, 2008], that larger magnitude earthquakes than presently known, may well characterize many of the subduction zones shown in Figure 17.4.

Following the work by *McCaffrey* [2007, 2008] and *Goldfinger et al.* [2013], a recent detailed statistical study on the maximum Mw magnitude for subduction zone thrust earthquakes, which occurred from 1900 to 2012 in the world, *Schellart and Rawlinson* [2013] carried out tests on the dependence of Mw of these earthquakes, with the geometry, kinematics, dynamics, and geological characteristics of the 24 active subduction zones shown in Figure 17.4. The zones shown in this figure were segmented into a total of 241 trench segments, each with a 200 km trench-parallel extent, achieving equal weightage to each segment in the statistical analysis. The study included several subduction segments in which historical EME (Mw > 8.5) have been reported, such as those in 1700 in Cascadia, in 1833 on southern Sumatra, in 1877 in northern Chile and in 1868 in southern Peru; as well as other segments in which the four largest (instrumentally) recorded EME occurred, that is, the 1960 Mw 9.5 Chile [*Plafker and Savage*, 1970], the 1964 Mw 9.2 Alaska [*Plafker*, 1965], the 2004 Mw 9.1 Andaman and the 2011 Mw 9 Tohoku earthquakes.

Among other conclusions, *Schellart and Rawlinson* [2013] suggested that the probability of occurrence of EM subduction thrust earthquakes is associated with: (1) large-scale dynamics of the subducting plate, (2) overriding plate, (3) slab, and (4) ambient mantle. This is mainly due to the slab rollback/roll-forward processes, the subduction-induced mantle flow patterns, which control the relative motions of the subduction zone hinge and the overriding plate, determining the trench and slab curvatures. Also, the existence of buoyant features on the subducting plate, affect the local dip angle of the slab, which can cause local overriding plate shortening and compression at the subduction zone interface, generating a potential (nucleation) zone of EMEs.

The main result of the study of *Schellart and Rawlinson* [2013] is depicted in Figure 17.4, where the 200 km trench segments of the 24 active subduction zones analyzed have been ranked in terms of their predicted capability of generating extreme Mw > 8.5 magnitude subduction earthquakes. The segments have been ranked in terms of the following subduction zone parameters (S): (1) trench-normal overriding plate deformation rate, (2) trench normal velocity, (3) subduction thrust dip

angle, (4) subduction partitioning, (5) subduction thrust curvature, and (6) trench curvature angle. The highest (S = 6, identified by the red color in Figure 17.4) and the lowest (S = 0, identified by the light-blue color in Figure 17.4) possible scores of a particular trench segment imply a high and a low risk of producing a Mw > 8.5 magnitude earthquake in the 241 segment trench, respectively. It can be observed from Figure 17.4 that most of the length of the Mexican-Guatemalan region (identified by Me in the figure) is ranked as "high risk," that is, a region capable of generating EMEs with Mw > 8.5 magnitudes.

17.3.2. Maximum Magnitude and Frequency of Occurrence of Extreme Magnitude Subduction Earthquakes Worldwide

As mentioned in an earlier section, the other very important aspect to be considered regarding EME in the world is their frequency of occurrence or return period, which may vary from tens to thousands of years [*Stein and Wysession*, 2003]. The Gutenberg-Richter (GR) distribution, $\log_{10} N = a - bM$ (where N is the number of events having a magnitude $\geq M$, and a and b are constants, whose values are characteristic of the seismotectonic region considered), is widely used to compute the earthquake magnitude-frequency distributions (i.e., the frequency of occurrence) of the seismic regions in the world [*Gutenberg and Richter*, 1954; *Stein and Wysession*, 2003].

The GR distribution expresses the relationship between the magnitude and the total number of earthquakes in a specific seismic region and time period. The GR distribution implies an exponential decrease in the rate of large magnitude earthquakes and an exponential increase in their seismic moment (which is equal to the product of the (planar) fault rupture area of the earthquake by the slip of the fault and by the rigidity of the geological media where the earthquake occurs [*Stein and Wysession*, 2003]), which disagrees with the seismic observations, particularly at the tail of the GR distribution, that is, for the maximum magnitude earthquakes [*Stein and Wysession*, 2003].

In order to overcome this paradox, some authors have proposed to truncate, abruptly to zero, the GR distribution at a so-called cutoff maximum magnitude [*Frankel et al.*, 1996, 2002; *Petersen et al.*, 2008]. This means that earthquakes with magnitude larger than the latter are not considered in the seismic hazard analysis performed for the seismotectonic region of interest. However, due to the short time span of world historical earthquake catalogs, the reliable estimation of the cutoff magnitude becomes a difficult task; and this could lead to underestimation of the value of possible EME in some cases that a seismotectonic

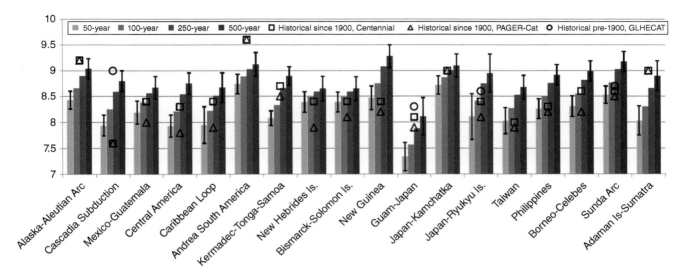

Figure 17.5 The vertical bars represent the estimated probable maximum magnitude $Mw_p(T) \geq 7$ in time interval T(years), for return periods T = 50, 100, 250, and 500 years for the world seismic subduction zones shown in Figure 17.4. The uncertainties (±1σ; black bars) are shown only for T = 50 and 500 years. The historical maximum magnitude earthquake data are from the Centennial [*Engdahl and Villaseñor*, 2002], PAGER-CAT [*Allen et al.*, 2009], and the GLHECAT [*Albini et al.*, 2014], catalogs [*Rong et al.*, 2014].

region could actually generate. This could lead to the underestimation of the corresponding seismic hazard for the region under consideration and its possible associated casualties and economic consequences, as illustrated by the cases of the 2011 Mw 9 Tohoku, Japan, the 2008 Mw 7.9 Wenchuan, China, and the 1985 Mw 8.01 Michoacan, Mexico EME.

In a recent study, *Rong et al.* [2014] applied maximum-likelihood methods constrained by tectonic information and the Tapered Gutemberg-Richter (TGR) distribution [*Kagan*, 1997; *Kagan and Schoenberg*, 2001; *Bird and Kagan*, 2004] to estimate the probability density function (PDF) and the corresponding cumulative distributions, of the probable maximum magnitude $Mw_p(T)$ expected in a given time interval T(years) for the subduction seismotectonic regions shown in Figure 17.4. *Rong et al.* [2014] argued that their choice of using the TGR distribution is supported by the following:

a. The results obtained by *Bell et al.* [2013] where the authors applied statistical tests on global seismicity information available and concluded that the frequency-magnitude size distributions found in their study converged to a TGR distribution;

b. Physically, the TGR distribution conforms better with the known behavior of dissipative physical dynamic systems that require a smooth transition of the magnitudes, as has been observed in different seismotectonic regions of the world [*Bird and Kagan*, 2004].

It is relevant to note that the $Mw_p(T)$ distributions proposed by *Rong et al.* [2014] contain information on the magnitude limit, and the occurrence rate of the extreme magnitude events for the circum-Pacific subduction regions shown in Figure 17.4. *Rong et al.* [2014] estimated that the $Mw_p(T)$ distributions for each of the subduction regions of Figure 17.4, and their estimates for any time period T is subject to natural variability. Therefore, $Mw_p(T)$ obtained represents the median of a probability density distribution estimated along with its uncertainty. The main results of the study are shown in Figure 17.5.

The results of *Rong et al.* [2014] presented in Figure 17.5 suggest that most of the circum-Pacific subduction zone shown in Figure 17.4 can generate Mw ≥ 8.5 earthquakes over a return period T = 250 years. For over a 500 year return period, most of the zones can generate Mw ≥ 8.8 earthquakes. For over a 10,000 year return period, almost all of the zones can generate Mw ≥ 9 earthquakes. It can be observed from Figure 17.5 that for the Mexico-Guatemala subduction zone region, for return periods T = 50, 100, 250, and 500 years, the estimated probable maximum magnitudes Mw_p are ~7.8, 8.3, 8.55, and 8.7, respectively.

17.3.3. Extreme Magnitude Subduction Earthquakes in Mexico

The seismotectonics of the Mexican subduction region is associated with the dynamics of the Cocos, Rivera, Caribbean, and North American plates (see Figure 17.6). The subduction of the Cocos and Rivera plates under the North American plate, historically, has generated the largest magnitude events in Mexico. Figure 17.6 shows

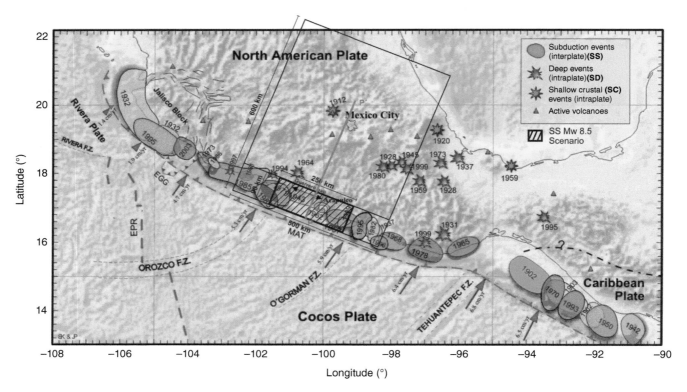

Figure 17.6 Historical seismicity (1900–2003) of Mexico including its subduction, deep and shallow crustal earthquakes, with magnitudes $M > 6.5$; the superficial projections (large rectangle) of the 3D volume (500 × 600 × 124 km³) and of the rupture area (hatched inner rectangle) used in the 3D Finite Differences Modeling of the wave propagation of the Mw 8.5 subduction earthquake scenario in the Guerrero region [modified, *Pacheco and Kostoglodov*, 1999 (updated in 2003)].

the historical seismicity (1900–2003) of Mexico including its subduction, deep and shallow crustal earthquakes with magnitudes $M > 6.5$. The year of occurrence and the rupture areas (which are proportional to the magnitude of the earthquake) of the subduction earthquakes are identified in Figure 17.6 by ellipsoidal shapes of different colors, located along the Pacific Ocean coast of Mexico. The epicenters of the deep and crustal superficial earthquakes are identified by red and blue stars, respectively.

We notice in Figure 17.6 that the dynamic interaction of the Cocos and the Rivera tectonic plates with the North American plate has generated in the last 115 years the largest subduction magnitude earthquakes in Mexico, such as the 3 June 1932 Ms 8.2 Jalisco, the 19 September 1985 Mw 8.01 Michoacan, and the 9 October 1995 Mw 8 Colima-Jalisco (CJ) earthquakes, whose rupture areas are located between latitudes 17° and 21° North, and longitudes −102° and −106° West (see the left side of Figure 17.6). The geometries of the subducting Cocos and Rivera, and the North American plates are shown in Figures 17.A1b and 17.B1b.

In order to obtain the probability of exceedance per year, λ_m (or its reciprocate, the return period T_r (years)) for the subduction earthquakes with magnitude $M \geq 6.4$

which have occurred in Mexico from 1900 to 2003, we used the last century catalogs of the Servicio Sismologico Nacional (SSN) of Mexico [*Pacheco and Kostoglodov*, 1999] and the one of *Engdahl and Villaseñor* [2002]. The data and the resulting λ_m are shown in Figure 17.7. λ_m (the continuous line in this figure) was obtained by applying a Bayesian technique (a statistical technique that aside of using observed data uses the a priori knowledge that we could have about the observations) to $M \geq 6.4$ observed earthquake magnitudes (identified by squares) to obtain the most likely λ_m fitting. We also included in the fitting of λ_m, the probable maximum (extreme) earthquake magnitude Mw$_p$ 9 value (which has a $T_r = 10,000$ years) suggested by *Rong et al.* [2014] for the Mexico-Guatemala subduction zone region (see Figure 17.5).

17.3.4. Extreme Mw 8.5 Magnitude Subduction Earthquake Scenarios for the Guerrero and the Colima-Jalisco Regions

The studies on the historical and expected occurrence of EME in the seismic subduction subzones of the circum-Pacific Belt by *McCaffrey* [2007, 2008], *Goldfinger et al.* [2013], *Schellart and Rawlinson* [2013], and *Rong*

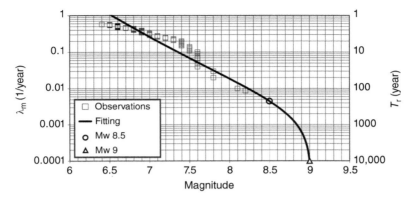

Figure 17.7 Rate of exceedance λ_m versus magnitude for superficial Ms/Mw ≥ 6.4 earthquakes that occurred in the subduction zone of Mexico from 1900 to 2003. The λ_m for the extreme Mw 8.5 magnitude scenario (obtained by the Bayesian fitting of the data) is identified by the circle (observed data (squares) from the Servicio Sismologico Nacional (SSN), Mexico, and *Engdahl and Villaseñor* [2002]). The triangle corresponds to the probable maximum (extreme) earthquake Mw_p 9 magnitude suggested for T_r = 10,000 years for the Mexico-Guatemala region by *Rong et al.* [2014].

et al. [2014] are shown in Figures 17.4 and 17.5. The results of Figure 17.5 suggest that for the Mexico-Guatemala subduction zone region (see Figure 17.4), the occurrence of earthquakes with maximum magnitudes Mw_p of 7.8, 8.3, 8.55, and 8.7 are expected in this region, with return periods T_r of 50, 100, 250, and 500 years, respectively.

From a statistical analysis of the historical information of large magnitude earthquakes that occurred in the Mexican subduction zone, *Nishenko and Singh* [1987] concluded that the Guerrero and the CJ subduction regions of Mexico should be considered as having high seismic hazard potential. With respect to the magnitudes and their frequency of occurrence, *Nishenko and Singh* [1987] suggested that in the Guerrero region "the occurrence of a Mw 8 earthquake is expected in the immediate future." They also suggested that in the CJ region, earthquakes with magnitudes Mw/Ms ≥ 8 should be expected with return periods varying from 77 to 126 years (incidentally, the last Ms 8.2 occurred in 1932 in this region).

From a study carried out by *Suarez and Albini* [2009] on the historical information of a large magnitude subduction earthquake that occurred in 1787 in southeastern Mexico, which produced a large tsunami that propagated up to 6 km inland in this region, it was concluded that this earthquake had an estimated Mw 8.6 magnitude. The occurrence of the tsunami associated with this EME was recently confirmed by *Ramirez-Herrera et al.* [2013], based on geological field work and laboratory tests (such as microfossils—foraminifera and diatoms, magnetic properties, and others) performed on samples (of the stratigraphic layers) found in a transect made in the mentioned region, with coring and test pits every 100 m from the Mexican Pacific ocean coastline up to 1.6 km inland.

It can be concluded from the results obtained in this study on the rate of exceedance (λ_m) of earthquakes with magnitude Ms/Mw ≥ 6.4 that occurred in the subduction zone of Mexico from 1900 to 2003 (see Figure 17.7) that an extreme Mw 8.5 earthquake scenario corresponds to a return period T_r ~225 years, which is close to T_r = 250 years suggested by *Rong et al.* [2014] for the Mexico-Guatemala region. The difference between the T_r values, reflects the fact that we used mainly the local data of the Servicio Sismologico Nacional (SSN) of Mexico, while *Rong et al.* [2014] used the worldwide earthquake catalogs mentioned in Figure 17.5.

Taking into account the results of the studies carried out by *McCaffrey* [2007, 2008], *Goldfinger et al.* [2013], *Schellart and Rawlinson* [2013], and *Rong et al.* [2014], on the historical and expected seismic activities of the circum-Pacific belt (see Figures 17.4 and 17.5), and on the results of similar studies on the subduction zone of Mexico (see Figure 17.6) by *Nishenko and Singh* [1987], *Pacheco and Kostoglodov* [1999], *Suarez and Albini* [2009], and *Ramirez-Herrera et al.* [2013] and Chapter 13 in this Monograph, two extreme Mw 8.5 magnitude subduction earthquake scenarios are proposed in this work: (1) one with an epicenter in the CJ region and (2) the other with an epicenter in the Guerrero region.

Also, considering the suggestion of *Suarez and Albini* [2009] on the occurrence of an extreme Mw 8.6 magnitude earthquake in 1787 with an epicenter in the Guerrero-Oaxaca Mexican Coasts, and the periods of recurrence T_r of 225 years (obtained in this study, see Figure 17.7) or 250 years (suggested by *Rong et al.* [2014], see Figure 17.5) for extreme Mw 8.5 magnitude subduction earthquake in the Mexico region, it can be concluded that extreme Mw 8+ magnitude, such as the two Mw 8.5

subduction earthquake scenarios proposed in this study, might occur from 2012 to 2037 (i.e., 1787 + 225 or 1787 + 250 years, respectively) in the Mexican earthquake subduction region.

The detailed characterizations of the proposed seismic scenarios for the Guerrero and the CJ regions are presented in the next sections.

17.4. SYNTHETIC ACCELEROGRAMS IN MEXICO CITY FOR AN EXTREME MW 8.5 MAGNITUDE SUBDUCTION EARTHQUAKE SCENARIO WITH AN EPICENTER IN THE GUERRERO REGION

17.4.1. Location and Rupture Area of an Extreme Mw 8.5 Magnitude Subduction Earthquake Scenario in the Guerrero Region

The location and the seismic rupture area proposed for the plausible occurrence of an extreme Mw 8.5 magnitude earthquake scenario, with an epicenter in the Guerrero region of the Mexican subduction zone, are represented by the inner hatched rectangle depicted in Figure 17.6. The proposed rupture area includes three sub-regions studied by *Nishenko and Singh* [1987]: (1) the so-called Guerrero gap region where the authors proposed that the occurrence of a Mw 8 earthquake is expected and therefore, should be considered of high seismic hazard potential in the "immediate future," (2) the Acapulco-San Marcos region where the same authors suggested that Ms ≥ 7.7 events are expected between 2013 and 2024, and (3) the Petatlan region where they proposed that Ms 7.6/7.7 events are expected in 2015.

We notice that the Guerrero gap region is located between the rupture areas of the 1979 Ms 7.6 Petatlan and the 1962 Ms 7.1/7.0 (Mw 7.3) Acapulco earthquakes (see Figure 17.6).

The surface projection of the rupture area for the Mw 8.5 earthquake scenario is represented by the inner hatched rectangle of 250 × 90 km² (see Figure 17.6). These dimensions were obtained by assuming a 90 km width for the Mw 8.5 earthquake scenario, similar to the observed width of the rupture areas of the 1932 Ms 8.2 and the 1985 Mw 8.01 earthquakes, and the widths suggested by *Ortiz et al.* [2000] for the 1957 Ms 7.5 and 1962 Ms 7.1 Acapulco earthquakes (see Figure 17.6). The 250 km length was obtained by following *Wells and Coppersmith* [1994] for the calculation of ~22,000 km² of the rupture area for a Mw 8.5 subduction earthquake (i.e., 22,000 km²/90 km = ~250 km).

It can be observed from Figure 17.6 that the 250 × 90 km² inner rectangle overlaps the rupture areas of the 1979 Ms 7.6, 1985bis Ms 7.5, 1962 Ms 7.1, 1957 Ms 7.5 and the 1989 Ms 6.8 subduction superficial earthquakes. The overlapping assumption is based on the following

observation: (1) the 1985 Mw 8.01/Ms 8.1Michoacan earthquake, whose rupture area overlapped partially the 1973 Ms 7.6 and totally the 1981 Ms 7.3 earthquakes, (2) the 1995 Mw 8 CJ earthquake which overlapped, partially the rupture area of the 1932-1 Ms 8.2, and totally one of the 1932-2 Ms 8 earthquakes, respectively (see Figure 17.6). A similar observation of the overlap of the rupture area of EME, on the "smaller" rupture areas of large historical Mw ≥ 8 magnitude earthquakes, is the case for the 2011 Mw 9 Tohoku, Japan earthquake [see Figure 17.D1; *Tajima et al.*, 2013].

17.4.2. Uncertainties on the Seismic Source Kinematic Slip of an Extreme Mw 8.5 Magnitude Subduction Earthquake Scenario in the Guerrero Region

The uncertainties surrounding the detailed spatial distribution of the kinematic slip on the seismic source of the proposed extreme Mw 8.5 earthquake scenario (see Figure 17.6) were taken into account by generating 10-synthetic slip distributions (Models 1–10) shown in Figure 17.8. (Incidentally, the number of synthetic slips could be increased to have a larger sample of slip distributions.) The synthetic slip distributions were obtained by using a kinematic slip model based on worldwide historical earthquake slip data of large magnitude subduction earthquakes [*Mai and Beroza*, 2002]. The worldwide slip data used by these authors included the slip distributions of the following large magnitude earthquakes that occurred in the Mexican subduction zone: 1979 Mw 7.4, 1981 Mw 7.25, 1985bis Mw 7.4, 1985 Mw 8.01 (14 September) 1995 Mw 7.3, and 1995 Mw 8 earthquakes.

It can be observed from Figure 17.8 that maximum slips of up to 30 m (deep red colors) were obtained for the synthetic slips, and that they included equally likely plausible seismic rupture patterns, some with large slips concentrated in a large area (Models 3, 5, 6), others with several slips distributed in the assumed rupture area (Models 1, 2, 4, 9) and other slip distributions patterns (Models 7, 8) and the location of their respective hypocenter (identified by a star in Figure 17.8).

17.4.3. Synthetic Accelerograms in Mexico City for an Extreme Mw 8.5 Subduction Earthquake Scenario in the Guerrero Region

The hybrid method described in Section 17.2.2 was used to generate synthetic accelerograms expected in Mexico City for the extreme Mw 8.5 subduction earthquake scenario presented in Figure 17.6. For the low-frequency modeling, a 500 (width) × 600 (length) × 124 (depth) km³ volume was used. The surface projection of the latter is shown in Figure 17.6. The physical and computational modeling parameters are identical to those used for the

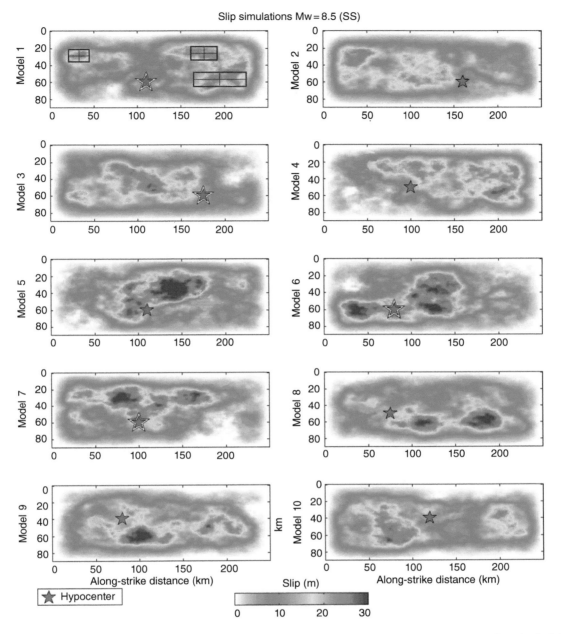

Figure 17.8 Slip simulations [based on *Mai and Beroza*, 2002] of the finite seismic sources used in the hybrid modeling of the extreme Mw 8.5 subduction superficial earthquake scenario. The star identifies the location of the hypocenter, that is, where the earthquake starts. The inner rectangles in Model 1 are an example of the finite sources used for the empirical Green function modeling.

successful modeling of the 1985 Michoacan earthquake discussed in Appendix 17.A (see Figures 17.A1b and 17.A2). However, the kinematic slips of Figure 17.8 were used to include 10 different possibilities of the rupture of the seismic source of the proposed scenario earthquake. The 3DWPFD code and the supercomputers KanBalam, HECToR and JUGENE were used for the tests and final runs of the low-frequency computation of the wave

propagation of the extreme Mw 8.5 earthquake scenario [*Cabrera et al.*, 2007; *Chavez et al.*, 2008, 2010, 2011].

For the high-frequency modeling, we used the EGF technique discussed in Section 17.2.2 [*Chavez et al.*, 2011], which allows us to generate high-frequency synthetic accelerograms. For the extreme Mw 8.5 earthquake scenario, the recorded accelerograms (of smaller magnitude events than the scenario earthquake) observed in Mexico

(a)

(b)

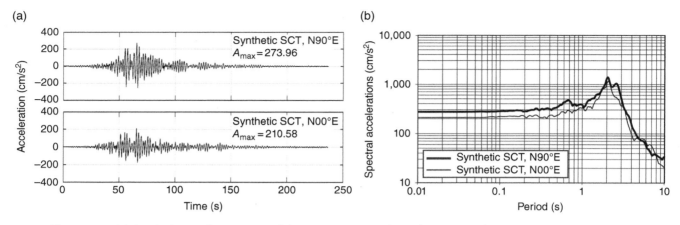

Figure 17.9 (a) Synthetic accelerograms and (b) response spectral accelerations in the west-east (N90°E), north-south (N00°E) directions for recording site SCT (Mexico City) for the Mw 8.5 earthquake scenario with the Model 1 kinematic slip of Figure 17.8.

(a)

(b)

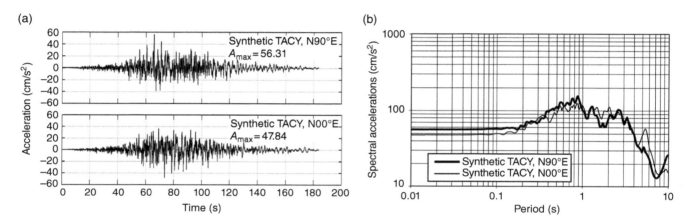

Figure 17.10 (a) Synthetic accelerograms and (b) response spectra acceleration in the west-east (N90°E), north-south (N00°E) directions for Mexico City recording site TACY for the Mw 8.5 earthquake scenario with the Model 1 kinematic slip of Figure 17.8.

City for the: (1) 14 March 1979 (Ms 7.6), (2) 19 September 1985 (Mw 8.01/Ms 8.1), (3) the 20 September 1985 (Ms 7.5), and (4) the 14 September 1995 (Mw 7.4), earthquakes were used—all of them with their rupture areas located inside or very close to the assumed rupture surface of the extreme Mw 8.5 magnitude earthquake scenario.

From the synthesis of the low- and high-frequency synthetic accelerograms (see Figure 17.1), the broadband (0.01–10 Hz) synthetics for the extreme Mw 8.5 magnitude earthquake scenario were obtained. Examples of the type of results obtained in this case corresponding to the kinematic slip rupture of the Model 1 shown in Figure 17.8, are presented in Figures 17.9a and 17.10a. These figures include the synthetic accelerograms in the N90°E (West-East) and N00°E (North-South) directions, for Mexico City SCT and TACY accelerographic recording sites, which are located in the compressible and firm

soil zones of Mexico City, respectively (see Figure 17.A6). It can be observed from Figures 17.9a and 17.10a that the maximum accelerations of the synthetics of the SCT site are ~4.9 and 4.4 times those of the TACY site for the N90°E and N00°E directions, respectively.

In Figures 17.9b and 17.10b, the response spectra of acceleration, Sa(5%), associated with accelerograms of Figures 17.9a and 17.10a are shown, respectively. The Sa(5%) is a plot of the maximum acceleration responses to ground motion accelerations, of idealized structural systems such as a one-floor construction with (1) different natural periods of vibration (i.e. the duration of one full cycle of the dynamic response of the system) and (2) the same structural damping (the energy dissipation capability of the system, in this case of 5% which allows the structural system to eventually stop oscillating once the ground motion accelerations acting on its foundation have completed [*Kramer*, 1996].

The different shapes and maximum values of the Sa(5%)'s of the synthetic accelerograms of SCT and TACY sites are shown in Figures 17.9b and 17.10b. One of the SCT sites has a maximum value of ~1200 cm/s² for a natural period $T = 2$ s, while the corresponding values for the TACY site are ~40 cm/s² for $0.5 \text{ s} \leq T < 0.9$ s and ~100 cm/s² for $1.0 \text{ s} \leq T \leq 3$ s. (The reciprocal value of the frequency 0.5 Hz is shown in the Fourier Amplitude Spectra in Figure 17.A4b for the 1985 Mw 8.01 earthquake.) From Figures 17.9b and 17.10b, we can conclude that the values of Sa (5%) for a specific natural period T_i of the SCT site can be obtained by multiplying the ordinates of Sa (5%) values for the same T_i of the TACY site (or other Mexico City firm soil site) by an Amplification Factor (AF).

The observation of the relationship between the firm and compressible soils Sa(5%) response spectra (and their associated Fourier Amplitude Spectra (FAS), see Figures 17.A4 and 17.A5) for the TACY and SCT recording sites discussed previously, can be generalized for all the sites located on the compressible soil zone of Mexico City, with respect to other site(s) located on the firm soil zone of Mexico City (see Figure 17.A6), as suggested, among others by: *Rosenblueth* [1953] by using unidimensional seismic wave propagation models for firm and viscoelastic soils representing Mexico City soils; *Zeevaert and Newmark* [1956] and *Zeevaert* [1960] by using seismological observations of earthquakes recorded in Mexico City at the Tacubaya (TACY) seismological station (in service since 1910) and geodynamic arguments on Mexico City compressible soils; *Rascón et al.* [1976, 1977] by the processing of acelerographic observations recorded from 1962 to 1968 on the firm and compressible Mexico City soils; *Singh et al.* [1988], *Ordaz et al.* [1988], *Rosenblueth and Arciniega* [1992], *Reinoso et al.* [1992], *Pérez-Rocha* [1998], *Reyes* [1999], and *Pérez-Rocha et al.* [2000] by processing with different techniques, large accelerographic data banks recorded after the 1985 Michoacan earthquake (i.e., when tens of new accelerographic stations were deployed in Mexico City).

17.4.3.1. Computation of the AF of the Response Spectra Sa(5%) for the 1985 Mw 8.01 Michoacan Earthquake Recordings in Mexico City by Using the Proposed RNN Technique

AF of the response spectra of acceleration Sa(5%) for $T = 0.2$ s for the 1985 Mw 8.01 Michoacan earthquake recordings in Mexico City (see Appendix 17.A), with respect to Sa(5%) for $T = 0.2$ s of TACY firm soil station, can be obtained by using the RNN technique presented in Section 17.2.3 as follows.

The RNN procedure (see Figure 17.2) was applied to Sa (5%) for $T = 0.2$ s of the accelerograms recorded in the E-W (and N-S) direction in the 10 stations indicated in Figure 17.11e. Sa (5%) for $T = 0.2$ s values of stations 1 (CDAF), 3 (CUIP), and 8 (TLHD) were not used in the RNN calculations, but were used to verify the RNN training results. For the RNN calculations a spatial distance $k = 0.1$ km was used (see Figure 17.2), compared with the distance of several kilometers among the Mexico City accelerographic recording stations shown in Figure 17.11e. In Figure 17.11, the surface of Mexico City of interest for the study, included inside the thick continuous lines, was discretized in square cells of ~0.7 km².

The results obtained by applying the RNN's scheme (see Figure 17.2) to estimate the spatial distribution of Sa(5%) for $T = 0.2$ s in Mexico City for the 1985 earthquake are shown in Figure 17.11a–e. In Figure 17.11a–d, the evolution of the RNN computations of Sa (5%) for $T = 0.2$ s patterns in the W-E direction are shown and in Figure 17.11e the final pattern is shown. The former figures include the evolution of isocurves of Sa (5%) for $T = 0.2$ s values in Mexico City, as well as their respective RNN values at the 10 recording stations, and the latter figure, the final estimated pattern of the Sa(5%) for $T = 0.2$ s isocurves, and their observed values during the 1985 earthquake at those stations.

From the ratios of Sa (5%) for $T = 0.2$ s values at any of the cells used to discretize Mexico City surface by the corresponding value of Sa(5%) for $T = 0.2$ s at the station (17.6) TACY of Figure 17.11e, their respective AFs were obtained and are shown in Figure 17.12. From this figure it can be concluded that the AF in Mexico City for the 1985 Michoacan earthquake in the W-E direction varied from ~0.5 to 4.5. Similar AF values were obtained for the N-S direction.

17.4.3.2. Uncertainties in the AF of the Response Spectra Sa (5%) on Mexico City Firm Soils to Compute Sa(5%) on Its Compressible Soils

As a very important objective of the hybrid procedure, proposed in Section 17.2.1, includes the explicit incorporation of the uncertainties in the steps (a)–(c) of the procedure to estimate the PEIs at a site, and taking into account that for Mexico City [*Pérez-Rocha*, 1998; *Pérez-Rocha et al.*, 2000], obtained the AFs for several earthquakes based on the ~100 recording Mexico City sites (and extrapolated their results for the whole of Mexico City surface), and also estimated their coefficients of variation (CV) [*Pérez-Rocha*, personal communication], we decided to use their suggested AF for Mexico City firm, transition, and compressible soil sites, with respect to the CU firm soil recording site (see Figure 17.A6). In this case, the CV of the AFs reflects the uncertainties in the quantity and quality of the data they used for different geotechnical subzones of Mexico City (see Figure 17.A6). The CV of the AFs obtained by these authors is shown in Figure 17.13 where the zones with larger CV values (>0.5) are those with less recording stations/km².

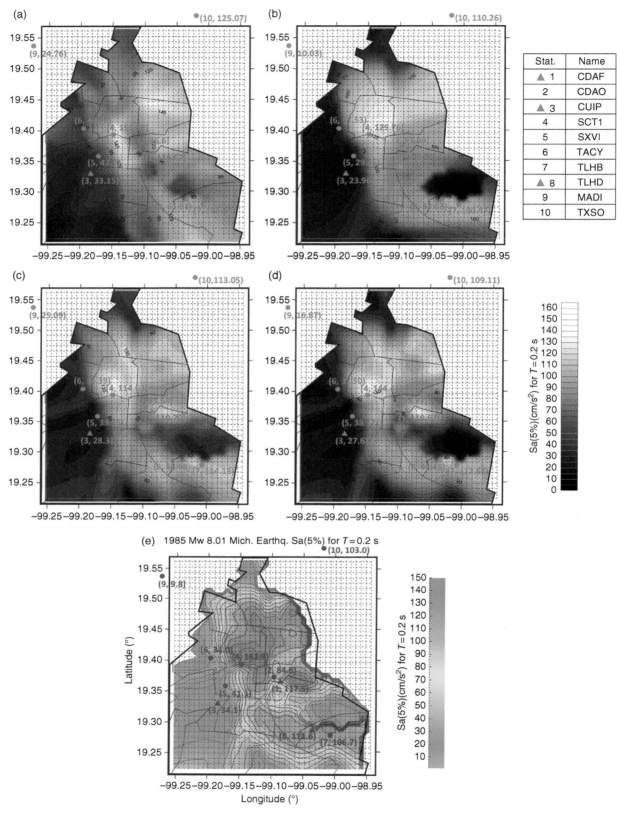

Figure 17.11 Evolution (a–d) and final (e) Sa(5%) for $T = 0.2$s patterns obtained with RNN computations by using the W-E direction accelerograms observed in Mexico City for the 1985 Mw 8.01 Michoacan earthquake; the location of the recording stations (1–10) of the 1985 event are identified by ●'s and ▲'s and by the first number in the parentheses; Sa(5%) for $T = 0.2$ s values by the second figure in the parentheses; Sa(5%) values of the ▲'s stations were used to verify the RNN training results.

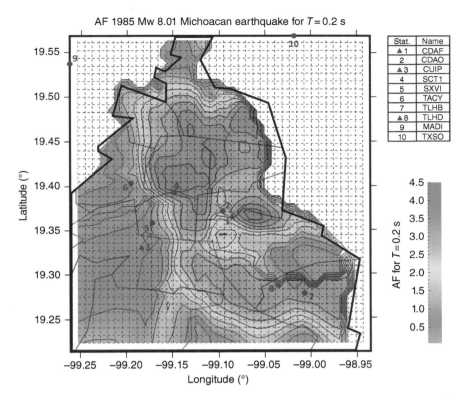

Figure 17.12 Amplification factor, AF, of the response spectra of acceleration Sa(5%) for $T = 0.2$ s for Mexico City firm, transition and compressible soils (see Figure 17.A6) with respect to Sa(5%) for $T = 0.2$ s of TACY firm soil station for the 1985 Mw 8.01 Michoacan earthquake obtained from the values of Figure 17.11 with RNN technique presented in Section 17.2.3.

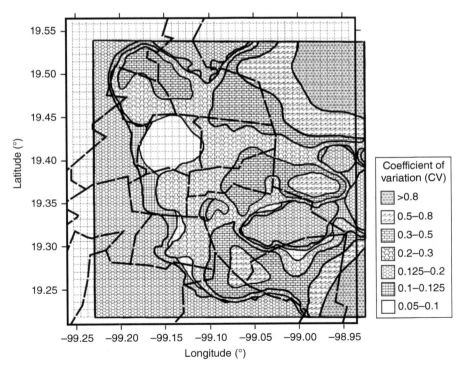

Figure 17.13 Coefficient of variation of the AF for the response spectra of acceleration Sa(5%) for Mexico City firm, transition and compressible soils (modified from *Pérez-Rocha* [1998] and personal communication *Pérez-Rocha* [2010]).

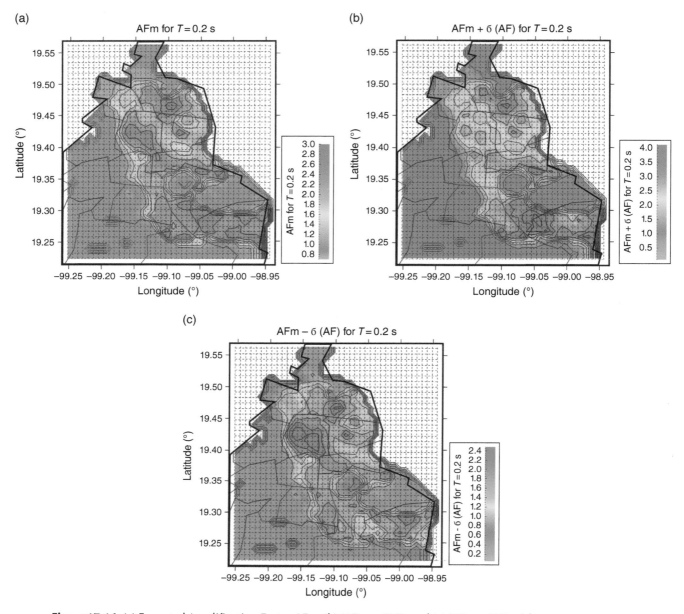

Figure 17.14 (a) Expected Amplification Factor AFm, (b) (AFm + δAF), and (c) (AFm − δAF) of the response spectra of acceleration Sa(5%) (for T = 0.2 s) for the Mexico City firm, transition and compressible soils with respect to Sa(5%) (for T = 0.2s) for TACY firm soil station (see Figure 17.A6).

Therefore, in this study, we adopted the superficial distribution of AFs suggested by *Pérez-Rocha* [1998], *Pérez-Rocha et al.* [2000], and *Pérez-Rocha* [personal communication], for Mexico City, multiplied by a factor that considers the reference firm soil station used in this work as TACY, instead of the station CU used as the firm soil reference station (see Figure 17.A6). For this purpose it is assumed that the mentioned AFs represent the expected values of these factors in what is referred as AFm, and we used the CVs of the AFs of Figure 17.13 to include the uncertainties of AF values, and then obtained their

respective AFm + δ_{AF} and AFm − δ_{AF} factors. As an example of the type of results obtained, the resulting surface distributions of the AFm, AFm + δ_{AF} and AFm − δ_{AF} factors in Mexico City for the natural period of vibration T = 0.2 s are shown in Figure 17.14a–c, respectively.

The values of AF, AFm + δ_{AF}, and AFm − δ_{AF} in the Mexico City surface of interest for the study, at each of the cells of ~0.7 km^2 area are respectively presented in Figure 17.14a–c. The AFm, AFm + δ_{AF} and AFm − δ_{AF} values at these cells vary from 0.9 to 3.0, 1.1 to 4 and 0.2

to 2.4, respectively. The inferior limits identified by the green-yellow zones correspond to the firm and transition soils, respectively. The superior limits of the compressible soils are represented by the orange-red areas. We notice that the AF values for the latter cover a wider range than those of the firm and transition soil zones (see Figure 17.A6).

Comparing the AF isovalues of Figures 17.12 and 17.14, it can be concluded that the AF of the former (computed with the RNN presented in Section 17.2.3) is similar to the superficial distribution of the AF of the Figure 17.14a, and that their minimum and maximum AF values are closer to those of Figure 17.14b.

17.5. ESTIMATION OF THE PRELIMINARY DIRECT ECONOMIC IMPACTS ON MEXICO CITY'S ONE- TO THREE-FLOOR DWELLING STOCK DUE TO THE OCCURRENCE OF AN EXTREME MW 8.5 MAGNITUDE SUBDUCTION EARTHQUAKE SCENARIO IN THE GUERRERO REGION

The objective of this section is to illustrate the application of the methodology proposed in Section 17.2.1 to obtain preliminary estimates of PEI, PEDEC and PML of Mexico City one- to three-floor dwelling constructions

due to the occurrence of the extreme Mw 8.5 magnitude earthquake scenario, with epicenter in the Guerrero region shown in Figure 17.6.

17.5.1. Preliminary Superficial Distribution of Mexico City Built Stock of One- to Three-Floor and Their Seismic Vulnerability

17.5.1.1. Preliminary Superficial Distribution of Mexico City One- to Three-Floor Dwelling Constructions

Figure 17.15 was generated based on the data retrieved from *INEGI* [2014] about the superficial distribution of Mexico City one- to three-floor dwelling constructions and complemented with the information suggested by *Castellanos* [2001]. In this figure, the area of Mexico City (also called Mexico Federal District) is shown. We notice that this figure only includes the urban areas more densely built and populated inside the Mexico City's external boundary identified by the continuous thick lines. Incidentally, the internal continuous lines correspond to the boundaries of the political division of Mexico City in 16 "Delegaciones."

The total Mexico City built area considered in Figure 17.15 is ~730 km². As mentioned earlier, each of the cells included in this figure in which this area was

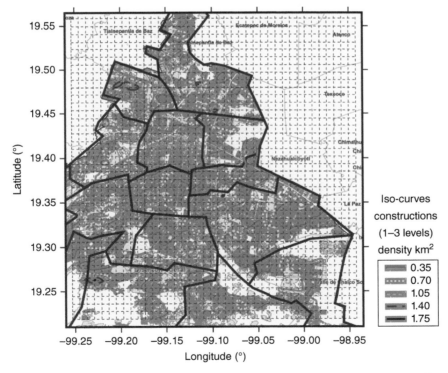

Figure 17.15 Preliminary isocurves of the density/km² of Mexico City one- to three-floor dwelling construction stock (the density is 0 km² in the cells in light blue) used for the estimation of the PEDEC for the extreme Mw 8.5 magnitude earthquake scenario; discretization of Mexico City in cells of 0.7 km² [modified *Castellanos*, 2001; *INEGI*, 2014].

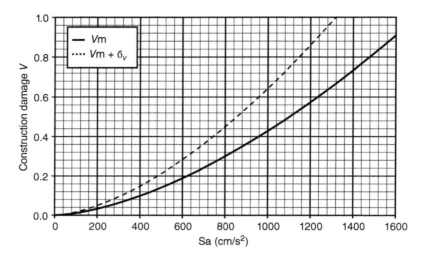

Figure 17.16 Expected seismic vulnerability functions (*V*m) and *V*m plus one standard deviation (*V*m + δ$_V$), of Mexico City dwelling construction stock of one to three floors used for the estimation of the PEDEC for the extreme Mw 8.5 earthquake scenario [modified, *Ordaz et al.*, 1994].

discretized corresponds to ~0.70 km². From Figure 17.15 it can be concluded that the density of the one- to three-floor constructions for most of the Mexico City built stock are ~0.35 and ~0.70 km². Furthermore, in order to approximately take into account the Mexico City areas without construction such as its avenues, streets, parks, and green areas, a reduction factor of 0.8 was applied to the mentioned figures.

17.5.1.2. Seismic Vulnerability and Behavior of Mexico City One- to Three-Floor Dwelling Constructions and Their Uncertainties

The seismic vulnerability (*V*) as a function of Sa(5%) for Mexico City one- to three-floor dwelling constructions, shown as the continuous curve in Figure 17.16, was observed for the 1985 Mw 8.01 Michoacan earthquake. This curve was suggested by *Ordaz et al.* [1994], and it is assumed in this study. It was mentioned that the *V*-curve of Figure 17.16 was obtained based on a small sample of the one- to three-floor constructions that were damaged due to the 1985 Mw 8.01 Michoacan earthquake, compared to the total number of those constructions existing in Mexico City at that time. We notice that the minimum and maximum values of *V* are 0 and 1, respectively. A *V* value of 0 means zero damage to the constructions, and a value 1 means that they are completely destroyed, these values can also be considered as percentages of dwelling constructions area damaged by the mentioned earthquake. The product of the damaged area by its actual cost/area can be considered as equal to the direct economic loss of rebuilding the constructions to their previous state before the earthquake. The direct economic loss does not include the costs associated with casualties, the

value of their contents, and disruption of the use of destroyed constructions.

Recently, *Reinoso et al.* [2015], in a study on the seismic code compliance of 150 Mexico City mid-rise dwellings constructions (i.e., with four to nine floors) built after 2004, which were designed with Mexico City's 2004 (actual) construction code, concluded that "many (constructions) would have inadequate performance during an intense earthquake, as they do not meet the minimum requirements (demanded) in the 2004 code." This indicates that, very likely, they are seismically more vulnerable than expected from the application of the latter.

Considering the uncertainties of the reduced sample of "the 1985 observed" data of the damage experienced by the one- to three-floor constructions of Mexico City reported by *Ordaz et al.* [1994], and the recent findings on the probable un-safe seismic behavior of Mexico City's mid-rise dwellings (designed with its 2004 Construction Code) during an "intense earthquake" reported by *Reinoso et al.* [2015], in this work, it is assumed that the continuous curve in Figure 17.16 represents, at best, the lower limit of the expected (mean) seismic vulnerability (*V*m) of Mexico City's one- to three-floor dwelling constructions, and assumed a standard deviation of *V*, δ$_V$ = 0.45 *V*. The latter is assumed here to include, in a mild fashion, the uncertainties on the vulnerability *V*, until improved and updated estimates of *V*m and its uncertainties are obtained. Therefore, the resulting vulnerability curve *V*m + δ$_V$, represented by the dashed curve of Figure 17.16 was also used in this study.

With respect to the seismic behavior of the one- to three-floor constructions of Mexico City, located on firm and compressible soils, based on a panel of experts opinions, *Ordaz et al.* [1994], suggested that the natural periods of vibration (the lapse (in seconds) that the top of a one-floor structural system last to return to its initial position when it is oscillating) for these types of Mexico City constructions were 0.05, 0.1, 0.2 s, and 0.2, 0.3, 0.5 s, depending on their location on firm or compressible soils (see Figure 17.A6), respectively.

In order to take into consideration the uncertainties on the detailed information about the age, type of materials used for their construction, and (particularly) actual seismic strength (especially after having experienced the 1985 Mw 8.01 earthquake, plus several events of magnitude Mw ~7.5 after 1985) of the one- to three-floor constructions existing in Mexico City, which is directly linked to their initial (when they were built) and their actual natural periods of vibration, in this work, it is assumed that the 0.05, 0.1, 0.2 s, and 0.2, 0.3, 0.5 s natural periods value (depending on their location on firm or compressible soils, respectively) suggested by *Ordaz et al.* [1994], are equally likely to represent the actual natural periods of vibration of those constructions in Mexico City. This means that the natural periods 0.05 and 0.2 s represent the initial or actual natural periods, and the 0.1, 0.2 s, 0.3, 0.5 s natural periods, other likely levels of the actual seismic strength (or vulnerability) of the one- to three-floor dwelling constructions located on Mexico City firm and compressible soils after 1985, respectively.

17.5.2. Estimation of the Probability of Exceedance of the (Expected) Intensities (PEI) in Mexico City for an Extreme Mw 8.5 Subduction Earthquake Scenario

As mentioned in Section 17.5.1, the seismic vulnerability of the one- to three-floor constructions of Mexico City (see Figure 17.16) depends on Sa (5%) values corresponding to the natural periods of vibration $T = 0.05$, 0.1, 0.2 s, and 0.2, 0.3, 0.5 s, of those constructions, depending on their location in on Mexico City's firm, transition, or compressible soils (see Figure 17.A6), respectively. The procedure presented in Appendix 17.E was applied to generate Sa(5%) for the corresponding (three) T values (depending on the type of soil in which they were located) at each of the cells in which Mexico City's surface was discretized (see Figure 17.15). From these values, PEI in Mexico City, corresponding to the extreme Mw 8.5 scenario earthquake of Figure 17.6 was obtained by carrying out the following steps.

From the 90 values of Sa(5%) which resulted by considering the 10 plausible seismic ruptures of the Mw 8.5 earthquake scenario (of Figure 17.8), the three AFs of Sa(5%) (similar to those of Figure 17.14), and the three values of the period of vibration of Sa(5%) obtained in step 4 of Appendix 17.E; the expected Sa(5%) value for each of the cells of Figure 17.15 were computed. With this information, the expected spatial distribution of Sa(5%) in Mexico City's firm and compressible soil zones due to the extreme Mw 8.5 magnitude scenario earthquake was generated (see Figure 17.17). In this figure, the green and yellow colors correspond to the expected Sa(5%) on firm and transition soils, respectively; and the orange and red colors to the expected Sa(5%) for Mexico City's compressible soils zone. We notice that the larger Sa(5%) values correspond to the compressible soil zone of Mexico City, which as mentioned in Section 17.4.3, amplifies the ground motions at certain frequencies, compared with the (smaller) ground motions experienced by its firm (and transition) soil zones.

The two sets of 90 values samples (one sample for the firm (and transition) and the other for the compressible, Mexico City soils) of Sa(5%) values for the Mexico City cells included in Figure 17.17, were used to obtain their respective histograms, their fitted loglogistic and Weibull PDF and their associated cumulative distributions. They are shown in Figure 17.18a–c, for Mexico City firm and transition soil zones, and in Figure 17.19a–c, for its compressible soil zone, respectively.

We notice that the fitted PDFs are different, that is, the loglogistic with its larger probability density value for Sa(5%) at ~59 cm/s^2 for the firm soils (see Figure 17.18a), and the Weibull distribution and the larger probability density values of Sa(5%) at ~175 cm/s^2 for the compressible soils (see Figure 17.19a).

The fitted distributions were truncated in both their left and right tails, at the minimum and maximum values of each respective sample (Figures 17.18b and 17.19b, respectively).

From the cumulative distributions of the fitted truncated distributions (Figures 17.18c and 17.19c, the PEIs of the expected Sa(5%) associated with the plausible Mw 8.5 earthquake scenario proposed for firm and transition, and for compressible soils can be obtained, respectively. From these figures, it can be concluded that, for example, there is a 10% probability of exceedance of the expected Sa(5%)s values of 70 and 210 cm/s^2 for the firm and transition, and the compressible Mexico City soils, respectively.

17.5.3. Estimation of the Probability Distribution of the Damage of the One- to Three-Floor Dwelling Constructions of Mexico City for an Extreme Mw 8.5 Magnitude Subduction Earthquake Scenario

As mentioned in the previous section, the seismic vulnerability curve Vm shown in Figure 17.16 can be associated with the direct economic loss of the one- to three-floor constructions of Mexico City, due to the occurrence of the 1985 Mw 8.01 Michoacan subduction earthquake. If it is assumed that these constructions are

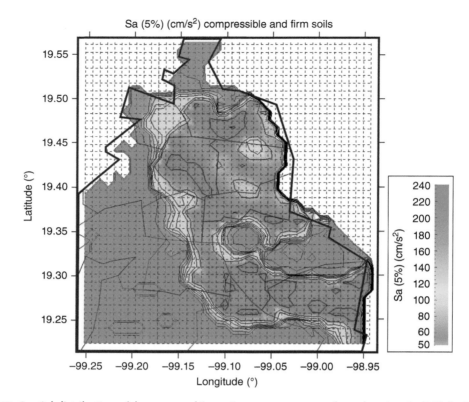

Sa (5%) (cm/s²) compressible and firm soils

Figure 17.17 Spatial distribution of the expected (mean) response spectra of acceleration Sa (5%) for Mexico City one- to three-floor dwelling constructions, with natural periods of vibration of 0.05, 0.10, 0.2 s and 0.2, 0.3, 0.5 s, located on its firm, transition and compressible soils, respectively; corresponding to the slip distributions of the 10 models of Figure 17.8 for the Mw 8.5 earthquake scenario of Figure 17.6 and the three Sa (5%) AF, of the type shown in Figure 17.14. The green and yellow colors correspond to Sa(5%) on Mexico City's firm and transition soils, and the orange to red colors to its compressible soils zone.

uniformly distributed per unit area in the cells (see Figure 17.15), the Vm curve of Figure 17.16 can be linked to the percentage of constructions (located on those cells) that could be damaged by the strong ground motions in Mexico City generated by other Mexican subduction earthquakes of similar Mw magnitude. Therefore, for any of the cells of Figure 17.15, the product of its seismic vulnerability (associated with a specific Sa(5%) value, for example for $T = 0.2$ s) multiplied by its built surface area, is equal to the damaged surface (in km²) of the one- to three-floor constructions of Mexico City built stock for that cell, due to the plausible occurrence, in this case, of the extreme Mw 8.5 magnitude earthquake scenario. In Appendix 17.F, the steps followed to obtain the probability distribution of the damage of those constructions due to the mentioned scenario is illustrated.

An example of the surface distribution of the expected (mean) damaged area (obtained in step 4 of Appendix 17.F) corresponding to the 180 values of the vulnerability, Vm & Vm + δ_V, for the one- to three-floor constructions of Mexico City's built stock, due to the extreme Mw 8.5 earthquake scenario of Figure 17.6, is presented in Figure 17.20. It can be observed from this figure that the

largest values of the damaged one to three floors of Mexico City built stock distribution, identified in orange and red colors in the figure correspond to the stock located on Mexico City's compressible soil zone, compared with the damaged stock on its firm and transition soil zones identified with the green and green-yellow colors. These results are in agreement with the observations on the location and density of the damaged constructions in Mexico City for the 1985 Mw 8.01 Michoacan earthquake [*Seed et al.*, 1988].

The histograms and the inverse-Gamma and logistic fitted probability density distributions obtained for the constructions of one to three floors of Mexico City built stock expected damaged areas, for the three samples' values (i.e., for vulnerabilities: Vm, Vm + δ_V and Vm & Vm + δ_V) for the firm and transition, and compressible soils, are shown in Figures 17.F1a–c and 17.F2a–c, respectively. Their corresponding truncated and cumulative distributions are included in Figures 17.21 and 17.22. We notice that the maximum values of each of the three truncated fitted probability densities distributions for both types of soils (see Figures 17.21a and 17.22a) are larger for those obtained for the vulnerability Vm, followed by

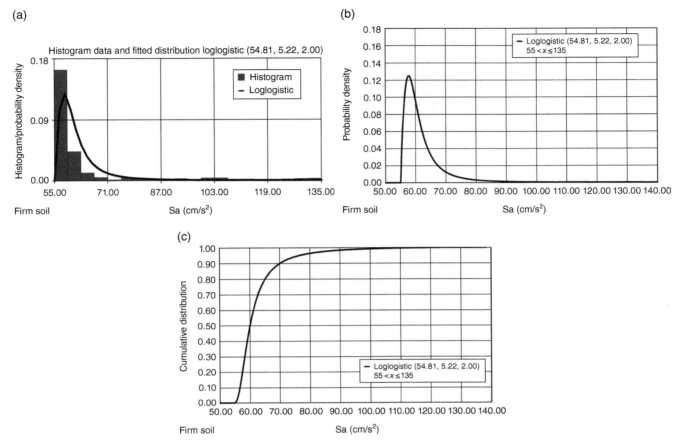

Figure 17.18 (a) Histogram and its fitted loglogistic probability density distribution of Sa (5%) for the one- to three-floor dwelling constructions of Mexico City on firm (and transition) soils, Mw 8.5 earthquake scenario, (b) truncated distribution of (a), and (c) cumulative distribution of (b).

those obtained for vulnerability Vm & $Vm + 6_V$, and last for the vulnerability $Vm + 6_V$.

With relation to the tails fatness of the truncated probability density distributions of Figures 17.21a and 17.22a, the fatter tail corresponds to the vulnerability $Vm + 6_V$, followed by the vulnerability Vm & $Vm + 6_V$ and last by the vulnerability Vm (see Figures 17.21a and 22a) Tail fatness relates here to potential lack of existence of second- or higher-order moments of the PDFs.

Figures 17.21b and 17.22b include the cumulative truncated distributions of damaged areas of the one- to three-floor constructions located on Mexico City firm and transition, and compressible soils, for the Mw 8.5 earthquake scenario, and vulnerabilities Vm, $Vm + 6_V$, and Vm & $Vm + 6_V$, respectively. From these two figures, it can be concluded that for a given probability of exceedance, the smaller, intermediate and larger damaged areas correspond to the vulnerabilities Vm, Vm & $Vm + 6_V$ and $Vm + 6_V$, respectively.

For example, for the firm and transition soil zones, for a probability of exceedance of 0.5 and 0.1 the estimated expected damaged areas are: 0.0015, 0.0023, 0.0029 and 0.0032, 0.0048, 0.0063 km², respectively. For the compressible soil zone, for the same probabilities of exceedance, the estimated expected damaged areas are: 0.0092, 0.0125, 0.0178 and 0.0137, 0.0201, 0.0263 km², respectively. We also notice from Figures 17.21b and 17.22b that the expected damaged areas estimated for the firm and transition soil zones are less or equal to ~0.5 than those for the compressible soil zone of Mexico City.

17.5.4. Estimation of the Probability of Exceedance of the Preliminary Direct Economic Consequences and the Probable Maximum Loss for the One- to Three-Floor Dwelling Constructions of Mexico City for an Extreme Mw 8.5 Magnitude Subduction Earthquake Scenario

17.5.4.1. Estimation of the PEDEC for the One- to Three-Floor Dwelling Constructions of Mexico City for an Extreme Mw 8.5 Magnitude Subduction Earthquake Scenario

The procedure applied to estimate the probability of exceedance of the preliminary PEDEC and PML, of the damaged areas of the one- to three-floor dwelling

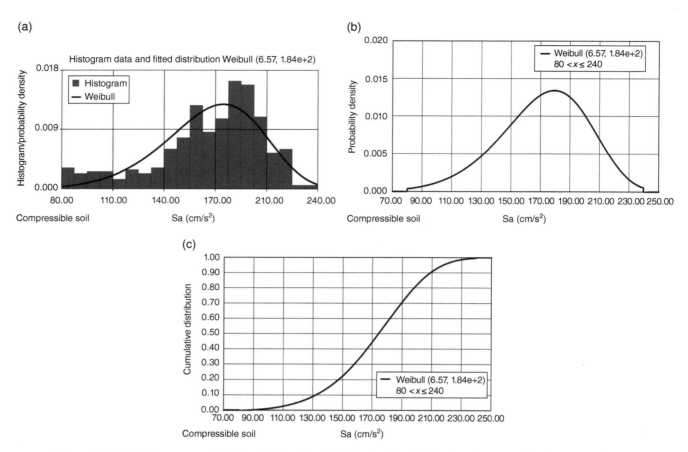

Figure 17.19 (a) Histogram and its fitted Weibull probability density distribution of Sa (5%), for the one- to three-floor dwelling constructions of Mexico City compressible soils, Mw 8.5 earthquake scenario, (b) truncated distributions of (a), and (c) cumulative distribution of (b).

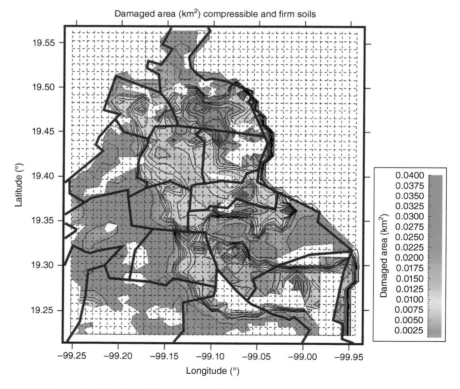

Figure 17.20 Preliminary distribution of the expected (mean) damaged dwelling constructions of one to three floors located on Mexico City firm and compressible soils due to the extreme Mw 8.5 earthquake scenario (in the cells in white there are no constructions of one to three floors), obtained from the 180 values sample of the vulnerability Vm & $Vm + \sigma_V$ (see Appendix 17.F).

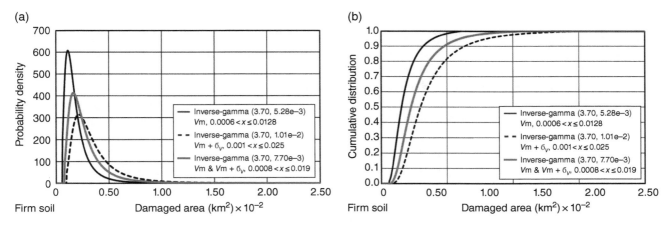

Figure 17.21 (a) Fitted inverse-gamma truncated probability density distribution of damaged areas of one- to three-floor dwelling constructions located on Mexico City firm and transition soils for the Mw 8.5 magnitude earthquake scenario, and vulnerability Vm, $Vm + 6_v$ and Vm & $Vm + 6_v$ (b) cumulative distribution of (a).

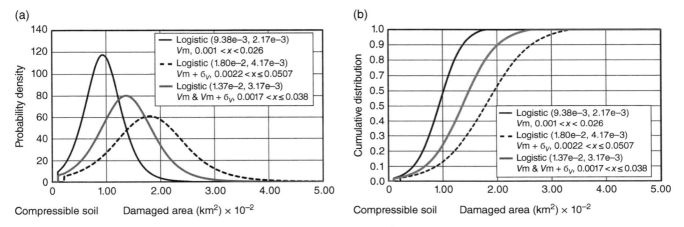

Figure 17.22 (a) Fitted logistic truncated probability density distribution of damaged areas of one- to three-floor dwelling constructions located on Mexico City compressible soils for the Mw 8.5 magnitude earthquake scenario and vulnerability Vm, $Vm + 6_v$ and Vm & $Vm + 6_v$ (b) cumulative distribution of (a).

constructions of Mexico City due to the extreme Mw 8.5 magnitude subduction earthquake scenario, consisted in multiplying, for each of the cells of Figure 17.15, their damaged areas (computed in Section 17.5.3) for each of the 90 and 180 values corresponding to the vulnerabilities Vm, $Vm + 6_v$ and Vm & $Vm + 6_v$, respectively, by an average unitary cost of 700 USD/m² suggested by *IMIC* [2013] and *SOFTEC* [2013], for this type of constructions in Mexico City and with the results obtained compute the associated PEDEC and PML.

The histograms together with their fitted lognormal probability density and cumulative distributions, of the direct costs (in billion USD) of the damaged areas obtained for the three vulnerabilities are shown in Figures 17.23, 17.24, and 17.25. The results are presented as follows: (1) in Figure 17.23a–c for the firm (and transition) soil zones of Mexico City, (2) in Figure 17.24a–c for

its compressible soil zone, and (3) in Figure 17.25a–c for the three types of soil zones (see Figure 17.A6).

In Figure 17.23a–c, it can be observed that the direct costs due to the estimated damages on constructions built on firm and transition soils vary from 0.36 to 1.64, 0.70 to 3.1 and 0.4 to 3.1 billion USD for construction vulnerabilities of Vm, $Vm + 6_v$ and Vm & $Vm + 6_v$, respectively. For the compressible soils the direct costs shown in Figure 17.24a–c vary from 0.59 to 8.01, 1.1 to 15.4, and 0.6 to 15.4 billion USD for construction vulnerabilities of Vm, $Vm + 6_v$ and Vm & $Vm + 6_v$, respectively. This means that the direct costs for constructions on the firm and transition soil zones are less or equal to ~0.2 of those corresponding to the cost for construction on the compressible soil zone of Mexico City. Finally from Figure 17.25a–c corresponding to the constructions located on the firm and transition, and compressible

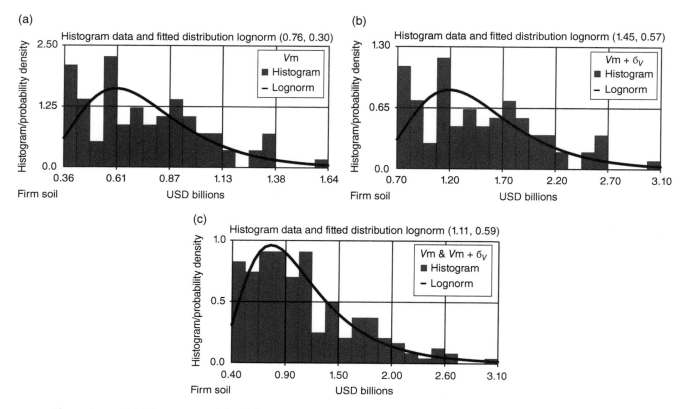

Figure 17.23 (a) Histogram and fitted lognormal probability density distribution of the preliminary direct economic costs of the one- to three-floor dwelling constructions located on Mexico City firm soils for the Mw 8.5 magnitude earthquake scenario, and vulnerability Vm, (b) same as (a) for vulnerability $Vm + 6_V$ and (c) same as (a) for vulnerability Vm & $Vm + 6_V$.

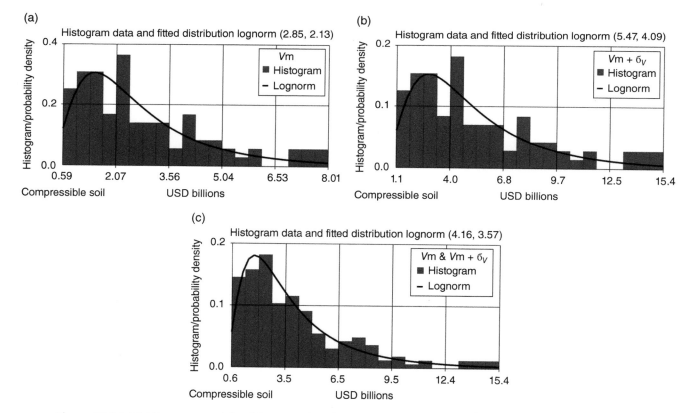

Figure 17.24 (a) Histogram and fitted lognormal probability density distribution of the preliminary direct economic cost of the one to three floors dwelling constructions located on Mexico City compressible soils for the Mw 8.5 magnitude earthquake scenario, and vulnerability Vm, (b) same as (a) for vulnerability $Vm + 6_V$ (c) same as (a) for vulnerability Vm & $Vm + 6_V$.

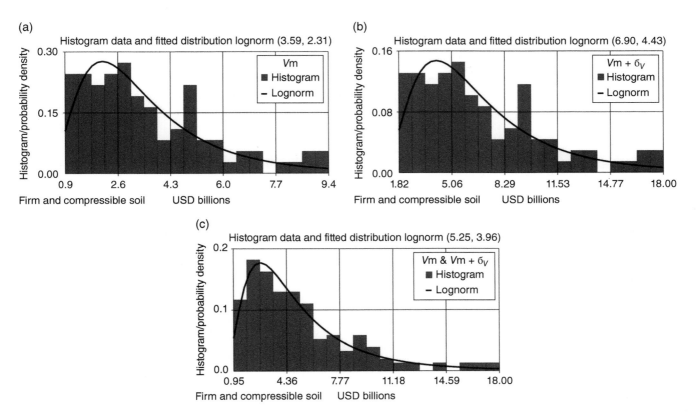

Figure 17.25 (a) Histogram and fitted lognormal probability density distribution of the preliminary direct economic costs of the one- to three-floor dwelling constructions located on Mexico City firm, transition and compressible soils for the Mw 8.5 magnitude earthquake scenario, and vulnerability Vm, (b) same as (a) for vulnerability $Vm + \delta_V$ and (c) same as (a) for vulnerability Vm & $Vm + \delta_V$.

Mexico City soil zones, the direct costs vary from 0.9 to 9.4, 1.82 to 18, and 0.95 to 18 billion USD, for construction vulnerabilities of Vm, $Vm + \delta_V$ and Vm & $Vm + \delta_V$ respectively. From these values, we can conclude that the minimum and maximum direct costs due to the destruction or damage of these constructions with vulnerability Vm are less or equal to ~0.5 of those with vulnerabilities $Vm + \delta_V$ and Vm & $Vm + \delta_V$.

The fitted unbounded lognormal probability density and cumulative distributions obtained for the preliminary direct economic costs of the one- to three-floor dwelling constructions located on Mexico City firm and transition and compressible soils of Mexico City for the Mw 8.5 earthquake scenario, and vulnerabilities Vm, $Vm + \delta_V$ and Vm & $Vm + \delta_V$ are presented in Figure 17.26a and b, respectively. The corresponding fitted truncated lognormal probability density and cumulative distributions are shown in Figure 17.27a and b, respectively.

From the comparison of Figures 17.26a and 17.27a, we notice that the maximum values of the PDFs of the latter are higher than those of the former. Also, from the comparison of Figures 17.26b and 17.27b, for the same chosen values of the probabilities of exceedance of, for instance, 0.5, 0.1, 0.05, and 0.0025, the respective economic costs of the truncated distributions are inferior to those estimated with the unbounded distributions.

17.5.4.2. Estimation of the Preliminary Probable Maximum Loss for the One- to Three-Floor Dwelling Constructions of Mexico City for an Extreme Mw 8.5 Subduction Earthquake Scenario

17.5.4.2.1. Preliminary Probable Maximum Loss Assuming that the Probability Density Functions of Sa(5%) and of the Damage Cost Are Statistically Independent

If it is assumed that Sa(5%) (see Figures 17.18 and 17.19) and the direct damaged costs C (see Figures 17.26 and 17.27) are independent random variables, the associated PML value can be selected from the cumulative lognormal truncated distribution of Figure 17.27b, or from Table 17.1. In this table, several PMLs are included for a few selected PEDEC values identified as C^a. For the cases analyzed, the PML could vary from 0.7 to 18 billion USD (see Figure 17.27a). For example, for PEDEC values of 0.5, 0.1, 0.01, 0.001, 0.0001 and vulnerabilities $Vm + \delta_V$, the corresponding PMLs are 5.65, 11.15, 15.56,

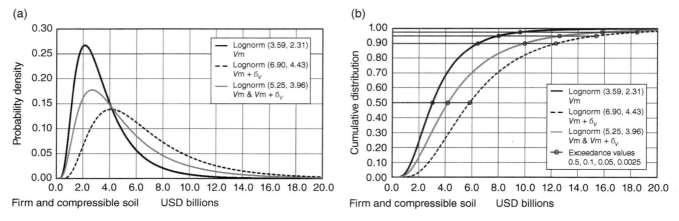

Figure 17.26 (a) Fitted lognormal probability density and cumulative distributions of the preliminary economic costs of the one- to three-floor dwelling constructions located on Mexico City firm and compressible soils for the Mw 8.5 magnitude earthquake scenario, and vulnerabilities Vm, Vm + 6$_v$ and Vm & Vm + 6$_v$ (b) cumulative distribution of (a).

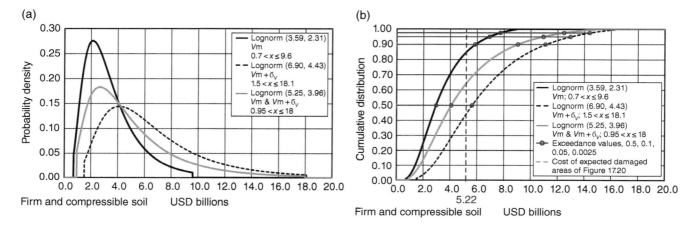

Figure 17.27 (a) Lognormal truncated probability density and cumulative distributions of the preliminary economic costs of the one- to three-floor dwelling constructions located on Mexico City firm and compressible soils for the Mw 8.5 magnitude earthquake scenario, and vulnerabilities Vm, Vm + 6$_v$ and Vm & Vm + 6$_v$ (b) cumulative distribution of (a).

16.46 and 16.56 billion USD, respectively, and the return period of a specific PML value is the reciprocal of its respective PEDEC.

Incidentally, if the PML values had been chosen from Figure 17.26b, where the cumulative distribution corresponds to the unbounded fitted lognormal density distribution, the respective PML values for the same selected PEDECs are 5.81, 12.33, 22.78, 35.67, and 51.62 billion USD, respectively; that is, the first two PML values are slightly larger than those of the truncated lognormal distribution, but the last three values are too large and unrealistic, therefore, it is strongly advised to avoid the use of unbounded probability distributions for this purpose. Also, care should be taken in considering a single expected value for the PML, such as that corresponding to the

expected (mean) damaged area for vulnerability Vm & Vm + 6$_v$ shown in Figure 17.20, which is of 5.22 billion USD (see Figure 17.27b). This PML corresponds to a probability of exceedance of 0.15, 0.37, and 0.56 for the distributions associated with constructions of vulnerabilities Vm, Vm & Vm + 6$_v$, and Vm + 6$_v$, respectively.

17.5.4.2.2. Preliminary Probable Maximum Loss Assuming that the Probability Density Functions of Sa (5%) and of the Damage Cost Are Statistically Dependent

If it is assumed that Sa (5%) values and the direct damage costs are dependent random variables, the PML value for the damaged areas of one- to three-floor dwelling constructions of Mexico City due to the extreme Mw 8.5

Table 17.1 Preliminary Direct Economic Costs of Damage to Mexico City Dwelling Constructions of One to Three Floors Due to the Extreme Mw 8.5 Magnitude Earthquake Scenario for Several Probabilities of Exceedance (PEDEC), Vulnerabilities Vm, $Vm + \delta_V$ and Vm & $Vm + \delta_V$

Direct Economic Costs (Billion USD)

PEDEC/ (T_r years)	Cumulative LN (Figure 17.26b) C^a			Cumulative LN Truncated (Figure 17.27b) C^a/Copula (Figures 17.29 and 17.30) $C^{b,c,d}$		
	Vm	$Vm + \delta_V$	Vm & $Vm + \delta_V$	Vm	$Vm + \delta_V$	Vm & $Vm + \delta_V$
0.50/(2)	3.02[a]	5.81[a]	4.19[a]	2.95[a] 2.75[b]	5.65[a] 5.25[b]	4.09[a]
0.10/(10)	6.42[a]	12.33[a]	9.91[a]	5.89[a] 6.38[b]	11.15[a] 12.50[b]	9.05[a]
0.05/(20)	7.95[a]	15.26[a]	12.64[a]	6.91[a] 7.51[b]	12.99[a] 14.52[b]	10.91[a]
0.025/(40)	9.57[a]	18.36[a]	15.62[a]	7.72[a] 2.12[c]	14.39[a] 4.12[c]	12.42[a]
0.010/(100)	11.87[a]	22.78[a]	19.97[a]	8.41[a] 4.38[c]	15.56[a] 8.35[c]	13.77[a]
0.005/(200)	13.75[a]	26.37[a]	23.61[a]	8.70[a] 6.03[c]	16.03[a] 11.33[c]	14.36[a]
0.0044/(225)	14.08[a]	27.01[a]	24.27[a]	8.74[a] 6.22[c]	16.09[a] 11.64[c]	14.43[a]
0.0042/(237)	14.24[a]	27.30[a]	24.56[a]	8.75[a] 6.28[c]	16.11[a] 11.81[c]	14.46[a]
0.004/(250)	14.38[a]	27.58[a]	24.85[a]	8.77[a] 6.38[c]	16.14[a] 12.14[c]	14.48[a]
0.0025/(400)	15.75[a]	30.21[a]	27.57[a]	8.87[a]7.21[c] 2.38[d]	16.30[a] 13.52[c] 4.76[d]	14.68[a]
0.001/(1000)	18.61[a]	35.67[a]	33.35[a]	8.97[a]8.51[c]4.63[d]	16.46[a] 16.25[c] 8.87[d]	14.90[a]
0.0001/(10,000)	26.95[a]	51.62[a]	50.85[a]	9.03[a]	16.56[a]	15.03[a]

[1] By considering Sa (5%) and costs are statistically independent (identified by C^a).

[2] By considering that Sa(5%) and costs are statistically dependent and interarrival times of the Mw 8.5 earthquake scenario of 1 year (C^b), 25 years (C^c), and 225 years (C^d).

magnitude subduction scenario earthquake, can be obtained by using the Gumbel-Hoogard copula, which provides a convenient framework for modeling the joint probability distribution of Sa(5%) and the direct damage costs. Hence, the Gumbel-Hoogard copula modeling is adopted here to assess the joint probabilistic risk associated with the occurrence of EME intensities represented by Sa(5%) and of their direct economic costs C. This implies that we apply Equations 17.24 and 17.30 to their respective marginal probability density distributions presented in the previous subsections. The results of applying these equations are presented in Figures 17.28, 17.29, and 17.30, respectively.

In Figure 17.28, the joint event probability density distributions and contours of Sa (5%) and the costs for vulnerabilities Vm (panels a, c), $Vm + \delta_V$ (panels b and d) of Mexico City one- to three-floor dwelling constructions due to the extreme Mw 8.5 magnitude earthquake scenario are depicted. From these figures, we notice that the maximum values of the joint probability densities (JPD) occurs in a narrow band of Sa(5%) and costs values of a volume with ellipsoidal shape cross section, as shown in their JPD perspectives, included in Figure 17.28a and b, and in their respective contours shown in Figure 17.28c and d, for vulnerabilities Vm and $Vm + \delta_V$ respectively. We also notice in these figures that the JPD values for Sa(5%) of <100 cm/s^2 were not included, because their associated JPDs are smaller that 10^{-4} outside the narrow band. Therefore, their contribution to the corresponding

joint event cumulative (JEC) probability is close to zero outside this band.

In Figure 17.29, the JEC and the contours of the probability distributions of Sa(5%) and the direct cost for vulnerabilities Vm (panels a, c), and $Vm + \delta_V$ (panels b and d) of Mexico City one- to three-floor dwelling constructions due to the extreme Mw 8.5 magnitude earthquake scenario are presented. From these figures, we can conclude that, as expected, the maximum values of the JEC correspond to the maximum values of Sa(5%) and cost.

Finally, in Figure 17.30 the joint event return period and its contours of Sa(5%) and costs for vulnerabilities Vm (panels a, c, and e) and $Vm + \delta_V$ (panels b, d, and f) of Mexico City's one- to three-floor dwelling constructions due to the extreme Mw 8.5 magnitude earthquake scenario, for an expected time interval $E(L)$ between the occurrence of the Mw 8.5 scenario of 1 year (panels a and b), 25 years (panels c and d) and 225 years (panels e and f), are shown.

In order to compare the results obtained, assuming Sa(5%) and the costs are independent or dependent random variables, in Table 17.1, several PMLs for the latter case are included for a few selected PEDEC values. The corresponding costs are identified by C^b, C^c, C^d, for expected time intervals $E(L)$ between the occurrence of the Mw 8.5 scenario of 1, 25, and 225 years, respectively.

From the ratios C^a/C^b, C^a/C^c, C^a/C^d of the cost values included in Table 17.1 the following conclusions can be drawn: (1) for an interarrival time of 1 year and joint

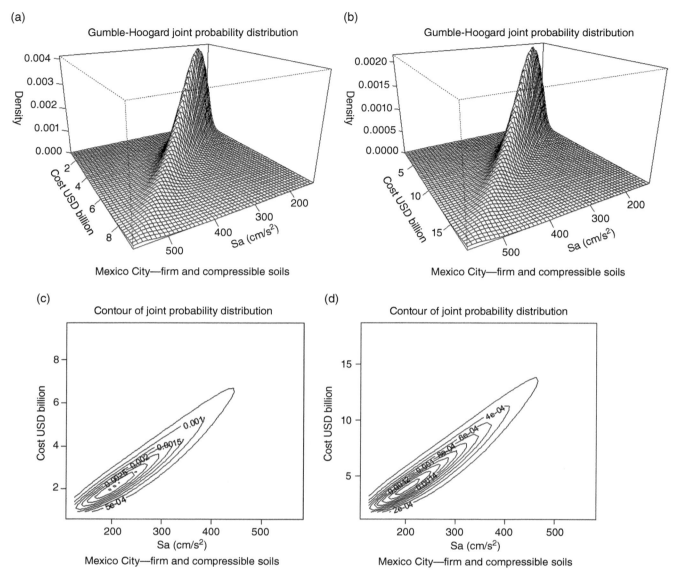

Figure 17.28 Joint event and contours of the probability density distribution of Sa (5%) and the preliminary cost of damage for vulnerabilities Vm (a and c), and Vm + σ_V (b and d) of Mexico City dwelling constructions of one to three floors due to the extreme Mw 8.5 magnitude subduction earthquake scenario.

event return periods of 2, 10, and 20 years the PML costs C^a vary from 0.9 to 1.08 of those of C^b, for joint event return periods of 20 and 2 years, respectively; (2) for an interarrival time of 25 years and joint event return periods of 40, 100, 200, 225, 237, 250, 400, and 1000 years, the PML costs C^a vary from 1.01 to 3.64 of those of C^c, for joint event return periods of 1000 and 40 years, respectively; (3) for an interarrival time of 225 years and joint event return periods of 400 and 1000 years, the PML costs C^a vary from 1.85 to 3.72 of those of C^d, for

joint event return periods of 1000 and 400 years, respectively; (4) from conclusions (1), (2), and (3) the statistical dependence of Sa(5%) and the costs, and the interarrival times of the considered EME scenario, become critical to decide about the final chosen value of PML in the seismic risk assessment exercise; (5) the PML cost C^a values of Table 17.1 represent a preliminary upper bound for the PML of the one- to three-floor dwelling constructions of Mexico City, due to the extreme Mw 8.5 magnitude earthquake scenario analysed.

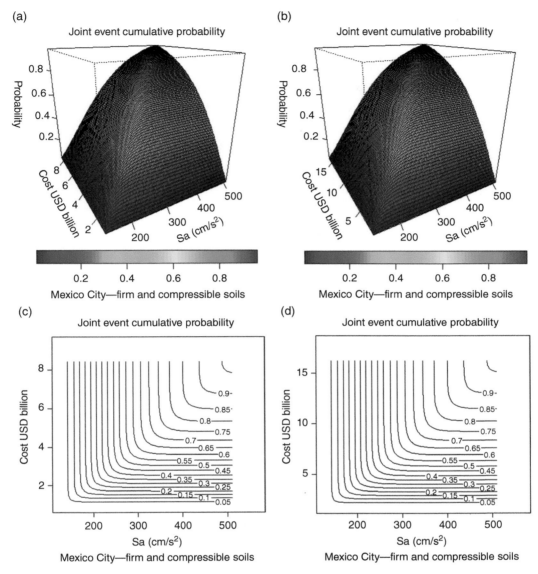

Figure 17.29 Joint event cumulative and contours of the probability distributions of Sa(5%) and preliminary cost of damage for vulnerabilities Vm (a and c), and $Vm + \sigma_V$ (b and d) of Mexico City dwelling constructions of one to three floors due to the extreme Mw 8.5 magnitude subduction earthquake scenario.

17.5.5. Risk Mitigation Retrofitting Policies to Minimize the Probable Maximum Loss and Casualties Derived from the Damage of One- to Three-Floor Constructions of Mexico City Subject to an Extreme Mw 8.5 Magnitude Subduction Earthquake Scenario

In *Aguilar et al.* [1996], the ex-post structural retrofitting measures, implemented in 12 high-rise buildings located in Mexico City damaged (except two of them) by the 1985 Mw 8.01 Michoacan earthquake, are thoroughly described. In particular, those authors mentioned that 2 out of the 12 buildings analyzed, which were retrofitted

before the 1985 Mw 8.01 Michoacan earthquake, performed "very well in the event" (i.e. experienced very slight damages). This observation, strengthens the argument that it would be relevant to analyze the impact, of the possible ex-ante implementation of seismic risk mitigation retrofitting policies for the one- to three-floor dwelling constructions of Mexico City built stock, based on the PML values estimated in Section 17.5.4 for those constructions, due to an extreme Mw 8.5 magnitude subduction earthquake scenario.

In particular, the objective of the ex-ante analysis includes the estimation of the costs of the seismic

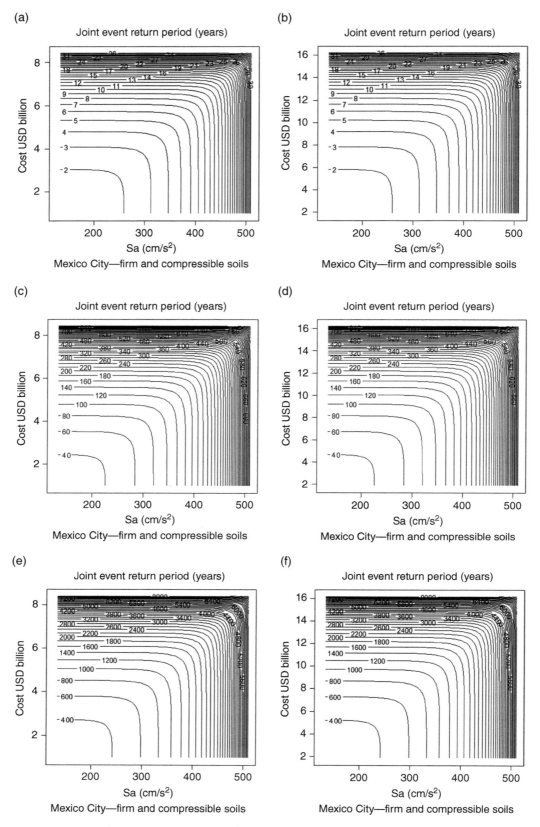

Figure 17.30 Contours of joint event return period of Sa (5%) and preliminary cost of damage for vulnerabilities *V*m (a, c, and e), and *V*m + δ$_V$ (b, d, and f) of Mexico City dwelling constructions of one to three floors due to the extreme Mw 8.5 magnitude subduction earthquake scenario, for an expected time interval *E*(*L*) between the occurrence of the Mw 8.5 scenario of 1 year (a and b), 25 years (c and d), and 225 years (e and f).

retrofitting of the mentioned constructions, in order to reduce their seismic vulnerability, at least, from $Vm + 6_V$ to Vm (see Figure 17.16), and as a consequence, to shift from the cumulative distribution corresponding to the former vulnerability, to the one of the latter vulnerability for a given probability of exceedance (see Figure 17.27b). The economic consequences of this action would mean a reduction of the PML's costs of construction with vulnerabilities $Vm + 6_V$, with respect to those with vulnerabilities Vm (see Figure 17.16).

If the statistical independence of the EME intensity (represented by Sa(5%)) and the associated direct economic cost (identified by C^a in Table 17.1) are assumed, upper bound values of the PML expected for Mexico City one- to three-floor dwelling constructions can be estimated. For example, for a probability of exceedance of 0.005 the PMLs are 16.03 and 8.70 billion USD, for constructions with vulnerabilities $Vm + 6_V$, and Vm, respectively, that is a difference of 7.33 billion USD (see Table 17.1). The latter cost should be compared with the seismic retrofitting costs, in order to take an informed economical decision in terms of time and available economic resources, the convenience of implementing a seismic retrofitting program for the one- to three-floor constructions of Mexico City built stock, which could include all the stakeholders involved, such as the Mexico City inhabitants, the government officers, the insurance companies.

In a recent work, *Jafarzadeh et al.* [2014] developed a model that allows the estimation of the construction seismic retrofitting costs, *CR* (in thousands of USD) of (mainly) one to three floors of confined masonry constructions (similar to those of interest for this study), located on earthquake-prone regions, as a function of the construction total plan area, *A* (in m²); the model is expressed as $CR = KA^B$, where the constants *K* and *B* were obtained by a multilinear regression analysis of seismic retrofitting (reliable) data of 183 constructions. The authors remarked that, compared with others, their model has the advantage of making reliable estimate of the construction cost of a retrofit project, with minimum information about the construction of interest; that is, its built surface *A*, whose value is usually known.

As for the constructions of interest in this study, an expression for *CR* is not available for the time being, in the present study, as a first approximation to quantify *CR* for the one- to three-floor dwelling constructions of Mexico City built stock; we will use the expression proposed by *Jafarzadeh et al.* [2014], $CR = 0.207 A^{0.823}$ to analyze the impact of the possible implementation of ex-ante mitigation retrofitting policies on these constructions, on the PMLs estimates (C^a values of Table 17.1) obtained in Section 17.5.4.2.1.

According to *INEGI* [2011], the information of 2010 census indicate that in Mexico City there are 2,453,031 dwelling constructions, inhabited by an average of 3.6 persons, and a population of 8,830,912 inhabitants. Approximately 1,070,000 of those dwelling constructions are of one to three floors. With respect to the cost and surface of the average residential house in Mexico City, based on the reports by the *IMIC* [2013] and *SOFTEC* [2013] for the mentioned constructions in Mexico City, an average unitary cost of 700 USD/m² and an average surface of 200 m² per dwelling were adopted in the analysis. The latter value was selected by considering average surfaces of 100, 200, and 300 m² for the one-, two-, and three-floor constructions of Mexico City. Therefore, the total cost per dwelling is 140,000 USD and the construction seismic retrofitting cost, $CR = 0.207 \times (200)^{0.823} = 16,207$ USD/dwelling.

As mentioned before, for a probability of exceedance of 0.005, the PML's for vulnerabilities $Vm + 6_V$ and Vm are 16.03 and 8.70 billion USD (i.e., a difference of 7.33 billion USD) (see Table 17.1), which correspond to damaged areas of 22.72 and 12.34 km², respectively. The latter figures divided by the assumed average surface of 200 m² per dwelling, correspond to 113,600 and 61,700 dwellings, respectively. Therefore, if mitigation retrofitting actions are taken to bring the constructions from vulnerability $Vm + 6_V$ to Vm (see Figure 17.16), 113,600 − 61,700 = 51,900 dwellings could be saved. And the cost of this action would be 16,207 USD/dwelling × 51,900 dwellings = 0.841 billion USD. This retrofitting total cost represents about 12% of 7.33 billion USD, that is, 6.489 billion USD could be saved by the possible implementation of ex-ante mitigation retrofitting policies on the one- to three-floor dwelling constructions of Mexico City built stock due an extreme Mw 8.5 magnitude subduction earthquake scenario.

Incidentally, the potential number of casualties that could be spared by the possible implementation of ex-ante mitigation retrofitting policies on the one- to three-floor dwelling constructions of Mexico City built stock would be 51,900 dwellings × 3.6 persons per dwelling = 186,840 casualties, which represents 2.1% of the total Mexico City inhabitants [*INEGI*, 2011]. This number of casualties can be compared with the official figure of 9500 casualties or missing reported in the aftermath of the 1985 Mw 8.01 Michoacan earthquake [*Swiss Re*, 2006].

In the United States, there are several risk mitigation programs that have been implemented to minimize the threat posed by hurricane and earthquake. For instance, as reported by *GAO-07-403* [2007], "in Florida, private insurance companies are required by law to offer a discount for structures that incorporate wind mitigation components. In California, state law requires the California Earthquake Authority (CEA)—a privately financed but publicly managed state agency—to offer a 5% discount on retrofitted homes that were built before 1979 and that meet other specifications." Another example of seismic mitigation policies are those implemented in the city of Berkeley, California, which encourages private property owners to conduct seismic retrofit activities by allowing them to use a portion of the transfer tax on the sale of a property to fund seismic retrofit work, and by waiving building permit fees on seismic retrofit projects [*GAO-07-403*, 2007]. From these experiences, *GAO-07-403* [2007] concluded that insurance premium discounts can promote mitigation by rewarding property owners for actions they take to reduce the effects of natural hazards.

This means that with the participation of all the stakeholders concerned by the consequences of seismic and hurricane hazards, several towns in the United States are making progress in sustainably increasing resilience [*GAO-07-403*, 2007]. These experiences should be taken into account in the analyses of initiating a seismic risk mitigation retrofitting program for Mexico City one- to three-floor dwelling constructions, considering the hazard posed by the likely occurrence in the lapse 2012–2037 of an extreme Mw $\geq 8^+$ such as the Mw 8.5 subduction earthquake scenario proposed in this study.

17.6. SYNTHETIC ACCELEROGRAMS IN GUADALAJARA FOR AN EXTREME MW 8.5 MAGNITUDE SUBDUCTION EARTHQUAKE SCENARIO WITH AN EPICENTER IN THE COLIMA-JALISCO REGION

17.6.1. Location and Rupture Area of an Extreme Mw 8.5 Magnitude Subduction Earthquake Scenario in the Colima-Jalisco Region

In the last ~80 years five subduction superficial, damaging earthquakes have occurred in the CJ region of Mexico, two in 1932, and one in 1973, 1995, and 2003 (see Figures 17.6 and 17.B1). The most relevant for this study are the events of the 3 June 1932 magnitude Ms 8.2 (the largest instrumentally recorded in Mexico) and the one on the 9 October 1995 Mw 8/Ms 7.4. The epicenters of these two large magnitude earthquakes were located at ~250 km from Guadalajara (the second largest town in Mexico). Only for the CJ1995 event, strong ground motions were recorded in the near, intermediate and far fields, especially in the far field at 11 accelerographic stations of Guadalajara [*Chavez et al.*, 2011, 2014].

By following the arguments already discussed in Sections 17.3.4 and 17.4.1 for the CJ Mw 8.5 earthquake scenario, and by applying the Mw–Mo (moment magnitude) and the Mw–rupture area relationships suggested for subduction events by *Wells and Coppersmith* [1994], an estimated seismic moment Mo of 6.92×10^{21} Nm and

a rupture area of 288 (length) × 90 (width) km^2 were obtained. Note that this width is the same as the one assumed for the Guerrero Mw 8.5 extreme earthquake scenario. The location and the kinematic rupture area proposed for the plausible extreme CJ Mw 8.5 magnitude earthquake scenario, with epicenter in the CJ region of the Mexican subduction zone are shown in Figure 17.31. We notice in this figure that the rupture area of the scenario event overlaps the events of the 3 June and 18 June 1932, the 9 October 1995, and a small part of the 22 January 2003, earthquakes. The latter assumption took into account the fact that in the CJ region and in its vicinity, the rupture areas of larger events generally overlap each other (and also those of the smaller events), as it has been observed for the rupture areas of the 1985 Michoacan (Mw 8.01, Ms 8.1) and the 1995 CJ (Mw 8) (see Figures 17.6 and 17.31).

With respect to the return period of large magnitude events in the CJ Mexican subduction zone, by using large magnitude earthquake historical data of Mexico, *Nishenko and Singh* [1987] suggested for the CJ region that an event with M 8^+ can be expected in this region with a return period of 77–126 years. Therefore, as the last one was the 1932 Ms 8.2 event, probably the next M 8^+ earthquake can be expected in the CJ region any time in the lapse 2009–2056, which includes the lapse 2012–2037 (based on the results shown in Figures 17.5 and 17.7) mentioned in Section 17.3.4.

17.6.2. Seismic Source Kinematic Slip of an Extreme Mw 8.5 Magnitude Subduction Earthquake Scenario in the Colima-Jalisco Region

The finite seismic source adopted for the Mw 8.5 magnitude subduction earthquake scenario in the CJ region consisted of 12 subevents with rupture areas of 30×36 km^2 (see Figure 17.31). The latter dimensions and their location took into account the results of *Escobedo et al.* [1998] for the location and dimensions of the four subevents representing the seismic source of the 1995 Mw 8 CJ event, as well as ~50% of the 288 (length) × 90 (width) km^2 assumed rupture area would be rupturing in the Mw 8.5 CJ scenario event. Each of the 12 subevents had an average Mo of 5.77×10^{20} Nm (which results in dividing the Mo 6.92×10^{21} Nm of the Mw 8.5 scenario event by 12 subevents), and a strike, dip, and rake source mechanism of 340°, 17°, and 90°. The latter values are based on the findings of *Bandy et al.* [1999], and *Escobedo et al.* [1998] on the seismic source parameters of the CJ Mw 8 CJ earthquake [*Chavez et al.*, 2011].

The source ruptures of the 12 subevents were kinematically simulated, radially propagating outward with a constant velocity of rupture (Vr) of 2.2 km/s in agreement with *Escobedo et al.* [1998], and the results of *Chavez*

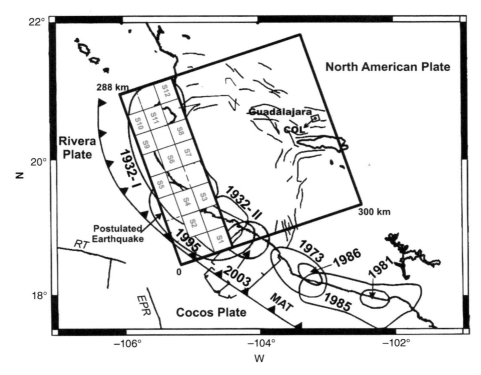

Figure 17.31 Rupture areas for the Ms 8.2 3 June (1932-I), Ms 8 18 June (1932-II), Mw 8/Ms 7.6 9 October 1995, and other large subduction earthquakes; and rupture area of the extreme Mw 8.5 magnitude subduction scenario earthquake, S1–S12 (in gray) depict the location of its assumed 12 subevents. Surface projection of the volume used for the 3D low-frequency simulation.

et al. [2011]; see Figure 17.32. The slip rate function used for all sources was an isosceles triangle with a rise time of 1 s as in *Chavez et al.* [2011]. The focal mechanisms used in the modeling for the 12 subevents were purely thrust mechanisms, as suggested by *Escobedo et al.* [1998] for the 1995 Mw 8 CJ earthquake.

We considered the three rupture scenarios shown in Figure 17.32 for the postulated Mw 8.5 scenario earthquake: (1) starting their rupture at subevent S1 (southern), (2) at subevent S7 (central), and (3) at subevent S12 (northern); see Figure 17.31. Table 2 and figure 9 of *Chavez et al.* [2011] summarizes the numerical parameters, and the minimum V_p, V_s, and the densities of the considered geological structure (see Figure 17.B1b).

17.6.3. Synthetic Accelerograms in Guadalajara for an Extreme Mw 8.5 Magnitude Subduction Earthquake Scenario in the Colima-Jalisco Region

The hybrid method described in Section 17.2.2 was applied to generate synthetic accelerograms expected in Guadalajara for the CJ extreme Mw 8.5 magnitude subduction earthquake scenario presented in Figure 17.31. For the low-frequency modeling, a 300 (length) × 288 (width) × 300 (depth) km³ volume was used. The surface projection of the latter is shown in Figure 17.31. The

physical and computational modeling parameters are similar to those used for the successful modeling of the 1995 Mw 8 CJ earthquake [*Chavez et al.*, 2011, 2014] discussed in Appendix 17.B (see Figure 17.B2). The rupture kinematic slips of Figure 17.32 were used to include three different possibilities of the rupture of the seismic source of the proposed extreme Mw 8.5 scenario earthquake. The 3DWPFD code and the supercomputers KanBalam, Miztli, HECToR, and JUGENE were used for the tests and final runs of the low-frequency computation of the wave propagation of the extreme Mw 8.5 earthquake scenario [*Chavez et al.*, 2011, 2014].

For high frequencies, the EGF technique discussed in Section 17.2.2 [*Chavez et al.*, 2011] was used to generate the high-frequency synthetic accelerograms at Guadalajara for the CJ extreme Mw 8.5 magnitude earthquake scenario. We used as EGFs the recorded accelerograms observed in Guadalajara for the 9 October 1995 Mw 8/Ms 7.6 CJ earthquake [*Chavez et al.*, 2014] (see Figure 17.B4). The elementary sources of the Mw 8.5 earthquake correspond to the 12 subevents shown in Figure 17.31.

From the synthesis of the low- and high-frequency synthetic accelerograms (see Figure 17.1), the broadband (0.01–15 Hz) synthetics for the CJ extreme Mw 8.5 magnitude earthquake scenario were obtained for Guadalajara.

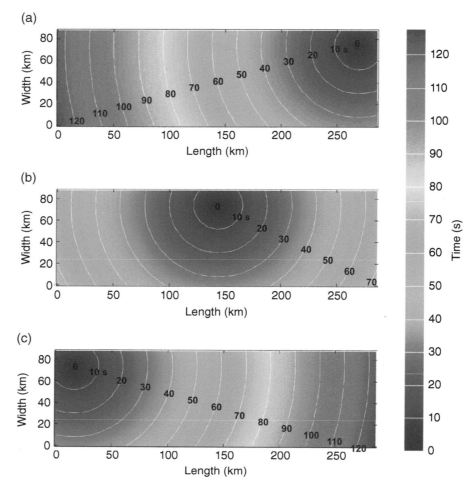

Figure 17.32 Three assumed finite source ruptures for the Mw 8.5 earthquake scenario of Figure 17.31, starting their rupture at: (a) subevent S1 (southern), (b) at subevent S7 (central), and (c) at subevent S12 (northern), see Figure 17.31. The numbers inside the rectangles are the rupture time elapsed from the initial rupture of the event.

Examples of the type of results obtained for the finite source rupture shown in Figure 17.32b are presented in Figure 17.33. This figure includes the synthetic accelerograms in the North-South (NS) direction obtained for the 11 accelerographic recording sites of Guadalajara. In panels (a), (b), and (c) of Figure 17.33, we grouped the synthetic accelerograms corresponding to the sites located in the geotechnical subzones I–IV (also called 1–4 in the following) shown in Figure 17.B4, respectively. In the subzones 3–4, the depth to rock of Guadalajara sandy layers is larger than 20 m, and for subzones 1–2, the depth to rock of the layers is <20 m.

We notice that the maximum amplitudes (i.e., the peak ground accelerations, PGAs) of the synthetic accelerograms in the subzones 1–2 are about 0.3–0.5 than the PGAs of the synthetics of the subzones 3–4, this is due to the local soil effects of Guadalajara sandy soil layers; as the depth to the rock of the layers increases, a larger amplification of the superficial strong ground motions is observed, as discussed in *Chavez et al.* [2014]. Incidentally, the maximum amplitudes of the synthetic accelerograms, corresponding to the finite source ruptures of Figures 17.32a and c, are smaller than those associated with ruptures of Figure 17.32b, presented in Figure 17.33; therefore, in what follows we will use the synthetic accelerograms obtained with the latter.

17.7. ESTIMATION OF THE DIRECT ECONOMIC IMPACTS IN GUADALAJARA ONE- TO THREE-FLOOR DWELLING STOCK DUE TO THE OCCURRENCE OF AN EXTREME MW 8.5 MAGNITUDE SUBDUCTION EARTHQUAKE SCENARIO IN THE COLIMA-JALISCO REGION

In this section, the hybrid methodology proposed in Section 17.2 is applied to obtain preliminary estimates of PEI, PEDEC, and PML for the metropolitan zone of Guadalajara (in what follows called "Guadalajara")

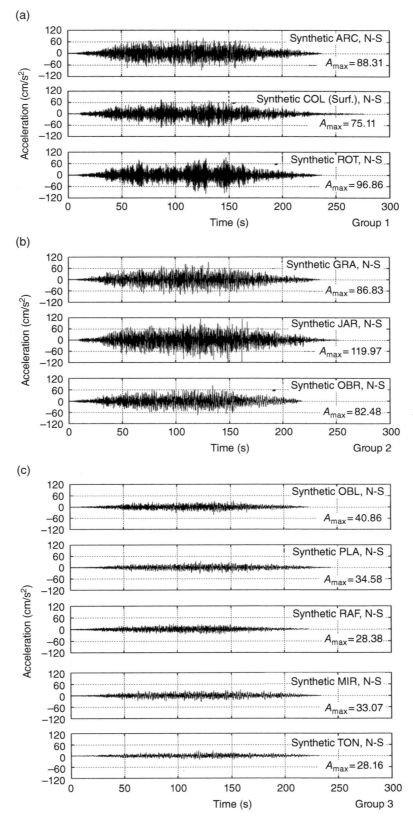

Figure 17.33 Broadband synthetics accelerograms for the Mw 8.5 central rupture earthquake scenario (see Figure 17.32) for the North-South (NS) component of the recording site stations of Guadalajara (see Figure 17.B4). The synthetics of panels (a), (b), and (c) correspond to the geotechnical subzones 3–4 and 1–2, respectively.

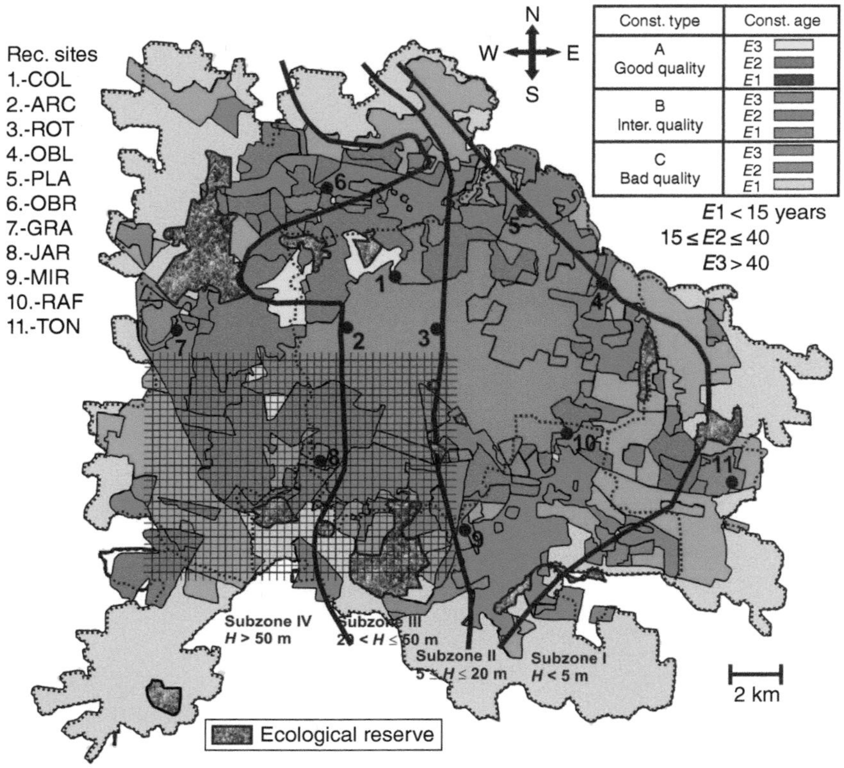

Figure 17.34 Guadalajara's: (i) Preliminary distribution of its one- to three-floor dwelling stock characterized by their construction quality and age [*Garcia-Rubio*, 1994; *Chavez*, 1995; *INEGI*, 2014]; (ii) geotechnical microzonation (*H*(m) depth to rock of Guadalajara sandy soils) [*Chavez et al.*, 1995, 2011]; (iii) Location of its accelerographic network which recorded the 1995 Mw 8 Colima-Jalisco earthquake (Appendix 17.B); and (iv) example of the discretization of its urban surface by square cells of (~0.287 × 0.287 km²).

dwelling built stock of one to three floors, associated with the plausible occurrence of the CJ extreme Mw 8.5 magnitude earthquake scenario shown in Figure 17.31. It is important to recall that for Guadalajara the only strong ground motion recordings available for large magnitude earthquakes are those of the 1995 Mw 8 CJ event (see Appendix 17.B). This fact has been taken into consideration in the application of the hybrid methodology to estimate its seismic hazard and risk posed by the extreme Mw 8.5 magnitude earthquake scenario with epicenter in the CJ region.

17.7.1. Superficial Distribution of Guadalajara One- to Three-Floor Dwelling Stock and Their Seismic Vulnerability

17.7.1.1. Superficial Distribution of Guadalajara One- to Three-Floor Dwelling Stock

Based on the information of the superficial distribution of Guadalajara built stock suggested by *Garcia-Rubio* [1994] and *Chavez* [1995], updated with information retrieved from the *INEGI* [2014], Figure 17.34 was

generated. In this figure the superficial distribution of the built dwelling stock of one- to three-floor constructions of Guadalajara metropolitan zone is presented, taking into account its construction quality and age. With respect to the quality of construction three categories are suggested: good (A), intermediate (B), and bad (C). These categories correspond to those constructions which very likely followed seismic construction recommendations (A), those which partially followed seismic recommendations (B), and those which did not follow any seismic recommendations (C), respectively. Concerning the age of the constructions, three construction ages were considered: <15 years (*E*1), between 15 and 40 years (*E*2), and more than 40 years (*E*3).

Also, in Figure 17.34 the geotechnical microzonation proposed for Guadalajara in four subzones [Chavez *et al.*, 1995, 2014] and the location of the accelerographic network of Guadalajara, which recorded the Mw 8 CJ are included. (Incidentally, this network stopped functioning in 1997 due to the lack of interest and economical support of the local, state, and federal authorities, *Chavez et al.*, 2011, 2014.)

The total urban (built) area of Guadalajara included in Figure 17.34 is ~500 km². This surface was discretized in 6024 square cells with an area of ~0.083 km² (i.e., each cell ~0.288 × 0.288 km²). An example of the discretization is shown in Figure 17.34. Furthermore, in order to approximately consider the areas of Guadalajara without constructions, such as its avenues, streets, and green areas, a reduction factor of 0.8 was applied to the mentioned areas.

In Table 17.2 a synthesis of the areas of the one- to three-floor built dwelling stock of Guadalajara characterized by their construction quality and age, and their location with respect to Guadalajara's geotechnical microzonation is presented. From the table, we can conclude that the one- to three-floor dwelling stock of Guadalajara can be characterized as follows: (1) its total area is ~400 km², (2) from which ~ 73, 139, and 188 km² are of quality A (good), B (intermediate), and C (bad), respectively; (3) that by their age ~ 112, 211, and 78 km² are of <15 years, between 15 and 40 years, and more than 40 years, respectively; (4) that ~ 74, 106, 77, and 144 km² are located in the geotechnical subzones I, II, III, and IV(or 1 to 4), respectively.

The expected (mean) cost, C, per square kilometer (in billion USD), and C plus or minus one standard deviation (σ_c) of the one- to three-floor dwelling stock in the surface of Guadalajara suggested by the *IMIC* [2013] are presented in Table 17.3. A CV of 0.15 of the cost values was also suggested by the *IMIC* [2013], and is included in the values of C shown in Table 17.3. We notice in the latter that the cost/km² of the constructions of quality A are ~2 and ~4 times higher than those of dwelling constructions with construction quality B and C, respectively.

The distribution of the unitary mean cost/km² on the surface of Guadalajara are shown in Figure 17.35. We notice in the latter that the lower costs are located in the central and the periphery of Guadalajara, and the higher costs are mainly located in the west subzones, reflecting the historical urban development of Guadalajara, as discussed by *Chavez* [1995].

By applying the unitary expected (mean) cost values of Figure 17.35 to the surface of Guadalajara included in Figure 17.34, we obtain the results shown in Figure 17.36. In this figure it can be observed that the mean lower cost/km² (identified by the green and pale yellow colors) correspond to the central and eastern zones of Guadalajara, and that the mean higher cost/km² (identified by the orange and red colors) are those located in the western part and the periphery of Guadalajara, and its total expected cost is of 139.32 billion USD.

The synthesis of the costs of the actual dwelling built stock of one to three floors of Guadalajara by quality and age of construction in the four geotechnical subzones are included in Table 17.4. From this table it can be concluded that the expected (mean) costs $C \pm \sigma_c$ are 174.152 and 104.491 billion USD, respectively. We notice in the latter that the total mean costs of the one- to three-floor Guadalajara constructions in the geotechnical subzone IV, represents ~2.6, 1.8, and 2.25 than those of the constructions located in the geotechnical subzones I, II, and III, respectively.

17.7.1.2. Seismic Vulnerability of Guadalajara One- to Three-Floor Dwelling Stock

The seismic vulnerabilities (V) as a function of PGA adopted for Guadalajara one- to three-floor dwelling constructions are shown in Figure 17.37. These curves were obtained by adapting the vulnerability curves as a function of MMIs suggested by *Cochrane and Schaad* [1992] to the MMI and PGAs observed in Guadalajara (see Figure 17.38) for the CJ 1995 Mw 8 earthquake [Chavez M. and Martinez, A. 1996, Isosistas en la zona metropolitan de Guadalajara del sismo de Colima-Jalisco Mw 8 del 9 de Octubre de 1995, unpublished report]. In this figure the 1995 Guadalajara's observations of MMIs and recorded PGAs (see Appendix 17.B) were complemented by the maximum MMI and PGA observed in Mexico City at the SCT compressible soil site for the Michoacan 1985 earthquake (see Appendix 17.A). The fitting of the mentioned observations is represented by the continuous curve of Figure 17.38. In this figure the relationship between MMI and PGA suggested by the USGS is also shown with a dashed curve.

The vulnerability curves of *Cochrane and Schaad* [1992] were obtained from a large sample of earthquake-damaged constructions observed (mainly for dwelling constructions) in Colombia, Chile and Mexico, which have construction practices similar to those of Guadalajara. The observations in Colombia correspond to the 1983 Popayan Ms 5.5 (hypocenter depth of 5.5 km) earthquake [*Lomnitz and Hashizume*, 1985], in which 14,000 buildings were damaged, the majority of them in the city's historic center where 2470 houses collapsed, 6885 of them suffered damage >50% of their structure and 4,500 experienced minor damage [*Cruz Hoyos*, 2013]. The earthquake construction damage data of Chile was gathered after the 1985 Ms 7.8 Chile earthquake, in which 45,000 dwelling constructions were destroyed and 76,000 heavily damaged [*USGS*, 1985]. The construction damage observations for Mexico were obtained for the 1985 Mw 8.01 Michoacan earthquake, already discussed in Section 17.1.

In Figure 17.37, 0.01 and 1 values imply that a minimum and a total damage to the dwelling construction can be experienced if the PGA values generated by an earthquake reach ~15 to ~200 cm/s², respectively. The V values can also be considered as percentages of the dwelling construction areas damaged by an earthquake depending

Table 17.2 Preliminary Surface (km²) of Guadalajara Dwelling Built Stock of One to Three Floors by Geotechnical Subzone, Quality (A, B, C), and Age (E1, E2, E3) of Its Construction (see Figure 17.34)

| | Surface of Dwelling Stock of One- to Three-Floor Constructions in Guadalajara (km²) | | | | | | | | | | | | |
| Quality of Construction | Geotechnical Subzone I, $H < 5$ m | | | Geotechnical Subzone II, $5 \leq H \leq 20$ m | | | Geotechnical Subzone III, $20 < H \leq 50$ m | | | Geotechnical Subzone IV, $H > 50$ m | | | Σ |
	E1	E2	E3	E1	E2	E3	E1	E2	E3	E1	E2	E3	E1
A	0	0.528	0	0	11.22	0	0	13.134	3.828	0	42.636	1.848	73.194
B	0	10.560	3.366	0	32.472	34.254	0	14.256	22.110	0	12.738	9.504	139.26
C	38.610	19.734	0.924	6.006	21.846	0.396	17.094	6.930	0.132	50.160	25.674	1.320	188.826
Σ	38.610	30.822	4.290	6.006	65.538	34.650	17.094	34.320	26.070	50.160	81.048	12.672	401.280

Construction quality: A (good), B (intermediate), and C (bad); construction age: E1 < 15 years; 15 ≤ E2 ≤ 40 years, and E3 > 40 years; depth to rock of Guadalajara sandy soils H(m).

Table 17.3 Preliminary Mean, Mean Plus or Minus One Standard Deviation of the Costs/km² of Guadalajara Dwelling Built Stock of One to Three Floors by Quality and Age of Construction in the Four Geotechnical Subzones (see Figure 17.34)

| Construction Cost (Billion USD/km²) | Construction Quality | Construction Cost (Billion USD/km²) of Guadalajara | | | | | | | | | | | |
| | | Geotechnical Subzone I, $H < 5$ m | | | Geotechnical Subzone II, $5 \leq H \leq 20$ m | | | Geotechnical Subzone III, $20 < H \leq 50$ m | | | Geotechnical Subzone IV, $H > 50$ m | | |
		E1	E2	E3	E1	E2	E3	E1	E2	E3	E1	E2	E3
$\bar{c}$	A	0.958	0.679	0.228	0.958	0.679	0.228	0.958	0.679	0.228	0.953	0.679	0.228
	B	0.573	0.406	0.136	0.573	0.406	0.136	0.573	0.406	0.136	0.573	0.406	0.136
	C	0.329	0.233	0.078	0.329	0.233	0.078	0.329	0.233	0.078	0.329	0.233	0.078
$\bar{c} + \sigma_c$	A	1.197	0.849	0.285	1.197	0.849	0.285	1.197	0.849	0.285	1.197	0.849	0.285
	B	0.716	0.508	0.170	0.716	0.508	0.170	0.716	0.508	0.170	0.716	0.508	0.170
	C	0.411	0.291	0.098	0.411	0.291	0.098	0.411	0.291	0.098	0.411	0.291	0.098
$\bar{c} - \sigma_c$	A	0.718	0.509	0.171	0.718	0.509	0.171	0.718	0.509	0.171	0.718	0.509	0.171
	B	0.430	0.305	0.102	0.430	0.305	0.102	0.430	0.305	0.102	0.430	0.305	0.102
	C	0.246	0.175	0.059	0.246	0.175	0.059	0.246	0.175	0.059	0.246	0.175	0.059

Construction quality: A (good), B (intermediate), and C (bad); construction age: E1 < 15 years; 15 ≤ E2 ≤ 40 years and E3 > 40 years; depth to rock of Guadalajara sandy soils H(m).

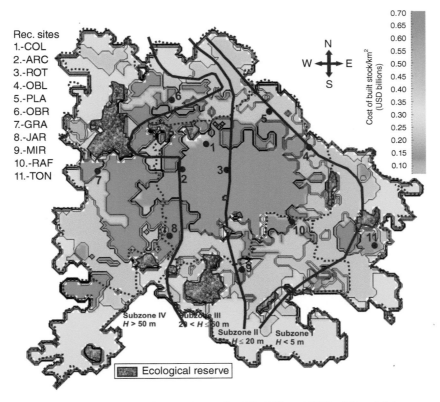

Figure 17.35 Preliminary unitary expected (mean) costs/km² (in billion USD) of Guadalajara one- to three-floor dwelling constructions.

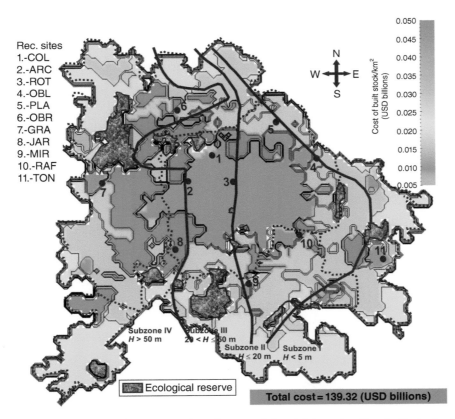

Figure 17.36 Preliminary expected (mean) and total costs of Guadalajara dwelling built stock of one to three floors by quality and age of construction located in its four geotechnical subzones, corresponding to the mean costs/km² included in Table 17.3.

Table 17.4 Preliminary Mean, Mean Plus or Minus One Standard Deviation Costs of Actual Guadalajara Dwelling Built Stock of One to Three Floors by Quality and Age of Construction in the Four Geotechnical Subzones (see Figure 17.34)

Construction Cost (Billion USD)	Construction Quality	Geotechnical Subzone I, $H < 5$ m			Geotechnical Subzone II, $5 \leq H \leq 20$ m			Geotechnical Subzone III, $20 < H \leq 50$ m			Geotechnical Subzone IV, $H > 50$ m			Σ
		E1	E2	E3	E1	E2	E3	E1	E2	E3	E1	E2	E3	
$\bar{c}$	A	0.000	0.359	0.000	0.000	7.622	0.000	0.000	8.922	0.872	0.000	28.963	0.421	47.159
	B	0.000	4.292	0.459	0.000	13.198	4.668	0.000	5.794	3.013	0.000	5.177	1.295	37.896
	C	12.687	4.599	0.072	1.974	5.092	0.031	5.617	1.615	0.010	16.483	5.984	0.103	54.267
	Σ	12.687	9.250	0.531	1.974	25.912	4.699	5.617	16.332	3.895	16.483	40.125	1.819	139.322
$\bar{c} + \sigma_c$	A	0.000	0.448	0.000	0.000	9.527	0.000	0.000	11.153	1.090	0.000	36.204	0.526	58.949
	B	0.000	5.365	0.573	0.000	16.497	5.835	0.000	7.243	3.766	0.000	6.472	1.619	47.370
	C	15.859	5.749	0.090	2.467	6.365	0.039	7.021	2.019	0.013	20.603	7.480	0.129	67.834
	Σ	15.859	11.563	0.664	2.467	32.390	5.873	7.021	20.415	4.869	20.603	50.156	2.274	174.152
$\bar{c} - \sigma_c$	A	0.000	0.269	0.000	0.000	5.716	0.000	0.000	6.692	0.654	0.000	21.723	0.316	35.369
	B	0.000	3.219	0.344	0.000	9.898	3.501	0.000	4.346	2.260	0.000	3.883	0.971	28.422
	C	9.515	3.450	0.054	1.480	3.819	0.023	4.213	1.211	0.008	12.362	4.488	0.077	40.700
	Σ	9.515	6.938	0.398	1.480	19.434	3.524	4.213	12.249	2.921	12.362	30.093	1.364	104.491

Construction quality: A (good), B (intermediate), and C (bad); construction age: $E1 < 15$ years, $15 \leq E2 \leq 40$ years, and $E3 > 40$ years; depth to rock of Guadalajara sandy soils H(m).

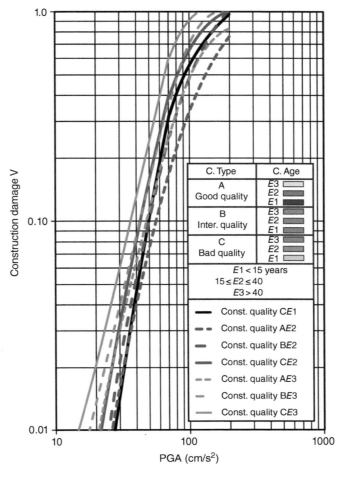

Figure 17.37 Preliminary vulnerability (*V*) of Guadalajara dwelling constructions of one to three floors (see Figure 17.34) as a function of PGA and their construction quality and age [adapted from *Cochrane and Schaad*, 1992].

on the PGA generated by the latter at a specific site; and the product of the damaged area by a cost/km² of those constructions, can be considered as equal to the direct economic loss of rebuilding the constructions to their previous state before the earthquake. The direct economic loss does not include the costs associated with casualties, the value of their contents, and the disruption of the use of the destroyed constructions.

We notice that the seismic vulnerability curves (*V*) shown in Figure 17.37 take into account the "actual" characteristics with respect to the quality and the age of the one- to three-floor dwelling constructions existing in Guadalajara (presented in Section 17.7.1.1). Therefore, as a first approach (until the respective studies on their *V* are carried out) to the seismic vulnerability issue of Guadalajara dwelling constructions, we assume here that the *V*–PGA functions of Figure 17.37 represent their expected *V* values, with a coefficient of variation equal to zero. It can be observed from the figure that the *V* red or

blue color curves correspond to the combination of the quality and age characteristics of the one- to three-floor dwelling constructions of Guadalajara.

17.7.2. Estimation of the Probability of Exceedance of the Intensities in Guadalajara for an Extreme Mw 8.5 Subduction Earthquake Scenario

As mentioned in Section 17.7.1.2, the seismic vulnerability of the one- to three-floor constructions of Guadalajara (see Figure 17.37) depends on the PGA values of the geotechnical subzone where they are located, as shown in Figure 17.B4. The RNN procedure of Section 17.2.3 (see Figure 17.2) was applied to the 11 PGA values (in the NS direction) of Figure 17.33 (and then to those in the EW direction) corresponding to the synthetic accelerograms obtained for the extreme Mw 8.5 subduction earthquake scenario of Figure 17.31 and the finite source rupture indicated in Figure 17.32b.

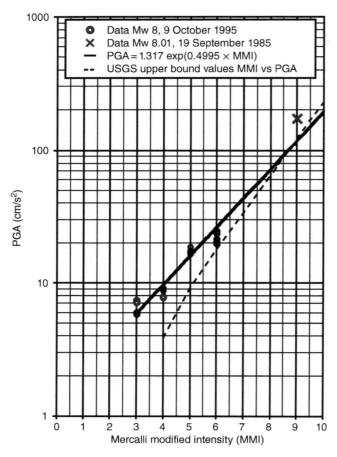

Figure 17.38 Peak ground acceleration versus MMI relationship obtained from the observations in Guadalajara for the 1995 Mw 8 Colima-Jalisco earthquake (o) and in Mexico City for the 1985 Mw 8.01 (Ms 8.1) Michoacan earthquake (X).

The PGA value of stations ROT was not used in the RNN calculations, but to verify the RNN training results. In the RNN calculations a spatial distance $k = 0.1$ km was used (see Figure 17.2) compared to the distances of several kilometers among the Guadalajara accelerographic recording stations shown in Figure 17.34. The evolution of the RNN calculations is shown in Figures 17.39 and 17.40.

The final result of the application of the RNN procedure for the NS and WE direction is shown in Figures 17.41 and 17.42 respectively. As the larger PGA values are those of the NS direction, in what follows we use only these. From Figure 17.41, the values of the PGA at each of the cells in which Guadalajara surface was discretized were used to obtain their respective histograms, their fitted loglogistic and lognormal PDFs and their associated cumulative distributions. They are shown in Figure 17.43a–c, for Guadalajara geotechnical subzones 1 and 2, and in Figure 17.44a–c, for the geotechnical subzones 3 and 4, respectively. From these values, the

probability of exceeding the PGA intensities (PEI) in Guadalajara, corresponding to the extreme Mw 8.5 scenario earthquake of Figure 17.31 was obtained.

We notice that the fitted probability density distributions are different, that is, the loglogistic with its larger probability density value for a PGA is ~32 cm/s² for the geotechnical subzones 1 and 2 (see Figure 17.43a) and the lognormal distribution with its larger probability density value for PGA ~105 cm/s² for its geotechnical subzones 3 and 4 (see Figure 17.44a). The fitted distributions were truncated in both their left and right tails, at the minimum and maximum values of each sample (Figures 17.43b and 17.44b, respectively).

The cumulative distributions of the fitted truncated distributions shown in Figures 17.43c and 17.44c are the PEIs of the PGA values associated with the plausible extreme Mw 8.5 magnitude earthquake scenario of Figure 17.31. From these figures, it can be concluded that there is a 10% probability of exceedance of the PGA value of 42 and 130 cm/s² for the geotechnical subzones 1–2, and 3–4, respectively.

17.7.3. Estimation of the Probability Distribution of the Cost of Damage/km² and the Total Cost of the One- to Three-Floor Dwelling Constructions of Guadalajara Built Stock for an Extreme Mw 8.5 Magnitude Subduction Earthquake Scenario

As mentioned in Section 17.7.1.2 the seismic vulnerability curves shown in Figure 17.37 can be associated with the direct economic loss of the one- to three-floor dwelling constructions of Guadalajara. If it is assumed that these constructions are uniformly distributed per unit area in the cells of Figure 17.34, the V curves of Figure 17.37 can be linked to the percentage of constructions located on those cells that could be damaged by the PGA values shown in Figure 17.41 (generated by the strong ground motions of Figure 17.33) due to the extreme Mw 8.5 magnitude earthquake scenario of Figure 17.31 and the finite seismic source rupture of Figure 17.32b.

The surface distribution of V for the constructions of interest associated with the PGA values of Figure 17.41 is presented in Figure 17.45. We notice in this figure that the larger V values correspond to the cells located in geotechnical subzones 3 and 4, compared to those located in subzones 1 and 2. For any of the cells in Figure 17.34, the product of its seismic vulnerability V multiplied by its built surface area is equal to the damaged surface (in km²) of the one- to three-floor constructions of Guadalajara built stock for that cell, due to the plausible occurrence, in this case, of the extreme Mw 8.5 magnitude earthquake scenario of Figure 17.31.

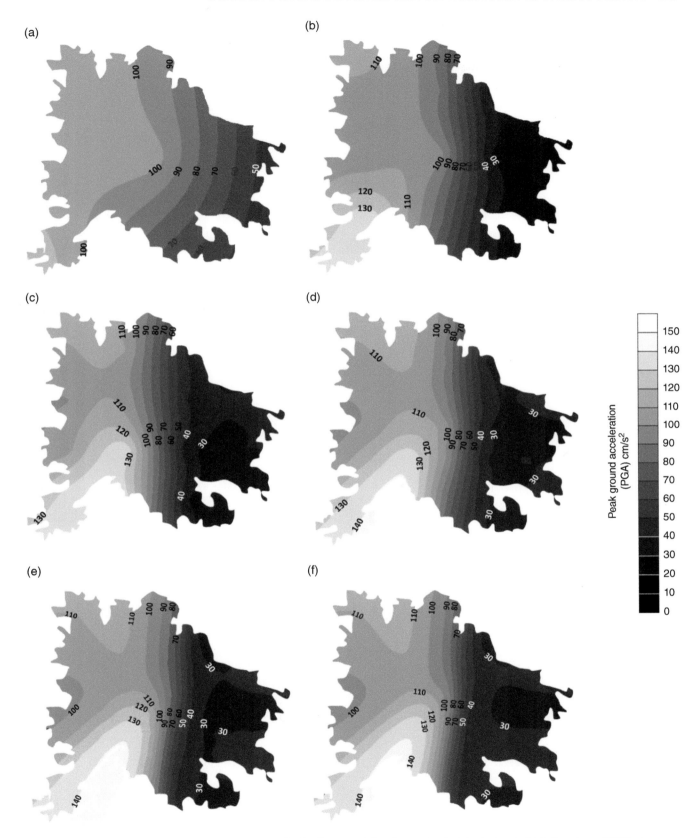

Figure 17.39 Recurrent neural network results for the spatial distribution in the North-South (NS) direction of PGA at Guadalajara for the extreme Mw 8.5 magnitude central rupture earthquake scenario (see Figures 17.31 and 17.32b).

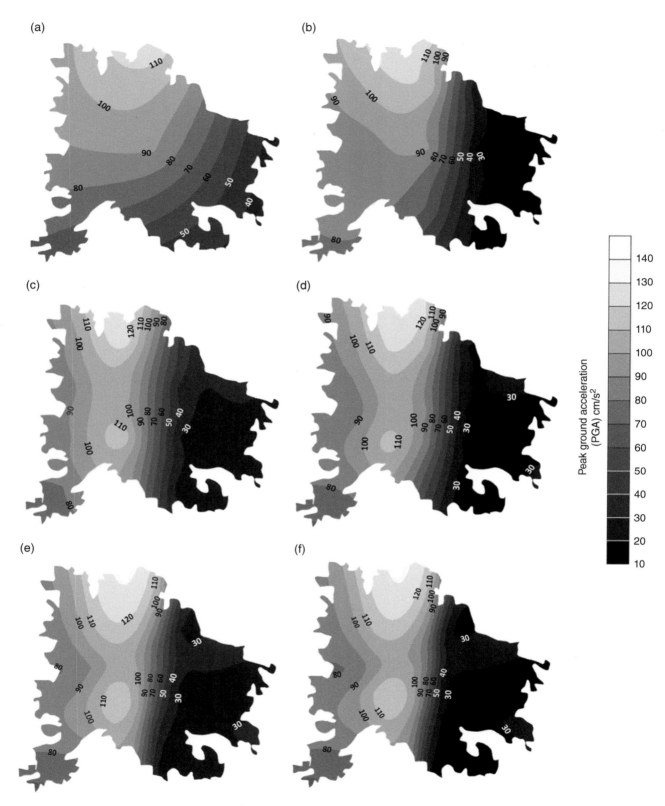

Figure 17.40 Recurrent neural network results for the spatial distribution in the West-East (WE) direction of PGA at Guadalajara for the extreme Mw 8.5 magnitude central rupture earthquake scenario (see Figures 17.31 and 17.32b).

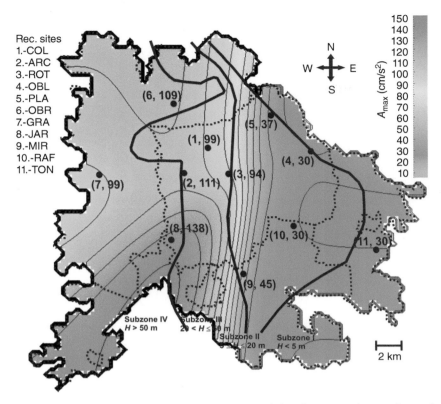

Figure 17.41 Recurrent neural network final result for the spatial distribution in the North-South (NS) direction of PGA at Guadalajara for the extreme Mw 8.5 magnitude central rupture earthquake scenario (see Figures 17.31 and 17.32b).

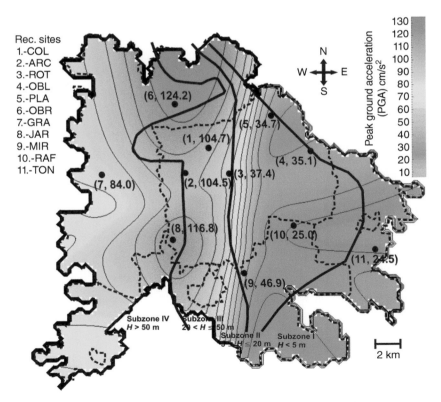

Figure 17.42 Recurrent neural network final result for the spatial distribution in the West-East (WE) direction of PGA at Guadalajara for the extreme Mw 8.5 magnitude central rupture earthquake scenario (see Figures 17.31 and 17.32b).

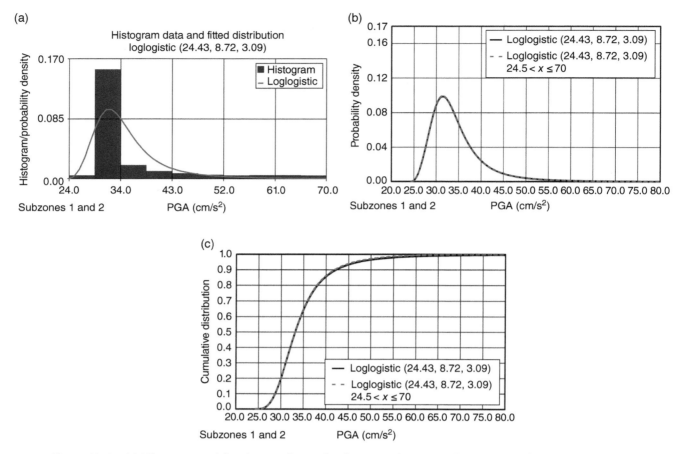

Figure 17.43 (a) Histogram and fitted PDF of PGA for the (central rupture of Figure 17.32b) extreme Mw 8.5 magnitude earthquake scenario for geotechnical subzones 1 and 2, (b) unbounded and truncated PDF of (a), and (c) cumulative distribution of (b).

The surface distribution of the expected (mean) damaged area for the one- to three-floor constructions of Guadalajara built stock, associated with the plausible occurrence of the extreme Mw 8.5 earthquake scenario of Figure 17.31, is presented in Figure 17.46. We notice in this figure that the largest values correspond to the stock located mainly on its geotechnical subzones 3 and 4, identified in orange-red colors in the figure, compared with the damaged stock located on subzones 1 and 2, identified with the blue colors. These results are in agreement with the MMI observations in Guadalajara for the 1995 Mw 8 magnitude CJ earthquake discussed in Appendix 17.B and *Chavez et al.* [2014]. Indeed, the MMI (and PGA) values of 3 and 4, and 5 and 6 used in Figure 17.38, were observed in geotechnical subzones 1–2 and 3–4, respectively [Chavez M. and Martinez, A. 1996, Isosistas en la zona metropolitan de Guadalajara del sismo de Colima-Jalisco Mw 8 del 9 de Octubre de 1995, unpublished report].

A synthesis of the damaged surface of Figure 17.46 as a function of the construction quality and age for each of the geotechnical subzones of Guadalajara is presented in Table 17.5. It can be observed in this table that (1) the total damaged surface is of ~148 km², which represents ~0.37 of the 401 km² of the one- to three-floor built stock of the dwelling constructions of Guadalajara (see Table 17.2); (2) ~4.5, 12.5, 43.8, and 86.7 km² of the damaged constructions corresponding to geotechnical subzones 1, 2, 3, and 4, respectively; (3) ~26.2, 46.6, and 74.7 km², this is ~0.18, 0.32, and 0.50 of the 148 km² of the total damaged surface are associated with Guadalajara's dwelling stock with construction quality A, B, and C, respectively (see Figure 17.34).

The surface distribution of the expected (mean) costs (see Table 17.3) of the damaged surface of Figure 17.46 can be obtained by the product of the damaged surface of the type of dwelling construction of a particular cell of Guadalajara (see Figure 17.34) and its respective unitary cost included in Table 17.3. The result obtained for all the cells of Guadalajara is shown in Figure 17.47. We notice in this figure that: (1) the total mean damage cost is 48.87 billion USD; (2) the largest values of the costs/km² of the damaged one to three floors of Guadalajara

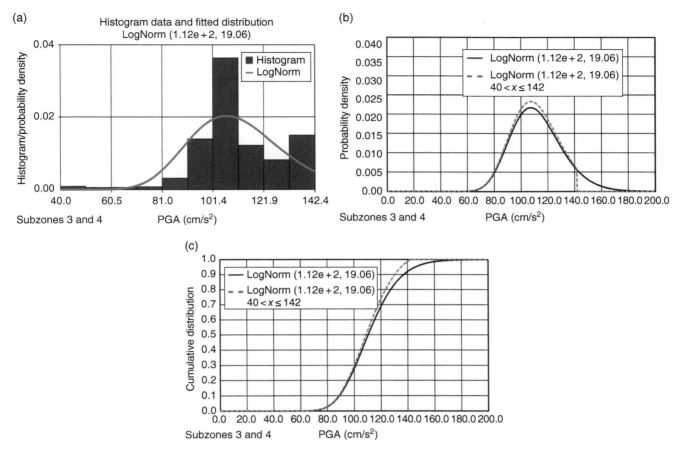

Figure 17.44 (a) Histogram and fitted PDF of PGA for the (central rupture of Figure 17.32b) extreme Mw 8.5 magnitude earthquake scenario for geotechnical subzones 3 and 4; (b) unbounded and truncated PDF of (a); and (c) cumulative distribution of (b).

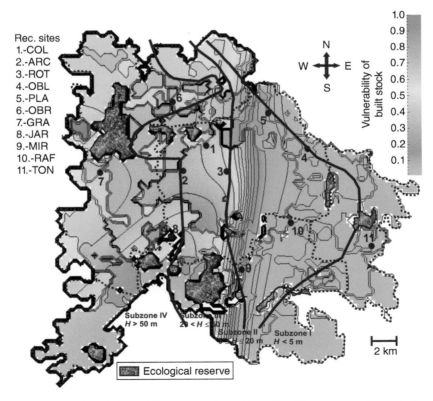

Figure 17.45 Preliminary vulnerability of the one- to three-floor dwelling constructions of Guadalajara for the extreme Mw 8.5 magnitude earthquake scenario of Figure 17.31.

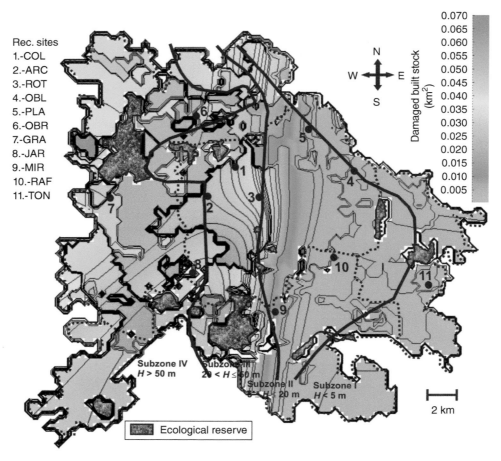

Figure 17.46 Preliminary surface distribution of damage of the one- to three-floor dwelling constructions of Guadalajara for the extreme Mw 8.5 magnitude earthquake scenario of Figure 17.31.

built stock distribution, identified in orange-red colors in the figure, correspond to the stock located mainly on its geotechnical subzones 3 and 4, compared with the damaged stock located on subzones 1 and 2, identified with the blue colors. A synthesis of the cost of construction damaged (see Figure 17.47), as a function of construction quality and age for each of the geotechnical subzones of Guadalajara is presented in Table 17.6. It is observed in this table that the total mean, mean plus and minus one standard deviation of the cost of the damaged surface of the dwelling constructions of one to three floors of Guadalajara for the extreme Mw 8.5 magnitude earthquake scenario of Figure 17.31 are: ~48.87, 61.09, and 36.65 billion USD, respectively.

17.7.4. Estimation of the Preliminary PEDEC/km² for the One- to Three-Floor Dwelling Stock for an Extreme Mw 8.5 Subduction Earthquake Scenario

The histograms, the fitted inverse-Gamma, the lognormal probability density, and the cumulative distributions of the expected (mean) costs/km² for the one- to three-floor

constructions damaged areas of Figure 17.47, located in geotechnical subzones 1–2 and 3–4, are shown in Figures 17.48a–c and 17.49a–c, respectively. The unbounded and truncated PDFs and cumulative distributions are included in Figures 17.48b,c and 17.49b,c, respectively. We notice that the maximum values of the fitted inverse-Gamma and the lognormal PDFs are 0.0004 and 0.01 billion USD/km², respectively.

17.7.4.1. PEDEC Assuming that the Probability Density Functions of PGA and the Preliminary Damage Cost are Statistically Independent

If it is assumed that the PGA (see Figures 17.43 and 17.44) and costs of damage/km² (see Figures 17.48 and 17.49) are independent random variables, the PEDEC for the damaged areas of one- to three-floor dwelling built stock of Guadalajara due to the extreme Mw 8.5 magnitude earthquake scenario of Figure 17.31, can be selected from the truncated cumulative inverse-gamma and lognormal distributions shown in Figures 17.48c and 17.49c, which correspond to geotechnical subzones 1–2 and 3–4, respectively, or from Table 17.7.

Table 17.5 Preliminary Damage Surface of Guadalajara Dwelling Built Stock of One to Three Floors by Soil Subzone, Quality of Construction and Age (see Figure 17.34) Due to the Extreme Mw 8.5 Magnitude CJ Earthquake Scenario

	Construction Damaged of Guadalajara (km^2)												
	Geotechnical Subzone I, $H < 5$ m			Geotechnical Subzone II, $5 \leq H \leq 20$ m			Geotechnical Subzone III, $20 < H \leq 50$ m			Geotechnical Subzone IV, $H > 50$ m			Σ
Constructions Type	$E1$	$E2$	$E3$	$E1$	$E2$	$E3$	$E1$	$E2$	$E3$	$E1$	$E2$	$E3$	$E1$
A	0.000	0.009	0.000	0.000	0.750	0.000	0.000	4.825	1.981	0.000	17.657	0.984	26.205
B	0.000	0.259	0.136	0.000	2.435	6.040	0.000	7.645	16.071	0.000	6.767	7.196	46.549
C	1.447	2.568	0.065	0.948	2.344	0.025	8.279	4.828	0.132	33.828	19.035	1.237	74.736
Σ	1.447	2.836	0.201	0.948	5.529	6.064	8.279	17.298	18.184	33.828	43.459	9.417	147.491

Construction quality: A (good), B (intermediate), and C (bad); construction age: $E1$ < 15 years, 15 ≤ $E2$ ≤ 40 years, and $E3$ > 40 years; depth to rock of Guadalajara sandy soils H(m).

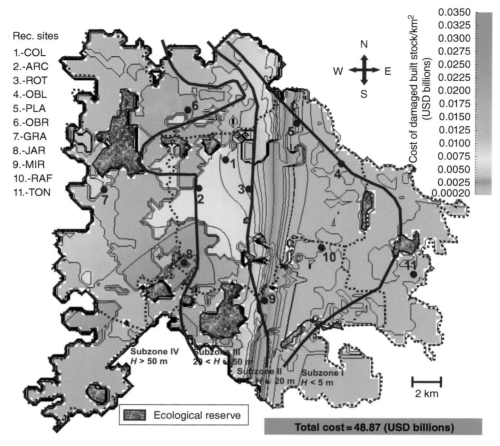

Figure 17.47 Preliminary mean cost of damage/km² and total cost of the one- to three-floor dwelling constructions of Guadalajara for the extreme Mw 8.5 magnitude earthquake scenario of Figure 17.31.

In Table 17.7, several PEDECs are included for a few selected PEDEC values identified by C^a. For example, for the one to three floors dwelling built stock located in geotechnical subzones 1 and 2 and for a PEDEC of 0.5, 0.1, 0.01, 0.001, 0.0001 the associated costs/km² are: 0.00071, 0.00261, 0.01160, 0.04754, 0.1145 and 0.00068, 0.00213, 0.00432, 0.00493, 0.00500 billion USD, for the unbounded and truncated PEDECs, respectively, and the return period of a specific PEDEC value is the reciprocal of the respective PEDEC. We notice that the first two PEDEC the cost values for the unbounded cumulative distribution are slightly larger than those corresponding to the truncated inverse-gamma distributions, but for the last three PEDECs, the cost values are too large and unrealistic.

For the one- to three-floor dwelling built stock located in geotechnical subzones 3 and 4 and for a PEDEC of 0.5, 0.1, 0.01, 0.001, and 0.0001, the costs/km² (see Table 17.7) are 0.01226, 0.02153, 0.03406, 0.04765, 0.06282 and 0.01218, 0.02099, 0.02987, 0.03286, 0.003327 billion USD for the unbounded and the truncated PEDECs, respectively, and the return period of a specific PEDEC is the reciprocal of the latter. We notice that the

first two PEDECs the cost values for the unbounded lognormal distribution are slightly larger than those of the truncated distribution, but for the last three values are too large and unrealistic.

17.7.4.2. PEDEC Assuming that the Probability Density Functions of PGA and the Preliminary Damage Cost Are Statistically Dependent

If it is assumed that the PGA (see Figures 17.43 and 17.44) and the costs of damages/km² (see Figures 17.48 and 17.49) are dependent random variables, their joint PEDECs can be obtained by the Gumbel-Hoogard copula, which provides a convenient framework for its modeling in the context of this study. Hence, for Guadalajara the Gumbel-Hoogard copula model is adopted to assess the joint probabilistic risk associated with the occurrence of EME intensities represented by PGA and their direct economic costs. This implies that we should apply Equations 17.20, 17.24, and 17.30 to their respective marginal probability density distributions presented in the previous sections. The results are presented in Figures 17.50, 17.51, and 17.52.

Table 17.6 Preliminary Mean, Mean Plus or Minus One Standard Deviation of the Costs of the Damage Surface of Guadalajara Dwelling Built Stock of One to Three Floors by Soil Subzone, Quality of Construction and Age (see Figure 17.34) Due to the Extreme Mw 8.5 Magnitude CJ Earthquake Scenario

Cost of Construction	Construction Quality	Cost of Construction Damage of Guadalajara (Billion USD)													
		Geotechnical Subzone I, $H < 5$ m			Geotechnical Subzone II, $5 \leq H \leq 20$ m			Geotechnical Subzone III, $20 < H \leq 50$ m			Geotechnical Subzone IV, $H > 50$ m			Σ
		$E1$	$E2$	$E3$	$E1$	$E2$	$E3$	$E1$	$E2$	$E3$	$E1$	$E2$	$E3$	
$\bar{c}$	A	0.000	0.006	0.000	0.000	0.509	0.000	0.000	3.277	0.451	0.000	11.995	0.224	16.463
	B	0.000	0.105	0.019	0.000	0.990	0.823	0.000	3.107	2.190	0.000	2.751	0.981	10.965
	C	0.475	0.599	0.005	0.312	0.546	0.002	2.720	1.125	0.010	11.116	4.437	0.097	21.444
	Σ	0.475	0.710	0.024	0.312	2.046	0.825	2.720	7.510	2.652	11.116	19.182	1.301	48.872
$\bar{c} + \sigma_c$	A	0.000	0.007	0.000	0.000	0.637	0.000	0.000	4.097	0.564	0.000	14.994	0.280	20.578
	B	0.000	0.132	0.023	0.000	1.237	1.029	0.000	3.884	2.737	0.000	3.438	1.226	13.706
	C	0.594	0.748	0.006	0.389	0.683	0.002	3.400	1.407	0.013	13.895	5.546	0.121	26.805
	Σ	0.594	0.887	0.030	0.389	2.557	1.031	3.400	9.388	3.314	13.895	23.977	1.627	61.090
$\bar{c} - \sigma_c$	A	0.000	0.004	0.000	0.000	0.382	0.000	0.000	2.458	0.338	0.000	8.996	0.168	12.347
	B	0.000	0.079	0.014	0.000	0.742	0.617	0.000	2.330	1.642	0.000	2.063	0.735	8.224
	C	0.357	0.449	0.004	0.234	0.410	0.001	2.040	0.844	0.008	8.337	3.327	0.073	16.083
	Σ	0.357	0.532	0.018	0.234	1.534	0.619	2.040	5.633	1.989	8.337	14.386	0.976	36.654

Construction quality: A (good), B (intermediate), and C (bad); construction age: $E1 < 15$ years, $15 \leq E2 \leq 40$ years, and $E3 > 40$ years; depth to rock of Guadalajara sandy soils H(m).

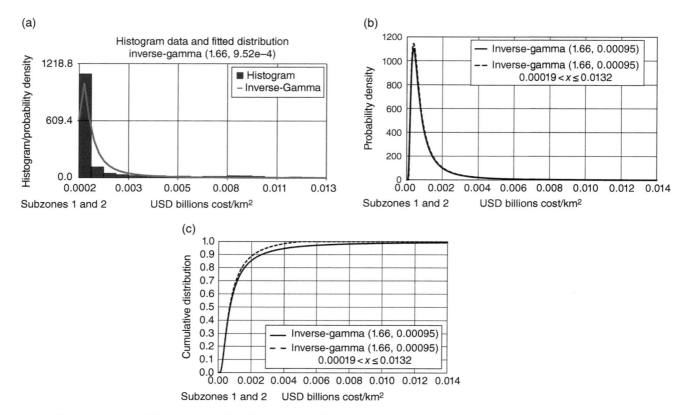

Figure 17.48 (a) Histogram and fitted PDF of the damage costs/km² for the central rupture (see Figure 17.32) Mw 8.5 earthquake scenario for geotechnical subzones 1 and 2; (b) unbounded and truncated PDFs of (a); and (c) cumulative distributions of (b).

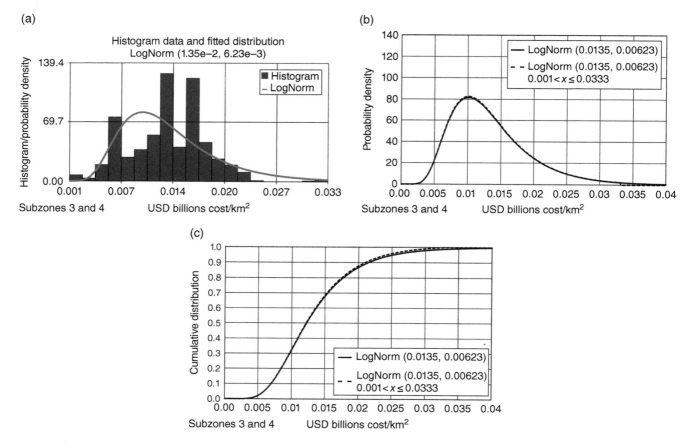

Figure 17.49 (a) Histogram and fitted PDF of the damage costs/km² for the central rupture (see Figure 17.32) Mw 8.5 earthquake scenario for geotechnical subzones 3 and 4; (b) unbounded and truncated PDFs of (a); and (c) cumulative distributions of (b).

Table 17.7 Preliminary Direct Economic Costs/km² of Damage of Guadalajara One- to Three-Floor Dwelling Constructions Due to the Extreme Mw 8.5 Magnitude CJ Earthquake Scenario for Several PEDEC

	Economic Costs (Billion USD/km²)				
	Cumulative Distribution (Figures 17.48c and 17.49c)		Cumulative Distribution Truncated (Figures 17.48c, 17.49c, and 17.52)		
PEDEC (T_r Years)	Geotechnical Subzone 1–2 Inverse-Gamma	Geotechnical Subzone 3–4 LogNormal	Geotechnical Subzone 1–2 inverse–gamma	Geotechnical Subzone 3–4 LogNormal	
0.50 (2)	0.00071[a]	0.01226[a]	0.00068[a]	0.01218[a]	0.01005[b]
0.10 (10)	0.00261[a]	0.02153[a]	0.00213[a]	0.02099[a]	0.02007[b]
0.05 (20)	0.00417[a]	0.02525[a]	0.00290[a]	0.02419[a]	0.02500[b]
0.025 (40)	0.00652[a]	0.02900[a]	0.00363[a]	0.02700[a]	0.00760[b]
0.010 (100)	0.01160[a]	0.03406[a]	0.00432[a]	0.02987[a]	0.01500[c]
0.005 (200)	0.01780[a]	0.03801[a]	0.00464[a]	0.03132[a]	0.01900[c]
0.0044 (225)	0.01926[a]	0.03875[a]	0.00468[a]	0.03152[a]	0.02117[c]
0.0042 (237)	0.01982[a]	0.03902[a]	0.00470[a]	0.03159[a]	0.02181[c]
0.004 (250)	0.02042[a]	0.03930[a]	0.00471[a]	0.03166[a]	0.02215[c]
0.0025 (400)	0.02722[a]	0.04207[a]	0.00482[a]	0.03222[a]	0.02368[c]
0.001 (1000)	0.04754[a]	0.04765[a]	0.00493[a]	0.03286[a]	0.01500[d]
0.0001 (10,000)	0.19145	0.06282[a]	0.00500[a]	0.03327[a]	0.02700[d]

By considering that (1) the PGA and costs are statistically independendent (identified by C^a), (2) PGA and costs are statistically dependent and the interarrival times of the Mw 8.5 earthquake scenario are 1 year (C^b), 25 years (C^c), and 225 years (C^d).

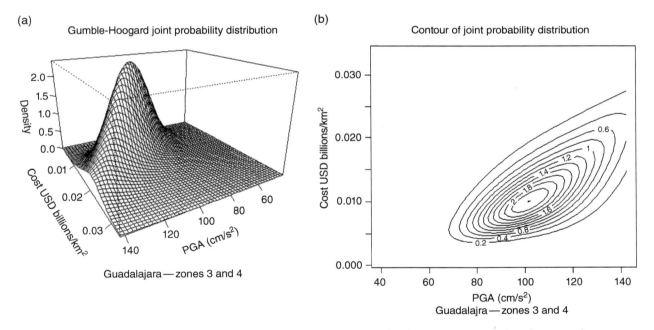

Figure 17.50 Joint event and contours of the probability density distribution of PGA and preliminary damage costs/km² for Guadalajara one- to three-floor dwelling constructions located on geotechnical subzones 3 and 4, due to the extreme Mw 8.5 earthquake scenario.

In Figure 17.50a and b, the probability density distribution of the joint event and its contours of PGA and the costs/km² for vulnerabilities V (see Figure 17.37) of Guadalajara one- to three-floor dwelling built stock located on geotechnical subzones 3 and 4, due to the extreme Mw 8.5 magnitude earthquake scenario (of Figure 17.31) are shown, respectively. From Figure 17.50a and b, we notice that the maximum values of the joint probability

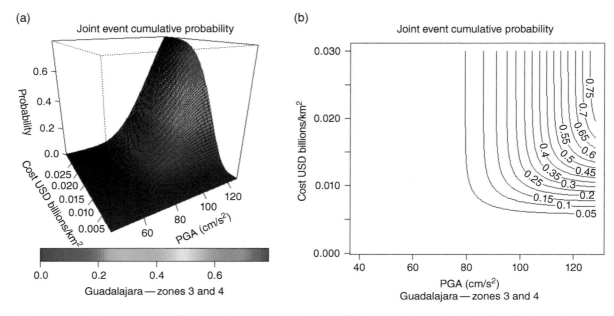

Figure 17.51 Joint event cumulative and contours of the probability distributions of PGA and preliminary damage costs/km² for Guadalajara one- to three-floor dwelling constructions located on geotechnical subzones 3 and 4 due to the extreme Mw 8.5 earthquake scenario.

density occurs in a band of values of PGA (70–140 cm/s²) and the costs/km² (0.004–0.025 billion USD).

In Figure 17.51a and b, the joint event cumulative and its contours of PGA and cost/km² of Guadalajara one- to three-floor dwelling built stock due to the extreme Mw 8.5 earthquake scenario are presented. Finally, in Figure 17.52 the joint event return period and its contours, of the PGA and the costs/km² of Guadalajara one- to three-floor dwelling built stock due to the extreme Mw 8.5 earthquake scenario, for an expected time interval $E(L)$ between the occurrence of the Mw 8.5 scenario of 1 year (panel a), 25 years (panel b), and 225 years (panel c) are shown.

In order to compare the results obtained by assuming that PGA and the damage cost/km² are independent random variables, or that they are statistically dependent, in Table 17.7 the joint event cumulative PEDEC's values for the one- to three-floors dwelling built stock located in geotechnical subzones 3 and 4 of Guadalajara are included. They are identified by C^b, C^c, C^d for expected time intervals between the occurrence of the Mw 8.5 scenario of 1 year, 25 years, and 225 years, respectively.

From the ratios C^a/C^b, C^a/C^c, C^a/C^d of the costs/km² values included in Table 17.7, the following conclusions can be drawn: (1) for an interarrival time of 1 year and joint event return periods of 2, 10, 20 and 40 years, the economic costs/km² C^a are 1.21, 1.045, 0.96, and 3.55 times of those of C^b, respectively; (2) for an interarrival time of 25 years and joint event return periods of 100, 200, 225, 237, 250, and 400 years, the costs/km² C^a

are 1.99, 1.65, 1.49, 1.45, 1.43, and 1.36 times of those of C^c, respectively; (3) for an interarrival time of 225 years and joint event return periods of 1000 and 10,000 years, the costs/km² C^a are 2.19–1.23 times of those of C^d; (4) from conclusions (1), (2), and (3) the statistical dependence of PGA, costs, and the interarrival times of the considered extreme Mw 8.5 magnitude earthquake scenario become critical in the seismic risk assessment exercise.

17.7.5. Preliminary Probable Maximum Loss for Guadalajara Dwelling Stock of One to Three Floors Due to the Extreme Mw 8.5 Magnitude Earthquake Scenario

If it is assumed that the PGA and the direct damaged costs C are independent random variables, the upper bound values of the PML can be selected from Table 17.6. In this table the mean, mean plus or minus one standard deviation of the costs of the damaged surface of Guadalajara one- to three-floor dwelling built stock by soil subzone, quality of construction and age (see Figure 17.34) due to the extreme Mw 8.5 CJ earthquake scenario are included. From this table, the following conclusions can be drawn: (1) the total mean, mean plus or minus one standard deviation PML costs of the damaged surface of considered dwelling built stock of Guadalajara due to the Mw 8.5 CJ scenario event are: 48.872, 61.090, and 36.654 billion USD, respectively; which represent ~0.35 of the 139.32, 174.15, and 104.49 billion USD, of

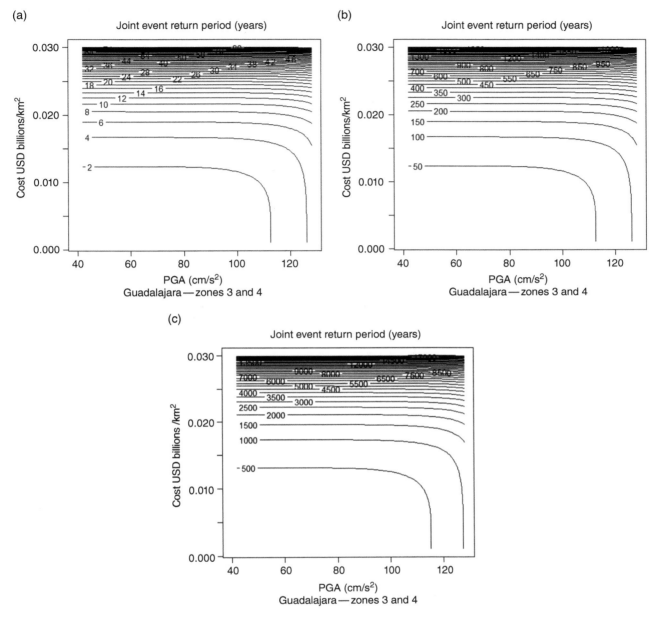

Figure 17.52 Joint event return period and contours of PGA and preliminary damage costs/km² for Guadalajara one- to three-floor dwelling constructions located on geotechnical subzones 3 and 4, due to the extreme Mw 8.5 earthquake scenario for expected time intervals of the scenario of 1 year (a), 25 years (b), and 225 years (c).

the mean, mean plus and minus one standard deviation of their actual cost (see Table 17.4); (2) ~0.025, 0.065, 0.263, and 0.647 of the total respective PML costs of the damaged constructions correspond to geotechnical subzones 1, 2, 3, and 4, respectively; (3) ~0.34, 0.22, and 0.44 of the mean, mean plus and minus one standard deviation of the total PML cost of the damaged surface of Guadalajara are associated with the dwelling stock with construction quality A, B, and C, respectively (see Figure 17.34).

17.7.6. Risk Mitigation Retrofitting Policies to Minimize the Preliminary Probable Maximum Loss and Casualties Derived from the Damage of One- to Three-Floor Constructions of Guadalajara Subject to an Extreme Mw 8.5 Magnitude Subduction Earthquake Scenario

By following the arguments mentioned in Section 17.5.5, the possible ex-ante implementation of seismic risk mitigation retrofitting policies for the one- to three-floor constructions built stock of Guadalajara are analyzed. The analysis is based on the PML values estimated in Section 17.7.5 for those constructions due to an extreme Mw 8.5 magnitude subduction earthquake scenario.

In particular, the objective of the ex-ante analysis for Guadalajara dwelling constructions includes the estimation of the costs of the seismic retrofitting of the mentioned constructions to reduce their seismic vulnerability, at least, from the quality of construction C to B, and as a consequence, to reduce the vulnerabilities of the former, to those of the latter constructions (see Figure 17.37). The economic consequences of this action would mean a reduction in the PML costs of damage of the constructions with construction quality C (see Table 17.6). The latter cost should be compared with the seismic retrofitting costs, in order to take an informed economic decision, in terms of time and available economic resources, about the convenience of implementing a seismic retrofitting program for the one- to three-floor constructions of Guadalajara built stock, which could include all the stakeholders involved, such as the Guadalajara inhabitants, government officers, and insurance companies, among others.

As for the constructions of interest in this study an expression for the retrofitting cost CR is not available for the time being, as a first approximation to quantify the latter cost for the one- to three-floor constructions of Guadalajara built stock, we will also use the expression proposed by $Jafarzadeh\ et\ al.$ [2014], $CR = 0.207\ A^{0.823}$ (where A is the construction surface in m^2) to analyze the impact of the possible implementation of ex-ante mitigation retrofitting policies on these constructions and on the PML estimates obtained in Section 17.7.5.

With respect to the cost and the surface of the average of the one- to three-floor dwelling constructions in Guadalajara, based on the reports by the $IMIC$ [2013] the unitary costs included in Tables 17.3 and 17.4, and an average surface of $300\ m^2$ per dwelling were assumed in the analysis. Therefore, the total costs per dwelling of construction quality A, B, C and ages $E1$, $E2$, and $E3$ (see Table 17.3) are 65,800, 46,600, and 15,600 USD, respectively, and their construction seismic retrofitting cost, $CR = 0.207 \times (300)^{0.823} = 22,627$ USD.

The total mean, mean plus or minus one standard deviation PML costs of the damaged construction quality C of Guadalajara due to the extreme Mw 8.5 magnitude earthquake scenario event are 21.444, 26.805, and 16.083 billion USD, respectively (see Table 17.6), which correspond to a damaged surface of 74.73 km² (see Table 17.5). The latter figure divided by the assumed average surface of $300\ m^2$ per dwelling, correspond to 248,871 dwellings. Therefore, if mitigation retrofitting actions are taken to bring those constructions from vulnerability C to B (see Figure 17.37), then a number of dwellings of Guadalajara

could be spared if a potential extreme Mw 8.5 magnitude earthquake scenario occurs. The total cost of implementing the retrofitting of those dwellings is 22,627 USD/dwelling × 248,871 dwellings equals 5.631 billion USD. This retrofitting total cost represents about 26.2%, 21%, and 35% of the total mean, mean plus or minus one standard deviation of the PML costs (see Table 17.6) of the one- to three-floor damaged constructions quality C of Guadalajara.

Incidentally, the potential number of casualties that could be spared by the possible implementation of ex-ante mitigation retrofitting policies on the one- to three-floor constructions of Guadalajara built stock would be 248,871 dwellings × 4 persons per dwelling = 995,484 casualties, which represents 22.4% of the 4,434,878 inhabitants of the metropolitan zone of Guadalajara reported by the INEGI census of 2010.

From the experiences reported by $GAO-07-403$ [2007], mentioned in Section 17.5.5 by rewarding property owners with, among others, reductions in their taxes for actions they take to reduce the effects of natural hazards, we can promote mitigation to the risks posed by the latter. These experiences should be taken into account in the analyses on the convenience of initiating a seismic risk mitigation retrofitting program for Guadalajara constructions (dwellings) of one to three floors, considering the hazard posed by the likely occurrence in the lapse 2012–2037, of an extreme Mw ≥ 8⁺ such as the Mw 8.5 subduction earthquake scenario proposed in this study.

17.8. CONCLUSIONS

1. Recent studies suggest that most of the circum-Pacific subduction zone can generate extreme magnitude earthquakes (EME) with magnitude Mw ≥ 8.5, 8.8, and 9 with return periods (T_r) of 250, 500, and 10,000 years, respectively. The Mw 9 EME occurred on 11 March 2011 in north-eastern Japan, which led to a large number of casualties, a nuclear accident, and huge economic losses, shows that the seismic (and tsunami) hazard and risk estimations in this seismotectonic region were grossly underestimated.

2. A hybrid method which uses both observations and modeling of the earthquake phenomena and its effects on the built environment is proposed to estimate the probabilities of exceeding the intensities (PEI) and the direct economic consequences (PEDEC) of EME at a site. The PEIs are obtained from synthetic ground motion samples for the 3D wave propagation of EME (plausible) scenarios and machine learning techniques. The PEDECs are computed by using cadastral information, direct costs, and appropriate seismic vulnerability functions of the infrastructure of interest, combined with the ground motion intensity samples of EME scenarios.

3. With the proposed methodology the uncertainties (and future updates) associated with the following issues can be included: the stochastic and fractal character of the EME (finite) seismic source, the source to site path geology, the local soil conditions at the site where the infrastructure is located, the seismic vulnerability functions, the seismic response, and the direct costs of the infrastructure of interest.

4. Taking into account conclusion (1), 3D synthetic ground motion samples expected in Mexico City and Guadalajara were obtained for two EME scenarios with Mw 8.5 magnitudes, and epicenters located in the Guerrero and the Colima-Jalisco subduction zone of Mexico, respectively. From those samples, their respective PEIs were computed.

5. By using cadastral information and seismic vulnerability functions of the one- to three-floor dwelling constructions of Mexico City and Guadalajara, and the samples of the synthetics mentioned in conclusion (4), preliminary estimates of the damage areas of these constructions due to the extreme Mw 8.5 earthquake scenarios were computed; and by using unitary direct cost of the damaged areas, their respective preliminary PEDECs were obtained.

6. The importance of estimating the PEIs and PEDECs by using bounded (truncated) marginal probability distributions, and considering their stochastic dependence by using Copula models, from which their associated joint return period probabilities can be derived for decision-making purposes are highlighted. The interarrival times of the Mw 8.5 magnitude EME scenarios, is a critical issue to be considered in the seismic risk assessment.

7. By assuming statistical independence of the PEIs and PEDECs, preliminary upper bound values of the probable maximum loss (PML) expected for Mexico City and Guadalajara due to the Mw 8.5 magnitude EME scenarios were obtained. For Mexico City, the preliminary PML can vary from 0.7 to 18 billion USD, and for Guadalajara (metropolitan zone) from 37 to 61 billion USD.

8. If ex-ante mitigation retrofitting actions are taken to reduce the vulnerability of the one- to three-floor dwelling constructions of Mexico City and Guadalajara, then to minimize the seismic risk posed by the likely occurrence in the lapse 2012–2037 of extreme Mw 8^+ magnitudes subduction earthquakes, such as the proposed Mw 8.5 scenarios, ~52,000 and ~250,000 dwellings could be spared, by investing ~0.8 and ~5.6 billion USD, versus potential PMLs of ~7 and ~22 billion USD, respectively.

ACKNOWLEDGMENTS

We would like to thank J.L. Gordillo, the Supercomputing staff of DGTIC, UNAM, and M. Ambriz, L. Alcantara, L. Ramirez and A. Soto of the Institute of Engineering, UNAM. We also acknowledge the support rendered by R. Madariaga and M. Mai of the ENS, Paris and KAUST of Saudi Arabia, respectively; and A. Rubalcava formerly at the Faculty of Engineering of the University of Guadalajara and G. Suarez of the Institute of Geophysics, UNAM. Thoughtful reviews from anonymous reviewers significantly improved the manuscript. We acknowledge DGTIC, UNAM for its support to use KanBalam and Miztli supercomputers, the STFC Daresbury Laboratory to use HECToR and BGQ Supercomputers, and the PRACE European project to use the JUGENE supercomputer. The first author acknowledges the partial support of the Institute of Engineering, UNAM, and of the SCAT project through Europe Aid contract II-0537-FC-FA (http://www.scat-alfa.eu).

APPENDIX 17.A. MODELING OF THE WAVE PROPAGATION OF THE 1985 MW 8.01 MAGNITUDE MICHOACAN, MEXICO EARTHQUAKE

The most frequent and damaging earthquakes in Mexico, especially for Mexico City constructions, are the interplate ones which occur in the subduction zone of Mexico (i.e., where the Cocos Plate descends under the North American plate), compared to the damaging effects of Mexico's intraplate (i.e., occurring inside the Cocos plate) or shallow depth cortical (occurring at shallow depths in the North American plate) earthquakes, respectively (see Figure 17.A1a and b). Figure 17.A1a includes: the rupture areas (the elliptical shapes of different colors), the location of epicenters (red and blue stars) and the year of occurrence of the large magnitude interplate, intraplate and cortical earthquakes that occurred during the twentieth century in Mexico; Figure 17.A1a also shows the location of Mexico's active volcanoes (the red triangles), respectively.

Incidentally, the size of the rupture as shown in Figure 17.A1a is proportional to the magnitude of the corresponding earthquakes, for example, the rupture area of the 3 June 1932 Ms 8.2 magnitude Jalisco earthquake (the largest yellow elliptical shape shown in the top left part of Figure 17.A1a) is the largest instrumentally ever recorded in Mexico, compared to the rest of the subduction events shown in Figure 17.A1a, all of them with Ms ≤ ~8, where the magnitude Ms is another objective measure of the energy released by an earthquake calculated from the maximum amplitude of the recorded ground motion [*Stein and Wysession*, 2003].

In Figure 17.A1b, the profile PP′ (see Figure 17.A1a for its location) includes the thicknesses and mechanical properties of geological layers of the earth crust up to a depth of 124 km. In this case, these properties are represented by the so-called V_p and V_s wave propagation velocities [*Stein and Wysession*, 2003], respectively; and the

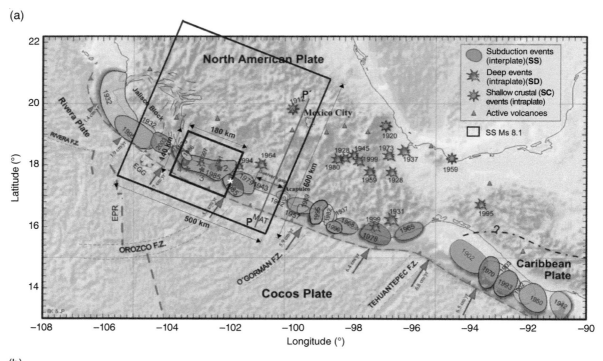

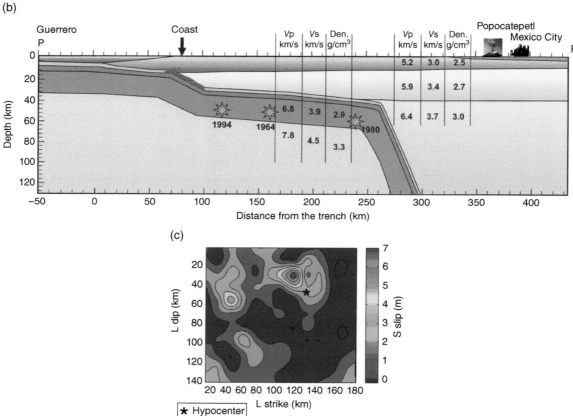

Figure 17.A1 (a) The elliptical shapes of different colors and their enclosed numbers indicate the rupture areas and the year of occurrence of historical (1900–2003) large magnitude subduction earthquakes in México, respectively. The red and blue stars and the triangles identify the epicenters of the large magnitude events occurred within the downgoing Cocos plate in the same period (see Figure A1b), the shallow depth crustal events, and the active quaternary volcanoes, of México, respectively. The large and small rectangles represent the surface projections of the 500 × 600 × 124 km³ earth crust volume discretization, and of the rupture area used in the modeling of the wave propagation of the 1985 Mw 8.01 magnitude Michoacan earthquake, respectively; (b) profile P-P'; (c) kinematic slip (distribution) of the 140 × 180 km² modeled rupture area of the 1985 earthquake; [A1a and b, modified, *Pacheco and Kostoglodov*, 1999 and *Pérez-Campos et al.*, 2008; A1c, modified, *Mendoza and Hartzell*, 1989].

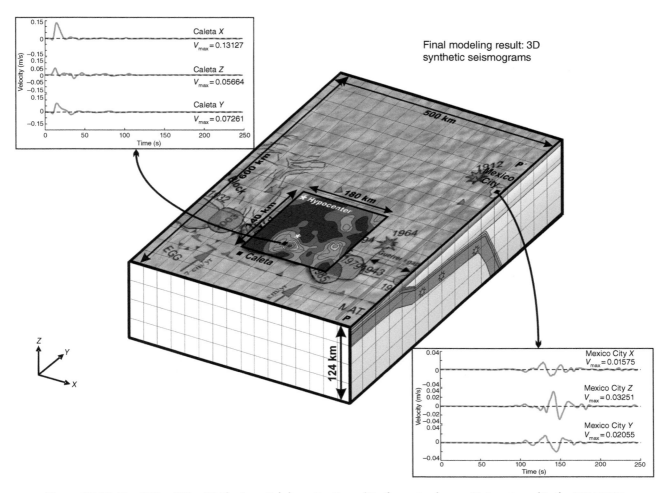

Figure 17.A2 The 500 × 600 × 124 km³ spatial discretization of Earth crust volume of interest used in the 3DWPFD code to model the low frequency propagation of the 1985 Mw 8.01 magnitude Michoacan earthquake; inner rectangle is the surface projection of the kinematic slip distribution of the rupture area of the event [*Mendoza and Hartzell*, 1989]; the earthquake hypocenter is indicated by the white star. Synthetic velocity seismograms obtained in the *x*, *y*, *z* directions at Caleta (coast) and TACY (Mexico City) recording sites.

density (weight) of the materials making up the geological layers of this region of Mexico. Notice that (usually) the values of V_p, V_s, and the density of the layers increases with depth. The zone where the large magnitude subduction events of Mexico occur is identified by the dense cloud of full red circles of Figure 17.A1b, which roughly correspond to the location of the contact surface between the Cocos and North American plates.

In Figures 17.A1 and 17.A2, the main input information used in the 3DWPFD code for the modeling of the low-frequency wave propagation of the 1985 Mw 8.01 magnitude Michoacan earthquake is shown. In Figure 17.A1a, the surface projection of the three dimensions 500 × 600 × 124 km³ earth crust volume (see Figure 17.A2) used in the modeling is shown. This 3D finite continuum physical domain was discretized (divided) by using 3D cells of

0.25 km in the *x*, *y*, and *z* directions, and the total duration of 250 s (selected for the synthetic ground motions) was divided in time steps of 0.01 s. The inner rectangle in Figure 17.A1a represents the surface projection (of 180 × 140 km²) of the finite seismic fault rupture area suggested by *Mendoza and Hartzell* [1989] for the 1985 Michoacan earthquake [*Cabrera et al.*, 2007, 2008].

The rupture area and the kinematic slip of the 1985 Michoacan earthquake suggested by *Mendoza and Hartzell* [1989] were assumed in this work (see Figure 17.A1c). Among other features of the kinematic slip of this earthquake, the length and width dimensions of the rupture area were 180, and 140 km, respectively. The distributions of the kinematic slip on the rupture area of the 1985 event varied from 0.01 to ~7 m; and its maximum values were from ~4 to ~7 m, in two well-defined zones, at a distance of ~90 km

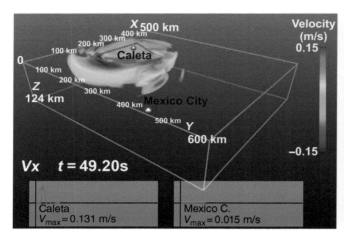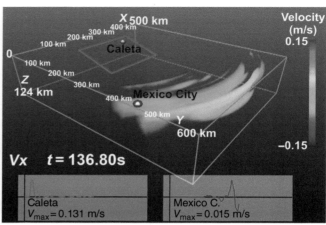

Figure 17.A3 3D Snapshots (at t = 49.20 s and 136.80 s) of the synthetic velocities wavefield (f < 0.3 Hz) in the x direction for the 1985 Mw 8.01 magnitude Michoacan earthquake. Also, the velocity seismograms in the same direction, for the Caleta, Michoacan, and TACY, Mexico City recording sites are shown.

between them (identified by the orange and red colors in Figure 17.A1c). In Figure 17.A2 are shown: (1) the spatial discretization of the 500 × 600 × 124 km³ finite earth crust volume selected to model the low-frequency seismic wave propagation of the 1985 Mw 8.01 Michoacan earthquake; (2) the surface projection of the kinematic slip distribution of the latter (see Figure 17.A1c); and (3) the synthetic ground motion velocities in the x, y, and z directions, obtained for the Caleta recording site station, located on the surface of firm soil layers in the epicentral zone of the 1985 earthquake, and those obtained for the Tacubaya (TACY) recording (firm soil) site, located in Mexico City at a distance of ~400 km from the Caleta site. Also, it can be observed from Figure 17.A2 that the synthetic ground motion velocities in the Caleta site start ~5 s after the initiation of the seismic rupture of the 1985 Michoacan earthquake, the time that the first seismic wave lasted to propagate from the hypocenter (located at a depth of 20 km) to the nearby Caleta site, compared with the synthetic ground motion velocities at the TACY site, which are different from zero at ~100 s after the initiation of the earthquake, the time that the first seismic wave of the 1985 earthquake, originating at the hypocenter of the 1985 Michoacan earthquake, located under the Caleta site region, lasted to propagate up to the TACY site in Mexico City.

Also note in Figure 17.A2 that the synthetic ground motion velocities in the Caleta site have maximum amplitudes of 0.131, 0.072, and 0.056 m/s, in the x, y, and z directions, respectively; and that those of the TACY site are 0.015, 0.020, and 0.032 m/s, respectively (i.e. ~0.1 to 0.5 than those of the Caleta site). This is due to the so-called attenuation (decrease) of the amplitudes of seismic waves, while they propagated through the geological layers of the earth crust, in this case, from a depth of ~20 km under the Caleta region up to the superficial (firm soil) TACY recording site in Mexico

City (see Figure 17.A1b) at ~400 km from the hypocenter of the Michoacan 1985 event. The attenuation of the seismic waves discussed here can also be observed in Figure 17.A3, in which two 3D snapshots, at two different wave propagation times (t = 49.20 s and 136.80 s) of the synthetic velocities wavefield at low frequencies (f < 0.3 Hz) in the x direction for the 1985 Mw 8.01 Michoacan earthquake are shown. The complexity (manifested by the mixed pattern, range and intensity of colors) and large amplitudes of the propagation wavefield occurring in the hypocentral region (nearby Caleta), at t = 49.2 s after the initiation of the earthquake, compared with the well-differentiated blue and yellow color patterns, and smaller amplitudes of the wavefield experienced by the region nearby Mexico City, at t = 136.80 s after the start of the earthquake.

The modeling of the high-frequency synthetics of the 1985 Mw 8.01 magnitude earthquake was obtained by applying the EGF method described in Section 17.2.2 (see Figure 17.2.1). For this purpose, the recordings of the ground motion accelerations observed in Mexico City for the 1979 Mw 7.5, 1985 Mw 7.6, and 1995 Mw 7.8 earthquakes (see Figure 17.A1a) were used as the EGFs.

Finally the synthesis of the low- and high-frequency synthetics was carried out by using matched pair of filters. A couple of examples of the type of results obtained with the mentioned synthesis are shown In Figures 17.A4a and A5a the accelerograms recorded in Mexico City's SCT and TACY sites for the 1985 Mw 8.01 magnitude Michoacan earthquake and their synthetic accelerograms are shown, respectively. The SCT and TACY sites are located in the so-called compressible and firm soils of Mexico City's geotechnical zoning, respectively (see Figure 17.A6). The synthetic accelerograms of these figures were generated by using the hybrid procedure and a supercomputer to run the 3DWPFD code.

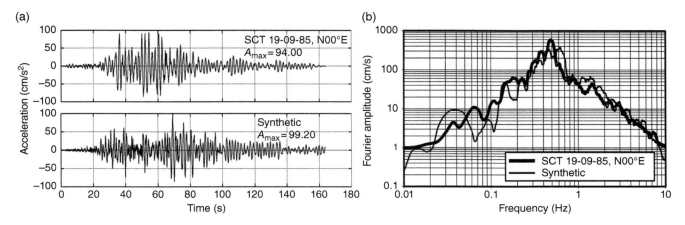

Figure 17.A4 (a) Observed and synthetic broadband accelerograms in the north-south (N00°E) direction at Mexico City recording site SCT and (b) their corresponding FAS, for the 1985 Mw 8.01 magnitude Michoacan, Mexico, earthquake.

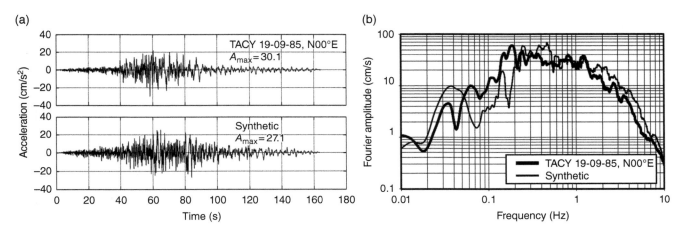

Figure 17.A5 (a) Observed and synthetic broadband accelerograms in the north-south (N00°E) direction at Mexico City recording site TACY and (b) their corresponding FAS, for the 1985 Mw 8.01 magnitude Michoacan, Mexico, earthquake.

It can be observed from Figures 17.A4a and 17.A5a that the general features, the amplitudes and the maximum values of the recorded accelerograms are preserved in the synthetic ones. The (FAS of the accelerograms of Figures 17.A4a and 17.A5a presented in Figures 17.A4b and 17.A5b, respectively, remark that the FAS of the synthetic and the observed accelerograms are also similar. The FAS (which result from a mathematical representation of a time signal by the sum of sines and cosines of various amplitudes and frequencies) allows us to visualize for which frequencies, the amplitudes of a time signal (in this case the observed and synthetic accelerograms of Figures 17.A4a and 17.A5a) are more important (i.e., have the largest values, *Stein and Wysession*, 2003).

In the case of the SCT recording site for the 1985 Mw 8.01 magnitude Michoacan earthquake, the maximum amplitudes observed in the N00°E (North-South) direction accelerogram were ~100 cm/s², these large amplitudes lasted for ~40 s (see Figure 17.A4a); and have a dominant

frequency of ~0.5 Hz, as shown in Figure 17.A4b (i.e., the largest value of its FAS amplitudes, ~650 cm/s, occurs at the mentioned frequency).

These observations are in contrast with those of the TACY site accelerogram in the same North-South direction, for which the maximum accelerations were ~30 cm/s² (i.e., ~3 times less than for the SCT site) and maximum FAS amplitudes were ~60 cm/s (i.e. ~10 times less than for the SCT site) from ~0.15 to 2 Hz, see Figure 17.A5a and b, respectively.

The ~0.5 Hz dominant frequency observed for the accelerogram of the STC site (see Figure 17.4a and b) is the result of the filtering and amplifying effects of Mexico City's compressible soils (i.e., due to the so-called local soil site conditions), on the seismic waves arriving during an earthquake to the rock layers found under those soils. The amplifying effects also occur, but to a considerably lesser degree for the TACY recording site, which, as shown in Figure 17.A6, is located on Mexico City's firm soil

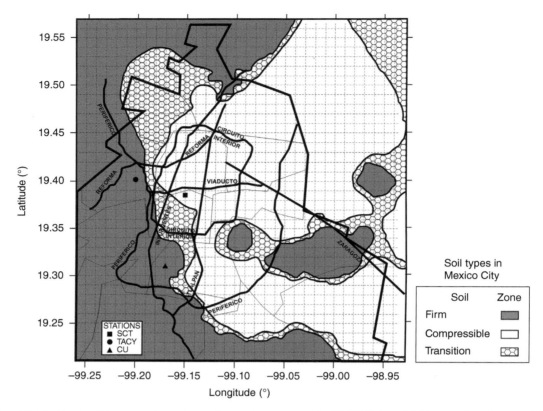

Figure 17.A6 Mexico City geotechnical zonation and location of the TACY, CU, and SCT recording sites [modified, *Marsal et al.*, 1953; *Marsal and Mazari*, 1959].

layers, whose seismic behavior is close to that of the rock basement which support them. This observation is also valid for the so-called transition soil layers zone of Mexico City (see Figure 17.A6). Incidentally, this type of observation about the plausible seismic behavior of Mexico City's firm and compressible soils was first reported by *Rosenblueth* [1953], *Zeevaert and Newmark* [1956], and *Zeevaert* [1960].

From the results discussed in this section, it can be concluded that by using the hybrid method proposed by *Chavez et al.* [2011] it is possible to generate realistic synthetic accelerograms and to study the wave propagation of the seismic waves arriving in Mexico City, due to the occurrence of large magnitude superficial subduction earthquakes such as the 1985 Mw 8.01 magnitude Michoacan event.

During the 1985 Mw 8.01 magnitude Michoacan earthquake, the ~0.5 Hz dominant frequency of the observed accelerogram at SCT (see Figure 17.A4b) matched the so-called natural frequency of vibration (or its reciprocal the natural period of vibration, $T = \sim 2$ s, where T is the lapse that the top of a structural system (such as a one-floor construction) lasts to return to its initial repose position when it is oscillating) of constructions located nearby the SCT site (or other Mexico City's compressible soil zone sites, see Figure 17.A6). Many of these constructions were

destroyed or experience severe structural damage during the 1985 Mw 8.01 magnitude Michoacan earthquake [*Seed et al.*, 1988; *Aguilar et al.*, 1996]. This was mainly due to the phenomena of mechanical resonance of the constructions, that is, the tuning of the dominant frequencies of vibration of the constructions, with those of the accelerograms of the 1985 Mw 8.01 earthquake, to which their foundations were subjected, and therefore, the maximum seismic response amplitudes of the constructions (such as their displacements or accelerations) were considerably larger than what they were seismically designed to resist [*Aguilar et al.*, 1996].

APPENDIX 17.B. MODELING OF THE WAVE PROPAGATION OF THE 9 OCTOBER 1995 MW 8.0 MAGNITUDE COLIMA-JALISCO, MEXICO EARTHQUAKE

The hybrid modeling procedure described in Section 17.2.2 was applied to the 1995 Mw 8.0 magnitude CJ earthquake, see Figure 17.B1a and b. This figure includes the seismic rupture areas for the 3 June Ms 8.2 and 18 June Ms 8 1932, 31 January 1973 Ms 7.6, 9 October 1995 Mw 8, 22 January 2003 Mw 7.6, and 19 September 1985 Mw 8.01, earthquakes. The main geotectonic and

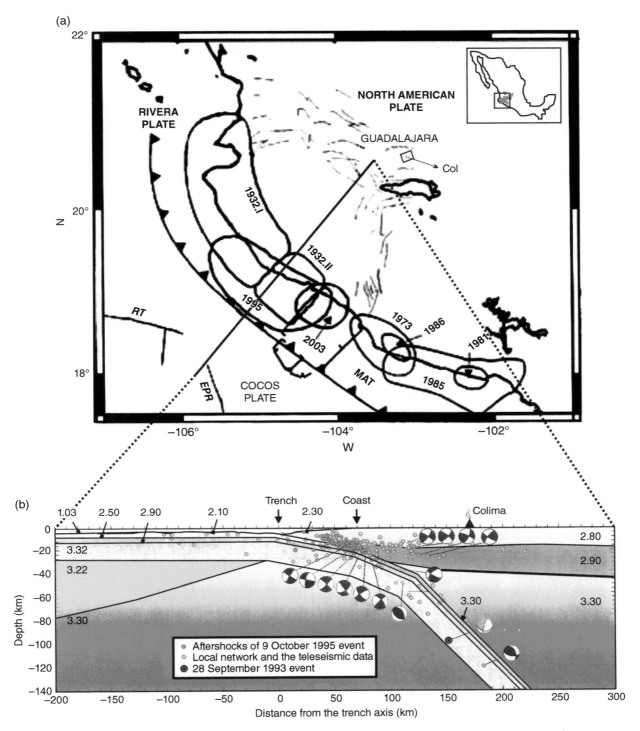

Figure 17.B1 (a) Location of the CJ region in Mexico; seismic rupture areas for the: 3 June (Ms 8.2) and 18 June (Ms 8) 1932, 31 January 1973 (Ms 7.6), 9 October 1995 (Mw 8), 22 January 2003 (Mw 7.6), and 19 September 1985 (Mw 8.01) earthquakes; RT: Rivera Trench; EPR: East Pacific Rise; MAT: Middle American Trench [modified from *Pacheco and Kostoglodov*, 1999]; (b) geological structure of the CJ region including the densities (g/cm³) of the Rivera (subducting) and North American (subducted) plates layer [modified *Bandy et al.*, 1999; *Chavez et al.*, 2011].

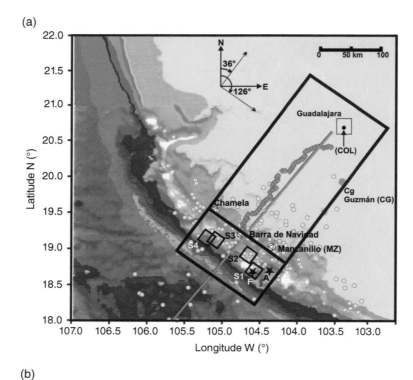

(a)

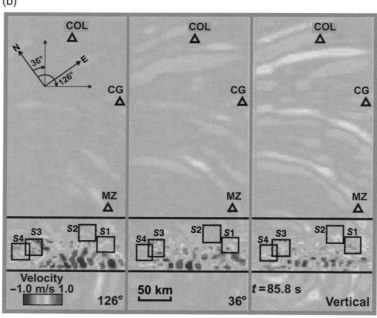

(b)

Figure 17.B2 (a) Surface projection (large rectangle) of the low-frequency model of the 1995 Mw 8.0 CJ earthquake. The rupture area of the considered seismic source is depicted by the small rectangle. S1–S4 (small dashed squares) depict the location and dimension of the four subevents proposed by *Escobedo et al.* [1998] to represent the earthquake, F is the largest foreshock, and A is the largest aftershock (stars). (b) Surface velocity snapshots at time 85.6 s of the synthetic velocity wavefield propagation pattern, for frequencies <0.5 Hz along 126° and 36° and the vertical component [*Chavez et al.*, 2011].

geometric characteristics of the Rivera and North American plates in the region (see Figure 17.B1b). The epicentral locations of the main event, and of its largest fore- and aftershocks, and the four subevents proposed by *Escobedo et al.* [1998] to represent the earthquake, are presented in Figure 17.B2a; a synthesis of the main seismotectonic characteristics of the CJ region is presented in *Chavez et al.* [2011].

For the low-frequency modeling of this event a 354.6 km (length) × 163.8 km (width) × 163.2 km (depth) km³ volume was used, some modeling parameters are included in Figures 17.B1b and 17.B2a, and others in *Chavez et al.* [2011]. In Figure 17.B2b, three snapshots (for $t = 85.8$ s) of the synthetic velocities wavefields for low frequencies ($f < 0.5$ Hz) along 126°, 36° and the vertical directions, for the 1995 Mw 8 CJ earthquake are shown, respectively. The complexity (manifested by the range and

intensity of the colors) and large amplitudes of the propagation wavefield occurring in the hypocentral region (nearby the MZ recording site), compared with the relative simplicity and smaller amplitudes of the wavefield experienced in the region near the recording site COL (at Guadalajara) is observed [*Chavez et al.*, 2011].

For the high-frequency modeling of the 1995 Mw 8 magnitude CJ earthquake, the accelerograms recorded at the stations COL (surface) for its largest Mw 5.75 fore (*F*)- and

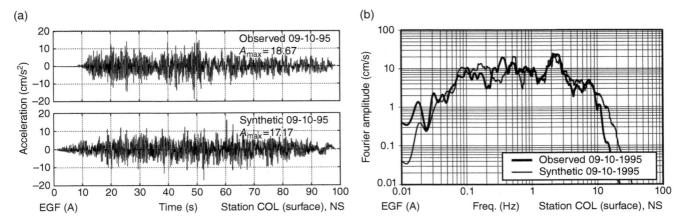

Figure 17.B3 (a) Observed and synthetic accelerograms and (b) their corresponding FAS in the north-south direction at station COL (Guadalajara) for the 1995 Mw 8 magnitude CJ earthquake [*Chavez et al.*, 2011].

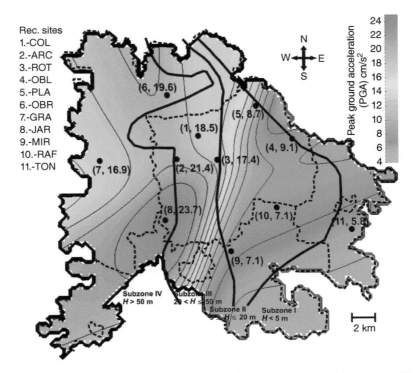

Figure 17.B4 Estimated PGA pattern in the north-south (NS) direction for Guadalajara for the Mw 8 magnitude CJ 1995 earthquake, obtained by applying the proposed RNN procedure (with a distance $k = 0.3$ km; see Figure 17.2) to the 10 recorded PGA values, included beside the dots identifying the recording stations. The PGA value of station ROT was used to verify the RNN training results [*Chavez et al.*, 2014].

Mw 5.92 after (*A*)- shocks, were used (the epicentral locations of the *F* and *A* events are shown in Figure 17.B2a) as the EGF time series, $u(t)$, required in Equation 17.6 [*Chavez et al.*, 2011].

In Figure 17.B3a and b, the observed and synthetic accelerograms (in the N-S direction) for the COL (Guadalajara) recording site for the 1995 Mw 8.0 magnitude CJ earthquake and their corresponding FAS are presented, respectively. From these figures we can conclude that the agreement between the observed and the synthetic accelerograms, both in time and frequency domains is satisfactory.

Similar results were obtained for other accelerographic recording stations sites of Guadalajara (see Figure 17.B4). The peak ground accelerations (PGA) at these sites and the estimated PGA pattern in the North-South (NS) direction for Guadalajara for the Mw 8 magnitude CJ 1995 earthquake was obtained by applying the proposed RNN procedure of Section 17.2.3 (by using a distance $k = 0.3$ km; see Figure 17.2) to the 10 recorded PGA values [see Figure 17.B4; *Chavez et al.*, 2014]. We observe in this figure that there are two well-defined subzones with respect to the PGA values, one with PGA of <17 cm/s^2 identified by the blue and green colors (corresponding to geotechnical subzones 1 and 2) and the other with PGA larger than 17 cm/s^2 identified by the yellow-orange colors (associated with geotechnical subzones 3 and 4), as discussed in *Chavez et al.* [2014].

APPENDIX 17.C. MODELING OF THE WAVE PROPAGATION OF THE 2008 MW 7.9 WENCHUAN, CHINA EARTHQUAKE

The low-frequency modeling described in Section 17.2.2 (as implemented in the 3DWPFD code), was successfully applied to model the low-frequency wave propagation of the 9 May 2008 Mw 7.9 magnitude Wenchuan, China, earthquake. Figure 17.C1 includes: the location of the epicenter of the earthquake, and the ground motion recording stations CD2, GYA, and TIY. The superficial projections of the physical volume discretized (2400 × 1600 × 300 km^3), and of the earthquake rupture area (315 × 40 km^2) are also shown in Figure 17.C1. Further details on the low-frequency modeling of Wenchuan event can be found in *Chavez et al.* [2010].

Examples of the type of results obtained in the modeling of the wave propagation of the 2008 Mw 7.9 magnitude Wenchuan, China earthquake are shown in Figures 17.C2, 17.C3, and 17.C4. From Figure 17.C2, which includes the comparison between the observed and synthetic seismograms for the station sites MZQ, GYA, and TIY located at about 90, 500, and 1200 km from the epicenter of the Wenchuan event, respectively (see Figure 17.C1). It can be concluded that they are acceptable, especially those of stations MZQ and GYA.

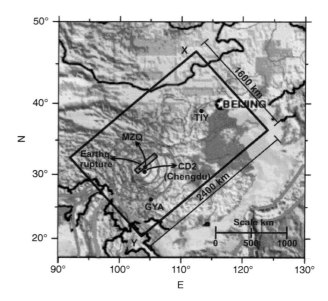

Figure 17.C1 The superficial projection of the 2400 × 1600 × 300 km^3 volume used to discretize the region of interest; the small rectangle represents the 315 × ~40 km^2 SW-NE directed rupture area of the 2008 Mw 7.9 magnitude Wenchuan, China earthquake; the red dot identifies the location of its epicenter; and the black dots the CD2, GYA and TIY seismographic stations sites and MZQ the accelerographic station site of the China Seismographic and Accelerographic Networks, respectively [*Chavez et al.*, 2010].

In Figure 17.C3, 3D snapshots (for $t = 24.24$ s, 43.44 s, 72.42 s, and 100.56 s) of the synthetic velocities wavefield ($f < 0.3$ Hz) in the y direction for the 2008 Wenchuan earthquake, and also the velocity synthetics at several sites of the epicentral region, are shown. Note that the maximum and minimum velocities are in the source rupture direction (x direction) and perpendicular to it (y direction), respectively. Also remark the very large amplitude of the velocity seismograms at location 5 (the town of Beichuan, which was destroyed by the 2008 Wenchuan earthquake) compared to those of the other six sites [*Chavez et al.*, 2010].

In Figure 17.C4, the comparison of the observed Mercalli Modified Intensity (MMI) for the Mw 7.9 magnitude Wenchuan earthquake, with the MMI obtained from the maximum synthetic velocities propagation pattern in the y direction are presented. It can be observed that the general agreement between the observed and synthetic MMIs, especially for the epicentral zone, and that the maximum MMI model is located around Beichuan, which was completely destroyed, that is which corresponds to MMI XI. Incidentally, this type of result, which covers an area, can be used as part of the information required for the estimation of the probable maximum (economic) loss (PML) in the region shown in Figure 17.C4 due to the Mw 7.9 magnitude Wenchuan event.

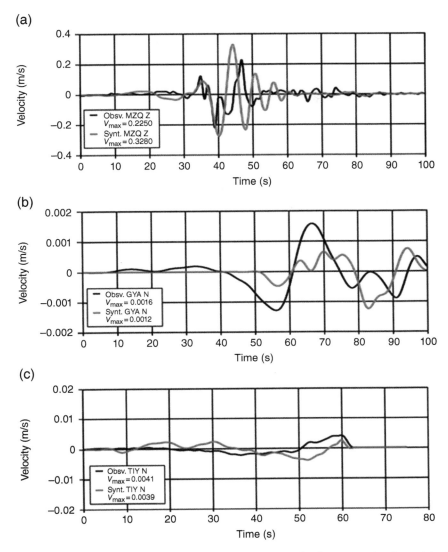

Figure 17.C2 Observed and synthetic velocity seismograms (≤0.3 Hz) for the 2008 Wenchuan Mw 7.9 magnitude earthquake: (a) in the vertical (z) direction for station MZQ, epicentral distance 90 km (see Figure 17.B1); (b) in the north (N) direction for station GYA, epicentral distance of 500 km (see Figure 17.B1); and (c) in the north (N) direction for station TIY, epicentral distance of 1200 km (see Figure 17.B1) [*Chavez et al.*, 2010].

From the results of this Appendix it can be concluded that the synthetic seismograms favorably compare with the observed ones for the station sites of the Seismological and Accelerographic Networks of China, such as MZQ, GYA, and TIY, located at about 90, 500, and 1200 km, respectively, from the epicenter of the Wenchuan event; that maximum of observed and synthetic (i.e., obtained from velocity synthetic patterns) MMI isoseists of the 2008 Wenchuan earthquake, are acceptable; that the 3D synthetic visualizations of the propagation of the Mw 7.9 magnitude Wenchuan event partially explain the extensive damage observed on the infrastructure and towns located in the neighborhood

of the Wenchuan earthquake rupture zone [*Chavez et al.*, 2010].

APPENDIX 17.D. PRELIMINARY MODELING OF THE WAVE PROPAGATION OF THE 2011 MW 9 TOHOKU, JAPAN EARTHQUAKE

The 11 March 2011 the Mw 9 magnitude Tohoku, Japan earthquake ruptured about 450 km of the boundary between the Pacific and the Okhotsk plates, in the Japan Trench off the coast of the Tohoku region (see Figure 17.D1). The main shock source had a seismic moment of 4.5×10^{22} Nm, equivalent to an Mw 9.0

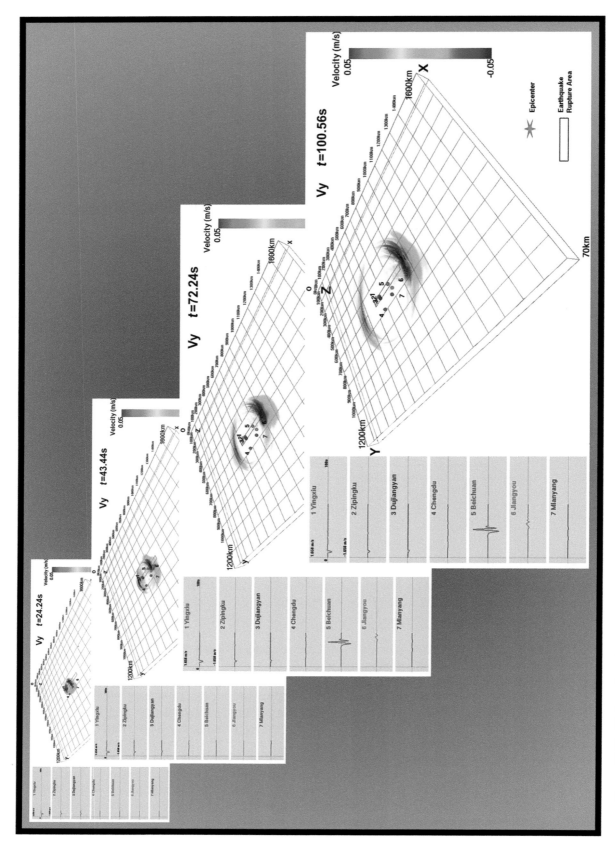

Figure 17.C3 3D Snapshots (at t = 24.24, 43.44, 72.42, and 100.56 s) of the synthetic velocities wavefield ($f < 0.3$ Hz) in the y direction for the 2008 Mw 7.9 magnitude Wenchuan earthquake, and examples of the velocity seismograms at locations 1–7 for each snapshot. Notice that the maximum and minimum velocities are in the source rupture direction (x) and perpendicular (y) to it, respectively, as well as the large amplitude of the seismograms at location 5 (Beichuan, which was destroyed by the earthquake) compared to those of the other sites [Chavez et al., 2010].

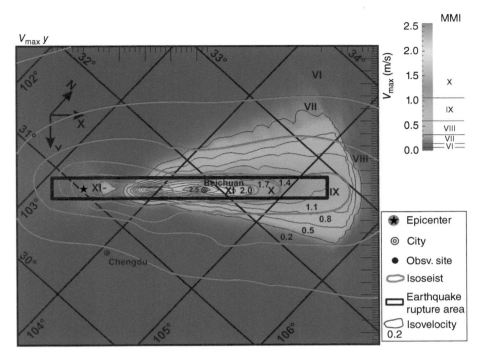

Figure 17.C4 Comparison of the observed MMI isoseists with the MMI obtained from the maximum synthetic velocities propagation pattern in the y direction of the 2008 Mw 7.9 magnitude Wenchuan, China earthquake [*Chavez et al.*, 2010].

magnitude, a seismic source duration of 150 s, and thrust focal mechanism (strike = 200°, dip = 13°, rake = 83°) [*Hayes et al.*, 2011]. A relevant observation about the 2011 Tohoku event is its large rupture area dimensions (~450 × 200 km^2) shown as a pink shade in Figure 17.D1, which fully or partially overlapped the rupture areas of several of the large magnitude historical events (i.e., earthquakes with Mw magnitudes from 7.1 to 8.2) occurred in the Tohoku region since 1896 (identified by the red line ellipses in Figure 17.D1). Some of these historical events with epicenters close to the Japan Trench also generated large tsunamis as the 2011 Tohoku earthquake [*Tajima et al.*, 2013]. It is relevant to remark that the magnitude of the latter follows *McCaffrey* [2007, 2008] suggestions about the probable occurrence of these EME in the circum-Pacific Belt.

For the preliminary modeling of the wave propagation of the 2011 Tohoku earthquake, a finite domain of 300 × 300 × 150 km^3 and the kinematic slip proposed by *Shao et al.* [2011] were adopted. Notice that a maximum slip of 55 m for the event, distributed in the red ellipsoid of Figure 17.D2 was suggested by these authors. Further detail of the modeling will be presented elsewhere [*Chavez et al.*, in preparation].

In Figures 17.D2 and 17.D3 the preliminary results obtained with the 3DWPFD code for the 2011 Mw 9 magnitude Tohoku, Japan earthquake are shown. In Figure 17.D2, the horizontal projection of the seismic rupture surface of this earthquake and its kinematic slip (i.e., the average slip experienced for the Tohoku earthquake when the Pacific tectonic plate subducted the Eurasian plate (slip symbology on the right side of Figure 17.D1)) are shown. In the same figure, the comparison of the observed MMI isoseists, with the MMI isoseists obtained from the modeled maximum synthetic velocities propagation pattern (see the relationship between the velocity and MMI on the left side of Figure 17.D2) in the x direction.

In Figure 17.D3 a detail of Figure 17.D2 is presented. There is a general agreement between the observed and the synthetic MMIs obtained with the simulation of the wave propagation of the 2011 Tohoku earthquake. Finally, in Figure 17.D4, the preliminary synthetic low-frequency wave velocity propagation pattern in the x direction of the Mw 9 Tohoku, Japan, earthquake at: (a) 33 s, (b) 36 s, and (c) 48 s, after the initial rupture (slip) of its seismic source is shown.

APPENDIX 17.E. COMPUTATION OF THE PEI FOR THE MW 8.5 EARTHQUAKE SCENARIO

As mentioned in Section 17.5.1 the seismic vulnerability of the one- to three-floor constructions of Mexico City shown in Figure 17.16 depends on Sa (5%) values that the strong ground motion acceleration that the cell in which they are located (see Figure 17.15) would experience

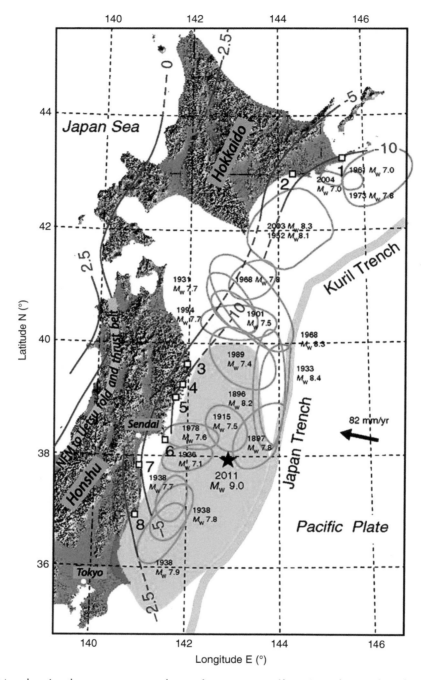

Figure 17.D1 Map showing the source areas and year of occurrences of large interplate earthquakes in the Northeast of Japan region. The source area and epicenter of the 2011 M_w 9.0 magnitude Tohoku earthquake are indicated by the pink shade and a star, respectively. The red lines indicate the source areas of earthquakes with M_w > 7 since 1896 in the region. NFM: Northern Fossa Magna [modified, *Goldfinger et al.*, 2013].

for the Mw 8.5 magnitude earthquake scenario, and on the construction's natural periods of vibration (i.e., $T =$ 0.05, 0.1, 0.2 s and 0.2, 0.3, 0.5 s) depending if the constructions are located on Mexico City's firm or compressible soils (see Figure 17.A6), respectively.

Therefore, the following procedure was carried out to generate Sa(5%) for the mentioned T values, at each of the cells in which Mexico City surface was discretized (see

Figure 17.15), and their probability of exceeding the intensities (PEI), corresponding to the extreme Mw 8.5 scenario earthquake of Figure 17.6:

1. The 10 plausible slip distributions for the extreme Mw 8.5 scenario earthquake shown in Figure 17.8 were used to generate 20 synthetic accelerograms for station site TACY (by applying the hybrid method discussed in Section 17.2.2) 10 for the north-south and 10 for the west-east directions,

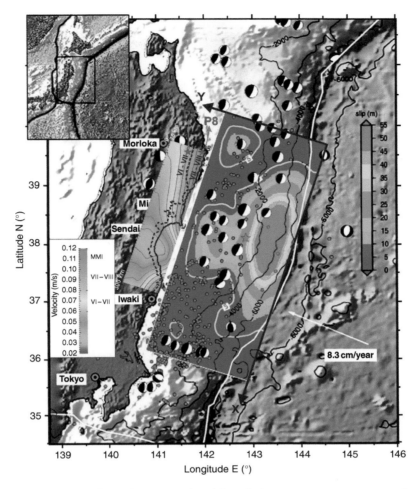

Figure 17.D2 Epicenter location (red star), kinematic slip of the Tohoku, Japan, 2011 Mw 9 magnitude earthquake [modified from *Shao et al.*, 2011] and comparison of the observed MMI isoseists (curves delimiting zones with the same MMI) with the MMI obtained from the maximum synthetic velocities propagation pattern in the *x* direction [*Chavez et al.*, in preparation].

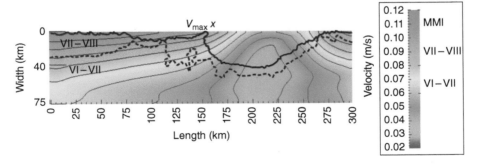

Figure 17.D3 Comparison of the observed MMI isoseists with the obtained from the maximum synthetic velocities propagation pattern in the *x* direction of the 2011 Mw 9 magnitude Tohoku, Japan earthquake [*Chavez et al.*, in preparation].

respectively. The results obtained for the slip model 1 of Figure 17.8 are shown in Figures 17.9 and 17.10, which includes two of their associated Sa(5%) response spectra.

2. The average Sa(5%) spectra for the TACY site (located on Mexico City firm soil) obtained in step 1 (for each of the 10 plausible scenarios of the slip of the extreme Mw 8.5 scenario earthquake) were computed from their corresponding two horizontal response spectra, and they were assumed as the 10 expected Sa(5%) for the TACY site for the Mw 8.5 scenario earthquake.

(a)

(b)

(c)

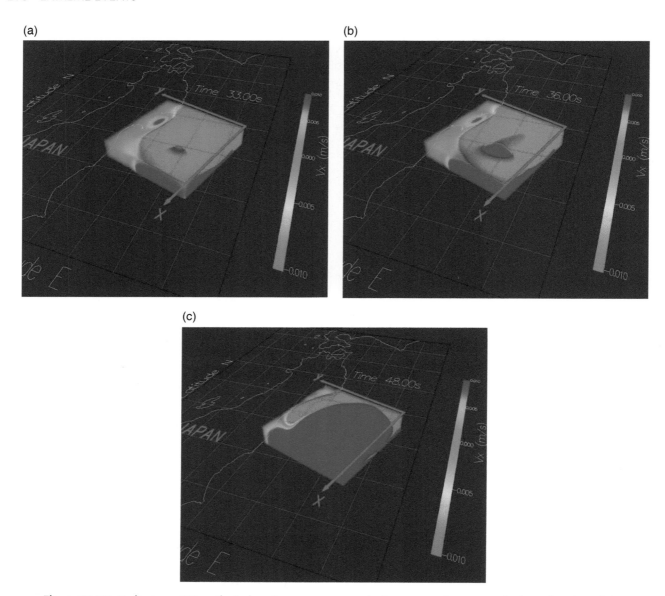

Figure 17.D4 Preliminary 3D synthetic low-frequency wave velocity propagation pattern in the x direction of the 2011 Mw 9 magnitude Tohoku, Japan earthquake at: (a) 33 s, (b) 36 s, and (c) 48 s after the initial rupture (slip) of its seismic source shown in Figure D2 [*Chavez et al.*, in preparation].

3. Each of the 10 Sa (5%) spectra of step (2) was multiplied by the amplification factors, AF of Sa(5%) of the TACY site (as those shown schematically in Figure 17.14 for the natural period $T = 0.2$ s) corresponding to 30 natural periods of Sa(5%) spanning from 0.005 to 5 s. Therefore, for each of the cells of Figure 17.15 and for each of the 10 plausible slip distributions of the Mw 8.5 scenario earthquake shown in Figure 17.8, the respective Sa(5%)m, Sa(5%)m + 6Sa(5%) and Sa (5%)m – 6Sa (5%) were obtained as those shown schematically in Figure 17.E1 for a natural period $T = 0.2$ s. This means that by taking into account the uncertainties in the AF factors (see Figure 17.13), we now have 30 scenarios, expressed in terms of Sa(5%), instead of the original 10 associated with the uncertainties on the plausible slips of the Mw 8.5 extreme earthquake scenario (see Figure 17.8).

4. From the 30 Sa(5%) obtained in step (3), at each cell of the figure located on the firm soil zone of Mexico City (see Figure 17.A6), we extracted Sa (5%) values for the natural periods $T = 0.05, 0.1, 0.2$ s, associated with the expected seismic behavior of the one- to three-floor constructions located on those soils (see Figures 17.15 and 17.A6); the same procedure was applied for each cell of Figure 17.15 located on Mexico City compressible soil zone, but in this case the extracted Sa (5%) values were for the natural periods $T = 0.2, 0.3, 0.5$ s. Therefore, a

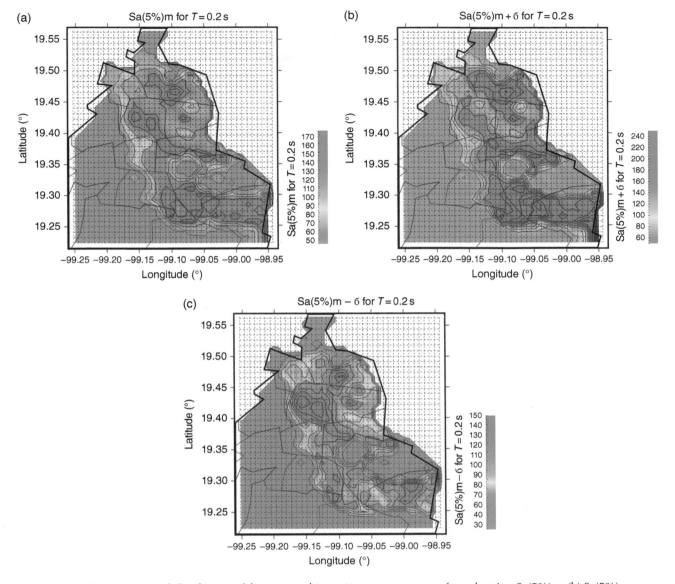

Figure 17.E1 (a) Spatial distribution of the expected (mean) response spectra of acceleration Sa(5%)m, (b) Sa(5%)m + 6Sa(5%), c) Sa(5%)m − 6Sa(5%) for natural period T = 0.2 s, of the one- to three-floor dwelling constructions of Mexico City corresponding to the slip distribution Model 1 (see Figure 17.8) of the Mw 8.5 magnitude earthquake scenario of Figure 17.6. The green and yellow colors correspond to Sa (5%) on Mexico City's firm and transition soils, and the orange to red colors to Sa(5%) on its compressible soils zone (see Figure 17.A6).

sample consisting of 90 values of Sa(5%) was obtained for each of the cells located on Mexico's City firm and compressible soil zones indicated in Figure 17.15.

5. From the 90 values (samples) of Sa(5%) obtained in step (4), we computed their expected Sa(5%) value for each of the cells of Figure 17.15; and with this information, we generated the expected spatial distribution of Sa(5%) in Mexico City (firm and compressible soil zones) due to the Mw 8.5 scenario earthquake of Figure 17.6. The resulting spatial distribution of the expected Sa(5%)

in Mexico City is shown in Figure 17.17. In this figure, the green and yellow colors correspond to the expected Sa (5%) on firm and transition soils, respectively; and the orange to red colors to the corresponding Sa(5%) for Mexico City's compressible soils zone. Notice that the larger Sa(5%) values correspond to the compressible soils zone of Mexico City, which, as mentioned in Section 17.4.3 and Appendix 17.A, amplifies the ground motions at certain frequencies, compared with the (smaller) ground motions experienced by its firm (and transition) soil zones.

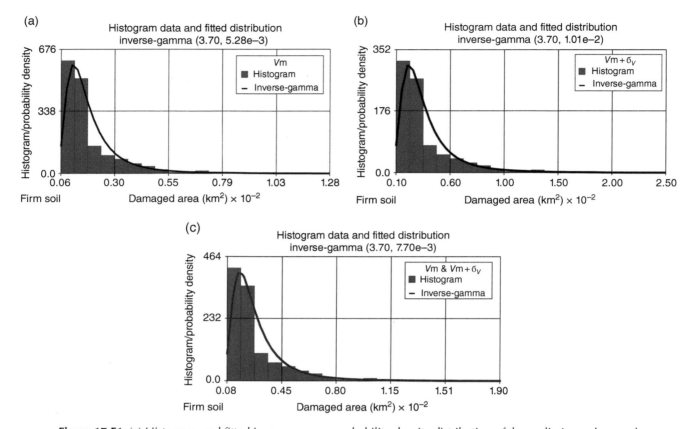

Figure 17.F1 (a) Histogram and fitted inverse-gamma probability density distribution of the preliminary damaged areas of one- to three-floor dwelling constructions located on Mexico City's firm and transition soils for the Mw 8.5 earthquake scenario, and vulnerability Vm, (b) for vulnerability $Vm + \delta_V$ and (c) for vulnerability Vm & $Vm + \delta_V$.

APPENDIX 17.F. COMPUTATION OF THE DAMAGE AREA FOR THE MW 85 EARTHQUAKE SCENARIO

The steps to obtain the probability distribution of the preliminary damage of Mexico City's one- to three-floor construction stock due to the extreme Mw 8.5 magnitude earthquake scenario are the following:

1. For each of the cells of Mexico City discretization (shown in Figure 17.15) located on the firm, transition, and compressible soil zones (see Figure 17.A6) and for each of its respective 90 Sa(5%) values computed in step 5 of Appendix 17.E, and the Vm vulnerability curve of Figure 17.16, their corresponding 90 seismic vulnerability values were obtained.

2. The 90 Vm values obtained in step 1 were multiplied by the construction density of each of the cells of Figure 17.15, and obtained for each of them, their respective 90 values sample of the estimated damage for the constructions located on the firm and transition, and for those on the compressible soils of Mexico City.

3. Steps (1) and (2) were also applied for the vulnerability curve $Vm + \delta_V$ of Figure 17.16 and their corresponding 90 values sample of the estimated damage for the

constructions on the firm and transition soils were obtained, and other 90 values for those on the compressible soils of Mexico City.

4. From the results of step (1)–(3), a 180 values sample of damage area was generated for each of the cells of Figure 17.15; the first 90 values of the 180 values sample were the estimated damaged areas for vulnerability Vm, and the second 90 values by those of the vulnerability $Vm + \delta_V$. The 180 values sample, which in what follows is called vulnerability "Vm & $Vm + \delta_V$" represents the impact that the uncertainties on the "1985 observed" vulnerability Vm has on the estimated damaged surface of the one- to three-floor constructions of Mexico City due to the extreme Mw 8.5 magnitude earthquake scenario.

5. The histograms and their fitted probability density, and cumulative distributions obtained for the constructions of one to three floors of Mexico City built stock expected damaged areas, for the three values sample (i.e., for vulnerabilities: Vm, $Vm + \delta_V$ and Vm & $Vm + \delta_V$) discussed earlier for the firm and transition, and compressible soils, are shown in Figures 17.F1a–c and 17.F2a–c, respectively.

In these figures, note that their fitted probability density distributions are different, that is, the inverse-gamma

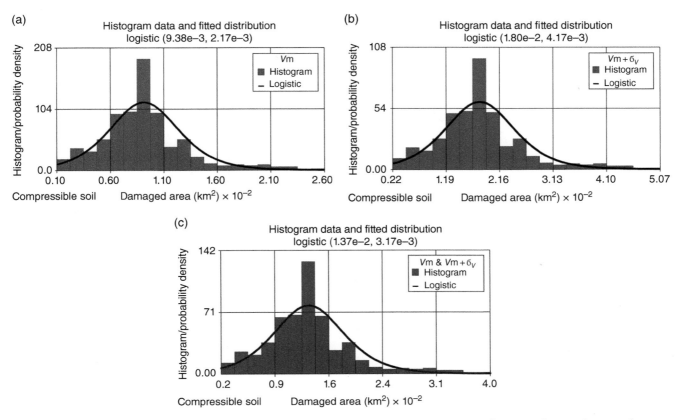

Figure 17.F2 (a) Histogram and fitted logistic probability density distribution of preliminary damaged areas of one- to three-floor dwelling constructions located on Mexico City's compressible soils for the Mw 8.5 earthquake scenario, and vulnerability Vm, (b) for vulnerability $Vm + \delta_V$ and (c) for vulnerability Vm & $Vm + \delta_V$.

probability density for the firm (and transition) soils with damaged area that varies from 0.0006 to 0.025 km² (Figure 17.F1a–c); and the logistic probability density distribution for the compressible soils with damaged area that varies from 0.001 to 0.050 km² (see Figure 17.F2a–c).

REFERENCES

Aguilar, J., S. F. Brena, E. Del Valle, J. Iglesias, M. Picado, and J. O. Jirsa (1996), *Rehabilitation of existing reinforced concrete buildings in Mexico City—Case Studies, PMFSEL*, Ferguson Structural Engineering Laboratory, The University of Texas at Austin.

Albini, P., R. M. W. Musson, A. Rovida, M. Locati, A. A. Gomez Capera, and D. Viganò (2014), The global earthquake history, *Earthq. Spectra, 30*, 607–624.

Allen, T. I., K. Marano, P. S. Earle, and D. J. Wald (2009), PAGER-CAT: A composite earthquake catalog for calibrating global fatality models, *Seismol. Res. Lett., 80*(1), 50–56.

Ammon, C. J., C. Ji, H. K. Thio, D. Robinson, S. Ni, V. Hjorleifsdottir, H. Kanamori, T. Lay, S. Das, D. Helmberger, G. Ichinose, J. Polet, and D. Wald (2005), Rupture process of the 2004 Sumatra–Andaman Earthquake, *Science, 308*, 1133–1139, doi:10.1126/science.1112260.

Bandy, W., V. Kostoglodov, H. Hurtado-Díaz, and M. Mena (1999), Structure of the southern Jalisco subduction zone Mexico, as inferred from gravity and seismicity, *Geofis. Int., 38*(3), 127–136.

Bell, A. F., M. Naylor, and I. G. Main (2013), Convergence of the frequency size distribution of global earthquakes, *Geophys. Res. Lett., 40*, 2585–2589, doi:10.1002/grl.50416.

Bird, P., and Y. Y. Kagan (2004), Plate-tectonic analysis of shallow seismicity: Apparent boundary width, beta, corner magnitude, coupled lithosphere thickness, and coupling in seven tectonic settings, *Bull. Seismol. Soc. Am., 94*(6), 2380–2399.

Cabrera, E., M. Chavez, R. Madariaga, N. Perea, and M. Frisenda (2007), 3D parallel elastodynamic modeling of large subduction earthquakes, in *Euro PVM/MPI 2007*, LNCS 4757, edited by F. Capello *et al.*, pp. 373–380, Springer-Verlag, Berlin/Heidelberg.

Castellanos, L. F. (2001), Metodos para zonacion sismica optima en varias dimensiones. MS Eng. thesis, Faculty of Engineering, UNAM, México.

Cerjan, C., D. Kosloff, R. Kosloff, and M. Reshef (1985), A nonreflecting boundary condition for discrete acoustic and elastic wave equations, *Geophysics, 50*(4), 707–708.

Chavez, M. (1995), Geotechnic, hazard and seismic safety of the Metropolitan zone of Guadalajara, Mexico, *Invited Opening Conference, X Pan-American Conference on Soil Mechanics and Engineering*, Vol. *4*, pp. 33–93, Guadalajara, Mexico.

Chavez, M., and D. de León E. (1983), Confiabilidad de marcos de concreto sujetos a temblores, *VI Congreso Nacional de Ingeniería Sísmica*, Puebla, México.

Chavez, M., and D. de León E. (1984), Reliability of nonlinear systems with uncertain parameters and random seismic excitation, *6th World Conference Earthquake Engineering*, Vol. *4*, pp. 435–442, San Francisco, CA.

Chavez, M., E. Cabrera, R. Madariaga, N. Perea, C. Moulinec, D. Emerson, M. Ashworth, and A. Salazar (2008), Benchmark study of a 3D parallel code for the propagation of large subduction earthquakes, in *Euro PVM/MPI 2008*, LNCS 5205, edited by A. Lastovesky *et al.*, pp. 303–310, Springer-Verlag, Berlin/Heidelberg.

Chavez, M., E. Cabrera, R. Madariaga, H. Chen, N. Perea, D. Emerson, A. Salazar, M. Ashworth, C. Moulinec, M. Wu, and G. Zhao (2010), Low Frequency 3D Wave Propagation Modeling of the Mw 7.9 Wenchuan 12 2008 Earthquake, *Bull. Seismol. Soc. Am.*, *100*(5B), 2561–2573, doi:10.1785/012009240.

Chavez, M., K. B. Olsen, E. Cabrera, and N. Perea (2011), Observations and Modeling of Strong Ground Motions for the 9 October 1995 Mw 8 Colima-Jalisco, Mexico, Earthquake, *Bull. Seismol. Soc. Am.*, *101*(5), 1979–2000, doi:10.1785/0120100200.

Chavez, M., S. Garcia, E. Cabrera, M. Ashworth, N. Perea, A. Salazar, E. Chavez, J. Saborio-Ulloa, and J. Saborio-Ortega (2014), Site effects and peak ground accelerations observed in Guadalajara, Mexico, for the 9 October 1995 Mw 8 Colima–Jalisco, earthquake, *Bull. Seismol. Soc. Am.*, *104*(5), 2430–2455, doi:10.1785/0120130144.

CIRC (2013), Quake to have limited impact on insurers, http://china.org.cn/china/2013-05/01/content_28702532.htm (accessed 23 September 2015).

Cochrane, S. W., and W. H. Schaad (1992), Assesment of earthquake vulnerability of buildings, *10th World Conference Earthquake Engineering*, Vol. *1*, pp. 497–503, Madrid, Spain.

Cruz Hoyos, S. (2013), Popayán conmemora los 30 años del terremoto que devastó la ciudad en 18 segundos, El País, Marzo 31.

Da Victoria L. N. (2010), Swiss Re: Financial mechanisms, insurance and reinsurance in case of disasters, *SELA Regional Seminar on Public Investment and Financial Mechanisms, Insurance and Reinsurance against Disasters in Latin America and the Caribbean: Recent Experiences Mexico City, Mexico 22 and 23 November 2010*, SP/SR-IPMFSRCDALC/Di N° 7-10.

EERI (2008), Special Earthquake Report—Learning from Earthquakes—The Wenchuan, Sichuan Province, China, Earthquake of May 12, 2008.

Egmont-Petersen, M., D. De Ridder, and H. Handels (2002), Image processing with neural networks—A review, *Pattern Recogn.*, *35*(10), 2279–2301, doi:10.1016/S0031-3203(01)00178-9.

Engdahl, E. R., and A. Villaseñor (2002), Global seismicity: 1900–1999, in *International Handbook of Earthquake Engineering and Seismology*, edited by W. K. Lee, H. Kanamori, P. C. Jennings, and C. Kisslinger, pp. 665–690, Academic Press, Amsterdam.

Escobedo, D., J. F. Pacheco, and G. Suárez (1998), Teleseismic body-wave analysis of the 9 October, 1995 (Mw 8.0), Colima–Jalisco, Mexico earthquake, and its largest foreshock and aftershock, *Geophys. Res. Lett.*, *25*(4), 547–550.

Frankel, A., C. Mueller, T. Barnhard, D. Perkins, E. Leyendecker, N. Dickman, S. Hanson, and M. Hopper (1996), National Seismic Hazard Maps—Documentation, U.S. Geology Survey, Open-File Report 96-532, 110 pp.

Frankel, A. D., M. D. Petersen, C. S. Mueller, K. M. Haller, R. L. Wheeler, E. V. Leyendecker, R. L. Wesson, S. C. Harmsen, C. H. Cramer, D. M. Perkins, and K. S. Rukstales (2002), Documentation for the 2002 update of the National Seismic Hazard Maps, U.S. Geology Survey, Open-File Report 2002-420, 39 pp.

GAO-07-403 (2007), *Natural Hazard Mitigation*, United States Government Accountability Office, Washington, DC.

Garcia-Rubio, L. (1994), Caracterizacion de las construcciones de la zona metropolitana de Guadalajara para evaluar su vulnerabilidad ante sismo, Tesis de Maestria en Ingenieria Civil, Universidad de Guadalajara, Guadalajara, Mexico.

Graves, A., M. Liwicki, S. Fernandez, R. Bertolami, H. Bunke, and J. Schmidhuber (2009), A novel connectionist system for improved unconstrained handwriting recognition, *IEEE Trans. Pattern Anal. Mach. Intell.*, *31*(5), 855–868.

Goldfinger, C., Y. Ikeda, R. S. Yeats, and J. Ren (2013), Superquakes and Supercycles, *Seismol. Res. Lett.*, *84*(1), 24–32.

Gutenberg, B., and C. F. Richter (1954), *Seismicity of the Earth and Associated Phenomena*, 2nd ed., Princeton University Press, Princeton, NJ.

Gottschaemmer, E., and K. B. Olsen (2001), Ground motion synthetics for spontaneous versus prescribed rupture on a 45° thrust fault, American Geophysical Union, Fall Meet. 2001, abstract #s42c-0667.

Hartzell, S. H. (1978), Earthquake aftershocks as Green's functions, *Geophys. Res. Lett.*, *5*, 1–4.

Hayes, G. P., P. S. Earle, H. M. Benz, D. J. Wald, and R. W. Briggs (2011), USGS/NEIC Earthquake Response Team, 2011. 88 hours: The U.S. Geological Survey National Earthquake Information Center response to the March 11, 2011 Mw 9.0 Tohoku earthquake, *Seismol. Res. Lett.*, *82*(4), 481–493.

Haykin, S. (1999), *Neural Networks: A Comprehensive Foundation*, 2nd ed., Prentice Hall, Upper Saddle River, NJ.

Hinton, G. E., S. Osindero, and Y. W. Teh (2006), A fast learning algorithm for deep belief nets, *Neural Comput.*, *18*(7), 1527–1554.

Hochreiter, S., Y. Bengio, P. Frasconi, and J. Schmidhuber (2001), Gradient flow in recurrent nets: The difficulty of learning long-term dependencies, in *A Field Guide to Dynamical Recurrent Neural Networks*, edited by J. F. Kremer and S. C. Kolen, pp. 237–243, IEEE Press, Piscataway, NJ.

IMIC (2013), Catalogo Nacional de Costos, Instituto Mexicano de Ingenieria de Costos, SA de CV, México D. F., México.

INEGI (2011), Panorama Sociodemografico del Distrito Federal, Instituto Nacional de Estadistica y Geografia.

INEGI (2014), Mapa Digital de México, Instituto Nacional de Estadistica y Geografia, http://www.inegi.org.mx/geo/contenidos/mapadigital/ (accessed October 2014)

Irikura, K. (1986), Prediction of strong acceleration motion using empirical Green's function, *Proceedings of the 7th Japan Earthquake Engineering Symposium*, Tokyo, Vol. *4*, pp. 151–156.

Irikura, K. (1998), Prediction of strong motions from future earthquakes in Osaka basin, *Proceedings of the Second International Symposium on The Effects of Surface Geology on Seismic Motion*, A. A. Balkema 1, pp. 171–188.

Jafarzadeh, R., J. M. Ingham, K. Q. Walsh, N. Hassani, and G. R. Ghodrati-Amiri (2014), Using statistical regression analysis to establish construction cost models for seismic retrofit of confined masonry buildings, *J. Constr. Eng. Manag.*, *141*(5),04014098,doi:10.1061/(ASCE)CO.1943-7862.0000968.

Kagan, Y. Y. (1997), Seismic moment-frequency relation for shallow earthquakes: Regional comparison, *J. Geophys. Res.*, *102*, 2835–2852.

Kagan, Y. Y., and F. Schoenberg (2001), Estimation of the upper cutoff parameter for the tapered Pareto distribution, *J. Appl. Probab.*, *38A*, 158–175.

Kamae, K., K. Irikura, and A. Pitarka (1998), A technique for simulating strong ground motion using hybrid green's function, *Bull. Seismol. Soc. Am.*, *88*(6), 357–367.

Kramer, S. L. (1996), *Geotechnical Earthquake Engineering*, Prentice Hall, Inc., Upper Saddle River, NJ.

Lomnitz, C., and M. Hashizume (1985), The Popayan, Colombia, earthquake of 31 March 1983, *Bull. Seismol. Soc. Am.*, *75*(5), 1315–1326.

Madariaga, R. (1976), Dynamics of an expanding circular fault, *Bull. Seismol. Soc. Am.*, *67*, 163–182.

Mai, P. M., and G. C. Beroza (2002), A spatial random-field model to characterize complexity in earthquake slip, *J. Geophys. Res.*, *107*(B11), 2308, doi:10.1029/2001JB000588.

Marsal, R., M. Mazari, and F. Hiriart (1953), Cimentaciones piloteadas en la Ciudad de Mexico, Ediciones ICA, Serie B, 16, ICA, Mexico DF, México.

Marsal, R. J., and M. Mazari (1959), *El subsuelo de la Ciudad de México*, UNAM, Mexico.

McCaffrey, R. (2007), The next great earthquake, *Science*, *315*, 1675–1676.

McCaffrey, R. (2008), Global frequency of magnitude 9 earthquakes, *Geology*, *36*, 263–266.

McNeil, A. J., and J. Neslehova (2009), Multivariate archimedean copulas, d-monotone functions and l1-norm symmetric distributions, *Ann. Stat.*, *37*, 3059–3097.

Mendoza, C., and S. Hartzell (1989), Slip distribution of the 19 september 1985 Michoacan, Mexico, earthquake: near source and telesismic constrains, *Bull. Seismol. Soc. Am.*, *79*, 655–669.

Minkoff, S. E. (2002), Spatial parallelism of a 3D finite difference, velocity-stress elastic wave propagation code, *SIAM J. Sci. Comput.*, *24*, 1–19.

Moczo, P., J. Kristek, and M. Galis (2014), *The Finite-Difference Modelling of Earthquake Motions: Waves and Ruptures*, pp. 365, Cambridge University Press, Cambridge.

NCDR (National Commission for Disaster Reduction), MOST (Ministry of Science and Technology of China) (2008), *Wenchuan Earthquake Disaster—A Comprehensive Analysis and Evaluation*, pp. 136–155, Science Press, Beijing.

Nelsen, R. B. (2006), *An Introduction to Copulas*, Springer Series in Statistics, Second ed., Springer, New York.

NIST, National Institute of Standards and Technology, http://www.nist.gov/el/disasterstudies/earthquake/earthquake_mexico_1985.cfm (accessed October 2014).

Nishenko, S. P., and S. K. Singh (1987), Conditional probabilities for the recurrence of large and great interplate earthquakes along the Mexican subduction zone, *Bull. Seismol. Soc. Am.*, *77*(6), 2095–2114.

OECD (2013), *OECD Reviews of risk management policies: Mexico 2013: Review of the Mexican National Civil protection System*, OECD Publishing, 10.1787/9789264192294-cn (accessed 30 August 2015).

Olsen, K. B., R. Madariaga, and R. J. Archuleta (1997), Three-dimensional dynamic simulation of the 1992 Landers earthquake, *Science*, *278*, 834–838.

Ordaz, M., S. K. Singh, E. Reinoso, J. Lermo, J. M. Espinosa, and T. Dominguez (1988), The Mexico Earthquake of September 19, 1985—Estimation of Response Spectra in the Lake Bed Zone of the Valley of Mexico, *Earthq. Spectra*, *4*(4), 815–834.

Ordaz, M., R. Meli, C. Montoya-Dulche, R. Sanchez, and L. E. Pérez-Rocha (1994), *Bases de datos para la estimación de riesgo sismico en la ciudad de Mexico*, CENAPRED, Mexico.

Ortiz, M., S. K. Singh, V. Kostoglodov, and J. Pacheco (2000), Source areas of the Acapulco-San Marcos, Mexico earthquakes of 1962 (M 7.1; 7.0) and 1957 (M 7.7), as constrained by tsunami and uplift records, *Geofis. Int.*, *39*(4), 337–348.

Pacheco, J., and V. Kostoglodov (1999), *Seismicity in Mexico from 1900 to 1999*, Servicio Sismologico Nacional, UNAM, Mexico.

Pérez-Campos, X., Y. H. Kim, A. Husker, P. M. Davis, R. W. Clayton, A. Iglesias, J. F. Pacheco, S. K. Singh, V. C. Manea, and M. Gurnis (2008), Horizontal subduction and truncation of the Cocos Plate beneath central Mexico, *Geophys. Res. Lett.*, *35*, L18303, doi:10.1029/2008GL035127.

Pérez-Rocha, L. E. (1998), Respuesta sismica estructural: efectos de sitio e interaccion suelo-estructura (aplicaciones al Valle de Mexico), PhD thesis, Faculty of Engineering, UNAM, Mexico.

Pérez-Rocha, L. E., F. J. Sánchez-Sesma, M. Ordaz, S. K. Singh, and E. Reinoso (2000), Strong ground motion prediction at Mexico City, *12th World Conference Earthquake Engineering*, Contribution 2693, 30 January to 4 February, Auckland.

Petersen, M. D., A. D. Frankel, S. C. Harmsen, C. S. Mueller, K. M. Haller, R. L. Wheeler, R. L. Wesson, Y. Zeng, O. S. Boyd, D. M. Perkins, N. Luco, E. H. Field, C. J. Wills, and K. S. Rukstales (2008), Documentation for the 2008 update of the United States National Seismic Hazard Maps, U.S. Geology Survey, Open-File Report 2008-1128, 61 pp.

Plafker, G. (1965), Tectonic deformation associated with the 1964 Alaska earthquake, *Science*, *148*, 1675–1687.

Plafker, G., and J. C. Savage (1970), Mechanism of the Chilean earthquakes of May 21 and 22, 1960, *Geol. Soc. Am. Bull.*, *81*, 1001–1030.

Ramirez-Herrera, M. T., M. Lagos, A. Goguitchaichrili, B. Aguilar, M. L. Machain-Castillo, M. Caballero, A. C. Ruiz-Fernandez, G. Suarez, M. Ortuno (2013), The Great 1787 Corralero, Oaxaca, Tsunami Uncovered, AGU Joint Meeting, Abstract NH41A-03, Cancun, Mexico.

Rascón, C. O. A., M. Chavez, L. Alonso, and V. Palencia (1976), Correccion de la linea base de registros de temblores, *Rev. Ingen. Sis.*, *16*(3), 75–123.

Rascón, C. O. A., M. Chavez, L. Alonso, and V. Palencia (1977), *Registros y espectros de temblores en las ciudades de México y Acapulco, 1961–1968*, Serie Azul No 385, Instituto de Ingeniería, UNAM, Mexico.

Reinoso, E., L. E. Pérez-Rocha, M. Ordaz, A. Arciniega (1992), Prediction of response spectra at any site in Mexico City, *10th World Conference Earthquake Engineering*, pp. 767–772, 19–24 July, Madrid, Spain.

Reinoso, E., M. A. Jaimes, and M. A. Torres (2015), Evaluation of building code compliance in Mexico City: Mid-rise dwellings, *Build. Res. Inf.*, doi:10.1080/09613218.2014.991622.

Reyes, C. (1999), El estado límite de servicio en el diseño sísmico de edificios, PhD thesis, Faculty of Engineering, UNAM, México.

Rong, Y., D. D. Jackson, H. Magistrale, and C. Goldfinger (2014), Magnitude Limits of Subduction Zone Earthquakes, *Bull. Seismol. Soc. Am.*, *104*(5), 2359–2377, doi:10.1785/0120130287.

Rosenblueth, E. (1953), *Teoria del diseno sismico sobre mantos blandos*, Ediciones Ingenieros Civiles Asociados, Serie B 14, pp. 3–12, ICA, Mexico, D.F., Mexico.

Rosenblueth, E., and A. Arciniega (1992), Response spectral ratios, *Earthq. Eng. Struct. Dyn.*, *21*(6), 483–492.

Schellart, W. P., and N. Rawlinson (2013), Global correlations between maximum magnitudes of subduction zone interface thrust earthquakes and physical parameters of subduction zones, *Phys. Earth Planet. Inter.*, *225*, 41–67.

Seed, H. B., M. P. Romo, J. I. Sun, A. Jaime, and J. Lysmer (1988), The Mexico earthquake of September 19, 1985—Relationships between soil conditions and earthquake ground motions, *Earthq. Spectra*, *4*(4), 687–730.

Serrano, A., E. Soria, and J. Martín (2009), Redes Neuronales Artificiales, Escuela Técnica Superior de Ingeniería, tesis de Licenciatura, Universitat de Valencia, Spain.

Shao, G., X. Li, C. Ji, and T. Maeda (2011), Focal mechanism and slip history of the 2011 Mw 9.1 off the Pacific coast of Tohoku Earthquake, constrained with teleseismic body and surface waves, *Earth Planets Space*, *63*, 559–564.

Shiau, J. T. (2006), Fitting drought duration and severity with two-dimensional copulas, *Water Resources Management*, *20*, 795–815, doi: 10.1007/s11269-005-9008-9.

Singh, S. K., J. Lermo, T. Domínguez, M. Ordaz, J. M. Espinosa, E. Mena, and R. Quaas (1988), The Mexico earthquake of September 19, 1985—A study of amplification of seismic waves in the Valley of Mexico with respect to a Hill Zone site, *Earthq. Spectra*, *4*(4), 653–674.

Sklar, A. (1959), Fonctions de répartition à n dimensions et leurs marges, *Publ. Inst. Stat. Univ. Paris*, *8*, 229–231.

SOFTEC (2013), *Dinamica del Mercado Inmobiliario Nacional*, SOFTEC, México, D. F., México.

Suarez, G., and P. Albini (2009), Evidence for great tsunamigenic earthquake (M 8.6) along the Mexican subduction zone, *Bull. Seismol. Soc. Am.*, *99*, 892–896, doi:10.1785/0120080201.

Stein, S., and M. Wysession (2003), *An Introduction to Seismology, Earthquakes, and Earth Structure*, Blackwell Publishing Ltd, Oxford.

Swiss Re (2006), Natural Catastrophes and man-made disaster 2005: high earthquake casualties, new dimension in windstorm losses, *Sigma*, *2*, 1–40.

Tajima, F., J. Mori, and B. L. N. Kennett (2013), A review of the 2011 Tohoku-Oki earthquake (Mw 9.0): Large-scale rupture across heterogeneous plate coupling, *Tectonophysics*, *586*, 15–34.

Theodoridis, S., and K. Koutroumbas (2008), *Pattern Recognition*, Fourth ed., Academic Press, Waltham, MA.

Tobler, W. R. (1970), A computer movie simulation of urban growth in the Detroit region, *Econ. Geogr.*, *46*, 234–240.

USGS (1985), Offshore Valparaiso, Chile 1985 March 03 22:47:07 UTC magnitude 7.8, *Earthq. Inf. Bull.*, *17* (5), September to October 1985.

Vervaeck, A., and J. Daniell (2012), *CATDAT Damaging Earthquakes Database 2011 – Annual Review*, Center for Disaster Management and Risk Reduction Technology, Karlsruhe.

Vigny, C., A. Socquet, S. Peyrat, J.-C. Ruegg, M. Métois, R. Madariaga, S. Morvan, M. Lancieri, R. Lacassin, J. Campos, D. Carrizo, M. Bejar-Pizarro, S. Barrientos, R. Armijo, C. Aranda, M. C. Valderas-Bermejo, I. Ortega, F. Bondoux, S. Baize, H. Lyon-Caen, A. Pavez, J. P. Vilotte, M. Bevis, B. Brooks, R. Smalley, H. Parra, J. C. Baez, M. Blanco, S. Cimbaro, and E. Kendrick (2011), The 2010 Mw 8.8 Maule Megathrust Earthquake of Central Chile, Monitored by GPS, *Science*, *332*, 1417–1421.

Wells, D. L., and K. J. Coppersmith (1994), New empirical relationships among magnitude, rupture length, rupture width, rupture area, and surface displacement, *Bull. Seismol. Soc. Am.*, *84*(4), 974–1002.

Zeevaert, L., and N. Newmark (1956), Aseismic design of Latino Americana Tower in Mexico City, *1st World Conference Earthquake Engineering*, pp. 35-1–35-11, Berkeley, CA.

Zeevaert, L. (1960), Base shear in tall buildings during the earthquake July 28, 1957 in Mexico City, *2nd World Conference Earthquake Engineering*, pp. 983–996, Tokyo and Kyoto, Japan.

18

Tropical Cyclones: From the Influence of Climate to Their Socioeconomic Impacts

Suzana J. Camargo[1] and Solomon M. Hsiang[2]

ABSTRACT

In the last few years, there has been tremendous interest in both the climate's influence on tropical cyclones and cyclones' influence on human societies. Much of this interest is driven by the notion that global climate change might alter tropical cyclone frequency or intensity, and that this response will in turn have important social impacts. Here, we summarize recent advances in our understanding of both these linkages.

We summarize the current state of the art for research on the link between tropical cyclones and climate at various timescales, from subseasonal to anthropogenic warming, using models of the global atmosphere and ocean. Improvements in computational capabilities have enabled the representation of tropical cyclones in these models to become much more realistic, primarily by increasing models' horizontal resolution, although there remain deficiencies in storm intensity. We also discuss the capability of the current models to forecast tropical cyclone activity at subseasonal and seasonal timescales. Our current understanding of the possible changes in tropical cyclone activity under global climate change is summarized and the remaining challenges are highlighted.

We then turn to recent progress in the quantitative modeling of tropical cyclones' socioeconomic impact. Advances in geospatial analysis have enabled researchers to link meteorological observations with socioeconomic data, allowing them to measure the effect that tropical cyclone exposure has on numerous human outcomes. New studies generally find that the social impact of tropical cyclones, both financially and using alternative measures of well-being, are larger than previously thought. While questions still outnumber results in this young field, several findings open the door for innovative strategies to manage tropical cyclone risk and losses in both current and future climates.

18.1. INTRODUCTION

Tropical cyclones are influenced by climate in various timescales, from intraseasonal to centennial. In different timescales, different climate modes are responsible for the modulation of tropical cyclone activity. There is variety in how the modulation occurs, with important regional distinctions. On top of the natural climate variability affecting tropical cyclones, in longer timescales (decadal to centennial), anthropogenic climate change can also impact tropical cyclone activity. Recent reviews of the modulation of tropical cyclones by natural and anthropogenic climate variability can be found in *Camargo et al.* [2010] and *Knutson et al.* [2010a, 2010b], respectively, here we emphasize papers that were published since then.

In the last few years, there has been a substantial increase in computer resources dedicated to climate models, which

[1]*Lamont-Doherty Earth Observatory, Columbia University, Palisades, NY, USA*

[2]*Goldman School of Public Policy, University of California Berkeley, Berkeley, CA, USA*

Extreme Events: Observations, Modeling, and Economics, Geophysical Monograph 214, First Edition.
Edited by Mario Chavez, Michael Ghil, and Jaime Urrutia-Fucugauchi.

has led to a huge advance in modeling tropical cyclones at timescales beyond a few days. While it is still not possible to simulate tropical cyclones (TCs) with realistic intensity beyond a few days, the advances in the last decade have been phenomenal.

Since the 1970s it has been known that even low-resolution climate models are able to produce vortices that have characteristics similar to those of observed TCs [*Manabe et al.*, 1970; *Bengtsson et al.*, 1982; *Krishnamurti*, 1988; *Krishnamurti et al.*, 1989]. These TC-like vortices in low-resolution models typically occur in the same location as the observed TCs and typically formed in the correct season, but tend to be much weaker and have much larger horizontal scale than observed ones. These biases are associated with the low-resolution of the models. There have been many studies of TC activity in low-resolution climate models, mainly focusing on their climatological characteristics [*Bengtsson et al.*, 1995; *Camargo and Sobel*, 2004], as well as seasonal [*Wu and Lau*, 2002; *Vitart et al.*, 1997; *Camargo and Zebiak*, 2002; *Camargo et al.*, 2005], and climate change timescales [*Broccoli and Manabe*, 1990; *Bengtsson et al.*, 1996; *Royer et al.*, 1998; *Krishnamurti et al.*, 1998; *Sugi et al.*, 2002].

Until a few years ago, only a few modeling groups invested resources in studying TC activity in climate models. Nowadays in most modeling groups analyzing the TC activity in climate models is becoming one of the staple diagnostics in their model diagnostic suite. With the computational and modeling advances in the last few years, many modeling groups started venturing in this area, and currently many modeling groups are doing research on the relationship between TCs and climate. The main effort is concentrated on the impacts of the climate change in TC activity. However, many groups are also exploring their model skill in other timescales, especially seasonal and intraseasonal.

In the first part of this chapter, we will review the factors that influence TCs in various timescales, from intraseasonal to centennial. We will then discuss the state of the art of modeling and forecasting in each of these timescales.

A major reason why physical scientists are interested in the climatic influence on TC activity is because changes in TC activity may have an acute effect on the well-being of exposed populations. Thus, the second part of this chapter is dedicated to a discussion of the social and economic impacts of TCs. Historically, the direct quantitative study of TCs social impact was difficult because of limited computing resources, data availability, and the various challenges posed by linking geospatial datasets. However, over the last decade progress has accelerated, motivated in part by concerns over changing patterns of TC risk caused by anthropogenic climate change.

There are many approaches to understanding the effect of TCs on society, ranging from qualitative ethnographic methods to quantitative analytical models of economic decision making. Each of these approaches offers their own unique perspective and contributes to our understanding of these events, however here we focus most of our attention on new findings that leverage recent advances in causal inference. Systematically identifying causal relationships in social systems is notoriously difficult; however, innovations in applied statistics [*Holland*, 1986; *Freedman*, 1991] led to the development of many quasi-experimental methods in the 1990s and 2000s [*Greenstone and Gayer*, 2009; *Angrist and Pischke*, 2010] that could reliably infer cause and effect relationships in complex social systems where many dimensions of social data are unobserved [*Angrist and Krueger*, 1999; *Chay and Greenstone*, 2003; *Deschenes and Greenstone*, 2007; *Schlenker and Roberts*, 2009]. These quasi-experimental approaches are well suited for the study of TC impacts because each TC event can be viewed as a "natural experiment" where an exposed population just prior to a TC event serves as a "control" for that same population just after a TC strikes, that is, after it is "treated." Because TC exposure is stochastic, it is unlikely that TC exposure is correlated with other confounding variables in large samples, so systematic differences between the "treatment" and "control" states of a given population can very likely be attributed to TC exposure.

The development of this approach is relatively recent in the social sciences and its application to measuring the impact of TCs has been slowed by the difficulty of incorporating TC data into the necessary statistical machinery. For these reasons the current literature is both young and relatively sparse, although we can make strong causal inferences with those studies that exist. We are hopeful that over the coming decade, the application of this quasi-experimental approach to TC impacts will continue to yield novel and important results, answering many of the remaining open questions.

In the second half of this chapter, we discuss the direct impacts of TCs, such as their physical damage and immediate mortality, as well as their indirect impacts, such as their influence on income, employment, migration, health, relief efforts, and adaptation. Despite the existence of a large literature on natural hazards generally, including non-TC events like earthquakes and droughts, we try to restrict our attention to TC impacts because it remains ambiguous whether the social impact of these various hazards are similar or not.

18.2. INTRASEASONAL TIMESCALES

In intraseasonal timescales, the Madden-Julian Oscillation [MJO; *Madden and Julian*, 1972, 1994; *Zhang*, 2005] is the strongest signal and the main source of predictability in the tropics. The MJO consists of large-scale coupled patterns of deep convection and atmospheric circulation with a 30–90 day period. The MJO has a coherent signal in many atmospheric variables in the tropics. The MJO usually initiates in the Indian Ocean and

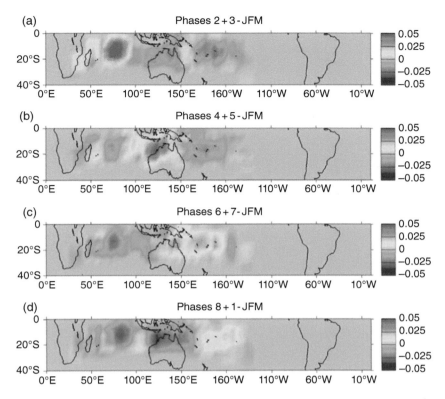

Figure 18.1 First position density anomalies for JFM during the period 1982–2007 for MJO phases (a) 2 and 3 (Indian Ocean), (b) 4 and 5 (Maritime Continent), (c) 6 and 7 (western Pacific), (d) 8 and 1 (western Hemisphere and Africa). Figure originally published in *Camargo et al.* [2009].

propagates eastward across the global tropics, with strong signature in deep convection in the Indian and western Pacific Oceans. In the eastern Pacific and Atlantic Oceans, the MJO signal is mainly apparent in wind fields. Another important characteristic of the MJO is that it is stronger in boreal winter than boreal summer [*Wang and Rui*, 1990].

The MJO modulates the TC activity in many regions [*Camargo et al.*, 2009]. When the MJO is in the enhanced convective or "active" phase in a certain region, there is a tendency for a higher frequency of TC formation in that region. Figure 18.1 shows the anomalies of the TC genesis density in various phases of the MJO in the southern hemisphere, January to March (JFM) TC season.

The MJO composites in Figures 18.1 and 18.2 were constructed using the phases of the MJO index developed by *Wheeler and Hendon* [2004], with phases 2 and 3 localized in the Indian Ocean, phases 4 and 5 in the Maritime Continent, phases 6 and 7 in the western Pacific, phase 8 in the western Hemisphere, and phase 1 in Africa. As the MJO progresses eastward, a positive anomaly of TC genesis shifts eastward. The MJO's eastward progression can be seen in Figure 18.2, as negative outgoing long-wave radiation (OLR) anomalies. Also shown in Figure 18.2 is the ability of a genesis potential index [*Emanuel and Nolan*, 2004; *Camargo et al.*, 2007a] to capture the enhancement of TC genesis when the MJO is active in

that region, reflecting the environmental changes related to the MJO which affect TC genesis.

The modulation of TCs by the MJO was first noticed in the western North Pacific and in the Indian Ocean [*Nakazawa*, 1988; *Liebmann et al.*, 1994]. Other regions with a strong modulation of TC activity by the MJO are the eastern North Pacific [*Molinari et al.*, 1997; *Molinari and Vollaro*, 2000; *Maloney and Hartmann*, 2000a, 2001; *Barrett and Leslie*, 2009], the Gulf of Mexico and northwestern Caribbean [*Maloney and Hartmann*, 2000b; *Aiyyer and Molinari*, 2008], North Atlantic main development region [*Mo*, 2000; *Klotzbach*, 2010], the south Indian Ocean [*Bessafi and Wheeler*, 2006; *Ho et al.*, 2006], and the Australian region and southwestern Pacific [*Hall et al.*, 2001; *Chand and Walsh*, 2010]. The modulation of TC genesis by the MJO leads to a relationship between the MJO phases and TC track types as well [*Camargo et al.*, 2007b, 2008; *Kossin et al.*, 2010; *Ramsay et al.*, 2012], similarly to what happens in decadal timescales [*Kossin and Camargo*, 2009]. *Li et al.* [2012] noticed a stronger modulation of the western North Pacific TCs by the MJO in the warm phase of the El Niño-Southern Oscillation (ENSO) than in neutral or La Niña years. This asymmetric modulation occurs because the MJO is stronger and extends further eastward during El Niño years. Furthermore, cyclogenesis is enhanced in the western North Pacific by a synchronization

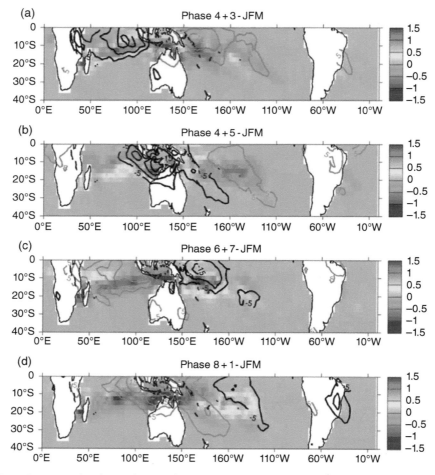

Figure 18.2 Genesis Potential Index (colors) and OLR (contours) anomalies for JFM during the period 1982–2007 for MJO phases (a) 2 and 3 (Indian Ocean), (b) 4 and 5 (Maritime Continent), (c) 6 and 7 (western Pacific), (d) 8 and 1 (western Hemisphere and Africa). Figure originally published in *Camargo et al.* [2009].

of the active MJO signal and favorable El Niño background conditions [*Li et al.*, 2012]. *Klotzbach* [2014] showed that in the MJO active phase there are more events with rapid intensification in the North Atlantic.

The active convective MJO phase environment is conducive to tropical cyclogenesis in a variety of ways. First, in the convective phase, the mid-level humidity and low-level vorticity are enhanced. Second, the frequent occurrence of convection can lead to more convective disturbances, which can potentially become TC precursors. An active MJO also provides a favorable region for wave accumulation mechanisms [*Sobel and Maloney*, 2000; *Aiyyer and Molinari*, 2003], by which large-scale convergence can amplify synoptic scale disturbances. In general, TC formation is strongly related to enhanced activity of many tropical waves [*Frank and Roundy*, 2006], for example, in the North Atlantic, ~70% of TCs are initiated from African easterly waves. However, the relationship of the waves with TC genesis has specific characteristics in different regions of the globe [*Schreck et al.*, 2011, 2012].

Given this strong relationship between the MJO phase and tropical cyclone genesis, statistical forecast models were developed for intraseasonal TC activity using the MJO phase as one of the predictors. *Leroy and Wheeler* [2009] developed a statistical forecast for the weekly probability of TC formation in the southern hemisphere using the MJO phase, as well as two leading modes of variability of sea surface temperature (SST) in the Indo-Pacific basin. Long-range probabilistic forecasts of TCs were also developed based on their association with various convectively coupled atmospheric waves and intraseasonal oscillations [*Frank and Roundy*, 2006; *Roundy and Schreck*, 2009].

Until recently, the representation of the MJO in most climate models has been quite poor [*Kim et al.*, 2009a], making the simulation of the MJO a difficult test for climate models [*Slingo et al.*, 1996; *Lin et al.*, 2006]. The quality of MJO simulation in climate models can sometimes be improved by changing specific aspects of the cumulus parametrization of the models [*Kim et al.*, 2011a], although in general, these changes tend to inhibit deep convection in the model [*Tokioka et al.*, 1998; *Wang and Schlesinger*, 1999; *Lin et al.*, 2008; *Kim et al.*, 2012a]. A systematic relationship between the model's MJO strength and a model mean bias has been noticed, probably leading to the rejection of these parameterizations by most modeling groups [*Kim et al.*, 2011a]. Using coupled atmospheric-ocean models instead of atmospheric models forced with prescribed SST is also fundamental, as it is important to represent the interaction of the atmosphere with the ocean in order to obtain more realistic MJO simulations [*Kim and Kang*, 2008; *Kim et al.*, 2008]. Even with all these issues, the predictability of the MJO in dynamical models is now at the same level or better than statistical models for the MJO, and a multimodel combination of statistical and dynamical forecasts provides a better skill than each of these approaches separately [*Kang and Kim*, 2010].

Given the existing biases of the MJO simulations in most climate models, the simulation of the relationship

between MJO and TCs is still far from being reproduced in most cases. However, a few models have been successful in simulating the MJO-TC connection. For instance, the Japanese high-resolution cloud-resolving model, NICAM, has successfully simulated an MJO event [*Liu et al.*, 2009] and its link to tropical cyclogenesis in the western North Pacific [*Oouchi et al.*, 2009]. One model that has made significant progress in modeling the MJO is the ECMWF (European Centre for Medium Range Weather Forecasts) model, using a seamless prediction approach from synoptic to decadal time series [*Bechtold et al.*, 2008]. The ECMWF model simulates the evolution of the MJO with skill up to 20 days and the model MJO teleconnections are consistent with observations [*Vitart and Jung*, 2010; *Vitart and Molteni*, 2010]. The modulation of TC activity by the MJO is simulated by the ECMWF model, as well as the relationship of landfall risk in Australia and North America with the MJO phase [*Vitart*, 2009]. Figure 18.3

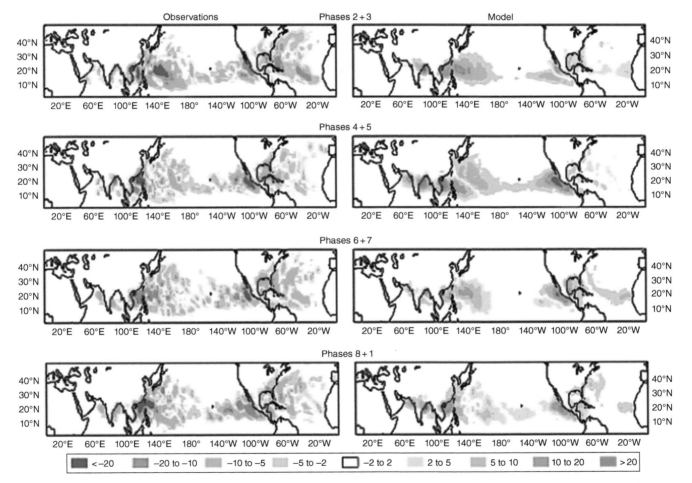

Figure 18.3 Tropical storm density anomalies (×1000) as a function of MJO phases in (left) observations and in the (right) ECMWF model hindcasts in the northern hemisphere for the period August to October 1989–2008. Yellow and red colors indicate an increase in TC activity. The blue colors indicate a reduction of TC activity. Figure originally published in *Vitart* [2009].

shows the modulation of TC activity by the MJO in the northern hemisphere in observations and in the ECMWF model hindcasts. Even in the northern hemisphere summer, when the MJO signal is weaker, the ECMWF model modulation of TC activity by the MJO is very clear.

Given the skill of the ECMWF in simulating MJO events and their relationship with TCs, the performance of the ECMWF model in real time during the 2008 and 2009 typhoon seasons was analyzed in *Elsberry et al.* [2010, 2011]. At least for the strongest typhoons during the peak season the ECMWF ensemble provided guidance of formation and tracks on 10–30 day timescales. The forecast of tracks when multiple cyclones occur simultaneously is still a challenge for the model, as well as late season weak storms [*Elsberry et al.*, 2011]. Analysis of the predictability of the monthly ECMWF system for forecasting North Atlantic tropical cyclone activity showed that the model skill is sensitive to the phase of the MJO and time of the model initialization [*Belanger et al.*, 2010].

A comparison of the performance of the ECMWF forecast system for weekly TC activity with the Leroy and Wheeler statistical model in the southern hemisphere was performed by *Vitart et al.* [2010], with the dynamical model performance better than the statistical model in the first two weeks. Figure 18.4 shows the reliability diagrams of the probability of TC occurrence in the southern hemisphere for the ECMWF model, the Leroy and Wheeler statistical model, and a simple calibrated version of ECMWF model. The calibration is done in two steps, in the first step, the forecast probability is set to zero in regions with no TCs in the observations in the climatological period of the study; in the second step the forecast probabilities are reduced so that the climatological model TC occurrence is equal to the observations (the model generates 30% more TCs than in observations). A simple multimodel combination of the calibrated dynamical model forecast and the statistical forecast (by simply averaging the forecast probabilities produced by the two models, with equal weights) exceeds the Brier skill scores of both models, similarly to improvements noticed in many other studies [*Krishnamurti et al.*, 1999; *Palmer et al.*, 2004; *Tippett and Barnston*, 2008; *DelSole et al.*, 2013].

The Geophysical Fluid Dynamics Laboratory (GFDL) High-Resolution Atmospheric Model (HiRAM) is able to reproduce the modulation of the MJO on TC activity in the eastern North Pacific very well [*Jiang et al.*, 2012a]. Initial results with the HiRAM forecasts on intraseasonal timescales are promising for the Atlantic basin [*Chen and Lin*, 2011; *Gall et al.*, 2011]. Figure 18.5 shows the time series of the 21 day tropical storm days for the HiRAM forecasts for the years 2006–2009. It is interesting to note though, that in a recent model intercomparison of the

(a)

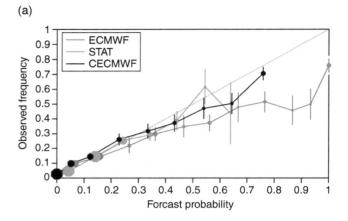

(b)

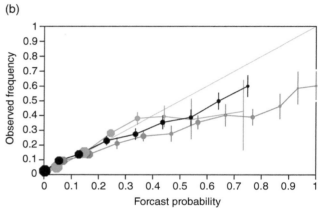

(c)

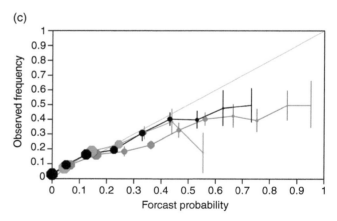

Figure 18.4 Reliability diagrams of the probability of TC occurrence in 20°×15° domains in the southern hemisphere for the forecast days (a) 1–7 (week 1), (b) 8–14 (week 2), and (c) 15–21 (week 3). The blue line corresponds to the statistical model of Leroy and Wheeler (STAT), the red line to the ECMWF model and the black line to the calibrated ECMWF model (CEMWF). In this graph the area of symbols (octagons) for each probability bin is proportional to the number of cases populating that bin. The error bars (95% level of confidence) were computed from a 10,000 bootstrap resampling procedure. Figure originally published in *Vitart et al.* [2010].

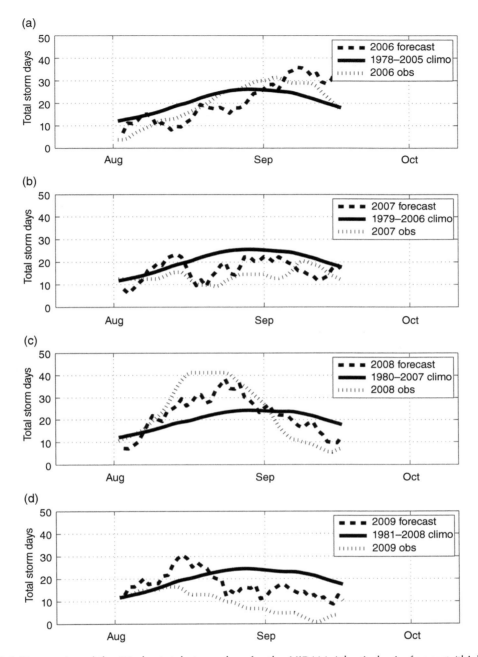

Figure 18.5 Time series of the 21 day total storm days for the HiRAM Atlantic basin forecast (thick dashed), observed (thin dashed), and preceding 28 year climatology (solid) for the period 2 August to 16 September for the years 2006–2009, respectively (a)–(d). Figure originally from *Gall et al.* [2011].

intraseasonal variability over the eastern Pacific, the HiRAM models was one of the models with best skill in simulating various characteristics of modes of intraseasonal variability [*Jiang et al.*, 2012b].

Other modeling groups are also making progress toward modeling the MJO-TC interaction and producing dynamical extended forecasts of TC activity, for example, *Fu and Hsu* [2010] who successfully simulated tropical cyclogenesis in the North Indian Ocean with a 2-week lead time. While there has been significant progress in using dynamical models for forecasting TC probability in intra seasonal timescales, there is still a need for improvement in this area. The development and improvement of intraseasonal tropical cyclone dynamical forecasts is certainly an area in which we expect substantial effort and progress in the next several years.

18.3. SEASONAL TIMESCALES

In seasonal timescales, the ENSO is the main climate mode in the tropics. ENSO is a coupled ocean-atmospheric climate mode that occurs in the tropical Pacific Ocean and is associated with changes in seasonal temperature, precipitation, and winds in various regions of the globe. The warm (El Niño) and cold (La Niña) phases usually occur every 3–7 years and last ~1 year.

ENSO dynamical forecasts were first developed in the 1980s [*Cane and Zebiak*, 1985]. Real-time statistical and dynamic ENSO forecasts are produced by many groups with range of skill levels [*Barnston et al.*, 2012; *Tippett et al.*, 2012]. ENSO forecasts are the basis of operational seasonal climate forecasts of temperature and precipitation [*Barnston et al.*, 1994, 2003; *Goddard et al.*, 2001, 2003].

The relationship between TCs and ENSO was first noted in the Australian region [*Nicholls*, 1979, 1984, 1985; *Evans and Allan*, 1992; *Basher and Zheng*, 1995; *Kuleshov et al.*, 2008; *Ramsay et al.*, 2008, 2012], followed by the North Atlantic basin [*Gray*, 1984; *Bove et al.*, 1998; *Landsea et al.*, 1999; *Pielke Jr. and Landsea*, 1999; *Tang and Neelin*, 2004; *Klotzbach*, 2011a, 2011b]. Since then,

the modulation of TC activity by ENSO has been examined in detail in all basins [*Camargo et al.*, 2007a, 2010]. ENSO affects TCs in various regions in different ways: ENSO can modulate TC activity by altering TC frequency, intensity, duration, genesis location, and track types. A global picture of the effect of ENSO on TC genesis and track density is shown in Figures 18.6 and 18.7 for August to October (ASO) and JFM seasons. In some basins, the frequency of TC occurrence decreases in warm ENSO events (North Atlantic, Australia, and Bay of Bengal), while in others there is an increase (eastern North Pacific, Central North Pacific, and South Pacific).

Recently, the differences between the impacts of central and eastern Pacific warm ENSO events on tropical cyclone activity have been explored in various studies. *Kim et al.* [2009b] examined the differences between the two types of El Niño North Atlantic TC activity and found higher frequency and landfall potential in Gulf of Mexico and Central America for a central Pacific warming. However, the small number of central Pacific ENSO events can be an important issue in determining the statistical significance of these results [*Lee et al.*, 2010], with a more recent paper arriving in an opposite conclusion regarding the impact of central Pacific ENSO on Atlantic TCs [*Larson et al.*, 2012].

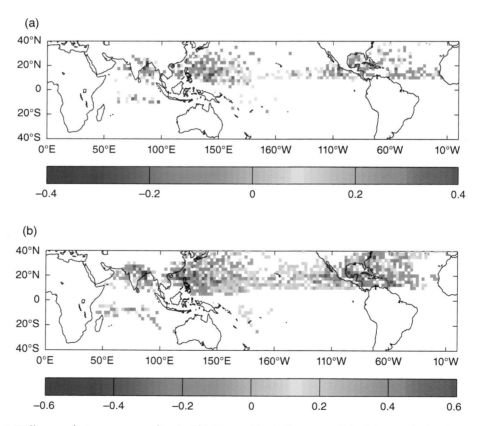

Figure 18.6 Difference between anomalies in El Niño and La Niña years of the (a) genesis density and (b) track density in August–October (ASO). Figure originally from *Camargo et al.* [2007a].

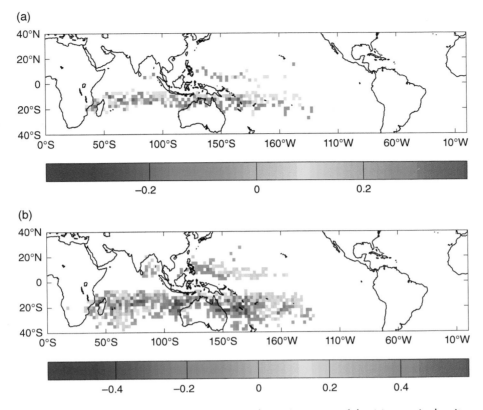

Figure 18.7 Difference between anomalies in El Niño and La Niña years of the (a) genesis density and (b) track density in January–March (JFM). Figure originally from *Camargo et al.* [2007a].

The different characteristics of typhoon activity for central and eastern Pacific ENSO events were also analyzed, as well as the changes in large-scale circulation associated with warming in different locations [*Kim et al.*, 2011b]. *Camargo et al.* [2007b] showed that different typhoon track types are associated with central and eastern Pacific warming, which exhibit larger differences in boreal autumn [*Hong et al.*, 2011]. Differences between the two El Niño types also have been found in typhoon frequency in the South China Sea [*Chen*, 2012] as well in other portions of the western North Pacific [*Chen and Tam*, 2010].

Although dominant, ENSO is not the only climate mode that influences TC activity in seasonal timescales. Other natural modes of climate variability have been associated with seasonal TC activity, for instance, the Atlantic Meridional Mode (AMM) and the Quasi-Biennial Oscillation (QBO). The AMM is an important mode of variability of the tropical Atlantic on seasonal timescales, with maximum variance in the boreal spring. The AMM is characterized by a meridional SST gradient in the tropical Atlantic, boundary layer winds that fluctuate toward the anomalously warmer water; and a meridional displacement of the intertropical convergence zone (ITCZ) toward the warmer hemisphere [*Servain et al.*,

1999; *Xie and Carton*, 2004; *Vimont and Kossin*, 2007]. There is a known relationship of the AMM with North Atlantic TC activity. The AMM is highly correlated with various environmental variables (SST, vertical shear, low-level vorticity and convergence, static stability, and sea level pressure) that cooperate to increase (warm SST anomaly in the North Atlantic) or decrease (cold SST anomaly in the North Atlantic) Atlantic hurricane activity [*Xie et al.*, 2005a, 2005b; *Kossin and Vimont*, 2007; *Vimont and Kossin*, 2007; *Kossin et al.*, 2010].

The stratospheric QBO is a quasi-periodic oscillation of the tropical winds in the stratosphere, dominating the interannual variability of the equatorial stratosphere and having alternating well-defined periods of ~28 months with easterly and westerly winds that descend with time [*Baldwin et al.*, 2001]. *Gray* [1984] pointed out an apparent influence of the QBO on North Atlantic TC activity: when the QBO was in its westerly phase, TC activity in the Atlantic was greater than when the QBO was in the easterly phase, with more intense Atlantic hurricanes occurring in the westerly QBO years. Possible reasons for the QBO influence on Atlantic TCs were discussed in *Shapiro* [1989] and *Arpe and Leroy* [2009]. However, the statistically significant relationship of the QBO with Atlantic TC frequency that was observed from the 1950s to the 1980s [*Gray*, 1984] is no longer present in more recent years [*Camargo and Sobel*, 2010]. The relationship of the QBO with TCs in the western North Pacific [*Chan*, 1995; *Ho et al.*, 2009], eastern North Pacific [*Whitney and Hobgood*, 1997], South Indian Ocean [*Jury*, 1993; *Jury et al.*, 1999], North Indian Ocean [*Balachandran and Guhathakurta*, 1999] tropical cyclone activity has also been discussed, with mixed results. *Camargo et al.* [2010] reviews the influence of natural climate variability on TC activity globally.

In most basins, the relationship of TC activity with ENSO led to the development of statistical TC seasonal forecasts, with varied success [*Nicholls*, 1979, 1992; *Gray*, 1984; *Chan et al.*, 1998, 2001]. One of the main issues is the ability to predict ENSO accurately and reliably, which then is used to predict TC activity. It should be noted that because ENSO predictability barrier occurs in northern spring, the skill of seasonal statistical forecasts of TC activity in the northern hemisphere increases significantly in June. (The northern spring predictability barrier is characterized by a drop in the skill of ENSO forecasts, so that in general ENSO forecasts for the second semester of the calendar year have no significant skill if initiated prior to March or April (Tippett et al. 2012)). Several studies have explored the spring barrier, but debate continues regarding its origin (Webster and Hoyos 2010).) It is relatively "easier" to predict TC activity in the southern hemisphere, as the peak TC season (January–March) typically happens once the ENSO state is well established. It is interesting to note that the QBO was used as one of the predictors of the Colorado State University seasonal Atlantic TC statistical forecasts for many years, but more recently these forecasts have ceased using QBO as a predictor [*Klotzbach*, 2007].

Our focus in this chapter is on the recent advances of modeling seasonal TC activity with climate models, as well dynamical and statistical-dynamical seasonal TC forecasts. We refer the reader to *Camargo et al.* [2007c, 2010] for information on statistical forecasts.

There are distinct ways of using climate models in producing TCs seasonal forecasts. The first and most used method is to detect and track tropical cyclone-like structures in the climate models using objective techniques. These techniques usually employ a criteria based on local maximum 850 hPa vorticity, local minimum sea-level pressure, evidence of a warm core, and wind speed above a certain threshold and system lifetime [*Bengtsson et al.*, 1982, 1995, 2007a, 2007b; *Tsutsui and Kasahara*, 1996; *Vitart et al.*, 1997; *Camargo and Zebiak*, 2002]. However, the criteria for locating and tracking storms in these different algorithms vary according to model resolution and statistics, which raises difficulties when comparing the results of different studies. Various suggestions have been proposed to deal with differences in detection in these algorithms, such as using a homogeneous resolution-based criteria for thresholds [*Walsh et al.*, 2007], or using a common low-resolution grid independent of the original model resolution [*Bengtsson et al.*, 2007a], modifying an algorithm widely applied to extra-tropical storms [*Hodges*, 1994, 1995, 1999], or using only large-scale parameters independent of model resolution and biases [*Tory et al.*, 2013a, 2013b].

Since the early 2000s, dynamical TC forecasts have been issued operationally in the ECMWF [*Vitart and Stockdale*, 2001; *Vitart et al.*, 2003] and the International Research Institute for Climate and Society [IRI; *Camargo and Barnston*, 2009] using algorithms that track TCs in climate models in various regions of the world. The ECMWF TC dynamical forecast system is based on a coupled ocean-atmospheric model, which has been constantly updated with increasingly higher resolution [*Vitart*, 2009], as well as multimodel techniques [*Vitart*, 2006; *Vitart et al.*, 2007]. In contrast, the IRI system is based on a two-tier approach: first a range of SST forecasts are obtained, which are then used to force the atmospheric model [*Camargo and Barnston*, 2009].

More recently, TC dynamical forecasts have been developed taking advantage of climate models with higher resolution, with a focus on the Atlantic region. The U.K. Met Office has been issuing Atlantic seasonal forecasts since 2007 using a multimodel approach [*Vitart et al.*, 2007] including the Met Office and the ECMWF coupled ocean-atmosphere systems [*Anderson et al.*, 2007; *Arribas et al.*, 2011]. The Florida State University (FSU) started issuing operational forecasts in, for the Atlantic, 2010 based on their atmospheric model [*LaRow et al.*, 2008, 2010].

The interannual variability of the number of tropical storms in the Atlantic generated by FSU model and observations is given in Figure 18.8. The model does a good job in capturing the interannual variability in that basin, although it did not generate enough storms in 2005.

As the dynamical models improve and the ability to do long high-resolution simulations increases, the ability of the models to represent TC activity has also significantly improved. Figure 18.9 shows global TC tracks in observations and simulated by the GFDL HiRAM model for the period 1981–2005. Although there are small biases that can be noticed in the model tracks, they are more realistic than low-resolution model tracks [*Camargo et al.*, 2005]. The HiRAM atmospheric model has very high skill in forecasting seasonal TC activity in the North Atlantic using 50 km [*Zhao et al.*, 2009] or 25 km horizontal resolution [*Chen and Lin*, 2011] and is now included in the National Oceanic and Atmospheric Administration (NOAA) Atlantic Hurricane Seasonal outlook. It should

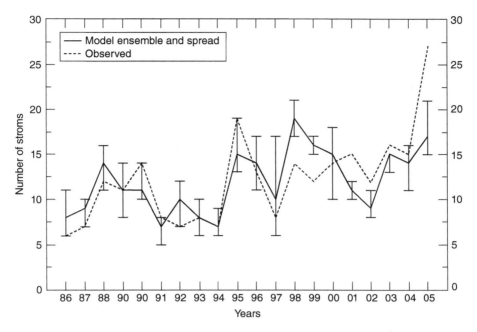

Figure 18.8 Interannual variability of Atlantic tropical storms during the period 1968–2005 in observations (dotted line), and in the FSU model. The model ensemble mean is shown in the solid line and the model ensemble spread in the vertical lines. Figure originally from *LaRow et al.* [2008].

be noted that, when the same model is forced with persisted (SST anomalies from the previous month are added to the climatological SST of the following months to construct "persisted" SST fields) SST [*Zhao et al.*, 2010], there is a significant degradation in skill, compared with the skill when the model is forced with observed SST [*Zhao et al.*, 2009]. *Zhao et al.* [2010] showed that the quality of the real-time seasonal forecasts will depend in large part on the model's ability to predict the difference between the SST in the Atlantic and the tropical SST [or relative SST; *Vecchi and Soden*, 2007]. Similarly, *LaRow* [2013] obtained significant better skill in hindcasts of number of TCs in the Atlantic when using bias-corrected SST.

A recent study with the ECMWF global climate model comparing various resolutions (up to 10 km) shows a significant improvement with resolution in simulating the TC intensity distribution and the structure of the most intense storms [*Manganello et al.*, 2012]. However, this improvement was not automatically translated in better simulation of the ENSO-TC relationship, with the caveat, that only one ensemble member was available for the simulation with highest horizontal resolution. The effect of model resolution on the ability of the model in simulating interannual variability of TC activity was also examined in *Strachan et al.* [2013] using the Hadley Center Global Environmental Model (HadGEM1). In this study, in the North Atlantic, a significant improvement of the model skill in interannual timescales (see Figure 18.10) was noticed, but the same was not true in other basins. *Caron*

et al. [2011] compared the impact of increasing resolution in TC activity in the Atlantic using the Global Environmental Multiscale (GEM) model. They found that the improvement in simulating Atlantic storms is partially due to a better representation of African Easterly waves.

The ability of coupled ocean-atmospheric models to reproduce the ENSO-TC relationship has also been analyzed. The model from the Japan Meteorological Agency with 60 km resolution is able to reproduce many of the features of the ENSO-TC relationship in the western North Pacific [*Iizuka and Matsuura*, 2008] and North Atlantic [*Iizuka and Matsuura*, 2009], even though the model ENSO has some deficiencies. *Shaman and Maloney* [2012] examined the ENSO-Atlantic TC relationship in a suite of low-resolution models and found that no model provides consistently a good representation of ENSO-related variability in the North Atlantic for variables associated with TC activity, due to an inaccurate representation of ENSO in the models, as well as biases in the ENSO response in the North Atlantic.

Regional climate models have been used to simulate seasonal TC activity on seasonal timescales [*Nguyen and Walsh*, 2001; *Landman et al.*, 2005; *Camargo et al.*, 2007d; *Feser and von Storch*, 2008; *Lavender and Walsh*, 2011; *Au-Yeung and Chan*, 2012]. There are improvements in the simulation of TC intensity in regional climate models due to the increase in resolution compared with the reanalysis or global climate model that is forcing the regional

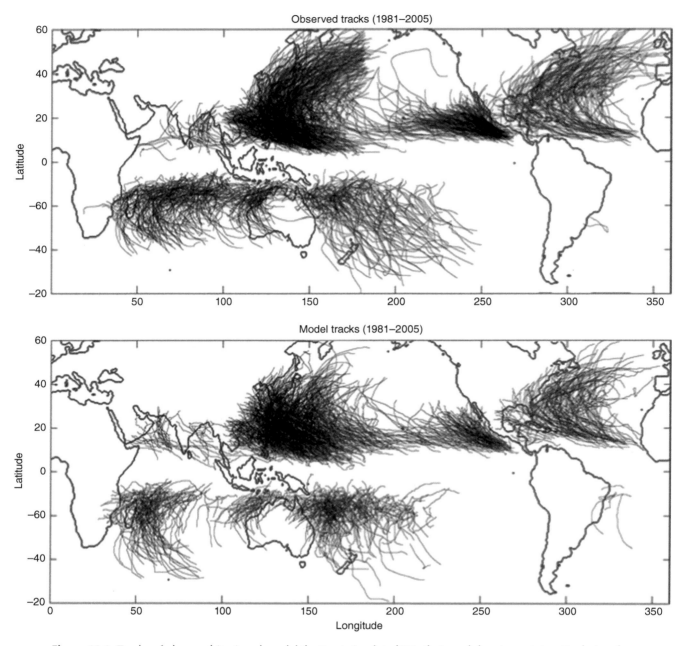

Figure 18.9 Tracks of observed (top) and model (bottom) simulated TCs that reach hurricane intensity during the period 1981–2005. The tracks were generated by the GFDL HiRAM model forced with observed SST. Figure originally from *Zhao et al.* [2009].

model. However, biases in a climate model's large-scale fields can lead to biases in the TC activity simulated by regional models [*Camargo et al.*, 2007d; *Lavender and Walsh*, 2011] and the location of domain boundaries can impact the results of simulations [*Landman et al.*, 2005]. As far as we are aware, no modeling center has been using regional climate models in real time to produce TC seasonal forecasts.

An alternative approach to examining the model TC-like structures is to consider the large-scale variables that are associated with TCs in the models. The advantage of this approach is that in many cases global climate models that are used to study TC activity have low-resolution, as it is desirable to have many ensemble members and long simulations when examining the TC-climate relationship. Given that the climate models' large-scale environment is in many

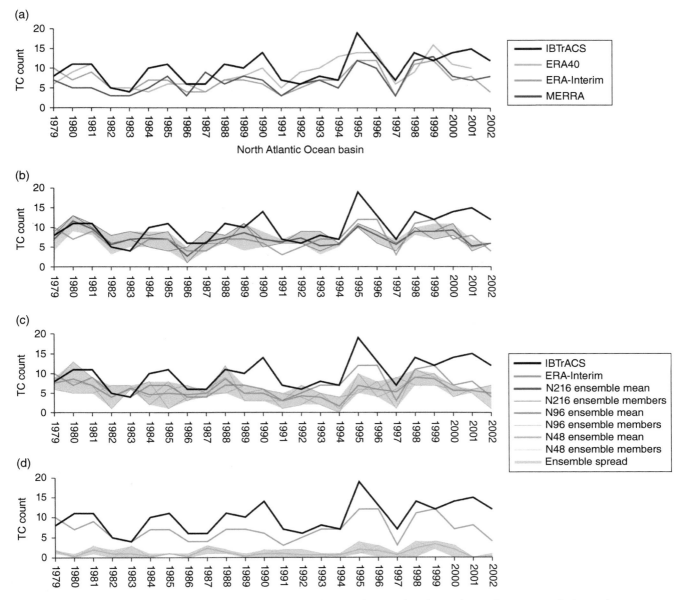

Figure 18.10 Tropical cyclone interannual variability for the North Atlantic basin for (a) reanalysis products: ERA-40 [ECMWF 40 year reanalysis; *Uppala et al.*, 2005], ERA-Interim [ECMWF Interim reanalysis; *Dee et al.*, 2011], and MERRA [Modern-Era Retrospective Analysis for Research and Applications Reanalysis; *Rienecker et al.*, 2011]; for the Hadley Center General Environmental Model Version 1 (HadGEM1) with horizontal resolution (b) N216 (~60 km), (c) N96 (~135 km), and (d) N48 (~270 km). The kilometer approximate values are given at 50°N. Figure originally from *Strachan et al.* [2013].

cases better simulated than the model TCs, this can be an attractive way of inferring TC activity in climate models.

It is also possible to use an empirical genesis index to infer the TC frequency in from climate models. There are many genesis indices available in the literature [*Gray*, 1979; *Ryan et al.*, 1992; *Watterson et al.*, 1995; *Thorncroft and Pytharoulis*, 2001; *Emanuel and Nolan*, 2004; *Emanuel*, 2010; *McGauley and Nolan*, 2011; *Tippett et al.*, 2011; *Bruyère et al.*, 2012; *Waters et al.*, 2012], and a recent comparison of many of these genesis indices for the various reanalysis products appeared in *Menkes et al.* [2011]. As an example of a genesis index we show here the *Tippett et al.* [2011] TC genesis index (TCGI):

$$\mu = \exp\left(b + b_\eta \eta + b_H H + b_T T + b_V V + \log \cos\Phi\right)$$

where μ is the expected number of TC genesis events per month and η, H, T, V, are, respectively, the absolute vorticity at 850 hPa (in $10^5 s^{-1}$), the relative humidity at 600 hPa in percent, the relative SST (difference of the local SST and the mean tropical SST) in degree centigrade, and the vertical wind shear between 850 and 200 hPa levels in m/s, Φ is the latitude, and b the coefficients obtained in the Poisson regression.

These genesis indices have been applied to many climate models, in most cases in relation to climate change [*Royer et al.*, 1998; *McDonald et al.*, 2005; *Chauvin et al.*, 2006]. In low-resolution models the quality of the relationship of the genesis potential index (GPI) and model TCs in the present climate is model, basin, and resolution dependent [*Camargo et al.*, 2007e]. *Caron et al.* [2011] showed that the GPI reliability as a predictor of model TC frequency in the North Atlantic improves with model horizontal resolution.

Recently, statistical-dynamical forecasts of TC activity have been developed for the North Atlantic, using the dynamical fields of climate models as predictors of a statistical scheme. *Wang et al.*'s [2009] statistical-dynamical forecast for Atlantic hurricanes is based on the fields from the National Centers for Environmental Prediction (NCEP) and Climate Forecast System (CSF) dynamical model. The predictors from the CSF model used in this scheme to forecast seasonal Atlantic hurricane frequency are: tropical Pacific SSTs and Atlantic main development region (MDR) SSTs, and vertical wind shear. *Vecchi et al.* [2011] also built a statistical-dynamical forecast for North Atlantic hurricane frequency, but used only two climate predictors: SST in the North Atlantic and the mean global tropics SST. The statistical model was trained in simulations of the high-resolution climate model (GFDL HiRAM) and considers initialized SST forecasts from the CSF system, as well as the GFDL CM2.1 experimental system. This dynamical-statistical system predicts the probability density function of North Atlantic hurricane frequency, explicitly including uncertainty estimates in the forecasts. Figure 18.11 shows the skill of *Vecchi et al.*'s [2011] statistical-dynamical forecast. Another North Atlantic tropical statistical-dynamical TC seasonal forecast was developed by *Kim and Webster* [2010] using the large-scale variables from the ECMWF system. In this case, the chosen predictors are North Atlantic SST and MDR vertical wind shear. The skill of these statistical-dynamical forecasts is competitive with current statistical forecast models, with the potential advantage that in retrospective forecasts they have shown skill earlier than the statistical models.

In the last few years, significant effort has been made by many modeling groups to examine the skill of high-resolution models in simulating TC activity in seasonal timescales. This effort led to the development of new seasonal forecast systems based directly on model storms or in the dynamical fields of climate models. Currently, these forecasts are focused on basin-wide variables, such as hurricane frequency. As models improve, we hope that the focus of these forecasts will start to shift toward variables that are more relevant to TC impacts, for example, landfall probabilities of storms in coastal regions.

18.4. DECADAL TIME-SCALES

In the last few years, decadal prediction appeared as a new field of study in climate science. This area has become a focal topic of research, with substantial effort in the climate community dedicated to this area. For instance, in order to examine in detail the decadal predictability question, a new suite of experiments was designed for the 5th Coupled Model Intercomparison Project (CMIP5) as part of the most recent Intergovernmental Panel on Climate Change assessment report, IPCC-AR5 [*Meehl et al.*, 2009; *Taylor et al.*, 2012].

The decadal prediction focus is on the next 10–30 years time frame and therefore is a bridge between the seasonal predictions and the climate change projections. In this time frame, the climate is strongly influenced by both anthropogenic forcing and natural variability. For skillful seasonal forecasts, a good climate model and accurate specification of the current state of the climate are fundamental. In contrast, in a climate change time frame, the projections are determined by anthropogenic forcing and significant changes in the climate (the "signal") are obtained by calculating averages over many years, and in this context the natural variability is the "noise" of the system. Furthermore, due to the chaotic characteristic of the atmosphere, the initial conditions do not influence the long-term climate projections. However, given that both natural variability and anthropogenic forcing are important for decadal predictions, in order to have accurate decadal predictions we must use both accurate initial conditions, as well as include anthropogenic greenhouse gases and aerosols forcing [*Cane*, 2010].

The reasons for a deliberately organized effort to determine the possibility of decadal predictions are twofold. First, there is demand from stakeholders and decision makers, who would like to incorporate these predictions in their planning and decision process, as infrastructure and resources planning is usually done on a decadal time frame [*Cane*, 2010]. Second, there are various spatial patterns of climate decadal variability identified in the observational record, such as the Atlantic Multidecadal Variability (AMV, also called in the literature Atlantic Multidecadal Oscillation or AMO), which could potentially be predicted [*Goddard et al.*, 2012]. Unfortunately, new challenges appear when one attempts to do decadal predictions, such as separating the natural and forced components of the climate in these timescales [*Ting et al.*, 2009; *DelSole et al.*, 2011; *Solomon et al.*, 2011]. An

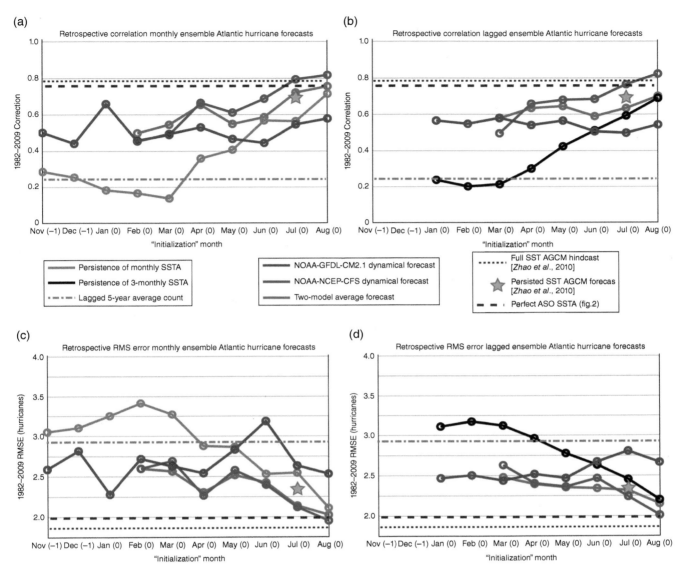

Figure 18.11 Performance of the seasonal dynamical-statistical hurricane frequency forecast system as a function of forecast lead time: (a) and (b) show correlations, (c) and (d) root-mean-square error for the monthly ensembles (a and c) and lagged ensemble schemes (b and d). The GFDL-CM2.1 is shown in red, the NCEP-CFS in blue, and the model average in violet. Null skill measures are also shown: a 5 year average (gray dashed-dotted line) and the model applied to persisted SST anomalies (solid gray for 1 month and black for 3 months persistence). Potential skill measures defined in the figure are model applied to observed SST (black dashed line) and performance of the HiRAM model forced with observed SST [black small dashes; *Zhao et al.*, 2009] and with persisted June SST anomaly [green star; *Zhao et al.*, 2010]. Figure originally from *Vecchi et al.* [2011].

important difference between seasonal and decadal prediction is the main source of variability: ENSO, a tropical phenomena, is dominant at the seasonal timescale, whereas AMV and Pacific Decadal Variability (PDV), mainly mid-latitude oceanic phenomena which may be linked to deeper oceanic processes than ENSO, dominate at longer time scales. The decadal modes do extend into the tropics, and it is expected that their impact could be

transmitted to the atmosphere through these tropical SST changes [*Goddard et al.*, 2012].

The AMV is a natural mode of variability on multidecadal timescales that was obtained from statistical analysis of observed SST after removing a linear trend [*Folland et al.*, 1986; *Delworth and Mann*, 2000]. The AMV is present in uninitialized coupled model simulations, with similar characteristics as the observed pattern [*Ting et al.*, 2011].

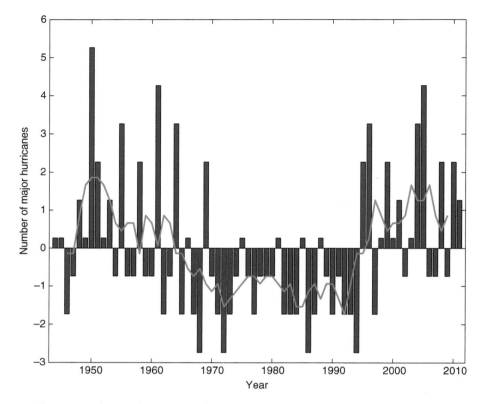

Figure 18.12 Difference in the number of major hurricanes per year in the North Atlantic and the mean number of major hurricanes (~2.7 per year) for the period 1944–2011 (blue bars). The 5 year running average is shown in the red line. Adapted from the original figure from *Goldenberg et al.* [2001].

However, the existence of the AMV as a natural climate mode of variability has been challenged by the argument that North Atlantic SST fluctuations in the 20th century were caused by a combination of external forcing, including greenhouse gases and industrial and volcanic aerosols [*Mann and Emanuel*, 2006]. In contrast, other analyses [*DelSole et al.*, 2011] indicate the existence of an Atlantic centered global pattern of internal multidecadal variability separated from the anthropogenic signal. The cause for the existence of the AMV is still a controversial topic in the scientific community and more research is necessary for a better understanding of this issue.

Pioneer hindcast experiments using initialized coupled models showed promising results for decadal predictions [*Smith et al.*, 2007; *Keenlyside et al.*, 2008]. More recently, positive results showed the possibility of predicting the AMV pattern on decadal timescales [*Yang et al.*, 2013] using a signal-to-noise method [*DelSole and Tippett*, 2009a, 2009b; *DelSole et al.*, 2011] and in agreement with idealized predictability analysis [*Msadek et al.*, 2010]. *Kim et al.*'s [2012b] analysis of a group of CMIP5 models [*Taylor et al.*, 2012] showed prediction skill for surface temperature up to 6–9 years over the Indian Ocean, North Atlantic, and the western North Pacific.

These models predicted AMV with significant skill, while the predictive skill for the PDV was relatively low for the same period.

The decadal variability of TC activity has been associated with natural modes of climate variability. The region that has attracted most attention in this topic is the North Atlantic, with the multidecadal variability in the number of major hurricanes in that region associated with the AMV through changes in vertical shear [*Gray et al.*, 1997; *Goldenberg et al.*, 2001; *Bell and Chelliah*, 2006]. Figure 18.12 shows the difference between the number of major hurricanes per year and the mean number of major hurricanes in the North Atlantic in the period 1944–2011 [adapted from *Goldenberg et al.*, 2001]. There are two very active eras, one in 1950s and early 1960s and the other one since 1995, with the period between them with a low in the number of major hurricanes. The U.S. landfall frequency and normalized U.S. hurricane damage also show similar modulation [*Klotzbach and Gray*, 2008; *Pielke Jr. et al.*, 2008]. *Wang et al.* [2008] suggest that the AMV influences Atlantic TC activity through the Atlantic Warm Pool, which includes the Gulf of Mexico, Caribbean Sea, and western tropical North Atlantic.

Smith et al. [2010] explored the possibility of issuing forecasts of TC frequency in the North Atlantic many years in advance using decadal predictions.

These decadal predictions are based on the concept that the climate system at decadal timescales is influenced from both natural climate modes as well as external forcing. They showed that their ensemble decadal prediction has skill in hindcast mode when initializing the prediction system with observed conditions. An almost identical system, which was initialized with random initial conditions, was used for skill comparison. In the second case, all the skill in the ensemble mean comes from external conditions, as the ensemble members' internal variability are not in phase with each other. Their decadal prediction system has higher skill in predicting 5 year mean North Atlantic TC frequency than similar systems with either random initial conditions or forced with persisted SST (see Figure 18.13). In this system, the source of most of the skill in the tropical North Atlantic comes from influence of remote regions (tropical Pacific and North Atlantic), as shown in Figure 18.14.

More recently, *Vecchi et al.* [2013b] examined retrospective forecasts of multiyear North Atlantic TC frequency using a dynamical-statistical system based on prediction systems that use initialized and noninitialized conditions. Similarly to *Smith et al.* [2010], the 5 year mean showed significant correlation when compared with the null hypothesis of a zero correlation. The correlations increase when using the ensemble of two models and by using a lagged-ensemble approach, in which past forecasts are used to augment the effective ensemble size.

Decadal variability in TC activity has been discussed not only in the North Atlantic, but in other regions as well. However, due to the short record of reliable observations in most regions, the results of these analyses need to be interpreted with caution. There are various studies analyzing the decadal variability of TC activity in the western North Pacific with a few of them identifying a modulation of intense typhoon occurrence and typhoon tracks by the PDV [*Ho et al.*, 2004; *Chan*, 2005, Chan, 2008; *Liu and Chan*, 2008]. Interestingly *Matsuura et al.* [2003] and *Yumoto et al.* [2003] could reproduce the mechanism of decadal variability in the typhoon activity using a high-resolution coupled atmospheric-ocean model. More recently, initialized experiments with high-resolution coupled atmospheric-ocean model successfully simulated the predictability of the SST in the Pacific, including the PDV [*Mochizuki et al.*, 2010] and the shifts from positive to negative phases of the PDV, which are associated with typhoon frequency changes in the region [*Chikamoto et al.*, 2012].

These encouraging results from decadal systems should be taken carefully. As discussed in *Vecchi et al.*

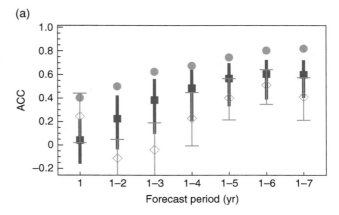

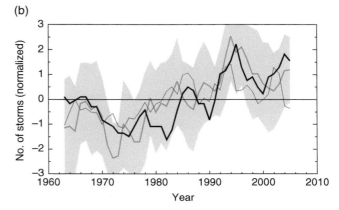

Figure 18.13 Multiannual hindcasts of Atlantic tropical storm frequency. (a) Anomaly correlation (ACC) for predictions of the number of Atlantic tropical storms for increasing forecast periods. Forecast period "1" is the first hurricane season (months 8–13 from November hindcasts), and "1–7" is the average of years 1–7 inclusive. Initialized predictions (red circles) are compared with externally forced (blue squares) and persistence (green diamonds), with the blue and green bars indicating the 5–95% confidence interval in which differences in skill from the initialized system are not significant. (b) Observed (black curve) and predicted with initialized system (red curve with gray shading showing the 5–95% confidence interval) normalized 5 year rolling mean number of Atlantic storms forming in the region 0°–25°N. Figure originally from *Smith et al.* [2010].

[2013b], the skill of the multiyear forecasts arise, in large part, from the persistence of the PDV phase in the initialized forecasts, rather than predicting its evolution per se. Furthermore, the experiments were performed for a relatively short period and there is a strong correlation of the time series, which could inflate the potential skill of these forecasts [*Vecchi et al.*, 2013b]. Another issue that was raised by *Vecchi et al.* [2013b] was the potential impact of changing of observing systems for the ocean and the atmosphere in the forecast system.

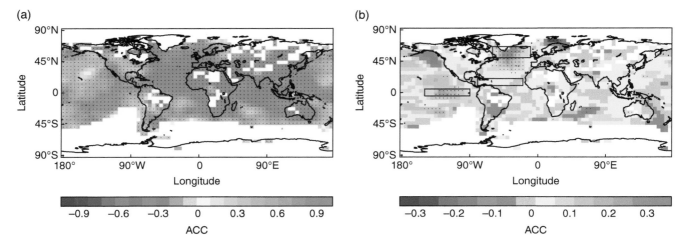

Figure 18.14 Skill and impact of initialization for 5 year mean surface temperature. (a) Anomaly correlation between predicted 5 year mean June–November surface temperature with initialized system and observations. Anomalies are relative to the 30 year mean preceding each hindcast period start date. (b) Anomaly correlation of the initialized system minus the random initialized system. Each 5° pixel represents the surrounding 15° region. The rectangles in (b) show the hurricane MDR, the subpolar gyre and the ENSO Nino3 region. Stippling denotes differences between initialized prediction and climatology (a) and the noninitialized system (b) exceeding the 5–95% confidence interval. Figure originally from *Smith et al.* [2010].

18.5. ANTHROPOGENIC CLIMATE CHANGE

The increased hurricane activity in the North Atlantic since the late 1990s has brought attention to TC variability in decadal timescales (10–30 years). While some attribute this increase to natural climate variability [*Goldenberg et al.*, 2001], there has been increased awareness of the important role of atmospheric aerosols in the variability of Atlantic TC activity in the last decades as well [*Mann and Emanuel*, 2006; *Evan et al.*, 2009]. Therefore it is fundamental to understand the role of both anthropogenic and natural variability in TC activity when discussing regional and global TC trends [*Camargo et al.*, 2013].

The impact of climate change in TC activity has been extensively examined. Due to the importance of the topic and the huge number of papers in the literature, review papers appear periodically, for example, *Henderson-Sellers et al.* [1998], *Walsh* [2004], and *Walsh et al.* [2009]. Two very recent comprehensive reviews of the literature in this topic were published recently [*Knutson et al.*, 2010a, 2010b].

Therefore, here we will summarize the main conclusions in these reviews and focus our discussion on modeling results that appeared after they were published.

There are two different issues that have been considered regarding changes in TC activity due to climate change. The first is the detection of long-term changes in the storm characteristics in the current observed record. The second is the projection of changes for future climates.

Given the large fluctuations in global TC frequency and intensity, the detection and attribution of changes

due to anthropogenic greenhouse gases forcing is very difficult. Furthermore, observational records of TC activity have well-known quality and availability issues [*Vecchi and Knutson*, 2008; *Landsea et al.*, 2010], which makes the detection of statistically significant small trends very problematic. When one considers an estimate for the missing hurricanes in the observed North Atlantic database, the trend in Atlantic hurricane frequency is not significant [*Vecchi and Knutson*, 2011]. These North Atlantic database issues are very important for short-duration storms (2 days or less); therefore when analyzing trends in TC frequency, short-lived storms should not be included in the analysis [*Villarini et al.*, 2011].

Emanuel [2005] associated recent trends (last 30 years) in Atlantic and western North Pacific power dissipation index (PDI; time integrated cube of estimated maximum wind speed) with trends in tropical SST. Similarly, *Webster et al.* [2005] found an increase of the proportion of storms reaching categories 4 and 5 in various regions. However, *Landsea et al.* [2006] pointed out problems with the intensity data in the early part of the record, which could be responsible for that trend. Some of these issues were addressed in a revised analysis in *Emanuel* [2007], the PDI in the North Atlantic and western North Pacific 20th century trends are shown in Figure 18.15. *Emanuel* [2007] attributed the increasing North Atlantic trend to decreasing vertical shear and increasing low-level vorticity and potential intensity in the same period. However, in the case of the western North Pacific, *Chan* [2006] attributed the increase in intensity typhoons to decadal variability. Another important point is

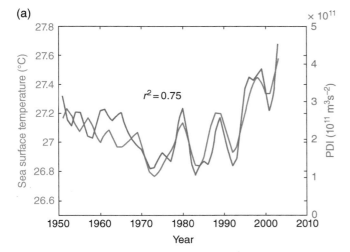

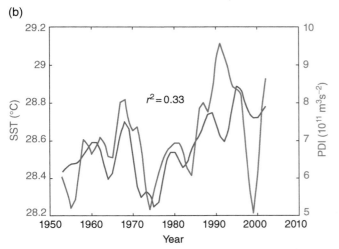

Figure 18.15 Power dissipation index (PDI, green) and scaled SST (blue) for the main development regions of the (a) North Atlantic and (b) western North Pacific. The time series have been smoothed using a filter to reduce the effect of interannual variability and highlight fluctuations on timescales if 3 years and longer. Figure originally from *Emanuel* [2007].

that if only the PDI for U.S. storms is considered, there is no significant trend in the historical record [*Landsea*, 2005]. Given the lack of consensus regarding the causes for the recent warming in the Atlantic Ocean (decadal variability or anthropogenic change), the attribution of the recent trend in the North Atlantic TC activity remains controversial [*Kunkel et al.*, 2013]. *Weinkle et al.* [2012] showed that there are no trends, globally or in individual basins, in the frequency and intensity of landfalling TCs with hurricane intensity of either minor (categories 1 and 2) or major (categories 3–5) strength. In contrast, *Chen et al.* [2011] observed a trend in the duration of a landfalling TCs while over land in China due to an increased survival time over land in the last 35 years.

More recently, a significant decrease in TC activity in the northern hemisphere was noticed, using ACE (accumulated cyclone energy time integrated square of estimated maximum wind speed) as measure of activity [*Maue*, 2009, 2011]. The decrease in the North Pacific TC activity was related to the PDV, and the known anti-correlation between the eastern North Pacific and North Atlantic is very clear in the last decade [*Frank and Young*, 2007], with the contribution of the North Atlantic ACE to the northern hemisphere ACE significantly increasing since 1995. An examination of the 20th century trend in Atlantic TC activity used storm surge statistics from tide gauges [*Grinsted et al.*, 2013]. A relationship between a surge index and landfalling TCs was obtained and a statistically significant positive trend was detected. However, it should be pointed though that winter storms also cause storm surge and that the record starts in a period of low TC activity.

It is interesting to note that the trend in North Atlantic tropical PI in the last few years is much larger than the trend of the local PI, which is actually relevant for Atlantic storms [*Kossin and Camargo*, 2009]. *Emanuel et al.* [2013] argued that the cooling near the tropical tropopause and associated decrease in TC outflow contributed to the observed increase in Atlantic PI since 1980, with the NCEP/NCAR reanalysis overestimating the cooling and therefore the increase in PI. The uncertainties in historical upper troposphere and tropical tropopause layer temperature trends are very large and could have important implications in our current understanding of the impacts of climate on TC activity [*Vecchi et al.*, 2013a].

Going beyond observed trends, TC intensity theory predicts that in a warmer world, intense TCs will occur more frequently [*Emanuel*, 1987; *Holland*, 1997]. TC maximum intensity is sensitive to SST, atmospheric temperatures, and humidity, which will all be increasing with global warming. Modeling studies support this theoretical result [*Knutson and Tuleya*, 2004; *Bender et al.*, 2010].

Projections of 21st century TC activity have been performed using various models and scenarios. A detailed summary of the model results appeared in *Knutson et al.* [2010a, 2010b]. Robust projections among a large array of models exist for global changes TC characteristics only: a slight reduction of TC global frequency and a small increase in the percentage of the most intense storms are expected by the end of the 21st century. Regional projections and other information about TC characteristics in TC activity in the future are still uncertain, as they are not robust across models. Even these global projections only became robust in the last few years due to increased computer capabilities available for modeling groups, which made it possible to have long climate simulations using high-resolution (50 km or less) climate models. It should be noted though that the magnitude of these changes frequency and intensity changes vary among these high-resolution models. The expected globally averaged intensity increases by 2100 are in the range of 2–11%, while the globally averaged frequency of storms is expected to reduce by 6–34% [*Knutson et al.*, 2010a]. The high-resolution models also project increased precipitation rate associated with the storms in the order of 20% [*Knutson et al.*, 2010a].

Murakami and Sugi [2010] examined the effect of model resolution on TC projections using one climate model in various horizontal resolutions. Overall, the simulations with high-resolution models are more realistic and reliable. Projections of changes in TC intensity could only be detected in the simulations with resolution of 60 km or higher. Furthermore, the geographical location of TCs is not expected to have significant changes in the future, although the SST threshold for deep tropical convection is projected to shift in a warming climate, there will not be an expansion of the regions with occurrence of deep tropical convection [*Evans and Waters*, 2012].

Ideally, in order to obtain statistically robust results, we would like to examine TCs in simulations spanning many years and scenarios. Even though the modeling community has made significant progress in this direction, simulating the most intense TCs with climate models is still challenging

and very few modeling groups have resources to do that. For instance, in the last CMIP5, only a couple of model groups have been able to do the long simulations of various future scenarios, as well as the present climate using high-resolution models. In most cases, the TC activity in these models is not very realistic in the present climate due to the low-resolution used [*Camargo*, 2013]. Therefore, in order to obtain long simulations of TC activity a strategy widely used is downscaling.

Dynamical downscaling with regional climate models has been used over various regions. For instance, recently, *Lavender and Walsh* [2011] focused on the Australian region using a regional climate model with 15 km resolution and obtained a 30% reduction of storms in that region by the end of the 21st century. *Bender et al.* [2010] used a complementary strategy: they downscaled each individual storm present in the regional climate model simulations of the North Atlantic [18 km resolution; *Knutson et al.*, 2008] using operational hurricane models. They obtained a doubling in category 4 and 5 storms by the end of the 21st century, despite the overall decrease in TC frequency in the region forced with 18 global climate-change projections (see Figure 18.16). *Zhao and Held*

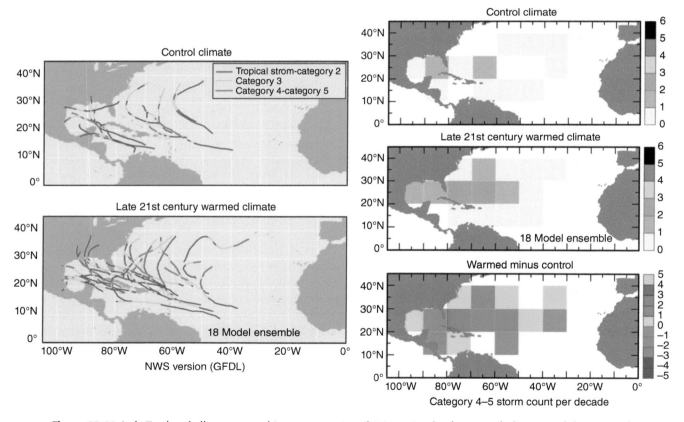

Figure 18.16 Left: Tracks of all storms reaching category 4 and 5 intensity, for the control climate and the warmed 18-model ensemble mean conditions using a hurricane model. Right: The spatial distribution of category 4 and 5 occurrences (scaled per storm counts per decade) for the control climate (top right), the combined warmed climate (middle right) and their difference (bottom right). Figure originally from *Bender et al.* [2010].

[2010] used a simple statistical refinement model to represent the strongest storms, which their global climate model with 50 km resolution cannot reproduce. They obtained an increase in storm maximum wind speed of 5–10 m/s for storms with intensities in the range of 30–60 m/s in 21st century.

An alternative method to downscale TCs from climate models generates a set of synthetic storm tracks using the large-scale circulation of the model. Then, a coupled ocean-atmospheric hurricane model is run for each track to determine the intensity of the storm, using the atmospheric and oceanic conditions of the climate model [*Emanuel*, 2006; *Emanuel et al.*, 2006]. Using this technique, TC activity in present and climate models can be generated and their characteristics compared. In *Emanuel et al.* [2010], a comparison of a very high-resolution global climate model (14 km) explicitly simulated TC activity and downscaled using the synthetic tracks technique was done. While in both cases an increase in the high-intensity storm occurs globally, the two methods disagree in the response of weaker storms to climate change, as well as in the response of storms in regional scales. The global warming effects on U.S. hurricane damage was examined using this synthetic storm technique, with increase damage occurring with global warming on timescales of 40 years or longer and increased probabilities of damage appearing in timescales as short as 25 years [*Emanuel*, 2011].

Another method to downscale TC activity is to use a statistical-dynamical approach, using the environmental fields of the climate models in statistical models. *Villarini and Vecchi* [2012] examined 21st-century projections of North Atlantic TC activity using SST, specifically tropical Atlantic SST, and mean tropical SST of the CMIP5 dataset as predictors of a simple statistical model for the number of Atlantic tropical storms using three different future scenarios, as shown in Figure 18.17. Their results show that in the first half of the 21st century, radiative forcing changes (probably aerosols) lead to an increase in the number of North Atlantic-named storms. However, trends over the entire 21st century are ambiguous and they attributed the uncertainties to the radiative forcing climate response, as well as the chaotic nature of the climate system.

There has been a significant effort to obtain robust projections of TC activity under climate-change scenarios. A few significant changes are expected: a small reduction in the global number of TCs, an increase in the percentage in the most intense storms, and the precipitation (mean and peak) associated with TCs. However, the projections are not yet robust for more regional analysis, as well as many other characteristics of future TC activity such as tracks and landfall frequency. We expect a continuous effort in improving future projections of TC activity under climate change in the next decade.

18.6. QUANTIFIED SOCIOECONOMIC IMPACTS

The socioeconomic impact of TCs can be decomposed into TC's *direct impact*, namely the physical damage and mortality that is induced immediately by the storm, and various *secondary impacts* that arise after the storm has passed. These indirect impacts of a storm emerge from the human reaction to a TC's direct impacts. For example, an individual may work less if their place of employment is destroyed in a TC, resulting in a low income. Firms, policymakers, and the media frequently focus on the direct impact of storms, since total mortality or insured losses are easy to observe; however a major contribution of academic research has been to demonstrate that many indirect impacts are large, often rivaling, and occasionally dwarfing, the more easily observed direct impacts of a TC. Here we describe some of the recent progress in systematically measuring both the direct and secondary impacts of TCs. Numerous case studies and qualitative studies provide detailed insights into the detailed mechanisms and contexts that contribute to these TC impacts, however we focus here on quantified patterns that are broadly consistent across numerous TC events.

18.6.1. Conceptual Framework

The general framework for quantitative studies of TC impact is the *dose-response* approach, commonly used in public health. The idea is to model the social *response* as a function of the "TC-*dosage*" that a population is exposed to. The social response that is modeled could be either a direct impact of TCs, such as total mortality, or an indirect impact, such as lost earnings.

The typical study attempts to recover the *dose-response function* $\mathbf{f}(.)$ where

$$\text{Social\_impact} = \mathbf{f}(\text{tropical\_cyclone\_incidence}) + \text{error} \quad (18.1)$$

using observed data when the form of $\mathbf{f}(.)$ is unknown. In general, this is accomplished by using multivariate statistical methods that regress social outcomes on measures of TC incidence, while controlling for the many factors that might influence the social outcome measure, such as a population's average income level, the political context, trends in forecast technology, or measures of the local cyclone climate. For a general discussion of the statistical techniques used in this kind of causal inference, we refer readers to *Freedman* [2009], *Angrist and Pischke* [2008], and *Wooldridge* [2001].

The systematic study of TC's indirect impacts arose in the social sciences relatively recently, so there is not

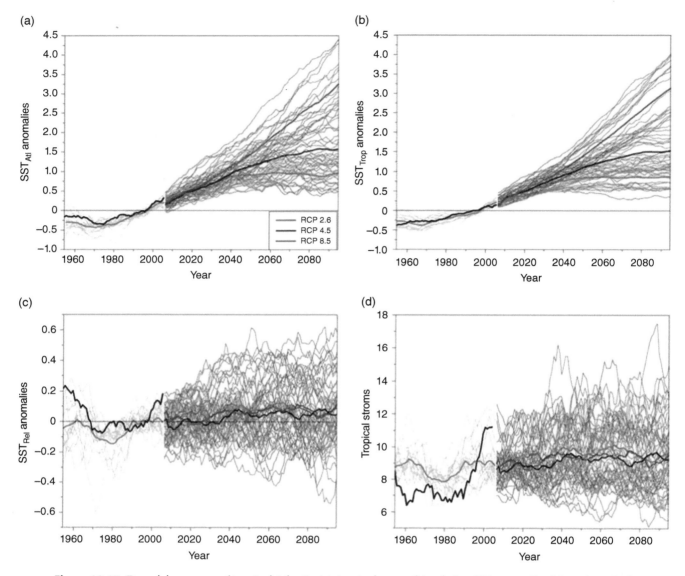

Figure 18.17 Decadal averages of tropical Atlantic (a), tropical mean (b), relative SST anomalies (c), and tropical storm projections (d) from 17 global climate models under the CMIP5 for three future scenarios (RCP2.6, RCP4.5, and RCP8.5). The thicker lines represent the mean for each scenario. The light gray lines (1950–2005) describe the historical simulations for the 17 global climate models, and the black lines the observations. The SST anomalies are computed over June–November with respect to 1986–2005; seasonal tropical storm frequency is derived with the statistical model of *Villarini et al.* [2010]. Figure originally from *Villarini and Vecchi* [2012].

yet an established technique for parameterizing *tropical-cyclone-incidence* in Equation 18.1. For example, several studies define a variable as either zero or one, depending on whether the eye of a storm passed over a given location, or they parameterize the intensity of a population's exposure using the maximum wind speed at landfall on the coast, regardless of the population's distance from the location of landfall. In both cases, these measures only coarsely describe what a population experiences during its exposure to a TC because

these approaches do not distinguish between strong and weaker levels of TC exposure. However, these measures are often sufficient for demonstrating that TC's have a causal effect on a particular outcome. Unfortunately, parameter estimates from these studies are context-specific because they lack a generalizable and physically based measure of exposure, so results from these studies are difficult to apply out of sample and are thus less informative for projections of impacts under climate change.

To produce an estimate of Equation 18.1 that is generalizable across locations and that can be projected into the future, it must describe the relationship between scale-invariant intensive variables that are independent of context and the scale at which social outcomes are aggregated. To achieve this, some researchers have moved toward using scale-invariant, physically based reconstructions of TC exposure, such as maximum experienced wind speed or cumulative energy dissipation at a location [*Sparks et al.*, 1994; *Hsiang*, 2010; *Anttila-Hughes and Hsiang*, 2013; *Strobl*, 2011; *Hsiang and Narita*, 2012; *Hsiang and Jina*, 2014]. These physically based metrics of TC exposure are more difficult to compute, but they allow researchers to recover how social outcomes at an arbitrarily small location (e.g., mortality risk at a pixel) respond to physical events at that specific location (in contrast to events at landfall, for example). Figure 18.18 displays an example of how location-specific wind exposure is computed in a recent study [*Hsiang and Jina*, 2014]. In theory, this approach will enable accurate climate change projections, although to date, projections of future outcomes have not yet utilized these scale-invariant analyses and instead rely on the properties of TCs at landfall.

An additional benefit of using scale-invariant variables is that point-specific relationships should be comparable across studies, allowing for cross-study validation and comparisons of results across contexts: for example, estimates of Equation 18.1 can be compared across countries of different geographical sizes if the specified relationship and defined variables are independent of geographical scales. Although in practise, only a few results can be quantitatively compared to one another because TC incidence is generally not parameterized in scale-invariant and physically comparable units throughout most of the literature. For further discussion of scale-invariant variables and their usage in this context, see *Hsiang and Narita* [2012] and *Hsiang and Jina* [2014].

18.6.2. Direct Impacts

The direct impacts of a TC are the losses that are suffered contemporaneous with a population's exposure to the physical TC event. Damage to public infrastructure, private assets, and immediate physical injury or loss of life are all direct impacts.

18.6.2.1. Physical Damage

It is obvious to even a casual observer that TCs cause physical damage, yet systematically quantifying this damage in the framework of Equation 18.1 is essential to the design of risk management strategies. The central challenge for researchers trying to recover this "dose-response" relationship is linking data on physical damage to data on physical exposure to a storm. *Sparks et al.*

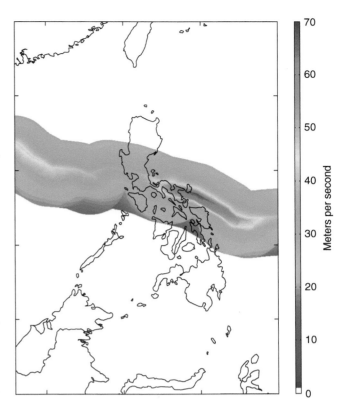

Figure 18.18 An example of how Best Track observations [*Knapp et al.*, 2010] are transformed into physically based and scale-invariant measures of human exposure to TCs. Maximum wind speed exposure at the surface in Super Typhoon Joan (Sening) over the Philippines (October 1970) computed with the Limited Information Cyclone Reconstruction and Integration for Climate and Economics (LICRICE) developed by *Hsiang* [2010]. Wind speed exposure is averaged over pixels, usually with area-weights, and used in Equation 18.1. To ensure that pixel-specific responses are recovered, the outcome variable (left-hand side of Equation 18.1) must be transformed so f(.) is linear [*Hsiang and Jina*, 2012]. Figure from *Hsiang and Jina* [2012].

[1994] matched detailed data on insured losses in South Carolina and Florida counties during Hurricanes Hugo (1989) and Andrew (1992) to estimates of wind exposure from reconnaissance aircraft flying through the storm. Sparks et al. demonstrated that damage to the individual exterior components of homes (e.g., the roof) tended to rise linearly with wind speed 0.13 percentage points per 1 m/s above a critical threshold (55 m/s), however total damage to a household's assets rose rapidly once the protective exterior envelope of a home was compromised, allowing water to enter and cause additional damage to its contents. Sparks et al. also showed that the distribution of damages, conditional on wind exposure, tended to follow a Poisson distribution with a rate parameter that increased with wind speed: a finding that suggests that the probability an individual asset is lost remains constant for each incremental period of exposure. *Anttila-Hughes and Hsiang* [2013] expand this approach to a new context by linking TC wind exposure to household surveys of assets in the Philippines (1985–2000), finding that household's report conspicuously lower rates of ownership for various durable assets (e.g., walls, toilets) just after their exposure to a TC. Anttila-Hughes and Hsiang assume that these missing assets are lost to TCs and estimate that the loss probability rises linearly by roughly 0.11 and 0.16 percentage points, for walls and toilets, respectively, per 1 m/s.

Huang et al. [2001] revisit the data of Sparks et al. to estimate how *total* insured damage rises with wind exposure and find that the increase in total losses, as a fraction of total insured value, increases exponentially with wind speed (measured in m/s):

$$\Pr(\text{loss}) = \frac{\text{Total insured loss}}{\text{Total insured value}} \propto e^{0.25 \times \text{wind\_speed}}$$

(18.2)

implying that losses rise 29% for each 1 m/s increase in maximum wind speed. This exponential increase in loss probability is more nonlinear than the roughly linear increase observed for individual components, a fact that the authors suggest is due to the loss of building contents that may occur after a building's envelope is breached. *Hsiang and Narita* [2012] extend this approach globally by linking total capital damages in the International Disaster Database [EM-DAT; *Guha-Sapir et al.*, 2015] to every TC in the IBTrACs archive [*Knapp et al.*, 2010]. Hsiang and Narita verify that the total reported damages at the national level, normalized by Gross Domestic Product [GDP; *Pielke Jr. et al.*, 2008], also rise exponentially with wind exposure (Figure 18.19).

Although they simultaneously examine all countries in the world, they find that the average rate at which damages increase with wind speed is somewhat lower than in Equation 18.2:

$$\Pr(\text{loss}) \approx \frac{\text{Total reported national loss}}{\text{Gross domestic product}} \propto e^{0.10 \times \text{wind\_speed}}.$$

(18.3)

However, when Hsiang and Narita account for global patterns of adaptations (see Section 18.6.3.5) they estimate that expected losses in a country with the cyclone risk, similar to that of the United States, should be proportional to $e^{0.10 \times \text{wind\_speed}}$, coming closer to Equation 18.2.

It remains unknown why total losses should be exponential in wind speed, while the probability that individual component failures are linear in wind speed. It is likely that individual component failures interact, for example, the failure of a roof may make the loss of a wall more

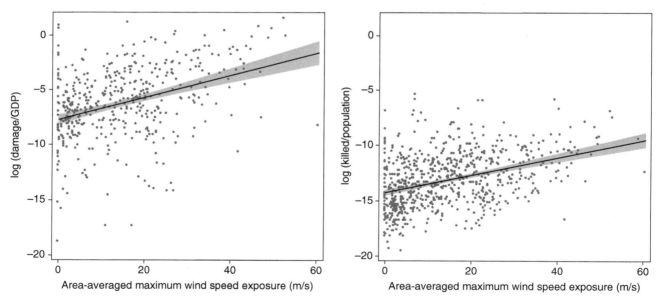

Figure 18.19 The global risk of direct loss conditional on TC wind exposure (1950–2008). Each observation is a county during 1 year when either economic damages or mortality are reported in the International Disaster Database (EM-DAT). The natural logarithm of damages/GDP (left) and killed/population (right) are plotted against maximum wind exposure (area-averaged across all pixels in a country). Regression lines are ordinary least squares with 95% confidence intervals. Reproduced using data from *Hsiang and Narita* [2012].

likely, causing total losses to climb nonlinearly. However, even if component failures are highly correlated, the empirically estimated failure rates [*Sparks et al.*, 1994; *Anttila-Hughes and Hsiang*, 2013] are not large enough to generate the observed nonlinearity [*Huang et al.*, 2001; *Hsiang and Narita*, 2012]. An alternative explanation may be that reports of total losses have high rates of human error or other biases that cause them to climb rapidly with TC intensity. For example, large storms may attract more media attention and thus greater scrutiny from government or private damage assessors. To our knowledge, these potential reporting biases are unexplored in the literature.

Nordhaus [2010] models total direct losses for the United States (1900–2008) as a function of wind speed at landfall, rather than the actual wind speed that populations are exposed to. Assuming that $f(.)$ from Equation 18.1 is a power-function of wind speed at landfall, Nordhaus uses estimates that

$$\Pr(\text{loss}) \approx \frac{\text{Total reported national loss}}{\text{Gross domestic product}}$$
$$\propto \text{wind\_speed\_at\_landfall}^9 \qquad (18.4)$$

Nordhaus calls the exponent of nine a "super-elasticity" because it is much higher than the value of 3 that is suggested by physical theory. *Mendelsohn et al.* [2012] replicate these results using a similar approach and similar data (1960–2009). Both Nordhaus and Mendelsohn et al. note these results as remarkable but do not explain why such a nonlinear result is physically justifiable, why a power-function is assumed, or how these results can be reconciled with the above results. However, reexamination of Nordhaus's data reveals that an exponential function similar to (18.3) fits the data equally as well as (18.4) while providing results that are more consistent with physics. Reanalysis of Nordhaus's data suggest that expected losses in the United States are proportional to $e^{0.11 \times \text{wind\_speed at landfall}}$, a finding that appears to be broadly consistent with results in Equations 18.2 and 18.3.

These and other empirical estimates, as well as wind tunnel experiments, are used to develop detailed simulations of TC impacts on buildings and other structures. Some simulations are probabilistic, specifying the joint distribution for the likelihood that different building components fail [*Pinelli et al.*, 2004], or they may be based on physical models of building structures [*Vickery et al.*, 2006]. Increasingly complex simulations contain greater detail and allow us to better understand the damage-generating process during TCs: for example, simulations that permit the components of multiple buildings to interact with one another during a simulated TC demonstrate the importance of wind-blown debris for causing damage [*Yau et al.*, 2011]. These modeling studies must explicitly simulate the different sensitivities of specific types of infrastructure (e.g., buildings vs. roads) and specific components of this infrastructure (e.g., roofs vs. windows) to TC exposure, however the large-scale statistical studies discussed earlier are generally unable to measure these differences systematically (Anttila-Hughes and Hsiang is an exception) and we expect future research to move in this direction.

These estimates have also been used to make projections of direct TC damages under anthropogenic warming [*Narita et al.*, 2009; *Nordhaus*, 2010; *Crompton et al.*, 2011; *Mendelsohn et al.*, 2012]. This is accomplished by linking an empirically estimated dose-response function similar to Equation 18.4 to a physical simulation of future TC exposure with and without anthropogenic forcing. Annual damages are computed for both simulated future trajectories and their difference is interpreted as expected additional direct damages that are attributable to anthropogenic climate forcing. However, to date this approach has only used a response function estimated with U.S. data (Eq. 18.4), which is then extrapolated globally: estimates using global data (Eq. 18.3) have not yet been developed. *Pielke Jr. and Landsea* [1998] and *Pielke Jr. et al.* [2008] take a different approach and examined historical damage data in the United States (1925–1995 and 1900–2005, respectively) to determine if an anthropogenic signal is apparent in historical damage trends. They find that there is no obvious long-term trend in direct TC damages once the total number of exposed assets is accounted for, a correction that follows directly from the Poisson-like distribution of component failure under uniform TC stress [*Sparks et al.*, 1994]. Refer to the Special Report on Managing the Risks of Extreme Events and Disasters [*IPCC*, 2012] for a discussion of historical trends in TC damages.

18.6.2.2. Mortality

Although widely reported by the media following TCs, mortality is not widely examined in the framework of Equation 18.1. To our knowledge, *Hsiang and Narita* [2012] is the only study to systematically evaluate mortality rates as a function of TC exposure. Following a similar approach to their analysis of physical damage, Hsiang and Narita find that globally, average mortality rates over a location also increase exponentially with wind speeds averaged over that location

$$\Pr(\text{death}) = \frac{\text{Total reported national mortality}}{\text{Total population}}$$
$$\propto e^{0.06 \times \text{wind\_speed}} \qquad (18.5)$$

although mortality increases more gradually with wind speed, rising 6% for each additional 1 m/s of wind exposure rather than the 10% per m/s rise in damages (see Figure 18.19). Importantly, this result is obtained without accounting for the physical properties of storms other than wind speed, such as the depth of flooding or the height of the storm surge, which are known to influence mortality. To the extent that these other factors are correlated with surface wind exposure, their influence will be described by Equation 18.2 where wind speed behaves as a proxy measure. Future work should develop independent datasets of these other physical processes to measure the extent to which their incidence is correlated with wind exposure and to quantify their influence on mortality.

Multiple studies have examined the socioeconomic determinants of mortality, although not all of these analyses account for the physical intensity of storm exposure. At the national level, average national income (GDP) is a strong and robust predictor of baseline mortality rates [*Kahn*, 2005; *Shultz et al.*, 2005; *Hsiang and Narita*, 2012; *Peduzzi et al.*, 2012], although it is not established whether income itself is the key determinant of risk or if some other factor that is correlated with income matters more, with income playing the role of proxy for this other factor. For example, infrastructure quality, average education levels, and government institutions are all correlated with income and are thought to influence mortality risk. Furthermore, case studies suggest that access to hardened (e.g., concrete) shelters and the presence of effective early warning systems, factors that are likely to be influenced but not fully determined by a population's income, are key determinates of whether individuals survive TC exposure [*Bern et al.*, 1993; *Shultz et al.*, 2005]. Aggregated country-level data suggests that, taken together, these types of protective investments are collectively effective. For example, *Hsiang and Narita* [2012] find that when two populations are exposed to physically similar TCs, mortality is lower in the country that is exposed to intense TCs more often. This result is consistent with the notion that populations exposed to greater TC risk invest more of their available resources to protect themselves and that these investments are effective (see Section 18.6.3.5).

18.6.3. Secondary Impacts

The secondary impacts of a TC are the losses that are suffered substantially after a population's physical exposure to a TC event stops. Lost income, unemployment, migration, political actions, and health impacts are all secondary impacts. Many of these secondary impacts arise because populations make adjustments to their behavior and economic decisions that compensate for the direct impact of a TC. Economic theory predicts that many of these secondary impacts should occur, such as changes in income, as price signals in different markets help restore the economy to a "general equilibrium"

[*Narita et al.*, 2009], although some secondary responses, such as relief aid, are more difficult to predict based on standard theory because they occur outside of formal markets.

18.6.3.1. Regional Income Losses and Economic Development

Concurrent with exposure to a TC, "business interruption" prevents populations from earning some fraction of immediate income. The cost of this interruption is usually included in estimates of total damages (Section 18.6.2.1) and is not itself a focus of research. However, loss of unearned income that accrues during the years following a TC is studied in a small but growing literature.

In general, the central challenge for this literature is to identify income that is never earned but would have been earned had a population escaped TC exposure. This task is difficult because, unlike physical damages or mortality, unearned income cannot be observed directly. Instead, these studies must reconstruct a counterfactual income trajectory that exposed populations would have followed in the absence of TC exposure. To accomplish this, researchers match the income trajectories of exposed populations to those of similar but unexposed populations, and then measure how the two differ. This procedure is complicated by the fact that no two populations are perfectly identical, so multivariate statistical models are used to correct for both observable and unobservable characteristics of both exposed and unexposed populations [*Wooldridge*, 2001; *Angrist and Pischke*, 2008; *Freedman*, 2009].

Early work by *Noy* [2009] on the immediate impact of natural hazards (including but not limited to TCs) found that disasters with large physical damages were associated with a significant decline in national income growth the year that the disaster occurred [also see *Loayza et al.*, 2009]. However, when Noy specifically examines the effect of TC wind speed at landfall, there is no discernible effect. A possible explanation for this inconsistency is the coarse nature of Noy's exposure measure, which has physically different implications for countries of different sizes and geographies: a Category 1 storm making landfall on a small island, like Jamaica, is not directly comparable to a Category 1 landfall for a large continental country, like the United States. In the former case, most of the country's population, capital and infrastructure will be exposed to intense winds, whereas only a fraction is exposed in the latter case.

To adjust for this, *Hsiang* [2010] developed a "power dissipation density index" that measures the amount of energy that a TC dissipates in a country per unit area of that country. This statistic is a scale-invariant intensive variable, so it is independent of country size while accounting for the trajectory and duration of a country's

TC exposure. Following the framework of Equation 18.1, Hsiang applies this approach to time series of per capita incomes in 28 Caribbean-basin countries (1970–2006) and finds

$$\underset{\propto\ e^{-0.03\times \text{power\_dissipation\_density\_index}}}{\text{Total GDP per capita}} \qquad (18.6)$$

where power dissipation is measured in standardized units. Equation 18.6 indicates that for every standard deviation increase in TC energy dissipation, average income temporarily falls by 0.3%. Equation 18.6 describes average effects on a country's entire economy, however responses in specific industries may be substantially larger in magnitude: income in *wholesale, retail, restaurants and hotels* temporarily declines by 0.9%, income in *agriculture, hunting and fishing* falls by 1.9%, and income in *mining and utilities* shrinks by 0.9%. These results are consistent with the decline in tourism revenue arising from a reduction in total visitors to these countries [*Hsiang*, 2010] as well as patterns of crop damage that has been observed in Japan [*Masutomi et al.*, 2012] and the United States [*Attaway*, 1999]. In contrast to these declines, Hsiang finds that income in construction industries rises by 1.4% for 2 years following TC exposure (see Figure 18.20).

Anttila-Hughes and Hsiang [2013] utilize a similar approach to examine the effect of TCs on household income in Philippine provinces. Anttila-Hughes and

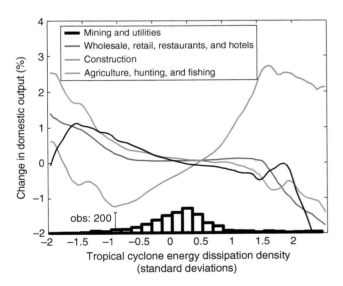

Figure 18.20 The average effect of TC exposure on national economic output in 28 countries in the Caribbean and Central America. Changes are relative to country-specific trends. Regression lines are nonparametric fits to the data and the histogram displays the distribution of the underlying data. From *Hsiang* [2010].

Hsiang find robust evidence that households' total income falls by 0.4% on average for each additional 1 m/s in wind exposure. This income loss is present across almost all industries (including construction) and, because of the Philippines intense TC climatology, amounts to an average income loss of 6.6% per year. Consistent with the patterns described in Section 18.6.2.2, these losses tend to be larger for low-income households.

Strobl [2011] and *Deryugina* [2013] examine income responses in coastal counties of the United States during 1970–2005 and 1980–1996, respectively. Following an approach similar to *Hsiang* [2010], Strobl finds that average income in a county declines: 0.5% for each standard deviation increase in TC energy exposure.

Deryugina models storm exposure as a binary event, instead of indexing events by wind speed, and finds that short-run average earnings rise by 0.6% in counties exposed to an average TC event, but these results that are not themselves statistically significant and are not statistically different from the analogous: 0.5% effect obtained by Strobl. In contrast to *Hsiang* [2010], which found that construction output in Caribbean-basin countries grew following TC events, Deryugina finds that construction output in United States counties falls after TCs.

The above studies focus on "short-run" losses that emerge in the year of TC exposure or in the few years that immediately follow. *Raddatz* [2009] proposed that "long-run" losses appearing many years after a TC might differ from these short-run effects. Unfortunately, similar to *Noy* [2009], Raddatz did not use a physical measure of storm exposure and could not recover evidence of a positive, null, or negative effect of TCs on long-run income. *Cavallo et al.* [2010] adopted a different statistical approach but used similar data and also could not determine whether long-run TC impacts exist. *Hsiang and Jina* [2014] then applied a physical model of wind speed exposure [following *Hsiang*, 2010] and were able to recover a large and statistically precise measure of TCs' long-run impact on national incomes. Hsiang and Jina find that globally, increasing a country's area-average wind speed exposure by 1 m/s linearly reduces national incomes by 0.37% two decades later. For levels of TC exposure measured at the 90th percentile, this amounts to a long-run loss of 7.4% of per capita income.

18.6.3.2. Employment, Wages and Migration

The changes in regional income described in the previous section arise from changes in large-scale patterns of economic activity. At the individual level, these large-scale patterns manifest as changes in the living conditions and economic opportunity for individuals and families. If economic output declines in the wake of a TC, it may be because either wages or employment is falling, or both. These declines in economic opportunity might cause

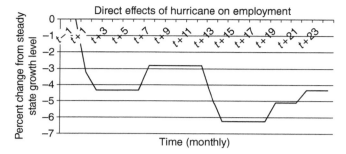

Figure 18.21 Average effects of a TC on employment in directly exposed Florida counties (1988–2005) over the 24 months following the TC strike. Changes are relative to country-specific trends. From *Belasen and Polachek* [2009].

some individuals to move, migrate, which may indirectly affect economic conditions in both the source and sink locations. If migrants bring with them valuable assets and skills, this will change the overall composition of both communities. In addition, the movement of workers to or from a community changes the nature of competition within the local workforce, raising wages, or employment in the case of worker out-migration and lowering wages or employment in the case of in-migration. Because changes in employment, wages, and migration may all affect one another, it is helpful to consider them as a system of interacting variables, rather than as independent responses to TCs.

In an early study, *Smith et al.* [2006] demonstrated that in the wake of Hurricane Andrew, a statistically significant fraction of middle-income households moved away from heavily damaged areas of Florida, presumably because they had the resources to do so, whereas low-income households moved into heavily damaged areas. Smith et al. demonstrate that the rental value of homes in heavily damaged locations declines, which they argue reflects falling living conditions [see also *Hallstrom and Smith*, 2005], encouraging the inward migration of low-income households. *Belasen and Polachek* [2008] and *Belasen and Polachek* [2009] studied employment and wage responses to TCs in Florida counties during 1988–2005, they found that employment rates fell on average in directly affected counties (Figure 18.21) but that per-worker wages rose slightly. This finding is consistent with the outmigration of workers and reduced competition among workers following lowered living conditions and reductions in economic output. Belasen and Polachek's second finding was that per-worker earnings in nearby but unaffected counties fall, with no significant change in employment rates, further supports this interpretation. Together, these results suggest that while workers leaving TC-affected counties may lower competition in the labor market of the county they leave, they raise competition within the neighboring counties that they move into.

Vigdor [2008] and *McComb et al.* [2011] also obtained similar results in their case studies of Hurricane Katrina's impact.

Deryugina [2013] and *Strobl* [2011] extend these analyses outside of Florida to all coastal counties in the United States. Deryugina does not find that the total population of counties exposed to a TC changes on average, but observes that the fraction of individuals younger than 20 years old gradually increases after a TC, while the fraction of senior citizens declines slowly. Strobl also finds evidence of migration into and out of counties affected by TCs, with those leaving a county having slightly higher average income than those entering. Deryugina also finds evidence that total federal unemployment benefits flowing into a county increases after a TC, indirectly suggesting that employment declines. Overall, both of these studies generally agree with *Smith et al.* [2006] and *Belasen and Polachek* [2008, 2009], extending their results beyond Florida to the rest of the United States.

Unfortunately, little is known about the TC response of employment, wages, and migration outside of the United States, since it tends to be more difficult to obtain detailed data on these measures in other TC-prone contexts. Migration and labor-market responses to TCs may differ substantially in contexts where labor-mobility is low or the geographical size of countries is small, relative to the size of TCs (e.g., island countries): in both of these cases, migration away from TC-affected areas may be more difficult or impossible, causing labor-market dynamics to differ from those characterized within the United States.

18.6.3.3. Transfers, Relief Aid, and Political Economy
Following TC exposure, relief aid or other types of support are often provided to affected populations. The transfer of assets from unaffected populations to affected populations is an important way that the cost of TC exposure is shared across large numbers of individuals, so understanding the scale and scope of these transfers is central to understanding the impact of TCs on the broader population.

Yang [2008] examined transfers between countries in the wake of TCs and found that when a TC strikes a developing country, official development assistance from developed countries and lending from multilateral institutions increase in the 3 years following exposure. Yang also finds that when the poorest developing countries (below median) are exposed to a TC, there is a substantial increase in the volume of migrant remittances that flow into the affected country, indicating that private transfers play an important role in sharing TC risk within populations of very low income. *Deryugina* [2013] examines transfers in the United States and finds that following an average TC, transfers of wealth through the public social safety net ($654 per capita in present discounted value) are almost twice as large as transfers through relief agencies ($356) and much larger than transfers from private insurance companies ($37). Because these nondisaster transfer payments have not previously been identified as a response to TCs, these results indicate that economic losses to TCs and their costs to an average American taxpayer are substantially larger than previously thought.

Because the supply of relief aid is usually an ad hoc process driven by government leaders, it is possible for two physically similar TC events to receive different amounts of aid. *Garrett and Sobel* [2003] show that in the United States, the allocation of relief aid (for all natural hazards) is partially influenced by political concerns: disaster declarations by the president are more likely in states that are politically important, and total expenditures are higher in states whose representatives oversee Federal Emergency Management Agency (FEMA). *Healy and Malhotra* [2009] demonstrate that this behavior may be rational for self-interested politicians since voters are more like to vote for an incumbent if postdisaster relief spending is abnormally high during the incumbent's previous term. *Viscusi and Zeckhauser* [2006] examine whether Americans think individuals other than themselves deserve governmental assistance after a disaster and find that support for disaster relief is lower among voters facing low personal risk and self-identified Republicans.

In a situation where the exposed population does not vote for leaders supplying relief, *Eisensee and Strömberg* [2007] examine international relief supplied by the United States and show that the availability of public news about a disaster is an important predictor of whether or not the United States supplies aid. Expanding on this approach, *Strömberg* [2007] studies the quantity of bilateral relief provided between pairs of countries in a global dataset and notes that disaster relief flows are also higher if an exposed country is a former colony, if it shares a common language with the donor country, if the geographical distance between the two countries is small, if they are strong trading partners, and if they are allies in the United Nations.

18.6.3.4. Health

The direct effect of TC exposure on mortality and injury is clearly a health issue, however there are additional health impacts that arise as secondary responses to TCs long after physical exposure to the TC event ends. In some cases, this is caused by the mechanical processes of the storm, such as the destruction of infrastructure or flooding: for example, cholera outbreaks following TC-induced flooding is frequently reported in regions that rely on surface waters and possess limited sanitation infrastructure [*Chhotray et al.*, 2002; *Bhunia and Ghosh*, 2011]. In other cases, the influence is through more subtle

mechanisms: *Currie and Rossin-Slater* [2012] show that mothers in Texas (1996–2008) who are affected by hurricanes during pregnancy are more likely to have complications with the delivery of their child, something which the authors suggest occurs because maternal stress during TC exposure may affect the health of the fetus.

The direct impacts may also translate into secondary health impacts through the reactions of people to a TC's aftermath: *Anttila-Hughes and Hsiang* [2013] show that in the Philippines (1979–2008), after households lose assets and income to TCs, they compensate by reducing spending on health care and nutritious foods and as a result infant mortality rises in the year after TC exposure. Roughly half of the infants that die in association with TC exposure are not yet conceived at the time the household is exposed to a TC, and mortality is focused among female infants in households where these infants must compete with older siblings for household resources, implicating household decision-making as a mediating mechanism. This Philippine example clearly illustrates the importance of secondary health impacts when considering the overall impact of a TC, as the surge in infant mortality exceeds official reports for direct mortality suffered during the storm by a factor of 15.

18.6.3.5. Learning and Adaptation

After experiencing exposure to a TC, populations learn more about the TC impacts that they experience and sometimes incorporate this new information into their actions. For example, the National Flood Insurance Program (NFIP) arose as a response to direct damage in TC-related floods and is designed to limit the extent of secondary impacts. Following unprecedented losses during Hurricane Katrina, the United States learned how the design of the NFIP and similar programs can be improved to further reduce risk [*Kunreuther and Michel-Kerjan*, 2011; *Michel-Kerjan*, 2010]. Tropical cyclone forecasts produced by government agencies, firms, and research centers are another form of adaptation that is widely utilized by policymakers, firms, and households, with individuals gradually learning how to incorporate imperfect forecast information into their decision making [*Emanuel et al.*, 2012; *Kelly et al.*, 2012]. Some types of learning and adaptation may be subconscious or unintentional, for example *Cameron and Shah* [2012] find that individuals in Indonesia who were recently exposed to natural hazards exhibit less risky behavior; and *Das and Vincent* [2009] find that the preservation of mangroves in India had the unintended benefit of reducing TC mortality.

These and other examples [see *Kousky*, 2012 for a review] indicate there are a large number of actions that individuals and communities take to reduce their risk from TCs; however, it is difficult to measure the overall effect that these numerous actions have on overall levels of risk within a society, particularly when many actions are taken privately and are not observable. To address this, *Hsiang and Narita* [2012] propose a method for empirically measuring the cumulative effectiveness of all adaptive actions without directly observing these numerous individual decisions: they measure the overall sensitivity of populations to TC exposure (Eq. 18.1) and examine whether different populations are more or less sensitive when they are exposed to physically similar TC events. Hsiang and Narita find that populations with more TC experience, that is, populations with intense TC climatologies, suffer lower direct damages and lower mortality per metre per second of wind exposure than similar populations with less TC experience. *Anttila-Hughes and Hsiang* [2013] and *Hsiang and Jina* [2014] apply this approach and replicate these results in alternative contexts.

Hsiang and Narita develop a simple decision-theory model to explain this result. Populations choose to make protective investments, such as developing early warning systems or building cyclone shelters, if the benefits of these investments outweigh their costs. The *costs* of these investments, regardless of whether they are private or public, are incurred before storms arrive and are not affected by the local TC climatology: for example, the cost of elevating a coastal home 2 m above the ground (to protect it from a TC storm surge) does not depend on the local risk of TC strikes. However, the *benefits* from these investments only emerge when the population making these investments is exposed to an actual TC: in the example, the contents of an elevated home might survive the storm surge of a TC that would destroy the contents of a normal home. Thus, in locations with higher TC risks, the benefits from adaptive investments are higher, but the costs remain the same. This causes populations in higher-risk climates to have a higher ratio of benefits to costs for the same protective investment, leading them to invest more in protection. Because these high-risk populations have invested more in protection, we observe their losses to be lower when they are exposed to actual TC events.

18.7. CONCLUSIONS

In this review, we give an overview of the state of the art of relationship of TC activity and climate in various timescales, from intraseasonal to climate change. In the last few years a significant improvement in the representation of TCs in climate models occurred, due to increased availability of powerful computers, which allowed the modeling groups to do long climate simulations with high-resolution climate models. As a consequence, many modeling groups started to analyze the characteristics of their TC simulations in various timescales, with varying

success. We expect that this trend will continue, and that in the near future skillful forecasts of intraseasonal and seasonal TC activity will be available. As these forecasts improve, hopefully coastal communities could better prepare for TC impacts. On longer timescales, infrastructure and planning could be influenced by decadal TC variability as well a possible changes in TC activity in a warmer climate.

In parallel to advances in modeling the physical dynamics of TCs, the last decade has seen several advances in the detection, measurement, and modeling of their social and economic impact. Expanding access to large datasets and the computing power needed to analyze them, in conjunction with growing support for the study of coupled human and natural systems, has accelerated the rate at which new TC impacts are explored, identified, and measured using quantitative methods. Because this vein of inquiry is young and complex societies possess many dimensions, there currently exist only a handful of studies that examine any particular type of social outcome. However, these small clusters of studies tend to suggest a similar storyline: the social and economic impact of TCs extends well beyond the commonly cited tallies of immediate physical damage and mortality, as large and important as those numbers are. We expect that future research will continue to use statistical inference to uncover previously unmeasured TC impacts, these impacts will be incorporated into dynamic economic models, and these models will in turn be linked to physical projections of TC activity under future climate changes. Our rational management of current and future TC risk must leverage policies and institutions, such as insurance systems and infrastructure investments, whose efficacy and value can only be determined through continued, systematic evaluation of TC's social cost.

GLOSSARY

AMM	Atlantic Meridional Mode
AMV	Atlantic Multidecadal Variability also known as AMO
AMO	Atlantic Multidecadal Oscillation
ASO	August to October
CM2.1	Climate Model version 2.1
CMIP5	5th Coupled Model Intercomparison Project
CSF	Climate Forecast System
ECMWF	European Centre for Medium Range Weather Forecasts
EM-DAT	International Disaster Database
ENSO	El Niño-Southern Oscillation
FEMA	Federal Emergency Management Agency
FSU	Florida State University

GEM	Global Environmental Multiscale Model
GFDL	Geophysics Fluid Dynamics Laboratory
GPD	Gross Domestic Product per capita
GPI	Genesis Potential Index
HadGEM1	Hadley Center Global Environmental Model Version 1
HiRAM	High-resolution Atmospheric Model
IBTrACS	International Best Track Archive for Climate Stewardship
IPCC-AR5	Intergovernmental Panel on Climate Change Assessment Report 5
IRI	International Research Institute for Climate and Society
ITCZ	Inter-Tropical Convergence Zone
JFM	January to March
MDR	Main Development Region
MJO	Madden–Julian Oscillation
NCEP	National Centers for Environmental Prediction
NFIP	National Flood Insurance Program
NICAM	Nonhydrostatic Icosahedral Atmospheric Model
OLR	Outgoing Long-Wave Radiation
PDV	Pacific Decadal Variability
QBO	Quasi-biennial Oscillation
SST	Sea Surface Temperature
TC	Tropical Cyclone
TCGI	Tropical Cyclone Genesis Index
U.K. Met Office	United Kingdom Meteorological Office (National Weather Service)
U.S.	United States

REFERENCES

Aiyyer, A. and J. Molinari (2003), Evolution of mixed Rossby-gravity waves in MJO type environments, *J. Atmos. Sci.*, *60*, 2837–2855.

Aiyyer, A. and J. Molinari (2008), MJO and tropical cyclogenesis in the Gulf of Mexico and eastern Pacific: Case study and idealized numerical modeling, *J. Atmos. Sci.*, *65*, 2691–2704.

Anderson, D., T. Stockdale, M. Balmaseda, L. Ferranti, F. Vitart, F. Molteni, F. Doblas-Reyes, K. Mogensen, and A. Vidard (2007), Development of the ECMWF seasonal forecast system-3, ECMWF Technical Memorandum, No. 503, pp. 56.

Angrist, J. D. and A. B. Krueger (1999), Empirical strategies in labor economics, in *Handbook of Labor Economics*, vol. *3*, pp. 1277–1366, Elsevier, New York.

Angrist, J. D. and J. S. Pischke (2008), *Mostly Harmless Econometrics: An Empiricist's Companion*, Princeton University Press, Princeton, NJ.

Angrist, J. D. and J.S. Pischke (2010), The credibility revolution in empirical economics: How better research design is taking the con out of econometrics, NBER Working Paper 15794, National Bureau of Economic Research.

Anttila-Hughes, J. K. and S. M. Hsiang (2013), Destruction, disinvestment, and death: Economic and human losses following environmental disaster. http://ssrn.com/abstract=2220501 (accessed 10 September 2015).

Arpe, K. and S. A. G. Leroy (2009), Atlantic hurricanes – Testing impacts of local SSTs, ENSO, stratospheric QBO – Implications for global warming, *Quat. Int.*, *195*, 4–14.

Arribas, A., M. Glover, A. Maidens, K. Peterson, M. Gordon, C. MacLachlan, R. Graham, D. Fereday, J. Camp, A. A. Scaife, P. Xavier, P. McLean, A. Colman, and S. Cusack (2011), The GloSea4 ensemble prediction system for seasonal forecasting, *Mon. Weather Rev.*, *139*, 1891–1910.

Attaway, J. (1999), *Hurricanes and Florida agriculture*, Florida Science Source, Lake Alfred, FL.

Au-Yeung, A. Y. M. and J. C. L. Chan (2012), Potential use of a regional climate model in seasonal tropical cyclone activity predictions in the western North Pacific, *Clim. Dyn.*, *39*, 783–794.

Balachandran, S. and P. Guhathakurta (1999), On the influence of QBO over North Indian Ocean and depression tracks, *Meteor. Atmos. Phys.*, *70*, 111–118.

Baldwin, M. P., L. J. Gray, T. J. Dunkerton, K. Hamilton, P. H. Haynes, W. J. Randel, J. R. Holton, M. J. Alexander, I. Hirota, T. Horinouchi, D. B. A. Jones, J. S. Kinnersley, C. Marquardart, K. Sato, and M. Takahashi (2001), The quasi-biennial oscillation, *Rev. Geophys.*, *39*, 179–229.

Barnston, A. G., H. M. van den Dool, S. E. Zebiak, T. P. Barnett, M. Ji, D. R. Rodenhuis, M. A. Cane, A. Leetmaa, N. E. Graham, C. F. Ropelewski, V. E. Kousky, E. A. O'Lenic, and R. E. Livezey (1994), Long-lead seasonal forecasts—Where do we stand?, *Bull. Am. Meteorol. Soc.*, *75*, 2097–2114.

Barnston, A. G., S. J. Mason, L. Goddard, D. G. deWitt, and S. E. Zebiak (2003), Increased automation and use of multi-model ensembling in seasonal climate forecasting at the IRI, *Bull. Am. Meteorol. Soc.*, *84*, 1783–1796.

Barnston, A. G., M. K. Tippett, M. L. L'Heureux, S. Li, and D. G. deWitt (2012), Skill of real- time seasonal ENSO model predictions during 2002–2011: Is our capability increasing?, *Bull. Am. Meteorol. Soc.*, *93*, 631–651.

Barrett, B. S. and L. M. Leslie (2009), Links between tropical cyclone activity and Madden–Julian Oscillation phase in the North Atlantic and Northeast Pacific basins, *Mon. Weather Rev.*, *137*, 727–744.

Basher, R. and X. Zheng (1995), Tropical cyclones in the southwest Pacific: Spatial patterns and relationships to the Southern Oscillation and sea surface temperature, *J. Clim.*, *8*, 1249–1260.

Bechtold, P., M. Kohler, T. Jung, F. Doblas-Reyes, M. Leutbecher, M. J. Rodwell, F. Vitart, and G. Balsamo (2008), Advances in simulating atmospheric variability with the ECMWF model: From synoptic to decadal time-scales, *Q. J. Roy. Meteor. Soc.*, *134*, 1337–1351.

Belanger, J. I., J. A. Curry, and P. J. Webster (2010), Predictability of North Atlantic tropical cyclone activity on intraseasonal time scales, *Mon. Weather Rev.*, *138*, 4632–4274.

Belasen, A. and S. Polachek (2008), How hurricanes affect wages and employment in local labor markets, *Am. Econ. Rev.*, *98*, 49–53.

Belasen, A. and S. Polachek (2009), How disasters affect local labor markets, *J. Hum. Resour.*, *44*, 251–276.

Bell, G. D. and M. Chelliah (2006), Leading tropical modes associated with interannual and multidecadal fluctuations in North Atlantic hurricane activity, *J. Clim.*, *19*, 590–612.

Bender, M. A., T. R. Knutson, R. E. Tuleya, J. J. Sirutis, G. A. Vecchi, S. T. Garner, and I. M. Held (2010), Modeled impact of anthropogenic warming on the frequency of intense Atlantic hurricanes, *Science*, *327*, 454–458.

Bengtsson, L., H. Böttger, and M. Kanamitsu (1982), Simulation of hurricane-type vortices in a general circulation model, *Tellus*, *34*, 440–457.

Bengtsson, L., M. Botzet, and M. Esch (1995), Hurricane-type vortices in a general circulation model, *Tellus*, *47A*, 175–196.

Bengtsson, L., M. Botzet, and M. Esch (1996), Will greenhouse gas-induced warming over the next 50 years lead to higher frequency and greater intensity of hurricanes?, *Tellus*, *48A*, 57–73.

Bengtsson, L., K. I. Hodges, and M. Esch (2007a), Tropical cyclones in a T159 resolution global climate model: Comparison with observations and re-analysis, *Tellus*, *59A*, 396–416.

Bengtsson, L., K. I. Hodges, M. Esch, N. Keenlyside, L. Kornblueh, J.-J. Luo, and T. Yamagata (2007b), How many tropical cyclones change in a warmer climate?, *Tellus*, *59A*, 539–561.

Bern, C., J. Sniezek, G. Mathbor, M. Siddiqi, C. Ronsmans, A. Chowdhury, A. Choudhury, K. Islam, M. Bennish, and E. Noji (1993), Risk factors for mortality in the Bangladesh cyclone of 1991, *Bull. World Health Organ.*, *71*, 73–78.

Bessafi, M. and M. C. Wheeler (2006), Modulation of South Indian Ocean tropical cyclones by the Madden–Julian oscillation and convectively coupled equatorial waves, *Mon. Weather Rev.*, *134*, 638–656.

Bhunia, R. and S. Ghosh (2011), Waterborne cholera outbreak following cyclone aila in sundarbans area of West Bengal, India, 2009, *Trans. R. Soc. Trop. Med. Hyg.*, *105*(4), 214–219.

Bove, M. C., J. J. O'Brien, J. B. Elsner, C. W. Landsea, and X. Niu (1998), Effect of El Niño on U.S. landfalling hurricanes, revisited, *Bull. Am. Meteorol. Soc.*, *79*, 2477–2482.

Broccoli, A. J. and S. Manabe (1990), Can existing climate models be used to study anthropogenic changes in tropical cyclone climate?, *Geophys. Res. Lett.*, *17*, 1917–1920.

Bruyère, C. L., G. J. Holland, and E. Towler (2012), Investigating the use of a genesis potential index for tropical cyclones in the North Atlantic basin, *J. Clim.*, *25*, 8611–8626.

Camargo, S. J. (2013), Global and regional aspects of tropical cyclone activity in the CMIP5 models, *J. Clim.*, *26*, 9880–9902.

Camargo, S. J. and S. E. Zebiak (2002), Improving the detection and tracking of tropical cyclones in atmospheric general circulation models, *Weather Forecast.*, *17*, 1152–1162.

Camargo, S. J. and A. H. Sobel (2004), Formation of tropical storms in an atmospheric general circulation model, *Tellus*, *56A*, 56–67.

Camargo, S. J., A. G. Barnston, and S. E. Zebiak (2005), A statistical assessment of tropical cyclone activity in atmospheric general circulation models, *Tellus*, *57A*, 589–604.

Camargo, S. J., K. A. Emanuel, and A. H. Sobel (2007a), Use of a genesis potential index to diagnose ENSO effects on tropical cyclone genesis, *J. Clim.*, *20*, 4819–4834.

Camargo, S. J., H. Li, and L. Sun (2007b), Feasibility study for downscaling seasonal tropical cyclone activity using the NCEP regional spectral model, *Int. J. Climatol.*, *27*, 311–325.

Camargo, S. J., A. G. Barnston, P. J. Klotzbach, and C. W. Landsea (2007c), Seasonal tropical cyclone forecasts, *WMO Bull.*, *56*, 297–309.

Camargo, S. J., A. W. Robertson, S. J. Gaffney, P. Smyth, and M. Ghil (2007d), Cluster analysis of typhoon tracks: Part II: Large-scale circulation and ENSO, *J. Clim.*, *20*, 3654–3676.

Camargo, S. J., A. H. Sobel, A. G. Barnston, and K. A. Emanuel (2007e), Tropical cyclone genesis potential index in climate models, *Tellus*, *59A*, 428–443.

Camargo, S. J., A. W. Robertson, A. G. Barnston, and M. Ghil (2008), Clustering of eastern North Pacific tropical cyclone tracks: ENSO and MJO effects, *Geochem. Geophys. Geosyst.*, *9*, Q06V05.

Camargo, S. J., and A. G. Barnston (2009), Experimental seasonal dynamical forecasts of tropical cyclone activity at IRI, *Weather Forecast.*, *24*, 472–491.

Camargo, S. J., M. C. Wheeler, and A. H. Sobel (2009), Diagnosis of the MJO modulation of tropical cyclogenesis using an empirical index, *J. Atmos. Sci.*, *66*, 3061–3074.

Camargo, S. J. and A. H. Sobel (2010), Revisiting the influence of the quasi-biennial oscillation on tropical cyclone activity, *J. Clim.*, *23*, 5810–5825.

Camargo, S. J., A. H. Sobel, A. G. Barnston, and P. J. Klotzbach (2010), The influence of natural climate variability, and seasonal forecasts of tropical cyclone activity, in *Global Perspectives on Tropical Cyclones, from Science to Mitigation*, World Scientific Series on Earth System Science in Asia, vol. *4*, 2nd ed., edited by J. C. L. Chan and J. D. Kepert, pp. 325–360, World Scientific, London.

Camargo, S. J., M. Ting, and Y. Kushnir (2013), Influence of local and remote SST on North Atlantic tropical cyclone potential intensity, *Clim. Dyn.*, *40*, 1515–1529.

Cameron, L. and M. Shah (2012), Risk-taking behavior in the wake of natural disasters, IZA Discussion Paper 6756, SSRN Working Paper 2157898.

Cane, M. A. (2010), Climate science: Decadal predictions in demand, *Nat. Geosci.*, *3*, 231–232.

Cane, M. A. and S. E. Zebiak (1985), A theory for El Niño and the Southern Oscillation, *Science*, *228*, 1085–1087.

Caron, L.-P., C. G. Jones, and K. Winger (2011), Impact of resolution and downscaling technique in simulating recent Atlantic tropical cyclone activity, *Clim. Dyn.*, *37*, 869–892.

Cavallo, E., S. Galiani, I. Noy, and J. Pantano (2010), *Catastrophic Natural Disasters and Economic Growth*, IDB, Washington, DC.

Chan, J. C. L. (1995), Tropical cyclone activity in the western North Pacific in relation to the stratospheric quasi-biennial oscillation, *Mon. Weather Rev.*, *123*, 2567–2571.

Chan, J. C. L. (2005), Interannual and interdecadal variations of tropical cyclone activity over the western North Pacific, *Meteorol. Atmos. Phys.*, *89*, 143–152.

Chan, J. C. L. (2006), Comment on "Changes in tropical cyclone number, duration, and intensity in a warming environment", *Science*, *311*, 1713.

Chan, J. C. L. (2008), Decadal variations of intense typhoon occurrence in the western North Pacific, *Proc. R. Meteorol. Soc. Ser. A.*, *464*, 249–272.

Chan, J. C. L., J. Shi, and C. M. Lam (1998), Seasonal forecasting of tropical cyclone activity over the western North Pacific and the South China Sea, *Weather Forecast.*, *13*, 997–1004.

Chan, J. C. L., J. E. Shi, and C. M. Lam (2001), Improvements in the seasonal forecasting of tropical cyclone activity over the western North Pacific, *Weather Forecast.*, *16*, 491–498.

Chand, S. S., and K. J. E. Walsh (2010), The influence of the Madden–Julian Oscillation on tropical cyclone activity in the Fiji region, *J. Clim.*, *23*, 868–886.

Chauvin, F., J.-F. Royer, and M. Déqué (2006), Response of hurricane-type vortices to global warming as simulated by ARPEGE-Climate at high resolution, *Clim. Dyn.*, *27*, 377–399.

Chay, K. and M. Greenstone (2003), The impact of air pollution on infant mortality: Evidence from geographic variation in pollution shocks induced by a recession, *Q. J. Econ.*, *118*, 1121–1167.

Chen, G. H. (2012), How does shifting Pacific Ocean warming modulate on tropical cyclone frequency over the South China Sea?, *J. Clim.*, *24*, 4695–4700.

Chen, G. H. and C.-Y. Tam (2010), Different impacts of Pacific Ocean warming on tropical cyclone frequency over the western North Pacific, *Geophys. Res. Lett.*, *37*, L01803.

Chen, J.-H. and S.-J. Lin (2011), The remarkable predictability of inter-annual variability of Atlantic hurricanes during the past decade, *Geophys. Res. Lett.*, *38*, L11804.

Chen, X. Y., L. G. Wu, and J. Y. Zhang (2011), Increasing duration of tropical cyclones over China, *Geophys. Res. Lett.*, *38*, L02708.

Chhotray, G., B. Pal, H. Khuntia, N. Chowdhury, S. Chakraborty, S. Yamasaki, T. Ramamurthy, Y. Takeda, S. Bhattacharya, and G. Balakrish Nair (2002), Incidence and molecular analysis of vibrio cholerae associated with cholera outbreak subsequent to the super cyclone in Orissa, India, *Epidemiol. Infect.*, *128*, 131–138.

Chikamoto, Y., M. Kimoto, M. Ishii, M. Watanabe, T. Nozowa, T. Mochizuki, H. Tatebe, T. T. Sakamoto, Y. Komuro, H. Shiogama, M. Mori, S. Yasunaka, Y. Imada, H. Koyama, M. Nozu, and F.-F. Jin (2012), Predictability of a stepwise shift in Pacific climate during the late 1990s in hindcast experiments using MIROC, *J. Meteorol. Soc. Jpn.*, *90A*, 1–21.

Crompton, R. P., R. A. Pielke Jr., and K. J. McAneney (2011), Emergence timescales for detection of anthropogenic climate change in US tropical cyclone loss data, *Environ. Res. Lett.*, *6*, 014003.

Currie, J. and M. Rossin-Slater (2012) Weathering the storm: Hurricanes and birth outcomes, NBER Working Paper 18070, National Bureau of Economic Research.

Das, S. and J. Vincent (2009), Mangroves protected villages and reduced death toll during Indian super cyclone, *Proc. Nat. Acad. Sci.*, *106*, 7357–7360.

Dee, D. P., S. M. Uppala, A. J. Simmons, P. Berrisford, P. Poli, S. Kobayashi, U. Andrea, M. A. Balmaseda, G. Balsamo, P. Bauer, P. Bechtold, A. C. M. Beljaars, L. van de Berg, J. Bidlot, N. Bormann, C. Delsol, R. Dragani, M. Fuentes, A. J. Geer, L. Haimberger, S. B. Healy, H. Hersbach, E. V. Hólm, L. Isaksen, P. Kållberg, M. Köhler, M. Matricardi, A. P. McNally, B. M. Monge-Sanz, J.-J. Morcrette, B.-P. Park, C. Peubey, P. de Rosnay, C. Tavolato, J.-N. Thépaut, and F.

Vitart (2011), The ERA-Interim reanalysis: Configuration and performance of the data assimilation system, *Q. J. Roy. Meteorol. Soc.*, *137*, 553–597.

DelSole, T. and M. K. Tippett (2009a), Average predictability time. Part I: Theory, *J. Atmos. Sci.*, *66*, 1172–1187.

DelSole, T. and M. K. Tippett (2009b), Average predictability time. Part II: Seamless diagnosis of predictability on multiple time scales, *J. Atmos. Sci.*, *66*, 1188–1204.

DelSole, T., M. K. Tippett, and J. Shukla (2011), A significant component of unforced multidecadal variability in the recent acceleration of global warming, *J. Clim.*, *24*, 909–926.

DelSole, T., X. Yang, and M. K. Tippett (2013), Is unequal weighting significantly better than equal weighting for multi-model forecasting?, *Q. J. Roy. Meteorol. Soc.*, *139*, 176–183.

Delworth, T. L., and M. E. Mann (2000), Observed and simulated multidecadal variability in the Northern Hemisphere, *Clim. Dyn.*, *16*, 661–676.

Deryugina, T. (2013), The role of transfer payments in mitigating shocks: Evidence from the impact of hurricanes, http://ssrn.com/abstract=2314663 (accessed 10 September 2015).

Deschenes, O. and M. Greenstone (2007), The economic impacts of climate change: Evidence from agricultural output and random fluctuations in weather, *Am. Econ. Rev.*, *97*, 354–385.

Eisensee, T. and D. Strömberg (2007), News droughts, news floods, and us disaster relief, *Q. J. Econ.*, *122*, 693–728.

Elsberry, R. L., M. S. Jordan, and F. Vitart (2010), Predictability of tropical cyclone events on intraseasonal timescales with the ECMWF monthly forecast model, *Asia-Pac. J. Atmos. Sci.*, *46*, 135–153.

Elsberry, R. L., M. S. Jordan, and F. Vitart (2011), Evaluation of the ECMWF 32-day ensemble predictions during the 2009 season of the western North Pacific tropical cyclone events on intraseasonal timescales. Asia-Pacific, *J. Atmos. Sci.*, *47*, 305–318.

Emanuel, K. (1987), The dependence of hurricane intensity on climate, *Nature*, *326*, 483–485.

Emanuel, K. (2005), Increasing destructiveness of tropical cyclones over the past 30 years, *Nature*, *436*, 686–688.

Emanuel, K. (2006), Climate and tropical cyclone activity: A new model downscaling approach, *J. Clim.*, *19*, 4797–4802.

Emanuel, K. (2007), Environmental factors affecting tropical cyclone power dissipation, *J. Clim.*, *20*, 5497–5509.

Emanuel, K. (2010), Tropical cyclone activity downscaled from NOAA–CIRES Reanalysis, 1908–1958, *J. Adv. Model. Earth Syst.*, *2*, doi:10.3894/JAMES.2010.2.1.

Emanuel, K. (2011), Global warming effects on U.S. hurricane damage, *Weather Clim. Soc.*, *3*, 261–268.

Emanuel, K. and D. S. Nolan (2004): Tropical cyclone activity and the global climate system, *Proceedings of the 26th AMS Conference on Hurricanes and Tropical Meteorology*, 3–7 May 2004, Miami, FL, #10A.2, pp. 240–241.

Emanuel, K., S. Ravela, E. Vivant, and C. Risi (2006), A statistical deterministic approach to hurricane risk assessment, *Bull. Am. Meteorol. Soc.*, *87*, 299–314.

Emanuel, K., K. Oouchi, M. Satoh, H. Tomita, and Y. Yamada (2010), Comparison of explicitly simulated and downscaled tropical cyclone activity in a high-resolution global climate model, *J. Adv. Model Earth Syst.*, *2*, doi:10.3894/JAMES.2010.2.9.

Emanuel, K., F. Fondriest, and J. Kossin (2012), Potential economic value of seasonal Hurricane forecasts, *Weather Climate Soc.*, *4*, 110–117.

Emanuel, K., S. Solomon, D. Folini, S. Davis, and C. Cagnazzo (2013), Influence of tropical tropopause layer cooling on Atlantic hurricane activity, *J. Clim.*, *26*, 2288–2301.

Evan, A. T., D. J. Vimont, R. Bennartz, J. P. Kossin, and A. K. Heidinger (2009), The role of aerosols in the evolution of tropical North Atlantic Ocean temperature, *Science*, *324*, 778–781.

Evans, J. L. and R. J. Allan (1992), El Niño/Southern Oscillation modification to the structure of the monsoon and tropical cyclone activity in the Australasian region, *Int. J. Climatol.*, *12*, 611–623.

Evans, J. L. and J. J. Waters (2012), Simulated relationships between sea surface temperature and tropical convection in climate models and their implications for tropical cyclone activity, *J. Clim.*, *25*, 7884–7895.

Feser, F. and H. Von Storch (2008), A dynamical downscaling study for typhoons in southeast Asia using a regional climate model, *Mon. Weather Rev.*, *5*, 1806–1815.

Folland, C. K., T. N. Palmer, and D. E. Parker (1986), Sahel rainfall and worldwide sea temperatures, *Nature*, *320*, 602–607.

Frank, W. M. and P. E. Roundy (2006), The role of tropical waves in tropical cyclogenesis, *Mon. Weather Rev.*, *134*, 2397–2417.

Frank, W. M. and G. S. Young (2007), The interannual variability of tropical cyclones, *Mon. Weather Rev.*, *135*, 3587–3598.

Freedman, D. A. (1991), Statistical models and shoe leather, *Sociol. Methodol.*, *21*, 291–313.

Freedman, D. A. (2009), *Statistical Models: Theory and Practice*, Cambridge University Press, Cambridge.

Fu, X. H. and P.-C. Hsu (2010), Extended range ensemble forecasting of tropical cyclogenesis in the northern Indian Ocean: Modulation of Madden–Julian Oscillation, *Geophys. Res. Lett.*, *38*, L15803.

Gall, J. S., I. Ginis, S.-J. Lin, T. P. Marchok, and J.-H. Chen (2011), Experimental tropical cyclone prediction using the GFDL 25-km-resolution global atmospheric model, *Weather Forecast.*, *26*, 1008–1019.

Garrett, T. and R. Sobel (2003), The political economy of FEMA disaster payments, *Econ. Inq.*, *41*, 496–509.

Greenstone, M. and T. Gayer (2009), Quasi-experimental and experimental approaches to environmental economics, *J. Environ. Econ. Manag.*, *57*, 21–44.

Goddard, L., S. J. Mason, S. E. Zebiak, C. F. Ropelewski, R. E. Basher, and M. A. Cane (2001), Current approaches to seasonal to interannual climate predictions, *Int. J. Climatol.*, *21*, 1111–1152.

Goddard, L., A. G. Barnston, and S. J. Mason (2003), Evaluation of the IRI's "Net Assessment" seasonal climate forecasts: 1997–2001, *Bull. Am. Meteorol. Soc.*, *84*, 1761–1781.

Goddard, L., J. W. Hurrell, B. P. Kirtman, J. Murphy, T. Stockdale, and C. Vera (2012), Two time scales for the price of one (almost), *Bull. Am. Meteorol. Soc.*, *93*, 621–629.

Goldenberg, S. B., C. W. Landsea, A. M. Mestas-Nuñez, and W. M. Gray (2001), The recent increase in Atlantic hurricane activity: Causes and implications, *Science*, *293*, 474–479.

Gray, W. M. (1979), *Hurricanes: Their Formation, Structure and Likely Role in the Tropical Circulation. Meteorology Over the Tropical Oceans*, Royal Meteorological Society, Bracknall.

Gray, W. M. (1984), Atlantic seasonal hurricane frequency. Part I: El Niño and 30 mb Quasi-Biennial Oscillation influences, *Mon. Weather Rev.*, *112*, 1649–1668.

Gray, W. M., J. D. Sheaffer, and C. W. Landsea (1997), Climate trends associated with multidecadal variability of Atlantic hurricane activity, in *Hurricanes: Climate and Socioeconomic Impacts*, edited by H. F. Diaz and R. S. Pulwarty, pp. 15–53, Springer-Verlag, Berlin.

Grinsted, A., J. C. Moore, and S. Jevrejeva (2013), Homogeneous record of Atlantic hurricane surge threat since 1923, *Proc. Nat. Acad. Sci.*, *110*, 5369–5373.

Guha-Sapir, D., R. Below, and Ph. Hoyois (2015), EM-DAT: The CRED/OFDA International Disaster Database, Université Catholique de Louvain, Brussels, www.emdat.be (accessed 10 September 2015).

Hall, J. D., A. J. Matthews, and D. J. Karoly (2001), The modulation of tropical cyclone activity in the Australian region by the Madden–Julian oscillation, *Mon. Weather Rev.*, *129*, 2970–2982.

Hallstrom, D. and V. Smith (2005), Market responses to hurricanes, *J. Environ. Econ. Manag.*, *50*, 541–561.

Healy, A. and N. Malhotra (2009), Myopic voters and natural disaster policy, *Am. Polit. Sci. Rev.*, *103*, 387–406.

Henderson-Sellers, A., H. Zhang, G. Berz, K. Emanuel, W. Gray, C. Landsea, G. Holland, J. Lighthill, S.-L. Shieh, P. Webster, and K. McGuffie (1998), Tropical cyclones and global climate change: A post–IPCC assessment, *Bull. Am. Meteorol. Soc.*, *79*, 19–38.

Ho, C.-H., J.-J. Baik, J.-H. Kim, D.-Y. Gong, and C.-H. Sui (2004), Interdecadal changes in summertime typhoon tracks, *J. Clim.*, *17*, 1767–1776.

Ho, C.-H., J.-H. Kim, J.-H. Jeong, and H.-S. Kim (2006), Variation of tropical cyclone activity in the South Indian Ocean: El Niño–Southern Oscillation and Madden–Julian Oscillation effects, *J. Geophys. Res.*, *111*, D22191.

Ho, C.-H., H.-S. Kim, J.-H. Leong, and S.-W. Son (2009), Influence of stratospheric Quasi-Biennial Oscillation on tropical cyclone tracks in the western North Pacific, *Geophys. Res. Lett.*, *36*, L06702.

Hodges, K. I. (1994), A general method for tracking analysis and its application to meteorological data, *Mon. Weather Rev.*, *122*, 2573–2586.

Hodges, K. I. (1995), Feature tracking on the unit sphere, *Mon. Weather Rev.*, *123*, 3458–3465.

Hodges, K. I. (1999), Adaptive constraints for feature tracking, *Mon. Weather Rev.*, *127*, 1362–1373.

Holland, G. J. (1997), The maximum potential intensity of tropical cyclones, *J. Atmos. Sci.*, *54*, 2519–2541.

Holland, P. W. (1986), Statistics and causal inference, *J. Am. Stat. Assoc.*, *81*, 945–960.

Hong, C.-C., Y.-H. Li, T. Li, and M.-Y. Lee (2011), Impacts of central Pacific and eastern Pacific El Niños on tropical cyclone tracks over the western North Pacific, *Geophys. Res. Lett.*, *38*, L16712.

Hsiang, S. (2010), Temperatures and cyclones strongly associated with economic production in the Caribbean and Central America, *Proc. Nat. Acad. Sci.*, *107*, 15367–15372.

Hsiang, S. M. and D. Narita (2012), Adaptation to cyclone risk: Evidence from the global cross-section, *Clim. Change Econ.*, *3*, 1250011-1–12500011-28.

Hsiang, S. M. and A. S. Jina (2014), The causal effect of environmental catastrophe on long-run economic growth: Evidence from 6,700 cyclones, NBER Working Paper 20352.

Huang, Z., D. Rosowsky, and P. Sparks (2001), Hurricane simulation techniques for the evaluation of wind-speeds and expected insurance losses, *J. Wind Eng. Ind. Aerodyn.*, *89*, 605–617.

Iizuka, S. and T. Matsuura (2008), ENSO and western North Pacific tropical cyclone activity simulated ina CGCM, *Clim. Dyn.*, *30*, 815–830.

Iizuka, S. and T. Matsuura (2009), Relationship between ENSO and North Atlantic tropical cyclone frequency simulated in a coupled general circulation model, in *Hurricanes and Climate Change*, edited by J. B. Elsner and T. H. Jagger, pp. 323–338, Springer, New York.

IPCC (2012), *Managing the Risks of Extreme Events and Disasters to Advance Climate Change Adaptation. A Special Report of Working Groups I and II of the Intergovernmental Panel on Climate Change*, edited by C. B. Field, V. Barros, T. F. Stocker, D. Qin, D. J. Dokken, K. L. Ebi, M. D. Mastrandrea, K. J. Mach, G.-K. Plattner, S. K. Allen, M. Tignor, and P. M. Midgley, pp. 582, Cambridge University Press, Cambridge.

Jiang, X., M. Zhao, and D. E. Waliser (2012a), Modulation of tropical cyclones over the eastern Pacific by the intraseasonal variability simulated in an AGCM, *J. Clim.*, *25*, 6524–6538.

Jiang, X. N., D. E. Waliser, D. Kim, M. Zhao, K. R. Sperber, W. F. Stern, S. D. Schubert, G. J. Zhang, W. Q. Wang, M. Khairoutdinov, R. B. Neale, and M.-I. Lee (2012b), Simulation of the intraseasonal variability over the eastern Pacific ITCZ in climate models, *Clim. Dyn.*, *39*, 617–636.

Jury, M. R. (1993), A preliminary study of climatological associations and characteristics of tropical cyclones in the SW Indian Ocean, *Meteorol. Atmos. Phys.*, *51*, 101–115.

Jury, M. R., B. Pathack, and B. Parker (1999), Climatic determinants and statistical prediction of tropical cyclone days in the Southwest Indian Ocean, *J. Clim.*, *12*, 1738–1746.

Kang, I.-S. and H.-M. Kim (2010), Assessment of MJO predictability for boreal winter with various statistical and dynamical models, *J. Clim.*, *23*, 2368–2378.

Kahn, M. E. (2005), The death toll from natural disasters: The role of income, geography, and institutions, *Rev. Econ. Stat.*, *87*, 271–284.

Keenlyside, N. S., M. Latif, J. Jungclaus, L. Kornblueh, and E. Rockner (2008), Advancing decadal-scale climate prediction in the North Atlantic sector, *Nature*, *453*, 84–88.

Kelly, D. L., D. Letson, F. Nelson, D. S. Nolan, and D. Solís (2012), Evolution of subjective hurricane risk perceptions: A Bayesian approach, *J. Econ. Behav. Organ.*, *81*, 644–663.

Kim, D., K. Sperber, W. Stern, D. Waliser, I.-S. Kang, E. Maloney, W. Wang, K. Weickmann, J. Benedict, M. Khairoutdinov, M.-I. Lee, R. Neale, M. Suarez, K. Thayer-Calder, and G. Zhang (2009a), Application of MJO simulation diagnostics to climate models, *J. Clim.*, *22*, 6413–6436.

Kim, D., A. H. Sobel, E. D. Maloney, D. M. W. Frierson, and I.-S. Kang (2011a), A systematic relationship between intra-seasonal variability and mean state bias in AGCM simulations, *J. Clim.*, *24*, 5506–5520.

Kim, D., A. H. Sobel, A. D. Del Genio, Y. Chen, S. J. Camargo, M.-S. Yao, M. Kelley, and L. Nazarenko (2012a), The tropical subseasonal variability simulated in the NASA GISS general circulation model, *J. Clim.*, *25*, 4641–4659.

Kim, H.-M., C. D. Hoyos, P. J. Webster, and I.-S. Kang (2008), Sensitivity of MJO simulation and predictability to sea surface temperature variability, *J. Clim.*, *21*, 5304–5317.

Kim, H.-M. and I.-S. Kang (2008), The impact of ocean-atmosphere coupling on the predictability of boreal summer intraseasonal oscillation, *Clim. Dyn.*, *31*, 859–870.

Kim, H.-M., P. J. Webster, and J. A. Curry (2009b), Impact of shifting patterns of Pacific Ocean warming on North Atlantic tropical cyclones, *Science*, *325*, 77–80.

Kim, H.-M. and P. J. Webster (2010), Extended-range seasonal hurricane forecast for the North Atlantic with a hybrid dynamical-statistical model, *Geophys. Res. Lett.*, *37*, L21705.

Kim, H.-M., P. J. Webster, and J. A. Curry (2011b), Modulation of North Pacific tropical cyclone activity by the three phases of ENSO, *J. Clim.*, *24*, 1839–1849.

Kim, H.-M., P. J. Webster, and J. A. Curry (2012b), Evaluation of short-term climate change prediction in multi-model CMIP5 decadal hindcasts, *Geophys. Res. Lett.*, *39*, L10701.

Klotzbach, P. J. (2007), Revised prediction of seasonal Atlantic basin tropical cyclone activity from 1 August, *Weather Forecast.*, *22*, 937–949.

Klotzbach, P. J. (2010), On the Madden–Julian Oscillation—Atlantic hurricane relationship, *J. Clim.*, *23*, 282–293.

Klotzbach, P. J. (2011a), The influence of El Niño–Southern Oscillation and the Atlantic Multi-Decadal Oscillation on Caribbean tropical cyclone activity, *J. Clim.*, *24*, 721–731.

Klotzbach, P. J. (2011b), El Niño–Southern Oscillation's impact on Atlantic basin hurricanes and U.S. landfalls, *J. Clim.*, *24*, 1252–1263.

Klotzbach, P. J. (2014), The Madden-Julian Oscillation's impacts on worldwide tropical cyclone activity, *J. Clim.*, *27*, 2317–2330.

Klotzbach, P. J. and W. M. Gray (2008), Multi-decadal variability in North Atlantic tropical cyclone activity, *J. Clim.*, *21*, 3929–3935.

Knapp, K. R., M. C. Kruk, D. H. Levinson, H. J. Diamond, and C. J. Neumann (2010), The International Best Track Archive for Climate Stewardship (IBTrACS): Unifying tropical cyclone best track data, *Bull. Am. Meteorol. Soc.*, *91*, 363–376.

Knutson, T. R. and R. E. Tuleya (2004), Increased hurricane intensities with CO2-induced warming on simulated hurricane intensity and precipitation: Sensitivity to choice of climate model and convective parametrization, *J. Clim.*, *17*, 3477–3495.

Knutson, T. R., J. J. Sirutis, S. T. Garner, G. A. Vecchi, and I. M. Held (2008), Simulated reduction in Atlantic hurricane frequency under twenty-first-century warming conditions, *Nat. Geosci.*, *1*, 359–364.

Knutson, T., C. Landsea, and K. Emanuel (2010a), Tropical cyclones and climate change: A review, in *Global Perspectives on Tropical Cyclones, from Science to Mitigation*, World Scientific Series on Earth System Science in Asia, vol. *4*, 2nd ed., edited by J. C. L. Chan and J. D. Kepert, pp. 243–284, World Scientific, London.

Knutson, T. R., J. L. McBride, J. Chan, K. Emanuel, G. Holland, C. Landsea, I. Held, J. P. Kossin, A. K. Srivastava, and M. Sugi (2010b), Tropical cyclones and climate change, *Nat. Geosci.*, *3*, 157–163.

Kossin, J. P. and D. J. Vimont (2007), A more general framework for understanding Atlantic hurricane variability and trends, *Bull. Am. Meteorol. Soc.*, *88*, 1767–1781.

Kossin, J. P. and S. J. Camargo (2009), Hurricane track variability and secular potential intensity trends, *Clim. Change*, *9*, 329–337.

Kossin, J. P., S. J. Camargo, and M. Sitkowski (2010), Climate modulation of North Atlantic hurricane tracks, *J. Clim.*, *23*, 3057–3076.

Kousky, C., 2012: Informing climate adaptation: A review of the economic costs of natural disasters, their determinants, and risk reduction options, RFF Discussion Paper, pp. 12–28.

Krishnamurti, T. N. (1988), Some recent results on numerical weather prediction over the tropics, *Aust. Meteorol. Mag.*, *36*, 141–170.

Krishnamurti, T. N., D. Oosterhof, and N. Dignon (1989), Hurricane prediction with a high resolution global model, *Mon. Weather Rev.*, *117*, 631–669.

Krishnamurti, T. N., R. Correa-Torres, M. Latif, and G. Daughenbaugh (1998), The impact of current and possibly future sea surface temperature anomalies on the frequency of Atlantic hurricanes, *Tellus*, *50A*, 186–210.

Krishnamurti, T. N., C. M. Kishtawal, T. E. LaRow, D. R. Bachiochi, Z. Zhang, C. E. Williford, S. Gadgil, and S. Surendan (1999), Improved weather and seasonal climate forecasts from a multi-model super-ensemble, *Science*, *286*, 1548–1550.

Kuleshov, Y., L. Qi, R. Fawcett, and D. Jones (2008), On tropical cyclone activity in the Southern Hemisphere: Trends and the ENSO connection, *Geophys. Res. Lett.*, *35*, L14S08.

Kunkel, K. E., T. R. Karl, H. Brooks, J. Kossin, J. H. Lawrimore, D. Arndt, L. Bosart, D. Changnon, S. L. Cutter, N. Doesken, K. Emanuel, P. Ya Groisman, R. W. Katz, T. Knutson, J. O'Brien, C. J. Paciorek, T. C. Peterson, K. Redmond, D. Robinson, J. Trapp, R. Vose, S. Weaver, M. Wehner, K. Wolter, and D. Wuebbles (2013), Monitoring and understanding trends in extreme storms: State of knowledge, *Bull. Am. Meteorol. Soc.*, *94*, 499–514.

Kunreuther, H. C. and E. O. Michel-Kerjan (2011), *At War with the Weather: Managing Large-Scale Risks in a New Era of Catastrophes*, pp. 464, MIT Press, Cambridge, MA.

Landman, W. A., A. Seth, and S. J. Camargo (2005), The effect of regional climate model domain choice on the simulation of tropical cyclone-like vortices in the Southwestern Indian Ocean, *J. Clim.*, *18*, 1253–1274.

Landsea, C. W. (2005), Meteorology: Hurricanes and global warming, *Nature*, *438*, E11–E12.

Landsea, C. W., R. A. Pielke Jr., A. M. Mesta-Nuñez, and J. A. Knaff (1999), Atlantic basin hurricanes: Indices of climatic changes, *Clim. Change*, *42*, 89–129.

Landsea, C. W., B. A. Harper, K. Horau, and J. A. Knaff (2006), Can we detect trends in extreme tropical cyclones? *Science*, *313*, 452–454.

Landsea, C. W., G. A. Vecchi, L. Bengtsson, and T. R. Knutson (2010), Impact of duration thresholds on Atlantic tropical cyclone counts, *J. Clim.*, *23*, 2508–2519.

LaRow, T. E. (2013), The impact of SST bias correction on North Atlantic hurricane retrospective forecasts, *Mon. Weather Rev.*, *141*, 490–498.

LaRow, T. E., Y.-K. Lim, D. W. Shin, E. P. Chassignet, and S. Cocke (2008), Atlantic basin seasonal hurricane simulations, *J. Clim.*, *21*, 3191–3206.

LaRow, T. E., L. Stefanova, D.-W. Shin, and S. Cocke (2010), Seasonal Atlantic tropical cyclone hindcasting/forecasting using two sea surface temperature datasets, *Geophys. Res. Lett.*, *37*, L02804.

Larson, S., S.-K. Lee, C. Z. Wang, E.-S. Chung, and D. Enfield (2012), Impacts of non-canonical El Niño patterns on Atlantic hurricane activity, *Geophys. Res. Lett.*, *39*, L14706.

Lavender, S. L. and K. J. E. Walsh (2011), Dynamically downscaled simulations of Australian region tropical cyclones in current and future climates, *Geophys. Res. Lett.*, *38*, L10705.

Lee, S.-K., C. Wang, and D. B. Enfield (2010), On the impact of central Pacific warming events on Atlantic tropical storm activity, *Geophys. Res. Lett.*, *37*, L17702.

Leroy, A. and M. C. Wheeler (2009), Statistical prediction of weekly tropical cyclone activity in the southern hemisphere, *Mon. Weather Rev.*, *136*, 3737–3654.

Li, R. C. Y., W. Zhou, J. C. L. Chan, and P. Huang (2012), Asymmetric modulation of western North Pacific cyclogenesis by the Madden–Julian Oscillation under ENSO conditions, *J. Clim.*, *25*, 5374–5385.

Liebmann, B., H. H. Hendon, and J. D. Glick (1994), The relationship between tropical cyclones of the western Pacific and Indian oceans and the Madden–Julian oscillation, *J. Meteorol. Soc. Jpn.*, *72*, 401–411.

Lin, J.-L., G. N. Kiladis, B. E. Mapes, K. M. Weickman, K. R. Sperber, W. Lin, M. C. Wheeler, S. D. Schubert, A. Del Genio, L. J. Donner, S. Emori, J.-F. Gueremy, F. Hourdin, P. J. Rasch, E. Roeckner, and J. F. Scinocca (2006), Tropical intraseasonal variability in 14 IPCC AR4 climate models. Part I: Convective Signals, *J. Clim.*, *19*, 2665–2690.

Lin, J.-L., M.-I. Lee, D. Kim, I.-S. Kang, and D. M. W. Frierson (2008), The impacts of convective parametrization and moisture triggering on AGCM-simulated convectively coupled equatorial waves, *J. Clim.*, *21*, 883–909.

Liu, K. S. and J. C. L. Chan (2008), Interdecadal variability of western North Pacific tropical cyclone tracks, *J. Clim.*, *21*, 4464–4476.

Liu, P., M. Satoh, B. Wang, H. Fudeyasu, T. Nasuno, T. Li, H. Miura, H. Taniguchi, H. Masunaga, X. Fu, and H. Annamalai (2009), An MJO simulated by the NICAM at 14- and 7-km resolutions, *Mon. Weather Rev.*, *137*, 3254–3268.

Loayza, N., E. Olaberria, J. Rigolini, and L. Christiaensen (2009), Natural disasters and growth: Going beyond the averages, World Bank Policy Research Working Paper 4980.

Madden, R. A. and P. R. Julian (1972), Description of global circulation cells in the tropics with a 40–45 day period, *J. Atmos. Sci.*, *29*, 1109–1123.

Madden, R. A. and P. R. Julian (1994), Observations of the 40–50-day tropical oscillation—A review, *Mon. Weather Rev.*, *122*, 814–837.

Manabe, S., J. L. Holloway, and H. M. Stone (1970), Tropical circulation in a time–integration of a global model atmosphere, *J. Atmos. Sci.*, *27*, 580–613.

Manganello, J. V., K. I. Hodges, J. L. Kinter, B. A. Cash, L. Marx, T. Jung, D. Achuthavarier, J. M. Adams, E. L. Altschuler, B. Huang, E. K. Jin, C. Stan, P. Towers, and N. Wedi (2012), Tropical cyclone climatology in a 10-km global atmospheric GCM: Toward weather-resolving climate modeling, *J. Clim.*, *25*, 3867–3893.

Maloney, E. D. and D. L. Hartmann (2000a), Modulation of eastern Pacific hurricanes by the Madden–Julian oscillation, *J. Clim.*, *13*, 1451–1460.

Maloney, E. D. and D. L. Hartmann (2000b), Modulation of hurricane activity in the Gulf of Mexico by the Madden–Julian oscillation, *Science*, *287*, 2002–2004.

Maloney, E. D. and D. L. Hartmann (2001), The Madden–Julian oscillation, barotropic dynamics and North Pacific tropical cyclone formation. Part I: Observations, *J. Atmos. Sci.*, *58*, 2545–2558.

Mann, M. E. and K. A. Emanuel (2006), Atlantic hurricane trends linked to climate change, *EOS Trans. Am. Geophys. Union*, *87*, 233–241.

Masutomi, Y., T. Iizumi, K. Takahashi, and M. Yokozawa (2012), Estimation of the damage area due to tropical cyclones using fragility curves for paddy rice in Japan, *Environ. Res. Lett.*, *7*, 024012, doi:10.1088/1748--9326/7/2/024012.

Matsuura, T., M. Yumoto, and S. Tizuka (2003), A mechanism of interdecadal variability of tropical cyclone activity over the western North Pacific, *Clim. Dyn.*, *21*, 105–117.

Maue, R. N. (2009), Northern hemisphere tropical cyclone activity, *Geophys. Res. Lett.*, *36*, L05805.

Maue, R. N. (2011), Recent historically low global tropical cyclone activity, *Geophys. Res. Lett.*, *38*, L14803.

McComb, R., Y. Moh, and A. Schiller (2011), Measuring long-run economic effects of natural hazard, *Nat. Hazard.*, *58*, 559–566.

McDonald, R. E., D. G. Bleaken, D. R. Cresswell, V. D. Pope, and C. A. Senior (2005), Tropical storms: Representation and diagnosis in climate models and the impacts of climate change, *Clim. Dyn.*, *25*, 19–36.

McGauley, M. G. and D. Nolan (2011), Measuring environmental favorability for tropical cyclogenesis by statistical analysis of threshold parameters, *J. Clim.*, *24*, 5698–5997.

Meehl, G. A., L. Goddard, J. Murphy, R. J. Stouffer, G. Boer, G. Danabasoglu, K. Dixon, M. A. Giorgetta, A. M. Greene, E. Hawkins, G. Hegerl, D. Karoly, N. Keenlyside, M. Kimoto, B. Kirtman, A. Navarra, R. Pulwarty, D. Smith, D. Stammer, and T. Stockdale (2009), Decadal prediction: Can it be skillful?, *Bull. Am. Meteorol. Soc.*, *90*, 1467–1485.

Mendelsohn, R., K. Emanuel, S. Chonabayashi, and L. Bakkensen (2012), The impact of climate change on global tropical cyclone damage, *Nat. Clim. Chang.*, *2*, 205–209.

Menkes, C. E., M. Lengaigne, P. Marchesiello, N. C. Jourdain, E. M. Vincent, J. Lefevre, F. Chauvin, and J.-F. Royer (2011), Comparison of tropical cyclogenesis indices on seasonal to interannual timescales, *Clim. Dyn.*, *38*, 301–321.

Michel-Kerjan, E. (2010), Catastrophe economics: The national flood insurance program, *J. Econ. Perspect.*, *24*, 165–186.

Mo, K. C. (2000), The association between intraseasonal oscillations and tropical storms in the Atlantic basin, *Mon. Weather Rev.*, *128*, 4097–4107.

Mochizuki, T., M. Ishii, M. Kimoto, Y. Chikamoto, M. Watanabe, T. Nozawa, T. T. Sakamoto, H. Shiogama, T. Awaji, N. Sigiura, T. Toyoda, S. Yasunaka, H. Tatebe, and M. Mori (2010), Pacific decadal oscillation hindcasts relevant to near-term climate prediction, *Proc. Nat. Acad. Sci.*, *107*, 1833–1837.

Molinari, J. and D. Vollaro (2000), Planetary- and synoptic-scale influences on eastern Pacific cyclogenesis, *Mon. Weather Rev.*, *128*, 3296–3307.

Molinari, J., D. Knight, M. Dickinson, D. Vollaro, and S. Skubis (1997), Potential vorticity, easterly waves, and eastern Pacific tropical cyclogenesis, *Mon. Weather Rev.*, *125*, 2699–2708.

Msadek, R., K. W. Dixon, T. L. Delworth, and W. Hurlin (2010), Assessing the predictability of the Atlantic meridional overturning circulation and associated fingerprints, *Geophys. Res. Lett.*, *37*, L19608.

Murakami, H. and M. Sugi (2010), Effect of model resolution on tropical cyclone climate projections, *SOLA*, *6*, 73–76.

Narita, D., R. S. J. Tol, and D. Anthoff (2009), Damage costs of climate change through intensification of tropical cyclone activities: An application of FUND, *Climate Res.*, *39*, 87–97.

Nakazawa, T. (1988), Tropical super clusters within intraseasonal variations over the western Pacific, *J. Meteorol. Soc. Jpn.*, *64*, 17–34.

Nguyen, K. C. and K. J. E. Walsh (2001), Interannual, decadal, and transient greenhouse simulation of tropical cyclone-like vortices in a regional climate model of the South Pacific, *J. Clim.*, *14*, 3043–3054.

Nicholls, N. (1979), A possible method for predicting seasonal tropical cyclone activity in the Australian region, *Mon. Weather Rev.*, *107*, 1221–1224.

Nicholls, N. (1984), The southern oscillation, sea-surface temperature, and interannual fluctuations in Australian tropical cyclone activity, *J. Climatol.*, *4*, 661–670.

Nicholls, N. (1985), Predictability of interannual variations of Australian seasonal tropical cyclone activity, *Mon. Weather Rev.*, *113*, 1144–1149.

Nicholls, N. (1992), Recent performance of a method for forecasting seasonal tropical cyclone activity, *Aust. Meteor. Mag.*, *40*, 105–110.

Nordhaus, W. D. (2010), The economics of hurricanes and implications of global warming, *Clim. Change Econ.*, *1*, 1, doi:10.1142/S2010007810000054.

Noy, I. (2009), The macroeconomic consequences of disasters, *J. Dev. Econ.*, *88*, 221–231.

Oouchi, K., A. T. Noda, M. Satoh, H. Miura, H. Tomita, T. Nasumo, and S.-i. Iga (2009), A simulated preconditioning of typhoon genesis controlled by a boreal summer Madden–Julian Oscillation event in a global cloud-system-resolving model, *SOLA*, *5*, 65–68.

Palmer, T. N., F. J. Doblas-Reyes, and R. Hagedorn (2004), Development of a European multimodel ensemble system for seasonal-to-interannual prediction (DEMETER), *Bull. Am. Meteorol. Soc.*, *85*, 853–872.

Peduzzi, P., B. Chatenoux, H. Dao, A. De Bono, C. Herold, J. Kossin, F. Mouton, and O. Nordbeck (2012), Global trends in tropical cyclone risk, *Nat. Clim. Chang.*, 2, 289–294.

Pielke, R. A., Jr., and C. W. Landsea (1998), Normalized Hurricane Damages in the United States: 1925–95, *Weather Forecast.*, 13, 621–631.

Pielke, R. A., Jr., and C. W. Landsea (1999), La Niña, El Niño and Atlantic hurricane damages in the United States, *Bull. Am. Meteorol. Soc.*, 80, 2027–2033.

Pielke, R. A., Jr., J. Gratz, C. W. Landsea, D. Collins, M. A. Saunders, and R. Musulin (2008), Normalized hurricane damage in the United States: 1900–2005, *Nat. Hazard. Rev.*, 9, 29–42.

Pinelli, J., E. Simiu, K. Gurley, C. Subramanian, L. Zhang, A. Cope, J. Filliben, and S. Hamid (2004), Hurricane damage prediction model for residential structures, *J. Struct. Eng.*, 130, 1685–1691.

Raddatz, C. (2009), The wrath of god: Macroeconomic costs of natural disastersm The World Bank Policy Research Working Paper Series 5039.

Ramsay, H. A., L. M. Leslie, P. J. Lamb, M. B. Richman, and M. Leplastrier (2008), Interannual variability of tropical cyclones in the Australian region: Role of large-scale environment, *J. Clim.*, 21, 1083–1103.

Ramsay, H. A., S. J. Camargo, and D. Kim (2012), Cluster analysis of tropical cyclone tracks in the southern hemisphere, *Clim. Dyn.*, 39, 897–917.

Rienecker, M. M., M. J. Suarez, R. Gelaro, R. Todling, J. Bacmeister, E. Liu, M. G. Bosilovich, S. D. Schubert, L. Takacs, G.-K. Kim, S. Bloom, J. Chen, D. Collins, A. Conaty, A. da Silva, W. Gu, J. Joiner, R. D. Koster, R. Lucchesi, A. Molod, T. Owens, S. Pawson, P. Pegion, C. R. Redder, R. Reichle, F. R. Robertson, A. G. Ruddick, M. Sienkiewicz, and J. Woollen (2011), MERRA: NASA's modern-era retrospective analysis for research and applications, *J. Clim.*, 24, 3624–3648.

Roundy, P. E. and C. J. Schreck III (2009), A combined wave-number-frequency and time- extended EOF approach for tracking the progress of modes of large-scale organized tropical convection, *Q. J. Roy. Meteorol. Soc.*, 135, 161–173.

Royer, J.-F., F. Chauvin, B. Timbal, P. Araspin, and D. Grimal (1998), A GCM study of the impact of greenhouse gas increase on the frequency of occurrence of tropical cyclones, *Clim. Change*, 38, 307–343.

Ryan, B. F., I. G. Watterson, and J. L. Evans (1992), Tropical cyclones frequencies inferred from Gray's yearly genesis parameter: Validation of GCM tropical climate, *Geophys. Res. Lett.*, 19, 1831–1834.

Schlenker, W. and M. J. Roberts (2009), Nonlinear temperature effects indicate severe damages to US crop yields under climate change, *Proc. Nat. Acad. Sci.*, 106, 15594–15598.

Schreck, C. J., J. Molinari, and K. Mohr (2011), Attributing tropical cyclogenesis to equatorial waves in the western North Pacific, *J. Atmos. Sci.*, 68, 195–209.

Schreck, C. J., J. Molinari, and A. Aiyyer (2012), A global view of equatorial waves and tropical cyclogenesis, *Mon. Weather Rev.*, 140, 774–788.

Servain, J. I., I. Wainer, J. P. McCreary, and A. Dessier (1999), Relationship between the equatorial and meridional modes of climatic variability in the tropical Atlantic, *Geophys. Res. Lett.*, 26, 485–488.

Shaman, J. and E. D. Maloney (2012), Shortcomings in climate model simulations of the ENSO-Atlantic hurricane teleconnection, *Clim. Dyn.*, 38, 1973–1988.

Shapiro, L. J. (1989), The relationship of the quasi-biennial oscillation to Atlantic tropical storm activity, *Mon. Weather Rev.*, 117, 1545–1551.

Shultz, J., J. Russell, and Z. Espinel (2005), Epidemiology of tropical cyclones: The dynamics of disaster, disease, and development, *Epidemiol. Rev.*, 27, 21–35.

Slingo, J. M., K. R. Sperber, J. S. Boyle, J.-P. Ceron, M. Dix, B. Dugas, W. Ebisuzaki, J. Fyfe, D. Gregory, J.-F. Gueremy, J. Hack, A. Harzallah, P. Inness, A. Kitoh, W. K.-M. Lau, B. McAvaney, R. Madden, A. Matthews, T. N. Palmer, C.-K. Park, D. Randall, and N. Renno (1996), Intraseasonal oscillations in 15 atmospheric general circulation models: Results from an AMIP diagnostic subproject, *Clim. Dyn.*, 12, 325–357.

Smith, D. M., S. Cusack, A. W. Colman, C. K. Folland, G. R. Harris, and J. M. Murphy (2007), Improved surface temperature prediction for the coming decade from a global climate model, *Science*, 317, 796–799.

Smith, D. M., R. Eade, N. J. Dunstone, D. Fereday, J. M. Murphy, H. Pohlmann, and A. A. Scaife (2010), Skillful multi-year predictions of Atlantic hurricane frequency, *Nat. Geosci.*, 3, 846–849.

Smith, V., J. Carbone, J. Pope, D. Hallstrom, and M. Darden (2006), Adjusting to natural disasters, *J. Risk Uncertain.*, 33, 37–54.

Sobel, A. H. and E. D. Maloney (2000), Effect of ENSO and the MJO on the western North Pacific tropical cyclones, *Geophys. Res. Lett.*, 27, 1739–1742.

Solomon, A., L. Goddard, A. Kumar, J. Carton, C. Deser, I. Fukumori, A. M. Greene, G. Hegerl, B. Kirtman, Y. Kushnir, M. Newman, D. Smith, D. Vimont, T. Delworth, G. A. Meehl, and T. Stockdale (2011), Distinguishing the roles of natural and anthropogenic forced decadal climate variability, *Bull. Am. Meteorol. Soc.*, 92, 141–156.

Sparks, P., S. Schiff, and T. Reinhold (1994), Wind damage to envelopes of houses and consequent insurance losses, *J. Wind Eng. Ind. Aerodyn.*, 53, 145–155.

Strachan, J., P. L. Vidale, K. Hodges, M. Roberts, and M.-E. Demory (2013), Investigating global tropical cyclone activity with a hierarchy of AGCMs: The role of model resolution, *J. Clim.*, 26, 133–152.

Strobl, E. (2011), The economic growth impact of hurricanes: Evidence from us coastal counties, *Rev. Econ. Stat.*, 93, 575–589.

Strömberg, D. (2007), Natural disasters, economic development, and humanitarian aid, *J. Econ. Perspect.*, 21, 199–222.

Sugi, M., A. Noda, and N. Sato (2002), Influence of global warming on tropical cyclone climatology: An experiment with the JMA global model, *J. Meteorol. Soc. Jpn.*, 80, 249–272.

Tang, B. H. and J. D. Neelin (2004), ENSO influence on Atlantic hurricanes via tropospheric warming, *Geophys. Res. Lett.*, 31, L24204.

Taylor, K. E., R. J. Stouffer, and G. A. Meehl (2012), An overview of CMIP5 and the experiment design, *Bull. Am. Meteorol. Soc.*, 93, 485–498.

Thorncroft, C. and I. Pytharoulis (2001), A dynamical approach to seasonal prediction of Atlantic tropical cyclone activity, *Weather Forecast.*, *16*, 725–734.

Ting, M., Y. Kushnir, R. Seager, and C. Li (2009), Forced and natural 20th Century SST trends in the North Atlantic, *J. Clim.*, *22*, 1469–1481.

Ting, M., Y. Kushnir, R. Seager, and C. Li (2011), Robust features of Atlantic multi-decadal variability and its climate impacts, *Geophys. Res. Lett.*, *38*, L17705.

Tippett, M. K. and A. G. Barnston (2008), Skill of multimodel ENSO probability forecasts, *Mon. Weather Rev.*, *136*, 3933–3946.

Tippett, M. K., S. J. Camargo, and A. H. Sobel (2011), A Poisson regression index for tropical cyclone genesis and the role of large-scale vorticity in genesis, *J. Clim.*, *24*, 2335–2357.

Tippett, M. K., A. G. Barnston, and S. Li (2012), Performance of recent multimodel ENSO forecasts, *J. Appl. Meteorol. Climatol.*, *51*, 637–654.

Tokioka, T., K. Yamazaki, A. Kitoh, and T. Ose (1988), The equatorial 30–60 day oscillation and the Arakawa–Schubert penetrative cumulus parametrization, *J. Meteorol. Soc. Jpn.*, *80*, 45–65.

Tory, K., S. S. Chand, R. A. Dare, and J. L. McBride (2013a), The development and assessment of a model-, grid-, and basin-independent tropical cyclone detection scheme, *J. Clim.*, *24*, 4096–4108, doi:10.1175/JCLI-D-12-00510.1.

Tory, K., S. S. Chand, R. A. Dare, and J. L. McBride (2013b), An assessment of a model-, grid-, and basin-independent tropical cyclone detection scheme in selected CMIP3 global climate models, *J. Clim.*, *26*, 5508–5522, doi:10.1175/JCLI-D-12-00511.1.

Tsutsui, J. I. and A. Kasahara (1996), Simulated tropical cyclones using the National Center for Atmospheric Research community climate model, *J. Geophys. Res.*, *101*, 15013–15032.

Uppala, S. M., P. W. Kållberg, A. J. Simmons, U. Andrae, V. da Costa Bechtold, M. Fiorino, J. K. Gibson, J. Haseler, A. Hernandez, G. A. Kelly, X. Li, K. Onogi, S. Saarinen, N. Sokka, R. P. Allan, E. Andersson, K. Arpe, M. A. Balmaseda, A. C. M. Beljaars, L. van de Berg, J. Bidlot, N. Bormann, S. Caires, F. Chevallier, A. Dethof, M. Dragosavac, M. Fisher, M. Fuentes, S. Hagemann, E. Hólm, B. J. Hoskins, L. Isaksen, P. A. E. M. Janssen, R. Jenne, A. P. McNally, J.-F. Mahfouf, J.-J. Morcrette, N. A. Rayner, R. W. Saunders, P. Simon, A. Sterl, K. E. Trenberth, A. Untch, D. Vasiljevic, P. Viterbo, and J. Woollen (2005), The ERA-40 re-analysis, *Q. J. Roy. Meteorol. Soc.*, *131*, 2961–3012.

Vecchi, G. A. and B. J. Soden (2007), Effect of remote sea surface temperature change on tropical cyclone potential intensity, *Nature*, *450*, 1066–1070.

Vecchi, G. A. and T. R. Knutson (2008), On estimates of historical North Atlantic tropical cyclone activity, *J. Clim.*, *21*, 3580–3600.

Vecchi, G. A. and T. R. Knutson (2011), Estimating annual numbers of Atlantic hurricanes missing from the HURDAT database (1878–1965) using ship track density, *J. Clim.*, *24*, 1736–1746.

Vecchi, G. A., M. Zhao, H. Wang, G. Villarini, A. Rosati, A. Kumar, I. M. Held, and R. Gudgel (2011), Statistical-dynam-ical predictions of seasonal North Atlantic Hurricane activity, *Mon. Weather Rev.*, *139*, 1070–1082.

Vecchi, G. A., S. Fueglistaler, I. M. Held, T. R. Knutson, and M. Zhao (2013a), Impacts of atmospheric temperature changes on tropical cyclone activity, *J. Clim.*, *26*, 3877–3891.

Vecchi, G. A., R. Msadek, W. Anderson, Y.-S. Chang, T. Delworth, K. Dixon, R. Gudgel, A. Rosati, W. Stern, G. Villarini, A. Wittenberg, X. Yang, F. Zeng, R. Zhang, and S. Zhang (2013b), Multi-year predictions of North Atlantic hurricane frequency: Promise and limitations, *J. Clim.*, *27*, 490–492, doi:10.1175/JCLI-D-12-00464.1.

Vickery, P., P. Skerlj, J. Lin, L. Twisdale Jr., M. Young, and F. Lavelle (2006), Hazus-mh hurricane model methodology. II: Damage and loss estimation, *Nat. Hazard. Rev.*, *7*, 94–103.

Vigdor, J. (2008), The economic aftermath of hurricane Katrina, *J. Econ. Perspect.*, *22*, 135–154.

Villarini, G., G. A. Vecchi, and J. A. Smith (2010), Modeling the dependence of tropical storm counts in the North Atlantic basin on climate indices, *Mon. Weather Rev.*, *138*, 2681–2705.

Villarini, G., G. A. Vecchi, T. R. Knutson, and J. A. Smith (2011), Is the recorded increase in short-duration North Atlantic tropical storms spurious?, *J. Geophys. Res.*, *116*, D10114.

Villarini, G. and G. A. Vecchi (2012), Twenty-first-century projections of North Atlantic tropical storms from CMIP5 models, *Nat. Clim. Chang.*, *2*, 604–607.

Vimont, D. J. and J. P. Kossin (2007), The Atlantic meridional mode and hurricane activity, *Geophys. Res. Lett.*, *34*, L07709.

Viscusi, W. and R. Zeckhauser (2006), National survey evidence on disasters and relief: Risk beliefs, self-interest, and compassion, *J. Risk Uncertain.*, *33*, 13–36.

Vitart, F. (2006), Seasonal forecasting of tropical storm frequency using a multi-model ensemble, *Q. J. Roy. Meteorol. Soc.*, *132*, 647–666.

Vitart, F. (2009), Impact of the Madden Julian Oscillation on tropical storms and risk of landfall in the ECMWF forecast system, *Geophys. Res. Lett.*, *36*, L15802.

Vitart, F., J. L. Anderson, and W. F. Stern (1997), Simulation of interannual variability of tropical storm frequency in an ensemble of GCM integrations, *J. Clim.*, *10*, 745–760.

Vitart, F. and T. N. Stockdale (2001), Seasonal forecasting of tropical storms using coupled GCM integrations, *Mon. Weather Rev.*, *129*, 2521–2537.

Vitart, F., D. Anderson, and T. Stockdale (2003), Seasonal forecasting of tropical cyclone landfall over Mozambique, *J. Clim.*, *16*, 3932–3945.

Vitart, F., M. R. Huddleston, M. Déqué, D. Peake, T. N. Palmer, T. N. Stockdale, M. K. Davey, S. Inenson, and A. Weisheimer (2007), Dynamically-based seasonal forecasts of Atlantic tropical storm activity issued in June by EUROSIP, *Geophys. Res. Lett.*, *34*, L16815, doi:10.1029/2007GL030740.

Vitart, F. and T. Jung (2010), Impact of the northern hemisphere extratropics on the skill in predicting the Madden Julian Oscillation, *Geophys. Res. Lett.*, *37*, L23805.

Vitart, F., A. Leroy, and M. C. Wheeler (2010), A comparison of dynamical and statistical predictions of weekly tropical cyclone activity in the southern hemisphere, *Mon. Weather Rev.*, *138*, 3671–3682.

Vitart, F. and F. Molteni (2010), Simulation of the Madden–Julian Oscillation and its teleconnections in the ECMWF forecast system, *Q. J. Roy. Meteorol. Soc.*, *136*, 842–855.

Walsh, K. (2004), Tropical cyclones and climate change: Unresolved issues, *Clim. Res.*, *27*, 77–83.

Walsh, K., D. Karoly, and N. Nicholls (2009), Detection and attribution of climate change effects on tropical cyclones, in *Hurricanes and Climate Change*, edited by J. B. Elsner and T. H. Jagger, pp. 1–20, Springer, New York.

Walsh, K. J., M. Fiorino, C. W. Landsea, and K. L. McInnes (2007), Objectively determined resolution-dependent threshold criteria for the detection of tropical cyclones in climate model and reanalyses, *J. Clim.*, *20*, 2307–2314.

Wang, B. and H. Rui (1990), Synoptic climatology of transient tropical intraseasonal convection anomalies: 1975–1985, *Meteorol. Atmos. Phys.*, *44*, 53–61.

Wang, C., S.-K. Lee, and D. B. Enfield (2008), Atlantic warm pool acting as a link between Atlantic Multidecadal Oscillation and Atlantic tropical cyclone activity, *Geochem. Geophys. Geosyst.*, *9*, Q05V03.

Wang, H., J.-K. Schemm, A. Kumar, W. Wang, L. Long, M. Chelliah, G. D. Bell, and P. Peng (2009), A statistical forecast model for Atlantic seasonal hurricane activity based on the NCEP dynamical seasonal forecast, *J. Clim.*, *22*, 4481–4500.

Wang, W. and M. E. Schlesinger (1999), The dependence on convection parametrization of the tropical intraseasonal oscillation simulated by the UIUC 11-layer atmospheric GCM, *J. Clim.*, *12*, 1423–1457.

Waters, J. J., J. L. Evans, and C. E. Forest (2012), Large-scale diagnostics of tropical cyclogenesis potential using environment variability metrics and logistic regression models, *J. Clim.*, *25*, 6092–6107.

Watterson, I. G., J. L. Evans, and B. F. Ryan (1995), Seasonal and inter-annual variability of tropical cyclogenesis: Diagnostics from large-scale fields, *J. Clim.*, *8*, 3052–3066.

Webster, P. J., G. J. Holland, J. A. Curry, and H.-R. Chang (2005), Changes in tropical cyclone number, duration and intensity in a warming environment, *Science*, *309*, 1844–1846.

Webster, P. J. and C. D. Hoyos (2010), Beyond the spring barrier?, *Nat. Geosci.*, *3*, 152–153.

Weinkle, J., R. Maue, and R. Pielke Jr. (2012), Historical global tropical cyclone landfalls, *J. Clim.*, *25*, 4729–4735.

Wheeler, M. C. and H. H. Hendon (2004), An all-season real-time multivariate MJO index: Development of an index for monitoring and prediction, *Mon. Weather Rev.*, *132*, 1917–1932.

Whitney, L. D. and J. Hobgood (1997), The relationship between sea surface temperature and maximum intensities of tropical cyclones in the eastern North Pacific, *J. Clim.*, *10*, 2921–2930.

Wooldridge, J. M. (2001), *Econometric Analysis of Cross Section and Panel Data*, pp. 1096, MIT Press, Cambridge, MA.

Wu, G. and N.-C. Lau (2002), A GCM simulation of the relationship between tropical–storm formation and ENSO, *Mon. Weather Rev.*, *120*, 958–977.

Xie, S.-P. and J. A. Carton (2004), Tropical Atlantic variability: Patterns, mechanisms and impacts, in *Earth's Climate: The Ocean–Atmosphere Interaction*, edited by C. Wang, S.-P. Xie, and J. A. Carton, pp. 121–142, AGU Press, Washington, DC.

Xie, L., T. Yan, and L. J. Pietrafesa (2005a), The effect of Atlantic sea surface temperature dipole mode on hurricanes: Implications for the 2004 Atlantic hurricane season, *Geophys. Res. Lett.*, *32*, L03701.

Xie, L., T. Yan, L. J. Pietrafesa, J. M. Morrison, and T. Karl (2005b), Climatology and interannual variability of North Atlantic hurricane tracks, *J. Clim.*, *18*, 5370–5381.

Yang, D. C. (2008), Coping with disaster: The impact of hurricanes on international financial flows, 1970–2002, *J. Econ. Anal. Policy*, *8*, 1–45, doi:10.2202/1935-1682.1903.

Yang, X., A. Rosati, S. Zhang, T. L. Delworth, R. G. Gudgel, R. Zhang, G. Vecchi, W. Anderson, Y.-S. Chang, T. DelSole, K. Dixon, R. Msadek, W. F. Stern, A. Wittenberg, and F. Zeng (2013), A predictable AMO-like pattern in GFDL's fully-coupled ensemble initialization and decadal forecast system, *J. Clim.*, *26*, 650–661.

Yau, S. C., N. Lin, and E. Vanmarcke (2011), Hurricane damage and loss estimation using an integrated vulnerability model, *Nat. Hazard. Rev.*, *12*, 184–189.

Yumoto, M., T. Matsuura, and S. Tizuka (2003), Interdecadal variability of tropical cyclone frequency over the western North Pacific in a high-resolution atmosphere-ocean coupled GCM, *J. Meteorol. Soc. Jpn.*, *81*, 1069–1086.

Zhang, C. (2005), Madden–Julian Oscillation, *Rev. Geophys.*, *43*, RG2003, doi:10.1029/2004RG000158.

Zhao, M., I. M. Held, S.-J. Lin, and G. A. Vecchi (2009), Simulations of global hurricane climatology, interannual variability, and response to global warming using a 50km resolution GCM, *J. Clim.*, *22*, 6653–6678.

Zhao, M. and I. M. Held (2010), An analysis of the effect of global warming on the intensity of Atlantic hurricanes using a GCM with statistical refinement, *J. Clim.*, *23*, 6382–6393.

Zhao, M., I. M. Held, and G. A. Vecchi (2010), Retrospective forecasts of the hurricane season using a global atmospheric model assuming persistence of SST anomalies, *Mon. Weather Rev.*, *138*, 3858–3868.

19

Impacts of Natural Disasters on a Dynamic Economy

Andreas Groth,[1,2] Patrice Dumas,[2,3,4] Michael Ghil,[5,6] and Stéphane Hallegatte[4,7]

ABSTRACT

This chapter presents a modeling framework for macroeconomic growth dynamics; it is motivated by recent attempts to formulate and study "integrated models" of the coupling between natural and socioeconomic phenomena. The challenge is to describe the interfaces between human activities and the functioning of the earth system. We examine the way in which this interface works in the presence of endogenous business cycle dynamics, based on a nonequilibrium dynamic model. Recent findings about the macroeconomic response to natural disasters in such a nonequilibrium setting have shown a more severe response to natural disasters during expansions than during recessions. These findings raise questions about the assessment of climate change damages or natural disaster losses that are based purely on long-term growth models. In order to compare the theoretical findings with observational data, we analyze cyclic behavior in the U.S. economy, based on multivariate singular spectrum analysis. We analyze a total of nine aggregate indicators in a 52 year interval (1954–2005) and demonstrate that the behavior of the U.S. economy changes significantly between intervals of growth and recession, with higher volatility during expansions.

[1] Department of Atmospheric & Oceanic Sciences, University of California, Los Angeles, CA, USA

[2] Environmental Research & Teaching Institute, Ecole Normale Supérieure, Paris, France

[3] Centre de coopération Internationale en Recherche Agronomique pour le Développement, Nogent-sur-Marne, France

[4] Centre International de Recherche sur l'Environnement et le Développement, Nogent-sur-Marne, France

[5] Geosciences Department, Environmental Research & Teaching Institute (CERES-ERTI), and Laboratoire de Meteorologie Dynamique (CNRS and IPSL), Ecole Normale Supérieure, Paris, France

[6] Department of Atmospheric & Oceanic Sciences and Institute of Geophysics & Planetary Physics, University of California, Los Angeles, CA, USA

[7] The World Bank, Climate Change Group, Washington, DC, USA

19.1. INTRODUCTION

The Fourth Assessment Report (AR4) of the Intergovernmental Panel on Climate Change (IPCC) [*IPCC*, 2007] provides further evidence for global warming and the significant contribution of anthropogenic greenhouse gases (GHGs) to this warming. Substantial uncertainties remain, however, regarding the degree of warming, and the part of natural variability in it. Even more controversial are the socioeconomic consequences of climate change, as well as the costs of reducing GHG emissions and of adapting to a changing climate.

There are numerous difficulties in trying to study the coupled behavior of the socioeconomic system and the climate system, each of which is highly complex and

Extreme Events: Observations, Modeling, and Economics, Geophysical Monograph 214, First Edition.
Edited by Mario Chavez, Michael Ghil, and Jaime Urrutia-Fucugauchi.
© 2016 American Geophysical Union. Published 2016 by John Wiley & Sons, Inc.

nonlinear, and possesses variability on a wide range of time and space scales. The assessment of interactions between the two systems posed a difficult organizational problem to the IPCC: socioeconomical scientists develop so-called emission scenarios that are passed on to the natural scientists to simulate climate change according to them and to derive the future range of temperature increases. The results of these future-climate simulations are then used in impact and adaptation studies to evaluate the associated damages.

Since no real feedbacks are taken into consideration in this exchange-of-information process, the IPCC requested the preparation of a new set of scenarios to facilitate future assessments of climate change. The introduction of Representative Concentration Pathways (RCPs) [*Moss et al.*, 2010] into the next Assessment Report (AR5) aims to improve the exchange of information among natural and social scientists. Although these RCPs expedite climate modeling in parallel with the development of socioeconomic and emission scenarios, the problems due to a lack of real feedbacks between the two systems, and due to lack of real communication between the research communities that study each of them separately [*Wittgenstein*, 2001; *Hillerbrand and Ghil*, 2008], persist. There are several truly coupled "integrated assessment models" [*Nordhaus and Boyer*, 1998; *Ambrosi et al.*, 2003; *Stern*, 2006], but they disregard variability and represent both climate and the economy as a succession of equilibrium states without endogenous dynamics.

The detailed dynamic modeling of the two systems is, however, still out of reach, as our understanding of the complex dynamics of either system, as well as of their coupling, is rather incomplete. For this reason, we advocate an approach based on a hierarchy of models, from simple, conceptual "toy models" all the way to complex detailed models. This approach has become fairly widespread in climate dynamics [*Ghil*, 2001; *Ghil et al.*, 2008a], and it allows us to give proper weight to the understanding of the underlying mechanisms given by the simpler models, on the one hand, and to the realism of the more detailed models, on the other hand. Modeling physicochemical, ecological, or socioeconomic processes means starting with toy models and climbing up the modeling ladder, rung by rung, toward more complex models, while always comparing the results with increasingly detailed observational data.

The work presented here describes, on the level of simple and highly idealized models, the impact of extreme climatic events on a nonequilibrium dynamic model (NEDyM) of the economy. After a brief description of the economic model and its business cycles in the next section, we consider in Section 19.3 the impact of natural disasters on this model's dynamical behavior, and present some recent results concerning a "vulnerability paradox" that arises from the presence of cyclic behavior, namely the greater impact of external shocks on a given,

out-of-equilibrium economy during expansions rather than during recessions.

This paradox suggests that a nonequilibrium version of fluctuation-dissipation theory (FDT) might be at work in such an idealized economy that possesses endogenous business cycles (EnBCs). Motivated by this conjecture and by the desire to validate the presence of EnBCs in real economies, we address in Section 19.4 the problem of extracting relevant information about business cycles from observational data. Singular spectrum analysis (SSA) is used on 52 years of U.S. economic indicators and the results appear to support the theoretical findings of phase-dependent vulnerability patterns. Finally, we conclude in Section 19.5 with a summary of results and an outlook on ongoing and future research.

19.2. BUSINESS CYCLE DYNAMICS

Ups and downs in prices and in economic activity have been discussed at least as far back as the seminal work of *Smith* [1776] and *Ricardo* [1810]. Beside a long-term upward drift, macroeconomic time series exhibit short-term fluctuations (Figure 19.1). There is a long history of attempts to study the characteristics and *stylized facts* of these fluctuations [*Burns and Mitchell*, 1946; *Kydland and*

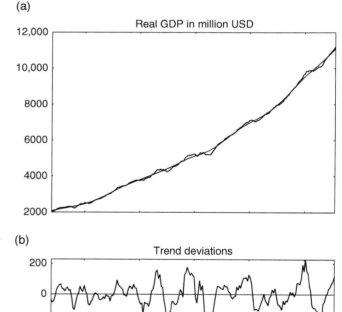

(a)

(b)

Figure 19.1 (a) Development of the real GDP in the United States (heavy curve) and a fitted trend (light curve). (b) Deviations of the GDP from the trend. The trend has been fitted using the *Hodrick and Prescott* [1997] filter with the parameter value $\lambda = 1600$.

Prescott, 1998]. To this day, the cyclic characteristics of economic behavior, referred to as business cycles, are explained by two main approaches that we briefly review in the following.

19.2.1. Real Business Cycles

The dominant approach today is known as *real business cycle (RBC)* theory and is implemented within stochastic-dynamic models called "general equilibrium models"; in this context, "real" refers to the nature of the goods involved, to distinguish them from monetary and financial aspects of the economy. RBC theory originated in the work of *Slutsky* [1927] and *Frisch* [1933], while *Kydland and Prescott* [1982] embedded this theory into the framework of general equilibrium modeling with rational expectations.

In RBC theory, it is assumed that economic fluctuations arise exclusively from exogenous shocks and that the economic system is otherwise stable, that is, that the fluctuations induced by the shocks will be damped to equilibrium. It follows that the system is entirely self-regulating and that there is no point in intervening in it.

19.2.2. Endogenous Business Cycles

The second approach is known as *endogenous business cycle (EnBC)* theory: it proposes that economic fluctuations are due to intrinsic processes that endogenously destabilize the economic system [*Kalecki* 1937; *Harrod*, 1939; *Samuelson*, 1939; *Kaldor*, 1940; *Hicks*, 1950; *Goodwin*, 1967; *Day*, 1982; *Grandmont*, 1985; *Chiarella et al.*, 2005]. These intrinsic processes may involve various instabilities and nonlinear feedbacks within the economic system itself. It follows that sociopolitical intervention might help control the mean, period, or other features of the cycles.

Both theories have their successes and shortcomings, but it is the RBC theory that garners consensus in the current economic literature.

The interplay between natural and economic variability depends to a considerable extent on the underlying economic mechanisms; therefore, overcoming the controversy between the EnBC and RBC theories could facilitate the study of interactions between the climatic and the economic system.

Exogenous shocks in real goods clearly play an important role in business cycles; for example, the strong economic expansion of the late 1990s was obviously driven by the rapid development of new technologies. Increasing interest in RBC models, since the work of *Kydland and Prescott* [1982], has led to good matches between multivariable, detailed versions of such models and actual historical data, which have been compiled and become widely available during this time interval [*King and Rebelo*, 2000].

Endogenous fluctuations, however, have their part in generating and shaping the cycles, too. Even within the neoclassical tradition, with perfect markets and rational expectations, *Day* [1982], *Grandmont* [1985], *Gale* [1973], and *Benhabib and Nishimura* [1979] proposed models in which endogenous fluctuations arise from savings behavior, wealth effects, and interest-rate movement, or from interactions between overlapping generations and between different sectors. Leading practitioners, like G. Soros, even blame the equilibrium paradigm for its role in helping bring about the current economic and financial crisis: "The currently prevailing paradigm, namely that financial markets tend towards equilibrium, is both false and misleading; our current troubles can be largely attributed to the fact that the international financial system has been developed on the basis of that paradigm" [*Soros*, 2008].

Market frictions, imperfect rationality in expectations, or aggregation biases can give rise to strongly destabilizing processes within the economic system. Numerous authors have proposed accounting for such processes and noted their importance. *Harrod* [1939] stated that the economy was unstable because of the absence of an adjustment mechanism between population growth and labor demand, although *Solow* [1956] suggested later that such a mechanism was provided by the producer's choice of the labor versus capital intensity.

Kalecki [1937] and *Samuelson* [1939] proposed simple business cycle models based on a Keynesian accelerator-multiplier effect and on delayed investing. Later on, *Kaldor* [1940], *Hicks* [1950], and *Goodwin* [1951, 1967] developed business cycle models in which the destabilizing process was still the Keynesian accelerator-multiplier, while the stabilizing processes were financial constraints, distribution of income, or the role of the reserve army of labor. In *Hahn and Solow* [1995, chapter 6], fluctuations can arise from an imperfect goods market, from frictions in the labor market, and from the interplay of irreversible investment and monopolistic competition.

EnBC theory was studied quite actively in the mid-twentieth century but much less so over the last quarter century or so. This fall from favor was due a shift toward rational expectations, that is, the assumption that all economic agents use all the available information, know perfectly the economic system, and anticipate as well as possible future economic variables [*Sargent*, 1971, 1973; *Lucas*, 1972, 1973]. In other terms, agents' predictions of the future value of all variables are not systematically biased, and all errors are random.

Still, *Hillinger* [1992], *Jarsulic* [1993], *Flaschel et al.* [1997], *Nikaido* [1996], *Chiarella and Flaschel* [2000], *Chiarella et al.* [2005], and *Hallegatte et al.* [2008], among many others, have recently proposed EnBC models and further investigated their properties. The business cycles in these models arise from nonlinear relationships between economic aggregates and are consistent with certain realistic features of actual business cycles.

Due to the relatively limited recent interest in EnBC models, less progress has been made so far in matching their results to the historical data. Even so, *Chiarella et al.* [2006] showed that their model is able to reproduce historical series when utilization data are taken as input. It is not surprising, moreover, that EnBC models with only a few state variables, typically less than a few dozen, were unable to reproduce the details of historical information that involves processes lying explicitly outside the scope of an economic model (e.g., geopolitical events).

19.2.3. EnBCs in a Nonequilibrium Model

The NEDyM of *Hallegatte et al.* [2008] is a neoclassical model with myopic expectations. Key features of the model are the adjustment delays that have been introduced into the clearing mechanisms of the labor and goods markets, as well as into the investment response to profitability signals. It is a highly idealized model that represents an economy with one producer, one consumer, and one type of goods that is used both to consume and invest.

NEDyM is based on the *Solow* [1956] model, in which all equilibrium constraints are replaced by dynamic relationships that involve adjustment delays. The model has eight state variables, which include production, capital, number of workers employed, wages, prices, inventory, liquid assets, and investment, and the evolution of these variables is modeled by a set of ordinary differential equations. In Appendix 19.A, we give a brief summary of the model equations; for a more detailed explanation, see *Hallegatte et al.* [2008].

NEDyM's main control parameter is the investment flexibility α_{inv}, which measures the adjustment speed of investments in response to profitability signals. This parameter describes how rapidly investment can react to a profitability signal: if α_{inv} is very small, investment decreases very slowly when profits are small; if α_{inv} is very large, investment soars when profits are high and collapses when profits are small. Introducing this parameter is equivalent to allocating an investment adjustment cost, as proposed by *Kydland and Prescott* [1982] and *Kimball* [1995], among others; these authors found that introducing adjustment costs and delays helps enormously in matching key features of macroeconomic models to the data.

In NEDyM, investment flexibility has a major influence on economic dynamics. For small α_{inv}, that is, slow adjustment, the model has a stable equilibrium, which has been calibrated to the economic state of the European Union (EU-15) in 2001 [*Eurostat*, 2002]. As the adjustment flexibility increases, this equilibrium loses its stability and undergoes a Hopf bifurcation, after which the model exhibits a stable periodic solution [*Hallegatte et al.*, 2008].

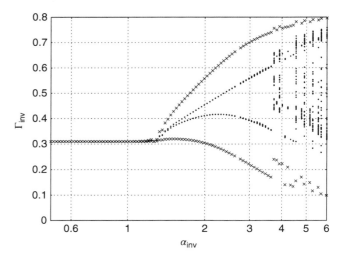

Figure 19.2 Bifurcation diagram of NEDyM, with the investment parameter α_{inv} on the abscissa and the investment ratio Γ_{inv} on the ordinate. The model has a unique, stable equilibrium for low values of α_{inv}, and the diagram shows the corresponding value of Γ_{inv}: small "x" symbols indicate, first the stable equilibrium and then the minima and maxima of the trajectory, and small dots the Poincaré intersections at $H = 0$, when the goods inventory H vanishes. With increasing α_{inv} a Hopf bifurcation at $\alpha_{inv} \approx 1.39$ leads to a limit cycle, while a transition to chaos occurs at $\alpha_{inv} \approx 3.8$.

Business cycles in NEDyM originate from the instability of the profit-investment relationship, which is quite similar to the Keynesian accelerator-multiplier effect. Furthermore, the cycles are constrained and limited in amplitude by the interplay of three processes: (1) A reserve army of labor effect, namely the increase of labor costs when the employment rate is high; (2) the inertia of production capacity; and (3) the consequent inflation in goods prices when demand increases too rapidly.

The model's bifurcation diagram is shown in Figure 19.2, here the values of the other parameters are given in table 3 of *Hallegatte et al.* [2008]. For somewhat greater investment flexibility, the model exhibits chaotic behavior, because a new constraint intervenes, namely limited investment capacity. In this chaotic regime, the cycles become quite irregular, with sharper recessions and recoveries of variable duration.

In this chapter, we concentrate, for the sake of simplicity, on model behavior in the purely periodic regime, that is, we have regular EnBCs, but no chaos. Such periodic behavior is illustrated in Figure 19.3.

The NEDyM business cycle is consistent with many stylized facts described in the macroeconomic literature, such as the phasing, or comovements of the distinct economic variables along the cycle. The model also reproduces the observed asymmetry of the cycle, with the

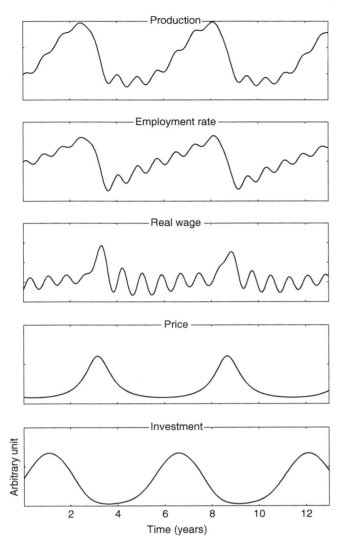

Figure 19.3 Limit cycle behavior of NEDyM for an investment flexibility of $\alpha_{inv} = 2.5$; all other parameter values as in table 3 of *Hallegatte et al.* [2008].

recession phase much shorter than the expansion phase. This typical sawtooth shape of business cycle is not well captured by RBC models, whose linear, auto-regressive character gives intrinsically symmetric behavior around the equilibrium. The amplitude of the price-wage oscillation, however, is too large in NEDyM, calling for a better calibration of the parameters and further refinements of the model.

In the setting of the recent economic and financial crisis, the banks' and other financial institutions' large losses have clearly reduced access to credit; this reduction obviously affects very strongly investment flexibility. The EnBC model considered herein can thus help explain how such a change in α_{inv} can seriously perturb the behavior of the entire economic system, by either increasing or

decreasing the variability in macroeconomic variables. Moreover, these losses also lead to a reduction in aggregated demand; this, in turn, can lead to a reduction in economic production and a full-scale recession. While the latter processes are captured by NEDyM, detailed predictions are way beyond the province of such a toy model, and would require, in particular, the "tuning" of its parameters to actual economic data, as currently done for RBC models.

19.3. NATURAL DISASTERS IN A DYNAMIC ECONOMY

The dynamics of reconstruction are a major concern when considering the socioeconomic consequences of natural disasters. Aside from the immediate damage caused by such a disaster, it is the length and other characteristics of the reconstruction period that will determine the disaster's full cost. Reconstruction may lead to an increase in productivity, by allowing for technical changes to be embedded into the reconstructed capital; technical changes could also sustain the demand and help economic recovery. At the same time, economic productivity may be reduced during reconstruction because some vital sectors are not functional, and reconstruction investments crowd out investment into new production capacity.

In this section, we briefly review recent findings on reconstruction costs using NEDyM [*Hallegatte and Ghil*, 2008] and show that it is especially the transition from equilibrium to nonequilibrium behavior that changes and complicates the response to exogenous shocks and the dynamics of reconstruction. This is a critical question in the assessment of natural disasters, since *Benson and Clay* [2004], among others, have suggested that the overall cost of a natural disaster might depend on the preexisting economic situation. As an example, the Marmara earthquake in 1999 caused destructions that amounted to 1.5–3% of Turkey's gross domestic product (GDP); its cost in terms of production loss, however, is believed to have been kept at a relatively low level by the fact that the country was experiencing a strong recession of −7% of GDP in the year before the disaster [*Bank*, 1999].

Even as simple a model as NEDyM shows that the long-term effects of a sequence of extreme events depend upon the behavior of the economy: an economy that is in stable equilibrium and has only very little flexibility or none ($\alpha_{inv} = 0$, cf. Figure 19.2) is more vulnerable than a more flexible economy, albeit still at or near equilibrium (e.g., $\alpha_{inv} = 1.0$). Clearly, if investment flexibility is null or very low, the economy is incapable of responding to the natural disasters through investment increases aimed at reconstruction; total production losses, therefore, are quite large. Such an economy behaves according to a pure

Solow [1956] growth model, where the savings, and therefore the investment, ratio is constant; see the comparative table 1 in *Hallegatte and Ghil* [2008].

When investment can respond to profitability signals without destabilizing the economy, that is when α_{inv} is nonzero but still lower than the critical bifurcation value of $\alpha_{inv} \simeq 1.39$, the economy has greater freedom to improve its overall state and thus respond to productive capital influx. Such an economy is much more resilient to disasters, because it can adjust its level of investment in the disaster's aftermath.

If investment flexibility α_{inv} is larger than its Hopf bifurcation value, the economy undergoes periodic EnBCs and, along such a cycle, NEDyM passes through phases that differ in their stability. This in turn leads to a phase-dependent response to exogenous shocks and consequently to a phase-dependent vulnerability of the economic system.

Hallegatte and Ghil [2008] investigated how the state of the economy may influence the consequences of natural disasters. In doing so, these authors introduced into NEDyM the disaster-modeling scheme of *Hallegatte et al.* [2007], in which natural disasters destroy the productive capital through a modified production function (see Appendix 19.A). Furthermore, to account for market frictions and constraints in the reconstruction process, the reconstruction expenditures are limited.

In this setting, *Hallegatte and Ghil* [2008] found a remarkable vulnerability paradox: the indirect costs caused by extreme events during a growth phase of the economy are much higher than those that occur during a deep recession. Figure 19.4 illustrates this paradox, by showing in its upper panel a typical business cycle and in the lower panel the corresponding losses for disasters hitting the economy in different phases of this cycle.

Such an apparent paradox, however, can be easily explained: disasters during high-growth periods enhance preexisting disequilibria. Inventories are low and cannot compensate the reduced production; employment is high, and hiring more employees induces wage inflation; and the producer lacks financial resources to increase his/her investment. The opposite holds during recessions, as mobilizing investment and labor is much easier.

As a consequence, production losses due to disasters that occur during expansion phases are strongly amplified, while they are reduced when the shocks occur during the recession phase. On average, however, (1) expansions last much longer than recessions, in our NEDyM model as well as in reality; and (2) amplification effects are larger than damping effects. It follows that the net effect of the cycle is strongly unfavorable to the economy, with an average production loss that is almost as large, for $\alpha_{inv} = 2.5$, as for $\alpha_{inv} = 0$; see table 1 in *Hallegatte and Ghil* [2008].

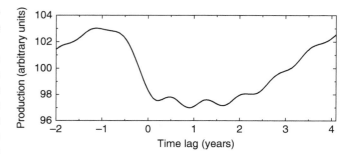

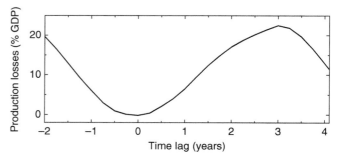

Figure 19.4 The effect of a single natural disaster on an EnBC. Upper panel: the business cycle in terms of annual production, as a function of time, starting at the cycle minimum (time lag = 0). Lower panel: total production losses due to a disaster that instantaneously destroys 3% of the GDP, shown as a function of the cycle phase in which the disaster occurs; phase measured as time lag with respect to cycle minimum. A disaster occurring near the cycle's minimum causes a limited indirect production loss, while a disaster occurring during the expansion leads to a much larger loss. From *Hallegatte and Ghil* [2008].

The results reviewed here suggest the existence of an optimal investment flexibility; this flexibility allows the economy to react in an efficient manner to exogenous shocks, without provoking endogenous fluctuations that would make it too vulnerable to such shocks. Therefore, according to the NEDyM model, stabilization policies may not only help prevent recessions from being too strong and costly, but they may also help control expansion phases, and thus prevent the economy from becoming too vulnerable to unexpected shocks, like natural disasters or other supply-side shocks. Examples of the latter are energy-price shocks, like the oil shock of the 1970s, and production bottlenecks, for instance, when electricity production cannot satisfy the demand from a growing industrial sector [*Hallegatte and Ghil*, 2008].

Applied to the specific issue of climate change, the results in this section highlight the importance of taking into account the presence of endogenous variability in assessing reconstruction costs in general, and the evolution of the economy through several EnBCs in particular. The inclusion of endogenous dynamics suggests that GDP losses may be larger than those obtained by the use of optimization strategies based on equilibrium models

[*Nordhaus and Boyer*, 1998; *Ambrosi et al.*, 2003; *Stern*, 2006]. Moreover, the allocation of capital between reconstruction and other types of investment after a large natural disaster can play an important role in both short- and long-term production losses. Optimizing this allocation, therefore, according to the state of the economy when disasters may strike is an important factor in dealing with the expected change in the distribution of extreme events, due to global warming.

19.4. VALIDATION WITH U.S. ECONOMIC INDICATORS

Besides a long-term trend in production and material well-being, macroeconomic time series exhibit short-term fluctuations with certain cyclic characteristic (see again Figure 19.1). In this section, we focus on the extraction of fundamental dynamical behavior from such time series and evaluate the consistency of the behavior so obtained with endogenous dynamics. This is an essential step in assessing the reliability of NEDyM results and especially of its behavior with respect to exogenous shocks.

In this context, it is of particular interest whether the predicted vulnerability pattern of NEDyM is also present in the data at hand. Indeed, the FDT of statistical physics [*Einstein*, 1905; *Kubo*, 1966] states that a system with many degrees of freedom near equilibrium reacts in the same way to an internal as well as to an external shock: the fluctuations to which the shock gives rise die out in the same way.

This property is very useful in estimating the response of such a system to an external shock, since one can compute its properties, in particular the dissipation rate of the fluctuations, from its long-term behavior while it is only subject to internal shocks. Furthermore, FDT for systems out of equilibrium indicates that similar properties hold under suitable assumptions, at least while the response is linear [*Ruelle*, 2009; *Chekroun et al.*, 2011].

19.4.1. Macroeconomic Dataset

The dataset we use here is quarterly U.S. macroeconomic data from the Bureau of Economic Analysis for 1954–2005; see http://www.bea.gov/. The nine time series we use are GDP, investment, consumption, employment rate (in %), total wage, change in private inventories, price, exports, and imports. As commonly done in econometrics, we first remove the trend and convert the data to relative values by dividing the data points by the corresponding trend values. A typical filter used in the economic literature for extracting the trend is the Hodrick-Prescott filter [*Hodrick and Prescott*, 1997]. Next, all time series are normalized by their standard deviation. The series, after being thus detrended and normalized, are shown in Figure 19.5a.

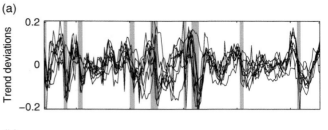

(a)

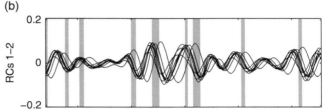

(b)

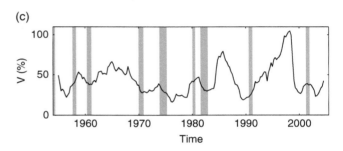

(c)

Figure 19.5 Time series of nine U.S. macroeconomic indicators, 1954–2005. (a) Normalized trend residuals; (b) data-adaptively filtered business cycle, captured by the leading oscillatory pair of M-SSA; and (c) local variance of fluctuations. The shaded vertical bars indicate the NBER-defined recessions.

All nine time series in the figure exhibit fluctuations of varying amplitude and period. These fluctuations could be induced by external shocks, such as political events and natural disasters, or by intrinsic macroeconomic processes. Whatever the causes, a predominantly cyclic behavior is clearly visible. In order to assess, from such a short and noisy time series, whether this cyclicity is significant or is merely due to chance, we decompose the full set of nine indicators into its spectral components with the help of multivariate singular spectrum analysis (M-SSA) and apply statistical Monte Carlo tests. Appendix 19.B contains a brief description and explanation of the M-SSA methodology.

19.4.2. Cyclic Behavior

The first result of the M-SSA decomposition procedure is the eigenvalue spectrum in Figure 19.6. These eigenvalues of the lag-covariance matrix of the dataset give the variances of the successive components.

The eigenvalues are plotted in Figure 19.6 versus their dominant frequency *f*, as suggested by *Allen and Smith*

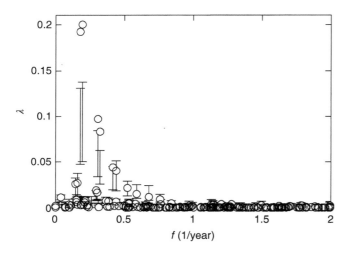

Figure 19.6 Spectrum of eigenvalues (circles) from M-SSA with a window width of $M = 24$. The error bars indicate the 2.5 and 97.5% percentile levels of significance, based on Monte Carlo SSA.

[1996], rather than versus their rank k, as originally proposed by *Vautard and Ghil* [1989]; see Appendix 19.B. We note, in this spectrum, a maximum of two nearly equal eigenvalues at the usually reported mean business cycle length of 5–6 years. According to M-SSA, such a pair of eigenvalues could be associated with a roughly periodic oscillation, rather than with a random fluctuation.

Since macroeconomic variables typically exhibit greater variance at lower frequencies, it is quite possible, however, to obtain such a high-variance *oscillatory pair* even though no truly oscillatory behavior occurs. To ensure that the eigenvalue pair associated with $f \simeq 0.2 \left(\text{year} \right)^{-1}$ is not merely a result of the detrending procedure and thus subject to the *Nelson and Kang* [1981] criticism of spurious cycles, we submit our set of indicators to Monte Carlo SSA [*Allen and Smith*, 1996]; the latter approach provides a robust statistical significance test for such oscillations.

Allen and Smith [1996] proposed to fit an autoregressive process of order one, AR(1), to a scalar, univariate time series, which replicates the variance and decorrelation time of the data, but in the absence of oscillations. It is then tested whether the eigenvalues of the given time series exceed the eigenvalue distribution of the AR(1) null hypothesis. The application of Monte Carlo SSA to the multivariate macroeconomic dataset at hand, however, requires certain modifications, and takes comovements and detrending effects into account; these necessary modifications are discussed by *Groth et al.* [2015].

The significance levels obtained in this manner are indicated as error bars in Figure 19.6. Like the time series' eigenvalues, the null hypothesis also exhibits a maximum at the 5 year period and many data eigenvalues do lie

between the error bars of the null hypothesis. The two largest eigenvalues, however, stand clearly out above the significance level and thus the related oscillation cannot be merely attributed to the detrending procedure.

Moreover, *Groth et al.* [2015] demonstrate that this oscillatory mode in the U.S. macroeconomic indicators gains further significance when taking multiple aggregate indicators into account. Indeed an analysis of GDP alone does not show any significant oscillations. The importance of taking the multivariate character of economic activity into account in our analysis is in full agreement with the U.S. National Bureau of Economic Research's (NBER) understanding of business cycles as an "activity spread across the economy" and demonstrates the advantage of M-SSA with respect to univariate methods. *Groth et al.* [2015] also show to what extent the presence of such significant oscillatory mode supports the idea of EnBC dynamics and the presence of deterministic, nonlinear effects.

19.4.3. Episodes of High Fluctuation Levels

Next, let us accept the results of Figure 19.6 and the conclusion that U.S. economic dynamics is indeed characterized by intrinsic oscillatory modes like those captured by the M-SSA *reconstructed components* (RCs) 1–2 in Figure 19.5b; see again Appendix 19.B for definitions. It is of interest then to evaluate its relative importance versus that of the residual "noise" associated with the rest of the variability in the dataset.

The eigenvalues provide only an average index of the total variance of the associated RCs over the entire time series. Next, we look into time-dependent aspects of the multivariate dataset's decomposition and the interplay between the deterministic oscillatory behavior of RCs 1–2 and the fluctuations in the remaining RCs 3–DM.

Groth et al. [2015] have analyzed the relative amplitude of the 5 year oscillatory activity by means of the *local variance fraction* as defined by *Plaut and Vautard* [1994]. This analysis shows a strong time dependency in the oscillation-fluctuation decomposition of the U.S. economy with much higher fluctuations during expansions. *Groth et al.* [2015] verified its statistical significance by means of Monte Carlo SSA against a simple stationary RBC model, and they came to the conclusion that random shocks alone, in the absence of endogenous dynamics, are not sufficient to explain such a strong time dependency in the oscillation-fluctuation decomposition of the U.S. economy.

This local variance fraction, however, is defined on PCs rather than on RCs, and measures the relative amplitude of oscillatory activity only in a window of the same length M as the one used in M-SSA. Furthermore, the transformation to PCs introduces frequency-dependent phase distortions and complicates the correct assignment of a given variance to a precise instant in time. A subsequent transformation to RCs, on the other hand, neutralizes this undesirable effect [*Groth and Ghil*, 2011].

For this reason, we propose here a geometric approach based on the RCs and analyze fluctuations perpendicular to a limit cycle; see Appendix 19.B. Figure 19.5c shows the local variance $V = V(t)$ of these fluctuations over a short window of length $L \leq M$, superimposed on the NBER-defined U.S. recessions. Starting after 1980, and in agreement with the findings of *Groth et al.* [2015], the variance of the fluctuations during expansions is much higher than during recessions, as suspected from applying FDT reasoning to the U.S. economy. We thus conclude that the vulnerability paradox obtained when subjecting NEDyM to a sequence of natural-hazard shocks is consistent with a mature economy's greater instability during expansions.

19.4.4. Reconstruction of Phase-Dependent Fluctuations

The fluctuation pattern of the U.S. macroeconomic indicators plotted in Figure 19.5 exhibits rapid changes on time scales that are below the M-SSA window length of $M = 24$ quarters. Is M-SSA flexible enough to detect changes in the dynamical system's behavior on time scales shorter than M? In the following example of a stochastically driven oscillator in the plane, we shall demonstrate that M-SSA is indeed capable of tracking such rapid changes; see Appendix 19.C for further details.

In polar coordinates (ρ, θ), this oscillator is given by

$$d\rho = \rho(\mu + c\rho)dt + \frac{\phi}{\pi}dW_1,$$

$$d\phi = \omega dt + dW_2. \tag{19.1}$$

We introduce phase-dependent variations in the stochastic forcing of the amplitude ρ in Equation 19.1 and try to reconstruct this variation.

Starting with the simple case of a circular limit cycle, we choose the parameters in Equation 19.1 as $\{c, \mu, \omega\} = \{-0.5, 1, 1\}$. Then system is integrated from $t = 0$ to $t = T = 16\pi$ with a small step size $\Delta t = 0.02$ by using a particular noise realization and the Euler-Maruyama scheme [*Kloeden and Platen*, 1992]. From this integration, we keep only every tenth sample value of the trajectory to get the final time series of length $N \simeq 500$. The sampling scheme results in a period length of about 31 samples, and a typical realization is shown in Figure 19.7a and b.

The window length $M = 50$ used in Figure 19.7 is chosen to cover more than one period of the oscillator, and it is not a critical parameter in this experiment. Besides $M = 50$, we have also tested $M = 100$ and 200 and found the same results.

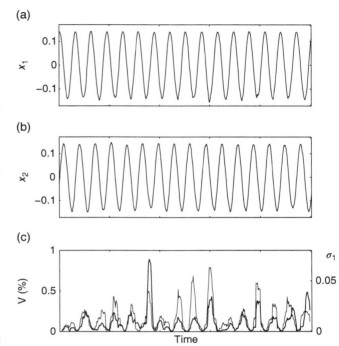

Figure 19.7 Changes in local variance of a simple, stochastically perturbed oscillator in Equation 19.1. (a and b) Typical realization of a solution of the stochastic oscillator, plotted in Cartesian coordinates (x_1, x_2); and (c) corresponding local variance $\sigma_1(t)$ of the stochastic forcing, as given by Equation 19.C5 (light solid), along with the estimated local variance $V(t)$ in a sliding window of length $L = 11$ (heavy solid). The M-SSA window length is $M = 50$.

The oscillatory mode can be reliably reconstructed by the first oscillatory pair RCs 1–2, and a test with Monte Carlo SSA confirms that only this pair is significant. The sum of the remaining RCs 3–DM, which represents the fluctuations, is projected on the local perpendiculars to the limit cycle described by RCs 1–2; see Appendix 19.B for details. The local variance $V(t)$ of these fluctuations agrees very well with the local variance $\sigma_1(t)$ of the stochastic forcing on ρ, cf. Figure 19.7c. Without the projection, $V(t)$ would represent a mixture of amplitude and phase forcing in Equation 19.1, and a reliable detection of variations in the former would not be possible (not shown).

Next, we wish to evaluate the consequences of a more complex limit cycle geometry, which resembles better than that of NEDyM's limit cycle, as shown in Figure 19.3. Instead of a simple circular limit cycle with constant amplitude, we introduce a phase-dependent amplitude, according to Equation (19.C7). This modification introduces higher harmonics of first and second order into the observed time series, and yields a sawtooth-shaped behavior in x_1, cf. Figure 19.8a.

(a)

(b)

(c)

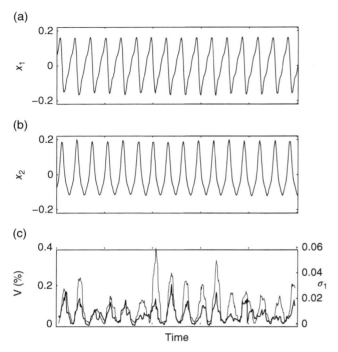

Figure 19.8 Same as Figure 19.7, but for a more complex limit cycle; see Equation 19.C7.

The presence of higher harmonics is also reflected in the M-SSA results: three significant oscillatory pairs are detected, and the corresponding RCs 1–6 give a good reconstruction of the limit cycle. The remaining RCs 7–DM still give a good approximation of the fluctuations, and the local variance $V(t)$ of the part that is orthogonal to the RCs 1–6 reflects very well the changes in the stochastic forcing on the amplitude, as shown in Figure 19.8c.

Although the geometric approach of local variance estimation by means of $V(t)$, in both Figures 19.7 and 19.8, provides a good distinction between epochs of small and large stochastic forcing, it gives only an approximate estimate of the correct variance. A better estimator, however, would require a more detailed knowledge about the underlying model dynamics and its response to exogenous shocks, and would lead to nonlinear inverse modeling, as reviewed, for instance, by *Kravtsov et al.* [2009]. This is, however, beyond the scope of the chapter and is left for future work.

19.5. CONCLUDING REMARKS

19.5.1. Summary

In this research-and-review chapter, we set out to combine three strands of research: (1) the formulation and study of a nonequilibrium dynamic model (NEDyM) of

endogenous business cycles (EnBCs) [*Hallegatte et al.*, 2008; *Dumas et al.*, 2015]; (2) the application of this NEDyM model to the investigation of the impact of global warming and extreme events on the economy [*Hallegatte et al.*, 2007; *Hallegatte and Dumas*, 2008; *Hallegatte and Ghil*, 2008]; and (3) the quantitative extraction of business cycles from macroeconomic data [*Groth and Ghil*, 2011; *Sella et al.*, 2013; *Groth et al.*, 2015], including the validation of the FDT hypothesis on the functioning of the U.S. economy.

In Section 19.2.3, we showed that NEDyM does indeed produce EnBCs, due essentially to the instability of the profit-investment relationship. NEDyM reproduces the observed asymmetry of business cycles, with the recession phase much shorter than the expansion phase (Figure 19.3); it is also consistent with many other stylized facts described in the macroeconomic literature, such as the phasing, or comovements, of the distinct macroeconomic variables along the cycle. The model's main control parameter is investment flexibility, α_{inv}. As this parameter increases, model solutions go from a single stable equilibrium, consistent with the *Solow* [1956] balanced-growth model, to regular, periodic business cycles and on to irregular, chaotic ones (Figure 19.2).

In Section 19.3, we have further shown that the response of a dynamic economy to natural disasters differs markedly from the one of an economy in generalized equilibrium or undergoing merely balanced growth. The state of an out-of-equilibrium economy may affect the consequences of natural disasters by interfering with reconstruction dynamics. When the investment flexibility favors the presence of business cycles, we found a remarkable *vulnerability paradox* in NEDyM: The indirect costs caused by extreme events during a growth phase of the economy exceed those that occur during a recession (Figure 19.4). The explanation of this apparent paradox is related to a greater instability of the economy during expansions.

Drawing a crude analogy between economic dynamics as the outcome of many interacting "particles," be they firms, individuals, or other entities [*Ghil et al.*, 2008b; *Soros*, 2008; *Coluzzi et al.*, 2011], and the particle systems of statistical physics, one might suspect that an out-of-equilibrium version [*Ruelle*, 2009; *Chekroun et al.*, 2011] of classical FDT [*Einstein*, 1905; *Kubo*, 1966] would apply. In particular, we expected to find greater variability during expansion phases in time series of macroeconomic indicators.

The macroeconomic data analysis in Section 19.4 dealt with multiple indicators for the U.S. economy from 1954 to 2005. Based on a systematic application of M-SSA, we have provided evidence for genuinely oscillatory, albeit not purely periodic, modes, which are pervasive in many aggregates. The application of Monte Carlo SSA thus allowed us to reject the hypothesis of purely random shocks generating business cycle dynamics in an otherwise stable economy.

We have compared the predicted vulnerability patterns of NEDyM with the recent findings of state-dependent fluctuations in the U.S. economy, as illustrated here in Figure 19.5c. *Groth et al.* [2015] have shown that the recession phase is dominated by a deterministic oscillatory mode, while the expansion phase exhibits more complex and irregular dynamics, in agreement with the FDT conjecture.

The latter suggests a higher volatility of business cycles during expansions, and we have demonstrated by introducing and analyzing here a simple nonlinear, stochastically perturbed oscillator that M-SSA is indeed able to track rapid changes in the variance of the stochastic forcing. It is a matter of some interest, as well as some puzzlement, that the more volatile response to external shocks occurs in a low-order model like NEDyM, while the FDT conjecture applies in principle to high-order, "multi-particle" systems. To further verify the greater instability of mature economies during an expansion phase, we have extended the analysis from *Groth et al.* [2015], and proposed in Sections 19.4.3 and B.2 here a simple geometric, M-SSA–based approach to estimate the local variance of irregular fluctuations along an otherwise deterministic trajectory.

19.5.2. Outlook

Our highly idealized macroeconomic model, however, is still lacking a suitable calibration of its parameters on economic data. The amplitude of the price-and-wage oscillation, for example, is still too large in NEDyM.

To estimate these parameters, we expect to rely on the *data assimilation* approach. Its use is common by now in many areas of the geosciences [*Bengtsson et al.*, 1981; *Ghil*, 1997; *Kondrashov et al.*, 2008]; it has also been used in the econometric context [*Harvey*, 1989], but is only starting to be applied to macroeconomic models [*Lemoine and Pelgrin*, 2004]. Preliminary results (not reported here) were obtained by applying data assimilation methods, such as Kalman filtering [*Kalman*, 1960; *Ghil et al.*, 1981] to the NEDyM model, using at first synthetic data produced by the model itself, the so-called identical-twin approach [*Bengtsson et al.*, 1981]; these results were encouraging but not conclusive.

Finally, work on truly coupled climate-economy models has started by coupling a very simple, linear climate model to a two-sector dynamic economic model [*Dumas*, 2006]. In this model, the infrastructure and housing sectors are separated from the rest of the economy; they are assumed to be vulnerable to extreme events but otherwise inert. While the macroeconomic modeling in this coupled climate-economy model is less advanced than in NEDyM, it allows one to represent, in one unified framework, climate prediction and adaptation to climate change impacts, while taking into account the natural variability of both the climate system and the economy.

Suitable calibration of NEDyM, combined with the development of multisector economic models along the same lines and the use of more advanced, nonlinear climate models, *Ghil* [2001]; *Ghil et al.* [2008a] should provide, eventually, a more advanced and realistic unified framework for the truly coupled study of climate and the economy.

ACKNOWLEDGMENTS

A.G. and P.D. have been supported by a grant from the Réseau de Recherche sur le Développement Soutenable (R2DS) of the Région Ile-de-France, while M.G. received partial support from NSF Grant No. DMS-1049253.

APPENDIX 19.A. NEDyM WITH SHOCKS

Our nonequilibrium dynamic model (NEDyM) builds on the key ideas of the classical *Solow* [1956] balanced-growth model, but it replaces the latter's static relationships by dynamic ones. NEDyM's long-term behavior reproduces the behavior of the Solow model with slowly evolving, perfect market equilibria. The introduction of adjustment delays, however, induces much richer, and arguably more realistic short-term dynamics.

The first part of this appendix gives a brief presentation of NEDyM; see *Hallegatte et al.* [2008] for a full description. In the second part, we summarize NEDyM modifications used to account for external shocks [*Hallegatte et al.*, 2007].

19.A.1. NEDyM Formulation

In the Solow model, the price p is determined by the equality of production Y and demand D, $Y = D$. In NEDyM, $Y \neq D$ and the goods inventory H is modeled as

$$\dot{H} = Y - D. \qquad (19.A1)$$

The demand D equals the sum of consumption C and investment I,

$$D = C + I. \qquad (19.A2)$$

Changes in the price p are driven by the ratio of H/D,

$$\dot{p} = -p\alpha_p \frac{H}{D}, \qquad (19.A3)$$

with the price adjustment coefficient α_p. As in the Solow model, the Cobb–Douglas [1928] production function is used,

$$Y = f(L,K) = AL^\lambda K^{1-\lambda}, \quad (19.A4)$$

where L stands for labor, more precisely the number of employed workers, and K for capital; we use the value $\lambda = 2/3$ for the capital-for-labor substitution parameter. The parameter A is the total productivity factor.

Instead of full employment $L = L_{full} = e_{full}L_{max}$ in the Solow model, the employment rate evolution follows:

$$\dot{L} = -\frac{1}{\tau_{empl}}(L - L_e), \quad (19.A5)$$

with a characteristic time τ_{empl}. The optimal labor demand L_e is chosen by the producer to maximize profits, as a function of real wage and marginal labor productivity,

$$\frac{w}{p} = \frac{\partial f}{\partial L}(L_e, K). \quad (19.A6)$$

The evolution of wages is related to the employment rate,

$$\dot{w} = \frac{w}{\tau_{wage}}\frac{L - L_{full}}{L_{full}}, \quad (19.A7)$$

with the characteristic time τ_{wage}. The wages essentially restore the full employment rate by increasing if the labor demand is higher than L_{full}, and decreasing when it is lower.

The capital K evolves here according to

$$\dot{K} = I - \frac{1}{\tau_{dep}}K, \quad (19.A8)$$

like in the classical Solow model, with the capital depreciation time τ_{dep}. In the latter's producer behavior, sales pD equal wages wL plus profits, and investment equals saving.

A key feature of NEDyM is the introduction of an investment module, inspired by *Kalecki* [1937]. Instead of equating investments and savings, it introduces a stock of liquid assets F, held by companies and banks; its evolution follows

$$\dot{F} = pD - wL + \gamma_{save}\alpha_M M - (1 - \Gamma_{inv})\alpha_F F - pI. \quad (19.A9)$$

The stock is filled by the difference between sales pD and wages wL, as well as by the consumers' savings $\gamma_{save}\alpha_M M$.

These assets are used to redistribute share dividends $(1 - \Gamma_{inv})\alpha_F F$ and to invest in the amount

$$pI = \Gamma_{inv}\alpha_F F. \quad (19.A10)$$

The consumer consumption

$$C = (1 - \gamma_{save})\frac{1}{p}\alpha_M M \quad (19.A11)$$

is linked to the consumer stock of money M, and it is fixed to a specific savings ratio γ_{save}. The companies and banks' stock of liquid assets F and the consumer stock of money M sum to a constant value, $F + M = $ const. The evolution of F is linked with the investment ratio dynamics Γ_{inv}, which in turn follows

$$\dot{\Gamma}_{inv} = \begin{cases} \alpha_{inv}(\gamma_{max} - \Gamma_{inv})[\Pi_n/(pK) - v], & \text{if } \Pi_n/(pK) > v, \\ \alpha_{inv}(\Gamma_{inv} - \gamma_{min})[\Pi_n/(pK) - v], & \text{if } \Pi_n/(pK) \le v. \end{cases} \quad (19.A12)$$

The expected net profit $\Pi_n = pD - wL - \tau_{dep}^{-1}pK$ follows the accounting definition of *Copeland and Weston* [2003] and it is compared with a standard of profitability v; the producer increases or decreases the investments accordingly. The extrema $\gamma_{min} = 0$ and $\gamma_{min} = 0.8$ represent the positivity of investments and a cash-flow constraint, respectively.

The investment dynamics is further governed by the investment coefficient α_{inv}. Seven parameters determine the model equilibrium at $\alpha_{inv} = 0$; they are calibrated to reproduce the state of the European Union's economy in 2001, with 15 countries [*Eurostat*, 2002]. The other six parameters are chosen, up till now, in an empirical, ad hoc manner; they require calibration by data assimilation methods, as discussed in Section 19.5.2. All 13 parameter values are given in table 3 of *Hallegatte et al.* [2008].

19.A.2. Impacts of Natural Disasters

Natural disasters mainly destroy the stock of productive capital and cause disequilibrium effects in model behavior. *Hallegatte et al.* [2007] presented at some length the modifications of NEDyM that are necessary in order to correctly model disaster consequences.

A simple replacement of the productive capital K by $K - \Delta K$ leads one to underestimate the impact on the production Y. For this reason, the authors introduced a further variable ξ_K into the Cobb-Douglas production function of Equation 19.A4, namely

$$Y = \xi_K f(L,K) = \xi_K AL^\lambda K^{1-\lambda}. \quad (19.A13)$$

Furthermore, *Hallegatte et al.* [2007] introduced inertia into the reconstruction process by distinguishing between the investments I_n that increase the capital K, and reconstruction investments I_r that restore ξ_K to the standard value $\xi_K = 1$. Hence, the capital in Equation 19.A8 now evolves according to

$$\dot{K} = \frac{I_n}{\xi_K} - \frac{1}{\tau_{dep}} K, \qquad (19.A14)$$

and the empirical, shock-response variable ξ_K is modeled as follows:

$$\dot{\xi}_K = \frac{I_r}{\xi_K}. \qquad (19.A15)$$

The authors further limit I_r to a fraction f_{max} of the total available investment $I = I_r + I_n$, and let

$$I_r = \begin{cases} \min\{f_{max} I, (1 - \xi_K) K_0\}, & \text{if } \xi_K < 1, \\ 0, & \text{otherwise.} \end{cases} \qquad (19.A16)$$

A value of $f_{max} = 5\%$ means that the economy can mobilize about 1% of the GDP per year for the reconstruction.

APPENDIX 19.B. SINGULAR SPECTRUM ANALYSIS

Singular spectrum analysis (SSA) as well as multivariate SSA (M-SSA) rely on the classical Karhunen–Loève spectral decomposition of stochastic processes [*Loève*, 1945; *Karhunen*, 1946]. In the context of nonlinear dynamics, *Broomhead and King* [1986a, 1986b] applied this methodology, long familiar in the stochastic realm, to the reconstruction of a deterministic dynamical system's behavior from observed time series. For this purpose, Broomhead and King applied principal component (PC) analysis to the Mañé–Takens's idea [*Mañé*, 1981; *Takens*, 1981] of a time-delayed embedding, and provided a robust way to extract major directions in the system's phase space.

M. Ghil, R. Vautard and associates first proposed to apply the SSA methodology to the spectral analysis of short and noisy time series, for which standard methods derived from Fourier analysis do not work well [*Vautard and Ghil* 1989; *Ghil and Vautard*, 1991; *Vautard et al.*, 1992]. *Ghil et al.* [2002] provide an overview and a comprehensive set of references; see also their free software at http://www.atmos.ucla.edu/tcd/ssa/.

19.B.1. Reconstruction of Oscillatory Behavior

M-SSA operates on a multivariate time series

$$\mathbf{x} = \{x_d(n) : d = 1 \cdots D, n = 1 \cdots N\}, \qquad (19.B1)$$

with D channels of length N. Each channel is embedded into an M-dimensional phase space, by using lagged copies

$$\mathbf{X}_d(n) = (x_d(n), \ldots, x_d(n + M - 1)), \qquad (19.B2)$$

with $n = 1, \ldots, N - M + 1$. From this extended dataset one forms the full *augmented trajectory matrix*

$$\mathbf{X} = (\mathbf{X}_1, \mathbf{X}_2, \ldots, \mathbf{X}_D), \qquad (19.B3)$$

which has DM columns of length $N - M + 1$.

The M-SSA algorithm then computes the covariance matrix $\mathbf{C} = \mathbf{X}^\top \mathbf{X}$ of $\mathbf{X}$, where $(\cdot)^\top$ is the transpose. The sample covariance matrix $\mathbf{C}$ contains all the auto- and cross-covariance information on $\mathbf{X}$, up to a time lag of $M - 1$. Due to the finite length of the time series, the matrix $\mathbf{C}$ may deviate slightly from symmetry. Therefore we use here the Toeplitz approach proposed by *Vautard and Ghil* [1989].

In the algorithm's next step, the Toeplitz matrix $\mathbf{C}$ is diagonalized

$$\Lambda = \mathbf{E}^\top \mathbf{C} \mathbf{E} \qquad (19.B4)$$

to yield a diagonal matrix Λ that contains the real eigenvalues λ_k along the diagonal, and a unitary matrix $\mathbf{E}$ whose columns are the associated eigenvectors $\mathbf{e}_k$. These eigenvectors form a new orthogonal basis in the embedding space of $\mathbf{X}$, and the corresponding eigenvalues λ_k give the variance in the direction of $\mathbf{e}_k$. This decomposition helps us find major components of the system's dynamical behavior and reconstruct a robust "skeleton" of the underlying structure. Essentially, these components can be classified into trends, oscillatory patterns, and noise.

By projecting the embedded time series $\mathbf{X}$ onto the eigenvectors $\mathbf{E}$,

$$\mathbf{A} = \mathbf{X} \mathbf{E}, \qquad (19.B5)$$

we get the PCs arranged as columns in $\mathbf{A}$. We denote the elements of the k-th PC by $a_k(n)$.

Finally, one can reconstruct that part of the time series that is associated with a particular eigenvector $\mathbf{e}_k$ by using the RCs introduced by *Ghil and Vautard* [1991] and *Vautard et al.* [1992], in the single-channel and by

Keppenne and Ghil [1993] and *Plaut and Vautard* [1994] in the multichannel case,

$$r_{dk}(n) = \frac{1}{M} \sum_{m=1}^{M} a_k(n-m+1) e_{dk}(m). \qquad (19.B6)$$

The notation $\mathbf{e}_k = \{e_{dk}(m) : 1 \le d \le D, 1 \le m \le M\}$ reflects the special structure of the eigenvectors [*Groth and Ghil*, 2011]; formulas for $r_{dk}(n)$ near the endpoints of the time series are given in *Vautard et al.* [1992] and *Ghil et al.* [2002].

Given any subset $\mathcal{K}$ of eigenelements $\{(\lambda_k, \mathbf{e}_k) : k \in \mathcal{K}\}$, we obtain the corresponding reconstruction $r_{d\mathcal{K}}$ by summing the RCs r_{dk} over $k \in \mathcal{K}$,

$$r_{d\mathcal{K}}(n) = \sum_{k \in \mathcal{K}} r_{dk}(n). \qquad (19.B7)$$

Typical choices of $\mathcal{K}$ may involve (1) $\mathcal{K} = \{k : 1 \le k \le S\}$, where S is the *statistical dimension* of the time series, cf. *Vautard and Ghil* [1989], that is, the number of statistically significant components, commonly referred to as the signal, as opposed to the noise; or (2) a so-called oscillatory pair $\mathcal{K} = \{k_1, k_2\}$, which might capture a possibly cyclic mode of behavior of the system [*Vautard and Ghil*, 1989; *Plaut and Vautard*, 1994].

Information about oscillatory modes can help detect clusters of phase- and frequency-locked oscillators even in the presence of high observational noise [*Groth and Ghil*, 2011]. Summing over the whole set of RCs, $\mathcal{K} = \{k : 1 \le k \le DM\}$, gives the complete reconstruction of the time series.

19.B.2. Reconstruction of Fluctuations

Here, we propose M-SSA as a tool to help quantify the intensity of fluctuations along a limit cycle. Our proposal relies on the smooth behavior of the band-limited RCs, which enables a quantification of the fluctuations that are orthogonal to the system's supposedly deterministic trajectory.

Let us assume that RCs 1–S represent this deterministic part and the remaining RCs represent irregular fluctuations. We denote the two parts by $\mathbf{r}_{\mathcal{K}} = (r_{1\mathcal{K}}, \ldots, r_{D\mathcal{K}})$ and $\mathbf{r}_{\mathcal{K}'} = (r_{1\mathcal{K}'}, \ldots, r_{D\mathcal{K}'})$, respectively, with $\mathcal{K} = \{k : 1 \le k \le S\}$ and $\mathcal{K}' = \{k : S+1 \le k \le DM\}$. From this we determine the part of the fluctuations $\mathbf{r}_{\mathcal{K}'}(n)$ that is orthogonal to the temporal evolution $\Delta \mathbf{r}_{\mathcal{K}}(n) = \mathbf{r}_{\mathcal{K}}(n-1) - \mathbf{r}_{\mathcal{K}}(n+1)$ of the deterministic part:

$$\mathbf{r}_{\mathcal{K}'}^{\perp}(n) = \mathbf{r}_{\mathcal{K}'}(n) - \frac{\langle \mathbf{r}_{\mathcal{K}'}(n), \Delta \mathbf{r}_{\mathcal{K}}(n) \rangle}{\|\Delta \mathbf{r}_{\mathcal{K}}(n)\|^2} \cdot \Delta \mathbf{r}_{\mathcal{K}}(n); \qquad (19.B8)$$

the notations $\langle \cdot, \cdot \rangle$ and $\|\cdot\|$ above refer to the scalar product and the norm, respectively.

Since the RCs are smooth, band-limited time series, $\Delta \mathbf{r}_{\mathcal{K}}$ gives a good approximation of the temporal evolution of the trajectory $\mathbf{r}_{\mathcal{K}}$. Once we have derived the orthogonal fluctuations $\mathbf{r}_{\mathcal{K}}^{\perp}$, this smoothness allows us to quantify the average amplitude of the fluctuations around the deterministic part with respect to the time series' expansion in a centered window of length $L \le M$, where $L = 2l+1$ is odd:

$$V(n) = \frac{\sum_{s=n-l}^{n+l} \|\mathbf{r}_{\mathcal{K}}^{\perp}(s)\|^2}{\sum_{s=n-l}^{n+l} \|\mathbf{x}(s)\|^2}. \qquad (19.B9)$$

APPENDIX 19.C. A RANDOMLY FORCED OSCILLATOR

Our oscillator's deterministic part is given, in Cartesian coordinates, by the equations

$$\begin{aligned} \dot{x}_1 &= \mu x_1 - \omega x_2 + c x_1 \left(x_1^2 + x_2^2\right) \\ \dot{x}_2 &= \mu x_2 + \omega x_1 + c x_2 \left(x_1^2 + x_2^2\right). \end{aligned} \qquad (19.C1)$$

For $c < 0$ and $\mu < 0$ the system has a unique, stable fixed point at the origin $(x_1, x_2) = (0,0)$. At $\mu = 0$ it undergoes a supercritical Hopf bifurcation to a stable limit cycle with frequency ω.

Transformation to polar coordinates, $x_1 + ix_2 = \rho^{1/2} \exp\{i\phi\}$, reduces (19.C1) to the more transparent form

$$\begin{aligned} \dot{\rho} &= \rho(\mu + c\rho), \\ \dot{\theta} &= \omega. \end{aligned} \qquad (19.C2)$$

We perturb this oscillator in the plane by two independent Wiener processes $W_{1,2}$, each of which has independent increments $dW_{1,2}$ of variance $\{0.4dt, 0.02dt\}$. We further introduce a phase-dependent variation of the forcing on ρ, and obtain the stochastic model

$$\begin{aligned} d\rho &= \rho(\mu + c\rho)dt + \frac{\phi}{\pi}dW_1, \\ d\phi &= \omega dt + dW_2. \end{aligned} \qquad (19.C3)$$

In order to compare the stochastic forcing on ρ with the M-SSA results, we keep track of the effective shocks on ρ in each interval between two sampling times, $t_n \le t \le t_{n+1}$,

$$\Delta W_1(n) = \pi^{-1} \int_{t_n}^{t_{n+1}} \phi(t) dW_1. \qquad (19.C4)$$

and estimate the local variance in a centered window whose length $L = 2l+1 \le M$ is odd-valued by

$$\sigma_1(n) = L^{-1} \sum_{s=n-l}^{n+l} \Delta W_1^2(s). \qquad (19.C5)$$

The observations on system (19.C3) are in polar coordinates and, prior to applying M-SSA, we have to transform them back into Cartesian coordinates. This is done in one of two distinct ways:

$$x_1 = \rho^{1/2} \cos\phi,$$
$$x_2 = \rho^{1/2} \sin\phi; \qquad (19.C6)$$

or

$$x_1 = \rho^{1/2}\left(1 + \sin\phi + \sin^2\phi\right)\cos\phi,$$
$$x_2 = \rho^{1/2}\left(1 + \sin\phi + \sin^2\phi\right)\sin\phi. \qquad (19.C7)$$

The first transformation (19.C6) yields a circular limit cycle, according to Equation (19.C1), while the second transformation (19.C7) introduces a phase-dependent amplitude and leads to a deformation of the circular structure.

REFERENCES

Allen, M. R. and L. A. Smith (1996), Monte Carlo SSA: Detecting irregular oscillations in the presence of colored noise, *J. Clim.*, *9*, 3373–3404, doi:10.1175/1520-0442(1996)009 ⟨3373:MCSDIO⟩ 2.0.CO;2.

Ambrosi, P., J.-C. Hourcade, S. Hallegatte, F. Lecocq, P. Dumas, and M. Ha-Duong (2003), Optimal control models and elicitation of attitudes towards climate change, *Environ. Model. Assess.*, *8*(3), 135–147, doi:10.1023/A:1025586922143.

Bank, W. (1999), *Turkey: Marmara Earthquake Assessment*, vol. *27380*, Turkey Country Office, The World Bank, Washington, DC.

Bengtsson, L., M. Ghil, and E. Källén (Eds.) (1981), *Dynamic Meteorology: Data Assimilation Methods*, pp. 330, Springer-Verlag, New York.

Benhabib, J. and K. Nishimura (1979), The Hopf-bifurcation and the existence of closed orbits in multi-sectoral models of optimal economic growth, *J. Econ. Theory*, *21*, 421–444.

Benson, C. and E. Clay (2004), *Understanding the Economic and Financial Impact of Natural Disasters*, The International Bank for Reconstruction and Development/The World Bank, Washington, DC.

Broomhead, D. S. and G. P. King (1986a), Extracting qualitative dynamics from experimental data, *Phys. D*, *20*(2–3), 217–236, doi:10.1016/0167-2789(86)90031-X.

Broomhead, D. S. and G. P. King (1986b), On the qualitative analysis of experimental dynamical systems, in *Nonlinear Phenomena and Chaos*, edited by S. Sarkar, pp. 113–144, Adam Hilger, Bristol.

Burns, A. F. and W. C. Mitchell (1946), *Measuring Business Cycles*, NBER, New York.

Chekroun, M. D., D. Kondrashov, and M. Ghil (2011), Predicting stochastic systems by noise sampling, and application to the El Niño-Southern Oscillation, *Proc. Natl. Acad. Sci. U. S. A.*, *108*(29), 11766–11771, doi:10.1073/pnas.1015753108.

Chiarella, C. and P. Flaschel (2000), *The Dynamics of Keynesian Monetary Growth*, Cambridge University Press, Cambridge.

Chiarella, C., P. Flaschel, and R. Franke (2005), *Foundations for a Disequilibrium Theory of the Business Cycle*, Cambridge University Press, Cambridge.

Chiarella, C., R. Franke, P. Flaschel, and W. Semmler (2006), *Quantitative and Empirical Analysis of Nonlinear Dynamic Macromodels*, pp. 277, Elsevier, Amsterdam.

Cobb, C. W. and P. H. Douglas (1928), A theory of production, *Am. Econ. Rev.*, *18*(1), 139–165.

Coluzzi, B., M. Ghil, S. Hallegatte, and G. Weisbuch (2011), Boolean delay equations on networks in economics and the geosciences, *Int. J. Bifurcation Chaos*, *21*, 3511–3548.

Copeland, T. E. and J. F. Weston (2003), *Financial Theory and Corporate Policy*, 3rd ed., Pearson Education International, Prentice Hall, Upper Saddle River, NJ.

Day, R. (1982), Irregular growth cycles, *Am. Econ. Rev.*, *72*, 406–414.

Dumas, P. (2006), L'évaluation des dommages du changement climatique en situation d'incertitude: l'apport de la modélisation des coûts de l'adaptation, Thèse de doctorat, École des Hautes Études en Sciences Sociales, Paris.

Dumas, P., M. Ghil, A. Groth, and S. Hallegatte (2015), Dynamic coupling of the climate and macroeconomic systems, *Math. Soc. Sci.*, in press.

Einstein, A. (1905), Über die von der molekularkinetischen Theorie der Wärme geforderte Bewegung von in ruhenden Flüssigkeiten suspendierten Teilchen, *Ann. Phys.*, *322*(8), 549–560, doi:10.1002/andp.19053220806.

Eurostat (2002), *Economic Portrait of the European Union 2001*, European Commission, Brussels.

Flaschel, P., R. Franke, and W. Semmler (1997), *Dynamic Macroeconomics: Instability, Fluctuations and Growth in Monetary Economies*, MIT Press, Cambridge, MA.

Frisch, R. (1933), Propagation problems and impulse problems in dynamic economics, in *Economic Essay in honor of Gustav Cassel*, pp. 171–206, George Allen and Unwin, London.

Gale, D. (1973), Pure exchange equilibrium of dynamic economic models, *J. Econ. Theory*, *6*, 12–36.

Ghil, M. (1997), Advances in sequential estimation for atmospheric and oceanic flows, *J. Meteorol. Soc. Jpn*, *75*(1B), 289–304.

Ghil, M. (2001), Hilbert problems for the geosciences in the 21st century, *Nonlinear Process. Geophys.*, *8*, 211–222.

Ghil, M., S. Cohn, J. Tavantzis, K. Bube, and E. Isaacson (1981), Applications of estimation theory to numerical weather prediction, in *Dynamic Meteorology: Data Assimilation Methods*, edited by L. Bengtsson, M. Ghil, and E. Källén, pp. 139–224, Springer-Verlag, New York.

Ghil, M. and R. Vautard (1991), Interdecadal oscillations and the warming trend in global temperature time series, *Nature*, *350*(6316), 324–327, doi:10.1038/350324a0.

Ghil, M., M. R. Allen, M. D. Dettinger, K. Ide, D. Kondrashov, M. E. Mann, A. W. Robertson, A. Saunders, Y. Tian, F. Varadi, and P. Yiou (2002), Advanced spectral methods for climatic time series, *Rev. Geophys.*, *40*(1), 1–41, doi:10.1029/2000RG000092.

Ghil, M., M. Chekroun, and E. Simonnet (2008a), Climate dynamics and fluid mechanics: Natural variability and related uncertainties, *Phys. D*, *237*, 2111–2126.

Ghil, M., I. Zaliapin, and B. Coluzzi (2008b), Boolean delay equations: A simple way of looking at complex systems, *Phys. D*, *237*(23), 2967–2986, doi:10.1016/j.physd.2008.07.006.

Goodwin, R. (1951), The non-linear accelerator and the persistence of business cycles, *Econometrica*, *19*, 1–17.

Goodwin, R. (1967), A growth cycle, in *Socialism, Capitalism and Economic Growth*, edited by C. Feinstein, pp. 54–58, Cambridge University Press, Cambridge.

Grandmont, J.-M. (1985), On endogenous competitive business cycles, *Econometrica*, *5*, 995–1045.

Groth, A. and M. Ghil (2011), Multivariate singular spectrum analysis and the road to phase synchronization, *Phys. Rev. E*, *84*, 036206, doi:10.1103/PhysRevE.84.036206.

Groth, A., M. Ghil, S. Hallegatte, and P. Dumas (2015), The role of oscillatory modes in the U.S. business cycle, *OECD J. Bus. Cyclic Meas. Anal.*, in press.

Hahn, F. and R. Solow (1995), *A Critical Essay on Modern Macroeconomic Theory*, MIT Press, Cambridge, MA.

Hallegatte, S., J.-C. Hourcade, and P. Dumas (2007), Why economic dynamics matter in assessing climate change damages: Illustration on extreme events, *Ecol. Econ.*, *62*, 330–340, doi:10.1016/j.ecolecon.2006.06.006.

Hallegatte, S. and P. Dumas (2008), Can natural disasters have positive consequences? Investigating the role of embodied technical change, *Ecol. Econ.*, doi:10.1016/j.ecolecon.2008.06.011.

Hallegatte, S. and M. Ghil (2008), Natural disasters impacting a macroeconomic model with endogenous dynamics, *Ecol. Econ.*, *68*(1–2), 582–592, doi:10.1016/j.ecolecon.2008.05.022.

Hallegatte, S., M. Ghil, P. Dumas, and J.-C. Hourcade (2008), Business cycles, bifurcations and chaos in a neo-classical model with investment dynamics, *J. Econ. Behav. Organ.*, *67*(1), 57–77, doi:10.1016/j.jebo.2007.05.001.

Harrod, R. (1939), An essay on dynamic economic theory, *Econ. J.*, *49*, 1433.

Harvey, A. C. (1989), *Forecasting, Structural Time Series Models and the Kalman Filter*, Cambridge University Press, Cambridge.

Hicks, J. (1950), The cycle in outline, in *A Contribution to the Theory of the Trade Cycle*, pp. 95–107, Oxford University Press, Oxford.

Hillerbrand, R. and M. Ghil (2008), Anthropogenic climate change: Scientific uncertainties and moral dilemmas, *Phys. D*, *237*, 2132–2138, doi:10.1016/j.physd.2008.02.015.

Hillinger, C. (1992), *Cyclical Growth in Market and Planned Economies*, Oxford University Press, New York.

Hodrick, R., and E. Prescott (1997), Postwar U.S. business cycles: An empirical investigation, *J. Money Credit Bank.*, *29*(1), 1–16.

IPCC (2007), *Climate Change 2007: The Physical Science Basis*, pp. 996, Cambridge University Press, Cambridge, contribution of Working Group I to the Fourth Assessment Report of the Intergovernmental Panel on Climate Change.

Jarsulic, M. (1993), A nonlinear model of the pure growth cycle, *J. Econ. Behav. Organ.*, *22*(2), 133–151.

Kaldor, N. (1940), A model of the trade cycle, *Econ. J.*, *50*, 78–92.

Kalecki, M. (1937), A theory of the business cycle, *Rev. Econ. Stud.*, *4*, 77–97.

Kalman, R. E. (1960), A new approach to linear filtering and prediction problems, *Trans. ASME J. Basic Eng.*, *82*, 5–45, Series D.

Karhunen, K. (1946), Zur Spektraltheorie stochastischer Prozesse, *Ann. Acad. Sci. Fenn. Ser. A1 Math. Phys.*, *34*, 1–7.

Keppenne, C. L., and M. Ghil (1993), Adaptive filtering and prediction of noisy multivariate signals: An application to subannual variability in atmospheric angular momentum, *Int. J. Bifurcation Chaos*, *3*, 625–634.

Kimball, M. S. (1995), The quantitative analytics of the basic neomonetarist model, *J. Money Credit Bank.*, *27*, 1241–1277.

King, R. and S. Rebelo (2000), Resuscitating real business cycles, in *Handbook of Macroeconomics*, edited by J. Taylor and M. Woodford, pp. 927–1007, North-Holland, Amsterdam.

Kloeden, P. E. and E. Platen (1992), *Numerical Solutions of Stochastic Differential Equations*, Applications of Mathematics 23, pp. 632, Springer, New York.

Kondrashov, D., C. Sun, and M. Ghil (2008), Data assimilation for a coupled ocean-atmosphere model. Part II: Parameter estimation, *Mon. Weather Rev.*, *136*, 5062–5076, doi:10.1175/2008MWR2544.1.

Kravtsov, S., D. Kondrashov, and M. Ghil (2009), Empirical model reduction and the modeling hierarchy in climate dynamics, in *Stochastic Physics and Climate Modelling*, edited by T. N. Palmer and P. Williams, pp. 35–72, Cambridge University Press, Cambridge.

Kubo, R. (1966), The fluctuation-dissipation theorem, *Rep. Prog. Phys.*, *29*, 255–284.

Kydland, F. and E. Prescott (1982), Time to build and aggregate fluctuations, *Econometrica*, *50*(6), 1345–1370.

Kydland, F. E. and E. C. Prescott (1998), Business cycles: Real facts and a monetary myth, in *Real Business Cycles: A Reader*, edited by K. D. S. James, E. Hartley, and K. D. Hoover, Routledge, London.

Lemoine, M. and F. Pelgrin (2004), Introduction aux modèles espace-état et au filtre de Kalman, *Revue l'OFCE*, *86*, 272.

Loève, M. (1945), Fonctions aléatoires de second ordre, *Comptes Rendus Acad. Sci. Paris*, *220*, 380.

Lucas, R. E., Jr. (1972), Expectations and the neutrality of money, *J. Econ. Theory*, *4*(2), 103–124.

Lucas, R. E., Jr. (1973), Some international evidence on output-inflation tradeoffs, *Am. Econ. Rev.*, *63*(3), 326–334.

Mañé, R. (1981), On the dimension of the compact invariant sets of certain non-linear maps, in *Dynamical Systems and Turbulence*, Lecture Notes in Mathematics, vol. *898*, pp. 230–242, Springer, Berlin, doi:10.1007/BFb0091916.

Moss, R. H., J. A. Edmonds, K. A. Hibbard, M. R. Manning, S. K. Rose, D. P. van Vuuren, T. R. Carter, S. Emori, M. Kainuma, T. Kram, G. A. Meehl, J. F. B. Mitchell, N. Nakicenovic, K. Riahi, S. J. Smith, R. J. Stouffer, A. M. Thomson, J. P. Weyant, and T. J. Wilbanks (2010), The next generation of scenarios for climate change research and assessment, *Nature*, *463*, 744–756, doi:10.1038/nature08823.

Nelson, C. R. and H. Kang (1981), Spurious periodicity in inappropriately detrended time series, *Econometrica*, *49*(3), 741–751.

Nikaido, H. (1996), *Prices, Cycles, and Growth*, pp. 285, MIT Press, Cambridge, MA.

Nordhaus, W. D. and J. Boyer (1998), *Roll the DICE Again: The Economics of Global Warming*, Yale University, New Haven, CN.

Plaut, G. and R. Vautard (1994), Spells of low-frequency oscillations and weather regimes in the northern hemisphere, *J. Atmos. Sci.*, *51*(2), 210–236, doi:10.1175/1520-0469(1994)051 ⟨0210:SOLFOA⟩ 2.0.CO;2.

Ricardo, D. (1810), *The High Price of Bullion, a Proof of the Depreciation of Bank Notes*, John Murray, London.

Ruelle, D. (2009), A review of linear response theory for general differentiable dynamical systems, *Nonlinearity*, *22*, 855–870.

Samuelson, P. (1939), A synthesis of the principle of acceleration and the multiplier, *J. Polit. Econ.*, *47*, 786–797.

Sargent, T. J. (1971), A note on the "accelerationist" controversy, *J. Money Credit Bank.*, *3*(3), 721–725.

Sargent, T. J. (1973), Rational expectations, the real rate of interest, and the natural rate of unemployment, *Brook. Pap. Econ. Act.*, *1973*(2), 429–480.

Sella, L., G. Vivaldo, A. Groth, and M. Ghil (2013), Economic cycles and their synchronization: A spectral survey, Technical Report 105, Fondazione Eni Enrico Mattei (FEEM).

Slutsky, E. (1927), The summation of random causes as a source of cyclic processes, III(1), Conjuncture Institute, Moscow, *Econometrica*, *5*, 105–146.

Smith, A. (1776), *An Inquiry into the Nature and Causes of the Wealth of Nations*, London.

Solow, R. M. (1956), A contribution to the theory of economic growth, *Q. J. Econ.*, *70*, 65–94.

Soros, G. (2008), *The New Paradigm for Financial Markets: The Credit Crisis of 2008 and What It Means*, BBS, Public Affairs, New York.

Stern, N. (2006), *The Economics of Climate Change. The Stern Review*, vol. *712*, Cambridge University Press, Cambridge.

Takens, F. (1981), Detecting strange attractors in turbulence, in *Dynamical Systems and Turbulence, Lecture Notes in Mathematics*, vol. *898*, pp. 366–381, Springer, Berlin.

Vautard, R. and M. Ghil (1989), Singular spectrum analysis in nonlinear dynamics, with applications to paleoclimatic time series, *Phys. D*, *35*(3), 395–424, doi:10.1016/0167-2789(89)90077–8.

Vautard, R., P. Yiou, and M. Ghil (1992), Singular-spectrum analysis: A toolkit for short, noisy chaotic signals, *Phys. D*, *58*(1–4), 95–126, doi:10.1016/0167-2789(92)90103-T.

Wittgenstein, L. (2001), *Philosophical Investigations*, pp. 246, Wiley-Blackwell, Oxford.

Part VI
Prediction and Preparedness

20

Extreme Tsunami Events in the Mediterranean and Its Impact on the Algerian Coasts

Lubna A. Amir,[1] **Walter Dudley,**[2] **and Brian G. McAdoo**[3]

ABSTRACT

The West Mediterranean region is subject to seismic and tsunami hazards. In this chapter, a tsunami modeling is carried out in North Algeria for extreme tsunami events. The West Mediterranean Sea is narrow and it takes less than 13 minutes for tsunami waves to reach the Spanish coasts. Calculated tsunami water heights triggered by magnitude 7.5 earthquakes with epicenters in the Oran and Algiers coasts are up to 2 m in height. As for the submarine tsunami slides sources, the extreme model tests performed in this study show that water heights can reach above 5 m in the Western Algerian coast. Calculations of tsunami energies and tsunami waves' celerity are presented, and the economical impact of extreme tsunami and earthquake events in the Algerian coast are also discussed. This study shows the challenge that North Algeria would face in case of an extreme magnitude destructive earthquake triggering a tsunami. Finally, the importance of the immediate, full implementation of actions in the framework of the North-East Atlantic and Mediterranean Seas Tsunami Warning System (NEAMTWS) for the prevention and awareness of tsunami hazard and risk in the Mediterranean earthquake-prone region are highlighted.

20.1. INTRODUCTION

The damaging 2004 Sumatra-Andaman tsunami has shown the importance of implementing a warning system for the Indian Ocean. A total of 250,000 people died and much damage could have been avoided if people had been informed and evacuated in due time. On March 2005, a scientific consortium decided to establish a tsunami alert program for the Indian Ocean within the International Oceanographic Commission framework. It was also an opportunity to create a warning system for the Mediterranean region. Tsunami warning systems are dedicated to prevent loss of life. The near-field tsunamis induced by earthquakes are challenging topics where the question is about the combination of the tsunami's and the earthquake's potential damage for vulnerable areas. The North-East Atlantic and Mediterranean Seas Tsunami Warning System (NEAMTWS) includes three types of message. The Tsunami Watch (red level) is for tsunami waves that can reach beyond 15 cm in height with a run-up above 1 m. The Tsunami Advisory (orange level) is for tsunami waves lower than 15 cm in height with a run-up lower than 1 m. Finally, the Tsunami Information

[1]Department of Geophysics, Faculty of Earth Sciences, University of Earth Sciences and Technology, Bab Ezzouar, Algiers, Algeria

[2]Marine Science Department, University of Hawaii at Hilo, Hilo, HI, USA

[3]Department of Geography, Vassar College, Poughkeepsie, NY, USA

Extreme Events: Observations, Modeling, and Economics, Geophysical Monograph 214, First Edition.
Edited by Mario Chavez, Michael Ghil, and Jaime Urrutia-Fucugauchi.

messages are to inform about a major seismic event but with no threat of tsunami.

The European Commission supported the development of a series of early detection and warning systems for early action (http://www.jrc.ec.europa.eu). For instance, the public document on the Humanitarian Early Warning System (HEWS II) states that the HEWS II *aims to enable humanitarian decision makers to respond proactively to risks through collaborative monitoring and analysis. It assists humanitarian aid agencies in anticipating and planning for unexpected crisis for which warning signs often exist but are overlooked or not acted upon by providing (1) A continuously updated global summary of emerging socio-political threats, (2) Earlier warning of threats that warrant action, (3) Inter-agency consensus on threats in real time, (4) Increased efficiency via shared automated monitoring of open source information* (http://www.jrc.ec.europa.eu). Decision-making policies should target a broader aspect of who and what is defined as at risk. People at risk are those who are exposed because of (1) their position by the time of the shaking/flood (under a bridge, at home, in a beach, or a harbor, etc.), (2) poorly constructed homes, or (3) their own vulnerability (disability, ill-health, etc.). To consider both social and geophysical risk, a new tsunami risk scale was developed in *Amir et al.* [2013a]. The understanding of tsunami generation and propagation mechanisms is complex and is in constant progress. Meanwhile, scientists have to address efficiency issues regarding tsunami warning systems in order to avoid "false" alarms. The Nias Islands Mw 8.7 earthquake, located near the devastating December 2004 earthquake, had triggered a massive evacuation in the surrounding Indian Ocean countries, but failed to generate a significant tsunami [*Song et al.*, 2008]. The 2005 west California Mw 7.1 and the 2007 Kuril Islands Mw 8.1 earthquakes also created large-scale tsunami alarms and panic in surrounding countries, but did not generate destructive waves [*Song et al.*, 2008]. DART systems are now widely implemented in the Pacific and Indian oceans. Thanks to the DART buoys, every tsunami warning has proved to be for an actual tsunami with waves that could have been dangerous if there had been no evacuations. Nevertheless, in the western Mediterranean, there is still no DART system.

In this chapter, a tsunami modeling is performed for worst case scenarios in the Algerian coast. The economical impact of disasters on the Algerian coast is discussed. The first section presents the seismic hazard and the tsunami occurrence in the West Mediterranean. The second section aims to develop the methodology used. Then, the results section presents the simulated parameters that are discussed for disasters' impact issues afterward.

20.2. TSUNAMI AND SEISMIC HAZARD IN THE MEDITERRANEAN

20.2.1. Tsunami History in the Mediterranean

Historical data record that in the Mediterranean Sea several tsunamis occurred (Figure 20.1). 3500 BP, the collapse of the Santorini caldera caused giant tsunami waves in the Ionian basin in eastern Mediterranean region [*Cita and Aloisi*, 2000]. The Italian peninsula and the Sicily Island are prone to tsunami hazard due to earthquakes, slides (land or sea slides), and volcanic eruptions. The National Geophysical Data Center (NGDC) database reports 119 tsunamis from 79 BC to present day (http://www.ngdc.noaa.gov).

The database uses the Imamura Scale (tsunami magnitude scale) and range between −1 and 4). The intensities range from 1 to 6 (Soloviev and Go tsunami intensity scale) [*Soloviev and Go*, 1974]. The tsunamis reported are mainly triggered by earthquakes (77%). However, volcanoes and landslides are sources to be considered for far-field tsunamis that could affect the Algerian coast (12% and 8%, respectively). Moreover, when earthquakes and landslides are combined, history shows that the maximum water height can reach above 15 m. The 1783 tsunami was triggered in the Calabrian Arc, in the Messinian straits, and induced waves up to 16 m in height. In 1908, in Messina (Italy), a destructive earthquake and tsunami killed at least 72,000 people. These tsunami waves could then affect the Algerian coast and be considered as far-field tsunami sources for Northern Africa.

In Algeria, minor tsunamis were also observed and recorded. The latest was triggered in 2003 by an earthquake of 6.8 magnitude offshore Boumerdes, about 50 km east of Algiers (*USGS-NEIC*). Run-up of 2 m in height was observed in the Balearic Islands, in Spain. However, the Spanish tide gauging stations recorded 1 m waves' height. The highest wave height reported for historical tsunamis is located in Bejaia after a destructive earthquake in 1856. The epicenter was located offshore Jijel [*Yelles-Chaouche et al.*, 2009]. The harbor of Jijel was flooded and in Bejaia, *Soloviev et al.* [2000] reported that *the sea receded after the earthquake in Bougie by approximately and then rose 5 m and flooded the shore 5–6 times* (Plate 20.1). Sources for near-field tsunamis in Algeria are mainly earthquakes (83%). Nevertheless, 17% of tsunamis were generated by landslides (http://www.ngdc.noaa.go).

20.2.2. Tsunami Hazard in Northern Algeria

The convergence between Africa and Europe resulted in the orogeny of the Alps and the Tell. Located at the limit between the convergent plates, Northern Algeria is subjected to moderate to important and shallow seismicity. The observed and recorded data and information

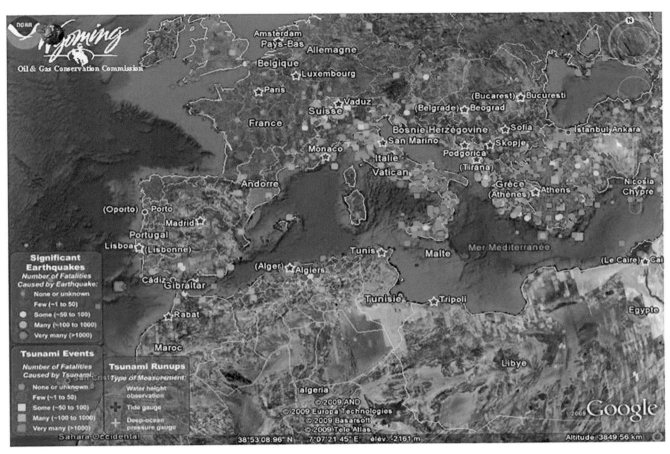

Figure 20.1 Tsunami history in the Mediterranean (NGDC database: Google Earth).

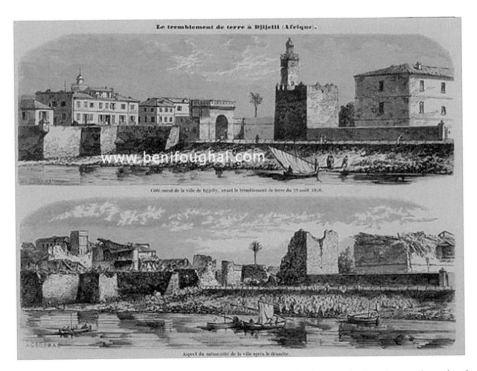

Plate 20.1 Photograph of the Jijel harbor (Eastern coast of Algeria) before and after the earthquake that triggered a tsunami in 1856 (www.benifoughal.com).

from historical seismology to present day show that the magnitude of earthquakes can reach 7–7.5. In 1365, the city of Algiers was totally destroyed after an earthquake of intensity X (EMS scale). Tsunami waves were observed and reports show that the lower part of the city was partly flooded [*Ambraseys and Vogt*, 1988]. In 1790, a destructive earthquake (Io = X) hit Oran and the tremors were felt as far as the Spanish coastal regions. This event triggered a tsunami that propagated all across the Alboran Sea [*Amir*, 2014]. In 1856, an earthquake of intensity Io = IX flooded the harbor of Jijel by tsunami waves. Run-ups in Jijel of 2–3 m in height are reported [*Harbi et al.*, 2003]. In 1980, a 7.3 magnitude earthquake totally destroyed the El Asnam city. It caused about 3000 deaths and 400,000 were made homeless [*Maouche et al.*, 2008]. Reports indicate that phone cables were broken and tsunami waves recorded [*Boudiaf*, 1996]. The 2003 Zemmouri Mw = 6.8 earthquake caused 2278 deaths, made 250,000 homeless and damaged 6000 buildings and 20,800 housing units [*Maouche et al.*, 2008]. It also triggered a small tsunami. Run-ups were recorded in Southern Europe and a temporary retreat of the sea was observed in Dellys (east of Algiers). The ascent of the seafloor was about 15 cm in the Dellys harbor. Finally, "killer waves" caused the deaths of 12 swimmers in the beach of Mostaganem (west of Algeria) in August 2007 [*Amir et al.*, 2013b].

The Algiers region is marked by the Thenia fault system [*Boudiaf*, 1996] in the East and the Sahel anticline in the West [*Boudiaf*, 1996; *Maouche et al.*, 2008]. The existence of the Sahel blind fault reverse fault is one of the most dangerous active faults in the south of Algiers. This fault is linked to the Sahel anticline [*Meghraoui*, 1991]. The 2003 Zemmouri magnitude 6.8 earthquake revealed an active thrust faulting offshore [*Deverchere et al.*, 2005]. The 1980 magnitude 7.3 El Asnam earthquake and the Zemmouri magnitude 6.8 earthquake induced phone cable failure and revealed that submarine slides were also associated with the earthquakes. The 1980 strong earthquake destabilized the unconsolidated sediment of the continental slope inducing turbidity currents [*El Robrini et al.*, 1985]. Debris flow carried lower downslope were identified in the Algerian submarine valley [*Giresse et al.*, 2006]. They estimated that the accumulation thickness is about 230 cm and suggested that this debris flow was linked to the major 1891 earthquake located at Gouraya. Turbidity currents were observed as well, from multibeam bathymetry, down the Dellys and Sebaou submarine canyons after the 2003 Zemmouri earthquake [*Savoye et al.*, 2007]. They suggested a multiple source for turbidity currents rather than a single source. Swath bathymetric map and seismic reflection profiles made also possible the imaging of headwall scars in four shallow slides, in the Eivissa channel, along the Balearic margin [*Lastras et al.*, 2004]. Earthquakes may have triggered these slides.

20.3. METHODOLOGY

20.3.1. The Hydrodynamic Modeling

Tsunami hazard can be investigated through hydrodynamic modeling. Tsunami waves are long water waves generated from undersea earthquakes, submarine slides, landslides, or volcanic activity. Generation and propagation of triggered water waves are simulated with a nonlinear shallow water code called SWAN [*Mader*, 2004]. The SWAN code solves the two-dimensional Eulerian equations with a finite difference scheme and includes the Coriolis and Frictional effects. These are written as follows:

$$\frac{\partial U_x}{\partial t} + U_x \frac{\partial U_x}{\partial x} + U_y \frac{\partial U_x}{\partial x} + g \frac{\partial H}{\partial x}$$
$$= FU_y + F^{(x)} - g \frac{U_x \left(U_x^2 + U_y^2 \right)^{\frac{1}{2}}}{C^2 \left(D + H - R \right)} \quad (20.1)$$

$$\frac{\partial U_y}{\partial t} + U_x \frac{\partial U_y}{\partial x} + U_y \frac{\partial U_y}{\partial y} + g \frac{\partial H}{\partial y}$$
$$= -FU_x + F^{(y)} - g \frac{U_y \left(U_x^2 + U_y^2 \right)^{\frac{1}{2}}}{C^2 \left(D + H - R \right)} \quad (20.2)$$

$$\frac{\partial H}{\partial t} + \frac{\partial \left(D + H - R \right) U_x}{\partial x}$$
$$+ \frac{\partial \left(D + H - R \right) U_y}{\partial y} - \frac{\partial R}{\partial t} = 0 \quad (20.3)$$

With U_x = velocity in the x-direction, U_y = velocity in the y-direction, g = gravity acceleration, t = time, H = water height above the sea level, R = sea bottom motion, F = Coriolis parameter, C = Chezy coefficient, D = depth, and $F^{(x)}$ and $F^{(y)}$ = functions for the meteorological effect.

The triggering of a tsunami is estimated from the source parameters. In the case of earthquakes, tsunami codes usually assume the instantaneous vertical translation of co seismic displacement to the free water surface as the initial condition that generates tsunami waves. Nevertheless, the tectonic rupture process is much more complex. Long-lasting rupture of a large earthquake often appears as a sequence of multiple events [*Trifunac et al.*, 2002]. Uncertainties in tsunami source parameters also relate to the submarine slides associated to the seismic events. The velocities of underwater landslides are one to two orders smaller than the velocities associated with the earthquakes' dislocations [*Trifunac and Todorovska*, 2002]. Uncertainties in tsunami source parameters also relate to the submarine slides associated with the seismic events. The velocities of underwater landslides are one to two orders smaller than the velocities associated with the earthquakes' dislocations [*Trifunac and Todorovska*, 2002]. Tsunamis induced from landslides are classically simulated based on the source volume displaced and the morphology and slope failures.

20.3.2. Tsunami Generation and Propagation

The western Mediterranean has been shaped by the successive steps of the eastward migration of the Apennines-Maghrebides subduction arc [*Guegen et al.*, 1998]. Among the main features inherited from the geodynamic processes that took place in the region during the Neogene and Plio-Quaternary times, a series of sub-basins developed from West to East. The western Mediterranean is a narrow sea where the maximum water depth is about 2900 m. A series of seamounts have been well imaged by the diverse offshore surveys [*Domzig et al.*, 2006, 2009]. Therefore undersea bottom displacement can be either triggered by sedimentary or mass-movements or by a co seismic displacement source.

In this work, the tsunami modeling was carried out from a 1-arc minute and 2-arc minute grid domain that covers the southern part of western Mediterranean [*Amante and Eakins*, 2009]. The time step calculation for the tsunami waves' generation and propagation is 5 minutes and the Coriolis' effect was neglected during the computation.

20.3.2.1. Earthquake Scenarios
Scientists expect an important earthquake near the Algiers and Oran harbor marked by a seismic gap. For magnitude in the range of order of 7, the return period is 475 years. Based on the regional seismotectonic analysis [*Meghraoui*, 1991; *Boudiaf*, 1996; *Mauffret*, 2007], the source considered for both cases are a pure NE-SW thrusting fault.

The tsunami source parameters for the earthquake were deduced from the classical empirical seismological relationships to estimate the fault plane geometry [*Kanamori and Anderson*, 1975; *Wells and Coppersmith*, 1994]. The co seismic displacements are simulated from the Okada analytic formula [*Okada*, 1992] within the topographical grid.

The results performed for Algiers and Oran case studies were published in Amir et al. [2012, 2014]. These were related to a single earthquake source offshore Algiers and Oran harbors. The earthquake for Algiers was located at 3.1°E, 36.8°N. The magnitude was 7.5 and the focal depth was 7 km. The active fault considered was oriented 55° in

the north direction (strike), dipping 40° in the south-east direction. As for the Alboran modeling, the epicenter was located at 0.58°W, 35.76°N. The magnitude was 7.5 as well, and the focal depth was 5 km. The fault was oriented 65° in the north direction (strike), dipping 45° in the south-east direction. In this chapter, we will only present them to support the discussion regarding the economical impact of disasters in the Algerian coast.

20.3.2.2. Submarine Slides Scenarios
Induced coastal or submarine slides due to instable slope failures in the Mediterranean are as well a factor for additional turbidity currents and tsunami waves. For that purpose, several submarine slide sources were tested offshore in several locations in the Algerian coasts. To fairly represent a submarine slide motion, tests were computed using simplified geometries to represent the sedimentary motion uplifted in the seabed. For the Algiers case study, a single source of 2 m sedimentary mass uplifted was considered. Finally, an attempt to reproduce the 2007 killer breaking waves in Mostaganem [*Amir et al.*, 2013b] was the motivation of modeling combined slides sources offshore western part of Algeria.

In August 2007, a moderate 4.5 earthquake was recorded by the European Mediterranean Seismological Center [*Amir et al.*, 2013b]. Based on what might have triggered the potential slide source for this breaking wave, an uplift of 3 m was considered while combining distinct areas of sliding in the western coast of Algeria. First, in Mostaganem, the Khadra Canyon is considered to be a candidate for underwater slides [*Domzig et al.*, 2009]. The dimension of the slide introduced in the SWAN code was 30 by 25 cells. Each cell was 1.8 km in both directions (x-axis × y-axis). The second source introduced in the SWAN code was located at the entrance of Arzew harbor, in respect of the geomorphology of the seabed in the region. The dimension of the source introduced in the program was 20 by 22 cells (x-axis × y-axis). There again, the size of the cell was 1.8 km in both directions. A third slide source was defined nearby the Yusuf-Habibas ridge that marks well the neotectonic in Alboran. The active fault is a strike-slip and cannot generate a significant tsunami. Nevertheless, the morphology of the ridge and the seamounts are a threat for water waves triggered by slides due to gravitational and tectonic stress. Another motivation for selecting another slide source in this location was the presence of the Habibas Island known for its unique ecosystem in the region. The dimension of the slide was 19 by 24 cells (cell size: 1.8 km).

20.3.3. Tsunami Energy and Tsunami Waves' Celerity

Humanitarian and economical impact of tsunami waves or destructive earthquakes are related to the damage that result from the disasters (natural or man-made if social vulnerability is considered). While approaching the coast, the tsunami waves velocity decreases, the water height increases. Due to the conservation laws that describe the fluid dynamics during the waves' propagation, the tsunami energy is a parameter that illustrates the strength of the current and the sources that generate current impacting vessels, infrastructures, and at the origin of debris that can then flow and become an additional source of damage. The tsunami celerity is distinct from the tsunami waves' velocity. The tsunami celerity depends on the bathymetry. The water height waves generated by the sea bottom motion due to the earthquake are not included. In this work, we only present the tsunami wave celerity estimated for the whole western Mediterranean. The bathymetry considered was extracted from the 1-minute ETOPO database [Amante and Eakins, 2009]. The calculation used the formula $c = \sqrt{gh}$, where c is the celerity wave, g is the gravitational constant, and h is the water depth.

In 2003, Okal and Synolakis reviewed the fundamental parameters controlling the energy dissipated into the tsunami wave [Okal and Synolakis, 2003]. They examined the seismic dislocations and the underwater slumps. In this chapter, we used the theoretical formalism and discussions they developed to provide orders of magnitude of the amount of energy potentially disseminated into the tsunami waves.

For a dislocation source, the energy of the tsunami can be evaluated with the following equation:

$$E_T = 7 \times 10^{-17} M_0^{4/3} \qquad (20.4)$$

The tsunami energy is expressed in ergs and the seismic moment is expressed in dyn-cm. In this work, the tsunami energy was calculated for earthquakes with magnitudes ranging from 4.5 to 7.5. The seismic moment was deduced from the Kanamori laws [Kanamori and Anderson, 1975].

As for the slump source, Okal and Synolakis [2003] highlighted the velocity acquired by the slumping mass is controlled by the gravity field g. They proposed a formula to estimate the maximum velocity reached during a slumping event on an inclined plane (Equation 20.5). The inclined plane is defined from the topography. The geometry of the plane was determined from the canyon's parameters identified from the swath bathymetry offshore the Algerian coast [Domzig et al., 2009; Cattaneo et al., 2010]. The slope gradients are steep and range between 20° and 40°. Mass volume for one single slide is about 0.8 km³. These parameters helped to propose a value for the maximum vertical extent z traveled by the slumping material. Then, the energy for the mass sliding can be evaluated using the classical kinetic energy formula.

$$v = \sqrt{2gz} \qquad (20.5)$$

In this chapter, the seismic energy triggered by a series of earthquakes with Mw magnitudes ranging from 4.5 to 7.5 is determined as well. For that purpose, the seismological relationship below is used [Kanamori and Anderson, 1975]. The energy in Equation 20.6 is expressed in ergs:

$$\log E = 1.5 \text{Mw} + 11.8 \qquad (20.6)$$

20.4. RESULTS

20.4.1. Tsunami Modeling Offshore Algiers

Figure 20.2 displays the location of the scenario tested (Figure 20.2a) and the calculated vertical sea bottom motion due to the earthquake (Figure 20.2b). The tsunami results are represented in Figures 20.3 and 20.4. First, the sea bottom deformation due to a 7.5 magnitude earthquake in the entrance of the Algiers harbor shows a maximum co seismic uplift of 2.6 m.

The second tsunami source (uplift of 2 m offshore Algeria) is represented in Figure 20.3a. Due to the 2 m bottom uplift, the tsunami waves reach the Algiers coast in less than 10 minutes after the tsunami source (Figure 20.3b). The water waves propagate in a wider area along the Algerian coast 17 minutes later. It takes 25 minutes for the tsunami to reach the Balearic Islands (Figure 20.3d). From 38 minutes, the tsunami wave front heads to France and Italy.

The calculated wave profiles near Algiers and in the Balearic Islands (Ibiza) are shown in Figure 20.4. Results represent the two scenarios tested. On the whole, those results show that maximum run-ups are as low as 2 m in height.

The sea level rises up to 0.5 m in height in Algiers just a few minutes after the 2 m uplift offshore Algiers (Figure 20.4a). As for the Ibiza (Balearic Islands), the tsunami waves arrive 30 minutes later. The results show a series of waves reaching lower than 0.4 m. Then, a maximum run-up is estimated for the fifth wave (0.5 m) (Figure 20.4c). The modeling of the water waves induced by an earthquake of magnitude 7.5 is represented in Figure 20.4b and d. The results also show the sea suddenly rises up to 1.4 m near Algiers. As for the Ibiza Island, the waves reach the coast 30 minutes after the earthquake and the water heights do not exceed 1 m.

20.4.2. Tsunami Modeling Offshore Western Algeria

In this work, tsunami hazard offshore Western Algeria is presented for two extreme events that were reported in Oran, as for a tsunami triggered by a destructive earthquake in 1790, and in Mostaganem in 2007; while the tsunami source is still being investigated [Amir, 2014]. Figure 20.5 shows the water height simulated in Oran for a 7.5 magnitude earthquake where the epicenter is located at the harbor entrance.

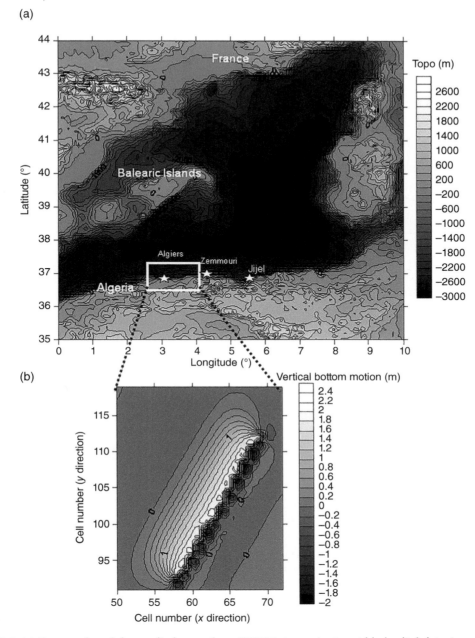

Figure 20.2 (a) Topography of the studied zone from ETOPO two minute gridded relief data (source: NOAA/NGDC). The black rectangle represents the area for the tested tsunami sources location. (b) Estimation of the vertical sea bottom motion computed for a 7.5 magnitude earthquake in the Algiers harbor. The seismic moment magnitude Mo is 2.21×10^{20} °N.m. The length and width of the fault plane is 73.3 by 29.2 km. The fault is a pure thrust striking N55° and dipping 40° to SE. The slip is 3.45 m.

The results obtained confirm the water height could have reached about 2 m in height in the Oranie coast [*Amir*, 2014].

The Figure 20.6 shows the water heights simulated for the Mostaganem beach (0.46°E, 36.23°N, water depth: −2 m) (Figure 20.6a) and for Oran harbor (0.4°W, 35.9°N, water depth: −15 m) (Figure 20.6b). The results represented here are for all the slides' combinations tested.

The simulations computed at the Mostaganem beach successfully showed the water height could reach above 8 m for slides introduced in (1) the Khadra Canyon (green curve) and (2) the Khadra Canyon and Arzew region (combined) (Figure 20.6a). At the entrance of Oran harbor (Figure 20.6b), the water heights is lower than those simulated in Mostaganem. Nevertheless, these are significant

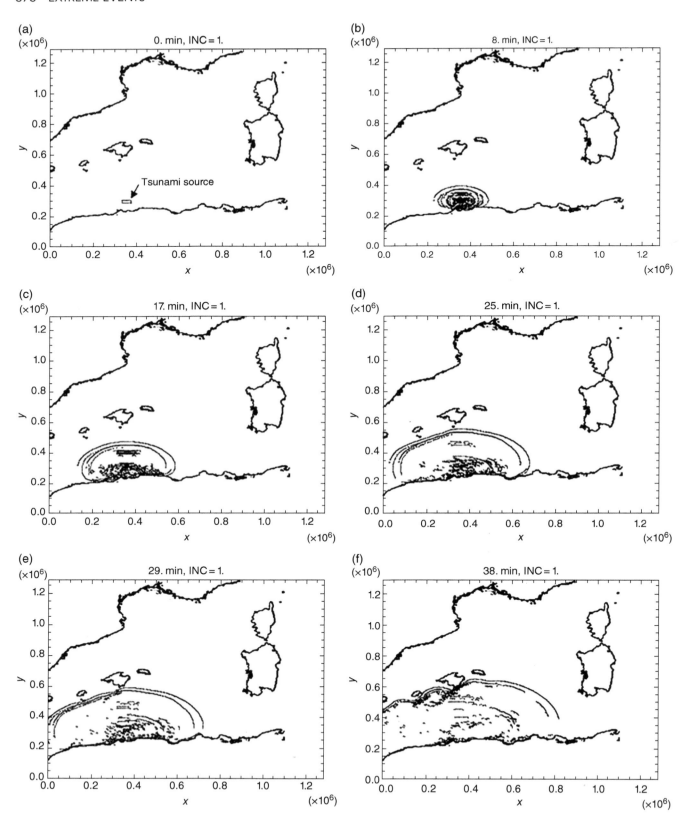

Figure 20.3 Tsunami generation and propagation computed with the SWAN code [*Mader*, 2004]. The source is a 2 m bottom uplift offshore Algiers. (a) Introduction of the bottom motion for the tsunami generation; (b–f) Snapshots of the tsunami wave propagation at 8, 17, 25, 29, and 38 minutes. The *x* and *y* axis are in meters.

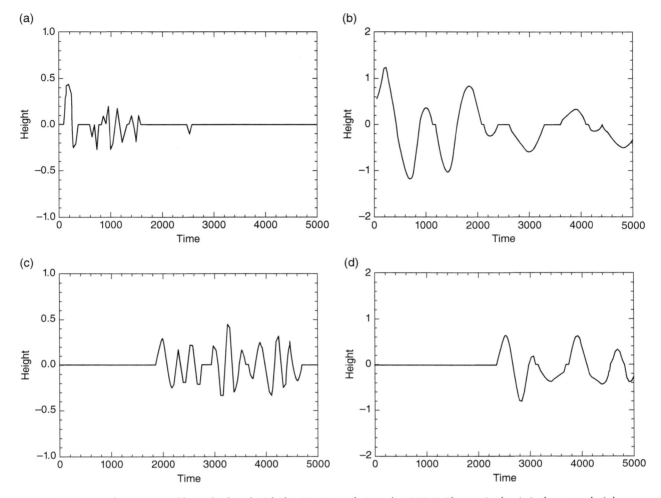

Figure 20.4 The wave profiles calculated with the SWAN code [*Mader*, 2004]. The vertical axis is the water height in meters and the horizontal axis is the time in seconds. (a and b) Water height computed for the Algiers coast (water depth is 21 m) for a bottom uplift of 2 m offshore Algiers, and for a 7.5 magnitude earthquake in the Algiers harbor, respectively. (c and d) Water height computed for the Balearic Islands (Ibiza) (water depth is 36 m) for the bottom uplift of 2 m offshore Algiers and the earthquake of magnitude of 7.5 in the Algiers harbor, respectively.

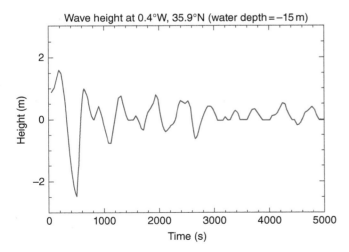

Figure 20.5 Water height profiles computed for a 7.5 magnitude at the entrance of Oran harbor [*Amir*, 2014].

(above 5 m). Further field investigations should be carried out to check any abnormal waves' behavior noticed or tsunami deposits in the sedimentary layers.

20.4.3. Energy Waves and Tsunami Wave Celerity: Economical Impact of Disasters in the Algerian Coast

The tsunami energy and the seismic energy calculated for earthquakes with magnitudes ranging from 4.5 to 7.5 are reported in Figure 20.7 hereafter. The slumping kinetic energy is as well displayed. The values estimated for the three sources of energy highlight that the seismic energies are the highest ones for magnitude above 7. The tsunami energies determined from the seismic moment values are low in comparison to the seismic and the slumping kinetic energies. Nevertheless, the tsunami energy estimated from the earthquakes' parameters only, and do not reflect the energy acquired through the waves' propagation in the

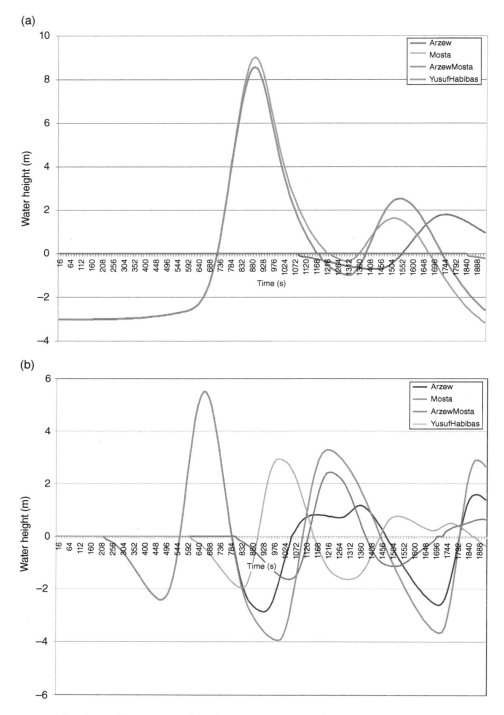

Figure 20.6 Water height profiles computed for distinct combined slides scenario in the western Mediterranean. (a) for Mostaganem beach location (0.46°E, 36.23°N) and (b) for Oran location (0.4°W, 35.9°N).

ocean. More research needs to be done on the amount of energy transferred from the tsunami sources' to the tsunami waves' that propagate and reach the coast. Sea bottom vertical displacements estimated from the Okada analysis [*Okada*, 1992] for magnitude above 7 are comparable to extreme events for underwater slumps under certain conditions. Therefore, the results presented in the Figure 20.7 could provide a new insight on how to analyze the impact of distinct tsunami sources not only on the shoreline, but also on offshore as well as for vessels and oil-related infrastructures.

Figure 20.8 illustrates the tsunami wave celerity estimated for the whole western Mediterranean. The results

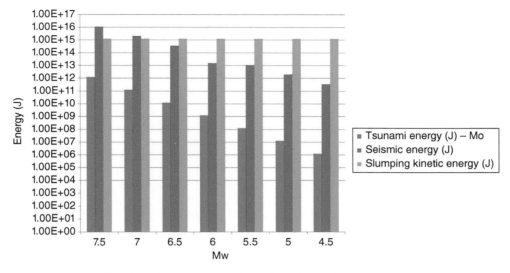

Figure 20.7 Energies calculated for distinct magnitude earthquakes and underwater slumps.

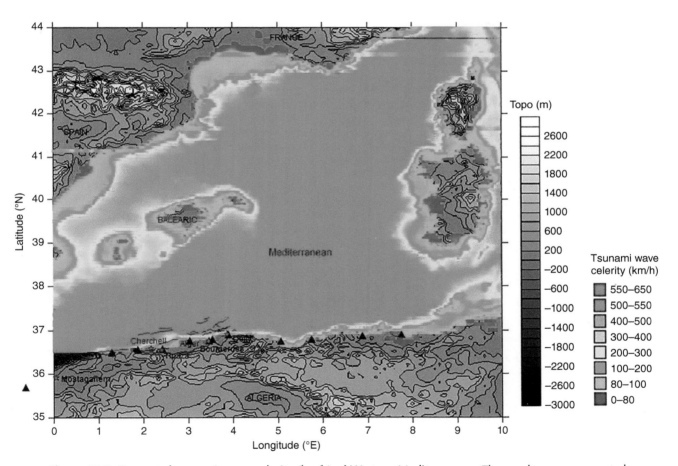

Figure 20.8 Computed tsunami wave celerity (km/h) of Western Mediterranean. The results are represented with the GIS Mapinfo software and the waves celerities' layers are superposed on the topographical/bathymetry map of the western Mediterranean. Black triangles correspond with the historical tsunami events reported for the Algerian coast in the NGDC database and documented by *Soloviev et al.* [2000]. The black lines in the central northern Algeria are offshore faults compiled after *Mauffret* [2007]. The red stars represent the main coastal cities.

well represent the correlation between the geomorphology and bathymetry and the wave celerity. In the open sea (central part of the western Mediterranean), tsunami waves are fast and travel at a speed around 500–620 km/h for water depths ranging around 2500 m. Although the tsunami waves celerity reduces when waves hit the coast, their velocities are to be considered for awareness and prevention in addition to the water height computed or observed. Beaches and harbors are immediately affected by waves travelling at a speed around 20–60 km/h. It can have an impact on human loss or infrastructure damages. Numerous slides triggered by earthquakes offshore Algiers or in the Eivissa channel may play a role as for broken cables (telephone, pipeline, etc.). The rate the tsunami wave reduces along the coastlines and the energy that is conservative all along the tsunami propagation is a real issue for ships carrying dangerous products such as oil between Europe and Northern Africa. Oil spills have already occurred in the past and environmental damages would be another disaster to be considered.

Moreover, numerous small harbors along the northern coast are important for the livelihoods of many coastal inhabitants. The impact of tsunami waves for these communities (including the protection/preservation of their boats/ships) is a serious issue as well.

20.5. DISCUSSION

20.5.1. The Tsunami Modeling and the Coastal Risk

The results presented here are constrained by simplified assumptions, the tsunami source location, the geometry and the size of the tsunami source, and some other limits.

The bathymetry of the West Mediterranean Sea is flat with maximum depths around 2500 m and the continental slopes of Algeria are steep (Figure 20.2). In comparison with the Indian and Pacific case studies, the West Mediterranean topography and the size of the tsunami sources attenuate the tsunami hazard in the Algerian coastline. Other published studies related to tsunami hazard in Zemmouri (east of Algiers) and in Jijel (East of Algeria) showed the run-ups calculated are less than 2 m in height [*Wang and Liu*, 2005; *Yelles-Chaouche et al.*, 2009]. The Italy case study shows the necessity to develop a regional tsunami alert program specific to the West Mediterranean. In 1908, a tsunami occurred in the Ionian and Tyrrhenian sea after a devastating earthquake ($M = 7$) that hit Messina in north-west of Sicily [*Piatanesi et al.*, 1999]. Nevertheless, the tsunami source in Italy is mostly related to volcanic and landslide events. A volcanic event is predicted from the increasing frequencies of seismic tremors. In such a case, people evacuate without confusion. But in North Africa, the major difficulties are due to the earthquake's disaster. The effect of a tsunami

Plate 20.2 Photograph of streets of the Casbah District after the 2003 Zemmouri earthquake (Algiers). Photo Credit: L. Amir.

watch or a tsunami alert is viewed differently by the population from the north and the south Mediterranean. A 7 magnitude or intensity Io (EMS) = X earthquake will induce damage and human loss. Moreover, such seismological events are followed by aftershock sequences with earthquakes of comparable or slightly lower magnitude. Damage would be severe and panic reactions cannot be avoided.

The Algerian coast is marked by fast urban development. However, safety standard rules for construction are not respected. Moreover, Algiers city is an old city, the rehabilitation of the construction and the infrastructure should be considered for disaster management. Plates 20.2–20.4 illustrate districts with a high density of buildings and inhabitants in Algiers. These places have been affected after the 2003 Boumerdes earthquake. Plate 20.2 shows the narrowness of the streets and the short space between dwellings in the Casbah area. The deterioration of the buildings is such that even heavy rains make them collapse. Plates 20.3 and 20.4 correspond to the Belouizdad district, damages are either due to the 2003 earthquake, regular heavy rains during the winter or due to the state of degradation of the buildings.

Plate 20.3 Photograph of the state of dwellings and constructions in the Belouizdad district (Algiers, after the 2003 Boumerdes earthquake, Mw = 6.9). Photo Credit: L. Amir.

Plate 20.4 Photograph illustrating the state of dwellings and construction in the Belouizdad district (Algiers, after, the 2003 Boumerdes Earthquake, Mw = 6.9). Photo Credit: L. Amir.

20.5.2. How to Evaluate Costs of the Civil and Industrial Infrastructure Generated by Extreme Events in the Algerian Coasts?

Several studies and Non-Governmental Organizations consider the GDP criteria to evaluate the economy's disaster. Then based on a quantitative estimation of the costs of the civil and the industrial infrastructures generated by the disaster, the challenge is to rebuild buildings and cities. The GDP per capita is defined by the World Bank as "*the gross domestic product divided by mid-year population. GDP is the sum of gross value added by all resident producers in the economy plus any product taxes and minus any subsidies not included in the value of the products.*

It is calculated without making deduction for depreciation of fabricated assets or for depletion and degradation of natural resources" (http://data.worldbank.org/indicator/NY.GDP.PCAP.CD).

In Algeria, the main income of the country is from the oil industry. In fact, Algeria is the leading natural gas producer in Africa and the second-largest natural gas supplier to Europe (http://www.eia.gov). Oil companies drill offshore the Mediterranean, very close to the Algerian shorelines. While knowing the risk and the disaster history in the Mediterranean and in the North Africa coast, the will to work for an economical growth is above the considerations related to the earthquake and the tsunami hazard. The questions then are as follows:

1. How can we evaluate with GDP per capita the costs of civil and infrastructure generated by extreme events?

2. What is really the cause of a disaster?

3. What really damaged those who are exposed?

4. How far were they really vulnerable prior to the disaster?

5. How can we evaluate the health issues with GDP per capita, especially the nonvisible ones, such as those suffering from post-trauma stress and those who need to find back an employment or a social network. Not all the aspects of damage are yet considered when risk is defined and evaluated. The neurosciences have developed new applications to better understand the role of the pollution, lack of clean water supply, and appropriate sanitary and security facilities for the neurological diseases developed by those who still live in refugees' shelters or poor districts [*Mateen*, 2010]. The Tohoku disaster in 2011 is a perfect example that illustrates the long-term effect of a disaster, for example, people facing cancer threats, disabilities because of the nuclear power plant leakage, and the radioactivity contamination.

6. How can we evaluate the number of infrastructure damage if those who are not totally destroyed will be sooner or later by less powerful events and are not considered when the goal is to rebuild a resilient and sustainable coastal place?

7. How can we evaluate the number of dead people? Sometimes the death may not be immediate, but there are situations when victims of the earthquake or the tsunami do not survive longer than the next 15 years because of the long-term consequences.

Tsunami warning systems can prevent loss of life in real time if all elements are correctly and effectively implemented (DART buoys, a good coordination between the government and the organizations in charge of spreading the message, and the scientists' warnings), however, one cannot prevent damage. It is long-term planning and mitigation measures that can reduce damage. And hence this is at first a political will. The Haiti earthquake in 2010 was a very good example of how colonialism inheritance, urbanism issue, and poor governance could be at the origin of the disaster [*McAdoo and Paravisini-Gebert*, 2011]. Preventing the present-day vulnerability and considering the ancestral cultural legacy and knowledge for the land, the ecosystem and coastal management will provide a new perspective to assess the natural risk triggered by extreme events.

20.5.3. Disaster Planning and Risk Awareness

In Northern Algeria, the coastal urbanism raises several issues regarding evacuations and emergency planning. Hence, tsunami mitigation and prevention measures help to improve warning systems. The challenge while managing the disaster is always the same, that is, the access to secure places for those located at the points of interest/focal points where a risk has been identified. Efficient and fast disaster responses rely on a good coordination between institutions and people on the ground. The vulnerability to destruction is considered more and more in interdisciplinary research related to tsunami mitigation, but not yet in the warning procedures. Therefore, to efficiently reduce vulnerability for tsunami warning system, it is very important to implement policies for coastal planning and coastal management. The western Mediterranean could learn from the lessons experienced in the Pacific and in the Indian regions. During an emergency, preparedness programs could reduce the risk for the vulnerable communities (disabled, old people, or those who need assistance).

Oregon Emergency Management has facilitated and helped to implement a special neighborhood preparedness program known as "The Tsunami Buddy System." First envisioned by Mrs. Betty Johnson for her community of Yachats, Oregon, the system has now spread to other areas of Oregon and has been successfully implemented as far away as coastal villages in Thailand. It cannot be assumed that emergency personnel will be available to help everyone who needs assistance during a tsunami emergency. This program is designed for the community to take care of one another during a tsunami evacuation by:

1. Identifying persons in the community who need help in getting out of the evacuation zone to a safe area.

2. Assigning a responsible "Buddy" within a four block radius to help their neighbor or family member, who needs assistance, to evacuate.

3. Issuing a window placard to those in need of assistance to identify their residences or businesses if located in an evacuation zone.

Finally, managing a disaster in real time is about preventing from long-term consequences. Unfortunately, new communities at risk and social vulnerability usually develop after a disaster. Emergency shelters become parts of new poor urban districts with unemployment or health issues and marginalization of victims after the disaster crisis.

20.5.4. The Social Progress Index Model and the Risk Reduction

The impact of natural hazards such as earthquakes, tsunamis, or associated landslides is linked to soil occupation in coastal areas. Several indices are developed to measure the "health" of an economy or a society. Most of the time, during a disaster, the level of damage is due to prior vulnerabilities, for example, degradation of the coastal ecosystem and the quality of life of the exposed communities. Nowadays, more and more economists tend to include in their studies new tools and parameters such as the Social Progress Index (SPI) or the Human Development Index (HDI) [*Stiglitz et al.*, 2009]. Hence, beyond the GDP per capita that only measures the growth of nations, the challenge is to include the health and quality of life of individuals living within a community in a location prone to natural hazards inherent to the cycle of the Earth and that happened long time before the building of "*an economy for the prosperity of a nation….*"

A report published by the Social Progress Imperative [*Porter et al.*, 2013] developed the concepts and elements of the Social Progress Index model that is now incorporated in the United States in late 2012 with already operational headquarters in Washington DC (http://socialprogressimperative.org). In fact, the Social Progress Imperative defines the social progress as "*the capacity of a society to meet the basic human needs of its citizens, establish the building blocks that allow citizens and communities to enhance and sustain the quality of their lives, and create the conditions for all individuals to reach their full potential*" [*Porter et al.*, 2013]. The basic architecture of the model involves the following criteria:

1. Basic Human Needs: the corresponding indicators are nutrition and basic medical care; air, water, and sanitation; and shelter and personal safety.

2. Foundations of Well-being: the corresponding indicators are access to basic knowledge; access to information and communications; health and wellness; and ecosystem sustainability.

3. Opportunity: the corresponding criteria are personal rights; access to higher education; and personal freedom and choice and the equity and inclusion.

At length, the SPI is to "*provide useful insights that will help stakeholders to make better choices, prioritize investments, and strengthen implementation capacity to improve the lives of citizens*" [*Porter et al.*, 2013].

A great challenge is then to establish a social database that reflects as much as possible the real needs of each member of the society. In that context, there is a need to redefine the role of a civil society in the 21st century. Thanks to the advancement of information and communication, and due to social media, every human being can play a role and influence policymakers and stakeholders. Crowd-sourcing using social network is the future of new ways to think about disaster planning and risk reduction by giving to the "voiceless" and the vulnerable group a place and a role in disaster management, awareness, and preparedness.

20.6. CONCLUSION

Tsunami warning system involves a series of stage, from the simple watch bulletin to the alert stage. People should be informed on the content of a tsunami warning program and the multiple risk and vulnerabilities due to combined hazards where a threat of breaking waves are estimated from historical database and modeling studies (geophysical, geological, and social). Otherwise, the panic reactions and the tsunami fear and the stress the community at risk may feel during the aftershocks' sequence could develop new vulnerability factors for disasters that are inherent to the coastal places. To efficiently reduce vulnerability for tsunami warning system, it is very important to implement an interdisciplinary policy for coastal planning, coastal and disaster risk real-time management (geophysical, geological, environmental, and social index parameters). Preserving coastlines from erosion due to human activities is necessary and assist in protecting from tsunami waves. Specificity of countries due to the ratio tsunami hazard (THD) related to the seismic damage (SHD) should be considered in tsunami alert program for near-field regions. Maps of potential inundated coastal areas should include information related to the ratio THD/SHD, the population density, and the existence and location of evacuation places with the implementation of a "buddy system" for those who need assistance.

ACKNOWLEDGMENTS

Discussions with Professor H. Benhallou who passed away in October 2011 was the main motivation to write this chapter. The first author acknowledges Dr. Charles L. Mader of Mader Consulting Company (HI, USA) for his assistance with the SWAN code. We are thankful to the editors and reviewers for their comments. The first author is really grateful to the Editor Mario Chavez for all the constructive remarks during the revision of the manuscript.

REFERENCES

Amante, C. and Eakins, B.W., 2009: ETOPO 1 Arc-Minute Global Relief Model: Procedures, Data Sources and Analysis. NOAA Technical Memorandum NESDIS NGDC-24, 19 pp.

Ambraseys, N. N. and J. Vogt (1988), Material for the investigation of the seismicity of the region of Algiers, *European Earthquake Engineering*, 3, 16–29.

Amir, L. (2014), Tsunami hazard assessment in the Alboran Sea for the Western Coast of Algeria, *Journal of Shipping and Ocean Engineering*, 4, 43–51.

Amir, L. A., A. Cisternas, J.-L. Vigneresse, W. Dudley, and B. G. McAdoo (2012), Algeria's vulnerability to tsunamis from near-field seismic sources, *Science of Tsunami Hazards*, *31*(1), 82–98.

Amir, L. A., A. Cisternas, W. Dudley, B. G. McAdoo, and G. Pararas-Carayanis (2013a), A new tsunami risk scale for warning systems-Application to the bay of Algiers in Algeria, West Mediterranean Sea, *Science of Tsunami Hazards*, *32*(2), 116–130.

Amir, L., Cisternas, A., Dudley, W., McAdoo, B.G., 2013b: Coastal Impact of tsunami in Industrial harbors: Study case of the Arzew-Mostaganem Region (Western Coast of Algeria, North Africa), Proceedings of the 3rd Specialty conference on Disaster Prevention and Mitigation, Montreal, Quebec, 20 May to 1 June.

Boudiaf, A. 1996: Etude sismotectonique de la region d'Alger et de la Kabylie (Algerie): Utilisation des Modeles Numeriques de Terrain (MNT) pour la reconnaissance des structures tectoniques actives: Contribution à l'évaluation de l'aléa sismique, PhD Thesis, 268 pp., University of Montpellier, France.

Cattaneo, A., N. Babonneau, G. Dan, J. Déverchère, A. Domzig, A. Gaullier, B. Lepillier, B. Mercier de Lepinay, A. Nougues, P. Strzerzynski, N. Sultan, and K. Yelles (2010), Submarine landslides along the Algerian Margin: A review of their occurrence and potential link with tectonic structures, in Submarine mass movements and their consequences, *Advances in Natural and Technological Hazards Research*, 28, 515–525.

Cita, M. B. and G. Aloisi (2000), Deep-sea tsunami deposits triggered by the explosion of Santorini (3500 y BP) eastern Mediterranean, *Sedimentary Geology*, 135, 181–203.

Deverchere, J., Yelles, K., Domzig, A., Mercier de Lepinay, B., Bouillin, J.P., Gaulier, V., Bracene, R., Calais, E., Savoye, B., Kherroubi, A., Le Roy, P., Pauc, H., Dan, G., 2005: Active thrust faulting offshore Boumerdes, Algeria, and its relation to the 2003 Mw 6.9 earthquake, *Geophysical Research Letters*, *32*: doi:10.1029/2004GL021646

Domzig, A., K. Yelles, C. Le Roy, J. Deverchere, J.-P. Bouillin, R. Bracene, B. Mercier de Lepinay, P. Le Roy, E. Calais, A. Kherroubi, V. Gaullier, B. Savoye, and H. Pauc (2006), Searching for the Africa–Eurasia Miocene boundary offshore western Algeria (MARADJA'03 cruise), C.R, *Geoscience*, *338*, 80–91.

Domzig, A., V. Gaullier, P. Giresse, H. Pauc, J. Deverchere, and K. Yelles (2009), Deposition processes from echo-character mapping along the western Algerian margin, (Oran - Tenes), *Western Mediterranean*, 26, 673–694.

El Robrini, M., M. Genesseaux, and A. Mauffret (1985), Consequences of the El Asnam earthquakes; turbidity currents and slumps on the Algerian margin (western Mediterranean), *Geo-Marine Letters*, 5, 171–176.

Giresse, P., Pauc, H., Savoye, B., Dan, G., Deverchere, J., Yelles, K., Gaullier, V.; the Maradja Shipboard, 2006: Depositional setting of gravity flow deposits on the western Algerian margin, Geophysical Research Abstracts, 8, EGU-Vienna, EGU06-A-06088.

Guegen, E., C. Doglioni, and M. Fernandez (1998), On the post-25 Ma geodynamic evolution of the western Mediterranean, *Tectonophysics*, *298*, 259–269.

Harbi, A., D. Benouar, and H. Benhallou (2003), Re-appraisal of seismicity and seismotectonics in the north-eastern Algeria Part I: Review of historical seismicity, *Journal of Seismology*, 7, 115–136.

Kanamori, H. and D. Anderson (1975), Theoretical basis of some empirical relations in seismology, *Bulletin of Seismological Society of America*, 65(5), 1073–1095.

Lastras, G., G. Canals, R. Urgeles, J. E. Hughes-Clarke, and J. Accosta (2004), Shallow slides and pockmark swarms in the Eivissa Channel, western Mediterranean Sea, *Sedimentology*, 51, 833–850.

Mader, C. L. (2004), *Numerical Modelling of Water Waves*, 2nd ed., pp. 269, CRC Press, Boca Raton, FL.

Maouche, S., A. Harbi, and M. Meghraoui (2008), Attenuation of Intensity for the Zemmouri Earthquake of 21 May 2003 (Mw 2008): Insights for the Seismic Hazard and Historical Earthquake Sources in Northern Algeria, in *Historical Seismology, Interdisciplinary Studies of Past and Recent Earthquakes*, edited by J. Frechet, M. Meghraoui, and M. Stucchi, pp. 327–350, Springer.

Mateen, F. J. (2010), Neurological disorders in complex humanitarian emergencies and natural disasters, *Annals of Neurology*, 68(3), 282–294.

Mauffret, A. (2007), The northwestern (Maghreb) boundary of the Nubia (Africa) Plate, *Tectonophysics*, *429*, 21–24.

Meghraoui, M. (1991), Blind reverse faulting system associated with the Mont Chenoua-Tipaza earthquake of 29 October 1989 (north central Algeria), *Terra Nova*, *3*, 84–94.

McAdoo, B. G. and L. Paravisini-Gebert (2011), Not the earthquake's fault, *Nature Geoscience*, 4, 210–211.

Okada, Y. (1992), Internal deformation due to shear and tensile faults in a half-space, *Bulletin of Seismological Society of America*, 82(2), 1018–1040.

Okal, E. A. and C. E. Synolakis (2003), A theoretical comparison of tsunamis from dislocations and landslides, *Pure and Applied Geophysics*, 160, 2177–2188.

Piatanesi, A., S. Tinti, and E. Bortolucci (1999), Finite-element simulations of the 28 December straits (Southern Italy) tsunami, *Physics and Chemistry of the Earth*, 24(2), 145–150.

Porter, M.O., Scott, S., Artavia, L.R., 2013: *Social Progress Index*, Social Progress Imperative, Washington, DC, 10 pp.

Savoye, B. Cattaneo, A., Babonneau, N., Deverchere, J., Dan, G., Matougi, R., 2007: Evidences that the May 2003 Boumerdes Earthquake reactivated the Dellys and Sebaou Submarine Canyons (Central Algeria Margin). Submarine Mass Movements and Their Consequences-3rd International Symposium, UNESCO-IGCP-511, Abstract, p. 46.

Song, Y. T., L.-L. Fu, V. Zlotnicki, C. Ji, V. Hjorleifsdottir, C. K. Shum, and Y. Yi (2008), The role of horizontal impulses of the faulting continental slope in generating the 23 December tsunami, *Ocean Modelling*, 20, 362–379.

Soloviev, S. L. and C. N. Go (1974), *A Catalogue of Tsunamis on the Western Shore of the Pacific Ocean*, Academy of Sciences of USSR, pp. 310, Nauka Publishing House, Moscow.

Soloviev, S. L., N. Olga, C. N. Solovieva, K. S. K. Go, and N. A. Shchetnikov (2000), *Tsunamis in the Mediterranean Sea 2000 B.C. –2000 A.D.*, Advances in Natural and Technological Hazards Research, vol. *13*, pp. 237, Kluwer Academic Publishers, Dordrecht.

Stiglitz, J.E., Sen, A., Fitoussi, J.-P., 2009: The measurement of economic performance and social progress revisited, Columbia University, IEP, OFCE Working Paper, 64 p.

Trifunac, M. D. and M. I. Todorovska (2002), A note on differences in tsunami source parameters for submarine slides and earthquakes, *Soil Dynamics and Earthquake Engineering*, *22*, 143–155.

Wang, X. and P. L.-F. Liu (2005), A numerical investigation of Boumerdes-Zemmouri (Algeria) Earthquake and Tsunami, *Computer Modeling in Engineering and Sciences*, *10*(2), 171–183.

Wells, D. L. and K. J. Coppersmith (1994), New empirical relationships among magnitude, rupture, length, rupture width, rupture area, and surface displacement, *Bulletin of Seismological Society of America*, *84*(4), 974–1002.

Yelles-Chaouche, A. K., J. Roger, J. Deverchere, R. Bracene, A. Domzig, H. Hebert, and A. Kherroubi (2009), The 1856 Tsunami of Djidjelli (Eastern Algeria): Seismotectonics, Modelling and Hazard Implications for the Algerian Coast, *Pure and Applied Geophysics*, *166*, 283–300.

21

High-Tech Risks: The 2011 Tôhoku Extreme Events

Heriberta Castaños[1] and Cinna Lomnitz[2]

ABSTRACT

The 2011 Fukushima nuclear accident was an extreme event by design. Engineers, geophysicists, and social scientists disagreed about the causation. Reports on this disaster were published by the Japanese government, the Lower-House legislature of Japan, the U.S. National Research Council, and nuclear utilities of both countries. The earthquake of 11 March 2011 of magnitude 9.0 was a megaquake followed by a mega-tsunami that caused more than 18,000 fatalities in Eastern Japan. Severe shaking of the ground damaged substations and shut down transmission lines as 11 nuclear reactors scrammed automatically. TEPCO, the owner of Fukushima-Daiichi nuclear power plant, was unable to borrow power from neighboring Kansai Electric Power Company because the two grids run on different frequencies (50 and 60 Hz). Shutdown cooling water and spent fuel-pool cooling were lost and three reactors experienced meltdown. We review the reports of Japanese and American official commissions and we introduce some ideas about tsunami landscapes and risk theory.

21.1. INTRODUCTION: CONFLICTING INTERPRETATIONS

As Arnold Gundersen famously stated, "Nuclear power is a technology that can have forty good years and one bad day." This statement gives the misleading impression that the extreme events of 11 March 2011 in Northeastern Japan were well understood. Here we examine the possibility that the Fukushima accident was largely caused by some lingering misconceptions about the Earth sciences.

The world's consumption of clean energy is expected to double by 2040 (Exxon, http://www.worldoil.com/Exxon-sees-energy-demand-rising-35-by-2040.html). The Asia-Pacific region will account for about 75% of the increase, most of it in the form of nuclear power. Japan depends on nuclear power for 30% of its total power consumption.

The Fukushima accident has been investigated by four official committees:

1. The *Investigation Committee on the Accident at the Fukushima Nuclear Power Stations* (ICANPS) appointed by the Japanese government. It issued its final report in July 2012;

2. The *Independent Investigation Commission* (NAIIC) appointed by the *National Diet (Parliament) of Japan*, also issued its final report in July 2012;

3. The *Committee on the Nuclear Accident at the Fukushima Daiichi Nuclear Power Station* appointed by the *Institute of Nuclear Power Operations* (INPO) represents U.S. nuclear power operators. It issued its report in November 2011;

4. The *United States National Research Council* issued a "Special Report on Lessons Learned from the Fukushima

[1]*Instituto de Investigaciones Económicas, Universidad Nacional Autónoma de México, México, DF, México*
[2]*Instituto de Geofísica, Universidad Nacional Autónoma de México, México, DF, México*

Extreme Events: Observations, Modeling, and Economics, Geophysical Monograph 214, First Edition.
Edited by Mario Chavez, Michael Ghil, and Jaime Urrutia-Fucugauchi.

Accident (LLFA) for Improving Safety of U.S. Nuclear Power Stations," published in July 2014.

These four reports cover substantially the same ground, but reach conclusions. There appears to be reasonable agreement on the following points: the Fukushima-Daiichi nuclear power plant was irretrievably damaged by a megaquake of magnitude 9.0 followed by a 14 m high tsunami that exceeded the design basis of the plant. The resulting station blackout caused a meltdown at three reactors.

Interpretation A: The accident was caused by a tsunami of unforeseen and possibly unforeseeable size that exceeded the design basis of the plant.

However, as numerous videos have shown, the tsunami wave was only 1 or 2 m high as it approached the coast. The 14 m run-up was attributable to the ocean-floor profile and the shape of the beach.

Interpretation B: The accident was caused by the corporate culture of Japan and other cultural factors.

However, Japan enjoyed years of economic "miracle" after the Second World War due to the same cultural factors, including the economic interventionism of the Japanese government.

Reports (1), (3), and (4) tend to agree with interpretation (A), whereas report (2) tends to agree with interpretation (B). We provide an evaluation of both interpretations. We find that the immediate cause of the accident was a tsunami of unforeseen magnitude but this interpretation is too narrow. The geographical features of the northeast coast of Japan (here called "tsunami landscape") should have been evaluated prior to construction of the plant. One year after the Fukushima-Daiichi accident, the Oyster Creek nuclear power plant in the United States went through a similar flooding emergency. High-water conditions reached less than 2 m. Both plants were of the boiling-water reactor (BWR) type. We argue that the magnitude of the flooding was immaterial: the design basis was exceeded in both plants. The design error consisted in placing the backup generators in a basement room below grade. The design of BWR nuclear power plants contains a serious flaw of design.

The sea walls in front of the Fukushima nuclear power plant were supposed to protect the plant against a tsunami of 5.7 m above mean sea level, as large as the 1960 Chile tsunami. But this was the high-water mark produced by the 1960 Chile tsunami at Japanese ports, after the wave had crossed the Pacific Ocean. The actual run-up at Chilean ports was much higher, for example, the maximum run-up at Corral exceeded 10 m above mean sea level [*Servicio Hidrográfico y Oceanográfico de la Armada*, 2000].

The seafaring people of old Japan discovered that tsunamis originate locally at beaches and inside bays. The Japanese term *tsunami* means "port wave," as distinct from waves observed on the open sea. When the sailors returned to port they found that the wave had wrecked everything. This basic feature of the phenomenon should have been evaluated at the time when the Fukushima-Daiichi nuclear power plant was sited. Tsunamis are nonlinear surface waves, also known as solitons [*Infeld and Rowlands*, 2000]. According to Newton's Third Law, they are caused at subduction boundaries by backlash or recoil of the subducted plate (Figure 21.4). The "overwhelming devastations" [*Konagai*, 2012] along the Sanriku coast of Northeastern Japan are observed recurrently because of the presence of tsunami landscapes between latitudes 36° and 41° north (Figure 21.1). In conclusion, the Fukushima-Daiichi accident should have been foreseen.

The same conclusion was independently reached by the report of the investigation commission chaired by

Figure 21.1 Tsunami landscape along the Sanriku coast between Otsuchi and Kamaishi, Japan. Note the drowned streams or *rias*. After Google Earth.

Professor Kiyoshi Kurokawa, Science Advisor to the Japanese cabinet.

Actually the Fukushima nuclear power plant was designed in the United States. However, the attribution of the accident to cultural traits should not be taken lightly. Richard A. Meserve, a former chairman of the U.S. Nuclear Regulatory Commission (NRC) and president emeritus of the Carnegie Institution for Science in Washington, D.C., was a star witness at the 5th meeting of the Kurokawa commission held at the National Diet of Japan on 27 February 2012.

In short, we propose that both interpretations "A" and "B" be taken seriously, but both should be supplemented and revised. The BWR nuclear power station was not designed against the occurrence of flooding as expected in tsunamis, typhoons, cyclones, winter storms, inundations, and other atmospheric phenomena. Most of these emergencies would also be likely to interrupt service of the local or regional power grid. In other words, a flooding emergency is likely to be combined with a power outage, as was the case at Fukushima and Oyster Creek.

21.2. COMPARISON WITH OYSTER CREEK

Engineers and social scientists are rediscovering the concept of risk. Risk is still defined as the product of *hazard times vulnerability*, where "hazard" is the probability of some accident occurring, and "vulnerability" is the expected loss. But this definition is not widely accepted: eight dictionaries provided eight different definitions of "risk."

Late sociologist *Niklas Luhmann* [1991] attributed risk to the process of making or omitting to make *decisions*. He made no distinction between good and bad decisions; on the contrary, he stressed the fact that there is no such thing as a risk-free decision. All decisions are risky, including the avoidance of decisions. We translate a relevant passage found in Luhmann's book on risk:

...a common feature of high-risk technologies is the fact that one can only understand them by using them, that is, by actually installing and testing them. These systems are too complex to admit a reliable forecast of their behavior. Research can be more risky than the eventual application of the results of research (viz. Wilhelm Röntgen and his manipulation of X-rays), as risks and how to prevent them are not known at the outset and must first be found out and learned about. Also, the experience with efforts at "taming" risk must be shared with the general user so that control over contexts that might involve new risks, such as the participation of less experienced or less creative technicians, or because the technology is made to work over longer time intervals, is forfeited. Besides, there are safety procedures or rules of supervision or warning that may turn out to be risky simply because one cannot exclude the possibility that they might be used in some unforeseen or inappropriate manner that induces a false sense of security. Impressive examples may be found in the reports on major accidents such as Three Mile Island or Bhopal. It turns out that such errors are often made even when a spectacular accident does not actually occur.

These considerations suggest that risk may originate in the technology itself, simply because it is non-nature, or differs from nature. Moreover, risk peaks when it becomes the object of technical research. It appears that there are limitations to the efforts at using technology to prevent technological risk... Technology is a boundary, yet has no bounds: it may eventually fail to conquer, not nature but itself. [*Luhmann*, 1991, p. 102]

Luhmann carefully distinguished between risky safety procedures and risk induced by a false sense of security. Fukushima is an example of the latter. The owner and operator of the plant rested on the false assumption that the procedure of defense-in-depth used in the United States was 100% safe as intended.

Report (4) by the U.S. National Research Council attempted to derive explicit lessons from the Fukushima accident that might be applicable to U.S. nuclear power plants. According to the interpretation by NRC:

1. Failure of the plant owner (Tokyo Electric Power Company) and the principal regulator (Nuclear and Industrial Safety Agency) to protect critical safety equipment at the plant from flooding in spite of mounting evidence that the plant's current design basis for tsunamis was inadequate.

But what is meant by a design basis for tsunamis? The NRC defines "design-basis events" as

1. Those natural and human-induced events that are reasonably likely to occur regularly, moderately frequently, or one or more times before permanent closure of the geological repository operations area; and

2. Other natural and man-induced events that are considered unlikely, but sufficiently credible to warrant consideration, taking into account the potential for significant radiological impacts on public health and safety.

This way of defining risk might mislead analysts to conclude that "nuclear plants situated outside known geological danger zones could pose greater accident threats in the event of an earthquake than those inside." If the design basis for tsunamis was inadequate because the plant was within a geological danger zone, the question arises as to whether or not this was known.

Consider an actual example. On 29 October 2012, the Oyster Creek, New Jersey, nuclear power plant declared an alert due to unforeseen flooding of the water intake structure. High intake structure water levels are of concern "as excessive levels can flood the diesel backup generators and render normal cooling systems inoperable." How did the operators know this? Because it had been the direct cause of the Fukushima disaster the year before. Oyster Creek is a BWR of the same design as Fukushima Daiichi. Both stations had similar safety systems. They had the same access to information about any inadequacy of the plant's current design basis for flooding.

The Oyster Creek operators declared an alert because they realized that the normal cooling systems were about to fail, as they did at Fukushima. The Oyster Creek site was experiencing a station blackout and shutdown cooling and spent fuel pool cooling were temporarily lost, as they were at Fukushima. The water level at the intake structure was about 6 ft. The emergency diesel generators started "as designed" and supplied power to the emergency electrical busses, but they were flooded, as they were at Fukushima.

Yet Oyster Creek terminated the alert at 3:52 a.m. EDT on the next day. Six hours and seven minutes later, "the licensee restored one line of off-site power via a start-up transformer." Offsite power was eventually recovered after the busses were reenergized. Water level dropped below 4.5 ft, as it did at Fukushima: and, the operators concluded, "no safety systems were adversely affected by the high intake level."

What was so different about Oyster Creek? What exactly was the lesson we ought to learn? Flooding of backup generators is a common problem: it can be produced by tsunamis, winter storms, hurricanes, typhoons, and possibly by other causes as yet unknown or indeterminate. Oyster Creek was neither flooded by a tsunami nor was there an earthquake. The station blackout was produced by Hurricane Sandy. The backup diesel generators started as designed, as they did at Fukushima, but they kept on running; Fukushima's did not. Fukushima diesel generators were not waterproof; Oyster Creek had waterproof diesel generators, and so do all American nuclear power plants [*Lipscy et al.*, 2013].

We conclude that waterproof diesel generators should be a required safety feature in BWR nuclear power stations because they can help prevent core melt accidents. But they may not be sufficient: flooding can damage the connections in the electrical system and the seawater pumps. Flooding should not be treated as a "beyond design-basis event" as it can be foreseen and nuclear power plants *can* be adequately designed for preventing core-melt accidents caused by such events.

21.3. THE TSUNAMI LANDSCAPE

Niklas Luhmann warned against trespassing on the boundaries of our understanding of complex high-risk technological systems. In the Earth sciences, there are some holistic concepts that may help identify hazardous interactions between natural and man-made factors. A *landscape* is a combination of geographical features at a site. It involves relief, vegetation, hydrology, weather, geological history, geophysical processes, land use and culture. The Pacific coast of Northeastern Japan, between latitudes 36° and 41° north, is a typical tsunami landscape. Consider the Sanriku coast of Iwate, Miyagi, and Fukushima Prefectures (Figures 21.1– 21.3). It features 36 elongated inlets technically known as *rias*, or drowned river valleys. The tsunami of 11 March 2011 was not the first disastrous tsunami to hit the Sanriku coast. Tsunami hazard is well recognized in Japan, about half the coast of Japan is protected by seawalls.

The typical morphology of peninsulas and rias alternating with marine terraces is sometimes described as "dendritic" or tree-like. In the planning and siting stage

Figure 21.2 The Otsuchi ria seen from Highway 231, looking south toward the collapsed railroad bridge. Remains of the seawall are visible at the center of the picture. Notice the typical tsunami landscape of low hills and terraces that channeled the tsunami toward the town. After Google Earth.

Figure 21.3 Looking downstream from the location of Figure 21.2 toward the Western abutment of the collapsed railway bridge. Note the marine terraces in the middle ground. After Google Earth.

Figure 21.4 Fukushima-Daiichi nuclear power plant before the accident. Notice the wetlands of the Izumida estuary and the wooded marine terraces along the waterfront. The standby generators of Units 1–4 are located in the basement of the elongated white turbine buildings facing the ocean. From Google Earth.

of Fukushima-Daiichi nuclear power plant it struck the trained observer that a minor stream known as the Izumida River created a tsunami landscape a few kilometers north of the selected site. The sediment load from the Izumida is dumped right in front of the plant (Figure 21.4). Tsunami waves from the open sea will impinge frontally upon the waterfront.

All along this coast there are numerous marine terraces of Pliocene age (about 3 million years B.P.). They are 30–40 m high, as the Pliocene mean sea level was about 25 m higher than at present. Unfortunately, most human settlements are in the rias, not on the terraces where they might be safe from tsunami hazard. Consider the small ocean-side fishing village of Otsuchi in Iwate Prefecture (Figures 21.1, 21.2, and 21.3). The town was destroyed five times by tsunamis; in 869, in 1611, in 1896, in 1933, and in 2011 [*Konagai*, 2012]. It is located on the Otsuchi River estuary, a deeply incised ria. Technical commissions repeatedly proposed relocating the town to the adjacent marine terraces but zoning recommendations were mostly ignored.

Otsuchi, Kamaishi, and similar coastal towns were believed to be protected against tsunami risk by seawalls built across the rias at a cost of up to 1.5 billion USD each. Most of these structures collapsed in the tsunami of 11 March 2011 and the towns were flooded.

The distal, or landward, end of a ria is the most exposed area in terms of tsunami risk: this is where human settlements are mostly found. Alternative locations are available on marine terraces at elevations of 30 m above mean sea level or more. The Fukushima Daiichi nuclear power plant was planned to be sited on such a marine terrace, but it was bulldozed down to sea level prior to construction.

21.4. TSUNAMIS AS GUIDED WAVES

A megaquake is a large earthquake capable of exciting a nonlinear water wave called a soliton. Solitons can propagate across oceans to large distances because they are essentially one-dimensional surface waves. They are guided waves and they travel along linear features such as canals, oceanic trenches, or rift valleys, with little dispersion [*Infeld and Rowlands*, 2000; *Craig*, 2006]. They may be obtained as solutions of the Korteweg–de Vries equation [1895]

$$\frac{\partial u}{\partial t} + u \frac{\partial u}{\partial x} + \frac{\partial^3 u}{\partial x^3} = 0 \qquad (21.1)$$

instead of the familiar linear three-dimensional wave equation. *Lord Rayleigh* [1877] first suggested that guided surface waves are obtained whenever one spatial dimension is dropped from the wave equation. Thus Rayleigh waves travel in two dimensions along a free surface. One-dimensional guided solitons propagate with less dispersion than two-dimensional waves. Thus solitons generated off the coast of Chile cross the Pacific Ocean and cause damage in Hawaii and Japan. Superposition of stable soliton modes produces wave packets with the tallest wavelet in front and the short wavelengths at the rear [*Infeld and Rowlands*, 2000].

Now whenever two tectonic plates interact along a megathrust boundary, the active lower plate (also called the "subducting plate") transfers momentum to the passive upper plate (also called the "subducted plate"). According to Newton's Third Law, the action in the lower plate generates an equal and opposite reaction in the upper plate. In ballistics this reaction is known as "recoil." As the lower plate moves landward the upper plate moves seaward, thus generating the tsunami. The momenta of the two interacting plates add up to zero (Figure 21.5).

As the tsunami reaches the coast it penetrates the shallows of a ria and travels inland. Because the energy travels with the group velocity, the height of the wave increases and the wavelength is shortened, an effect known as

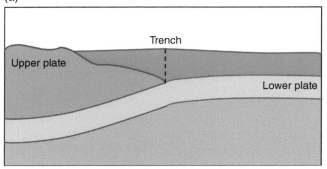

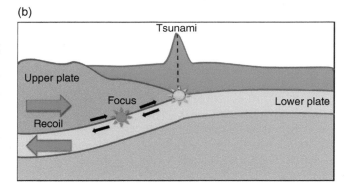

Figure 21.5 (a) Diagram of a subduction plate boundary prior to rupture. (b) Origin of a tsunami. A megaquake originates at the focus. As the lower plate (*yellow*) slides under the continental plate (*brown*), the upper plate recoils in the opposite direction and transfers momentum to the ocean at the trench.

shoaling. The wave is funneled toward the far end of the ria as the water depth tends to zero. The low-lying flatlands around the estuary are flooded.

The Izumida river flows into the Pacific Ocean less than a kilometer north of the Fukushima nuclear power plant (Figure 21.4). Its estuary features brackish wetlands nested between marine terraces. Similar drowned landscapes were described by Darwin in Chile; he attributed them to alternating periods of tectonic uplift and subsidence.

21.5. THE HUMAN SETTING

As Kurokawa suggested, economic conditions are part of the tsunami landscape. The Japanese economy stagnated after 1990; many industrial concerns packed up and left. The Sanriku coast became an economically disadvantaged region where salaries for technicians fell to a level comparable to that of part-time help at McDonald's [*Brinsley and Ito*, 2011]. Many young people migrated to Tokyo and other large cities even before the tsunami. Thus the 2011 tsunami struck an area of Japan ravaged by an economic and social crisis.

An estimated 18,000 people drowned in the 2011 tsunami. Damage amounted to 16,400 billion yen. The Kamaishi sea wall, world's largest, collapsed; the overturning moment of the structure had been underestimated. Other sea walls failed in the region, one after another. The early-warning system provided tsunami warnings within 3 minutes of the earthquake but the signal somehow missed the urgency of an adequate disaster response. As a result, half the population chose to stay home and risk drowning rather than seeking safety on high ground.

People seemed stunned, their behavior was unexpected. Known to psychiatrists as *post-traumatic stress disorder* (PTSD), this reaction was attributed to an ineffectual management of the nuclear crisis. An overwhelming proportion of damage and fatalities was due to the tsunami rather than the earthquake [*Konagai*, 2012].

What went wrong? The large magnitude of the earthquake (Mw = 9.0) placed it squarely among the largest tsunami earthquakes of the world. According to Japanese Police, 92.4% of the earthquake victims died due to drowning. Most of them (65.2%) were aged 60 and over, and 46% were over 70. Special protection must always be provided to vulnerable segments of the population, such as children, the elderly, and the ill [*National Research Council*, 2014]. But this is not what was seen in the 2011 disaster. School children led by their teachers were safely evacuated to nearby heights, but too many survived as orphans when their parents refused to abandon their endangered homes.

21.6. STRATEGIES OF SURVIVAL: AUTONOMY AND CASCADING FAILURES

After the Second World War the U.S. Navy commissioned 168 nuclear submarines, nine nuclear cruisers, and six nuclear aircraft carriers. All U.S. submarines are nuclear, they have an excellent safety record. But civilian nuclear power plants are vulnerable to floods, hurricanes, typhoons, winter storms, tsuyu rainfall, earthquakes, tsunamis, power outages, and terrorist attacks. They cannot use their own power generation capacity to control an emergency. The plants continue to generate heat, cooling fluids must be kept circulating in the reactors, meaning that power generation is turned off when it is most needed.

Professor Kurokawa reserved his most damning language for a critique of Japanese corporate culture (Figure 21.6). To make his point, he cited some hoary stereotypes formerly used to explain Japanese economic success, such as obedience to authority and "regulatory capture," meaning the cozy relationship between TEPCO and the regulating *Nuclear and Industrial Safety Agency*. He mentioned four famous U.S. technological disasters: the 1979 Three-Mile Island nuclear accident; the two space shuttle accidents of 1986 and 2003; and the 2001

Figure 21.6 Presentation of the Report of the *Independent Investigation Commission* by Professor Kiyoshi Kurokawa (*left*) to Mr Takahiro Yokomichi, Speaker of the House of Representatives. An aspect of Japanese culture is illustrated. From *The Guardian* (*Naoko Shimazu*, 2012).

World Trade Center attacks in New York. Kurokawa argued that these technological failures should have warned Japanese scientists and engineers about the fallibility of high-risk technological solutions. He claimed that Fukushima was "a disaster made in Japan." But the plant was designed in Schenectady, NY.

21.7. CONCLUSION: A COMPLEX FAILURE

The operators of Oyster Creek nuclear power plant declared an alert because (1) they were empowered to do so, (2) they knew that high water levels in the intake structure "can flood the diesel backup generators," and (3) heavy rainfall from Hurricane Sandy was flooding the basement of the turbine building where the diesel backup generators were located. This hazardous condition could "render normal cooling systems inoperable."

But the flooding at Oyster Creek was only 6 ft (2 m) above the normal water level at the intake structure. Therefore interpretation (A) is not valid, if flooding of the generators was potentially sufficient for rendering normal cooling systems "inoperable" the Fukushima accident could have been produced by a 2 m tsunami. Using waterproof generators was not enough, it did not immunize the plant against flooding. The Fukushima emergency could be produced by any of the five historical tsunamis recorded on the Sanriku coast. But BWR nuclear power stations were not designed against flooding.

The Fukushima nuclear power plant was designed under a strategy known as "defense-in-depth." This was originally a military strategy consisting of delaying the progress of an enemy force by trading casualties for space. As applied to the design of nuclear power plants, the design procedure consisted of adding subsystems construed as layers of redundant technology around the reactor core. This approach implied that nuclear safety is conditioned by a risky constellation of subordinated technologies.

Backup systems alone do not guarantee the safety of a complex system. The backups can be less reliable than the systems they are supposed to replace. Backup generators can be more vulnerable to flooding than the power grid. Sound conservative methods of risk assessment tend to be replaced with probabilistic methods of doubtful validity. The behavior of the resulting complex systems cannot be fully predicted and the proliferation of probability methods "creates a fictive reality, a second-order reality, a parallel reality, when nothing occurs by chance" [*Luhmann*, 1991, p. 195].

The mechanism of the 2011 tsunami may be reconstructed as follows. The Okhotsk Plate (labeled "1") moved bodily in an ESE direction by about of 5.3 m (Figure 21.7). This motion is attributable to recoil of the

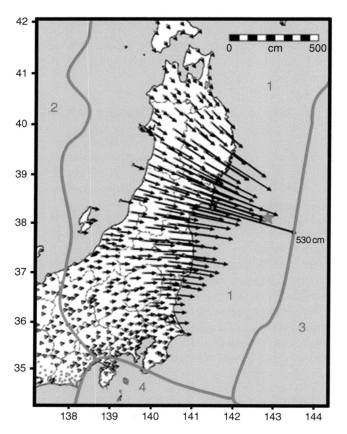

Figure 21.7 GPS horizontal displacement vectors due to recoil of the upper plate in the 2011 Japan megaquake. 1. Okhosk Plate, 2. Amurian Plate, 3. Pacific Plate, 4. Philippine Sea Plate. *Red star,* location of epicenter. From the Geonet GPS network, Geographical Survey Institute, http://www.gsi.go.jp/common/000059672.pdf

Okhotsk plate as referred to the Global Positioning System (GPS), a space-based satellite navigation system. Plate 3 (the Pacific Plate) is inferred to have subducted Plate 1 in the opposite direction. Thus the tsunami was generated by Plate 1 impacting the body of water along the Japan Trench. The recoil of the Okhotsk Plate may be observed in real time on the GPS network and the coastal population can be alerted well in advance of the arrival of the tsunami.

The flooding emergency at Fukushima-Daiichi was produced by a combination of high water levels plus station blackout. The Tōhoku power grid suffered a long-term outage over the entire coastal region of Iwate, Miyagi, and Fukushima prefectures. The power outage also affected the tsunami early-warning system. All four high-voltage power lines into the Fukushima-Daiichi nuclear power plant were lost, including the 66 kV Yonomori Line which could have enabled a connection with Tokyo and with the Fukushima-Daini nuclear power plant via the Shin-Fukushima Substation.

After an emergency repair of this substation was completed, it was realized that Tower #27 of the Yonomori Line had collapsed in the earthquake. In the meantime several hydrogen explosions in the plant produced a dangerous level of radiation. It took 10 days to repair the collapsed tower and to re-establish the Yonomori connection.

The diesel power generators in the basement of the turbine buildings only worked for an hour. They were cooled by sea water and they were vulnerable to flooding. A single air-cooled generator sited on a terrace behind reactor 6 remained operational.

Defense-in-depth consists of a hierarchical deployment of different levels of equipment and procedures "in order to maintain the effectiveness of physical barriers ... to provide a graded protection against a wide variety of transients, incidents and accidents, including equipment failures and human errors within the plant and events initiated outside the plant" (INSAG-10 of the International Atomic Energy Agency). Basically it consists of surrounding the reactor core with a set of multiple, redundant, and independent layers of safety systems. The Fukushima accident proved that a loss-of-coolant accident (LOCA) can be generated by a compound risk produced by a chain of catastrophic failures [*Perrow*, 1999]. Errors in design, such as placing the backup generators of BWR nuclear power stations in a basement room, are not easily reversed; moving the generators to higher ground and providing watertight electrical switchgear was contemplated but the idea was dropped.

A nuclear power station should be autonomous in terms of excess heat disposal and water supply. But experience gathered at one plant is not easily translated into design policy. Thus the accident of 27 December 1999 at Le Blayais, France (a pressurized water nuclear power plant) also involved flooding but the situation was somewhat different [*Birraux, 2000*].

This review chapter started out with a critique of siting. The Fukushima-Daiichi nuclear power plant was sited in a tsunami landscape. A backup reservoir in the Sanriku hills could have provided the critical water reserve to prevent the Fukushima-Daiichi incident from escalating into a full-blown LOCA.

ACKNOWLEDGMENT

We are indebted to Eduardo Muñiz for his valuable discussions and his editorial support, and Erick Minero for improving the figures. Funding by research project PAPIIT IG-300114 is gratefully acknowledged.

REFERENCES

Birraux, C. (2000), Report to Assemblée Nationale, Paris, ISBN 2-11-109242-8.

Brinsley, J. and A. Ito (2011), McDonald's wage for nuclear job shows Japan towns may fade, *Bloomberg News*, April 10, 2011, www.bloomberg.com/ news/2011-04-10/mcdonald-s-wage-for-nuclear-job-shows-some-japan-towns-may-fade.html (accessed 7 September 2015).

Craig, W. (2006), Tsunamis and ocean waves, *Symposium on tsunamis: their hydrodynamics and their impact on people*, AAAS Annual Meeting, St. Louis, MO, February 19, 2006.

Infeld, E. and G. Rowlands (2000), *Nonlinear Waves, Solitons and Chaos*, 2nd ed., Cambridge University Press, Cambridge.

Konagai, K. (2012), Overview of massive destruction caused by the March 11th, 2011 off the Pacific coast of Tohoku earthquake and impact that the quake and tsunami had on earthquake engineering experts, *Bulletin of ERS No. 45*, Institute of Industrial Sciencie, University of Tokyo.

Korteweg, D. J. and G. de Vries (1895), On the change of form of long waves advancing in a rectangular canal, and on a new type of long stationary waves, *Philosophical Magazine*, *39*(240), 422–443.

Lipscy, P. Y., K. E. Kushida, and T. Incerti (2013), The Fukushima disaster and Japan's nuclear plant vulnerability in comparative perspective, *Environ. Sci. Technol.*, *47*, 6082–6088.

Luhmann, N. (1991), *Soziologie des Risikos*, Walter de Gruyter, Berlin.

Naoko Shimazu (2012), The Fukushima report hides behind the cultural curtain, *The Guardian*, http://www.theguardian.com/commentisfree/2012/jul/06/fukushima-report-disaster-japan (accessed 7 September 2015).

National Diet of Japan (2012), The Fukushima Nuclear Accident Independent Investigation Commission.

National Research Council (2014), *Lessons Learned from the Fukushima Nuclear Accident for Improving Safety of U.S. Nuclear Plants*, The National Academies Press, Washington, DC.

Perrow, C. (1999), *Normal Accidents: Living with High-risk Technologies*, 2nd ed., pp. 451, Princeton University Press, Princeton, NJ.

Rayleigh, J. S. (1877), *The Theory of Sound*, vol. *I*, Macmillan, London.

Servicio Hidrográfico y Oceanográfico de la Armada (2000), *El maremoto del 22 de mayo de 1960 en las costas de Chile*, 2nd ed., Valparaíso, Chile.

22

On Predictive Understanding of Extreme Events: Pattern Recognition Approach; Prediction Algorithms; Applications to Disaster Preparedness

Vladimir Keilis-Borok,[1,2] Alexandre Soloviev,[2] and Andrei Gabrielov[3]

ABSTRACT

We describe a uniform approach in predicting different extreme events, also known as critical phenomena, disasters, or crises. The following types of extreme events are considered in this chapter: strong earthquakes, economic recessions (their onset and termination), surges of unemployment, surges of crime, and electoral changes of governing party. A uniform approach is possible due to the common feature of these events: each of them is generated by a certain hierarchical dissipative complex system. After a coarse-graining, such systems exhibit regular behavior patterns; among them we look for the *premonitory patterns* that signal approach of an extreme event. We introduce methodology, based on the optimal control theory, assisting disaster management in choosing optimal set of disaster preparedness measures undertaken in response to a prediction. Predictions with their currently realistic (limited) accuracy do allow preventing a considerable part of the damage by a hierarchy of preparedness measures. Accuracy of prediction should be known, but not necessarily high.

22.1. INTRODUCTION

22.1.1. Prediction Problem

Targets of prediction are individual extreme events that are rare but make big impact. Prediction is formulated as a discrete sequence of alarms, each indicating the time window and space where an extreme event is expected (Figure 22.1). An alarm is correct if an extreme event occurs within the predicted time and space; otherwise the alarm is false. Failure to predict is the case where an extreme event occurs outside an alarm.

This approach is complementary to the classical Kolmogoroff-Wiener problem that is concerned with the prediction of a random time series $x(t)$ based on observations available with some time delay τ by the time $t - \tau$.

At the heart of our problem is the absence of a complete theory that would unambiguously define a prediction algorithm. Overcoming that difficulty did require an intense collaboration of experts in mathematics, statistics, exploratory data analysis, and also in the specific extreme events considered. Previous applications have inevitably involved teams of such experts, as can be seen from the list of references. For example, prediction of homicide surges was developed jointly with police officers

[1] Institute of Geophysics & Planetary Physics and Department of Earth & Space Sciences, University of California, Los Angeles, CA, USA

[2] Institute of Earthquake Prediction Theory & Mathematical Geophysics, Russian Academy of Sciences, Moscow, Russia

[3] Departments of Mathematics & Earth and Atmospheric Sciences, Purdue University, West Lafayette, IN, USA

Extreme Events: Observations, Modeling, and Economics, Geophysical Monograph 214, First Edition.
Edited by Mario Chavez, Michael Ghil, and Jaime Urrutia-Fucugauchi.
© 2016 American Geophysical Union. Published 2016 by John Wiley & Sons, Inc.

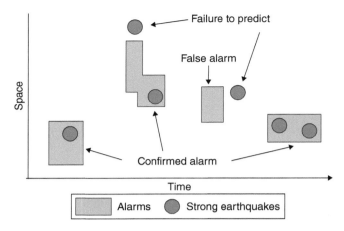

Figure 22.1 Possible outcomes of prediction.

in active service; prediction of unemployment: with experts in labor relations, etc.

Developing a prediction algorithm is naturally divided into the following interconnected stages:

1. *Choosing prediction targets.* These might be either given a priori (e.g., outcome of elections or the start of a recession as it is established by the National Bureau of Economic Research, NBER) or defined independently by data analysis (e.g., strong earthquakes or starting points of homicide surge).

2. *Choosing the background fields where we hope to detect precursors.* For example, prediction of strong earthquakes was based on seismicity patterns in lower magnitude range; prediction of recessions was based on six leading economic indicators. Any potentially relevant field can be considered.

3. *Formulation of a hypothetical prediction algorithm.* That is done by the *pattern recognition of rare events:* the methodology developed by the school of *I. Gelfand* for studying rare events of highly complex origin [*Bongard,* 1970; *Gelfand et al.,* 1976; *Keilis-Borok and Lichtman,* 1993; *Press and Allen,* 1995; *Keilis-Borok et al.,* 2000, 2003, 2005].

4. *Validation of prediction algorithm by prediction in advance.*

Prediction quality is characterized by three scores: rate of false alarms, rate of failures-to-predict, and total space-time occupied by alarms (as percentage of total space-time considered). These characteristics are important to decision makers choosing what, if any, preparedness measures to undertake in response to an alarm.

22.1.2. Predictability

Extreme events targeted by our predictions have a consequential common feature: they are generated by complex (chaotic) systems such as seismically active

lithosphere, society, or economy. Complex systems are often regarded as unpredictable in principle. Actually, after a coarse-graining, on a not-too-detailed scale, such systems do exhibit certain regular behavior patterns. Among them are *premonitory patterns* that emerge more frequently as an extreme event approaches. Thus extreme events become predictable up to a limit.

Premonitory patterns might be either "perpetrators" contributing to the triggering of the extreme event, or "witnesses" merely signaling that the system has become unstable, ripe for such an event. An example of a witness is proverbial straws in the wind preceding a storm.

The need for coarse-graining is illustrated in Figure 22.2: a crack is visible only on a less detailed scale. "It is not possible to understand chaotic system by breaking it apart" [*Crutchfield et al.,* 1986].

Taking a holistic approach, "from the whole to details" circumvents the actual complexity and the chronic imperfection of the data. Moreover, it allows to take advantage of the considerable universality of precursors. Quoting *M. Gell-Mann* [1994], *"… if the parts of a complex system or the various aspects of a complex situation, all defined in advance, are studied carefully by experts on those parts or aspects, and the results of their work are pooled, an adequate description of the whole system or situation does not usually emerge. … The reason, of course, is that these parts or aspects are typically entangled with one another. …We have to supplement the partial studies with a transdisciplinary crude look at the whole."*

The general scheme of prediction is illustrated in Figure 22.3. Bold vertical lines mark times of extreme events targeted for prediction. Fine vertical lines show a time series where premonitory patterns are looked for. It is robustly described by the functions $F_k(t)$, $k = 1, 2, …$ usually defined on a sliding time window $(t-s, t)$. Each function captures emergence of a certain pattern. An alarm is triggered when a certain combination of patterns emerge.

In the language of pattern recognition, the "object of recognition" is the time t. The problem is to recognize whether it belongs to the time interval Δ preceding a strong earthquake. That interval is often called the *TIP* (an acronym for the *time of increased probability* of a strong earthquake). Such prediction is aimed not at the whole dynamics of seismicity, but only at the rare extraordinary phenomena, strong earthquakes.

Development of a prediction algorithm by that approach starts with the learning stage where the "learning material," sample of past critical events and the time series hypothetically containing premonitory patterns, is analyzed. This analysis comprises the following steps:

Each time series considered is robustly described by the functions $F_k(t)$, $k = 1, 2, …$, capturing hypothetical

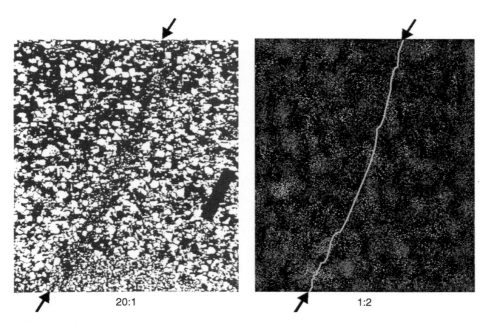

Figure 22.2 The need for coarse-graining (courtesy of *A. Johnson*). A sample with a crack is shown on different scales: more detailed (left) and less detailed (right). The crack is explicitly visible on a less detailed scale.

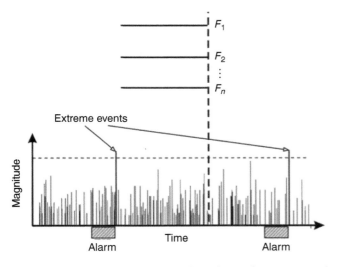

Figure 22.3 General scheme of earthquake prediction. Vertical solid lines show background earthquakes (height of a line is proportional to the event magnitude). A vertical dotted line marks a certain time t at that functions $F_k(t)$, $k = 1, 2, ..., n$, are calculated using the information on background seismicity before time t. An alarm is declared at time t when the number of capturing hypothetical patterns functions for that $F_k(t) \geq C_k$. is greater than a specified threshold.

patterns (Figure 22.3). These patterns are selected based on the universal models of complex systems, models of specific systems considered, exploratory data analysis, and practical experience, even if it is intuitive. Pattern recognition of rare events provides an efficient common framework for formulating and testing such hypotheses, their diversity notwithstanding.

Emergence of a premonitory pattern is defined by the condition $F_k(t) \geq C_k$. The threshold C_k is usually defined as a certain percentile of the functional $F_k(t)$. Thus the time series $F_k(t)$ is presented on the lowest-binary-level of resolution.

An alarm is triggered at a time t_a, when a certain combination of patterns occurs; this combination is determined by application of the pattern recognition procedure.

Detailed description of pattern recognition methodology can be found in *Bongard* [1970], *Gelfand et al.* [1976], *Keilis-Borok and Lichtman* [1993], and *Keilis-Borok and Soloviev* [2003].

Four paradigms on premonitory patterns [*Keilis-Borok*, 2002] provide a guidance for the choice of functions $F_k(t)$.

Paradigm 1: Basic types of premonitory patterns. These are illustrated in Figure 22.4. As an extreme event draws near, the background activity becomes more intense and clustered in space-time, while the correlation range in space increases and size distribution (scaling relation) shifts in favor of relatively stronger events.

Paradigm 2: Large size of precursor manifestation area. Generation of an extreme event is not localized in its vicinity. For example, according to *Press and Allen* [1995], the Parkfield, California earthquake with the characteristic source dimension 10 km "...*is not likely to occur until activity picks up in the Great Basin or the Gulf of California,*" about 800 km away. Numerous evidences for that paradigm are described also by *Mogi* [1968], *Aki* [1996], *Press and*

Safe stage   **Pre-disaster stage**

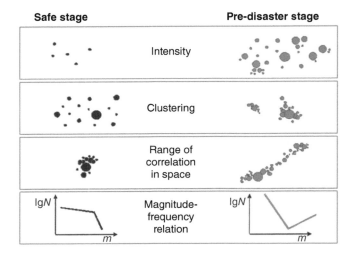

Figure 22.4 Four types of premonitory patterns.

Briggs [1975], *Keilis-Borok and Press* [1980], *Ma et al.* [1990], *Romanowicz* [1993], etc. In the case of seismicity these correlations may be explained by several mechanisms that range from microfluctuations of large-scale tectonic movements to impact of migrating fluids [*Barenblatt et al.,* 1983; *Barenblatt,* 1993; *Press and Allen,* 1995; *Sornette and Sammis,* 1995; *Aki,* 1996; *Bowman et al.,* 1998; *Pollitz et al.,* 1998; *Turcotte et al.,* 2000]. An example of the long-range correlation in a socioeconomic system is surge of ethnic violence in a French suburb, preceded by a rise in ethnic delinquency countrywide [*Bui Trong,* 2003].

Paradigm 3: Similarity. Quantitative definition of prediction algorithms is self-adjusting to regional conditions. For example, earthquake prediction algorithms developed for seismicity of California demonstrate the applicability to other active regions, with the magnitude of the target event varying from 3.0 to 6.6, for starquakes, and, at the other end of the spectrum, for fracturing in engineering constructions and laboratory samples [*Keilis-Borok et al.,* 1980; *Aki,* 1996; *Rotwain et al.,* 1997, 2006; *Keilis-Borok and Shebalin,* 1999; *Kossobokov et al.,* 2000; *Keilis-Borok and Soloviev,* 2003; *Kossobokov and Shebalin,* 2003]. The energy of a target event in these applications ranges from ergs (microfracture) to 10^{26} ergs (major earthquake), and even to 10^{41} ergs (starquake). Another example is an algorithm for predicting the surge of unemployment, applicable "as is" to the United States, France, Germany, and Italy [*Keilis-Borok et al.,* 2005].

Paradigm 4: Dual nature of premonitory patterns. The premonitory patterns shown in Figure 22.4 are "universal," common for hierarchical complex systems of different origin. They can be reproduced in the models of dynamic clustering [*Gabrielov et al.,* 2008], branching diffusion [*Gabrielov et al.,* 2010], percolation [*Zaliapin et al.,* 2005, 2006], direct, inverse, and colliding cascades [*Allègre*

et al., 1982; *Narkunskaya and Shnirman,* 1994; *Shnirman and Blanter,* 1999, 2003; *Gabrielov et al.,* 2000; *Zaliapin et al.,* 2003; *Yakovlev et al.,* 2005], as well as in certain system-specific models [*Soloviev and Ismail-Zadeh,* 2003; *Sornette,* 2004].

22.1.3. Coping with Risk of Data Fitting

Since our prediction algorithms cannot be defined unambiguously by an existing theory, they inevitably include some adjustable elements, from selecting the data used for prediction to the values of numerical parameters. These elements are adjusted retrospectively by "predicting" past extreme events.

Such data-fitting might be self-deceptive: As *J. von Neumann* put it *"with four exponents I can fit an elephant."* Hence, the following tests are performed.

Sensitivity analysis: predictions should not be too sensitive to variations in adjustable parameters.

Out-of-sample analysis: application of an algorithm to past data that has not been used in the algorithm's development. The test is considered successful if the accuracy of prediction does not drop too much.

Prediction in advance is the ultimate test.

22.2. PREDICTING INDIVIDUAL EXTREME EVENTS

22.2.1. Earthquakes

Relatively better tested are the algorithms based on premonitory seismicity patterns [*Keilis-Borok,* 1990, 2002; *Keilis-Borok and Shebalin,* 1999; *Keilis-Borok and Soloviev,* 2003; *Kossobokov and Shebalin,* 2003; *Peresan et al.,* 2005]. The predictions are filed in advance on the following websites: http://www.mitp.ru/predictions.html; http://users.ictp.it/www_users/sand/index_files/DevelopmentofPrediction.html; and http://rtptest.org/.

Access to yet unexpired alarms on these websites is limited to about 200 scientists and professional experts worldwide. This is done in compliance with the UNESCO guidelines, since public release of prediction might trigger disruptive anxiety of population and profiteering. Predictions are made available for general public after a strong earthquake occurs or alarm expires, whichever comes first.

22.2.1.1. M8 and MSc Algorithms [Kossobokov and Shebalin, 2003]

Algorithm M8 provides intermediate-term predictions. Characteristic duration of an alarm is about 5 years. That algorithm was first developed for predicting the largest earthquakes ($M \geq 8$) worldwide. The algorithm MSc ("Mendocino Scenario") provides a second approximation to M8, considerably reducing the alarm area. Figure 22.5 shows an example of prediction by both algorithms.

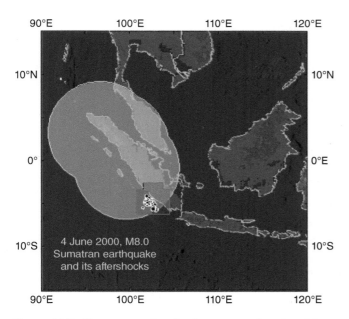

Figure 22.5 Alarms capturing the Sumatra earthquake, 4 June 2000. The yellow oval curve bounds the area of alarm by M8, put on record in July 1996, to expire on 1 July 2001. Red rectangle is its reducing made by MSc, put on record in January 1998. White circles indicate epicenters of Sumatra earthquake and its first-month aftershocks.

Table 22.1 Scoring of M8 and M8 and MSc Pedictions, 1992–2010

Algorithm	Total Number of Target Earthquakes	Number of Predicted Earthquakes	Space-Time Volume of Alarm (%)
M8	17	12	29
M8 and MSc	17	8	15

22.2.1.1.1. Scoring

Thus far, the algorithms have had most success in predicting future earthquakes in the magnitude range 8–8.5 (Table 22.1). Statistical significance of predictions exceeds 99%.

22.2.1.2. "Second Strong Earthquake" (SSE) Algorithm [Levshina and Vorobieva, 1992; Vorobieva, 1999, 2009]

That algorithm is applied when a strong earthquake of a certain magnitude M has occurred. The algorithm predicts whether a second strong earthquake with magnitude $(M-1)$ or more will occur within 18 months of the first one, within a distance $R = 0.03 \times 10^{0.5M}$ km that is one and a half of the characteristic linear size of the after-shock area for an earthquake with magnitude M [*Tsuboi*, 1956]. Figure 22.6 shows an example of SSE prediction

made after the Landers earthquake, 28 June 1992, $M = 7.6$. Prediction was released in EOS, October 1992, with alarm ending on 28 December 1993. A second strong earthquake $M \geq 6.6$ was predicted to occur within the yellow circle. On 17 January 1994, 20 days after the alarm expired, the Northridge earthquake ($M = 6.8$) did occur and resulted in 57 deaths, more than 5000 injuries, and more than 20 billion USD in property damage. For the sake of rigorous scoring, this earthquake was counted as not predicted. On the practical side, escalation of prepar-edness measures in response to this prediction would be fully justified.

22.2.1.2.1. Scoring

Since 1989 the SSE algorithm is being tested in 10 regions worldwide [*Vorobieva*, 1999, 2009], with the mag-nitude of the first events ranging from 5 or above in the Dead Sea Rift region, to 7 or above in the Balkans. In total, 31 first events have been considered. Eight of them were followed by a second strong earthquake within 18 months; 6 have been predicted and 2 missed. For the remaining 23 single events, 19 correct predictions and 4 false alarms have been made. Statistical significance of these predictions is above 99%.

22.2.1.3. "Reverse Tracing of Precursors" (RTP) Algorithm [Shebalin et al., 2004, 2006; Keilis-Borok et al., 2004a]

The algorithm is aimed at predictions about 9 months in advance, much shorter than by the M8 and SSE algorithms. This algorithm, as its name suggests, traces precursors in the reverse order of their formation. First it identifies "candidates" for short-term precursors. These are long, quickly formed chains of earthquakes in the background seismicity. Such chains reflect an increase in the earthquake correlation range (Figure 22.7). Next, each chain is examined to determine whether there had been any preceding intermediate-term precursors in its vicinity within the previous five years. If so, the chain triggers an alarm.

22.2.1.3.1. Scoring

Since 2003, the RTP algorithm has been tested by predicting future earthquakes in five regions of the world (California and adjacent regions; Central and Northern Italy with adjacent regions; Eastern Mediter-ranean; Northern Pacific, Japan and adjacent regions). Till 2012, five out of seven target earthquakes have been predicted (captured by alarms) and two missed. Out of 19 alarms, 5 were correct and 14 false, 2 of the latter being near misses occurring close to alarm areas. The data are still insufficient for rigorous estimation of statis-tical significance.

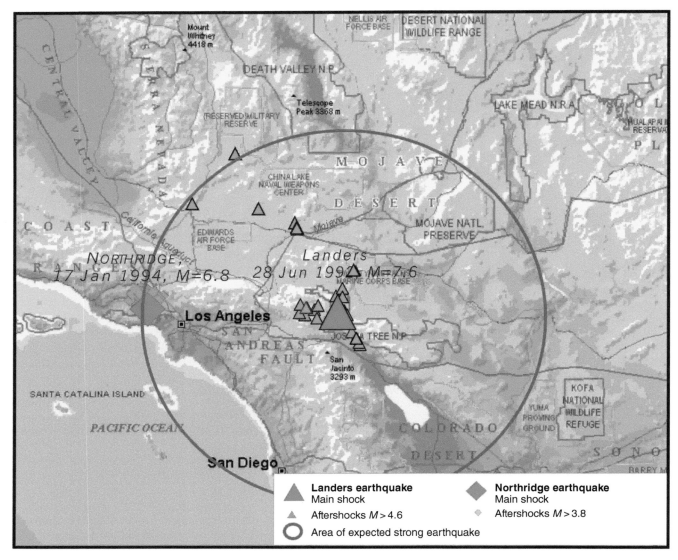

Figure 22.6 Prediction of Northridge, California earthquake by SSE algorithm.

22.2.2. Presidential Elections in the United States

Tradition regards American elections as a trial by battle, where the goal of the competitors is to attract a maximum number of voting blocks with minimal alienation of other blocks. The outcome depends strongly on manipulation of public opinion and last-minute sensations. Accordingly, that tradition ascribes the victory of *George H.W. Bush* in 1988 to three brilliant campaigners: speechwriter Peggy Noonan, who improved his image overnight by the New Orleans speech; two hardball politicians staged mass-media exposure of failure of *M. Dukakis* as a Governor of Massachusetts. Furthermore *M. Dukakis* fired a good campaigner. As a result, he lost the elections, which were in his grasp (he led by 17% in opinion polls).

This notion tells us that a huge mass of voters can reverse its opinion through the influence of three campaigners and the loss of one, in a "for-want-of-a-nail-the-war-was-lost" fashion. In other words, it portrays Jane/Joe Voter as an excitable simpleton, manipulated by commercials, reversing the vote for transient reasons, irrelevant to the essence of the electoral dilemma. American elections deserve a more dignified explanation.

An alternative view, contrasting with that described above, was developed by holistic approach, understanding electorate as a hierarchical complex system [*Keilis-Borok and Lichtman*, 1981]. Here, election outcome depends on coarse-grained socioeconomic and political factors of the common-sense type. These factors were given a robust definition by means of the questionnaire (with *yes/no* responses) shown in Table 22.2. The data on the past 31 elections, 1860–1980 were considered. The actual electoral dilemma is found to be whether an incumbent party will win or lose rather than whether the

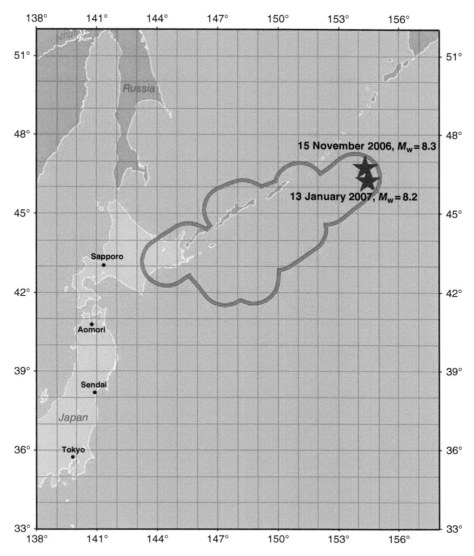

Figure 22.7 RTP prediction of the 2006–2007 Simushir earthquakes in Kuril Islands. Red contour: area of alarm issued on October 2006 for 9 months. This was confirmed by the earthquake of 15 November 2006, $M = 8.3$. Stars: predicted earthquakes.

Table 22.2 Keys Used for Prediction of the Outcome of the Presidential Elections in the United States

Key #	Relevance	Statement to Favor the Reelection of the Incumbent Party
1	Party mandate	After the midterm elections, the incumbent party holds more seats in the U.S. House of Representatives than it did after the previous midterm elections.
2	Contest	There is no serious contest for the incumbent-party nomination.
3	Incumbency	The incumbent-party candidate is the sitting president.
4	Third party	There is no significant third party or independent campaign.
5	Short-term economy	The economy is not in recession during the election campaign.
6	Long-term economy	Real per-capita economic growth during the term equals or exceeds mean growth during the previous two terms.
7	Policy change	The incumbent administration effects major changes in national policy.
8	Social unrest	There is no sustained social unrest during the term.
9	Scandal	The administration is untainted by major scandal.
10	Foreign/military failure	The administration suffers no major failure in foreign or military affairs.
11	Foreign/military success	The administration achieves a major success in foreign or military affairs.
12	Incumbent charisma	The incumbent-party candidate is charismatic or a national hero.
13	Challenger charisma	The challenging-party candidate is not charismatic or a national hero.

Republicans or Democrats will win. A victory of a challenger party is considered as an extreme event. *The prediction algorithm [Lichtman and Keilis-Borok, 1989; Keilis-Borok and Lichtman, 1993; Lichtman, 1996, 2000, 2005] was developed by pattern recognition analysis of the data. The extreme event (victory of the challenger) is predicted if the number of answers no, on the questions listed in Table 22.2, is 6 or more.*

Results of retrospective analysis and advance predictions made by *A. Lichtman* for eight subsequent elections, 1984–2012, are shown in Table 22.3. All advance predictions happened to be correct. That includes *Al Gore's* victory by popular vote, which was reversed by electorate; this happened three times through the whole history. Timing and source of the advance predictions are listed in Table 22.4.

22.2.2.1. What have we Understood about the Elections?

Uniformity of prediction rules transcends the diversities of situations prevailing in individual elections. Accordingly, the same pattern of the choice of president

has prevailed since 1860, that is, since election of *A. Lincoln*, throughout all the overwhelming changes of these 140 years. And in particular, note that the electorate of 1860 did not include the groups making up 75% of the present electorate: no women, blacks, or most of the citizens of Latin American, South European, East European, and Jewish descent (*Lichtman*, 2000). In a nutshell, we have found that the outcome of a presidential election is determined by collective estimation of performance of incumbent administration over the previous 4 years.

22.2.3. Surges in Unemployment

Here we describe uniform prediction of the sharp and long-term rise in unemployment in France, Germany, Italy, and the United States [*Keilis-Borok et al.*, 2005]—we term this FAU, which is an acronym for "Fast Acceleration of Unemployment." The data comprise macroeconomic indicators of national economy. In stability tests a variety of other indicators were also analyzed. Figure 22.8 shows retrospective alarms. Exactly the same self-adjusting algorithm was applied to all four countries.

Table 22.3 Prediction of US Presidential Election Years when the Incumbent Won Are Shown in Italic; Years when the Challenger Won, in Bold

0	1	2	3	4	5	6	7	8	9
\multicolumn{10}{c}{Number of answers *yes* on questions listed in Table 22.2}
\multicolumn{10}{l}{Predictions (published months in advance)}
					2000[a]				
	1984	*1988*	*2004*		*1996*	**1992**	**2012**	**2008**	
\multicolumn{10}{l}{Retrospective analysis}
		1964						**1980**	
		1928						**1976**	
		1916						**1968**	
		1908						**1952**	
		1944	*1900*	*1972*				**1932**	
	1956	*1940*	*1872*	*1924*	*1948*	**1912**	**1884**	**1920**	**1960**
1904	*1936*	*1868*	*1864*	*1880*	*1888*[a]	**1892**	**1860**	**1896**	**1876**[a]

[a]Years when popular vote was reversed by electoral vote.

Table 22.4 Timing and Source of Predictions

Election	Date of Prediction	Source
1984	April 1982	"How to Bet in '84," *Washingtonian Magazine*, April 1982
1988	May 1988	"How to Bet in November," *Washingtonian Magazine*, May 1988
1992	September 1992	"The Keys to the White House," *Montgomery Journal*, 14 September 1992
1996	October 1996	"Who Will Be the Next President?" *Social Education*, October 1996
2000	November 1999	"The Keys to Election 2000," *Social Education*, November/December 1999.
2004	April 2003	"The Keys to the White House," *Montgomery Gazette*, April 25, 2003
2008	February 2006	"Forecast for 2008," *Foresight*, February 2006,
2012	March 2010	"Allan Lichtman's prediction: Obama wins re-election in 2012," *Gazette.net*, Friday, 26 March 2010.

Prediction-in-advance has been in progress since 1999, so far only for the United States. Two recent episodes of FAU have been predicted correctly, without failures to predict or false alarms (Figure 22.9).

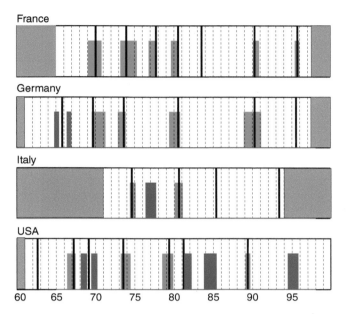

Figure 22.8 FAUs and alarms in the four countries. Vertical lines: prediction targets (FAUs). Red bars: correct alarms. Purple bars: alarms triggered within the periods of unemployment surge. Blue bars: false alarms. The 1968 alarm is scored as false since it expired 1 month before FAU.

22.2.4. US Economic Recessions

Prediction targets are the peaks and troughs of economic activity, that is, the first and last months of each recession as identified by the NBER. The data used in the prediction algorithm comprise six monthly leading economic indicators, reflecting interest rates, industrial production, inventories, and job market [*Keilis-Borok et al.*, 2000, 2008].

Retrospective alarms and recessions are shown together in Figure 22.10. We see that five recessions occurring between 1961 and 2000 were preceded by alarms. The sixth recession started in April 2001, one month before the corresponding alarm. In practice, this is not a failure-to-predict, since recessions are usually declared by NBER much later than they begin. The duration of each alarm was 1–14 months. Total duration of all alarms was 38 months, or 13.6% of the time interval considered. There was only one false alarm in 2003.

According to the NBER announcement issued in December 2008, the last recession in the United States began in January 2008. Our algorithm gave an alarm started in May 2008, that is, 4 months after the recession start but 7 months before the NBER announcement.

The same six macroeconomic indicators have been used to develop an algorithm for prediction of the recovery from a recession [*Keilis-Borok et al.*, 2008]. The algorithm declares alarms within 6 months before the end of each American recession since 1960 and at no other time during these recessions (Figure 22.10). This study is a natural

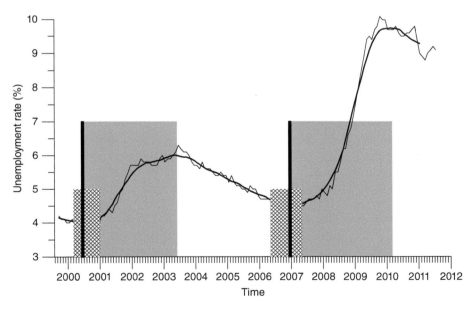

Figure 22.9 Advance predictions of *FAU*s. A thin curve shows the monthly unemployment rate in the United States, according to the data of the Bureau of Labor Statistics, U.S. Department of Labor (http://data.bls.gov). The thick curve shows this rate with seasonal variation smoothed out. Vertical lines: prediction targets (*FAU*s). Gray bars: periods of unemployment growth. Checkered bars: periods of alarms.

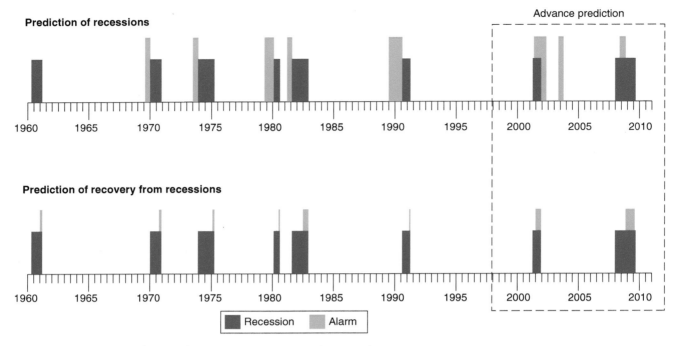

Prediction of recessions

Advance prediction

1960   1965   1970   1975   1980   1985   1990   1995   2000   2005   2010

Prediction of recovery from recessions

1960   1965   1970   1975   1980   1985   1990   1995   2000   2005   2010

■ Recession   ■ Alarm

Figure 22.10 Prediction of economic recessions in the United States.

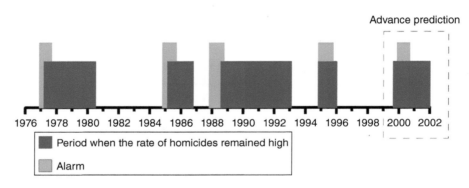

Advance prediction

1976 1978 1980 1982 1984 1986 1988 1990 1992 1994 1996 1998 2000 2002

■ Period when the rate of homicides remained high

■ Alarm

Figure 22.11 Prediction of homicide surges in Los Angeles.

continuation of the previous one, aimed at predicting the start of a recession. Comparing these cases we find that precursory trends of financial indicators are opposite during transition to a recession and recovery from it. To the contrary, precursory trends of economic indicators happen to have the same direction (upward or downward) but are steeper during recovery. The algorithm declares an alarm starting in November 2008 for the end of the last recession.

22.2.5. Homicide Surge

Prediction target is the start of a sharp and lasting rise ("a surge") of the homicide rate in an American mega-city, Los Angeles.

Data comprise monthly rates of 11 types of low-level crimes: burglaries, assaults, and robberies. Statistics of these types of crime in Los Angeles over the period 1975–2002 has been analyzed to find an algorithm for predicting such a surge of the homicide rate [*Keilis-Borok et al.*, 2003].

Premonitory patterns include: first— an escalation of burglaries and assaults, but not of robberies; closer to a homicide surge, robberies also escalate.

It has been found in retrospective analysis that this algorithm is applicable through all the years considered despite substantial changes, both in socioeconomic conditions and in the procedure for the counting of crimes. Alarms and homicide surges are plotted together in Figure 22.11. In total, alarms occupy 15% of the time considered. Moreover, the algorithm gives satisfactory results for the prediction of homicide surges in New York city as well.

22.3. PREMONITORY TRANSFORMATION OF SCALING LAW

Here, we compare the scaling laws in the background activity of a complex system in the time periods of three kinds: **D,** preceding an extreme event; **X,** following it; and **N,** others (Figure 22.12). The background activity of a system is described by background events with sizes (magnitudes) that are defined for different complex systems by different ways. Scaling law is defined as $P(m) = N(m)/N^T$, where $N(m)$ is the number of background events of the size $\geq m$, N^T is the total number of background events (obviously, $P(m)$ is equivalent to the statistical distribution function). Changing in scaling law before strong events is analyzed by comparison of functions $P(m)$ obtained separately for D- and N-periods (functions $P^D(m)$ and $P^N(m)$, respectively).

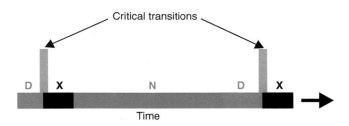

Figure 22.12 Division of time into intervals: **D**—preceding an extreme event; **X**—following it; **N**—others.

Figure 22.13 shows functions $P^D(m)$ and $P^N(m)$ in the case of the largest (with magnitude $M \geq 8.0$) of the world as extreme events and worldwide seismicity main shocks in lower magnitude range as background events. Magnitude of a background event or the number of its aftershocks is used as its size.

Figure 22.14 shows functions $P^D(m)$ and $P^N(m)$ in the case of the start of socioeconomic crises (economic recessions in the United States, unemployment surges in the United States, and homicide surges in Los Angeles) as extreme events. Background events are defined as changes in trends of indicators describing a relevant system: U.S. monthly industrial production for recessions and unemployment and the monthly number of assaults with firearms in Los Angeles for homicides. Sizes of background events are proportional to changes in relevant trends. The detailed definition of these background events is given by *Keilis-Borok and Soloviev* [2010] and *Ghil et al.* [2011].

Figure 22.15 shows functions $P^D(m)$ and $P^N(m)$ for three countries, in the case of months with extremely large score of casualties (killed and wounded) caused by terrorism as extreme events. Here **D**-period before only one extreme event (indicated in Figure 22.3) is considered for each country and background events are months when there are casualties caused by terrorism with the numbers of the casualties as event sizes.

In each case function $P^D(m)$ has distinctly higher ("heavier") tails at large m than $P^D(m)$, and extends to larger values of m. This demonstrates predictive power of scaling law. Similarity of this effect in so different systems suggests looking for universal definition of premonitory patterns in different complex systems.

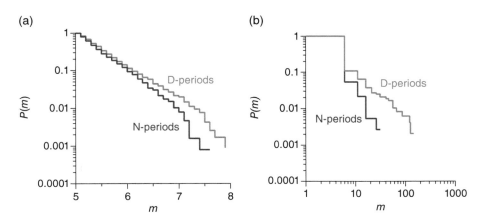

Figure 22.13 Premonitory transformation of a scaling law: earthquakes. Extreme events: main shocks with magnitude $M \geq 8$ worldwide, 1985–2002. Red curves correspond to D-periods and blue curves correspond to N-periods. Background activity: seismicity in lower magnitude range; m is magnitude of individual main shocks (a) or number of aftershocks (b). Courtesy of *L. Romashkova*.

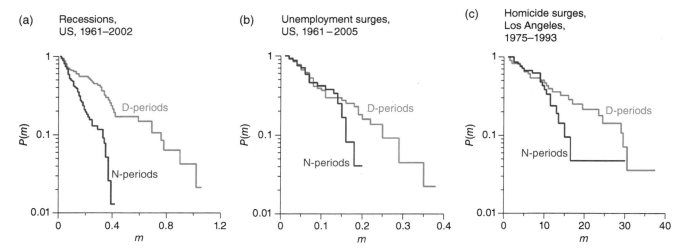

Figure 22.14 Premonitory transformation of scaling law: socioeconomic crises. Extreme events: starting points of respective crises. Red curves correspond to D-periods and blue curves correspond to N-periods. Background activity, change in trend of a monthly indicator: (a and b) denote industrial production and (c) denotes assaults with firearms.

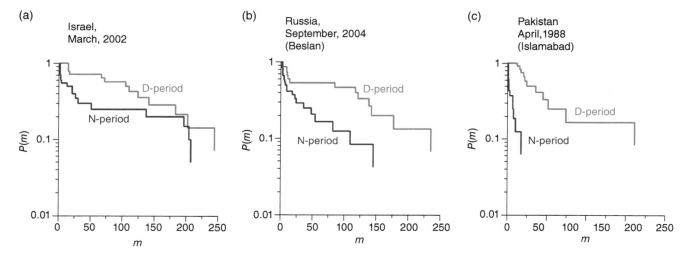

Figure 22.15 Premonitory transformation of scaling law: terrorism. Extreme events are the months with extremely large score of casualties (killed and wounded). Background activity is represented by the monthly number m of casualties.

22.4. PREDICTION AND DISASTER PREPAREDNESS

> Of course, things are complicated… But in the end every situation can be reduced to a simple question: Do we act or not? If yes, in what way?
>
> [*E. Burdick*, "480"]

What, if any, preparedness actions to undertake in response to a prediction, given its inherently limited accuracy? Methodology assisting decision maker in choosing optimal response to earthquake prediction is developed in *Kantorovich et al.* [1974], *Molchan* [1991, 1997, 2003],

Keilis-Borok et al. [2004b], *Davis et al.* [2007, 2010], and *Molchan and Keilis-Borok* [2008].

Earthquakes might hurt population, economy, and environment in many different ways, from destruction of buildings, lifelines, and other constructions, to triggering other natural disasters, economic, and political crises. That diversity of damage requires a hierarchy of preparedness measures, from public safety legislation and insurance to simulation alarms, preparedness at home, and red alert. Different measures can be implemented on different time-scales, from seconds to decades. They should be implemented in areas of different size, from selected sites to large regions; should be maintained for different time periods; and should belong to different levels of jurisdiction, from local to international. Such measures might complement, supersede, or mutually exclude each other. For this reason, optimizing preparedness involves comparison of a large number of combinations of possible measures [*Davis et al.*, 2007, 2010].

Disaster management has to take into account the cost/benefit ratio of possible preparedness measures. No single measure alone is sufficient. However, many efficient measures are inexpensive and do not require high accuracy of prediction. As is the case for all forms of disaster preparedness, including national defense, a prediction can be useful if its accuracy is known, even if it is not high.

Decision depends on specific circumstances in the area of alarm. At the same time, it depends on the prediction quality that can be described by two characteristics: n, rate of failures-to-predict (in percents) and τ, percent of total space-time considered occupied by alarms. Their values are determined as follows. Consider a prediction algorithm applied during the time period T. A certain number of alarms A are declared. N extreme events did occur, and N_f of them have been missed by alarms. Altogether, the alarms cover the time D. Then $\tau = (D \cdot 100\%)/T$ and $n = (N_f \cdot 100\%)/N$.

The choice of preparedness measures is not unique. Different measures may supersede or mutually exclude one another, leaving certain freedom of choice to a decision maker [*Keilis-Borok et al.*, 2004b; *Davis et al.*, 2007, 2010]. Designer of a prediction algorithm has certain freedom to choose the tradeoff between different characteristics of its accuracy (duration of alarms, and rate of failures to predict) by varying adjustable elements of the algorithm.

Accordingly, prediction and preparedness should be optimized jointly; *there is no "best" prediction per se* [*Molchan*, 1997, 2003; *Molchan and Keilis-Borok*, 2008]. A framework for such optimization is shown in Figure 22.16. Earthquake prediction strategies (composite strategies are meant) are characterized by points at (τ, n)—diagram and an envelope of these points (curve Γ) is constructed. If there is a loss function depending on τ and n, then the contours ("loss curves") with the constant value γ of this function can be constructed. Optimal strategy is the tangent point of contours Γ and γ [*Molchan*, 1997]. Thus disaster preparedness would be more flexible and efficient if prediction would be carried out in parallel with several versions of an algorithm. This has not yet been done.

Other software and know-how for assisting decision makers in choosing the best combination is described by *Kantorovich et al.* [1974], *Molchan* [1991, 2003], *Keilis-Borok* [2003], and [*Davis et al.*, 2010].

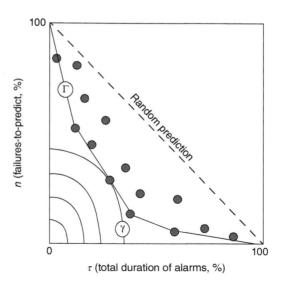

Figure 22.16 Joint optimization of prediction and preparedness based on theory of optimal control. Dots show points corresponding to results of application of different earthquake prediction strategies. Γ is their envelope. Thin contours (γ) show "loss curves" with constant value of a prevented "loss." Optimal strategy is the tangent point of contours Γ and γ. After *Molchan* [2003].

22.5. CONCLUSION

Major results of the studies described in the earlier sections could be summarized as follows:

1. *Prediction algorithms* are developed for the extreme events of each type considered. As required in complexity studies these algorithms are robust and self-adjusting to the scale of the system, level of its background activity, magnitude of prediction targets, etc. Accuracy of prediction is defined by the rate of false alarms, rate of failures to predict, and total time-space occupied by the alarms. The algorithms allow to choose the trade-off between these characteristics.

2. *New understanding of the origin of the extreme events* considered is also developed.

3. *Linking prediction with disaster preparedness.*

These results have large potential for further development. A wealth of available and highly relevant data, models, and practical experience for disaster prediction and preparedness remains as yet untapped. Further, less immediate results within reach [*Keilis-Borok and Soloviev*, 2006; *Keilis-Borok*, 2007] include, for example, considerable increase in prediction accuracy; prediction of other kinds of disasters and crises; and with luck, new tools for disaster control.

In the general scheme of things, the problems considered here belong to a much wider field of predictive understanding and control of crises and disasters: a key for the survival and sustainability of our civilization.

REFERENCES

Aki, K. (1996), Scale dependence in earthquake phenomena and its relevance to earthquake prediction, *Proc. Nat. Acad. Sci.*, *93*, 3740–3747.

Allègre, C. J., J.-L. Le Mouël, and V. Provost (1982), Scaling rules in rock fracture and possible implications for earthquake prediction, *Nature*, *297*, 47–49.

Barenblatt, G. I., V. I. Keilis-Borok, and A. S. Monin (1983), Filtration model of earthquake sequence, *Trans. (Doklady) Acad. Sci. SSSR*, *269*, 831–834.

Barenblatt, G. I. (1993), Micromechanics of fracture, in *Theoretical and Applied Mechanics*, edited by E. R. Bodner, J. Singer, A. Solan, and Z. Hashin, Elsevier, Amsterdam, pp. 25–52.

Bongard, M. M. (1970), *Pattern Recognition*, Spartan Books, New York.

Bowman, D. D., G. Ouillon, G. G. Sammis, A. Sornette, and D. Sornette (1998), An observational test of the critical earthquake concept, *J. Geophys. Res.*, *103*, 24359–24372.

Bui Trong, L. (2003), Risk of collective youth violence in French suburbs, in *Risk Science and Sustainability*, NATO Science Series. II. Mathematics, Physics and Chemistry, vol. *112*, edited by T. Beer and A. Ismail-Zadeh, pp. 199–221, Kluwer Academic Publishers, Boston, MA.

Crutchfield, J. P., J. D. Farmer, N. H. Packard, and N. H. Shaw (1986), Chaos, *Sci. Am.*, *255*, 46–57.

Davis, C., K. Goss, V. Keilis-Borok, G. Molchan, P. Lahr, and C. Plumb (2007), Earthquake prediction and tsunami preparedness, *Workshop on the Physics of Tsunami, Hazard Assessment Methods and Disaster Risk Management*, 14–18 May 2007, Trieste: ICTP.

Davis, C. A., V. Keilis-Borok, G. Molchan, P. Shebalin, P. Lahr, and C. Plumb (2010), Earthquake prediction and disaster preparedness: Interactive analysis, *Nat. Hazard. Rev.*, *11*(4), 173–184.

Gabrielov, A. M., I. V. Zaliapin, W. I. Newman, and V. I. Keilis-Borok (2000), Colliding cascade model for earthquake prediction, *Geophys. J. Int.*, *143*(2), 427–437.

Gabrielov, A., V. Keilis-Borok, Y. Sinai, and I. Zaliapin (2008), Statistical properties of the cluster dynamics of the systems of statistical mechanics, in *Boltzmann's Legacy*, ESI Lectures in Mathematics and Physics, edited by G. Gallavotti, W. L. Reiter, and J. Yngvason, pp. 203–215, European Mathematical Society, Zurich.

Gabrielov, A., V. Keilis-Borok, S. Olsen, and I. Zaliapin (2010): Predictability of extreme events in a branching diffusion model. arXiv:1003.0017, January 2010.

Gelfand, I. M., S. A. Guberman, V. I. Keilis-Borok, L. Knopoff, F. Press, E. Y. Ranzman, I. M. Rotwain, and A. M. Sadovsky (1976), Pattern recognition applied to earthquake epicenters in California, *Phys. Earth Planet. Inter.*, *11*, 227–283.

Gell-Mann, M. (1994), *The Quark and the Jaguar: Adventures in the Simple and the Complex*, Freeman and Company, New York.

Ghil, M., P. Yiou, S. Hallegatte, B. D. Malamud, P. Naveau, A. Soloviev, P. Friederichs, V. Keilis-Borok, D. Kondrashov, V. Kossobokov, O. Mestre, C. Nicolis, H. W. Rust, P. Shebalin, M. Vrac, A. Will, and I. Zaliapin (2011), Extreme events: dynamics, statistics and prediction, *Nonlinear Process. Geophys.*, *18*, 295–350.

Kantorovich, L. V., V. I. Keilis-Borok, and G. M. Molchan (1974), Seismic risk and principles of seismic zoning, In *Seismic Design Decision Analysis*. Internal Study Report 43, Department of Civil Engineering, MIT, Cambridge (Mass).

Keilis-Borok, V. I., L. Knopoff, and I. M. Rotwain (1980), Bursts of aftershocks, long-term precursors of strong earthquakes, *Nature*, *283*, 258–263.

Keilis-Borok, V. I. and F. Press (1980), On seismological applications of pattern recognition, in *Source Mechanism and Earthquake Prediction Applications*, edited by C. J. Allegre, pp. 51–60, Editions du Centre National de la Recherché Scientifique, Paris.

Keilis-Borok, V. I. and A. Lichtman (1981), Pattern recognition applied to presidential elections in the United States 1860-1980: Role of integral social, economic and political traits, *Proc. Nat. Acad. Sci.*, *78*(11), 7230–7234.

Keilis-Borok, V. I. (1990), The lithosphere of the Earth as a nonlinear system with implications for earthquake prediction, *Rev. Geophys.*, *28*, 19–34.

Keilis-Borok, V. I. and A. Lichtman (1993), The self-organization of American society in presidential and senatorial elections, in *Limits of Predictability*, edited by Yu. A. Kravtsov, pp. 223–237, Springer-Verlag, Berlin-Heidelberg.

Keilis-Borok, V. I. and P. N. Shebalin (Eds.) (1999), Dynamics of lithosphere and earthquake prediction, *Phys. Earth Planet. Inter.*, *111*(3–4 special issue).

Keilis-Borok, V., J. H. Stock, A. Soloviev, and P. Mikhalev (2000), Pre-recession pattern of six economic indicators in the USA, *J Forecast.*, *19*, 65–80.

Keilis-Borok, V. I. (2002), Earthquake prediction: State-of-the-art and emerging possibilities, *Annu. Rev. Earth Planet. Sci.*, *30*, 1–33.

Keilis-Borok, V. I. and A. A. Soloviev (Eds.) (2003), *Nonlinear Dynamics of the Lithosphere and Earthquake Prediction*, pp. 337, Springer-Verlag, Berlin-Heidelberg.

Keilis-Borok, V. I. (2003), Basic science for prediction and reduction of geological disasters, in *Risk Science and Sustainability*, NATO Science Series. II. Mathematics, Physics and Chemistry, vol. *112*, edited by T. Beer and A. Ismail-Zadeh, pp. 29–38, Kluwer Academic Publishers, Boston, MA.

Keilis-Borok, V. I., D. J. Gascon, A. A. Soloviev, M. D. Intriligator, R. Pichardo, and F. E. Winberg (2003), On predictability of homicide surges in megacities, in *Risk Science and Sustainability*, NATO Science Series. II. Mathematics, Physics and Chemistry, vol. *112*, edited by T. Beer and A. Ismail-Zadeh, pp. 91–110, Kluwer Academic Publishers, Boston, MA.

Keilis-Borok, V., P. Shebalin, A. Gabrielov, and D. Turcotte (2004a), Reverse tracing of short-term earthquake precursors, *Phys. Earth Planet. Inter.*, *145*(1-4), 75–85.

Keilis-Borok, V., C. Davis, G. Molchan, P. Shebalin, P. Lahr, and C. Plumb (2004b), Earthquake prediction and disaster preparedness: Interactive algorithms, *Eos. Trans. AGU*, *85*(47 Fall Meeting Suppl., Abstract S22B-02).

Keilis-Borok, V. I., A. A. Soloviev, C. B. Allègre, A. N. Sobolevskii, and M. D. Intriligator (2005), Patterns of macroeconomic indicators preceding the unemployment rise in Western Europe and the USA, *Pattern Recogn.*, *38*(3), 423–435.

Keilis-Borok, V. and A. Soloviev (2006) Earthquakes prediction: "The paradox of want amidst plenty", *26th IUGG Conference on Mathematical Geophysics*, 4–8 June 2006, Sea of Galilee, Israel. Book of Abstracts, p 28.

Keilis-Borok, V.I. (2007), Earthquake prediction: paradigms and opening possibilities, *Geophysical Research Abstracts*, Volume 9, 2007. Abstracts of the Contributions of the EGU General Assembly 2007, Vienna, Austria, 15–20 April 2007 (CD-ROM): EGU2007-A-06766.

Keilis-Borok, V. I., A. A. Soloviev, M. D. Intriligator, and F. E. Winberg (2008), Pattern of macroeconomic indicators preceding the end of an American economic recession, *J. Pattern Recogn. Res.*, *3*(1), 40–53.

Keilis-Borok, V. I. and A. A. Soloviev (2010), Variations of trends of indicators describing complex systems: Change of scaling precursory to extreme events, *Chaos*, *20*, 033104.

Kossobokov, V. G., V. I. Keilis-Borok, and B. Cheng (2000), Similarities of multiple fracturing on a neutron star and on the Earth, *Phys. Rev. E*, *61*(4), 3529–3533.

Kossobokov, V. and P. Shebalin (2003), Earthquake prediction, in *Nonlinear Dynamics of the Lithosphere and Earthquake Prediction*, edited by V. I. Keilis-Borok and A. A. Soloviev, pp. 141–207, Springer-Verlag, Berlin-Heidelberg.

Lichtman, A. J. and V. I. Keilis-Borok (1989), Aggregate-level analysis and prediction of midterm senatorial elections in the United States, 1974-1986, *Proc. Nat. Acad. Sci.*, *86*(24), 10176–10180.

Lichtman, A. J. (1996), *The Keys to the White House*, Madison Books, Lanham, MD.

Lichtman, A. J. (2000), *The Keys to the White House*, Lexington Books Edition, Lanham, MD.

Lichtman, A. J. (2005), The keys to the White House: Forecast for 2008, *Foresight*, *3*, 5–9.

Levshina, T. and I. Vorobieva, 1992: Application of algorithm for prediction of a strong repeated earthquake to the Joshua Tree and Landers, Fall Meeting AGU, Abstracts, p. 382.

Ma, Z., Z. Fu, Y. Zhang, C. Wang, G. Zhang, and D. Liu (1990), *Earthquake Prediction: Nine Major Earthquakes in China*, Springer-Verlag, New York.

Mogi, K. (1968), Migration of seismic activity, *Bull. Earthq Res. Inst. Univ. Tokyo*, *46*(1), 53–74.

Molchan, G. (1991), Structure of optimal strategies in earthquake prediction, *Tectonophysics*, *193*, 267–276.

Molchan, G. M. (1997), Earthquake prediction as a decision-making problem, *Pure Appl. Geophys.*, *149*, 233–237.

Molchan, G. M. (2003), Earthquake prediction strategies: A theoretical analysis, in *Nonlinear Dynamics of the Lithosphere and Earthquake Prediction*, edited by V. I. Keilis-Borok and A. A. Soloviev, Springer-Verlag, Berlin-Heidelberg, pp. 209–237.

Molchan, G. and V. Keilis-Borok (2008), Earthquake prediction: probabilistic aspect, *Geophys. J. Int.*, *173*(3), 1012–1017.

Narkunskaya, G. S. and M. G. Shnirman (1994), On an algorithm of earthquake prediction, in *Computational Seismology and Geodynamics*, vol. *1*, edited by D. K. Chowdhury, pp. 20–24, AGU, Washington, DC.

Peresan, A., V. Kossobokov, L. Romashkova, and G. F. Panza (2005), Intermediate-term middle-range earthquake predictions in Italy: a review, *Earth Sci. Rev.*, *69*(1-2), 97–132.

Pollitz, F. F., R. Burgmann, and B. Romanowicz (1998), Viscosity of oceanic asthenosphere inferred from remote triggering of earthquakes, *Science*, *280*, 1245–1249.

Press, F. and P. Briggs (1975), Chandler wobble, earthquakes, rotation and geomagnetic changes, *Nature*, *256*, 270–273.

Press, F. and C. Allen (1995), Patterns of seismic release in the southern California region, *J. Geophys. Res.*, *100*(B4), 6421–6430.

Romanowicz, B. (1993), Spatiotemporal patterns in the energy-release of great earthquakes, *Science*, *260*, 1923–1926.

Rotwain, I., V. Keilis-Borok, and L. Botvina (1997), Premonitory transformation of steel fracturing and seismicity, *Phys. Earth Planet. Inter.*, *101*, 61–71.

Rotwain, I., G. De Natale, I. Kuznetsov, A. Peresan, and G. F. Panza (2006), Diagnosis of time of increased probability (TIP) for volcanic earthquakes at Mt. Vesuvius, *Pure Appl. Geophys.*, *163*(1), 19–39.

Shebalin, P., V. Keilis-Borok, I. Zaliapin, S. Uyeda, T. Nagao, and N. Tsybin (2004), Advance short-term prediction of the large Tokachi-oki earthquake, September 25, 2003, M = 8.1. A case history, *Earth Planets Space*, *56*(8), 715–724.

Shebalin, P., V. Keilis-Borok, A. Gabrielov, I. Zaliapin, and D. Turcotte (2006), Short-term earthquake prediction by reverse analysis of lithosphere dynamics, *Tectonophysics*, *413*, 63–75.

Shnirman, M. G. and E. M. Blanter (1999), Mixed hierarchical model of seismicity: Scaling and prediction, *Phys. Earth Planet. Inter.*, *111*(3-4), 295–303.

Shnirman, M. G. and E. M. Blanter (2003), Hierarchical models of seismicity, in *Nonlinear Dynamics of the Lithosphere and Earthquake Prediction*, edited by V. I. Keilis-Borok and A. A. Soloviev, pp. 37–69, Springer-Verlag, Berlin-Heidelberg.

Soloviev, A. and A. Ismail-Zadeh (2003), Models of dynamics of block-and-fault systems, in *Nonlinear Dynamics of the Lithosphere and Earthquake Prediction*, edited by V. I. Keilis-Borok and A. A. Soloviev, pp. 71–139, Springer-Verlag, Berlin-Heidelberg.

Sornette, D. and C. G. Sammis (1995), Complex critical exponents from renormalization group theory of earthquakes: Implications for earthquake predictions, *J. Phys. I France*, *5*, 607–619.

Sornette, D. (2004), *Critical Phenomena in Natural Sciences: Chaos, Fractals, Selforganization, and Disorder. Concept and Tools*, 2nd ed., Springer-Verlag, Berlin-Heidelberg.

Tsuboi, C. (1956), Earthquake energy, earthquake volume, aftershock area and strength of the Earth's crust, *J. Phys. Earth*, *4*, 63–69.

Turcotte, D. L., W. I. Newman, and A. Gabrielov (2000), A statistical physics approach to earthquakes, in *Geocomplexity and the Physics of Earthquakes*, pp. 83–96, AGU, Washington, DC.

Vorobieva, I. A. (1999), Prediction of a subsequent large earthquake, *Phys. Earth Planet. Int.*, *111*, 197–206.

Vorobieva, I. (2009), Prediction of subsequent strong earthquake. Advanced School on Non-Linear Dynamics and Earthquake Prediction, 28 September to 10 October, 2009, Trieste: ICTP, 2060-49, 37 pp.

Yakovlev, G., W. I. Newman, D. L. Turcotte, and A. Gabrielov (2005), An inverse cascade model for self-organized complexity and natural hazards, *Geophys. J. Int.*, *163*, 433–442.

Zaliapin, I., V. Keilis-Borok, and M. Ghil (2003), A Boolean delay equation model of colliding cascades. Part II: Prediction of critical transitions, *J. Stat. Phys.*, *111*, 839–861.

Zaliapin, I., H. Wong, and A. Gabrielov (2005), Inverse cascade in percolation model: hierarchical description of time-dependent scaling, *Phys. Rev. E*, *71*, 066118.

Zaliapin, I., H. Wong, and A. Gabrielov (2006), Hierarchical aggregation in percolation model, *Tectonophysics*, *413*, 93–107.

INDEX

Accumulated cyclone energy (ACE), 321
ACF. *See* Autocorrelation function
Acid rain, 104
Adaptation, 331–32
Aeromagnetic surveys, 98, 99
AF. *See* Amplification factor
Aguilar, J., 253
Air-sea interaction, 64
Akaike, H., 39
Akhmediev, N., 157
Aki, K., 393
Alaska, 230
Albini, P., 233
Alboran modeling, 367
Algeria, 2, 5, 363
    economical impact of tsunami in, 371–74, 373f
      Northern, 364–66, 365f
      Western, 368–71, 369f, 370f, 371f
Algorithm M8, 394–95, 395t
Algorithm MSc, 394–95, 395t
Allen (hurricane), 130
Allen, C., 393
Allen, M. R., 349, 350
Alpine Mountain System, 189, 192
Alvarez, L. W., 94, 103, 104
Amazon rainforest, 51
Amir, L., 5, 364, 367
AMM. *See* Atlantic Meridional Mode
AMO. *See* Atlantic Multidecadal Oscillation
AMOC. *See* Atlantic meridional overturning circulation
Amphora coffeaeformis, 171
Amplification factor (AF), 237, 239f, 240f, 241
AMV. *See* Atlantic Multidecadal Variability
Andrew (hurricane), 212, 325, 330
Angrist, J. D., 323
Anomalies, 37, 64
Anthropogenic climate change, 320–23, 322f
Anthropogenic warming, 303, 316
Anttila-Hughes, J. K., 326, 329, 331, 332
Apennines-Maghrebides subduction arc, 367
Apennines Mountain System, 189, 192
AR. *See* Autoregressive models
AR(1) model, 39–40, 48, 49, 350
    empirical skill of, 44–45
    raw and post-processed ensemble forecast
      compared to, 45–46
    theoretical skill of, 43–44
AR4. *See* Fourth Assessment Report

Arbell, H., 158
Archimedean copulas, 227–28
Arctic sea ice, 51, 53
Arenillas, I., 102
Arpe, K., 311
ASO. *See* August to October
Asteroids. *See also* Chicxulub asteroid impact
    NEAs, 106, 106f
Atlantic Hurricane Seasonal outlook, 312
Atlantic Meridional Mode (AMM), 311, 332
Atlantic meridional overturning circulation (AMOC), 52
Atlantic Multidecadal Oscillation (AMO), 316, 332
Atlantic Multidecadal Variability (AMV), 316–17, 332
Atlantic thermohaline circulation, 56
Atlantic Warm Pool, 318
Atmosphere-ocean coupling strength, 66, 69f
Atmosphere-ocean systems, 37
Atmospheric aerosols, 320
Atmospheric pollution, 197
Attenuation of seismic waves, 284
AUC value, 46, 48, 48f
August to October (ASO), 310, 332
Auroral currents, 81–82
Auroras, 81, 83
Australia, 305, 307, 310
Autocorrelation, 38f
Autocorrelation function (ACF), 58–59
Autoregressive models (AR), 13, 39f
Avicennia trees, 145

Backup systems, 388
Bacro, J. N., 18
Balearic Islands, 364
Banda Aceh, Indonesia, 137, 139–42, 148–49
    impact of tsunami at, 145–46
    inundation processes in, 147
    mangroves in, 146, 148, 149f
Bandy, W., 256
Barrett, B. S., 103
Base rate model, 38–39, 48
    CEBR, 39, 43, 43f, 44
    theoretical skill of, 42–43
Battisti, D. S., 74
Bauer, F., 116
Bayesian analysis, 198
Becker, E. J., 122
Belasen, A., 330
Belcher, C. M., 104

Extreme Events: Observations, Modeling, and Economics, Geophysical Monograph 214, First Edition.
Edited by Mario Chavez, Michael Ghil, and Jaime Urrutia-Fucugauchi.
© 2016 American Geophysical Union. Published 2016 by John Wiley & Sons, Inc.